Administrative Law
and Procedure

Paralegal Titles from Delmar Publishers

Legal Research, Steve Barber, Mark McCormick, 1996
Wills, Estates, and Trusts, Jay Gingrich, 1996
Criminal Law and Procedure, 2E, Daniel Hall, 1996
Introduction to Environmental Law, Harold Hickock, 1996
Civil Litigation, 2E, Peggy N. Kerley, Paul A. Sukys, Joanne Banker Hames, 1996
Client Accounting for the Law Office, Elaine Langston, 1996
Law Office Management, 2E, Jonathan Lynton, Donna Masinter, Terry Mick
    Lyndall, 1996
Foundations of Law: Cases, Commentary, and Ethics, 2E, Ransford C. Pyle, 1996
Administrative Law and Procedure, Elizabeth Richardson, 1996
Legal Research and Writing, David J. Smith, 1996

Legal Research and Writing, Carol M. Bast, 1995
Federal Taxation, Susan Covins, 1995
Everything You Need to Know About Being a Legal Assistant, Chere B. Estrin, 1995
Paralegals in New York Law, Eric Gansberg, 1995
Ballentine's Legal Dictionary and Thesaurus, Jonathan Lynton, 1995
Legal Terminology with Flashcards, Cathy Okrent, 1995
Wills, Trusts, and Estate Administration for Paralegals, Mark A. Stewart, 1995
The Law of Contracts and the Uniform Commercial Code, Pamela Tepper, 1995
Life Outside the Law Firm: Non-Traditional Careers for Paralegals, Karen Treffinger,
    1995

An Introduction to Paralegal Studies, David G. Cooper, 1994
Administrative law, Daniel Hall, 1994
Ballentine's Law Dictionary: Legal Assistant Edition, Jack Handler, 1994
The Law of Real Property, Michael Kearns, 1994
Ballentine's Thesaurus for Legal Research and Writing, Jonathan Lynton, 1994
Legal Ethics and Professional Responsibility, Jonathan Lynton, Terri Mick Lyndall, 1994
Criminal Law for Paralegals, Daniel J. Markey, Jr., 1994
Family Law, Ransford C. Pyle, 1994
Paralegals in American Law: Introduction to Paralegalism, Angela Schneeman, 1994
Intellectual Property Richard Stim, 1994

Legal Writing for Paralegals, Steve Barber, 1993
Administration of Wills, Trusts, and Estates, Gordon W. Brown, 1993
Torts and Personal Injury Laws, William Buckley, 1993
Survey of Criminal Law, Daniel Hall, 1993
The Law of Corporations, Partnerships, and Sole Proprietorships, Angela Schneeman,
    1993

Administrative Law and Procedure

Elizabeth C. Richardson, J.D.

Adjunct Faculty
Central Piedmont Community College

Delmar Publishers

 I**T**P An International Thomson Publishing Company

Albany • Bonn • Boston • Cincinnati • Detroit • London • Madrid • Melbourne
Mexico City • New York • Pacific Grove • Paris • San Francisco • Singapore • Tokyo
Toronto • Washington

NOTICE TO THE READER

Background by Jennifer McGlaughlin
Design by Douglas J. Hyldelund / Linda C. DeMasi

Delmar Staff:

Acquisitions Editor: Christopher Anzalone
Developmental Editor: Jeffrey D. Litton
Project Editor: Eugenia L. Orlandi

Production Coordinator: Jennifer Gaines
Art & Design Coordinator: Douglas J. Hyldelund

Copyright © 1996
By Delmar Publishers and Lawyers Cooperative Publishing
divisions of International Thompson Publishing Inc.

Printed in the United States of America

For more information, contact:

Delmar Publishers
3 Columbia Circle, Box 15015
Albany, New York 12212-5015

International Thomson Editores
Campos Eliseos 385, Piso 7
Col Polanco
11560 Mexico D F Mexico

International Thomson Publishing Europe
Berkshire House 168 - 173
High Holborn
London WC1V 7AA
England

International Thomson Publishing GmbH
Königswinterer Strasse 418
53227 Bonn
Germany

Thomas Nelson Australia
102 Dodds Street
South Melbourne, 3205
Victoria, Australia

International Thomson Publishing Asia
221 Henderson Road
#05 - 10 Henderson Building
Sinapore 0315

Nelson Canada
1120 Birchmount Road
Scarborough, Ontario
Canada M1K 5G4

International Thomson Publishing - Japan
Hirakawacho Kyowa Building, 3F
2-2-1 Hirakawacho
Chiyoda-ku, Tokyo 102
Japan

1 2 3 4 5 6 7 8 9 10 xxx 01 00 99 98 97 96 95

Library of Congress Cataloging-in-Publication Data

Richardson, Elizabeth C.
  Administrative law and procedure / Elizabeth C. Richardson.
    p. cm.
    Includes bibliographical references and index.
    ISBN: 0-8273-7468-2
  1. Administrative law—United States. 2. Administrative procedure—United States. I. Title.
KF5402.R53 1996
342.73'06—dc20
[347.3026]
                                                                95-23056
                                                                CIP

CONTENTS

IIII **CHAPTER 7**   **Administrative Procedures and Appeals:**
How to File Applications with Administrative Agencies
and Appeal Administrative Decisions   251

IIII **Chapter 8**   **Adjudications: A Closer Look at Administrative**
Hearings   295

IIII **CHAPTER 9**   **Judicial Review: Understanding the Extent**
to Which Courts Control Agency Actions   337

DELMAR PUBLISHERS INC.

 AND

LAWYERS COOPERATIVE PUBLISHING

ARE PLEASED TO ANNOUNCE THEIR PARTNERSHIP TO CO-PUBLISH COLLEGE TEXTBOOKS FOR PARALEGAL EDUCATION.

DELMAR, WITH OFFICES AT ALBANY, NEW YORK, IS A PROFESSIONAL EDUCATION PUBLISHER. DELMAR PUBLISHES QUALITY EDUCATIONAL TEXTBOOKS TO PREPARE AND SUPPORT INDIVIDUALS FOR LIFE SKILLS AND SPECIFIC OCCUPATIONS.

LAWYERS COOPERATIVE PUBLISHING (LCP), WITH OFFICES AT ROCHESTER, NEW YORK, HAS BEEN THE LEADING PUBLISHER OF ANALYTICAL LEGAL INFORMATION FOR OVER 100 YEARS. IT IS THE PUBLISHER OF SUCH RENOWNED LEGAL ENCYCLOPEDIAS AS **AMERICAN LAW REPORTS, AMERICAN JURISPRUDENCE, UNITED STATES CODE SERVICE, LAWYERS EDITION,** AS WELL AS OTHER MATERIAL, AND FEDERAL- AND STATE-SPECIFIC PUBLICATIONS. THESE PUBLICATIONS HAVE BEEN DESIGNED TO WORK TOGETHER IN THE DAY-TO-DAY PRACTICE OF LAW AS AN INTEGRATED SYSTEM IN WHAT IS CALLED THE "TOTAL CLIENT-SERVICE LIBRARY (TCSL). EACH LCP PUBLICATION IS COMPLETE WITHIN ITSELF AS TO SUBJECT COVERAGE. YET ALL HAVE COMMON FEATURES AND EXTENSIVE CROSS-REFERENCING TO PROVIDE LINKAGE FOR HIGHLY EFFICIENT LEGAL RESEARCH INTO VIRTUALLY ANY MATTER AN ATTORNEY MIGHT BE CALLED UPON TO HANDLE.

INFORMATION IN ALL PUBLICATIONS IS CAREFULLY AND CONSTANTLY MONITORED TO KEEP PACE WITH AND REFLECT EVENTS IN THE LAW AND IN SOCIETY. UPDATING AND SUPPLEMENTAL INFORMATION IS TIMELY AND PROVIDED CONVENIENTLY.

FOR FURTHER REFERENCE, SEE:

AMERICAN JURISPRUDENCE 2D: AN ENCYCLOPEDIC TEXT COVERAGE OF THE COMPLETE BODY OF STATE AND FEDERAL LAW.

AM JUR LEGAL FORMS 2D: A COMPILATION OF BUSINESS AND LEGAL FORMS DEALING WITH A VARIETY OF SUBJECT MATTERS.

AM JUR PLEADING AND PRACTICE FORMS, REV: MODEL PRACTICE FORMS FOR EVERY STAGE OF A LEGAL PROCEEDING.

AM JUR PROOF OF FACTS: A SERIES OF ARTICLES THAT GUIDE THE READER IN DETERMINING WHICH FACTS ARE ESSENTIAL TO A CASE AND HOW TO PROVE THEM.

AM JUR TRIALS: A SERIES OF ARTICLES DISCUSSING EVERY ASPECT OF PARTICULAR SETTLEMENTS AND TRIALS WRITTEN BY 180 CONSULTING SPECIALISTS.

UNITED STATES CODE SERVICE: A COMPLETE AND AUTHORITATIVE ANNOTATED FEDERAL CODE THAT FOLLOWS THE EXACT LANGUAGE OF THE STATUTES AT LARGE AND DIRECTS YOU TO THE COURT AND AGENCY DECISIONS CONSTRUING EACH PROVISION.

ALR AND ALR FEDERAL: SERIES OF ANNOTATIONS PROVIDING IN-DEPTH ANALYSES OF ALL THE CASE LAW ON PARTICULAR LEGAL ISSUES.

U.S. SUPREME COURT REPORTS, L ED 2D: EVERY REPORTED U.S. SUPREME COURT DECISION PLUS IN-DEPTH DISCUSSIONS OF LEADING ISSUES.

FEDERAL PROCEDURE, L ED: A COMPREHENSIVE, A-Z TREATISE ON FEDERAL PROCEDURE—CIVIL, CRIM- INAL, AND ADMINISTRATIVE.

FEDERAL PROCEDURAL FORMS, L ED: STEP-BY-STEP GUIDANCE FOR DRAFTING FORMS FOR FEDERAL COURT OR FEDERAL AGENCY PROCEEDINGS.

FEDERAL RULES SERVICE, 2D and 3D: REPORTS DECISIONS FROM ALL LEVELS OF THE FEDERAL SYSTEM INTERPRETING THE FEDERAL RULES OF CIVIL PROCEDURE AND THE FEDERAL RULES OF APPELLATE PROCEDURE.

FEDERAL RULES DIGEST, ED: ORGANIZES HEADNOTES FOR THE DECISIONS REPORTED IN FEDERAL RULES SERVICE ACCORDING TO THE NUMBERING SYSTEMS OF THE FEDERAL RULES OF CIVIL PROCEDURE AND THE FEDERAL RULES OF APPELLATE PROCEDURE.

FEDERAL RULES OF EVIDENCE SERVICE: REPORTS DECISIONS FROM ALL LEVELS OF THE FEDERAL SYSTEM INTERPRETING THE FEDERAL RULES OF EVIDENCE.

FEDERAL RULES OF EVIDENCE NEWS

FEDERAL PROCEDURE RULES SERVICE

FEDERAL TRIAL HANDBOOK, 2D

FORM DRAFTING CHECKLISTS: AM JUR PRACTICE GUIDE

GOVERNMENT CONTRACTS: PROCEDURES AND FORMS

HOW TO GO DIRECTLY INTO YOUR OWN COMPUTERIZED SOLO PRACTICE WITHOUT MIS-SING A MEAL (OR A BYTE)

JONES ON EVIDENCE, CIVIL AND CRIMINAL, 7TH

LITIGATION CHECKLISTS: AM JUR PRACTICE GUIDE

MEDICAL LIBRARY, LAWYERS EDITION

MEDICAL MALPRACTICE—ALR CASES AND ANNOTATIONS

MODERN APPELLATE PRACTICE: FEDERAL AND STATE CIVIL APPEALS

MODERN CONSTITUTIONAL LAW

NEGOTIATION AND SETTLEMENT

PATTERN DEPOSITION CHECKLISTS, 2D

QUALITY OF LIFE DAMAGES: CRITICAL ISSUES AND PROOFS

SHEPARD'S CITATIONS FOR ALR

SUCCESSFUL TECHNIQUES FOR CIVIL TRIALS, 2D

STORIES ET CETERA—A COUNTRY LAWYER LOOKS AT LIFE AND THE LAW

SUMMARY OF AMERICAN LAW

THE TRIAL LAWYER'S BOOK: PREPARING AND WINNING CASES

TRIAL PRACTICE CHECKLISTS

2000 CLASSIC LEGAL QUOTATIONS

WILLISTON ON CONTRACTS, 3D AND 4TH

FEDERAL RULES OF EVIDENCE DIGEST: ORGANIZES HEAD-NOTES FOR THE DECISIONS REPORTED IN FEDERAL RULES OF EVIDENCE SERVICE ACCORDING TO THE NUMBERING SYSTEM OF THE FEDERAL RULES OF EVIDENCE.

ADMINISTRATIVE LAW: PRACTICE AND PROCEDURE

AGE DISCRIMINATION: CRITICAL ISSUES AND PROOFS

ALR CRITICAL ISSUES: DRUNK DRIVING PROSECUTIONS

ALR CRITICAL ISSUES: FREEDOM OF INFORMATION ACTS

ALR CRITICAL ISSUES: TRADEMARKS

AMERICANS WITH DISABILITIES: PRACTICE AND COMPLIANCE MANUAL

ATTORNEYS' FEES

BALLENTINE'S LAW DICTIONARY

CONSTITUTIONAL LAW DESKBOOK

CONSUMER AND BORROWER PROTECTION: AM JUR PRACTICE GUIDE

CONSUMER CREDIT: ALR ANNOTATIONS

DAMAGES: ALR ANNOTATIONS

EMPLOYEE DISMISSAL: CRITICAL ISSUES AND PROOFS

ENVIRONMENTAL LAW: ALR ANNOTATIONS

EXPERT WITNESS CHECKLISTS

EXPERT WITNESSES IN CIVIL TRIALS

FORFEITURES: ALR ANNOTATIONS

FEDERAL LOCAL COURT RULES

FEDERAL LOCAL COURT RULES

FEDERAL LOCAL COURT FORMS

FEDERAL CRIMINAL LAW AND PROCEDURE: ALR ANNOTATIONS

FEDERAL EVIDENCE

FEDERAL LITIGATION DESK SET: FORMS AND ANALYSIS

PREFACE

"Administrative law is not for sissies."[1] Administrative law instructors know that this is not an easy course to teach. Administrative law is simply different from other courses in paralegal curricula. There are certain broad topics that most administrative law texts address; however, without a unifying theme and practical applications, administrative law is not only difficult but dull. *Administrative Law and Procedure* rescues students and instructors by making administrative law an interesting and practical subject.

A Practical Approach to Administrative Law

This textbook addresses all the major subjects in administrative law, from delegation of authority to judicial review. What sets this text apart from other administrative law texts? *Administrative Law and Procedure* includes not only theory, but also procedure, substantive law, and practical applications. The textbook achieves the successful integration of these critical elements by concentrating on four federal administrative agencies and the statutes they administer. The text concentrates on the Social Security Act, with an emphasis on disability benefits; the Immigration and Nationality Act, with an emphasis on naturalization and political asylum; Title VII of the 1964 Civil Rights Act, with an emphasis on the prohibition against retaliation; and the Resource Conservation and Recovery Act. Students also learn procedure, such as the steps in appealing unfavorable determinations of applications for Social Security disability. Students read the actual statutes and regulations, and the text walks students through important statutes such as the Administrative Procedure Act, the Freedom of Information Act, the Privacy Act, and the National Environmental Policy Act.

Administrative Law and Procedure uses real-life examples throughout the text to bring the theoretical aspects of administrative law to life. The textbook has four sample cases that are used to illustrate the principles of administrative law throughout. In each chapter, these sample cases and other real-life examples are used in the Practical Applications exercises so that students can apply the theory to the facts. In addition to Practical Applications, each chapter contains a Summary and Review Questions. Further, each chapter contains a Case Analysis, in which students read portions of a case and answer questions that reinforce the

---

1. Antonin Scalia, Judicial Deference to Administrative Interpretations of Law, 1989 Duke L.J. 511, 511.

concepts of administrative law taught in that chapter. Throughout, students read and interpret the primary sources of administrative law.

Contents

Chapter 1 provides an introduction to administrative law. In addition to explaining in an understandable manner just what administrative law is, Chapter 1 explains how administrative agencies fit into the United States system of government, which is a practical introduction to the important subject of delegation of authority and the separation of powers. Chapter 1 then examines the mission of representative federal agencies and gives an overview of state administrative agencies. Chapter 2 examines in detail the sources of administrative law and procedure. The important concept of due process is introduced in the section on the United States Constitution. Chapter 2 examines statutes that govern federal administrative agencies, including the Administrative Procedure Act, the Freedom of Information Act, the Privacy Act, and the National Environmental Policy Act. The text then turns to enabling statutes, regulations, case law, and presidential documents, all important sources of administrative law. Chapters 3 and 4 explain the substantive law of four important areas of administrative law that provide ample job opportunities for paralegals—Social Security disability, employment discrimination (Title VII's prohibition against retaliation), immigration law (naturalization), and environmental law (hazardous waste management).

Chapter 5 introduces the important functions of federal administrative agencies, including rulemaking, enforcement and sanctions, agency information and advice, and investigations and monitoring. Chapter 5 also discusses alternative dispute resolution in the context of administrative law. Chapter 6 examines the controls on agency actions, including controls exerted by the executive branch, Congressional control, and judicial review of agency actions. Chapter 6 then addresses the role of discretion and remedies for failure to act. Next is an extensive treatment of the critical topic of due process, followed by a discussion of the Federal Tort Claims Act. Chapter 7 teaches administrative procedures in a practical way, explaining how to file applications and appeal unfavorable determinations for Social Security disability benefits and applications for naturalization.

Chapter 8 addresses adjudications, examining in detail the nature of administrative hearings. This chapter walks students through a hearing before an Administrative Law Judge on the issue of Social Security disability and a deportation hearing before an Immigration Judge in which the defense is a claim for political asylum. Chapter 8 explains how administrative hearings differ from federal court trials, including the generally relaxed rules of evidence. The chapter includes an explanation of how to obtain information from federal agencies through the Freedom of Information Act. Chapter 9 discusses the important topic of judicial review of administrative agencies. The chapter begins with a practical discussion of the two sets of circumstances in which litigation with federal agencies ensues—*de novo* litigation, such as the defense in an employment discrimination claim, and judicial review, such as the review of the Social Security Administration's decision that a person is not entitled to disability benefits. Chapter 9 then explains the right to judicial review, the scope of judicial review, and the procedure for pursuing judicial review.

Chapter 10 covers an important topic overlooked by most administrative law—legal ethics. Administrative law raises specific issues not found in other areas of law. The regulations of some federal administrative agencies allow paralegals to represent people applying for certain benefits, such as Social Security disability benefits. The agency in turn has the power to sanction all representatives, both attorneys and non-attorneys. Further, paralegals who work for federal agencies must be aware that federal regulations set precise ethical guidelines for all employees of federal agencies. Chapter 9 gives an overview of the statutes and regulations specific to federal government employees.

The text contains the Administrative Procedure Act for ready reference, a decision issued by an Administrative Law Judge in one of the sample cases, and illustrations of numerous forms which paralegals will encounter when they deal with federal agencies. The text is replete with practical tips for paralegals, ranging from useful looseleaf services to professional organizations that keep members current with the rapid changes in many areas of administrative law.

Administrative law offers immense opportunities for paralegals. Students who complete this text will understand the theory and the practical applications of administrative law, and they will be able to hit the ground running from day one of an exciting career.

Acknowledgments

Writing this text was fun but arduous. I thank all my clients whom I have had the honor to serve in their cases before administrative agencies. I also thank all my students who enabled me over the years to learn how to teach administrative law and to keep them awake at the same time. The many people who shared their knowledge of administrative law are too numerous to name. Two people, however, were such an enormous help that I would be remiss in not naming them—Cynthia Aziz and Bill Shaw. All the reviewers who read the manuscript offered wise and kind insights, and I thank them. I extend a special thanks to Athena Putman, who patiently sent me immigration forms every time that I called to report that I had misplaced them in my study. Finally, I thank the most patient person in the United States, my husband, Michael Pawlyk. During this project, he not only put up with me and listened to my ideas, but he also reminded me to eat, sleep, and occasionally to hike in the mountains.

ABBREVIATIONS

ABA American Bar Association

ACUS Administrative Conference of the United States

ADR alternative dispute resolution

AILA American Immigration Lawyers Association

ALJ Administrative Law Judge

APA Administrative Procedure Act

BIA Board of Immigration Appeals

BLM Bureau of Land Management

CEQ Council on Environmental Quality

CERCLA Comprehensive Environmental Response, Compensation and Liability Act (Superfund)

CFR Code of Federal Regulations

DOT Department of Transportation

EA environmental assessment

EIS environmental impact statement

EEOC Equal Employment Opportunity Commission

EOIR Executive Office of Immigration Review

EPA Environmental Protection Agency

FDA Food and Drug Administration

FIFRA Federal Insecticide, Fungicide and Rodenticide Act

FOIA Freedom of Information Act

FONSI finding of no significant impact

FTC Federal Trade Commission

FTCA Federal Tort Claims Act

GAO General Accounting Office

GPO Government Printing Office

HHS Health and Human Services

HSWA Hazardous and Solid Waste Amendments of 1984

IJ Immigration Judge

IMFA Immigration Marriage Fraud Amendments of 1986

INA Immigration and Naturalization Act

INS Immigration and Naturalization Service

NEPA National Environmental Policy Act

NOSSCR National Organization of Social Security Claimants Representatives

OGE Office of Government Ethicds

OHA Office of Hearings and Appeals

OMB Office of Management and Budget

OPM Office of Personnel Management

OSC Order to Show Cause

OSHA Occupational Safety and Health Administration

PRW past relevant work

RCRA Resource Conservation and Recovery Act

RFC residual functional capacity

SSA Social Security Administration

SSI supplemental security income

TPS temporary protected status

TSCA Toxic Substances Control Act

TSD Facilities waste treatment, storage and disposal facilities

VE Vocational expert

TABLE OF CASES

Sample Case One

SOCIAL SECURITY DISABILITY

Ms. Garcia's client, Melinda Lewis, has applied for Social Security disability benefits. She applied for Title II benefits only, because her husband earns $35,000 a year.

In the initial interview with Ms. Garcia, Mrs. Lewis stated that she has been unable to work since March 1, 1992. Thus, her alleged onset date is March 1, 1992. Assume that Mrs. Lewis meets the insured status requirements of the Social Security Act.

Mrs. Lewis was born on January 3, 1940. Thus, she was fifty-two years old on her alleged onset date. She completed the eleventh grade. From June 1968 until March 1, 1992, she worked as a cashier at a small grocery store. She had to stand most of the time. She sometimes helped with stocking shelves but never lifted more than twenty pounds. From March 1960 until June 1968, Mrs. Lewis worked for a company that makes and packages Christmas ornaments. At this job she never lifted more than ten pounds, and she sat seven of the eight hours of her shift.

On March 1, 1992, Mrs. Lewis suffered a heart attack. She was hospitalized and underwent triple bypass grafting. After surgery, Mrs. Lewis continued to suffer from fatigue, and she has difficulty performing household tasks except for light activities such as dusting. In addition, Mrs. Lewis has a long history of back pain. Her orthopedic surgeon has confirmed that she suffers from degenerative disk disease at multiple levels. She has fairly constant low back pain that sometimes radiates into her right leg. X-rays have shown degenerative changes, but it remains unclear whether she has a herniated disk. She has been referred to a neurosurgeon for further evaluation of her back problem.

Sample Case Two

TITLE VII (Retaliation)

John Simon is the general manager of the Minos Group, Inc., an environmental consulting firm with fifty full-time employees. Minos serves a variety of companies, advising them on matters of environmental risk assessment and management. For instance, if a company wishes to purchase a site that may have been contaminated with hazardous wastes, Minos would provide advice about purchaser liability and potential cleanup costs.

In May 1991, John Simon hired Linda Watson and James Jones as environmental engineers with Minos. Both Watson and Jones completed and signed Minos's standard application form. At the bottom of the application is a section entitled "SIGNATURE, CERTIFICATION AND RELEASE OF INFORMATION." Next, in bold print, are these words: "YOU MUST SIGN THIS APPLICATION. Read the following carefully before you sign." Beneath the heading and statement are these sentences:

- A false statement on any part of your application may be grounds for not hiring you or for firing you after you begin work.
- I consent to the release of information about my ability and fitness for employment by employers, schools, law enforcement agencies, other individuals and organizations, and to other authorized employees of Minos.
- I certify that, to the best of my knowledge and belief, all of my statements are true, correct, complete, and made in good faith.

One question on the application form asked whether the applicant had been convicted of a felony, and both Jones and Watson wrote "no."

John Simon supervised Jones and Watson throughout the time they worked for Minos. After Jones and Watson had been employed with Minos for two years, a position as a senior engineer was announced, and both Jones and Watson applied. Jones, a white male, was chosen. Watson, a white female, was not promoted. Watson stated to other engineers that she felt Minos had violated Title VII by not promoting her. The job evaluations in her personnel file rated her performance as "minimally satisfactory" in every job review. Although it was not reflected in her personnel file, employees throughout the office had complained that she spent at least two hours a day making personal telephone calls. Jones received a rating of "fully satisfactory" in his first annual review and "excellent" in all subsequent reviews.

After Jones received the promotion in May 1993, Watson filed a charge of discrimination with the Equal Employment Opportunity Commission. The EEOC's investigation revealed some inter- esting facts that had previously been unknown. At the time Jones and Watson applied, no one had verified their educational credentials. An investiga- tion revealed that Jones had actually dropped out of college when he still had one semester left and that he did not in fact have a college degree. Watson held a B.S. degree as she reported on her application.

The Title VII charge was settled in the early stages of the investigation. The investigation had, however, raised some questions, so Simon requested police records for both employees. Police records revealed that Watson had pled guilty to a felony charge of check forgery several years before she was hired by Minos. Jones had no felony convictions.

In early September 1993, Simon discharged both Jones and Watson. Watson returned to the EEOC and filed another charge on the basis that she had been fired in retaliation for the earlier charge she filed with the EEOC.

Sample Case Three

NATURALIZATION

Massoud Kazemi is one of Ms. Garcia's immigration clients. Mr. Kazemi entered the United States in 1981 on a tourist visa. A citizen of Iran, he came to the United States to seek medical treatment of a heart condition. While Mr. Kazemi was in the United States, he learned from friends and family members that it was not safe to return to Iran because the Revolutionary Guards had come to his office to arrest him. Mr. Kazemi had been an outspoken opponent of Ayatollah Khomeini. Before he left Iran, he had participated in anti-Khomeini demonstrations and was a member of a group dedicated to the replacement of the Khomeini government by a democratic government, by peaceful means. Mr. Kazemi was granted political asylum in the United States. Pursuant to Immigration and Naturalization Service regulations, one year later he was allowed to become a lawful permanent resident of the United States.

Mr. Kazemi is now applying for naturalization. He is thirty-seven years old. He has resided continuously in the United States since 1981. He left the United States to visit friends in London for one month in 1990. His employer sent him to Germany to work for four months in 1991. He has had no absences since 1991. His use of the English language is very good, and he has adequate knowledge of United States government and history.

Sample Case Four

HAZARDOUS WASTE MANAGEMENT

Chaco Corporation is one of Susan Garcia's clients. Chaco is a company that manufactures chemicals. The chemicals it manufactures are used primarily in the textile and paper industries. For instance, Chaco makes wet strength resins, which are used in the manufacture of paper grocery bags and paper towels to keep the paper from falling apart. For the textile industry Chaco makes lubricants, which allow yarn machines to spin fibers into yarn without destroying the fibers. Without lubricants the heat and movement would melt or otherwise destroy the fibers.

Chaco's final products are not classified as hazardous waste. Chaco does, however, use some materials defined by the Environmental Protection Agency as hazardous waste in the process of manufacturing its final products. Further, some of its manufacturing processes produce by-products classified as hazardous waste. Chaco does not transport or dispose of hazardous waste.

Chaco has one manufacturing facility in Raleigh, North Carolina, and several other plants throughout the United States. The plant in Raleigh has about 100 employees.

||||

CHAPTER 1

AN INTRODUCTION TO ADMINISTRATIVE LAW AND PROCEDURE

You have just been hired as a paralegal with the law firm of McKethan and Garcia. This is a small law firm with a varied practice. You will be working for Susan Garcia, a partner in the law firm. Ms. Garcia told you during the initial interview that her practice includes several areas of administrative law. Ms. Garcia explained that her administrative law practice brings her into frequent contact with many federal agencies, including the Social Security Administration (SSA), the Immigration and Naturalization Service (INS), the Equal Employment Opportunity Commission (EEOC), and the Environmental Protection Agency (EPA). She deals with the SSA because she represents persons who have applied for Social Security disability benefits. She has a busy immigration law practice, which involves helping persons from different countries obtain visas to stay in the United States for a few months, a few years, or permanently. Her contacts with the EEOC arise when a client needs help with a charge involving employment discrimination. She also advises clients on compliance with environmental laws.

A Brief Overview of Administrative Law

You confessed that, like many people, you are confused by what the term "administrative law" means. Ms. Garcia explained that administrative law controls how governmental agencies deal with you and how you deal with them. For instance, if you apply for Social Security disability benefits, you must deal with the Social Security Administration, a federal administrative agency.

Statutes

Federal statutes are laws passed by Congress. There are federal statutes that give the Social Security Administration the authority to determine whether a person is entitled to disability benefits. The federal statutes also give broad definitions and criteria for determining disability. These federal statutes governing the actions of the Social Security Administration are part of the body of law known as administrative law.

BALLENTINE'S

federal statutes   Statutes enacted by Congress.

Regulations

For specific details, such as how to file an application, how to appeal an unfavorable determination, and how to submit medical evidence, you must follow the regulations of the Social Security Administration. **Regulations** are written statements issued by an administrative agency, explaining in detail the substantive law and the procedural requirements of the programs the agency administers. Regulations can best be understood as the "rules of the game," that is, the rules that both the person applying for disability benefits (the "claimant") and the Social Security Administration must follow. There are specific regulations that govern the procedures the claimant must follow in applying for benefits and in appealing unfavorable decisions. A claimant must pursue several levels of appeal within the Social Security Administration before seeking review by a federal court, and the regulations dictate the procedure for appeals. Although the federal statutes provide some general standards for determining whether a person is disabled, the regulations set forth the standards in far greater detail. These regulations are an important part of the body of law known as administrative law.

SIDEBAR

Paralegals frequently encounter the terms "substantive law" and "procedural law." **Substantive law** creates and defines the benefits that agencies dispense and the rules they enforce. The definition of "disability" in the Social Security statute and regulations is an example of substantive law. **Procedural law** describes the steps to follow to obtain a benefit from an agency or comply with the agency's rules. The process of filing an application for disability benefits and appealing a denial of the application is an example of procedural law.

—————————————BALLENTINE'S—————————————

regulation 1. A rule having the force of law, promulgated by an administrative agency; the act of rulemaking. 2. A rule of conduct established by a person or body in authority for the governance of those over whom they have authority.

substantive law Area of the law that defines right conduct, as opposed to procedural law, which governs the process by which rights are adjudicated.

procedural law The law governing the manner in which rights are enforced; law prescribing the procedure to be followed in a case. Also called adjective law; procedural law dictates *how* rights are *presented* for interpretation and enforcement, as distinguished from substantive law, which *creates* legal rights. The Federal Rules of Civil Procedure, the Federal Rules of Criminal Procedure, and rules are EXAMPLES of procedural laws.

Judicial Review

Another major component of administrative law is the courts' oversight of governmental agencies' actions, commonly called **judicial review**. Most agency decisions are reviewable by the courts. Some common grounds for seeking judicial review are that the agency acted in an unlawful manner, in a manner inconsistent with a constitutional right, or in a manner clearly inconsistent with the evidence.[1] Thus, after a claimant has exhausted all administrative appeals within the Social Security Administration, the claimant can file a lawsuit in federal court, asking the court to find that the agency's denial of benefits was not supported by substantial evidence or that the agency made some other error that warrants a reversal or remand of the case.[2]

It is important to remember that the statutes, regulations, and court decisions work together, not in isolation, to define the powers and procedures of agencies. Congress may pass a very broad statute giving an agency a specific power. The agency then formulates detailed regulations to implement the statute. A court decision may ultimately be necessary to clarify the meaning of the regulations or to determine whether the agency's actions in implementing the statute are valid.

This overview, which gives you a better idea of the meaning of the term "administrative law" can be summarized by defining **administrative law** as the "law concerning the powers and procedures of administrative agencies . . . ."[3]

Why Administrative Law Is Important

You are embarking upon the study of a vital and expanding area of law. As society becomes increasingly complex, governmental agencies affect everyone more and more. For instance, environmental regulations affect individuals and businesses daily. Numerous laws govern everyone in the workplace, in areas ranging from employment discrimination to workers' compensation for those injured on the job. The Internal Revenue Service (IRS) is an agency that touches all the lives of everyone at least once a year.

BALLENTINE'S

judicial review 1. Review by a court of a decision or ruling of an administrative agency. 2. Review by an appellate court of a determination by a lower court.

administrative law 1. The body of law that controls the way in which administrative agencies operate. 2. Regulations issued by administrative agencies.

Administrative Law Permeates the Lives of Individual and Corporate Clients

Even paralegals who do not work exclusively in an area of administrative law will face administrative law issues almost daily. Individual and corporate clients have regular dealings with federal, state, and local administrative agencies. For example, responding to a charge of employment discrimination would bring a corporate client into direct contact with the Equal Employment Opportunity Commission.

Administrative agencies permeate clients' daily activities in more indirect ways as well. For instance, a company must ensure that its building is in compliance with occupational safety standards developed by the Occupational Safety and Health Administration (OSHA). Perhaps your law firm will represent a real estate developer who wishes to build a small shopping center in an area not currently zoned for this particular type of land use. Your law firm may represent a group of citizens opposed to the location of a hazardous waste disposal facility near their neighborhood. In any of these situations, the attorney-paralegal team will have numerous contacts with a host of administrative agencies. Knowledge of administrative law will assist paralegals in virtually every area of law in which they work. This knowledge can only enhance your career.

Administrative Law Offers Employment Opportunities for Paralegals

Administrative law presents many job opportunities for paralegals, and those opportunities are increasing. Some of the fastest growing areas of law, such as environmental regulation, require extensive involvement with agencies on the federal, state, and local level. Administrative agencies employ paralegals in many capacities.

Paralegals often work for private law firms that represent clients who have dealings with administrative agencies, such as law firms that specialize in immigration law. There are also job opportunities for paralegals in private industry. For instance, a large corporation may employ paralegals to keep the company current with hazardous waste regulations.

How Administrative Agencies Fit into the United States System of Government

Administrative agencies have become an integral part of the system of government in the United States. The need for administrative agencies has grown as the United States government has become larger and the laws more complex.

Administrative agencies are responsible for enforcing laws passed by Congress that Congress does not have the time and expertise to enforce. As the United States has grown, Congress has passed new laws to address problems that have accompanied this growth.

Consider, for instance, the environmental problems that Congress has addressed in the past twenty years. A few examples of environmental legislation include the Resource Conservation and Recovery Act, the National Environmental Policy Act, the Clean Air Act, the Clean Water Act, and the Toxic Substances Control Act. These are complex laws, and their interpretation requires a great deal of expertise and detailed analysis. Members of Congress and their staffs do not have the expertise or the time to spell out the details of how these laws will be enforced. Instead, the implementation and enforcement power is given to the Environmental Protection Agency.

Administrative agencies are given broad powers to carry out their missions. The agencies occupy a unique position in our system of government because they have powers traditionally attributed to all three branches of our government—judicial, executive, and legislative. A brief review of the three branches will enhance your understanding of how administrative agencies fit into the United States system of government.

A Review of the Structure of the United States Government

Throughout this discussion, it will be helpful to refer to Figure 1–1, a chart that outlines the government of the United States. The United States Constitution establishes three branches of government.

The Legislative Branch

First is the legislative branch. Article I, Section 1 of the United States Constitution provides that "All legislative powers herein granted shall be vested in a Congress of the United States, which shall consist of a Senate and House of Representatives." Both the Senate and House of Representatives consider potential legislation in their committees and

FIGURE 1–1
The Government
of the United
States

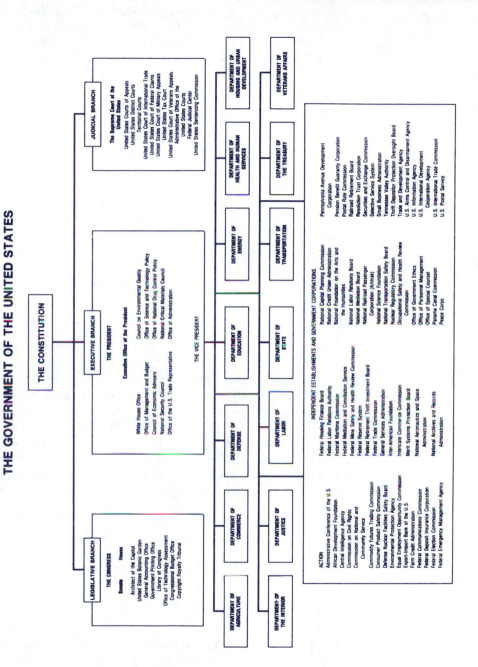

then vote on the proposed bills that are referred out of the committees and are debated on the floor of the Senate and House. The Senate also has special powers, including approving and disapproving Presidential appointments and approving treaties. The House of Representatives' special powers include originating all revenue bills.

The Executive Branch

Second is the executive branch. Article II, Section 1 of the United States Constitution states that "The executive power shall be vested in a President of the United States of America." The President is part of the executive branch, but the executive branch is far more extensive than many people realize. Refer to Figure 1–1, which shows the divisions of the executive branch. The executive branch includes numerous agencies, as well as the fourteen executive departments.[4] The heads of these departments are part of the President's Cabinet. Most of the heads of these fourteen executive agencies are called Secretaries, such as the Secretary of Health and Human Services. The head of the Justice Department is called the Attorney General of the United States.

The Judicial Branch

The third branch of the United States government is the judicial branch. Article III, Section 1 of the United States Constitution provides that "The judicial power shall be vested in one supreme court and in such inferior courts as the Congress may from time to time ordain and establish." The United States Supreme Court, the highest court in the land, is comprised of the Chief Justice and eight Associate Justices. Congress has established inferior, or lower, courts. These include the United States District Courts, which are the federal trial courts. Congress has also established the United States Courts of Appeal. These are the intermediate appellate courts, that is, the courts to which decisions of the United States District Courts are first appealed. In addition to the United States District Courts, Congress has also established specialized federal trial courts, such as the United States Tax Court and United States Court of International Trade.

The Hybrid Nature of Administrative Agencies

The United States Constitution directly grants specific powers to the three traditional branches of government—the legislative, executive, and judicial branches. Administrative agencies, however, do not always fit neatly into a specific branch of government. In fact, agencies can have powers which embrace aspects of all three branches of government. Congress can give an administrative agency powers that are legislative in nature, powers that are executive in nature, and powers that are judicial in nature.

The Immigration and Naturalization Service: An Agency with Legislative, Executive, and Judicial Powers

The powers granted to the Immigration and Naturalization Service (INS) are a good example. The Immigration and Nationality Act is administered and enforced by the INS. The actual language of the Immigration and Nationality Act charges the Attorney General of the United States with administering and enforcing the Act, but the Attorney General in turn has delegated these duties to the INS. The Immigration and Nationality Act provides many ways for persons from other countries to live in the United States temporarily or permanently.

Note that the legal term defining a person who is not a citizen or national of the United States is **alien**. While the choice of words is unfortunate, "alien" is the term used in immigration statutes and regulations.

One method for an alien to gain permanent residence in the United States is by applying for political asylum, a topic discussed in detail in subsequent chapters. Briefly, a person who is granted political asylum is given permission to enter or remain in the United States because that person is a refugee within the statutory meaning. The statutory definition of a **refugee** is a person who cannot return to his or her country of nationality because "of persecution or a well-founded fear of persecution on account of race, religion, nationality, membership in a particular social group or political opinion."[5] Assume that your law firm has a client who has fled her home country because of political persecution. She is now applying for political asylum in the United States. The INS exercises legislative, judicial, and executive powers in determining whether your client and other aliens are eligible for political asylum.

Political Asylum: Legislative Powers of the INS. The Immigration and Nationality Act provides that the Attorney General shall establish procedures for aliens present in the United States to apply for asylum.[6] The Attorney General in turn directs the INS to develop regulations detailing the procedure for applying for political asylum. The INS has

---

──────────────── BALLENTINE'S ────────────────

alien 1. Any person present within the borders of the United States who is not a U.S. Citizen. 2. Any foreigner.

refugee A person who cannot return to his or her country of nationality because "of persecution or a well-founded fear of persecution on account of race, religion, nationality, membership in a particular social group or political opinion."

formulated detailed regulations, which can be found in Title 8 of the **Code of Federal Regulations.** The regulations address the procedure for filing applications and additional details such as employment authorization while applications are pending, limitations on travel outside the United States, and how to appeal unfavorable decisions.

These regulations guide the procedure for applying for political asylum just as firmly as if Congress itself had passed statutes setting out the details. Congress has, however, deferred to the INS to cover these details. The enactment of regulations by the administrative agency is a legislative function, and thus the INS has been given legislative powers.

Political Asylum: Judicial Powers of the INS. There are two different avenues of applying for political asylum. Assume that the client was not already in deportation proceedings. Instead, she filed an application for political asylum with the INS Asylum Office shortly after she entered the United States on a valid visitor's visa. A **visa** is a document issued to aliens permitting them to enter the country.[7] An INS asylum officer will interview your client, consider the written evidence and testimony, and make the initial determination whether the client will be granted political asylum. The regulations require that the asylum officer issue a written decision. The regulations further provide that, in the case of an adverse decision, the asylum officer must state why asylum was denied and give an assessment of the applicant's credibility.[8]

These duties are similar to those of a judge in state or federal court. The asylum officer has the power to adjudicate claims, that is, to determine whether a person meets the criteria for political asylum. The power to adjudicate and decide controversies is considered a judicial function. The INS asylum officer has been delegated the authority to consider the testimony and written evidence and decide the claim, just as a judge would do. Political asylum is just one type of claim that INS employees adjudicate. The INS performs judicial-type duties in adjudicating a wide variety of visa applications.

Political Asylum: Executive Powers of the INS. The INS also has executive powers. The Immigration and Nationality Act provides for deportation of persons who are in the United States illegally. The Immigration and Nationality Act further authorizes the INS to apprehend and deport persons who are in the United States illegally.

————————————————————— BALLENTINE'S —————————————————————

Code of Federal Regulations An arrangement, by subject matter, of the rules and regulations issued by federal administrative agencies; commonly referred to as the CFR or abbreviated as C.F.R.

visa A stamp affixed to a passport by an official of a country one wishes to visit. It is a recognition of the validity of the passport and approval to enter the country.

Suppose the client were found not to be entitled to political asylum and had no other legal basis for remaining in the United States. The INS would have the authority to deport her because it has the authority to deport persons who have no legal basis to remain in the United States. This is part of the extensive enforcement authority granted to the INS.

The enforcement of laws is generally considered a function of the executive branch of government. The broad powers given to the INS to investigate whether persons are in the country illegally and to prosecute accordingly are generally considered executive functions.

Delegation of Authority and the Separation of Powers

Thus, administrative agencies have been given broad powers that span across the three branches of government. You may wonder whether this is constitutional because the United States Constitution contains no specific authorization to give the administrative agencies these powers.

Separation of Powers

The United States Constitution is based on the doctrine of **separation of powers**, that is, the principle that each branch of government should be limited to activities in the area assigned to it and should not encroach upon the powers given to the other branches. This means that the power to make laws rests with the legislative branch, the power to enforce laws rests with the executive branch, and the power to interpret laws and decide controversies rests with the judicial branch. This principle results in a system of **checks and balances**, that requires each branch to perform its duties and, in doing so, restrain the exercise of power by the other two branches.

BALLENTINE'S

separation of powers A fundamental principle of the Constitution, which gives exclusive power to the legislative branch to make the law, exclusive power to the executive branch to administer it, and exclusive power to the judicial branch enforce it. The authors of the Constitution believed that the separation of would make abuse of power less likely.

checks and balances The principle that each branch of government its duties and in doing so will provide restraints on the exercise of other two branches.

Administrative agencies have broad powers that cut across the lines traditionally drawn by the separation of powers. Thus, some critics over the years have asserted that the authority given the agencies violates the principle of separation. The administrative agencies at times seem to have attained the status of a "fourth branch" of government, which seems at odds with the traditional scheme of three branches of government.[9] This view was expressed by Justice Jackson in a 1952 United States Supreme Court decision:

> They (administrative agencies) have become a veritable fourth branch of the Government, which has deranged our three-branch legal theories much as the concept of a fourth dimension unsettles our three-dimensional thinking. Courts have differed in assigning a place to these seemingly necessary bodies in our constitutional system. Administrative agencies have been called quasi-legislative, quasi-executive, or quasi-judicial, as the occasion required, in order to validate their functions within the separation-of-powers scheme of the Constitution.[10]

Over the years administrative agencies have been given more powers. The agencies have become so integrated into the United States system of government that they no longer seem to "derange" the traditional three-branch system of government, but rather to be an integral part of it.

Delegation of Authority to Administrative Agencies

The grant of authority to the agencies by Congress is called **delegation**. Sometimes the terms **legislative delegation** and **delegation of authority** are used interchangeably with the word "delegation."

The Development of the Delegation Doctrine

The concern that agencies might disrupt the separation of powers doctrine spawned legal challenges concerning whether the broad grant of powers to agencies was constitutional. An examination of early court decisions concerning delegation demonstrates how the authority granted to agencies has developed and been refined and how the courts have become more receptive to the delegation of authority to administrative agencies.

————————————————— BALLENTINE'S —————————————————

delegation 1. The act of conferring authority upon, or transferring it to, another. USAGE: "By virtue of the delegation of powers contained in the Constitution, Congress is the branch of the federal government empowered to make laws."

legislative delegation Legislative powers are delegated to the legislative branch.

Remember that the tension is between delegating enough authority to the agencies to allow them to carry out their missions, while not granting them such broad, insufficiently defined authority that they can run rampant, unconstrained by the traditional checks and balances in our government. The delegation doctrine developed as the courts examined whether Congress had provided sufficient standards to limit the agency's discretion in carrying out the tasks broadly assigned to it.[11]

Early Court Decisions Defining the Bounds of Delegation. In early decisions concerning delegation, the United States Supreme Court upheld delegation of authority and stated in 1928, that a delegation of authority was permissible when it contained an "intelligible principle to which the (agency must) . . . conform."[12] The delegation debate heated up and the doctrine became more refined in the 1930s, when administrative agencies proliferated with the increase in federal agencies formed to implement programs instituted to bring the country out of the Great Depression. The National Industrial Recovery Act was enacted, and it granted broad but ill-defined authority to the National Recovery Administration (NRA) to establish "codes of fair competition" for certain industries if the code "tended to effectuate the policy of this title."

Owners of the Schechter Poultry Corporation had been convicted through the National Recovery Administration of violating the "codes of fair competition." The violations included, among other things, the sale of sick chickens at reduced prices. The Schechters appealed their convictions, culminating in the United States Supreme Court case of *Schechter Poultry Corp. v. United States*, frequently called the "sick chicken" case. The Schechters contended that the authority granted to establish industrial codes was unconstitutionally broad. The United States Supreme Court agreed. The Supreme Court found the delegation to be lacking in directives and in procedural safeguards. The Supreme Court wrote in part that:

> Section 3 of the Recovery Act . . . supplies no standards for any trade, industry or activity. It does not undertake to prescribe rules of conduct to be applied to particular states of fact determined by appropriate administrative procedure. Instead of prescribing rules of conduct, it authorizes the making of codes to prescribe them. For that legislative undertaking, Section 3 sets up no standards, aside from the statement of the general aims of rehabilitation, correction and expansion described in Section 1. In view of the scope of that broad discretion, and of the nature of the few restrictions that are imposed, the discretion . . . is virtually unfettered. We think that the codemaking authority thus conferred is an unconstitutional delegation of legislative power.[13]

It is important to understand that the protections that are now embodied in delegations of authority were not present in the codes at issue in the *Schechter* case. The delegating legislation did not provide for trial-type hearings or judicial review of unfavorable decisions by an agency. In short, the delegation of authority was not accompanied by sufficient standards to determine whether the delegated powers were being used as Congress intended.[14]

The same deficiencies in delegation were brought out in another case decided by the Supreme Court in 1935, *Panama Refining Co. v. Ryan*.[15] Here, the National Industrial Recovery Act had given the President the authority to regulate the interstate shipment of oil, prohibiting the shipment of contraband oil. As with *Schechter*, the legislation gave no guidance for the standards to use to determine whether the shipment of oil should be prohibited. The code prohibiting the shipment of contraband oil was found to be an unconstitutionally broad delegation of power.

The Contemporary Trend to Uphold Delegation of Authority. Aside from the *Schechter* and *Panama Refining* decisions, the United States Supreme Court has struck down no other legislation on the ground that it was an unconstitutional delegation of legislative authority. There are several reasons why even broad delegations of authority have been upheld since these two 1935 decisions. First, procedures have been developed to control agency actions without striking down the entire regulatory program. As discussed more fully in subsequent chapters, courts can review particular agency actions and impose controls on the agencies by invalidating particular actions, without invalidating the entire operating procedures of the agency. Second, Congress has become more attuned to setting some intelligible standards to be followed when it enacts enabling statutes. Third, both the Congress and the American people have seen the need for agencies that handle specialized functions that are too complex and time-consuming for Congress to handle.

The Necessity for Administrative Agencies

Administrative agencies sometimes seem to be too cumbersome and overbearing to work well. Yet even recognizing that the agencies are not perfect, the agencies are necessary instruments in a highly regulated society with complex laws.

Administrative Agencies Have Valuable Expertise

As noted above, members of Congress have to deal with a multitude of subjects, and they cannot become experts in every area governed by administrative agencies. For instance, it is unrealistic to expect every member of Congress to be able to identify every hazardous material regulated by the Environmental Protection Agency. It is the specialized domain of the EPA, assigned to that agency by Congress, to identify hazardous wastes, regulate their disposal, and impose fines for violators of the rules governing their disposal. The EPA employs engineers, chemists, and other experts to perform these specialized duties. The specialists in administrative agencies devote all their time to identifying and regulating problems within their agency's domain, and thus they develop the expertise to respond quickly and knowledgeably to problems in their designated areas.

Administrative Agencies Can Respond Efficiently

Many people feel that agencies do not handle problems quickly or efficiently. However, agencies are efficient when you consider how long it would take Congress or even a court to respond to the daily problems that agencies handle. It can take Congress months to move a bill out of committee to a vote. Imagine if Congress had to pass an individual bill to regulate the disposal of hazardous materials for every company that performs this task and if Congress also had to pass bills to solve every problem that each company caused or encountered.

Agencies can generally move faster than courts as well. In fact, administrative agencies often have mandatory time frames to complete their tasks. Litigation can go on for months or even years before a lawsuit is resolved. If every problem encountered with the disposal of hazardous waste had to be resolved through a lawsuit, the court system would be overwhelmed. It is more efficient to entrust the problems to experts at the agency who already have the background knowledge, including in-depth knowledge of the regulations.

Administrative hearings are less formal than trials in federal or state court. An administrative hearing, with relaxed rules of evidence, can resolve an issue in less time than a full-blown trial would require.

Because of their unique attributes, administrative agencies can handle a huge number of applications and claims. For instance, in 1993, the 793 administrative law judges with the Social Security Administration each issued approximately 39 decisions per month, and the total dispositions for all types of cases the judges heard was approximately 374,308.[16] In 1993, the Social Security Administration was responsible for payments of disability benefits to approximately 4.98 million beneficiaries, with payments totaling approximately $33.6 billion.[17] Obviously, specialized expertise is needed to administer programs of this magnitude.

Administrative Agencies Can Provide Efficient Supervision

Many agencies are entrusted with the supervision of a complex and highly regulated industry. For instance, the Nuclear Regulatory Commission must ensure that nuclear materials are used in a manner "consistent with the public health and safety, environmental quality, national security, and the antitrust laws."[18] The many technical responsibilities of the Nuclear Regulatory Commission include licensing the construction and operation of nuclear facilities, regulating the disposal of nuclear materials, investigating nuclear incidents, and conducting public hearings on nuclear safety.[19] Obviously these are tasks that cannot be performed by generalists in the judicial or legislative branches of government. Highly trained specialists within the agency are necessary to provide the close supervision required of the Nuclear Regulatory Commission.

The same is true for the regulation of other complex areas, such as the regulation of securities markets. The Securities and Exchange Commission regulates registration of securities, the conduct of securities brokers and dealers, and related areas that cannot effectively be supervised by the generalist.

Administrative Agencies Can Disseminate Information Widely

Because the actions of administrative agencies are so pervasive, at some point everyone has to obtain information from agencies. Trying to find the right person in the right agency to answer questions can at times be bewildering. It may be impossible to telephone a local office of the Immigration and Naturalization Service. You may have to go to the office in person to get an answer, and there may be only one office serving one or two entire states.

Compare the INS with the Social Security Administration, an agency for which everyone has questions ranging from the amount of retirement benefits to the procedure for applying for disability benefits. Although it may not be possible to telephone a local office directly, the SSA has developed a nationwide system of offices, with more than 1,300 field offices, making it more accessible than some other agencies.

A Closer Look at the Types and Organization of Federal Administrative Agencies

In gaining an overview of what agencies are and what they do, paralegals must become familiar with how the agencies fit into the structure of the government of the United States (Figure 1–1). The functions of a federal agency and the latitude it is given for operation are often the result of the agency's place in the scheme of government.

Executive Agencies

An important distinction is whether an agency is an executive agency or an independent agency. The chart from the *United States Government Manual* shows fourteen executive agencies. These are familiar agencies, such as the Department of Labor, Department of State, and Department of Health and Human Services. An **executive agency** operates directly under the executive branch and is typically headed by just one person, generally called the Secretary of that agency. The President appoints the head of the agency and can remove that person without cause. Thus, executive agencies generally operate with fairly direct supervision by the executive branch.

Independent Agencies

In contrast, there are numerous **independent agencies** that do not operate under any specific branch of government. Refer to Figure 1–1, which lists the most important independent agencies. Some of the most familiar independent agencies include the Equal Employment Opportunity Commission, the Environmental Protection Agency, the Small Business Administration, and the Securities and Exchange Commission. Independent agencies are generally headed by multimember boards rather than one agency head. For instance, the Securities and Exchange Commission is headed by a chairman and four other commissioners. Compare the organizational chart of the Department of Justice (Figure 1–2) with the chart for the Securities and

---

executive agency   An agency that operates directly under the President (chief of the executive branch of government), with one head, who can be terminated without cause.

independent agency   An agency that does not operate under a specific branch of government, usually headed by multi-member board, and considered less subject to direct Presidential control.

FIGURE 1–2
The Department of
Justice

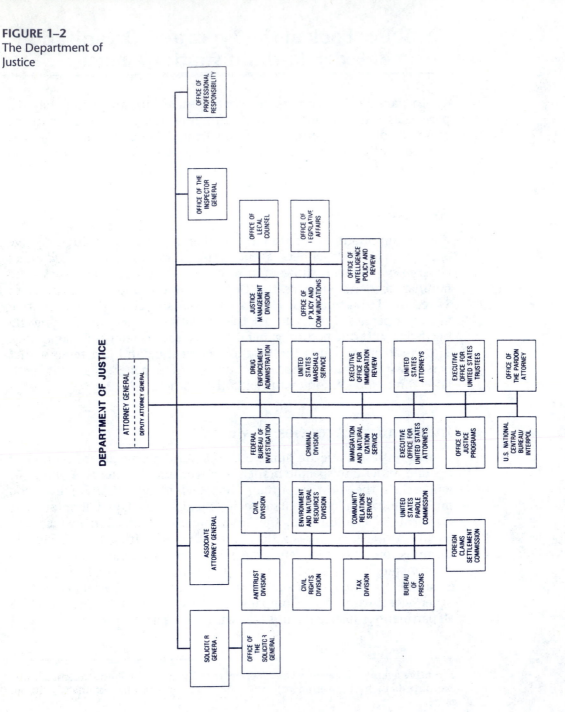

Source: United States Government Manual, 1993/94 (Washington, DC: U.S. Government Printing Office), p.365.

FIGURE 1–3
The Securities and
Exchange
Commission

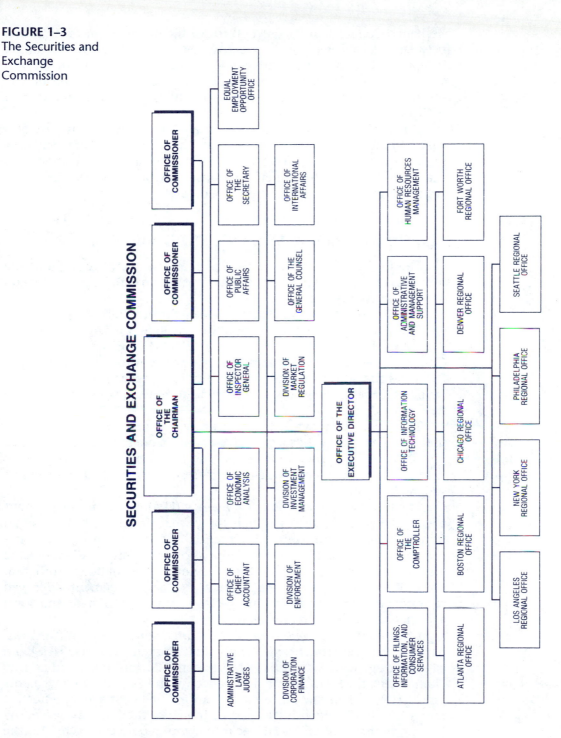

Source: United States Government Manual, 1993/94 (Washington, DC: U.S. Government Printing Office), p.724.

Exchange Commission (Figure 1–3) to see the difference in organization between a representative executive agency and a representative independent agency. The independent agencies are considered less subject to direct Presidential control, in part because they are headed by several persons who serve rotating terms and who cannot be dismissed without formal cause.

Do not become preoccupied with labeling an agency as part of a specific branch of government or as an independent agency. For now remember that agencies have specific functions assigned to them and that the successful fulfillment of those functions makes our entire system of government run more efficiently.

The Organization of SSA, INS, EEOC, and EPA

The four agencies that are the focus of discussion throughout the text provide an overview of the organization and functions of federal administrative agencies.

The Immigration and Naturalization Service (INS) is part of an executive agency, the Department of Justice. Refer to Figure 1–2, which illustrates how the INS fits in the Department of Justice. The Commissioner of the INS reports directly to the Attorney General. The INS has thirty-three districts and twenty-one border patrol sectors, as well as four regional offices that provide administrative support to the field offices.[20]

The Equal Employment Opportunity Commission (EEOC) is an independent agency, headed by five commissioners, a setup typical of multiheaded independent agencies. The EEOC operates through fifty field offices, each of which processes charges filed within its geographical area.[21]

The Environmental Protection Agency (EPA) is also an independent agency. Refer to Figure 1–4, which shows that the EPA is headed by an Administrator, with multiple branch heads reporting to the Administrator. The EPA has ten regional offices, which are responsible for "accomplishing, within their regions, the national program objectives established by the Agency."[22] They implement approved regional programs by maintaining close contact with state and local agencies, as well as with private industry.[23]

Until March 31, 1995, the Social Security Administration (SSA) was part of the Department of Health and Human Services (HHS), an executive agency. In August 1994, President Clinton signed Public Law No. 103-296, the Social Security Independence and Program Improvements Act of 1994.[24] This law made the SSA an independent agency, effective March 31, 1995. When it was part of the HHS, the SSA was headed by the Commissioner of Social Security, who reported directly to the Secretary of Health and Human Services. As an independent agency,

FIGURE 1–4
The Environmental
Protection Agency

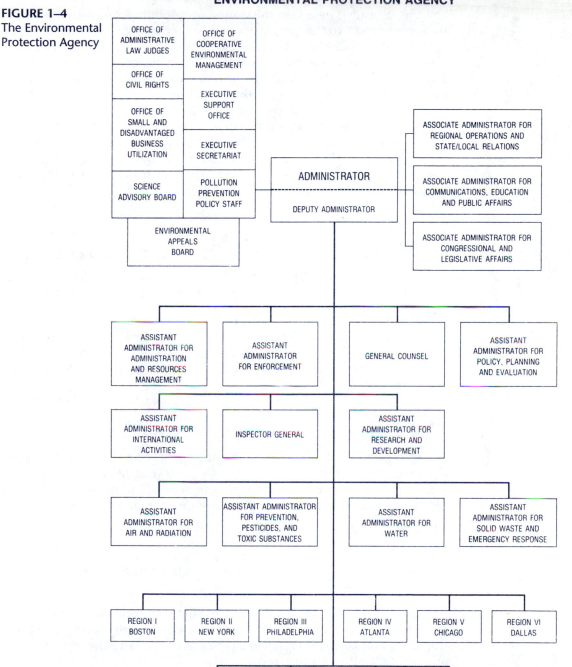

ENVIRONMENTAL PROTECTION AGENCY

OFFICE OF ADMINISTRATIVE LAW JUDGES

OFFICE OF COOPERATIVE ENVIRONMENTAL MANAGEMENT

OFFICE OF CIVIL RIGHTS

EXECUTIVE SUPPORT OFFICE

OFFICE OF SMALL AND DISADVANTAGED BUSINESS UTILIZATION

EXECUTIVE SECRETARIAT

SCIENCE ADVISORY BOARD

POLLUTION PREVENTION POLICY STAFF

ENVIRONMENTAL APPEALS BOARD

ADMINISTRATOR

DEPUTY ADMINISTRATOR

ASSOCIATE ADMINISTRATOR FOR REGIONAL OPERATIONS AND STATE/LOCAL RELATIONS

ASSOCIATE ADMINISTRATOR FOR COMMUNICATIONS, EDUCATION AND PUBLIC AFFAIRS

ASSOCIATE ADMINISTRATOR FOR CONGRESSIONAL AND LEGISLATIVE AFFAIRS

ASSISTANT ADMINISTRATOR FOR ADMINISTRATION AND RESOURCES MANAGEMENT

ASSISTANT ADMINISTRATOR FOR ENFORCEMENT

GENERAL COUNSEL

ASSISTANT ADMINISTRATOR FOR POLICY, PLANNING AND EVALUATION

ASSISTANT ADMINISTRATOR FOR INTERNATIONAL ACTIVITIES

INSPECTOR GENERAL

ASSISTANT ADMINISTRATOR FOR RESEARCH AND DEVELOPMENT

ASSISTANT ADMINISTRATOR FOR AIR AND RADIATION

ASSISTANT ADMINISTRATOR FOR PREVENTION, PESTICIDES, AND TOXIC SUBSTANCES

ASSISTANT ADMINISTRATOR FOR WATER

ASSISTANT ADMINISTRATOR FOR SOLID WASTE AND EMERGENCY RESPONSE

REGION I BOSTON

REGION II NEW YORK

REGION III PHILADELPHIA

REGION IV ATLANTA

REGION V CHICAGO

REGION VI DALLAS

REGION VII KANSAS CITY

REGION VIII DENVER

REGION IX SAN FRANCISCO

REGION X SEATTLE

Source: United States Government Manual, 1993/94 (Washington, DC: U.S. Government Printing Office), p.562.

the SSA is headed by a Commissioner and Deputy Commissioner, who no longer report to the Secretary of HHS. Like many other independent agencies, the SSA has a multimember bipartisan advisory board that makes policy recommendations to the Commissioner.

The purpose of making the SSA an independent agency was to make it function more effectively and to improve the overall administration of the programs delegated to the SSA. As part of the same legislation, Congress also enacted various program improvements, such as expansion of the SSA's authority to detect and terminate fraudulent claims. Congress did not alter the basic mission of the SSA, which is to administer benefits, such as retirement and disability benefits and supplemental security income, discussed in detail below.

A Closer Look at the Functions of Federal Administrative Agencies

Having examined the reasons that administrative agencies exist and the agencies' places in the scheme of the federal government, the discussion turns to questions fundamental to a practical understanding of administrative law: What do administrative agencies do? What are their functions?

Functions Differ According to the Mission of the Agency

The daily functions will differ from agency to agency, depending on the agency's mission. A federal agency's mission is the overall task that Congress has assigned the agency to perform. The missions of many federal agencies can be divided generally into three categories:

1. administration of benefits;
2. enforcement of laws;
3. the combination of administration of benefits and enforcement of laws.

These functions are best understood by examining specific agencies that exemplify the three categories—the Social Security Administration, the Equal Employment Opportunity Commission, and the Immigration and Naturalization Service, respectively.

There are other agencies that do not fit neatly into these three categories. The mission of some agencies is to provide and administer a comprehensive plan for governmental action in a particular area, such as protecting the environment. Such agencies include the Environmental Protection Agency.

Administration of Benefits: The Social Security Administration (SSA)

The Social Security Administration (SSA) is responsible for administering a wide variety of benefits programs, including the Old Age Survivors and Disability Insurance Program. This is the program that provides monthly benefit checks to retired persons who paid into the Social Security trust fund during their working careers. The SSA is responsible for maintaining that trust fund, keeping track of the contributions paid in by individuals and their employers, and sending out monthly benefit checks when the individuals retire. This same program provides monthly benefit checks to persons who qualify for disability insurance benefits because they are disabled within the meaning of the Social Security Act and thus qualify for benefits before they reach age sixty-five.

The SSA also administers the Supplemental Security Income (SSI) program for the aged, blind, and disabled. Individuals who apply for these benefits must have income, assets, and resources below a certain level in order to qualify. Supplemental security income benefits are paid out of a general revenue fund, not the special trust fund into which employees and employers make payments.

Persons who wish to receive any of these benefits must apply for them. This can be done by going to the local Social Security district office and completing forms. In addition, it is possible to apply by giving the information to Social Security employees over the telephone.

Like most agencies whose primary mission is to administer benefits, the SSA must provide a great deal of information to the public. Social Security employees across the country answer thousands of questions a day from people with inquiries about their entitlement to benefits, the amount of their benefits, and similar concerns.

The SSA provides information and services to the public through district offices, branch offices, and teleservice centers. The *United States Government Manual* describes the services rendered through the various offices as follows:

- informing people of the purposes and provisions of programs and their rights and responsibilities thereunder;

- assisting with claims filed for retirement, survivors, health, or disability insurance benefits, black lung benefits, or supplemental security income;

- developing and adjudicating claims;

- assisting certain beneficiaries in claiming reimbursement for medical expenses;

- conducting development of cases involving earnings, records, coverage, and fraud-related questions;

- making rehabilitation service referrals; and

- assisting claimants in filing appeals on Administration determinations of benefit entitlement or amount.[25]

Enforcement of Laws: The Equal Employment Opportunity Commission (EEOC)

The *United States Government Manual* states that the purpose of the Equal Employment Opportunity Commission (EEOC) is "to eliminate discrimination based on race, color, religion, sex, national origin, or age in hiring, promoting, firing, setting wages, testing, training, apprenticeship, and all other terms and conditions of employment . . . . The Commission also has oversight responsibility for all compliance and enforcement activities relating to equal employment opportunity among Federal employees and applicants, including discrimination against individuals with disabilities."[26]

The EEOC is specifically charged with enforcement of several statutes aimed at preventing the types of discrimination described above. These statutes include Title VII of the Civil Rights Act (42 U.S.C. § 2000e *et seq.*). Title VII prohibits employment discrimination on the basis of race, color, religion, sex, or national origin.

Since 1979, the EEOC has also enforced the Equal Pay Act (29 U.S.C. § 206(d)). The Equal Pay Act prohibits employers from paying unequal wages to members of the opposite sex for equal work. In addition, since 1979, the EEOC has enforced the Age Discrimination in Employment Act, which prohibits discrimination in employment against persons between the ages of forty and seventy). Another law enforced by the EEOC is the Pregnancy Discrimination Act, which prohibits unequal treatment of pregnant employees.

The EEOC has offices at numerous locations throughout the country. Suppose a woman feels that she has suffered employment discrimination on the basis of her gender. She can go to a local EEOC office and file a charge of discrimination. The EEOC then investigates the charge. If there is reasonable cause to believe that the charge of employment discrimination is true, the EEOC tries to reach an acceptable conciliation agreement with the employer. If conciliation fails and the EEOC decides to pursue litigation, the EEOC has the authority to file suit in federal court on behalf of the party charging discrimination.

Thus, the EEOC is largely an enforcement agency. Like most agencies, the EEOC is also responsible for disseminating information. For instance, the EEOC has collected data on the employment status of women and minorities. The EEOC shares the data with other agencies, such as the Department of Labor.[27]

Combined Mission of Administering Benefits and Enforcing Laws: The Immigration and Naturalization Service (INS)

The Immigration and Naturalization Service (INS) is part of the Justice Department, which "serves as counsel" for the citizens of the United States.[28] Under the direction of the United States Attorney General, the Department of Justice enforces myriad laws, covering diverse areas ranging from illegal drugs to consumer affairs. The INS is specifically charged with enforcing the Immigration and Nationality Act (8 U.S.C. § 1101).

The *United States Government Manual* describes the mission of the INS as being divided into four major areas of responsibility:

- facilitating the entry of persons legally admissible as visitors or as immigrants to the United States;

- granting benefits under the Immigration and Nationality Act, including providing assistance to those seeking permanent resident status or naturalization;

- preventing unlawful entry, employment, or receipt of benefits by those who are not entitled to them; and

- apprehending or removing those aliens who enter or remain illegally in the United States and/or whose stay is not in the public interest.[29]

Thus, the INS administers benefits by processing applications for visas for persons who wish to visit or to live and work in the United States. The other side of the dual mission of the INS is to enforce the laws prohibiting persons from entering the United States illegally, that is, without a visa. As part of its enforcement duties, the INS removes (deports) people who are in the United States illegally and are not eligible for any type of relief from deportation.

Like other federal agencies, the INS also has a duty to disseminate information regarding the laws it enforces and administers. The INS has regional offices throughout the United States. Anytime you go to an INS office, you will see persons asking for information about the immigration laws and getting the necessary forms to apply for immigration benefits. For instance, if a United States citizen who was originally a citizen of India wants to bring his mother to the United

States, he may be at the INS office picking up the appropriate forms to apply for a visa for his mother.

Information clerks at INS offices answer questions and give forms to the public and to attorneys and paralegals who assist persons with their immigration requests. INS offices also have an investigation unit which concentrates on arresting individuals who have no legal right to remain in the United States. At the INS office you will also find the INS examiners, who interview individuals applying for immigration benefits, review the applications and supporting documentation, and make an initial determination of whether a person will be granted the relief for which the person has applied. Thus, on a daily basis the INS employees enforce immigration laws, disseminate information, and process applications for immigration benefits.

An Integrated Approach to Pollution Control by Research, Standard Setting, and Enforcement: The Environmental Protection Agency (EPA)

The *United States Government Manual* describes the mission of the Environmental Protection Agency (EPA) as follows:

> The Environmental Protection Agency protects and enhances our environment today and for future generations to the fullest extent possible under the laws enacted by Congress. The Agency's mission is to control and abate pollution in the areas of air, water, solid waste, pesticides, radiation, and toxic substances. Its mandate is to mount an integrated, coordinated attack on environmental pollution in cooperation with State and local governments.[30]

Like the three agencies we have already discussed, an important function of the EPA is enforcement of statutes and regulations.

There are, however, several features of the functions of the EPA that stand apart from the three agencies we have already discussed. In addition to the EPA's enforcement functions, The *United States Government Manual* identifies three other functions crucial to the EPA's mission of effecting an integrated program to control pollution. These three functions are research, monitoring, and standard setting.

Research and technical support are integral to the EPA's mission. Within the EPA there is an Office of Research and Development which "is responsible for a national research program in pursuit of technological controls of all forms of pollution."[31] The EPA has national laboratories and regional laboratories. These research functions are necessary because the EPA oversees a technologically complex area of law.

The EPA develops national standards that affect every community, industry, and person in the United States. These include national standards for air quality, water quality, hazardous waste treatment and disposal, and standards for underground storage tanks, to cite just a few examples. The EPA then monitors and enforces the standards it has developed.

With all its functions, the EPA uses regional offices to work closely with local agencies, industries, and academic institutions. The locations of the ten regional offices are shown in Figure 1–4, which illustrates the organization of the entire EPA.

The EPA has more interaction with state and local governments than some agencies. As the mission statement reflects, one way that the EPA mounts an "integrated, coordinated attack" on pollution is by its close interaction with state and local governments. The EPA lends technological support to other federal, state, and local agencies. One distinguishing feature of environmental law, however, is that some statutes allow the state government to administer certain federal statutes. For instance, the Clean Air Act and Clean Water Act have set up "federal-state regulatory programs in which the states are given the opportunity to enact and enforce laws, meeting federal minimum criteria, to achieve the regulatory objectives which the Congress has established."[32] This stands in contrast to statutes such as Title VII, which are enforced solely by a federal agency.

An Overview of State Administrative Agencies

The numerous variations in state law make it difficult to present an overview of all states' administrative agencies. While the names and precise functions of agencies may vary from state to state, the basic principles of administrative law, such as delegation of authority and judicial review, apply to the administrative agencies of all states.

Sources of Law for State Administrative Agencies

Just as federal agencies' actions are created and directed by Congress, the actions of state agencies are created and directed by state legislatures. The sources of law that govern state administrative agencies include state constitutions, state laws, and judicial review by state courts. Thus, paralegals assigned the task of researching the question of whether a state agency was authorized to take a certain action must examine the state delegation statute and the applicable case law as well as any restraints (including due process) set forth in the state constitution. Further, paralegals must read the agency's regulations.

Just as the regulations of federal agencies are published in the *Code of Federal Regulations,* the regulations of state agencies are published in states' administrative codes.

Functions of State Administrative Agencies

Some state agencies administer benefits. Some types of benefits, such as workers' compensation, are solely state programs. Other types of benefits, such as Medicaid, are federal-state cooperative programs in which the funding comes largely from the federal government, but the daily functions, such as determining eligibility for benefits, are performed by state agencies. Thus, paralegals' direct contacts, such as appealing unfavorable eligibility determinations, are with the state agencies.

Many state agencies have enforcement functions. Indeed, just a brief look at case law regarding state agencies' authority will yield many references to the state's police power. The term **police power** is far broader than just law enforcement duties, such as highway patrol officers giving speeding tickets. The state's police power encompasses functions ranging from automobile safety inspections to standard placement of billboards or junkyards.

Licensing is an important regulatory function of state agencies. While federal agencies license large entities such as radio and television stations, state licensing has an even more immediate impact on individuals in their daily lives. For instance, individuals who wish to drive a car must obtain a driver's license. Thus, states seek to ensure safe operation of vehicles.

State agencies license entire professions—electricians, cosmetologists, lawyers, and plumbers, to name a few. Persons subject to state license requirements must obtain and keep current their license to engage in their professions. Thus, states seek to ensure certain standards to protect the public. Those who fail to maintain the required standards are subject to discipline or even the loss of their license. This is a potent means of regulation.

Additionally, paralegals will come into contact with state agency employees who administer state facilities such as prisons and universities. In the areas they regulate, the actions of state agencies are just as pervasive as the actions of federal agencies, therefore, paralegals will also have contact with state agencies, regardless of the area of law in which they work.

BALLENTINE'S

police power 1. The power of government to make and enforce laws and regulations necessary to maintain and enhance the public welfare and to prevent individuals from violating the rights of others.

A Closer Look at the Work of an Immigration Law Paralegal

You now have an overview of administrative law. An introductory chapter would not be complete without an overview of what you have to look forward to when you are a paralegal working in the area of administrative law. Rather than go through a dry list of paralegal work duties, a more interesting perspective comes from an interview with a paralegal working in the field of immigration law. Adriana Taylor has worked for several years exclusively in the area of immigration law. She has helped to prepare cases ranging from visas for executives of large foreign corporations to individual deportation cases. Her wealth of knowledge and experience should be an inspiration to you as aspiring paralegals.

You have worked exclusively in the area of immigration law for several years. Are there advantages to working in just one area of the law?

Working exclusively in immigration law has advantages, such as being able to learn in detail the many facets of a complex area of law. It is, however, important to remember that immigration law does not exist in a vacuum. Immigration law embraces almost every other kind of law in the final analysis. For instance, there are criminal law issues if the client has criminal convictions. These can have serious consequences in immigration law. Many issues addressing corporate law also arise, including some basic corporate matters such as contracts, as well as tax consequences for clients. Family law issues also arise, particularly when clients wish to adopt children born in foreign countries.

Tell us what you like about being a paralegal in the field of immigration law.

One very rewarding aspect of immigration law is the opportunity to deal with the broadest range of people, from Guatemalan farm workers to the president of a Fortune 500 corporation. Immigration law allows attorneys and paralegals to be creative. I do not mean this in the sense of being creative with the facts. The creativity comes with taking the facts and presenting them in a package that convinces the adjudicator to grant the benefit you request for the client. We will discuss this in more depth, but it is important to realize that immigration law paralegals do a lot more than fill out forms.

Another rewarding aspect of immigration law is the analytical depth required. Beyond just studying the statutes and regulations, you have to develop a strategy for each client. This makes interviewing clients very interesting, because you are continuously forming a strategy and formulating the right questions to ask so you can determine whether your strategy is likely to work. You must also consider strategies not just for the present application but for future applications your client might pursue. For instance, your client may seek a nonimmigrant visa as an investor, which involves establishing a major investment in the United States. The client may later wish to move to the United States permanently and thus seek an immigrant visa. If your client entertains the thought of eventually coming to live in the United States permanently, this involves long-range corporate planning. You must then consider the most effective way to set up the corporation and consider whether to maintain the preexisting foreign corporation.

There are positive aspects of being an immigration paralegal on the lighter side as well. We prepare labor certifications for foreign chefs, so we know the best restaurants in town for foreign cuisine.

You obviously have a lot of responsibility and participate in complex analysis and planning for your clients. Can you give us some idea of how you work in conjunction with supervising attorneys?

Obviously, the attorneys must review the work product and make the final decision regarding strategy. However, immigration law allows paralegals to participate directly in the strategy sessions with attorneys. Often the paralegal does the extensive fact gathering, research, drafts of applications, and presents them to the attorney for review and discussion. We then sit down and discuss the proposed strategy, and it is rewarding to know that you formulated the blueprint in a difficult case.

Are there any frustrating aspects to your job as an immigration paralegal?

It is often frustrating to see the limited perspective many people have regarding cultural differences. For instance, a birth certificate may be a crucial document for an application, but your client may come from a culture where birth certificates are not issued and birth records are difficult, if not impossible, to obtain. Sometimes the process from passing a statute to implementing regulations for a new program is very slow, and this is frustrating. For instance, congress may pass a statute setting up a special program for a duration of two to three years' for certain foreign nationals to gain immigrant visas. However, it may be eighteen months before the regulations are implemented and another six months before the exact procedures and forms are ready from the Immigration and Naturalization Service. Thus, it may be just a few months before the sunset of the program before the staff is in place and the forms are ready, so the opportunity is practically lost before it is available.

On the surface, one would say that immigration paralegals fill out visa petitions and other applications, but you do much more. Could you explain in more depth what immigration paralegals do?

We do fill out many forms. However, we participate in much fact-finding and analysis before any forms are filled out. First, I make sure I know everything necessary about the procedure and substantive issues. This includes reviewing the applicable regulations and statutes. I also review treatises that specifically address the applicable immigration issues and get a sense of what type of supporting documents and strategy have worked in similar cases. Next, I discover the facts by interviewing the clients and any other parties involved such as officers of the corporation that wishes to have the foreign national as an employee. I organize the information and prepare the documentation to support the petition. For instance, I may need brochures, financial statements, and other information about the corporation, as well as documentation of the foreign national's education and work experience. I then draft supporting documents, such as affidavits, establishing that all requirements as stated in the regulations are met. Along the way, I keep the attorneys advised of developments and prepare the documents for their final review.

It sounds as if your writing skills are crucial. Is that correct?

Writing is an essential aspect of my job. The ability to express facts in ways that appeal to the adjudicator, while remaining true to the facts, can definitely increase your success ratio. Simplicity and clarity of style are crucial, and the overall presentation of the package is important. Good writing skills are essential for immigration paralegals.

Summary

A Brief Overview of Administrative Law

Administrative law controls how governmental agencies deal with you and how you deal with them. It is the law that concerns the powers and procedures of administrative agencies. Three major sources of administrative law are federal statutes, the laws passed by Congress giving authority to agencies and defining terms broadly; regulations, written statements issued by an administrative agency explaining in detail the substantive law and procedural requirements of the programs the agency administers; and judicial review, the courts' review of agency action.

Why Administrative Law Is Important

Administrative law offers job opportunities for paralegals, particularly in some of the fastest growing areas, such as environmental law. In some fields, such as Social Security disability, the regulations allow paralegals to represent claimants, including appearing at hearings before Administrative Law Judges. As society becomes more highly regulated, the actions of administrative agencies permeate the lives of individuals and businesses more and more. Even if paralegals do not work exclusively in the area of administrative law, their clients will have problems involving federal and state agencies, requiring some familiarity with administrative law.

How Administrative Law Fits into the United States System of Government

The United States Constitution establishes three branches of government. The legislative branch makes the laws, the executive branch enforces the laws, and the judicial branch interprets the laws. Administrative agencies do not fit neatly into any one branch of government. In fact, agencies generally have legislative, executive, *and* judicial powers. For instance, the INS has the power to develop regulations that govern the granting of political asylum, a legislative power; the power to deport a person who loses a claim for political asylum and has no other valid ground for staying in the United States, an executive power; and the power to hold hearings and determine whether a person is entitled to political asylum, a judicial power.

Delegation of Authority and Separation of Powers

Fundamental to the United States system of government is the separation of powers, the principle that each branch of government should be limited to activities in the area assigned to it and should not encroach upon the powers given to the other branches. A related principle is that of checks and balances, the principle that each branch performs its duties and in doing so provides checks and balances on the exercise of power by the other two branches. Because administrative agencies have broad powers that cut across the lines traditionally drawn by the separation of powers, some critics have asserted, particularly in the early part of the century, that the agencies' authority violates the principle of separation of powers.

The grant of authority by Congress to agencies is called delegation. Synonymous terms are delegation of authority and legislative delegation. In two decisions in the 1930s, *Shechter* and *Panama Oil*, the United States Supreme Court struck down legislation delegating certain powers to administrative agencies. In both cases, the Court found that the delegation of authority was not accompanied by sufficient standards to determine whether the delegated powers were being used as Congress intended. In subsequent cases, the Court has upheld even broad delegations of authority for several reasons. Congress has become more adept at stating intelligible standards in delegating legislation. Further, there are now many limitations on agency actions, such as trial-type hearings and judicial review.

The Necessity for Administrative Agencies

Employees of administrative agencies develop expertise in very technical areas, because they usually work in one narrow area of agency operations. One function of agencies is to share this expertise with the public. Agency employees can respond efficiently. Due to their expertise, they can process applications and dispose of cases much more rapidly than a court could in the course of protracted litigation. Agency expertise is also necessary to enable agencies to supervise highly technical areas such as nuclear energy and pollution control.

A Closer Look at the Types and Organization of Federal Administrative Agencies

One important distinction in understanding administrative agencies is the difference between executive agencies and independent agencies. Executive agencies are subject to direct Presidential control; the heads of executive agencies are part of the President's cabinet and can be removed from office without cause. Independent agencies are usually headed by multimember boards whose members serve rotating terms and who can be removed only with cause. The Immigration and Naturalization Service is part of an executive agency, the Department of Justice. The Equal Employment Opportunity Commission, Social Security Administration, and Environmental Protection Agency are independent agencies.

A Closer Look at the Functions of Federal Administrative Agencies

The overall task assigned to a federal agency by Congress is called the agency's mission. The primary mission of the Social Security Administration is to administer benefits, including benefits programs such as retirement insurance benefits, disability insurance benefits, and supplemental security income. The overall mission of the Equal Employment Opportunity Commission is to enforce employment discrimination laws. The Immigration and Naturalization Service has a combined mission of administering benefits, that is, the processing of applications for visas, as well as extensive enforcement duties, such as deporting aliens who have no legal basis to remain in the United States. The Environmental Protection Agency has a more complex mission. It not only enforces environmental protection statutes, but also carries out wide-ranging research projects. Further, the EPA sets national standards for pollution control and has monitoring functions, all in an effort to take a comprehensive, integrated approach to pollution control.

An Overview of State Administrative Agencies

Because of the numerous variations in state laws, paralegals must become familiar with the sources of law that govern the state agencies with which they work. These sources include the state's constitution, statutes, and regulations, as well as the case law in which state courts review the agencies' actions. State agencies perform many functions, including administration of benefits such as workers' compensation and Medicaid. State administrative agencies also perform many regulatory functions. They regulate entire professions by enforcing licensing requirements.

A Closer Look at the Work of an Immigration Law Paralegal

This section enables you to take a first-hand look at the work an immigration law paralegal performs. The interview explains the challenging and exciting duties of an immigration law paralegal. Note the emphasis on writing skills.

Review Questions

1. The branch of the United States government that interprets the laws is
   _____.
   a. the judicial branch
   b. the executive branch
   c. the legislative branch
   d. none of the above

2. The branch of the United States government that enforces the laws is
   _____.
   a. the judicial branch
   b. the executive branch
   c. the legislative branch
   d. none of the above

3. The principle that each branch of government provides oversight and
   restraint of the activities of other branches is _____.
   a. due process
   b. delegation of authority
   c. checks and balances
   d. none of the above

4. The grant of authority to agencies by Congress is called _____.

5. The courts' review of agency decisions is called _____.

6. Written statements issued by an administrative agency explaining
   substantive law and procedural requirements of programs the agency
   administers are _____.

7. Executive agencies are headed by one person, generally called the
   Secretary.   True ___ / False ___

8. The President may replace a person on the board of an independent
   agency without cause.   True ___ / False ___

9. The principle that each branch of government should be limited to
   the area assigned to it by the Constitution is called separation of
   powers.   True ___ / False ___

10. The Equal Employment Opportunity Commission is an independent
    agency.   True ___ / False ___

11. The Immigration and Naturalization Service has the authority to enforce
    laws but not to interpret them.   True ___ / False ___

12. Discuss the meaning of the term "administrative law."

13. There are three branches of the United States government. Describe the
    function of each branch and explain why administrative agencies have
    been viewed by some as a "derangement" of the traditional governmental
    structure.

14. Describe succinctly the missions of the Social Security Administration, the Equal Employment Opportunity Commission, the Immigration and Naturalization Service, and the Environmental Protection Agency.

15. Based on the interview with Adriana Taylor, does immigration law strike you as an interesting area of law? Why or why not?

Practical Applications

Exercise 1

For each of the following federal agencies, if the agency is an executive agency, state the Executive Department (e.g., Department of Health and Human Services) of which the agency is a part. If the agency is independent, simply state that it is an independent agency. Refer to The *United States Government Manual*.

1. Coast Guard

2. Health Care Financing Administration

3. Bureau of Indian Affairs

4. Food and Drug Administration

5. Federal Bureau of Investigation

6. Peace Corps

7. Central Intelligence Agency

8. National Park Service

9. Forest Service

10. Veterans Benefits Administration

Exercise 2

The object of this exercise is to become familiar with a federal agency in addition to the four that you learned about in Chapter 1. Pick a large executive or independent agency, and answer the following questions. Note: The *United States Government Manual* is a good place to begin. Turn in your answers on a separate sheet of paper.

1. Describe the mission of the agency.

2. Is the agency an executive agency or an independent agency?

3. If the agency is an executive agency, describe the Department of which it is a part, such as Department of Health and Human Services.

4. State the title and name of the person who heads the agency. If the agency is headed by a multimember board, name the members.

5. Cite at least two statutes that Congress has delegated to the agency to administer or enforce.

6. State the address of the area, district, or regional office nearest the city in which you live.

7. Suppose your law firm is suing the agency, attacking the validity of an action of that agency. Pursuant to Rule 4 of the *Federal Rules of Civil Procedure,* you must deliver the summons and complaint to the United States attorney for the district in which the action is filed and serve by certified or registered mail the Attorney General of the United States. You must also serve the agency by certified or registered mail.
   a. What is the address of the United States Attorney General?
   b. What is the address of the head of the agency you are suing?

8. Assume that you wish to apply for a job with the agency. Where do you direct your inquiry? State the specific address, if possible.

9. Does the agency produce pamphlets, books, or other publications? If so, state two of the titles.

10. Suppose that you wish to order a publication from a federal agency. The Government Printing Office prints and distributes publications for federal agencies.
   a. What are the titles of two free catalogs of Government publications?
   b. Give the address and phone number for ordering a publication from the Government Printing Office.

Case Analysis

Read the excerpts below from *Narenji v. Civiletti,* 617 F.2d 745 (D.C. Cir. 1979), *cert. denied,* 446 U.S. 957 (1980) and answer the following questions.

NARENJI

v.

CIVILETTI
United States Court of Appeals,
District of Columbia Circuit
ROBB, Circuit Judge:

This is an appeal from a judgment of the District Court declaring unconstitutional a regulation promulgated by the Attorney General at the direction of the President. In the circumstances of this case the court has concluded that the challenged regulation, issued November 13, 1979, must be sustained.

Regulation 214.5 requires all nonimmigrant alien post-secondary school students who are natives or citizens of Iran to report to a local INS office or campus representative to "provide information as to residence and maintenance of nonimmigrant status." At the time of reporting each student must present his passport and evidence of his school enrollment, of payment of fees, of the number of course hours in which he is enrolled, of his good standing, and his current address in the United States. The regulation provides that failure to comply with the reporting requirement will be considered a violation of the conditions of the nonimmigrant's stay in the

United States and will subject him to deportation proceedings under section 241(a)(9) of the Act.

The regulation is within the authority delegated by Congress to the Attorney General under the Immigration and Nationality Act. That statute charges the Attorney General with "the administration and enforcement" of the Act, and directs him to "establish such regulations . . . and perform such other acts as he deems necessary for carrying out his authority under the provisions of" the Act. He is directed to prescribe by regulation the time for which any nonimmigrant alien is admitted to the United States, and the conditions of such an admission. Finally, the Act authorizes the Attorney General to order the deportation of any nonimmigrant alien who fails to maintain his nonimmigrant status or to comply with the conditions of such status. These statutory provisions plainly encompass authority to promulgate regulation 214.5.

Recognizing the broad authority conferred upon the Attorney General by the Immigration and Nationality Act the District Court nevertheless thought that the Act does not empower him to draw distinctions among nonimmigrant alien students on the basis of nationality. We do not accept this conclusion. The statute need not specifically authorize each and every action taken by the Attorney General, so long as his action is reasonably related to the duties imposed upon him. Furthermore, we note that the Act, 8 U.S.C. § 1303(a), does specifically authorize the Attorney General "to prescribe special regulations and forms for the registration and fingerprinting of . . . (5) aliens of any other class not lawfully admitted to the United States for permanent residence." Finally, failure to maintain nonimmigrant status or to comply with the conditions of such status is specified as a ground for deportation. We conclude that promulgation of regulation 214.5 is directly and reasonably related to the Attorney General's duties and authority under the Act.

The District Court concluded that even if authorized by statute regulation 214.5 is unconstitutional because it violates the Iranian students' right to equal protection of the laws. The court found no basis for the "discriminatory classifica-tion" of the students established by the regulation. Here again we must differ. Distinctions on the basis of nationality may be drawn in the immigration field by the Congress or the Executive. So long as such distinctions are not wholly irrational they must be sustained.

By way of an affidavit from the Attorney General we are informed that his regulation was issued "as an element of the language of diplomacy by which international courtesies are granted or withdrawn in response to actions by foreign countries. The action implemented by these regulations is therefore a fundamental element of the President's efforts to resolve the Iranian crisis and to maintain the safety of the American hostages in Tehran." The Attorney General refers of course to the lawless seizure of the United States Embassy in Tehran and the imprisonment of the embassy personnel as hostages. Those actions denied to our embassy and citizens the protection to which they are entitled under the Amity Treaty in force between the United States and Iran and under international law. The lawlessness of this conduct of the Iranian government was recognized by the decision of the World Court on December 15, 1979. Thus the present controversy involving Iranian students in the United States lies in the field of our country's foreign affairs and implicates matters over which the President has direct constitutional authority.

The District Court perceived no "overriding national interest" justifying the Attorney General's regulation: it found that "although defendants' regulation is an understandable effort designed to somehow reply to the Iranian attack upon this nation's sovereignty and the seizure of its citizens, it is one that does not support a legitimate national interest". In this we think the District Court erred.

As we have said, classifications among aliens based upon nationality are consistent with due process and equal protection if supported by a rational basis. The Attorney General's regulation 214.5 meets that test; it has a rational basis. To reach a contrary conclusion the District Court undertook to evaluate the policy reasons upon which the regulation is based. In doing this the court went beyond an acceptable judicial role.

> For reasons long recognized as valid, the responsibility for regulating the relationship between the United States and our alien visitors has been committed to the political branches of the Federal Government. Since decisions in these matters may implicate our relations with foreign powers, and since a wide variety of classifications must be defined in the light of changing political and economic circumstances, such decisions are frequently of a character more appropriate to either the Legislature or the Executive than to the Judiciary.

> This court is not in a position to say what effect the required reporting by several thousand Iranian students, who may be in this country illegally, will have on the attitude and conduct of the Iranian government. That is a judgment to be made by the President and it is not for us to overrule him, in the absence of acts that are clearly in excess of his authority.

> In view of the foregoing the judgment of the District Court is reversed with directions to dismiss the complaints and enter judgment for the defendants.

> *So ordered.*

1. Did the District of Columbia Court of Appeals find that the regulation in question (8 C.F.R. § 214.5) was within the authority delegated to the Attorney General by Congress?
2. The court cited three sections of the Immigration and Nationality Act that give the Attorney General the power to establish regulations. Summarize the powers given to the Attorney General in these three sections.
3. Did the court describe the authority delegated to the Attorney General as narrow or broad?
4. Did the court require that the action taken by the Attorney General be specifically authorized in the Immigration and Nationality Act? Why?
5. In addition to their assertions that the regulation was beyond the Attorney General's delegated authority, the plaintiffs argued that the regulation was unconstitutional because it deprived them of equal protection of the laws. Why did the court uphold the regulation in face of the challenge of constitutionality?

Notes

1. This is a partial list of grounds for review as set forth in section 706 of the Administrative Procedure Act.
2. An important principle in administrative law is exhaustion of administrative remedies, which provides that a person may not seek judicial review until he has gone through all avenues of appeal within the agency. This topic is discussed in Chapter 7.
3. Kenneth Culp Davis, *Administrative Law and Government* (St. Paul: West Publishing Co., 1975), at 6.
4. *United States Government Manual, 1993–94* (Washington, D.C.: U.S. Government Printing Office), at 91.
5. I.N.A. § 101(a) (42) (A), 8 U.S.C. § 1101(a)(42)(A) (1982).
6. I.N.A. § 208(a), 8 U.S.C. § 1158(a) (1982).
7. *United States v. Pizzarusso*, 388 F.2d 8, 9 (2d Cir. 1968).
8. 8 C.F.R. § 208.17.

[9] Ernest Gellhorn & Ronald Levin, *Administrative Law and Procedure in a Nutshell,* 3d ed. (St. Paul: West Publishing Co., 1990), at 10.

[10] *FTC v. Ruberoid Co.,* 343 U.S. 470, 487–88 (1952).

[11] Gellhorn & Levin, *supra* note 9, at 13.

[12] *Id.* at 14.

[13] 295 U.S. at 541–42.

[14] Gary Moore, Arthur Magaldi & John Gray, *The Legal Environment of Business: A Contextual Approach* (Cincinnati: South-Western Publishing Co., 1987), at 130.

[15] 298 U.S. 388 (1935).

[16] Social Security Administration's 1994 Annual Report to Congress, at 40.

[17] *Id.* at 37.

[18] *United States Government Manual, supra* note 4, at 692.

[19] *Id.* at 692.

[20] *Id.* at 391.

[21] *Id.* at 566.

[22] *Id.* at 564.

[23] *Id.*

[24] The citation is 42 U.S.C. § 901.

[25] *United States Government Manual, supra* note 4, at 319.

[26] *Id.* at 565.

[27] *Id.* at 569.

[28] *Id.* at 364.

[29] *Id.* at 391.

[30] *Id.* at 561.

[31] *Id.* at 563.

[32] J. Gordon Arbuckle *et al., Environmental Law Handbook,* 12th ed. (Rockville, MD: Government Institutes, Inc.), at 3, 4.

IIII
CHAPTER 2

SOURCES
OF ADMINISTRATIVE LAW
AND PROCEDURE

If you have already taken a course in legal research, you have studied sources of law and research strategies. You may not, however, have delved into administrative law material in detail. Chapter 2 reviews the sources of administrative law and procedure, including statutes, regulations, case law, and executive orders.

The primary sources for administrative law are the same sources that you study in a general legal research course. Recall that **primary authority**, what is generally considered the mandatory law, is comprised in large part of federal and state constitutions, statutes, and court decisions (also called cases or judicial opinions). Primary authority also includes sources commonly encountered in administrative law, such as administrative regulations and executive orders. All these are primary sources of law, whether you are considering an administrative law issue or any other legal issues. Administrative law focuses more on certain primary sources of law, such as an agency's regulations.

Recall that **secondary authority** includes a multitude of other sources, anything other than primary authority, which can be persuasive, though not mandatory, in interpreting a primary source of law. For instance, if a relevant statute or regulation is unclear and there is no applicable case law, paralegals look to secondary sources of law, such as law review articles. As with primary sources of law, the secondary sources are basically the same for administrative law as for other areas of law. Important secondary sources are treatises, legal periodicals such as law review articles, and legal encyclopedias such as *Corpus Juris Secundum* (C.J.S.) and *American Jurisprudence* (Am. Jur.). Another secondary source is *American Law Reports* (A.L.R.). A.L.R. annotations offer a good example of how to use the same sources for administrative law as for other areas of law, just with a different emphasis. Recall that the A.L.R. set is divided into the First through Fifth Series, with a separate series entitled *A.L.R. Federal,* which addresses strictly federal issues. An annotation addressing an aspect of Social Security disability benefits or immigration law, which are exclusively issues of federal law, would be found in *A.L.R. Federal.*

The following discussion of sources of administrative law is not a comprehensive review of legal research materials in general. The discussion concentrates only on the materials that are most important in helping paralegals gain an overview of the essential sources of administrative law and procedure. In-depth knowledge of administrative

---

primary authority The mandatory enforceable law, including federal and state constitutions, statutes, and court decisions.

secondary authority Sources other than primary authority, which can be persuasive, though not mandatory, in interpreting a primary source of law.

sources of law assists paralegals in performing effective legal research in their first assignment with a law firm or other employer.

Constitutions

Central to the federal government is the United States Constitution, the supreme law of the land.

Read the United States Constitution. You will see no mention of federal agencies. Yet, without naming any agency, the Constitution affects every administrative agency in a fundamental way. State constitutions are equally central to every state government and affect the actions of state agencies.

The United States Constitution

As noted in Chapter 1, the United States Constitution establishes the basic structure of the federal government and sets forth the powers granted to the three branches of government, with article I granting legislative powers to Congress. Article II vests the executive power in the President and grants the President the power to appoint judges, cabinet members, and a host of other "Officers of the United States." Article III vests the judicial power in the Supreme Court and inferior courts, specifying areas over which the federal courts have jurisdiction.

Constitutional Restraints on Administrative Agencies

Restraints on agency actions are discussed in detail in Chapter 6. It is appropriate at the outset, however, to consider some of the broad constraints imposed on the actions of every administrative agency by the United States Constitution.

Administrative Agencies Cannot Enforce Unconstitutional Regulations. Administrative agencies' regulations are primary sources of law. It is important to remember, however, that the Constitution is the supreme law of the land. No agency's regulations are valid if they are unconstitutional. Thus, Congress may pass a statute and direct a certain agency to enforce the law. The agency then promulgates regulations detailing how it will enforce the law; however, if the agency's regulations set forth procedures or definitions that are forbidden by the Constitution, those regulations are unconstitutional and must be rewritten. For instance, regulations have been challenged on the basis that they are unconstitutionally vague. While the vagueness challenges do not often prevail, regulations are subject to the same scrutiny that statutes receive regarding allegations of vagueness.

Administrative Agencies Cannot Enforce Unconstitutional Statutes. Congress may pass a statute that turns out to be unconstitutional. If an administrative agency tries to enforce the unconstitutional statute, the courts may enjoin the agency from enforcement. An example of such a statute was the Immigration Marriage Fraud Act of 1986. The statute was passed because of a concern that an alien might marry a United States citizen solely for the purpose of becoming a lawful permanent resident and then the couple might divorce as soon as the alien had received a green card. This statute set forth new and more restrictive requirements for an alien to receive a green card by virtue of marriage to a United States citizen. One part of the statute required that the couple return for an interview with the (INS) two years after their marriage so that an INS examiner could assess the validity of the marriage, that is, whether the couple married for bona fide reasons or whether they married solely in order that the alien could get a green card.

There was another, more controversial provision in the Immigration Marriage Fraud Act which was struck down by at least one federal court before Congress repealed the provision. This portion of the statute provided that if an alien married a United States citizen while the alien was in deportation proceedings, the alien must live outside the United States for two years before applying for a green card. This left the United States citizen spouse with the unfortunate choice of leaving family and job in the United States to reside abroad for two years or of living in the United States without his or her spouse for two years. A federal court struck down this provision as unconstitutional on the grounds that it violated the fifth amendment due process and equal protection requirements.[1] When a statutory provision is struck down as unconstitutional, then the administrative agency cannot enforce the provision.

Restraints on Agency Actions Imposed by the Bill of Rights

The Constitution has a direct bearing on the actions an agency can take. Prominent in placing restraints on administrative agencies are the protections contained in the **Bill of Rights**, the first ten amendments to the United States Constitution.

BALLENTINE'S

Bill of Rights The first 10 amendments to the United States Constitution. The Bill of Rights is the portion of the Constitution that sets forth the rights which are the fundamental principles of the United States and the foundation of American citizenship.

An Overview of the Protections in the Bill of Rights. All the protections against unwarranted governmental intrusion afforded in the Bill of Rights apply with equal force to administrative agencies. Of particular importance are the first, fourth, and fifth amendments.[2] Consider the Internal Revenue Service (IRS), which has the power to collect taxes and prosecute tax-related fraud. The IRS does not, however, have a completely free hand in accomplishing the duties delegated to it. The fifth amendment prohibition of compulsory self-incrimination and the fourth amendment prohibition of unreasonable searches and seizures apply with equal force to the IRS just as they apply to the local police investigating a crime.

A Fundamental Protection: Due Process. Perhaps the most fundamental constitutional protection in the area of administrative law is the due process clause of the fifth amendment. The fifth amendment provides that no person may "be deprived of life, liberty, or property, without due process of law." The fifth amendment applies to the federal government, but the fourteenth amendment makes the due process requirements applicable to the states as well.

Essentially, the **due process** requirement protects persons from having the government take away their life, liberty, or property without a valid reason and adequate procedural protection. Consider a person who is receiving Social Security disability benefits because he was in an automobile accident and fractured a leg and both arms. The Social Security Administration (SSA) cannot simply decide that, because one year has passed, he must be able to work again and on this basis cease his disability benefits without giving him an opportunity to prove that he is in fact still disabled. Instead, the SSA sends the claimant for a medical examination to assess his physical condition and consults his treating physician for information about the claimant's current condition and limitations. If the SSA then determines that the claimant is no longer disabled, the claimant can appeal the determination and

---

BALLENTINE'S

due process of law Law administered through courts of justice, equally applicable to all under established rules that do not violate fundamental principles of fairness. Whether a person has received due process of law can only be determined on a case-by-case basis. In all criminal cases, however, it involves, at the very least, the right to be heard by a fair and impartial tribunal, the defendant's right to be represented by counsel, the right to cross-examine witnesses against him, the right to offer testimony on his own behalf, and the right to have advance notice of trial and of the charge sufficient in detail and in point of time to permit adequate preparation for trial. Due process requirements for criminal prosecutions are considerably more rigorous than those for civil cases. "Due process of law" is guaranteed by both the Fifth Amendment and the Fourteenth Amendment. *See* due process clause.

follow an appeal process that includes a hearing before an administrative law judge.

This illustrates due process, which is essentially a test of whether an agency has dealt with a person in a fundamentally fair manner. The text addresses due process in detail in Chapter 6. For now, it is important to remember that the fifth and fourteenth amendments' guarantee of due process is a fundamental restraint on agency actions. The purpose of the due process requirement is to ensure fundamental fairness when an agency action affects a person's life, liberty, or property. This constitutional protection permeates administrative law and procedure and is the basis of many important court decisions.

How to Find the United States Constitution

The United States Constitution is published in the three compilations of federal statutes—*United States Code* (U.S.C.), *United States Code Annotated* (U.S.C.A.), and *United States Code Service* (U.S.C.S.). The text of the Constitution is also published in pamphlet editions and in the back of *Black's Law Dictionary*. Because the United States Constitution is not frequently amended, locating the current text is not difficult.

The annotated publications of the Constitution are most helpful, for the same reason that annotated publications of statutes are helpful. **Annotations** include paragraph summaries of court decisions, arranged by subject matter, which provide a crucial link between the text of the statute or section of the Constitution and the court decisions interpreting them. The annotations also provide references to law review and other periodical articles, as well as the legislative history.

Both U.S.C.A. and U.S.C.S. contain annotations to aid research for each article and amendment of the United States Constitution.[3] The annotations are extensive; both U.S.C.S. and U.S.C.A. devote several volumes to the United States Constitution.

State Constitutions

Every state has its own constitution. The purpose of state constitutions is the same as that of the United States Constitution—that is, to set forth the basic framework of the government and to establish certain protections

---

BALLENTINE'S

annotation 1. A notation, appended to any written work, which explains or comments upon its meaning. 2. A commentary that appears immediately following a printed statute and describes the application of the statute in actual cases. Such annotations, with the statutes on which they comment, are published in volumes known as annotated statutes or annotated codes. 3. A notation that follows an opinion of court printed in a court report, explaining the court's action in detail.

and obligations for citizens of that state. State constitutions frequently have more detailed provisions than the United States Constitution. State constitutions address subjects peculiar to state and local governments, such as higher education facilities. See Figure 2–1 for an excerpt from the North Carolina Constitution.

FIGURE 2–1
Excerpt from
North Carolina
Constitution

Sec. 12. Higher education facilities.

Notwithstanding any other provisions of this Constitution, the General Assembly may enact general laws to authorize the State or any State entity to issue revenue bonds to finance and refinance the cost of acquiring, constructing, and financing higher education facilities to be operated to serve and benefit the public for any nonprofit private corporation, regardless of any church or religious relationship provided at no cost incurred earlier than five years prior to the effective date of this section shall be refinanced. Such bonds shall be payable from any revenues or assets of any such nonprofit private corporation pledged therefor, shall not be secured by a pledge of the full faith and credit of the State or such State entity or deemed to create an indebtedness requiring voter approval of the State or such entity, and, where the title to such facilities is vested in the State or any State entity, may be secured by an agreement which may provide for the conveyance of title to, with or without consideration, such facilities to the nonprofit private corporation. The power of eminent domain shall not be used pursuant hereto. (1985 (Reg. Sess., 1986), c. 814.)

Constitutional Restraints on State Agencies

State constitutions affect the actions of state administrative agencies just as the United States Constitution affects the actions of federal agencies. A state agency cannot enforce a law passed by the state legislature if that law is unconstitutional, nor can it enforce regulations that would abrogate the constitution. The state constitution also imposes broad constitutional controls on local government entities such as a local school system or zoning commission.

The United States Constitution, however, also comes into play when considering state constitutions. Recall the hierarchy of the law—the United States Constitution is the supreme law of the land. Thus, a state constitution cannot contain provisions that would diminish protections granted by the United States Constitution. A state is free, however, to grant even more protections than those contained in the United States Constitution. A state or local agency must be mindful not to take actions that abrogate either that state's constitution or the United States Constitution.

The requirement of due process is just as important on the state and local level as on the federal level. Even if a state constitution makes no mention of due process, the due process requirement applies nevertheless, because the fourteenth amendment specifically makes the requirement applicable to the states. Thus, a local zoning commission cannot unilaterally determine that a large shopping mall would fit in nicely at the end of the cul de sac on which you and your neighbors live. Instead, due process would require hearings where you would be given an opportunity to explain why this is not a good idea. In summary, all the constraints on agency action contained in the United States Constitution apply with equal force to state and local agencies, but a state constitution may impose additional protections as well.

How to Find State Constitutions

State constitutions are generally published with the compilation of the state statutes. Annotated texts similar to those available for the United States Constitution are also available. Paralegals may also use computer data bases such as LEXIS or WESTLAW to locate state constitutions.

Statutes of Broad Application

Statutes are an essential source of administrative law and procedure. As discussed in Chapter 1, Congress delegates to agencies the authority to carry out their mission and sets out the substantive law that the agency enforces by means of **enabling statutes.** An enabling statute applies specifically to the agency it addresses. An example is the Social Security Act, which delegates to, or enables, the Social Security Administration to determine whether a person is disabled.

There are, however, several very important statutes that apply to most agencies, such as the Administrative Procedure Act, the Freedom of Information Act, the Privacy Act, and the National Environmental Policy Act. The text addresses the Freedom of Information Act and the Privacy Act in detail in Chapter 8. It is important at the outset, however, to gain an overview of the statutes that have broad applicability and furnish a framework for administrative law and procedure. The text focuses on the Administrative Procedure Act (APA), the Freedom of Information Act (FOIA), the Privacy Act, and the

---

enabling statutes Statutes by which Congress delegates to agencies the authority to carry out their mission and sets out the substantive law that the agency enforces.

National Environmental Policy Act (NEPA). There are other important statutes of broad applicability, but the selected statutes are of fundamental significance to administrative law.

An excellent source for examining these and other important statutes addressing administrative procedure is the *Federal Administrative Procedure Sourcebook* (2d ed.), published by the Administrative Conference of the United States.

SIDEBAR

The Administrative Conference of the United States (ACUS) is an independent federal agency. Its purpose is to develop improvements in the procedures by which federal agencies conduct regulatory programs and generally perform their functions. ACUS conducts research and issues reports to the President, federal agencies, and the judiciary concerning procedural reform.[4] ACUS produces a wide range of publications which frequently carry great influence as Congress and the agencies themselves explore new procedures to help administrative agencies carry out their missions effectively.

The Administrative Procedure Act

A fundamental statute addressing administrative procedure is the Administrative Procedure Act (APA). The APA was signed into law in 1946 and has remained a basic framework for administrative procedure to this day.

General Background

In the 1930s, the number of administrative agencies increased dramatically with the new programs implemented as part of the New Deal. It became apparent that all agencies must be held to uniform procedures to ensure fairness and impartiality. President Roosevelt directed the attorney general of the United States to form a committee to study the administrative procedures then in place and to recommend ways to improve and make uniform the procedures used by agencies.[5] The committee's extensive studies and congressional hearings culminated in the Administrative Procedure Act (APA), which was signed into law by President Truman in 1946. The next year saw the publication of *The Attorney General's Manual on the Administrative Procedure Act* (*Attorney General's Manual*), which "remains the principal guide to the structure and intent of the APA."[6] The text of the *Attorney General's Manual* is published in the *Federal Administrative Procedure Sourcebook*.

How to Find the APA

The text of the APA is easy to find because it is part of the United States Code, that is, the compilation of federal statutes. The APA comprises sections 551–559, 701–706, 1305, 3344, 5372, and 7521 of Title 5 of the United States Code. Sections 551–559 address agency procedures such as rule making and adjudications, and sections 701–706 address judicial review. The other sections cited above deal with administrative law judges.[7]

Other Acts that Are Part of the APA

One aspect of the content of the APA could cause confusion when you are first becoming acquainted with it. Several of the most important acts governing agency procedures are actually part of the APA. These acts carry separate names, but are in Title 5 of the United States Code and constitute part of the APA. The most important of these are the Freedom of Information Act (FOIA) (5 U.S.C. § 552), the Privacy Act (5 U.S.C. § 552a), and the Government in the Sunshine Act (5 U.S.C. § 552b). Two other important acts, the Administrative Dispute Resolution Act and the Negotiated Rulemaking Act, were enacted in 1990 and are part of the APA.

These acts govern important aspects of administrative procedure and thus their inclusion as part of the APA makes sense. These acts are referred to by their own names, and you seldom hear them referred to as part of the APA. Do not let this confuse you.

Scope of the APA

The word "scope" is used in many ways when studying any area of law. Here, the word "scope" means the breadth of the coverage of the APA—to which parts of the federal government does the APA apply? The *Attorney General's Manual* explains that the APA applies, with certain exceptions, to every agency of the United States government. The APA defines "agency" as "each authority . . . of the government of the United States other than Congress, the courts, or the governments of the possessions, Territories, or the District of Columbia." The definition specifically excludes Congress and the courts. There are some other exceptions stated in section 551 of the APA, such as military commissions. Because the APA gives a broad definition of "agency" and does not specifically list every entity that is considered an "agency," there has been some litigation on the issue of whether certain governmental entities are agencies within the APA definition. For instance, a court has stated that the Library of Congress is not an agency under the APA.[8] For now, remember that the APA applies to most federal administrative agencies. Some agencies may be exempted from certain provisions of the APA. Throughout the discussion of administrative agencies, any important exemptions will be pointed out.

What the APA Requires Federal Agencies to Do

The purposes of the APA are set forth in the *Attorney General's Manual* as follows:

1. to require agencies to keep the public currently informed of their organization, procedures, and rules;
2. to provide for public participation in the rule-making process;
3. to prescribe uniform standards for the conduct of formal rule-making and adjudicatory proceedings, that is, proceedings required by statute to be made on the record after opportunity for an agency hearing;
4. to restate the law of judicial review.[9]

APA Guidelines for Rule Making. The requirements set forth in the APA will surface in the discussion of almost every aspect of administrative law. Consider, for instance, the process known as rule making. **Rule making** is the procedure agencies follow to promulgate their regulations. In the detailed discussion of rule making in Chapter 5, you will see that the APA sets forth specific steps agencies must follow, such as publishing their proposed regulations in the *Federal Register* so that the public can comment on the regulations before they go into effect.

APA Guidelines for Adjudications. The APA also sets forth guidelines that agencies must follow in adjudications. Speaking generally, **adjudications** are trial-type proceedings that determine the rights of one person or a small group of persons with related interests. For instance, a hearing before an administrative law judge (ALJ) to determine whether a person is entitled to disability insurance benefits is an adjudication. The ALJ reviews the written evidence and the testimony at the hearing and then issues a written decision explaining why the ALJ has determined the claimant is either "disabled" or "not disabled." This is an adjudication to determine whether a person is

---

rule making The procedure agencies follow in formulating, amending, or repealing their regulations.

--------------------------------- BALLENTINE'S ---------------------------------

adjudication The final decision of a court, usually made after trial of the case; the court's final judgment.

entitled to disability benefits under the Social Security Act. The ALJ follows procedures dictated by the APA. Adjudication procedures are discussed in detail in Chapter 8.

SIDEBAR

Adjudications are sometimes referred to as "**order making**," because the trial-type hearing culminates in an order explaining the agency's decision.

APA Guidelines for Judicial Review. Judicial review is a court's examination of agency action to determine whether the action was proper and within the agency's authority. Multiple sections of the APA address judicial review, discussed in detail in Chapter 9.

APA Guidelines for Public Information. The APA's requirement that agencies inform the public of their organization, procedures, and rules affects agency actions in a multitude of ways. Most of the public information provisions are in section 552, which requires agencies to publish certain information in the *Federal Register,* to make certain information available for inspection and copying, and to make certain information available to the public on request.

The public information requirements of the APA are essential for everyone who deals with administrative agencies. The *Attorney General's Manual* states that the purpose of the public information section of the APA is "to assist the public in dealing with administrative agencies by requiring agencies to make their administrative materials available in precise and current form."[11] Paralegals can deal with administrative agencies effectively only when they know the agencies' rules, organization, and procedures.

State Administrative Procedure Acts

States have their own administrative procedure acts, ensuring uniformity among state agencies. For instance, the North Carolina Procedure Act is found in chapter 150B of the General Statutes of North Carolina. The North Carolina APA requires the state to publish the *North Carolina Register,* the counterpart of the *Federal Register*. The *North Carolina Register* must be published at least two times a month and

---

order making Another term for adjudications.

BALLENTINE'S
---

judicial review 1. Review by a court of a decision or ruling of an administrative agency. 2. Review by an appellate court of a determination by a lower court.

must contain notices of proposed adoptions of rules, executive orders of the Governor, and other matters of public interest. The North Carolina APA also requires compilation of all agency rules in the North Carolina Administrative Code and addresses other pertinent subjects such as adjudications. Paralegals need to be familiar with their state's APA and codification of agency rules.

Many state administrative procedure statutes follow the general provisions of the Model State Administrative Procedure Act, which has been adopted by the National Conference of Commissioners on Uniform State Laws. The major provisions in the Model State Administrative Procedure Act (1981) are Public Access to Agency Law and Policy, Rule Making, Adjudicative Proceedings, and Judicial Review and Civil Enforcement. Not every state statute bears the title "Administrative Procedure Act," but every state has statutes addressing administrative procedure. See Figure 2–2 for the citations for each state.

FIGURE 2-2
Citations for State Administrative Procedure Acts

State	Citation
Alabama	ALA. CODE §§ 41-22-1 to 41-22-27
Alaska	ALASKA STAT. §§ 44.62.010–44.62.650
Arizona	ARIZ. REV. STAT. ANN. §§ 41-1001 to 41-1066
Arkansas	ARK. STAT. ANN. §§ 25-15-201 to 25-15-214
California	CAL. CODE § 11370 *et seq.* (West)
Colorado	COLO. REV. STAT. §§ 24-4-101 to 24-4-108
Connecticut	CONN. GEN. STAT. §§ 4-166 to 4-189
Delaware	DEL. CODE ANN. §§ 10101–10161
District of Columbia	D.C. CODE ANN. §§ 1-1501 to 1-1510
Florida	FLA. STAT. ANN. §§ 120.50–120.73 (West)
Georgia	GA. CODE ANN. §§ 50-13-1 to 50-13-23
Hawaii	HAW. REV. STAT. §§ 91-1 to 91-18
Idaho	IDAHO CODE §§ 67-5201 to 67-5219
Illinois	ILL. ANN. STAT. ch. 127, §§ 1001–1021 (Smith-Hurd)
Indiana	IND. CODE ANN. § 4-22-2-13 *et seq.* (Burns)
Iowa	IOWA CODE ANN. §§ 17A.1–17A.23 (West)
Kansas	KAN. STAT. ANN. §§ 77-501 to 77-549
Kentucky	KY. REV. STAT. §§ 13A.010-13A.330
Louisiana	LA. REV. STAT. ANN. §§ 49:950–49:970 (West)
Maine	ME. REV. STAT. ANN. tit. 5, §§ 8001–11008
Maryland	MD. STATE GOV'T CODE § 10-201 *et seq.*
Massachusetts	MASS. ANN. LAWS ch. 30A, §§ 1–17 (Law. Co-op.)
Michigan	MICH. COMP. LAWS ANN. §§ 24.201–24.315 (West)
Minnesota	MINN. STAT. ANN. §§ 14.01–14.69 (West)
Mississippi	MISS. CODE ANN. §§ 25-43-1 to 25-43-19
Missouri	MO. ANN. STAT. §§ 536.010–536.150 (Vernon)

FIGURE 2–2
(continued)

Montana	MONT. CODE ANN. §§ 2-4-101 to 2-4-711
Nebraska	NEB. REV. STAT. §§ 84-901 to 84-920
Nevada	NEV. REV. STAT. §§ 233B.010–233B.150
New Hampshire	N.H. REV. STAT. ANN. §§ 541A:1–541A:22
New Jersey	N.J. STAT. ANN. § 52:14B-1 *et seq.* (West)
New Mexico	N.M. STAT. ANN. §§ 12-8-1 to 12-8-25
New York	N.Y. STATE LAW § 100 *et seq.* (McKinney)
North Carolina	N.C. GEN. STAT. §§ 150B-1 to 150B-53
North Dakota	N.D. CENT. CODE §§ 28-32-01 *et. seq.*
Ohio	OHIO REV. CODE ANN. §§ 119.01 *et. seq.*
Oklahoma	OKLA. STAT. ANN. tit. 75, §§ 250.3–250.5, 302–323 (West)
Oregon	OR. REV. STAT. § 183.310 *et seq.*
Pennsylvania	2 PA. CONS. STAT. ANN. §§ 501–508
Rhode Island	R.I. GEN. LAWS §§ 42-35-1 to 42-35-18
South Carolina	S.C. CODE ANN. §§ 1-23-310 to 1-23-400 (Law. Co-op.)
South Dakota	S.D. CODIFIED LAWS ANN. §§ 1-26-1 to 1-26-41
Tennessee	TENN. CODE ANN. § 4-5-101 *et seq.*
Texas	TEX. ADMIN. CODE tit. 10, §§ 20001.001–20001.902
Utah	UTAH CODE ANN. §§ 63-46a-1 to 63-46a-16, 63-46b-1 to 63-46b-22
Vermont	VT. STAT. ANN. tit. 3, §§ 801–849
Virginia	VA. CODE ANN. §§ 9-6.14:1 to 9-6.14:25
Washington	WASH. REV. CODE ANN. §§ 34.05.001–34.05.902
West Virginia	W. VA. CODE §§ 29A-1-1 to 29A-7-4
Wisconsin	WIS. STAT. ANN. §§ 227.01–227.60 (West)
Wyoming	WYO. STAT. §§ 16-3-101 to 16-3-115

The Freedom of Information Act (FOIA)

Most of the public information requirements are in section 552 of the APA, which is commonly called the Freedom of Information Act (FOIA) (5 U.S.C. § 552). FOIA is discussed in more detail in Chapter 8; however, because FOIA is integral to the study of administrative law, paralegals need to be familiar with the basic provisions from the outset.

General Background

The Freedom of Information Act (FOIA) was enacted into law in 1966. FOIA underwent substantial amendments in subsequent years, most notably in 1974. The amendments narrowed some exemptions to disclosure of information, such as national security and law enforcement exemptions, and broadened other exemptions, such as those for business records.[12] FOIA applies to all federal agencies. The lead agency for implementation of FOIA is the Justice Department.

What FOIA Requires

FOIA requires agencies to publish and make available for public inspection and copying a wide range of information, including the methods by which the public may obtain information from the agency. Agencies must also publish their rules of procedure and descriptions of the forms the agencies use, as well as instructions on how to obtain the forms. Details of the information that FOIA requires to be published are discussed in more detail in Chapter 8. It is important to realize at the outset, however, that because of the public information requirements of FOIA, agencies must publish their regulations—both those that explain the substantive law, such as the definition of disability, and those that address procedure, such as how to appeal an initial determination that a person is not disabled.

Each agency must also publish in its regulations an explanation of how the agency is organized and where persons can go to get information and publications. For instance, the Immigration and Naturalization Service publishes a list of its offices and a list of forms available there. Excerpts of the list of forms are reprinted in Figure 2–3.

FIGURE 2–3
Excerpt from 8 CFR 299.1, Prescribed INS Forms

PART 299—IMMIGRATION FORMS

Sec.
299.1 Prescribed forms.
299.2 Distribution of Service forms.
299.3 Forms available from the Superintendent of Documents.
299.4 Reproduction of forms by private parties.
299.5 Display of control numbers.

AUTHORITY: 8 U.S.C. 1101, 1103; 8 CFR part 2.

§ 299.1 Prescribed forms.

The forms listed below are hereby prescribed for use in compliance with the provisions of Subchapter A and B of this chapter. To the maximum extent feasible the forms used should bear the edition date shown or as subsequent edition date.

Form No., Title and description

AR-4 (8-30-72)—Alien Registration Fingerprint Chart.
AR-11 (3-21-79)—Alien's Change of Address Card.
CDC 4.417 (11-74)—(Formerly HSM-240 or PHS-124) Medical Certificate.
CDC 4.422-1 (10-84)—Statement in Support of Application for Waiver of Excludability under section 212(a)(1), Immigration and Nationality Act.
CDC 4.422-2 (10-84)—Statement in Support of Application for Waiver of Excludability under section 212(a)(3), Immigration and Nationality Act.

Administrative agencies produce a multitude of publications. Although some publications are more detailed or obscure than you would hope, there are many government publications that are veritable gold mines of useful information. For instance, many agencies produce manuals to guide their employees in interpreting the law and making adjudications. Such publications can help paralegals understand both the applicable law and the point of view of the agency adjudicators. FOIA requires agencies to make available administrative staff manuals that affect members of the public, as well as statements of policy not published in the *Federal Register*. In addition, agencies must make available final opinions issued in the adjudication of cases by the agency.

The shared characteristic of the publications addressed by FOIA is that they are not already available to the public through the *Federal Register* or some other means of general publication. It is important for paralegals to know that it is not necessary to file a FOIA request to receive agency information that is already generally available to the public. Agencies have numerous publications that are available for sale from the Government Printing Office. Further, much general information is published in the *Federal Register*.

How to Find FOIA and Guides to Finding FOIA

Like the APA, the Freedom of Information Act is a federal statute and thus can be found in the published compilations of federal statutes, such as *United States Code Annotated* (U.S.C.A.). As with any statute, the annotations can be particularly helpful in interpreting the statute.

There are a host of publications that provide information about using and interpreting FOIA. The United States Department of Justice publishes the *Freedom of Information Case List,* which includes court cases involving FOIA and a bibliography of journal articles addressing FOIA issues, and the Justice Department Guide to FOIA. For additional bibliography of FOIA publications, see *Federal Administrative Procedure Sourcebook* (2d ed.).[14]

The Privacy Act

In some ways the Privacy Act is the flip side of FOIA. While FOIA delineates information that agencies must disclose, the Privacy Act delineates information that agencies must not disclose.

The Privacy Act is discussed in detail in Chapter 8. Like FOIA, however, the Privacy Act is such an essential part of administrative law that paralegals need to know the basic requirements from the beginning of their study of administrative law.

General Background

Agencies must maintain information about individuals in order to administer the programs delegated to them. For instance, the Social Security Administration needs your Social Security number in order to credit earnings to your account so that you will have the correct amount credited when you draw retirement benefits. Although agencies should have the information they need, individuals do not want the agencies to harbor an inordinate amount of information that they may not need. Further, individuals do not want the agencies to have incorrect information in their records. The Privacy Act addresses these concerns.

In the years after the Freedom of Information Act was implemented, concerns mounted about the information the government kept and disseminated. These concerns culminated in the Privacy Act, which was enacted into law in 1974. The next year significant amendments were added. The Privacy Act applies to "executive branch agencies and certain government-controlled corporations," but not to the legislative branch of the government.

How to Find the Privacy Act and Guides to Using the Privacy Act

The statutory cite for the Privacy Act is 5 U.S.C. § 552a. As you now know, this and other federal statutes are easily found in the *United States Code Annotated* (U.S.C.A.). As with FOIA, there are many treatises, government publications, and journal articles on the use and interpretation of the Privacy Act. For a bibliography, see *Federal Administrative Procedure Sourcebook* (2nd ed.).[16]

The lead agency responsible for implementation and oversight of the Privacy Act is the Office of Management and Budget (OMB). Both the OMB and the Department of Justice have published overviews and guidelines regarding the Privacy Act, which are listed in the *Sourcebook* bibliography.

What the Privacy Act Requires

The Privacy Act requires administrative agencies to publish in the *Federal Register* a notice of the existence and character of the system of records they maintain. Examples of the information they must publish include the name and location of the system, the categories of records kept, and the routine use of the records contained in the system.

Administrative agencies are required to maintain accurate, complete, and timely records.[17] The statute states that the purpose of this requirement is to "assure fairness to the individual" when the agency uses this information to make some determination regarding the individual. Consider your earnings record, which is maintained by the Social Security Administration. The SSA must maintain an accurate record of your earnings so that you will receive the proper disability or retirement benefits.

A central purpose of the Privacy Act is to give individuals access to information kept about them. The Privacy Act requires agencies to allow individuals to copy the information kept about them, request amendment of erroneous information, and request an accounting from the agency of the disclosures made about the individual.

Another important provision of the Privacy Act is that agencies cannot disclose information about an individual without that person's written request or prior written consent. There are twelve exceptions to this provision, which are explored in more detail in Chapter 8. For now, remember that an important exception is disclosure of information "for routine use." Routine use is defined in the Privacy Act as "the use of such record for a purpose that is compatible with the purpose for which it was collected." Suppose Ms. Andrews applies for Social Security disability benefits when she is age fifty-five. The amount of her monthly benefit is based on her earnings record, and higher earnings yield higher monthly benefit amounts. Using the earnings record to determine the monthly amount is a routine use, that is, one of the purposes for which the information was collected.

In addition to the affirmative steps that the Privacy Act requires of administrative agencies, the Act also restricts the information that agencies can maintain about individuals. Agencies are allowed to maintain in their records "only such information about an individual as is relevant and necessary to accomplish a purpose of the agency. . . ."[18]

National Environmental Policy Act

The National Environmental Policy Act (NEPA) requires all federal agencies to analyze and consider the impact their actions have on the environment. NEPA is a short statute, but its effects are wide reaching.

General Background

NEPA, enacted in 1970, was a response to the growing concern of Congress about the impact of federal agency actions on the environment. The "Congressional declaration of national environmental policy" stated in NEPA reads as follows:

> The Congress, recognizing the profound impact of man's activity on the interrelations of all components of the natural environment . . . declares that it is the continuing policy of the Federal Government, in cooperation with State and local governments, and other concerned public and private organizations to use all practicable means and measures . . . in a manner calculated to foster and promote harmony,

and fulfill the social, economic, and other requirements of present and future generations of Americans.

The general policy statement goes on to state that "it is the continuing responsibility of the Federal Government to use all practicable means . . . to improve and coordinate Federal plans, functions, programs, and resources" in order to achieve certain goals. These goals are stated very generally, and include acting as trustee of the environment for succeeding generations, assuring aesthetically pleasing surroundings, preserving historic and natural aspects of the national heritage, achieving a balance between population and resource use, and approaching the maximum attainable recycling of depletable resources.

Obviously Congress has far-reaching goals in NEPA. Paralegals must examine the statute and related regulations more closely to gain an understanding of the practical effect that NEPA has on the daily workings of administrative agencies.

What NEPA Requires

The heart of NEPA is the requirement of environmental impact statements. NEPA requires agencies to prepare an environmental impact statement (EIS) to accompany "every recommendation or report on proposals for legislation and other major Federal actions significantly affecting the quality of the human environment."[19] The language of the statute is broad and subject to interpretation. There have been an enormous number of lawsuits to determine whether the language of the statute applies to specific agency actions. Lawsuits have addressed such actions as federal timber sales, federal livestock grazing, and federal issuance of dredge-and-fill permits.[20] For instance, in interpreting whether an agency action was "major," a court held that the sale of twenty-six acres of trees by the Forest Service was not a "major" act.[21] NEPA is an excellent example of a broad statute passed by Congress and subsequently interpreted by the courts.

In further examining what NEPA requires agencies to do, it is important to remember what NEPA does *not* require agencies to do. NEPA does not require agencies to reach a particular result after assessing environmental consequences of a proposed action. Instead, NEPA imposes *procedures* that agencies must follow to ensure that the agencies assess the likely environmental consequences.

NEPA obviously applies to certain actions which the agencies themselves propose to take. NEPA also applies to actions permitted or approved by the agency.[22] Thus, if a private citizen or corporation seeks to take an action that is regulated by an administrative agency, NEPA requires that the agency assess the environmental consequences of the action for which the private party seeks permission. Courts have held that an EIS was required in connection with a request for permission to sell timber, but was not required when a private concessioner sought permission for an advertising campaign to increase tourism in Yosemite National Park.[23]

It is important to note that agencies have the authority to determine that an EIS is not necessary. The agency's first step is to prepare an environmental assessment (EA). The EA has been described as "a kind of mini-EIS."[24] If after this preliminary analysis of likely environmental impact the agency decides that a full-blown EIS is not necessary, the agency issues a "finding of no significant impact." The preparation of an EIS is lengthy and expensive, so the "finding of no significant impact" (FONSI) is a determination of far-reaching consequence. A FONSI may, however, be challenged in court.

Timing and Content of Environmental Impact Statements. The NEPA statute provides that an EIS must include a "detailed statement" of:

> (i) the environmental impact of the proposed action,
> (ii) any adverse environmental effects which cannot be avoided should the proposal be implemented,
> (iii) alternatives to the proposed action,
> (iv) the relationship between local short-term uses of man's environment and the maintenance and enhancement of long-term productivity, and
> (v) any irreversible and irretrievable commitments of resources which would be involved in the proposed action should it be implemented.[25]

As frequently occurs in administrative law, the applicable statute gives the broad overview, and the applicable regulations give the details. For instance, the regulations state that the EIS should normally be less than 150 pages, and for proposals of unusual complexity, less than 300 pages.[26] In regard to actual content, the regulations require a discussion of adverse environmental effects that cannot be avoided if the proposal is implemented and any irreversible commitments of resources. See Figure 2–4 for an excerpt from these regulations, further detailing the content of the EIS.

FIGURE 2–4
40 CFR 1502.7

> **§ 1502.7   Page limits.**
>
> The text of final environmental impact statements (e.g., paragraphs (d) through (g) of § 1502.10) shall normally be less than 150 pages and for proposals of unusual scope or complexity shall normally be less than 300 pages.

The regulations also describe the parties to whom the EIS must be circulated, the parties from whom comments must be invited, and the means by which the agencies may respond to the comments. Further, the regulations require that after the agency has completed its analysis and reached a decision, it must prepare a public record of its decision stating the decision reached, the alternatives considered in reaching its decision, and whether all practicable means have been adopted to avoid or minimize environmental harm.

Summary of the Impact of NEPA on Agency Action. NEPA is a good example of a statute that affects all federal agencies. It is also a good example of how regulations fill in the details of a broad statute and how courts play their role in interpreting a statute.

While NEPA cannot prevent an agency from taking an action that harms the environment, it is a powerful tool for delaying agency action in order to force a careful analysis of environmental impact. One commentator has observed that "[f]ear of NEPA litigation has revolutionized agency decisionmaking by making environmental review the most significant condition precedent to the undertaking of a major federal action."[27]

How to Find NEPA and Guides to Using NEPA

NEPA is a federal statute and thus easily found in the *United States Code.* See 42 U.S.C. §§ 4321–4347. The regulations can be found in 40 CFR Parts 1500–1508.

When Congress enacted NEPA, it also created the Council on Environmental Quality (CEQ), which has the primary responsibility for overseeing NEPA. The CEQ is part of the Executive Office of the President, and is composed of three members appointed by the president. One duty of the CEQ is to prepare the annual environmental quality report, which NEPA requires the president to present to Congress. The CEQ also issues the regulations discussed above, which provide guidance on definitions such as "major federal action," as well as procedural guidance, such as the length and format of the EIS.

In addition to the regulations, which help to interpret the statute, the CEQ has provided ongoing guidance. Its publications include a "Memorandum to Agencies Containing Answers to 40 Most Asked Questions on NEPA Regulations." This memorandum is published in the ACUS *Sourcebook,* together with an extensive bibliography of government documents, books, and articles analyzing NEPA.[28]

Enabling Statutes

So far the discussion has focused on statutes that impose requirements on many, or all, administrative agencies. These statutes of broad application impose general requirements on how agencies operate. Regardless of the mission Congress has delegated to an agency, that agency must comply with these requirements. Thus, statutes such as FOIA and NEPA apply equally to the Social Security Administration, Immigration and Naturalization Service, Environmental Protection Agency, and Equal Employment Opportunity Commission.

In contrast, Congress also passes statutes that apply specifically to only one agency. These are the enabling statutes, the statutes by which Congress delegates to agencies the authority to carry out their missions.

Purposes of Enabling Statutes

Enabling statutes have two basic purposes—"to establish the agency and its powers and to set out the substantive rules of law the agency is to carry out."[29] Thus, in enabling statutes, Congress describes the person, such as the Administrator of the Environmental Protection Agency, who heads the agency. Congress also states broadly the substantive law, with key definitions, such as the meaning of "disabled" as used in the Social Security Act or the actions that may constitute retaliation within the meaning of Title VII.

SIDEBAR   Remember that statutory definitions can differ from your own understanding of what a word means in everyday life. For instance, when you read your disability insurance policy issued by a private insurance company, the policy probably defines "disability" as the inability to perform your job. In contrast, "disability" as defined in the Social Security Act means the inability to perform your job *or any other job* that exists in significant numbers in the national economy.

Examples of Enabling Statutes

Here is the section of the Social Security Act in which Congress delegates to the Social Security Administration the authority to determine whether a person is disabled:

FIGURE 2–5
42 U.S.C. § 405(a)

> SEC. 205. [42 U.S.C. 405] (a) The Secretary shall have full power and authority to make rules and regulations and to establish procedures, not inconsistent with the provisions of this title, which are necessary or appropriate to carry out such provisions, and shall adopt reasonable and proper rules and regulations to regulate and provide for the nature and extent of the proofs and evidence and the method of taking and furnishing the same in order to establish the right to benefits hereunder.
>
> (b)(1) The Secretary is directed to make findings of fact, and decisions as to the rights of any individual applying for a payment under this title. Any such decision by the Secretary which involves a determination of disability and which is in whole or in part unfavorable to such individual shall contain a statement of the case, in understandable language, setting forth a discussion of the evidence, and stating the Secretary's determination and the reason or reasons upon which it is based. . . .

In the following section of the Social Security Act, Congress defines "disability" as follows:

FIGURE 2–6
42 U.S.C. § 423(d)

> ### Definition of Disability
>
> (d)(1) The term "disability" means—
>
> (A) inability to engage in any substantial gainful activity by reason of any medically determinable physical or mental impairment which can be expected to result in death or which has lasted or can be expected to last for a continuous period of not less than 12 months; or
>
> (B) in the case of an individual who has attained the age of 55 and is blind (within the meaning of "blindness" as defined in section 216(i)(1)), inability by reason of such blindness to engage in substantial gainful activity requiring skills or abilities comparable to those of any gainful activity in which he has previously engaged with some regularity and over a substantial period of time.

The first thing you will note is that delegating statutes are very broad. After reading the enabling statute and the statutory definition of "disability," many questions remain unanswered. This is typical of enabling statutes and the statutes defining important terms in the programs that agencies administer and enforce.

A similar example from Title VII further illustrates this point. The section of Title VII that makes it unlawful for an employer to retaliate against an employee who opposes unlawful employment practices (42 U.S.C. § 2000e-3(a)) reads as follows:

FIGURE 2–7
42 U.S.C.
§ 2000e-3(a)

§ 2000e-3. Other unlawful employment practices

(a) It shall be an unlawful employment practice for an employer to discriminate against any of his employees or applicants for employment, for an employment agency, or joint labor-management committee controlling apprenticeship or other training or retraining, including on-the-job training programs, to discriminate against any individual, or for a labor organization to discriminate against any member thereof or applicant for membership, because he has opposed any practice made an unlawful employment practice by this subchapter, or because he has made a charge, testified, assisted, or participated in any manner in an investigation, proceeding, or hearing under this subchapter.

In the next section of Title VII (42 U.S.C. § 2000e-4), Congress created the Equal Employment Opportunity Commission. Refer to the excerpt in Figure 2–8.

FIGURE 2–8
42 U.S.C.
§ 2000e-4

§ 2000e-4. Equal Employment Opportunity Commission

(a) There is hereby created a Commission to be known as the Equal Employment Opportunity Commission, which shall be composed of five members, not more than three of whom shall be members of the same political party. Members of the Commission shall be appointed by the President by and with the advice and consent of the Senate for a term of five years. . . .

You have the same impression after reading portions of Title VII that you had after reading portions of the Social Security Act. Congress has delegated authority to the SSA and EEOC in a very broad manner. Reading the statutes alone leaves numerous unanswered questions. For instance, you still do not know the type of analysis that the SSA uses to determine whether a person falls within the statutory definition of disability. You do not know where to file an application or how to appeal an unfavorable determination by the SSA. In regard to Title VII, you still do not know how to file a charge with the EEOC when an employer has retaliated against an employee. You do not know what types of actions might constitute retaliation or the actions that the local EEOC employees must take before they are allowed to file a lawsuit on the employee's behalf in federal court.

Congress does not generally fill in the details when it passes legislation delegating authority to administrative agencies. At most, Congress generally states broadly the substantive law, creates the agency, and defines some key terms. Congress then leaves it to the agencies to fill in the details. This leads us to a discussion of one of the most fundamental sources of administrative law—regulations.

Regulations

Most paralegal students have a good understanding of statutes. They are comfortable with the fact that statutes are the laws that must be followed. Many paralegal students, however, do not grasp the significance of regulations without in-depth consideration of these questions—What are regulations? How do you find them? How do you find explanations and interpretations when the meaning of a regulation is not readily apparent?

What Regulations Are

Regulations are written statements issued by an administrative agency, explaining in detail the substantive law and the procedural requirements of the programs the agency administers. An example of substantive law is a detailed definition of a key term used in the enabling statute, such as the term "disability." An example of procedural law is a detailed description of how a person files an application and the steps for appealing an unfavorable determination by the agency. Agencies establish their rules of practice through regulations.

The purpose of regulations is to fill in the details that Congress did not address in the enabling legislation. Agency regulations frequently contain language that sounds similar to statutes. Regulations, however, are generally more detailed and technical.[30]

BALLENTINE'S

regulation 1. The act of regulating. 2. A rule having the force of law, promulgated by an administrative agency; the act of rule making. 3. A rule of conduct established by a person or body in authority for the governance of those over whom they have authority.

Regulations that Explain the Substantive Law

Now that you have some idea of the purpose and general content of regulations, it is instructive to read some actual regulations promulgated by the Social Security Administration. First, examine a regulation that explains a term used in the statute defining "disability." The statute defined "disability" as the "inability to engage in substantial gainful activity. . . ." The statutory definition, however, does not tell us what "substantial gainful activity" means. The statutory definition of "disability" has little meaning if you do not know what "substantial gainful activity" means. Here is the regulation that gives an explanation:

FIGURE 2–9
20 CFR 404.1572

---

§ 404.1572 What we mean by substantial gainful activity.
Substantial gainful activity is work activity that is both substantial and gainful:

(a) *Substantial work activity.* Substantial work activity is work activity that involves doing significant physical or mental activities. Your work may be substantial even if it is done on a part-time basis or if you do less, get paid less, or have less responsibility than when you worked before.

(b) *Gainful work activity.* Gainful work activity is work activity that you do for pay or profit. Work activity is gainful if it is the kind of work usually done for pay or profit, whether or not a profit is realized.

(c) *Some other activities.* Generally, we do not consider activities like taking care of yourself, household tasks, hobbies, therapy, school attendance, club activities, or social programs to be substantial gainful activity.

Although you may still have some questions about the term "substantial gainful activity," the regulation gives far more explanation than the statute. Note that the regulation is written in a rather conversational tone, rather than the compact and sometimes difficult style frequently encountered in statutes.

Regulations that Explain Procedure

The Social Security regulations contain a subpart explaining the procedure for filing an application for disability benefits. A **subpart** is simply a section of regulations addressing a common subject. Subpart G contains the regulations explaining how to file an application, subpart

---

subpart A section of regulations addressing a common subject.

H explains the types of evidence that the SSA considers, and so forth. It is fairly common to find a section at the beginning of a subpart that explains the definitions used in the subpart. For instance, 20 CFR 404.601 and 404.602 give the following definitions:

FIGURE 2–10
20 CFR 404.601
and 404.602

GENERAL PROVISIONS

§ 404.601   Introduction.

This subpart contains the Social Security Administration's rules for filing a claim for old-age, disability, dependents', and survivors' insurance benefits as described in subpart D of part 404. It tells what an application is, who may sign it, where and when it must be signed and filed, the period of time it is in effect and how it may be withdrawn. This subpart also explains when a written statement, request, or notice will be considered filed. Since the application form and procedures for filing a claim under this subpart are the same as those used to establish entitlement to Medicare benefits under 42 CFR part 405, persons who wish to become entitled to Medicare benefits should refer to the provisions of this subpart. Requirements concerning applications for the black lung benefits program are contained in part 410. Requirements concerning applications for the supplemental security income program are contained in part 416. Part 422 contains the requirements for applying for a social security number.

§ 404.602   Definitions.

For the purpose of this subpart—

Applicant means the person who files an application for benefits for himself or herself or for someone else. A person who files for himself or herself is both the *applicant* and the *claimant.*

Application refers only to an application on a form described in § 404.611.

Benefits means any old-age, disability, dependents', and survivors' insurance benefits described in subpart D, including a period of disability.

Claimant means the person who files an application for benefits for himself or herself or the person for whom an application is filed.

We, us, or *our* means the Social Security Administration (SSA).

You or *your* means, as appropriate, the person who applies for benefits, the person for whom an application is filed, or the person who may consider applying for benefits.

The regulations that follow the definitions give instructions for the actual filing of an application for Social Security disability benefits. For instance, 20 CFR 404.611 states that "[you] must apply for benefits on an application we prescribe." The regulations also explain who may sign the application (20 CFR 404.612) and when an application is considered filed (20 CFR 404.614). This is a small sample of regulations that explain procedure.

General Characteristics of Regulations

Having read some regulations, paralegal students can now identify some common characteristics.

Regulations Have Broad Applicability

First, regulations have broad, general application. The Social Security regulations instruct everyone applying for disability benefits to follow a certain procedure.

Many applicants for disability benefits (claimants) will eventually have a hearing with an administrative law judge (ALJ), because this is the procedure for appeal provided by the regulations. The ALJ will then issue a decision *specifically for that individual claimant,* explaining whether that claimant is disabled. This is an adjudication, that is, a decision addressing the facts of a specific person's case and explaining why or why not that person is disabled, applying the applicable statutes and regulations. In contrast to regulations, which apply broadly to entire groups of persons, an adjudication is a decision that applies to a specific person.

Regulations Have Future Effect

Regulations prescribe procedures and interpretations of substantive law that will take effect after the regulations have been properly implemented. After the steps for implementing the regulations have been followed, the regulations become applicable to the situations they address. For instance, if the SSA issued regulations revising the analysis it uses to determine whether a person is disabled, then the revised method would be used for all future claimants.

One purpose of regulations is to give the public notice of the rules, definitions, and procedures agencies will use. Only when paralegals have access to the agencies' current regulations can they effectively seek benefits from an agency and comply with the rules that the agencies enforce. Thus, paralegals must know how to find the current regulations. There is an established procedure for publishing regulations.

How to Find Regulations

In order to understand how to find current regulations, paralegals must first have an overview of the process by which regulations are made. The process that agencies must follow in formulating, amending, or repealing a rule is called rule making, and the actual requirements for this process are established in the Administrative Procedure Act. For now, the text will address only the basic rule-making procedure, which is called **informal** or **notice-and-comment rule making.**

The Procedure for Informal Rule Making

Section 553 of the Administrative Procedure Act (APA) sets forth the procedure for informal rule making. There are three basic steps.

Notice. First, the agency must publish a notice of proposed rule making in the *Federal Register*. The notice must include the statutory authority for issuing the proposed regulations. The notice must describe "either the terms or substance of the proposed rule or a description of the subjects and issues involved."[31]

Comment. The agency must then give interested parties "an opportunity to participate in the rule making through submission of written data, views, or arguments . . . ."[32] The comments are usually submitted in writing, although the agency has the discretion to allow oral presentations. Proposed regulations state the name and address of the person to whom the written comments are mailed, and the period allowed for submission of comments is generally thirty days. Section 553(c) of the APA requires the agency to consider the written comments received. Sometimes the agency makes substantial revisions after considering the comments. For instance, in August 1987 the INS issued proposed regulations for the adjudication of asylum claims. These proposed regulations generated intense public debate and comment because the INS sought to remove immigration judges from the asylum adjudication process. The proposed regulations were revised, and the jurisdiction of immigration judges was retained.

Issuance of Final Regulations. After considering the public comments, the agency publishes its final rules. Section 553(c) of the APA requires that the agencies incorporate in the final rules "a concise general statement of their basis and purpose." This statement is

---

informal rule making A process for developing regulations that consists of publication of proposed regulations (notice), comment from the public, and publication of final regulations.

sometimes brief. For instance, final regulations addressing political asylum, issued in July 1990, stated that "[t]he Department believes that promulgation of this final rule will facilitate the adjudication of claims for asylum . . . in a manner consistent with the Refugee Act of 1980."

Publication of Regulations

The proposed regulations and the final regulations are published in the *Federal Register*. The *Federal Register* is published daily. Regulations are published in the *Federal Register* chronologically, as they are issued. After regulations become final, they are then published in the *Code of Federal Regulations* (CFR). The regulations in CFR are arranged by agency and subject matter. For instance, regulations issued by the INS are in the same volume, with the regulations governing political asylum grouped together. This process is similar to the publication of federal statutes. At the end of each congressional session, the federal laws enacted during that session are published in *Statutes at Large,* with the laws arranged chronologically. The laws are then published in *United States Code,* where they are arranged by subject matter. Obviously, the *Code of Federal Regulations* and *United States Code* are easiest to use, because it is so much easier to find materials arranged by subject matter.

A Closer Look at the *Federal Register*

Perhaps the best explanation of the purpose of the *Federal Register* is found in the introductory pages of the *Federal Register* itself: "The *Federal Register* provides a uniform system for making available to the public regulations and legal notices issued by Federal agencies." Remember that the purpose of publication is to give notice to parties who may be affected. Publication in the *Federal Register* is deemed sufficient to give the required notice.[33]

Contents of the *Federal Register*. As noted, the *Federal Register* contains agencies' proposed and final regulations. Many other documents are also in the *Federal Register*. As the preface to the *Federal Register* states, "[t]hese include Presidential proclamations and Executive Orders and Federal agency documents having general applicability and legal effect, documents required to be published by act of Congress and other Federal agency documents of public interest." Regulations and executive orders are published again in the *Code of Federal Regulations*. Some materials, however, are published only in the *Federal Register*. An example is the discussion of comments received about proposed regulations. An excerpt from the comments received about proposed regulations, published in the *Federal Register* on July 27,

1990, appears in Figure 2–11. These comments are useful in evaluating the meaning and purpose of the final regulations. Thus, although the *Federal Register* is published daily, its contents have permanent value.

FIGURE 2–11
Excerpt from Comments in *Federal Register* About Proposed Political Asylum Regulations (July 27, 1990)

II. Analysis and Discussion of Comments

(1) *8 CFR 208.1—General.* The final rule creates the position of Asylum Officer within the Office of Refugees, Asylum, and Parole ("CORAP") in INS; requires that such officers receive specialized training in the relevant fields of international relations and international law under the co-direction of the Assistant Commissioner, CORAP, and the Director of the Asylum Policy and Review Unit of the Department of Justice ("APRU"); and reflects the role of the Deputy Attorney General and APRU in providing those officers with current information as an ongoing component of their training. In addition, under § 208.1, the new standards and procedures established in the final rule will apply only to applications for asylum or withholding of deportation filed on or after the date the rule becomes effective, unless a motion to reopen or reconsider under the new rule is granted. In addition, it is provided that a documentation center shall be maintained for the collection and dissemination of information on human rights conditions. The creation of a documentation center is an addition to the rule. It was felt that this would be a very positive development in aiding Asylum Officers to maintain current knowledge of country conditions around the world. It also reflects recent developments in the methods used to aid in the adjudication of asylum cases in other countries, such as Canada.

Many comments on the previously published rules have raised the objection that the adjudication of asylum cases will remain within INS, since the Service is also responsible for enforcement functions. This regulation creates an asylum adjudications function which is separate from INS enforcement functions. The Asylum Officers will be directed and supervised by CORAP and will deal only with asylum cases.

(2) *8 CFR 208.2—Jurisdiction.* Under the final rule, affirmative applications for asylum or withholding of deportation are to be referred in the first instance to an Asylum Officer and adjudicated in a nonadversarial setting. At the same time, the final rule provides for continued adversarial adjudications of asylum and withholding of deportation applications by Immigration Judges for those applicants who are in exclusion or deportation proceedings. Paragraph (b) provides that the "Immigration Judge shall make a determination on such claims *de novo* regardless of whether or not a previous application was filed and adjudicated by an Asylum Officer prior to the initiation of exclusion or deportation proceedings." Thus the final rule maintains a system of adjudication parallel to that established in the 1980 interim rule with the exception that Asylum Officers reporting directly to CORAP will now assume the jurisdiction formerly exercised by District Directors.

How to Find and Cite Materials in the Federal Register. Legal research courses and publications give paralegals in-depth explanations of how to locate materials in the *Federal Register*. Paralegals simply need a reminder for purposes of the study of administrative law.

Although the *Federal Register* publishes items chronologically, there are some guidelines for the order within each volume. Generally, materials are grouped in the following order: presidential documents, rules and regulations, proposed rules, notices (such as deadlines for applications), and notices of Sunshine Act meetings.

Each day's issue of the *Federal Register* is published as a paperback pamphlet. Some libraries eventually bind the daily pamphlets into a hardbound volume for easier use. Each year's issues of the *Federal Register* constitute a volume. Within each volume, the pages are numbered consecutively throughout the year.

Citation Form The *Federal Register* itself states that the proper citation is to use the volume number and the page number. For example, the final regulations for political asylum, excerpts of which are in Figure 2–11, were published in Volume 55 of the *Federal Register,* beginning on page 30674. This was the issue published on Friday, July 27, 1990. The citation is 55 FR 30674. *A Uniform System of Citation,* rule 14, calls for a more expanded citation form for the *Federal Register.* You can read rule 14 and note the forms given for proposed regulations, notices of meetings, and other materials published in the *Federal Register.* Note that *A Uniform System of Citation* (commonly called the "Blue Book") uses the abbreviation "Fed. Reg." rather than "FR" and that it provides that the year should also be given. Thus, the citation "55 FR 30674" in "Blue Book" form would be 55 Fed. Reg. 30,674 (1990).

SIDEBAR

This textbook uses the citation forms given in *Federal Register* and the *Code of Federal Regulations.* Many instructors or employers may prefer the forms given in *A Uniform System of Citation.* Note that if you are appealing an administrative decision in federal court, you should comply with the federal court's local rules. Federal court rules for citation are often very exact and sometimes differ from *A Uniform System of Citation.*

Finding Aids. At the front of every issue of the *Federal Register* is a table of contents. This lists each agency in alphabetical order, followed by the proposed and final rules, notices, and other materials issued by that agency in that issue. A small excerpt appears in Figure 2–12. The government publishes *Federal Register Index,* cumulated monthly and yearly.

FIGURE 2–12
Excerpt of List of
Agencies and
Documents in the
Federal Register

Environmental Protection Agency
NOTICES
Clean Air Act:
  Oxygenated gasoline waiver applications—
    California, 21719
Drinking water:
  Public water supply supervision program—
    New Hampshire, 21719
Environmental statements; availability, etc.:
  Agency statements—
    Comment availability, 21720
    Weekly receipts, 21721
Meetings:
  Gulf of Mexico Program Citizens Advisory Committee, 21721
  Gulf of Mexico Program Management Committee, 21721
  Gulf of Mexico Program Policy Review Board, 21722
Superfund program:
  Confidential business information and data transfer to contractors,
    21722
Toxic and hazardous substances control:
  Premanufacture notices receipts, 21723
Water pollution control:
  Clean Water Act—
    State water quality standards; approval and disapproval lists and
      individual control strategies; availability, 21724

Executive Office of the President
See Trade Representative, Office of United States

Export Administration Bureau
NOTICES
Export privileges, action affecting:
  Pan Aviation, Inc., 21703
  Soghanalian, Sarkis, G., 21704

Paralegals can review the many texts available on legal research for further explanation of finding aids for administrative law materials. The explanation and illustration of every source for legal research is beyond the scope of this text.

Loose-leaf Services as a Finding Aid. Some attorneys and paralegals whose work requires daily interaction with administrative agencies review the *Federal Register* every day, especially if they work in a highly regulated area with rapidly changing regulations. Unless you read the *Federal Register* regularly, it may be difficult to find materials without a specific citation to take you to the right volume and page. Luckily, loose-leaf services are widely available for many areas of administrative law. A **loose-leaf service** is a set of volumes that gathers the sources of law, with explanatory text, for one particular area of law. Publishers use the loose-leaf format, generally three-ring binders, so that various sections can be removed easily and replaced with updated materials. Loose-leaf services and other specialized publications for areas of administrative law are discussed below, beginning on page 80.

A Closer Look at the *Code of Federal Regulations*

Before exploring in depth the content of the *Code of Federal Regulations,* it is essential to understand the relationship between the *Code of Federal Regulations* and the *Federal Register*. As noted, an agency publishes proposed regulations in the *Federal Register,* and, after reviewing comments received through the notice and comment process, the agency publishes the final regulations in the *Federal Register*. The public notice requirement has then been met, and the final regulations are ready for publication in the *Code of Federal Regulations*. Thus, the *Code of Federal Regulations* (CFR) contains only the agencies' final regulations.

The volumes of the CFR are updated and published once a year. Agency regulations, however, can change frequently. Thus, the regulations printed in the CFR may not be current. The *Federal Register* contains the current regulations. Obviously a publication that is issued daily is more reliable as the source for the current regulations than a publication issued yearly. The *Federal Register* is the research tool to use to check the status of the regulations and to make sure that you are using the current regulations. Just as attorneys and paralegals would not cite a court decision that has been overruled, they would not cite regulations that have been amended or rescinded. Only by using the CFR and the *Federal Register* together can paralegals be sure that they have the latest version of a regulation.

Contents of the *Code of Federal Regulations*. Perhaps the best explanation of the content and organization of the *Code of Federal Regulations* (CFR) is found in the CFR itself. The "Explanation" at the beginning of each volume states:

> The Code of Federal Regulations is a codification of the general and permanent rules published in the Federal Register by the Executive departments and agencies of the Federal Government. The Code is divided into 50 titles which represent broad areas subject to Federal regulation. Each title is divided into chapters which usually bear the

---

loose-leaf service A set of volumes that gathers the sources of law, with explanatory text, for one particular area of law.

name of the issuing agency. Each chapter is further subdivided into parts covering specific regulatory areas.

Format of CFR. The format for the CFR is more accessible than the *Federal Register*. As the Explanation states, the CFR is divided into fifty titles, with each title addressing an area subject to regulation by the federal government. For instance, Title 20 contains regulations of the Social Security Administration, Title 8 contains regulations of the Immigration and Naturalization Service, and so forth.

Every volume in the CFR is revised at least once each calendar year, with the revisions scheduled as follows:

Title 1 through Title 16	as of January 1
Title 17 through Title 27	as of April 1
Title 28 through Title 41	as of July 1
Title 42 through Title 50	as of October 1

The spine of each volume states the year in which it was issued, as well as the title(s) contained in that volume.

Each title is divided into chapters. The chapter number is not part of the citation, so paralegals and attorneys may use certain regulations daily without paying attention to the chapter number. The division into parts and sections, however, is important for citation purposes.

Citation Form. The *Code of Federal Regulations* states that to cite a regulation, you use title, part, and section number. Earlier the text discussed 20 CFR 404.1572. This is Title 20, part 404, section 1572.

A Uniform System of Citation (rule 14.2(a)) gives a slightly different form. The Blue Book form for Title 20, part 404, section 1572 is 20 C.F.R. § 404.1572 (1992). Thus, the Blue Book form puts periods in the CFR abbreviation, uses the section sign, and includes the year. As with the *Federal Register* citation, use the form requested by the court, your employer, or your instructor. This textbook uses the format given in the CFR itself.

How to Find Materials in CFR. When paralegals have the citation to a specific regulation, it is easy to find the regulation in the CFR. Consider, for instance, 20 CFR 404.1572. You simply look in the volume that includes Title 20 and find the part (404) and within the part, the section (1572). It is easy to find the parts and sections because they simply appear in numerical order. At the top of each even-numbered page is the part and section that appears first on that page. At the top of each odd-numbered page is the part and section that appears last on that page.

The key to finding a regulation in the CFR is to locate the citation in the first place. There are several finding aids. As with the *Federal Register,* often the easiest way to find the citation is through a loose-leaf service. The CFR has its own index prepared by the government publisher, the Office of the Federal Register. This index is a separate volume entitled *CFR Index and Finding Aids*. Indexes are also compiled by commercial publishers, such as *Index to the Code of Federal Regulations* published by Congressional Information Service.

Computer databases such as LEXIS and WESTLAW also provide access to the CFR and the *Federal Register*.

Sometimes paralegals find a statute on the subject matter they are researching and need to find the regulations that pertain to that subject matter. The *Index and Finding Aids* volume of CFR contains a Parallel Table of Statutory Authorities and Agency Rules (Table I). An excerpt is reprinted in Figure 2–13. Suppose your research involves 8 U.S.C. § 801. The Parallel Table shows that the related regulations are in 8 CFR Part 289.

FIGURE 2–13
Excerpt from CFR's
Parallel Table of
Statutory
Authorities and
Agency Rules

8 U.S.C.
  226a. . . . . .8 Part 289
  451. . . . . .8 Part 289
  801. . . . . .8 Part 349
  1101. . . . . 8 Parts 1,
            100, 101, 103, 204, 205, 207, 209, 211, 212, 214, 216, 221,
            231, 235, 245a, 247, 248, 258, 264, 270, 274a, 299, 343
                                                  20 Part 655
                                           22 Parts 41, 43, 44, 514
                                           29 Parts 501, 504, 507
                              34 Parts 425, 668, 674–676, 682, 692
  1101 note. . . . . 8 Parts 245, 324, 343a
                                                  22 Parts 42, 43
                                                  24 Part 49
  1102 . . . . .8 Part 212

Throughout the research process, paralegals should remember the common research tools such as A.L.R., especially A.L.R. Fed. The *Federal Digests* are also ripe sources for research in administrative law. Finally, paralegals will often find the citations for pertinent regulations while reading court opinions.

Case Law

In every area of law, judicial opinions are a critical source of law. Administrative law is no exception. Judicial review of administrative agencies' actions is critical to the study of administrative law. In fact, judicial review is so important that Chapter 9 is devoted entirely to this important subject.

Common Types of Litigation Involving Administrative Agencies

As you learned in Chapter 1, the principle of checks and balances is central to the federal government. Congress makes the laws that give agencies the authority to carry out their missions, including the power to promulgate regulations. The courts, however, are the ultimate authority to interpret the laws. Courts address a multitude of issues in cases involving administrative law. For instance, litigation may ensue when an agency tries to enforce a law that is arguably unconstitutional. A common ground for litigation is an agency's interpretation of its enabling statute. Agencies interpret their enabling statutes when they promulgate regulations, and the agencies' actions must remain within the authority given to them by Congress. A corporation may contend that an agency's regulation stems from too strict an interpretation of the applicable statutes. The corporation may then choose to ask a court to review the agency's action. The court's interpretation of the statutes and regulations, particularly newly enacted ones, forms an important part of administrative law. Thus, case law is critical in administrative law.

Case Reporters

This text's discussion of administrative law centers on federal agencies. Therefore, the focus is on federal courts. As you recall from legal research, the decisions of the United States Supreme Court are published in *United States Reports* (U.S.), *Supreme Court Reporter* (S. Ct.), and *United States Supreme Court Reports, Lawyers' Edition* (L. Ed., L. Ed. 2d). Decisions of the United States Courts of Appeals are in *Federal Reporter* (F., F.2d), and opinions of the United States district courts in *Federal Supplement* (F. Supp.). The study of administrative law, however, is enhanced by numerous specialized reporters. These and other specialized research aids for administrative law are discussed in the last section of this chapter.

Presidential Documents

Article II of the United States Constitution gives the president, as head of the executive branch of government, the power to execute the laws of the United States. Thus, after Congress passes a bill, the president must sign the bill in order for the bill to become law.

Types of Presidential Documents

The president may also act unilaterally to create law. Pursuant to either specific statutory authority or the inherent constitutional power of the president to execute the laws of the United States, the president can issue several types of documents to control the actions of administrative agencies. These documents include executive orders, proclamations, and reorganization plans. These means of executive control of administrative agencies are discussed more fully in Chapter 6. For now, the text focuses only on executive orders, perhaps the most common and direct means of presidential control over agencies.

Executive Orders

Executive orders are formal directives from the president to federal agencies or officials.[34] Executive orders may direct federal personnel to take very specific actions. For instance, Executive Order 12807, issued by President Bush in May 1992, ordered the secretary of state and the Coast Guard to take action to suspend the entry of all undocumented aliens into the United States by the high seas. This executive order was issued at a time when many undocumented aliens were fleeing Haiti and coming to Florida by boat. The order commanded the Coast Guard to stop and to board certain vessels, to inspect the documents of the persons on board, and to return the vessel and its passengers to the country from which it came, where there was a reasonable belief that "an offense is being committed against the United States immigration laws." See Figure 2–14 for excerpts of Executive Order 12807.

BALLENTINE'S

executive order An order issued by the chief executive officer (EXAMPLES the president of the United States; the governor of a state; the mayor of a city) of government, whether national, state, or local.

FIGURE 2–14
Excerpt from
Executive Order
12807

Executive order 12807 of May 24, 1992

Interdiction of Illegal Aliens

By the authority vested in me as President by the Constitution and the laws of the United States of America, including sections 212(f) and 215(a)(1) of the Immigration and Nationality Act, as amended (8 U.S.C. 1182(f) and 1185(a)(1)), and whereas:

(1) The President has authority to suspend the entry of aliens coming by sea to the United States without necessary documentation, to establish reasonable rules and regulations regarding, and other limitations on, the entry or attempted entry of aliens into the United States, and to repatriate aliens interdicted beyond the territorial sea of the United States;

(2) The international legal obligations of the United States under the United Nations Protocol Relating to the Status of Refugees (U.S. T.I.A.S. 6577; 19 U.S.T. 6223) to apply Article 33 of the United Nations Convention Relating to the Status of Refugees do not extend to persons located outside the territory of the United States;

(3) Proclamation No. 4865 suspends the entry of all undocumented aliens into the United States by the high seas; and

(4) There continues to be a serious problem of persons attempting to come to the United States by sea without necessary documentation and otherwise illegally;

I, GEORGE BUSH, President of the United States of America, hereby order as follows:

Section 1. The Secretary of State shall undertake to enter into, on behalf of the United States, cooperative arrangements with appropriate foreign governments for the purpose of preventing illegal migration to the United States by sea.

Sec. 2. (a) The Secretary of the Department in which the Coast Guard is operating, in consultation, where appropriate, with the Secretary of Defense, the Attorney General, and the Secretary of State, shall issue appropriate instructions to the Coast Guard in order to enforce the suspension of the entry of undocumented aliens by sea and the interdiction of any defined vessel carrying such aliens. . . .

Other executive orders direct all federal agencies to take certain actions that have a widespread effect on agencies and individuals. For instance, Executive Orders 12291 and 12498 have had a major impact on rule making by federal agencies. Together, these require executive agencies to submit an analysis of all their planned regulatory actions to the Office of Management and Budget (OMB). The executive agencies cannot issue a "major rule" without clearance from OMB. Further, the agencies must submit an annual report informing OMB of their regulatory goals for the coming year. OMB operates in close conjunction with the president and thus these executive orders give the president influence over agency actions. For instance, the president can curb regulations considered too intrusive or expensive.[35]

How to Find Executive Orders

Executive orders, like agency regulations, are first published in the *Federal Register*. The Office of the Federal Register assigns a number to each executive order, and this becomes the official means of identifying the order. They are then compiled and published annually in Title 3 of the *Code of Federal Regulations*. The Office of the Federal Register also publishes the *Codification of Presidential Proclamations and Executive Orders*. In addition, executive orders are published in the *U.S. Code Congressional and Administrative News*.

Specialized Research Aids for Administrative Materials

You have reviewed the basic sources of administrative law: statutes of general applicability, enabling statutes, regulations, case law, and executive orders. In legal research class, paralegals learn the common methods for finding and interpreting these sources. There are, however, some specialized research materials for administrative law with which you may not be familiar. These specialized materials make administrative law far more accessible and comprehensible.

Loose-Leaf Services

Loose-leaf services can be indispensable in areas of administrative law, especially those that change rapidly, such as immigration and environmental law. Loose-leaf services provide regular updates, which bring to paralegals' attention changes in the law of which they may otherwise be unaware.

A particularly useful loose-leaf service for Social Security is *Social Security Law and Practice*. There are multiple loose-leaf services for employment law, which encompasses Title VII. There is also a loose-leaf service entitled *Equal Employment Compliance Manual*. Publications addressing environmental law and immigration law abound. For a list of loose-leaf services, refer to part E of *A Uniform System of Citation*.

Specialized Court Reporters

Paralegals who work in areas of administrative law will find specialized court reporters very helpful. A specialized reporter includes judicial opinions in one particular area of law. This is more efficient and generally more affordable than perusing every volume of the reporters for the Supreme Court, circuit courts of appeals, and federal district courts.

Some specialized reporters are in loose-leaf service form. Others are published like regular reporters, with hardbound volumes and advance sheets. A particularly useful publication for employment discrimination cases is *Employment Practices Guide*. There are multiple reporters for environmental law, including *Environment Reporter*. *West's Social Security Reporting Service* is a helpful specialized reporter. There are also specialized reporters for immigration law. For a useful compilation of sources, refer to Appendix D in *Finding the Law* (1989).

Paralegals can find cases in specialized reporters that are not published in the common reporters such as *Federal Supplement*. Decisions by federal courts that are unpublished are frequently included in specialized reporters and loose-leaf services.

Administrative Agency Decisions

Many components of administrative agencies issue decisions that are not published in the traditional reporting services. An example is the Board of Immigration Appeals (BIA), which decides appeals from decisions of immigration judges. The BIA publishes precedent decisions in slip form in Interim Decisions (Int. Dec.), then in bound volumes in *Administrative Decisions Under Immigration and Nationality Laws* (I & N Dec.).

This is just one of many agency decision publications. Paralegal students may feel initially that they will never be able to learn all the special publications for specific areas of administrative law. This should not be a concern. There are numerous associations of legal professionals in various areas of administrative law that share such information both informally and through their publications.

Publications by Associations of Legal Professionals

There are numerous associations for legal professionals who practice in a particular area of administrative law. One such association is the American Immigration Lawyers Association (AILA). AILA members share information through newsletters and publications. For instance, *The Law of Asylum in the United States* is a useful book published through AILA.

The National Organization of Social Security Claimants' Representatives (NOSSCR) publishes newsletters that help attorneys and paralegals stay current with developments in Social Security disability. These are just a few examples. Paralegals who work in a specific area of administrative law will quickly find through their employers' libraries easy access to these and other publications.

Summary

This chapter addresses the sources of administrative law and procedure. Primary authority is the mandatory law, including statutes, regulations, and court decisions. Secondary authority is mandatory, but may be persuasive, and includes treatises, law review articles, legal encyclopedias, and A.L.R.

Constitutions

The United States Constitution is the supreme law of the land. It imposes restraints on administrative agencies, preventing them from enforcing unconstitutional statutes and regulations. The Bill of Rights provides important protection for individuals in their dealings with administrative agencies. Of particular importance is the due process clause of the fifth amendment, which precludes the government from depriving persons of life, liberty, or property without a valid reason and adequate procedural protection. State constitutions establish the framework of state government and extend protection to individuals. Like federal agencies, state agencies cannot deprive persons of life, liberty, or property without due process (the fourteenth amendment makes due process applicable to state actions). Unlike the United States Constitution, state constitutions sometimes have detailed provisions addressing state and local government.

Statutes of Broad Application

Two types of statutes are of particular concern in the study of administrative law. First are enabling statutes, which address one agency only. Through enabling statutes, Congress delegates to agencies the authority to carry out their missions. The second type are the statutes of broad application, which impose requirements on all or most federal agencies. These include the Administrative Procedure Act (APA), which seeks to ensure that federal agencies use uniform procedures. The APA requires agencies to keep the public informed of their current organization, procedures, and rules; to provide for public participation in the rule-making process; and to prescribe uniform standards for adjudications. The APA also addresses judicial review.

The Freedom of Information Act (FOIA) also applies to all agencies, requiring that they make public their regulations, organization, and other information, such as the forms they use. Persons may file FOIA requests to obtain information agencies have about them. In contrast to the disclosure requirements of FOIA, the Privacy Act requires that agencies not disclose information about individuals without their permission. The Privacy Act also requires agencies to keep only the information that they need for routine use and requires that the information be correct.

Another statute that applies to all agencies is the National Environmental Policy Act (NEPA). NEPA requires agencies to consider the environmental consequences of proposed actions that would have a significant effect on the quality of the environment. NEPA mandates that agencies prepare an environmental impact statement (EIS) before undertaking "major" actions. Agencies can first prepare an environmental assessment (EA), which obviates the need for an EIS if the agency concludes that the actions would have no significant impact. The interpretation of these terms has spawned much litigation.

Enabling Statutes and Regulations

Enabling statutes usually delegate authority to agencies in general terms. Regulations are necessary to fill in the details. Regulations explain the substantive law, as well as the procedures that agencies use. Regulations have broad applicability and future effect. This stands in contrast to adjudications, which affect the rights of one person or a group of persons with similar interests. The process that agencies use for formulating, amending, or repealing a regulation is called rule making. Most regulations are the product of informal rule-making, also called notice-and-comment rule making. This process requires first the publication of proposed regulations in the *Federal Register*. Then comes a period for the public to send in comments. Finally, the agency publishes the final regulations in the *Code of Federal Regulations*. As this process shows, regulations are published first in the *Federal Register*. The final regulations are then published in the *Code of Federal Regulations*. The CFR is divided into fifty titles, and each title is updated only once a year. Thus, for current regulations, paralegals must often consult the *Federal Register*, which is published daily. In addition to regulations, the *Federal Register* also contains other Presidential documents, such as executive orders, and federal agency documents that may not be published anywhere else. Review the text regarding how to locate current information in these two publications.

Case Law

Case law is an important source of administrative law. Judicial review of agency actions is important to the principle of checks and balances, which is central to the federal government. A ripe area of litigation is interpretation of enabling statutes. In addition to the traditional case reporters for federal court decisions, there are specialized case reporters, discussed below.

Presidential Documents

Presidential documents include executive orders, proclamations, and reorganization plans. Executive orders are formal directives from the President to federal agencies or officials. They may direct one agency to perform a certain task or impose far-reaching requirements on all federal agencies. Executive orders can be found in Title 3 of CFR.

Specialized Research Aids for Administrative Materials

The law changes quickly in many areas of administrative law. Most attorneys and paralegals do not read the *Federal Register* and all the new publications every day. Specialized research aids are helpful because they contain the current statutes, regulations, and case law, with commentary. One of the most common and useful aids is the loose-leaf service, which contains the current sources of law with commentary, usually in a binder, for ease of updating the materials. There are also specialized court reporters, which contain court decisions in one area of law only, such as Social Security disability. Some branches of some agencies publish their decisions, which are not published elsewhere. An example is the Board of Immigration Appeals. In many areas of administrative law there are professional organizations, such as the National Organization of Social Security Claimants Representatives, which publish valuable newsletters and other publications that allow paralegals to keep up with the current sources of law.

Review Questions

1. The United States Constitution may be found in _____.
   a. *Black's Law Dictionary*
   b. *United States Code*
   c. *United States Code Annotated*
   d. all of the above
   e. b and c only

2. Which of the following are purposes of enabling statutes?
   a. to establish the agency that enforces the statute
   b. to establish the powers of the agency that enforces the statute
   c. to set out substantive rules of law that the agency carries out
   d. all of the above
   e. b and c only

3. Which of the following are sources of secondary authority for administrative law?
   a. *Federal Digest*
   b. A.L.R. Fed.
   c. *American Jurisprudence*
   d. all of the above
   e. a and b only

4. State constitutions often have detailed provisions addressing local government issues.   True ___ / False ___

5. The Privacy Act is part of the APA.   True ___ / False ___

6. Regulations usually affect one person or a small group of persons with similar interests.   True ___ / False ___

7. The CFR is published daily.   True ___ / False ___

8. The APA provides guidelines for judicial review of agency actions.
                                                          True ___ / False ___

9. NEPA precludes federal agencies from taking any action that has an adverse impact on the environment.   True ___ / False ___

10. Administrative agencies' regulations are primary sources of law.
                                                          True ___ / False ___

11. The president has the authority to issue executive orders that impose requirements on all federal agencies.   True ___ / False ___

12. Discuss the difference between enabling statutes and statutes that apply to multiple agencies, such as the APA.

13. What is the purpose of the APA?

14. What limitations does the Privacy Act place on agencies?

15. NEPA requires agencies to prepare Environmental Impact Statements (EIS) about certain proposed actions. What information must an EIS contain?

Practical Applications

This exercise will help you to become more familiar with the format of the *Federal Register*. Read the following excerpt from the *Federal Register,* and answer the questions below.

DEPARTMENT OF JUSTICE

Immigration and Naturalization Service
8 CFR Parts 3, 103, 208, 235, 242, and 253
[Atty. Gen. Order No. 1435-90]
Aliens and Nationality; Asylum and Withholding of Deportation Procedures
AGENCY: Immigration and Naturalization Service, Justice.
ACTION: Final Rule.
SUMMARY: This final rule establishes procedures to be used in determining asylum under section 208 and withholding of deportation under section 243(h) of the Immigration and Nationality Act, as amended by the Refugee Act of 1980. The rule adopts with minor changes the revised proposed rule published on April 8, 1988 (53 FR 11300) which substantially modified an earlier proposed rule published on August 28, 1987 (52 FR 32552) and the interim rule published on June 2, 1980 (45 FR 37392). That modification responded to numerous and diverse comments received on the August 28, 1987 proposed rule, in particular a substantial number objecting to the original proposal to require that all asylum and withholding of deportation claims be adjudicated in a nonadversarial setting by Asylum Officers within the INS. The final rule provides for continued adversarial adjudications of asylum and withholding of deportation applications by Immigration Judges for those applicants who are in exclusion or deportation proceedings. At the same time, it preserves an opportunity, prior to the institution of proceedings, for adjudication of initial applications in a nonadversarial setting by a specially-trained corps of Asylum Officers.
EFFECTIVE DATE: October 1, 1990.
FOR FURTHER INFORMATION CONTACT:
Henry I. Curry, Director, Asylum Policy and Review Unit, Department of Justice, 10th and Constitution Ave., NW., room 6213, Washington, DC 20530. Telephone: (202) 514-2415; or

Ralph Thomas, Deputy Assistant Commissioner, Refugees, Asylum, and Parole, Immigration and Naturalization Service, 425 Eye Street, NW., Washington, DC 20538. Telephone: (202) 514-2361; or

Gerald Hurwitz, Counsel to the Director, Executive Office for Immigration Review, 5107 Leesburg Pike, suite 2800, Falls Church, Virginia 22041. Telephone: (703) 758-6470.

SUPPLEMENTARY INFORMATION:

I. Background

The Refugee Act of 1980 created a statutory basis for asylum in the United States and made withholding of deportation for those who qualify mandatory rather than discretionary. In passing the Act, Congress for the first time established a statutory definition of refugee based on the definition the United States accepted upon becoming a party to the 1967 Protocol to the UN Convention Relating to the Status of Refugees. It also established a regular procedure for the admission for refugees to the United States, thus largely eliminating the need to use the Attorney General's parole authority for this purpose, and required the Attorney General to establish a procedure through which aliens already in the United States could apply for asylum on the basis of refugee status.

Consistent with the UN refugee definition, under the Act a refugee is, in essence, someone who has been persecuted or who has a well-founded fear of persecution on account of race, religion, nationality, membership in a particular social group, or political opinion. Someone who meets the refugee definition and who has not been firmly resettled elsewhere is eligible for a discretionary grant of asylum, unless one of several specific exclusionary provisions applies (e.g., the applicant has been convicted of a serious non-political crime). The Attorney General is vested with the discretionary authority to grant or deny asylum to refugees physically present in the United States or at a land border or port of entry, irrespective of status.

Similarly, the Act specifically recognizes the obligation under the Convention and Protocol not to expel or return—*refouler*—those whose life or freedom would be threatened upon return to a country of claimed persecution except under strictly limited circumstances. Withholding of deportation is required by the statute for those who are clearly at such risk, unless the individual falls within a limited number of exclusion classes. Entitlement to withholding of deportation thus requires a showing that the life or freedom of the applicant would be threatened in the country of proposed deportation on account of race, religion, nationality, membership in a particular social group, or political opinion.

However, Congress did not legislate any particular method by which claims for asylum or withholding of deportation were to be adjudicated, directing instead that the Attorney General establish the necessary procedures for such adjudication. Interim regulations establishing procedures and standards governing applications under the provisions of the Refugee Act of 1980 were published on June 2, 1980. These interim regulations (hereafter referred to as the "1980 interim rule") were intended only to provide a temporary regulatory mechanism for adjudicating claims pending publication of permanent procedures following a period of deliberate study and analysis. After an appropriate period of experience under the interim rule, the Department of

Justice ("the Department"), including the Immigration and Naturalization Service ("INS") and the Executive Office for Immigration Review ("EOIR"), the Department of State, and other concerned administrative agencies of the United States Government conducted detailed reviews and discussions of the asylum process in order to formulate and implement a comprehensive and uniform asylum policy and procedure. Designed within the legislative framework established by the Refugee Act, that policy reflects two basic guiding principles: A fundamental belief that the granting of asylum is inherently a humanitarian act distinct from the normal operation and administration of the immigration process; and a recognition of the essential need for an orderly and fair system for the adjudication of asylum claims.

The internal policy and regulatory process itself consumed more than two years of effort, culminating with the Attorney General's creation of an Asylum Policy and Review Unit within the Office of Policy Development in the Department of Justice and the subsequent publication of a proposed rule on August 28, 1987 (hereafter referred to as the "August 28, 1987 rule"). Following a 60-day period of intense public debate and comment, the Department announced on December 12, 1987 (52 FR 46776) that it intended to modify that rule in order to provide for continued adversarial adjudications of asylum and withholding of deportation applications by Immigration Judges for those applicants who are in exclusion or deportation proceedings. That major substantive modification as well as other procedural modifications necessitated by that change were reflected in a revised proposed rule published on April 6, 1988 (hereafter referred to as the "April 6, 1988 revised proposed rule") which was opened for an additional 30-day public comment period. The final rule adopts with minor changes the April 6, 1988 revised proposed rule. The "Supplementary Information" section accompanying the April 6, 1988 revised proposed rule provides a complete discussion of the major substantive and other procedural modifications.

1. What is the name of the agency issuing these regulations?

2. Are these proposed or final regulations?

3. What is the date that the regulations became effective?

4. What law (statute) created a statutory basis for granting political asylum in the United States?

5. Is the definition of "refugee" in this statute consistent with the 1967 Protocol to the UN Convention Relating to the Status of Refugees?

6. Under section 208 of the Immigration and Nationality Act, what is the definition of "refugee"?

7. If a person meets the statutory definition of "refugee," is the grant of political asylum mandatory?

8. If it is not mandatory, state a factor that can preclude grant of political asylum.

9. To whom did Congress delegate the responsibility for establishing procedure to determine whether a person is eligible for political asylum?

10. These final regulations were issued after the notice and comment period on the proposed regulations had ended. On what date were the proposed regulations issued?

11. During the notice and comment period, did the proposed regulations generate many comments?

Case Analysis

Read the excerpts below from *Bob Marshall Alliance v. Hodel*, 852 F.2d 1223 (9th Cir. 1988), and answer the following questions.

BOB MARSHALL ALLIANCE
v.
HODEL
United States Court of Appeals, Ninth Circuit.
Decided Aug. 1, 1988.

REINHARDT, Circuit Judge:

This appeal involves the issuance of oil and gas leases on the area known as Deep Creek, located in Montana's Lewis and Clark National Forest. The Bob Marshall Alliance and the Wilderness Society (collectively "Marshall Alliance") brought suit against several federal agencies and the lessees, challenging issuance of the leases on several statutory grounds.

First, Marshall Alliance alleges that issuance of the leases violated the National Environmental Policy Act. NEPA mandates the preparation of an environmental impact statement ("EIS") for all "major Federal actions significantly affecting the quality of the human environment." In order to determine whether an EIS is required, the federal agency concerned prepares an environmental assessment. Based on that assessment the agency may conclude that the action will not significantly affect the environment and issue a "Finding of No Significant Impact" ("FONSI") in lieu of an EIS. We have held that an EIS is required at the point where a federal agency makes an "irreversible and irretrievable commitment of the availability of resources." Marshall Alliance contends that, because the leases in question here were issued without an EIS, the requirements of NEPA were not met.

Second, NEPA also requires that federal agencies "study, develop, and describe appropriate alternatives to recommended courses of action in any proposal which involves unresolved conflicts concerning alternative uses of available resources." Marshall Alliance contends that the alternative of not issuing the Deep Creek leases—the "no action alternative"—was not considered adequately, in violation of NEPA's mandate.

Marshall Alliance's third claim involves the Endangered Species Act. The ESA establishes a consultation process by which federal agencies ensure that their actions will not jeopardize a threatened or endangered species or damage the habitat of such a species. The statute requires preparation of a biological opinion based on "the best scientific and commercial data available" whenever a threatened or endangered species is present in the area of a proposed action. If the opinion concludes that the action would jeopardize a protected species, the action must be modified. Marshall Alliance alleges that the requirements of the ESA were not met before the Deep Creek leases were issued.

We hold that the defendant agencies violated the provisions of both NEPA and the ESA.

FACTS AND PROCEEDINGS BELOW

The Deep Creek Further Planning Area ("Deep Creek") comprises about 42,000 acres of wild, mountainous terrain. It is bounded to the west by three designated wilderness areas and to the east by three wilderness study areas. Deep Creek offers spectacular scenery and recreational opportunities for fishers, hikers, and outdoors enthusiasts of all kinds. Perhaps most important, it is home to a large and unique wildlife population. Deep Creek is an important refuge for four threatened or endangered species: the grizzly bear, the gray wolf, the peregrine falcon, and the bald eagle. In addition, bighorn sheep, elk, mule and white-tailed deer, black bear, moose, mountain goat and mountain lion abound in the area. At the same time, Deep Creek offers opportunities for resource developers. The area is located in the Overthrust Belt, an extensive geologic zone in which major discoveries of oil and natural gas have already been made.

In 1977, the United States Forest Service began reviewing national forest lands to determine which areas should be recommended for wilderness designation. Through this Roadless Area Review and Evaluation ("RARE II") process, the Forest Service classified areas as either wilderness, nonwilderness, or further planning. Those lands classified as further planning areas are open for all uses permitted under applicable land use plans—including oil and gas exploration—pending the development of management plans which will consider whether to recommend the area for inclusion in the wilderness system. In order to preserve the possibility of wilderness designation, the final RARE II environmental impact statement declared that development activities that might reduce the land's wilderness potential are prohibited in further planning areas.

The RARE II evaluation awarded Deep Creek the highest possible wilderness rating—a "perfect score" on the Wilderness Attribute Rating System. Deep Creek also received a very high rating on its potential for natural gas discovery. Because Deep Creek possesses both highly favorable wilderness characteristics and a high potential for the development of natural gas resources, it was classified as a further planning area.

Following this designation, the Bureau of Land Management ("BLM") of the Interior Department received sixteen applications for oil and gas leases on Deep Creek. The Forest Service prepared an environmental assessment of Deep Creek and concluded that such leasing would have no significant effect on the quality of the human environment. This FONSI absolved the agencies of the need to prepare an EIS on the sale of the leases. With regard to the requirements of the ESA, the Forest Service requested formal consultation with the Fish and Wildlife Service ("FWS") regarding the effects of the lease issuance on the threatened and endangered species in Deep Creek. The biological opinion issued by FWS concluded that the sale of leases in itself would not threaten the species in question, but found that there was insufficient information available to issue a comprehensive biological opinion beyond the initial leasing phase.

Beginning in January 1982, BLM issued the sixteen leases for which applications had been received; subsequently BLM issued three simultaneous oil and gas leases by lottery. Collectively these leases cover all of the land within Deep Creek. Some of the leases contain "no surface occupancy" ("NSO") stipulations, which prohibit the lessee from engaging in any surface-disturbing activity. Others contain various stipulations that allow the Secretary of the Interior to impose reasonable conditions on surface-disturbing activity. All of the leases contain "threatened or endangered species stipulations," which state that surface-disturbing activity may be restricted if it would have a detrimental effect on endangered or threatened species or their habitats.

In February 1982, following a series of administrative appeals, Marshall Alliance brought this action in federal district court to challenge the issuance of the Deep Creek leases. Specifically, Marshall Alliance alleged that NEPA required preparation of an EIS prior to the issuance of the leases; that the defendant agencies failed to consider the alternative of not issuing leases, again in violation of NEPA; that the leases would impair the wilderness character of Deep Creek in violation of Forest Service regulations; and that the consultation process mandated by the ESA had not taken place.

The district court awarded summary judgment for Marshall Alliance. The court held that the agencies violated NEPA and Forest Service regulations by failing to prepare an EIS for the Deep Creek leases, and that the stipulations (both NSO and non-NSO) were insufficient to comply with NEPA's mandate. The court also held that the agencies violated NEPA by failing to give meaningful consideration to the no-leasing alternative. Finally, the court held that the effects of leasing on threatened and endangered species in Deep Creek had not been properly assessed, as the ESA requires. The court set aside the actions of the agencies in issuing the leases and enjoined the agencies from issuing any leases on Deep Creek pending compliance with NEPA, the ESA, and agency regulations.

The defendants appeal from the district court's decision. They contend that both NEPA and the ESA are satisfied by a process of "staged consultation" under which the effects of surface-disturbing activity are analyzed as specific activities are actually proposed. They argue that ongoing NEPA evaluation and ESA consultation, combined with the various stipulations in the leases, will protect environmental interests as fully as the two statutes require.

DISCUSSION
I. The Decision in Conner

Some of the issues raised in this appeal are disposed of by our recent opinion in *Conner v. Burford*, 836 F.2d 1521 (9th Cir. 1988). That case also involved the sale of oil and gas leases on national forest lands in Montana. As in the instant case, the leases were issued without preparation of an EIS. Some of the leases contained NSO stipulations and some did not. Again as in the instant case, a comprehensive biological opinion was not prepared prior to issuing the leases. The plaintiffs challenged the lease sale, claiming violations of NEPA and the ESA.

On the NEPA claims, we held that the sale of an "NSO lease"—defined as a lease that "absolutely forbid[s] the lessee from occupying or using the surface of the leased land unless a modification of the NSO stipulation is specifically approved by the BLM"—does *not* constitute the "go/no go point of commitment at which an EIS is required."

However, we held that "non-NSO leases"—that is, leases which "do not reserve to the government the absolute right to prevent all surface-disturbing activity"—cannot be sold without preparation of an EIS, because non-NSO leases represent an irretrievable commitment of resources.

* * *

II. Preparation of an EIS

It is clear from our decision in *Conner* that sale of the Deep Creek leases required preparation of an EIS unless the lease "absolutely prohibits surface disturbance in the absence of specific government approval." No EIS was prepared on any of the leases. Following *Conner,* we affirm the district court's holding that the agencies violated NEPA by failing to prepare an EIS for the non-NSO leases, and reverse the district court's judgment insofar as it requires preparation of an EIS for the sale of NSO leases.

As in *Conner,* we cannot determine from the record which of the Deep Creek leases protect absolutely against surface-disturbing activity. Four of the leases apparently contain NSO stipulations covering the entire leased acreage; some of the others contain NSO stipulations covering part of the leased acreage; some leases contain both NSO stipulations and less strict stipulations regarding regulation of surface-disturbing activity. On remand, the district court may need to determine which of the Deep Creek leases are NSO leases—that is, leases in which "the language of the stipulation, construed with the rest of the lease, absolutely prohibits surface disturbance in the absence of specific government approval."

* * *

CONCLUSION

The defendant agencies violated NEPA by issuing non-NSO leases on Deep Creek without preparation of an EIS, and by issuing any leases at all on Deep Creek without adequate consideration of the no action alternative. They violated the ESA by issuing the leases without preparation of a comprehensive biological opinion which assesses the effects of leasing and post-leasing activities on threatened and endangered species in the Deep Creek area.

The proper remedy for substantial procedural violations of NEPA and the ESA is an injunction. The district court's opinion declared that "the actions of the defendant agencies, allowing the issuance of oil and gas leases in the Deep Creek Area, are HEREBY SET ASIDE. The defendant agencies are enjoined from making further recommendations to lease and issuing leases pending compliance with NEPA, agency regulations, and the ESA." The parties have raised some question as to the effect and appropriateness of the district court's order. In *Conner*, we found similar language to be unclear and undertook to clarify the order. Here we face an additional factor not present in *Conner*, namely the agencies' failure to consider the no action alternative. Under these circumstances we prefer to remand the action and allow the district court the first opportunity to clarify its order and to determine the specific steps to be taken with respect to the various Deep Creek leases. In doing so, the district court shall consider our decisions in this case and in *Conner*, as well as [other] recent opinions.

Pending the district court's clarification of its order, we enjoin all activities on Deep Creek lands conducted under the provisions of the Deep Creek oil and gas leases, and enjoin the sale of any additional leases on Deep Creek, until all statutory requirements are met.

AFFIRMED IN PART, REVERSED IN PART, AND REMANDED.

1. This court decision has many abbreviations for terms, as is common in administrative law. What do each of the following abbreviations stand for?
   a. EIS
   b. FWS
   c. NSO
   d. BLM
   e. FONSI
2. At least three agencies were involved in the environmental assessment of the Deep Creek and the issuance of oil and gas leases in the Deep Creek area. Name three agencies involved.
3. The plaintiff contended that in issuing the leases, the agencies had violated two statutes. Name the statutes.
4. On what specific ground did the plaintiffs contend that the agencies had violated the requirements of NEPA?
5. The court concluded that an EIS is necessary before the agencies can issue a non-NSO lease. Why?

Notes

[1] *Manwani v. U.S. Dep't of Justice, INS*, 736 F. Supp. 1367 (W.D.N.C. 1990).

[2] As noted below, the fourteenth amendment, while not part of the Bill of Rights, is also crucial, because it makes due process protection applicable to state actions.

[3] Morris Cohen et al., Finding the Law (St. Paul: West Publishing Co., 1989), at 198.

[4] Administrative Conference of the United States, *Federal Administrative Procedure Sourcebook*, 2d ed. (Office of the Chairman, 1992), inside front cover (hereinafter ACUS *Sourcebook*).

[5] ACUS *Sourcebook*, at 1.

[6] Id. at 2. The text of the Attorney General's Manual is published in the ACUS Sourcebook.

[7] *Id.* at 7.

[8] *Ethnic Employees of the Library of Congress v. Boorstin,* 751 F.2d 1405, 1416 (D.C. Cir. 1985).

[9] ACUS *Sourcebook,* at 75.

[10] *Id.* at 633.

[11] *Id.* at 83.

[12] *Id.* at 644–45.

[13] *Id.* at 648.

[14] *Id.* at 647.

[15] *Id.* at 864.

[16] *Id.* at 874ff.

[17] 42 U.S.C. § 552(a)(e)(5).

[18] 42 U.S.C. § 552(e)(1).

[19] 42 U.S.C. § 4332(s)(C).

[20] Jan Laitos & Joseph Tomain, *Energy and Natural Resources Law* (St. Paul: West Publishing Co., 1992), at 20.

[21] *Id.* at 225.

[22] *Id.*

[23] *Id.* at 225–26.

[24] *Id.* at 221.

[25] 42 U.S.C. § 4332(2)(C).

[26] The applicable regulations are 40 CFR 1500–1508.

[27] Laitos & Tomain, *supra* note 20, at 87.

[28] ACUS *Sourcebook,* at 685ff.

[29] Christina Kunz *et al., The Process of Legal Research* (Boston: Little, Brown and Company, 1989), at 156.

[30] *Id.* at 168.

[31] 42 U.S.C. § 553(b)(3).

[32] 42 U.S.C. § 553(c).

[33] Cohen, *supra* note 3, at 264.

[34] Ernest Gellhorn & Ronald Levin, *Administrative Law and Procedure in a Nutshell,* 3d ed. (St. Paul: West Publishing Co., 1990), at 61.

[35] See Chapter 5 for further discussion of Executive Orders 11291 and 12498.

IIII

CHAPTER 3

THE SUBSTANTIVE LAW OF SOCIAL SECURITY DISABILITY AND TITLE VII OF THE 1964 CIVIL RIGHTS ACT

You are now familiar with the sources of law that govern administrative law and procedure. With that knowledge, you are ready for an in-depth study of the substantive law that governs particular federal agencies. The text focuses on four agencies—the Social Security Administration, the Equal Employment Opportunity Commission, the Immigration and Naturalization Service, and the Environmental Protection Agency. Within each agency, the discussion focuses on one specific statute or program. With the Social Security Administration, the focus is on Social Security disability. With the Equal Employment Opportunity Commission, the discussion addresses Title VII, with an emphasis on the section that prohibits an employer from taking retaliatory action against an employee who opposes an employment practice which is unlawful under Title VII.

In Chapter 4, the text turns to immigration law, focusing on the requirements for becoming a United States citizen, a procedure called naturalization. The final area of substantive law addressed is environmental law, specifically the Resource Conservation and Recovery Act (RCRA), which governs the management (transportation, storage, and disposal) of hazardous waste. Through this discussion, you gain an understanding of the substantive law in four important areas of administrative law. Significantly, these are also areas that afford many job opportunities for paralegals.

The Substantive Law of Social Security Disability

Chapters 1 and 2 presented a brief look at Social Security disability benefits. The Social Security Administration (the SSA) administers a wide variety of benefits programs. Most persons are familiar with retirement insurance benefits for persons age sixty-five and older. Some persons, however, become unable to work before age sixty-five and qualify for disability insurance benefits. The Social Security Act also provides for retirement insurance benefits at age sixty-two, but the monthly amount is not as great as for people who wait until they are sixty-five years old to draw retirement insurance benefits.

There are different types of disability benefits. The text focuses on disability insurance benefits, often called Title II benefits.

 SIDEBAR   Paralegals should remember that clients may also be eligible for supplemental security income (SSI), authorized by Title XVI of the Social Security Act. As noted in Chapter 1, the SSI program provides benefits to persons who are over age sixty-five, blind, or disabled and who have income and resources below specified amounts. The definition of "disability" is the same for purposes of Title II and Title XVI benefits; therefore, claimants may apply for and be eligible for both types of benefits. Often claimants are eligible for Title II benefits only, because the amount of their Title II monthly payment exceeds the income cutoff for Title XVI benefits.

The Statutory Requirements for Entitlement to Title II Benefits

To determine the requirements for entitlement to Title II benefits, paralegals must turn to the applicable statutes and regulations, the standard sources in administrative law. The precise requirements for entitlement to disability insurance benefits are set forth in section 223 of the Social Security Act (42 U.S.C. § 423(a)(1)), which reads as follows:

> Every individual who—
> (A) is insured for disability insurance benefits (as determined under subsection (c)(1)),
> (B) has not attained retirement age (as defined in section 216(l)),
> (C) has filed application for disability insurance benefits, and
> (D) is under a disability (as defined in subsection (d)) shall be entitled to a disability insurance benefit. . . .

Two of the requirements are quite straightforward. Disability insurance benefits are for persons who have not reached retirement age, that is, persons under age sixty-five. Another simple requirement is that a person must file an application.

The other two eligibility factors—insured status and disability as defined in the Social Security Act—are more complex. A discussion of insured status is beyond the scope of this text. Briefly, in order to meet the insured status requirements of the Social Security Act, a claimant must have worked an aggregate of five years in the ten years before the claimant's alleged onset date. Paralegals should be alert for problems regarding insured status if their client has not worked in many years or has worked only sporadically. Refer to 20 CFR 404.110–404.146 for explanation of insured status.

Disability Within the Meaning of the Social Security Act

The fourth requirement for entitlement to Title II benefits is that the claimant must be **disabled** within the meaning of the Social

---

disabled In the context of Social Security disability, persons are disabled if they cannot perform their past relevant work or any substantial gainful activity because of medically determinable impairments which can be expected to result in death or to last for a period of twelve continuous months.

Security Act. The term "disability" as defined in the Social Security Act is not the definition to which you may be accustomed. Most people think of the definition in their private, long-term disability insurance policies, which generally states that persons are totally disabled when they are unable to perform the principal duties of their occupations. The definition of "disability" in the Social Security Act is substantially different—persons must be unable to perform their past work *or any other work*. To understand the definition of "disability" within the meaning of the Social Security Act, paralegals must turn to the applicable statutes and regulations.

SIDEBAR   In the foregoing discussion, the terms "disability" and "disabled" were put in quotations because they have a technical, statutory meaning rather than the meaning generally understood outside the discussion of Social Security disability. For ease of reading, in the remainder of text, the terms "disabled" and "disability" will not be placed in quotations. Throughout the chapter, quotations will not be used for regulatory terms after the term has been defined.

The Statutory Definition of Disability

Section 223(d)(1)(A) of the Social Security Act (42 U.S.C. § 423(d)(1)(A)) states the definition of disability. It is reprinted in Figure 3–1.

FIGURE 3–1
Section 223(d)(1)(A) of the Social Security Act: The Statutory Definition of Disability

Definition of Disability

(d)(1) The term "disability" means—

(A) inability to engage in any substantial gainful activity by reason of any medically determinable physical or mental impairment which can be expected to result in death or which has lasted or can be expected to last for a continuous period of not less than 12 months. . . .

Section 223(d)(2)(A) adds:

(2) For purposes of paragraph (1)(A)—

(A) An individual shall be determined to be under a disability only if his physical or mental impairment or impairments are of such severity that he is not only unable to do his previous work but cannot, considering his age, education, and work experience, engage in any other kind of substantial gainful work which exists in the national economy, regardless of whether such work exists in the immediate area in which he lives, or whether a specific job vacancy exists for him, or whether he would be hired if he applied for work. . . .

The statute states the basic requirements for disability. A person must have medically determinable impairments. The impairments must prevent a person from engaging in substantial gainful activity. Further, a person must be unable to perform his past work or any other substantial gainful activity which exists in the national economy.

It is important to note the language that requires that the impairments will either result in death or last for at least twelve continuous months. Generally, it is easy to identify impairments that will result in death, such as cancer that cannot be treated. It is sometimes difficult, however, to determine whether an impairment will last for twelve continuous months. If a claimant seeks disability because of fractures suffered in an automobile accident, it may be difficult to determine how long it will take the fractures to heal and thus how long it will be before the claimant regains the ability to work. The SSA relies heavily on the opinions of the claimant's treating physicians to determine whether the twelve-month duration requirement is met.

The statute provides that it is immaterial whether the person can actually get another job. Factors that go into determining whether a person can do his or her past work or any other work include the person's age, education, and work experience. The statute, however, leaves many questions unanswered.

The Regulatory Definition of Disability

The section of the regulations entitled "Basic definition of disability" is 20 CFR 404.1505(a). The pertinent portion is reprinted in Figure 3–2. The first sentence of 20 CFR 404.1505(a) essentially restates the statutory definition of disability. Like the statute, the regulations next state that in order to meet the statutory definition of disability, a person must be unable to perform his or her past work or any other work. This section of the regulations, however, does not answer the essential question: What is the analysis used to determine whether a person is disabled? This question is answered in 20 CFR 404.1520.

FIGURE 3–2
20 CFR 404.1505(a): The Regulatory Definition of Disability

> ### § 404.1505   Basic definition of disability.
>
> (a) The law defines disability as the inability to do any substantial gainful activity by reason of any medically determinable physical or mental impairment which can be expected to result in death or which has lasted or can be expected to last for a continuous period of not less than 12 months. To meet this definition, you must have a severe impairment, which makes you unable to do your previous work or any other substantial gainful activity which exists in the national economy. . . .

The Sequential Evaluation Process

In 20 CFR 404.1520 we find the specific procedure that the SSA uses to determine whether a person is disabled, called the sequential evaluation process. The **sequential evaluation process** is the Social Security Administration's response to its statutory duty to develop a procedure for determining whether a person is disabled within the meaning of the Social Security Act. The sequential evaluation process consists of five questions, culminating in an answer to the same question posed in the statute—whether a person can perform his or her past work or any other substantial gainful work. This is an example of how an agency promulgates regulations to carry out its statutory mandate.

Read 20 CFR 404.1520, which is reprinted as Figure 3–3. The regulation sets forth the sequential evaluation process in fairly straightforward language. As the regulation states, if a person can be found disabled or not disabled at any step in the sequential evaluation process, the inquiry stops at that step. For instance, a person who is engaging in substantial gainful activity will be found "not disabled" at the first step. Refer to Figure 3–4, which charts the five steps and the conclusions that can be reached at each step. The sequential evaluation process leads us full circle to answer the question posed by the statute and regulations to determine whether a person is disabled—can the person perform his or her past work or any other work?

FIGURE 3–3
20 CFR 404.1520:
The Sequential
Evaluation Process

§ 404.1520   Evaluation of disability in general.

(a) *Steps in evaluating disability.* We consider all evidence in your case record when we make a determination or decision whether you are disabled. When you file a claim for a period of disability and/or disability insurance benefits or for child's benefits based on disability, we use the following evaluation process. If you are doing substantial gainful activity, we will determine that you are not disabled. If you are not doing substantial gainful activity, we will first consider the effect of your physical or mental impairment; if you have more than one impairment, we will also consider the combined effect of your impairments. Your impairment(s) must be severe and meet the duration requirement before we can find you to be disabled. We follow a set order to determine whether you are

sequential evaluation process   The five-step evaluation process used by SSA to determine whether claimants are disabled within the meaning of the Social Security Act.

FIGURE 3–3
(continued)

disabled. We review any current work activity, the severity of your impairment(s), your residual functional capacity, your past work, and your age, education, and work experience. If we can find that you are disabled or not disabled at any point in the review, we do not review your claim further. Once you have been found entitled to disability benefits, we follow a somewhat different order of evaluation to determine whether your entitlement continues, as explained in § 404.1594(f)(6).

(b) *If you are working.* If you are working and the work you are doing is substantial gainful activity, we will find that you are not disabled regardless of your medical condition or your age, education, and work experience.

(c) *You must have a severe impairment.* If you do not have any impairment or combination of impairments which significantly limits your physical or mental ability to do basic work activities, we will find that you do not have a severe impairment and are, therefore, not disabled. We will not consider your age, education, and work experience. However, it is possible for you to have a period of disability for a time in the past even though you do not now have a severe impairment.

(d) *When your impairment(s) meets or equals a listed impairment in appendix 1.* If you have an impairment(s) which meets the duration requirement and is listed in appendix 1 or is equal to a listed impairment(s), we will find you disabled without considering your age, education, and work experience.

(e) *Your impairment(s) must prevent you from doing past relevant work.* If we cannot make a decision based on your current work activity or on medical facts alone, and you have a severe impairment(s), we then review your residual functional capacity and the physical and mental demands of the work you have done in the past. If you can still do this kind of work, we will find that you are not disabled.

(f) *Your impairment(s) must prevent you from doing any other work.* (1) If you cannot do any work you have done in the past because you have a severe impairment(s), we will consider your residual functional capacity and your age, education, and past work experience to see if you can do other work. If you cannot, we will find you disabled.

FIGURE 3–4
Flow Chart for
the Sequential
Evaluation
Process

SOCIAL SECURITY DISABILITY—THE SEQUENTIAL EVALUATION PROCESS
(20 CFR 404.1520)

Step One: Is the claimant engaging in
            substantial gainful activity?
            (See 20 CFR 1571 *et seq.*)   →→Yes = not disabled
                      ↓
            No: Go to Step Two.

FIGURE 3–4
(continued)

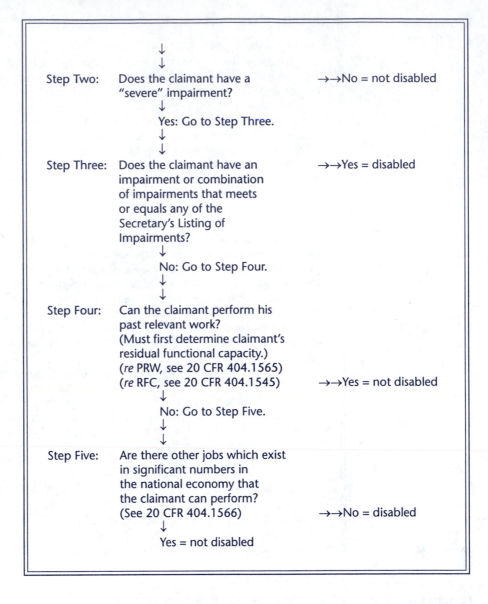

In order to understand the analysis set forth in the sequential evaluation process, paralegals must study in more detail the meaning of the terms used in each of the five steps. Paralegals must understand each step and then apply the regulations to the facts in the clients' cases.

SIDEBAR   It is important for paralegals to understand that the twelve-month duration requirement applies at every step in the sequential evaluation process. Thus, a claimant whose impairments are not severe for a period of twelve continuous months is found not to be disabled. Likewise, if a claimant became ill and recovered within six months, the duration requirement would not be met.

Step One: Is the Claimant Engaging in Substantial Gainful Activity?

If a person is engaging in substantial gainful activity, the person will be found "not disabled" at the first step in the sequential evaluation process, regardless of his or her medical condition. Thus the first term paralegals must understand is **substantial gainful activity.** Refer to 20 CFR 404.1572, which is reprinted in Figure 3–5. This section of the regulations essentially states that work is "substantial" if it involves significant physical or mental activities and is "gainful" if it is work usually performed for pay or profit.

FIGURE 3–5
20 CFR
404.1572:
Substantial
Gainful Activity

---

§ 404.1572   What we mean by substantial, gainful activity.

Substantial gainful activity is work activity that is both substantial and gainful:

(a) *Substantial work activity.* Substantial work activity is work activity that involves doing significant physical or mental activities. Your work may be substantial even if it is done on a part-time basis or if you do less, get paid less, or have less responsibility than when you worked before.

(b) *Gainful work activity.* Gainful work activity is work activity that you do for pay or profit. Work activity is gainful if it is the kind of work usually done for pay or profit, whether or not a profit is realized.

(c) *Some other activities.* Generally, we do not consider activities like taking care of yourself, household tasks, hobbies, therapy, school attendance, club activities, or social programs to be substantial gainful activity.

After reading this explanation, the meaning of substantial gainful activity remains far from clear. Luckily, the regulations offer more concrete guidance in 20 CFR 404.1574, which sets forth an amount of

---

substantial gainful activity A Social Security regulatory term which means work that involves significant mental or physical activity and is usually performed for pay or profit.

monthly earnings that raises a presumption that a person is engaging in substantial gainful activity. For instance, from January 1990 to the present, average earnings of more than $500 per month raise the presumption of substantial gainful activity. Separate rules apply to self-employed persons, and paralegals may find these rules in 20 CFR 404.1575.

The rationale behind the amounts in 20 CFR 404.1574 is that a person who is able to earn a certain amount of money per month is "not disabled." The monthly earnings in the regulations appear low. They reflect, however, an attempt to set out a general rule that will be applied to every person who applies for disability insurance benefits.

Paralegals should be aware that the SSA makes some allowances for persons who try to work after their alleged onset dates. The regulations allow a trial work period of nine months (20 CFR 404.1592). Further, if a claimant tries to return to work for a short period, such as two months, but is unable to sustain work because of his or her impairments, this is considered an unsuccessful work attempt and does not preclude a finding of disability.

Step Two: Does the Claimant Have Impairments That Are "Severe"?

Here is another word that has a specific meaning in the regulations, and that meaning differs from the common, nonregulatory meaning. In everyday parlance, people think of a severe problem as a very serious problem.

The regulations (20 CFR 404.1520(c)) state that an impairment is **severe** when, considered either alone or in combination with other impairments, it "significantly limits your physical or mental ability to do basic work activities." The regulations explain more about the meaning of severe and nonsevere impairments in 20 CFR 404.1521. This section reiterates the requirement that the impairments must interfere with a person's ability to perform basic work activities. The regulations then explain the meaning of basic work activities. The regulations then explain the meaning of **basic work activities.** Refer to Figure 3–6, which reprints 20 CFR 404.1521. Basic work activities include physical activities such as walking, standing, sitting, and lifting, as well as mental skills such as the ability to understand directions and use appropriate judgment.

---

severe impairment As used in the context of Social Security disability, an impairment that significantly limits a person's physical or mental ability to perform basic work activities; defined by courts as an impairment that has more than a minimal effect on a person's ability to work.

basic work activities In the context of Social Security disability, basic work activities include walking, standing, sitting, and lifting, as well as mental skills such as the ability to understand directions and use appropriate judgment.

FIGURE 3–6
20 CFR
404.1521:
Nonsevere
Impairments and
Basic Work
Activities

> **§ 404.1521   What we mean by an impairment(s) that is not severe.**
>
>   (a) *Non-severe impairment(s).* An impairment or combination of impairments is not severe if it does not significantly limit your physical or mental ability to do basic work activities.
>   (b) *Basic work activities.* When we talk about basic work activities, we mean the abilities and aptitudes necessary to do most jobs. Examples of these include—
>   (1) Physical functions such as walking, standing, sitting, lifting, pushing, pulling, reaching, carrying, or handling;
>   (2) Capacities for seeing, hearing, and speaking;
>   (3) Understanding, carrying out, and remembering simple instructions;
>   (4) Use of judgment;
>   (5) Responding appropriately to supervision, co-workers and usual work situations; and
>   (6) Dealing with changes in a routine work setting.

Judicial Interpretation of the Term "Severe" Impairment.   Although the regulations give some guidance as to the meaning of the term "severe" impairment, when paralegals face the task of analyzing whether the clients' impairments are "severe," they generally need guidance beyond that offered in the regulations and must look to court decisions for further interpretation.

The definition adopted by many courts is the standard enunciated by the Fourth Circuit Court of Appeals in *Evans v. Heckler.*[1] The Fourth Circuit has held that "[a]n impairment can be considered as 'not severe' if it is only a slight abnormality which has such a minimal effect on the individual that it would not be expected to interfere with the individual's ability to work, irrespective of age, education, or work experience."

SIDEBAR

There are some differences among the Circuit Courts of Appeal as to what constitutes a severe impairment. Paralegals must consult the case law for their circuit. A useful starting point is a compilation of cases, such as 80 A.L.R. Fed. 564.

As a practical matter, the sequential evaluation process seldom ends at the second step. Only very minor impairments are generally found to be "not severe." Consider, for instance, a claimant who states that she is nervous. An examination of her medical records reveals that she has been seen frequently by both her family doctor and her orthopedic doctor. The treatment records of neither doctor contain a diagnosis of anxiety or any other mental impairment. In fact, both doctors have completed forms on which they described the claimant's mental status as normal. The claimant was examined by a psychiatrist who reported that she has no mental impairments. She has never been treated in a psychiatric hospital or at a mental health center nor has been prescribed medications for anxiety or any other mental impairments. In this instance, it is reasonable to conclude that the claimant does not have a "severe" mental impairment. If a claimant had asserted only "nervousness" as an impairment, and the evidence showed no other impairment, then the sequential evaluation process would terminate at the second step with a finding of "not disabled" because the claimant did not have a "severe" impairment.

Step Three: Does the Claimant Have an Impairment or Combination of Impairments That Meets or Equals Any of the Secretary's Listing of Impairments?

The purpose of the third step is the converse of the purpose of the second step. In the second step, the SSA determines when impairments are "not severe" and thus screens out claimants with very weak claims. The third step is designed to render a finding of disability when it is obvious that a person cannot engage in substantial gainful activity. If the SSA determines that a claimant meets or equals one of the Secretary's Listing of Impairments, the claimant is determined to be "disabled," and the evaluation process terminates at the third step.

What Is the Listing of Impairments? The regulations state the purpose of the **Listing of Impairments** as follows:

> The Listing of Impairments describes, for each of the major body systems, impairments which are considered severe enough to prevent a person from doing any substantial gainful activity. Most of the listed impairments are permanent or expected to result in death . . . . 20 CFR 404.1525.

The best way to understand the nature of the Listings is to examine one particular Listing. Consider Section 1.11 of the Listings, which reads as follows:

> 1.11 *Fracture of the femur, tibia, tarsal bone or pelvis* with solid union not evident on X-ray and clinically solid, when such determination is feasible, and return to full weight-bearing status did not occur or is not expected to occur within 12 months of onset.

Listing of Impairments The section of the Social Security regulations that describes, for each of the major body systems, impairments that are considered severe enough to prevent a person from doing any substantial gainful activity.

To determine whether a claimant meets section 1.11, the SSA reviews the claimant's medical records with a focus on two points. Was a solid union of the fracture achieved and was the claimant able to return to full weight-bearing status within twelve months? The pertinent information is in hospital records and treatment records of the claimant's orthopedic surgeon. These records confirm whether the claimant fractured one of the bones to which section 1.11 applies. After a patient is released from the hospital, her orthopedist follows her progress and takes X-rays to determine when a solid union of the fracture is achieved. As the orthopedist tracks the claimant's progress, she records in her treatment notes the date on which the claimant is given permission to return to full weight-bearing status. If complications arise, such as infection or a fall that affects the fracture, the doctor may not give the claimant permission to bear her weight fully on the affected extremity for quite some time. If the claimant is restricted from full weight-bearing for twelve months, then she meets section 1.11.

How to Find and Use the Listings. The Listing of Impairments is part of the regulations in 20 CFR part 404, the regulations discussed throughout the overview of Social Security disability. The technical term for the Listing of Impairments is "Appendix 1 to Subpart P—Listing of Impairments." Thus, paralegals may hear the term "Appendix 1," "the Listing of Impairments," or simply "the Listings." Do not let the reference to "Subpart P" confuse you. Subpart P is simply the portion of the regulations addressing "Determining Disability and Blindness." Part A contains the Listings used for evaluation of persons age eighteen and older. Part B addresses the criteria used for children under age eighteen. This text discusses only part A.

SIDEBAR   Class action lawsuits have had an impact on the criteria the SSA uses to determine whether certain claimants are disabled. For instance, Sullivan v. Zebley,[2] was a class action lawsuit that prompted a change in the disability determination process for supplemental security income claims for disabled children. The SSA had required that a child meet or equal a Listing in order to be found disabled. The *Zebley* class action challenged this stringent standard. As a result, the SSA now uses a more individualized analysis.

Part A contains fourteen sections, each devoted to a separate body system. The body systems assigned a section include the musculoskeletal system, special senses and speech, respiratory system, cardiovascular system, digestive system, genito-urinary system, hemic and lymphatic system, skin, endocrine system, multiple body systems, neurological, mental disorders, and malignant neoplastic diseases (cancer), and the immune system. Within each section are a number of impairments, each with a specific set of criteria which the claimant must fit in order to meet that Listing. Examples of impairments in the musculoskeletal section, in addition to the section on leg fractures discussed above, include active rheumatoid arthritis, disorders of the spine, and soft tissue injuries of an upper or lower extremity.

Practical Application of the Listings to a Particular Client's Case. Paralegals can effectively use the Listings by determining whether the client has one of the impairments in any of the sections. Paralegals then must examine the specific criteria within the particular impairment to determine whether the client's medical records reflect those criteria. If the records show this, paralegals may then assert that the client meets one of the Listings and is entitled to a finding of disability at Step Three of the sequential evaluation process.

The Listings are a purely regulatory creature and may seem difficult at first. Once paralegals become familiar with the Listings, they will use them as an effective screening tool to identify impairments serious enough to merit a finding of disability at Step Three of the sequential evaluation process.

SIDEBAR   The regulations also embrace the concept of "equalling" a Listing. This occurs when a claimant does not precisely meet the criteria but other factors contribute to a finding that when all the claimant's impairments are considered together, a physician concludes that the claimant equals the criteria. This determination is made by a doctor. Paralegals may, however, contact the claimant's doctor to ask whether the doctor feels that the claimant equals a certain Listing.

Residual Functional Capacity

Before addressing Steps Four and Five, it is important to understand the term "residual functional capacity" because it is central to the determinations that the SSA makes in the last two steps of the sequential evaluation process. The regulations explain that "[y]our **residual functional capacity** [emphasis added] is what you can still do despite your limitations" (20 CFR 404.1545(a)).

SIDEBAR   The common abbreviation for residual functional capacity is RFC.

residual functional capacity   The work capacity that a person retains despite his or her impairments, categorized as the capacity for sedentary, light, medium, heavy, or very heavy work.

The regulations further explain that in assessing physical limitations, the SSA assesses a claimant's ability to sit, stand, walk, lift, carry, push, pull, as well as the ability to perform functions such as reaching, handling objects, stooping, or crouching (20 CFR 404.1545(b)). The SSA also assesses mental abilities such as understanding, remembering, and carrying out instructions (20 CFR 404.1545(c)).

In assessing physical limitations, the SSA determines what physical exertion requirements a claimant remains able to do. The regulations identify five levels of exertional capacity—sedentary, light, medium, heavy, and very heavy work. The exertional demands of each level are found in 20 CFR 404.1567, which is summarized in Figure 3–7. Thus, if a claimant cannot lift more than ten pounds at a time and cannot engage in prolonged standing and walking, that claimant is limited to sedentary work. In assessing a claimant's residual functional capacity, the SSA looks at the claimant's medical records, especially the treatment notes and reports of treating physicians.

FIGURE 3–7
The Five Levels of Exertional Capacity

Sedentary Work:	lifting no more than 10 pounds no prolonged standing and walking
Light Work:	lifting no more than 20 pounds with frequent lifting or carrying of weights up to 10 pounds
Medium Work:	lifting no more than 50 pounds with frequent lifting or carrying of weights up to 25 pounds
Heavy Work:	lifting no more than 100 pounds with frequent lifting or carrying of weights up to 50 pounds
Very Heavy Work:	lifting more than 100 pounds with frequent lifting or carrying of weights of 50 pounds or more

Once the SSA determines a claimant's residual functional capacity, the sequential evaluation process turns to the last two steps.

Step Four: Is the Claimant Able to Perform His or Her Past Relent Work?

If a claimant remains able to perform his or her past relevant work, the claimant is found "not disabled" at this, the fourth step in the sequential evaluation process.

What Is Past Relevant Work? A job performed by a claimant is considered to be **past relevant work** if it was performed within the last fifteen years, lasted long enough for the claimant to learn to do it, and was substantial gainful activity. Thus, if a claimant worked as an attorney for five years and earned $40,000 a year, this constitutes past relevant work experience. In contrast, if a claimant had worked as an attorney for only three months, this would not constitute past relevant work experience, because this is not considered sufficient time to learn to be an attorney. Consider a claimant who worked as a convenience store clerk for three weeks in 1992 and two weeks in 1993, earning about $450 each year. This does not constitute past relevant work because the claimant did not perform the job long enough to learn it and did not have earnings at a level that would be considered substantial gainful activity.

SIDEBAR   The common abbreviation for past relevant work is PRW.

When claimants file their application, they also complete a form called a Disability Report. See the sample Disability Report in Appendix B. A large portion of the Disability Report is devoted to a description of the claimant's past jobs. For each job, the claimant is asked how many hours during the work day the claimant was required to sit, stand, and walk, as well as how many pounds the claimant had to lift and whether the claimant had to bend, stoop, and so forth.

SIDEBAR   Often the SSA consults the *Dictionary of Occupational Titles* (DOT) for information on the requirements of certain jobs. The DOT describes various jobs in the United States and explains the exertional requirements and level of skill needed to perform the job. A full discussion of how to use the DOT is beyond the scope of this text, but paralegals who work in the areas of both Social Security disability and immigration law will use the DOT frequently.

How the SSA Determines Whether a Claimant Can Perform Past Relevant Work. Two factors are involved in this analysis. First, what is the claimant's residual functional capacity? Second, what residual functional capacity is required to perform the claimant's past relevant work? Assume that the claimant has a residual functional capacity for

past relevant work Work performed within the past fifteen years, which lasted long enough for the person to learn the job and generated wages high enough to indicate substantial gainful activity.

sedentary work. Further assume that the claimant's only past relevant work experience was as a secretary, performed at the "sedentary" exertional level. This claimant retains the residual functional capacity to perform past relevant work as a secretary. Thus, the claimant is not disabled within the meaning of the Social Security Act.

Consider another example. Suppose that during the past fifteen years the claimant had worked as a sales clerk in a department store, a job performed at the light exertional level. Due to back problems, the claimant is now limited to sedentary work. Light work requires more exertional capacity than the claimant can perform. Thus, the claimant can no longer perform past relevant work (PRW).

Step Five: Is the Claimant Able to Perform Any Other Work?

After determining that a claimant cannot perform past relevant work, the SSA reaches the fifth and final question—can the claimant perform any other work?

Several more factors now come into play. The claimant's residual functional capacity remains a critical factor. At the fifth step, however, the SSA considers additional factors—the claimant's age, education, and past relevant work experience.

SIDEBAR   Compare Step Four. If a claimant can perform past relevant work, the claimant is found not disabled regardless of his or her age and education. The claimant's age and education become critical factors only when Step Five is reached.

Regulatory Categories for Age.   Essentially, the older a claimant is, the greater likelihood that the claimant will be found disabled. The regulations establish four age categories (20 CFR 404.1563). Persons forty-nine years old and younger are "younger individuals." Persons age fifty through fifty-four are "persons approaching advanced age." Persons age fifty-five through fifty-nine are "persons of advanced age." Persons age sixty through sixty-four are "persons close to retirement age." Recall that when a person attains age sixty-five, the person receives retirement benefits, not disability benefits. Refer to Figure 3–8 for a chart of the age categories.

FIGURE 3–8
20 CFR
404.1563: Age
Categories

Under Age 50	Younger Person
50–54	Person Approaching Advanced Age
55–59	Person of Advanced Age
60–64	Person Close to Retirement Age

Regulatory Categories for Education. Another factor in the fifth step is the claimant's education. The less formal education a claimant has, the greater the likelihood the claimant will be found disabled. The regulations establish four levels of education (20 CFR 404.1564). A claimant unable to read and write is classified as "illiterate." A claimant with formal schooling at the sixth grade level or less has a "marginal" education. A claimant with a formal education at the seventh through eleventh grade level has a "limited" education. Claimants who completed high school or higher levels of formal education are classified as having a "high school and above" education. Refer to Figure 3–9 for a chart of the education categories.

FIGURE 3–9
20 CFR 404.1564:
Education
Categories

Unable to Read and Write	Illiterate
Formal Education = 6th Grade or Less	Marginal Education
Formal Education = 7th Through 11th Grade	Limited Education
Formal Education = 12th Grade or Above	High School and Above Education

Putting the Factors Together to Determine Whether a Claimant Can Perform Any Other Work. Suppose that a claimant has had a hearing with an administrative law judge, and the ALJ is ready to render a decision as to whether the claimant is disabled. The ALJ puts together the factors—residual functional capacity, age, education, past work experience, and transferability of skills—to determine whether the claimant can perform any work that exists in significant numbers in the national economy. The ALJ determines that the claimant is a person approaching advanced age, has a limited (tenth grade) education, and can perform only sedentary work. The claimant's past relevant work included only unskilled jobs; therefore, the claimant has no transferable skills.

The regulations provide the mechanism for putting these factors together to determine whether a claimant is disabled in the Medical-Vocational Guidelines, found in appendix 2 to subpart P of the regulations. The **Medical-Vocational Guidelines** are tables that categorize the vocational factors (residual functional capacity, age, education, and past work experience) and direct a conclusion whether a claimant who fits a certain combination of the vocational factors is

---

Medical-Vocational Guidelines Tables promulgated by the SSA which categorize the vocational factors—residual functional capacity, age, education, and past work experience—and direct a conclusion of "not disabled" or "disabled" when all the factors coincide.

disabled or not disabled. They are commonly called the **grids.** The reason for the term "grids" is clear when you examine the Medical-Vocational Guidelines, a portion of which is illustrated in Figures 3–10 and 3–11. The regulations explain that the grids reflect the analysis of the various vocational factors (i.e., age, education, and work experience) in combination with the individual's residual functional capacity in evaluating the individual's ability to engage in substantial gainful activity in other than his or her vocationally relevant past work. When the findings of fact made with respect to a particular individual's vocational factors and residual functional capacity coincide with all of the criteria of a particular rule, the rule directs a conclusion as to whether the individual is or is not disabled.

The use of the grids is best understood by direct application to particular claimants. Consider a claimant who has a residual functional capacity for sedentary work, is a person approaching advanced age, has a limited education, and has only unskilled work experience. Look at Figure 3–10 and find the rule that applies to this claimant. To find the appropriate rule, first locate the claimant's age in the "Age" column. Next, find the claimant's education level in the "Education" column. Finally, check the "Previous work experience" column to find the description that fits the claimant. Here, rule 201.09 applies because all the factors coincide. Look at the column entitled "Decision," and you see that rule 201.09 directs a conclusion that the claimant is disabled.

Compare a claimant who is forty-eight years old and has a residual functional capacity for sedentary work, a limited education, and unskilled work experience. Here, the factors coincide with rule 201.18, which directs a conclusion that the claimant is not disabled.

Now consider a claimant who can perform only sedentary work, has unskilled work experience, is forty-eight years old, but is illiterate. These factors coincide with rule 201.17, which directs a conclusion that the claimant is disabled. These examples show how the various factors combine to direct a conclusion that a claimant is disabled or not disabled.

SIDEBAR   The grids contain the term "do." This is simply an abbreviation for "ditto."

The examples above used only Table No. 1, which applies to persons with a residual functional capacity for sedentary work. The grids also contain Table No. 2, which applies to persons with a residual functional capacity for light work; and Table No. 3, which applies to

---

grids   A term synonymous with Medical-Vocational Guidelines.

persons with a residual functional capacity for medium work. See Figure 3–11, which illustrates Table No. 2. The application of factors is the same in all the tables. Find the applicable age, education, and previous work experience, and the rule directs a conclusion of either disabled or not disabled. Thus, when a claimant has a residual functional capacity for light work, is a person approaching advanced age, has a limited education, and has only unskilled work experience, rule 202.10 directs a conclusion that the claimant is not disabled. This illustrates the difference that a claimant's residual functional capacity makes. A claimant with these same factors, except that the claimant can only perform sedentary work, would be disabled pursuant to rule 201.09.

FIGURE 3–10
The Sedentary Grids

TABLE NO. 1—RESIDUAL FUNCTIONAL CAPACITY: MAXIMUM SUSTAINED WORK CAPABILITY LIMITED TO SEDENTARY WORK AS A RESULT OF SEVERE MEDICALLY DETERMINABLE IMPAIRMENT(S)				
Rule	Age	Education	Previous work experience	Decision
201.01	Advanced age	Limited or less	Unskilled or none	Disabled.
201.02	...do	...do	Skilled or semiskilled—skills not transferable [1].	Do.
201.03	...do	...do	Skilled or semiskilled—skills transferable [1].	Not disabled.
201.04	...do	High school graduate or more—does not provide for direct entry into skilled work [2].	Unskilled or none	Disabled.
201.05	...do	High school graduate or more—provides for direct entry into skilled work [2].	...do	Not disabled.
201.06	...do	High school graduate or more—does not provide for direct entry into skilled work [2].	Skilled or semiskilled—skills not transferable [1].	Disabled.
201.07	...do	...do	Skilled or semiskilled—skills transferable [1].	Not disabled.
201.08	...do	High school graduate or more—provides for direct entry into skilled work [2].	Skilled or semiskilled—skills not transferable [1].	Do.
201.09	Closely approaching advanced age.	Limited or less	Unskilled or none	Disabled.
201.10	...do	...do	Skilled or semiskilled—skills not transferable.	Do.
201.11	...do	...do	Skilled or semiskilled—skills transferable.	Not disabled.
201.12	...do	High school graduate or more—does not provide for direct entry into skilled work [3].	Unskilled or none	Disabled.
201.13	...do	High school graduate or more—provides for direct entry into skilled work [3].	...do	Not disabled.
201.14	...do	High school graduate or more—does not provide for direct entry into skilled work [3].	Skilled or semiskilled—skills not transferable.	Disabled.
201.15	...do	...do	Skilled or semiskilled—skills transferable.	Not disabled.
201.16	...do	High school graduate or more—provides for direct entry into skilled work [3].	Skilled or semiskilled—skills not transferable.	Do.
201.17	Younger individual age 45–49.	Illiterate or unable to communicate in English.	Unskilled or none	Disabled.
201.18	...do	Limited or less—at least literate and able to communicate in English.	...do	Not disabled.
201.19	...do	Limited or less	Skilled or semiskilled—skills not transferable.	Do.

FIGURE 3–10 (continued)

Rule	Age	Education	Previous work experience	Decision
201.20	...do	...do	Skilled or semiskilled—skills transferable.	Do.
201.21	...do	High school graduate or more	Skilled or semiskilled—skills not transferable.	Do.
201.22	...do	...do	Skilled or semiskilled—skills transferable.	Do.
201.23	Younger individual age 18–44.	Illiterate or unable to communicate in English.	Unskilled or none	Do.[4]
201.24	...do	Limited or less—at least literate and able to communicate in English.	...do	Do.[4]
201.25	...do	Limited or less	Skilled or semiskilled—skills not transferable.	Do.[4]
201.26	...do	...do	Skilled or semiskilled—skills transferable.	Do.[4]
201.27	...do	High school graduate or more	Unskilled or none	Do.[4]
201.28	...do	...do	Skilled or semiskilled—skills not transferable.	Do.[4]
201.29	...do	...do	Skilled or semiskilled—skills transferable.	Do.[4]

[1] See 201.00(f).
[2] See 201.00(d).
[3] See 201.00(g).
[4] See 201.00(h).

FIGURE 3–11
The Light Grids

TABLE NO. 2—RESIDUAL FUNCTIONAL CAPACITY: MAXIMUM SUSTAINED WORK CAPABILITY LIMITED TO LIGHT WORK AS A RESULT OF SEVERE MEDICALLY DETERMINABLE IMPAIRMENT(S)

Rule	Age	Education	Previous work experience	Decision
202.01	Advanced age	Limited or less	Unskilled or none	Disabled.
202.02	...do	...do	Skilled or semiskilled—skills not transferable.	Do.
202.03	...do	...do	Skilled or semiskilled—skills transferable.[1]	Not disabled.
202.04	...do	High school graduate or more—does not provide for direct entry into skilled work.[2]	Unskilled or none	Disabled.
202.05	...do	High school graduate or more—provides for direct entry into skilled work.[2]	...do	Not disabled.
202.06	...do	High school graduate or more—does not provide for direct entry into skilled work.[2]	Skilled or semiskilled—skills not transferable.	Disabled.
202.07	...do	...do	Skilled or semiskilled—skills transferable.[2]	Not disabled.
202.08	...do	High school graduate or more—provides for direct entry into skilled work.[2]	Skilled or semiskilled—skills not transferable.	Do.
202.09	Closely approaching advanced age.	Illiterate or unable to communicate in English.	Unskilled or none	Disabled.
202.10	...do	Limited or less—At least literate and able to communicate in English.	...do	Not disabled.
202.11	...do	Limited or less	Skilled or semiskilled—skills not transferable.	Do.
202.12	...do	...do	Skilled or semiskilled—skills transferable.	Do.
202.13	...do	High school graduate or more	Unskilled or none	Do.
202.14	...do	...do	Skilled or semiskilled—skills not transferable.	Do.
202.15	...do	...do	Skilled or semiskilled—skills transferable.	Do.
202.16	Younger individual	Illiterate or unable to communicate in English.	Unskilled or none	Do.
202.17	...do	Limited or less—At least literate and able to communicate in English.	...do	Do.
202.18	...do	Limited or less	Skilled or semiskilled—skills not transferable.	Do.
202.19	...do	...do	Skilled or semiskilled—skills transferable.	Do.
202.20	...do	High school graduate or more	Unskilled or none	Do.

FIGURE 3–11
(continued)

TABLE No. 2—RESIDUAL FUNCTIONAL CAPACITY: MAXIMUM SUSTAINED WORK CAPABILITY LIMITED TO LIGHT WORK AS A RESULT OF SEVERE MEDICALLY DETERMINABLE IMPAIRMENT(S)—Continued

Rule	Age	Education	Previous work experience	Decision
202.21	....do	....do	Skilled or semiskilled—skills not transferable.	Do.
202.22	....do	....do	Skilled or semiskilled—skills transferable.	Do.

¹ See 202.00(f).
² See 202.00(c).

Jobs Must Exist in Significant Numbers. At the fifth step, the burden of proof shifts to the SSA to show that there exist *a significant number of jobs in the national economy* that the claimant can perform. Application of the grids is one method the SSA uses to meet that burden. The regulations explain in the Introduction to the Medical-Vocational Guidelines that, in promulgating these rules, the SSA relied on the *Dictionary of Occupational Titles, Occupational Outlook Handbook,* and various surveys prepared by the SSA and the Bureau of the Census. Relying on the information in these sources, the SSA determined which combinations of vocational factors (age, education, and previous work experience) direct a conclusion of "disabled" and which combinations direct a conclusion of "not disabled." The grids can be applied to a claimant only when all vocational factors coincide.

To understand when the grids cannot be properly applied, paralegals must first understand the difference between exertional and nonexertional limitations. The regulations consider limitations to be exertional when they affect a claimant's ability "to meet the strength demands of jobs," that is, sitting, standing, walking, lifting, carrying, pushing, and pulling (20 CFR 404.1569a). Thus, a cardiac impairment that diminishes a claimant's ability to lift and to walk for prolonged periods is an exertional limitation.

Nonexertional limitations do not relate solely to bodily strength, but rather to limitations such as difficulty in seeing or hearing, and an intolerance of fumes. 20 CFR 404.1569a(b). Mental impairments often impose nonexertional limitations such as difficulty maintaining concentration.

When a claimant has nonexertional limitations, a determination may not properly be based on application of the grids. This is because all the vocational factors do not coincide. If a claimant has the strength to perform light work but has pulmonary impairments that limit the claimant to a work environment free of exposure to fumes or extreme temperature changes, that claimant cannot perform a full range of light work. Therefore, the grids cannot be applied. With such a claimant, an ALJ would take the testimony of a vocational expert to determine whether there exist a significant number of jobs that the claimant can perform. **Vocational experts** are persons who, through experience in vocational assessment and placement, know the exertional and nonexertional requirements of jobs and the incidence of jobs in the economy. They generally rely on the DOT, job surveys, and personal observations.

Summary.   In summary, at the final step of the sequential evaluation process, the SSA determines a person's age, education, past relevant work, and residual functional capacity. For claimants with solely exertional limitations, the grids direct a finding as to whether a person is disabled or not disabled. When a claimant has nonexertional limitations, then the opinion of a vocational expert is sought to determine whether there exist a significant number of jobs in the national economy which the claimant can perform. If there are a significant number of jobs, then the claimant is not disabled. If there are not a significant number of jobs, then the claimant is disabled.

Social Security disability addresses the problems of persons who are no longer able to work. Persons who do work often face problems on the job, such as discrimination because of their race or sex. Title VII of the 1964 Civil Rights Act is a powerful tool that the EEOC uses to eradicate employment discrimination.

The Substantive Law of Title VII of the 1964 Civil Rights Act

One of the principal statutes enforced by the Equal Employment Opportunity Commission (EEOC) is Title VII of the Civil Rights Act of 1964 (42 U.S.C. § 2000-e *et seq.*). The purpose of Title VII is to eliminate employment discrimination based on race, color, religion, sex, or national origin. Title VII has spawned a massive body of case law for several reasons. First, Title VII is such a far-reaching statute that it has prompted employees and the EEOC to invoke its protection in a wide array of circumstances. Second, the language of the statute itself is broad but sparse, inviting judicial interpretation. For instance, through case law, the meaning of "terms, conditions, or privileges of employment" has been clarified. Third, the applicable regulations are general and largely address procedure rather than the substantive law.

---

vocational expert   Person relied on by the SSA, when the grids cannot be directly applied, to state whether there exists a significant number of jobs a claimant can perform, considering the claimant's vocational factors.

The EEOC's regulations stand in contrast to the detailed Social Security disability regulations, providing far less guidance as to the substantive law. Thus, the attorney-paralegal team must rely heavily on case law.

The General Prohibitions of Title VII

The general prohibitions of Title VII are set forth in section 703(a)(1) (42 U.S.C. § 2000e-2), which states:

> It shall be an unlawful employment practice for an employer to fail or refuse to hire or to discharge any individual, or otherwise to discriminate against any individual with respect to his compensation, terms, conditions, or privileges of employment, because of such individual's race, color, religion, sex, or national origin . . . .

To Whom the Prohibitions Apply

Title VII prohibits "employers" from engaging in employment discrimination. Thus, to grasp the broad reach of Title VII, paralegals must know how the term "employer" is defined. Section 701 defines an employer as a person who is engaged in an industry affecting commerce. "Person" includes employers such as those that readily come to mind—corporations, partnerships, and even individuals. The term also includes employment agencies, labor unions, and religious and educational institutions. Further, federal, state, and local governments are included.[3]

Title VII exempts certain employers from coverage. Section 701 exempts from coverage employers who have fewer than fifteen employees for each working day in twenty or more calendar weeks in the prior or current calendar year.

Examples of Prohibited Employer Actions

It is important to note at the outset that if an employer discriminates against an employee for some reason other than race, color, religion, sex, or national origin, Title VII does not provide protection. Thus, in *Burrows v. Chemed Corp.*,[4] the Eighth Circuit found no sex discrimination when a female chemist was passed over for a promotion because her supervisor preferred research scientists over production testing chemists and there was a personality clash between the plaintiff and her supervisor.

Section 703 directly states that an employer is not allowed to discharge or to refuse to hire persons because of their race, color, religion, sex, or national origin. Section 703 also prohibits discrimination with respect to "compensation, terms, conditions or privileges of employment." Obviously, this prohibits an employer from paying a person less because of her race, color, religion, sex, or national origin. The meaning of the other terms is less evident, and paralegals must turn to the case law to understand the meaning of "terms, conditions, or privileges of employment." Case law reveals that fringe benefits and promotions are included. The United States Supreme Court has held that where an attorney joined a law firm as an associate, but with the promise that she would be considered for partnership in the firm, that promise was a "term, condition or privilege" of her employment.[5]

An Overview of the Remedies Afforded by Title VII

Before narrowing the focus to the prohibition against retaliation, it is instructive to take a brief look at the extensive remedies Title VII affords. Section 706(g) gives courts the power to enjoin employers from engaging in prohibited activities and the power to award a wide array of remedies to employees. For the exact language of section 706, see Figure 3–12. Section 706 specifies that courts may order employers to hire or to reinstate employees and may also award back pay as a remedy. The Civil Rights Act of 1991(28 U.S.C. § 1981a) expanded the available remedies to include compensatory and punitive damages.

FIGURE 3–12
Section 706(g) of Title VII (42 U.S.C. § 2000e-5(g))

(g) Relief available

(1) If the court finds that the respondent has intentionally engaged in or is intentionally engaging in an unlawful employment practice charged in the complaint, the court may enjoin the respondent from engaging in such unlawful employment practice, and order such affirmative action as may be appropriate, which may include, but is not limited to, reinstatement or hiring of employees, with or without back pay (payable by the employer, employment agency, or labor organization, as the case may be, responsible for the unlawful employment practice), or any other equitable relief as the court deems appropriate. Back pay liability shall not accrue from a date more than two years prior to the filing of a charge with the Commission. Interim earnings or amounts earnable with reasonable diligence by the person or persons discriminated against shall operate to reduce the back pay otherwise allowable.

(2)(A) No order of the court shall require the admission or reinstatement of an individual as a member of a union, or the hiring, reinstatement, or promotion of an individual as an employee, or the payment to him of any back pay, if such individual was refused admission, suspended, or expelled, or was refused employment or advancement or was suspended or discharged for any reason other than discrimination on account of race, color, religion, sex, or national origin or in violation of section 2000e-3(a) of this title.

FIGURE 3–12
(continued)

> (B) On a claim in which an individual proves a violation under section 2000e-2(m) of this title and a respondent demonstrates that the respondent would have taken the same action in the absence of the impermissible motivating factor, the court—
>
> (i) may grant declaratory relief, injunctive relief (except as provided in clause (ii)), and attorney's fees and costs demonstrated to be directly attributable only to the pursuit of a claim under section 2000e-2(m) of this title; and
>
> (ii) shall not award damages or issue an order requiring any admission, reinstatement, hiring, promotion, or payment, described in subparagraph (A).

In *Albemarle Paper Company v. Moody*,[6] the United States Supreme Court explained that one purpose of Title VII is to restore victims of unlawful employment practices to the position they would have been in were it not for the unlawful discrimination. Obviously, to accomplish these purposes, courts must have wide latitude in fashioning remedies.

There are, however, some restrictions on the remedies courts can order. For instance, section 706(g) provides that back pay can accrue only to the date two years prior to the filing of a charge with the EEOC. It states that the amount of back pay awarded must be offset by the amount of the plaintiff's interim earnings, that is, the amount the plaintiff earned performing another job during the course of the litigation. Thus, courts have denied an award of back pay when the plaintiff's interim earnings were higher than the amount the plaintiff would have earned if the employer had not discriminated against the plaintiff.[7]

Section 706(k) provides that courts may award attorney fees to the prevailing party. This is an important feature of Title VII. As paralegals may recall from litigation courses, the general rule in the United States is that each party pays its own attorney fees. Courts are allowed to order one party to pay the other party's attorney fees only when allowed by statute. Title VII is such a statute, and it is important to remember the attorney fee provision. Note that this applies only to private attorneys, not to the EEOC, which is a federal agency with attorneys on staff.

Title VII's Prohibition Against Retaliation

You now have an overview of the general prohibitions against employment discrimination under Title VII. To gain a practical understanding of Title VII, the text narrows the focus to section 704(a), which prohibits employers from retaliating against employees who have opposed activities made unlawful by Title VII. See Figure 3–13 for the language of section 704(a) of Title VII (42 U.S.C § 2000e-3(a)).

FIGURE 3–13
Section 704(a) of
Title VII (42
U.S.C.
§ 2000e-3(a))

---

§ 2000e-3.   Other unlawful employment practices

Discrimination for making charges, testifying, assisting, or participating in enforcement proceedings

(a) It shall be an unlawful employment practice for an employer to discriminate against any of his employees or applicants for employment, for an employment agency, or joint labor-management committee controlling apprenticeship or other training or retraining, including on-the-job training programs, to discriminate against any individual, or for a labor organization to discriminate against any member thereof or applicant for membership, because he has opposed any practice made an unlawful employment practice by this subchapter, or because he has made a charge, testified, assisted, or participated in any manner in an investigation, proceeding, or hearing under this subchapter.

Paralegals must understand the relationship of section 704(a) to the Title VII statute as a whole. Section 704(a) is part of Title VII. It prohibits a specific type of action by employers, that is, retaliation. Congress recognized that it must afford protection to those who seek the benefits of Title VII. If an employer had free rein to discharge or retaliate in some other form against employees who sought the protection of Title VII, then Title VII would not be an effective statute.

What Constitutes Retaliation

Speaking generally, **retaliation** occurs when an employee engages in a protected activity and an employer then takes an unlawful action against the employee.

Examples of Protected Activities. The statute and regulations do not spell out in detail what constitutes a protected activity. Thus, paralegals must turn to the case law for guidance. In most cases alleging retaliation, employees have observed and then reported activities made unlawful by section 703 of Title VII—discrimination on the basis of

---

retaliation In the context of title VII, retaliation occurs when an employee has engaged in a protected activity and an employer takes an unlawful action against the employee because of his or her action.

race, color, religion, sex, or national origin. The employees then complained about the activities directly to their employers or went to the EEOC and filed charges that their employers had engaged in unlawful employment practices.

An instructive case is *Sherrill v. J.P. Stevens and Co., Inc.*[8] Here, a black employee at a yarn manufacturing plant (the company) was denied promotion when he applied for various positions at the plant, including supervisory positions. After he was passed over for one promotion, Sherrill wrote a letter to the company and complained that he had been passed over because of his race. Sherrill then was called to a series of meetings with management. He was criticized and threatened by fellow employees. Sherrill requested a six-month leave to obtain further training and to take a vacation because of the pressures on him after he wrote his letter. Leave was denied, although leave had been granted to white employees with similar requests. Sherrill felt frightened after some further conferences with management, and he left the company, although he later expressed a desire to return to the company if afforded better opportunities.

Sherrill's lawsuit was certified as a class action, with the class including black employees and applicants affected by the alleged racially discriminatory employment practices. Thus, the *Sherrill* case involved violations of both section 703 for the alleged unlawful practices against black employees, and section 704(a) for alleged retaliation against Sherrill. The trial court found that the company had engaged in discriminatory actions against black employees and applicants in violation of section 703. In regard to the retaliation charge, the court found that "[t]he reprisals against plaintiff Sherrill which resulted in termination of his employment constitute[d] a violation of section 704(a) of Title VII . . . ." The actions considered reprisals by the court were the conferences into which Sherrill was called, threats and harassment by white employees, and denial of leave to study for a better job. As a remedy, the court ordered Sherrill's reinstatement with back pay.

Courts have found that employees engaged in protected activities when they reported alleged unlawful employment practices to officials in the company or the board of directors. The filing of formal charges with the EEOC is also a protected activity.[9] Section 704(a) also protects persons who participate in investigations and hearings regarding unlawful employment practices.[10]

Examples of Unlawful Actions Against Employees. Before examining actions that constitute retaliation, it is important to note that in order to constitute retaliation, the employer must have knowledge of the employee's participation in protected activities. Thus, where an employee alleged that she was transferred to a job she did not want, it was determined that this was not a retaliatory act, because the supervisor who transferred the employee did not know that the employee had filed a charge with the EEOC.[11]

When an employee is discharged from a job because the employee participated in a protected activity, this violates section 704(a). Other retaliatory actions include denial of a promotion, suspension from a job, or transfer to a different position.[12] Harassment has also been found to be retaliatory, as in the *Sherrill* case discussed above.

What Does Not Constitute Retaliation

It is equally instructive to examine cases where the courts found no retaliation within the meaning of section 703(a).

Activities That Are Not Protected. Not every action taken by an employee against an employer is protected. For instance, in *McDonnell Douglas Corp. v. Green,*[13] the employee had participated in a "stall-in," blocking the road that gave access to the work place during rush hour. He also participated in a "lock-in," where a chain and padlock were placed on a door to prevent employees from leaving. The United States Supreme Court stated that "[n]othing in Title VII compels an employer to absolve or rehire one who has engaged in such deliberate, unlawful activity against it."[14] Section 704(a) does not protect tortious or criminal activity or activity that "interferes with the work of the employer or other employees."[15]

Claims Without Foundation. Section 704(a) does not afford protection to baseless accusations. Although the law does not require that the employer actually be guilty of employment discrimination, the employee must have a good faith belief that the employment practices were unlawful.[16] Section 704(a) does not afford protection to employees who make unfounded claims of discrimination in order to excuse noncompliance with legitimate employer demands.[17]

Usually the question of whether section 704(a) affords protection is not so clear cut. There are often factual disputes. For instance, there may be conflicting evidence as to whether the employer had knowledge that the employee had opposed an allegedly unlawful employment practice. Frequently the trial court must determine whether an action was taken against an employee as a result of retaliation or for a legitimate, nondiscriminatory reason.

Sequence of Proof

The courts have fashioned a sequence of proof for retaliation cases, which is an adaptation of the sequence of proof prescribed in

McDonnell Douglas. The United States Circuit Court of Appeals for the District of Columbia explained in *Williams v. Boorstin* that "*McDonnell Douglas* applies in retaliation cases where employers discharge or fail to promote employees who have engaged in activities fighting discrimination."[18] The court described the sequence of proof as follows:

> The *McDonnell Douglas* approach directs a Title VII plaintiff to make out a *prima facie* case of retaliation, thus shifting to the defendant the burden of rebuttal. The employer then may demonstrate a legitimate and nonretaliatory reason for discharging or not promoting the plaintiff. Such a reason would dispel the inference of retaliation. . . . If the employer adduces a lawful reason for his adverse act, the employee may show, in the final step of the *McDonnell Douglas* analysis, that the employer's reason is merely a "pretext" covering up unlawful retaliation through the guise of innocent business planning.[19]

Because the plaintiff's first step is to establish a prima facie case, it is important for paralegals to know the elements necessary to establish a prima facie case. The plaintiff must establish that he or she engaged in protected activity, such as protesting an unlawful employment practice. The plaintiff must also establish that the plaintiff suffered adverse treatment as a result and that there was a causal link between the protected opposition and the adverse treatment.[20]

Refer to Figure 3–14 for a chart summarizing the sequence of proof and the elements of a prima facie case. Paralegals must read the case law to learn how to apply the sequence of proof framework. Exercises at the end of Chapter 3 and discussion in the remainder of the text will provide this opportunity.

FIGURE 3–14
Summary of Sequence of Proof for Retaliation Claim

1. The plaintiff has the initial burden to establish a prima facie case of retaliation. The three elements of the prima facie case are:

   a. the plaintiff engaged in protected activity;
   b. the plaintiff suffered adverse treatment thereafter; and
   c. there was a causal link between the protected activity and the adverse treatment.

2. The burden shifts to the employer to articulate a legitimate and nonretaliatory reason for its action.

3. The plaintiff has the opportunity to show that the articulated reason was a pretext.

Balancing the Interests of the Employee and Employer

Title VII, including the protection from retaliation established in section 704(a), seeks to protect employees without forcing employers to hire or retain unqualified or unfit employees. The Supreme Court explained in *McDonnell Douglas* that the purpose of Congress in enacting Title VII was "to assure equality of employment opportunities and to eliminate those discriminatory practices and devices which have fostered racially stratified job environments to the disadvantage of minority citizens."[21] The Court further stated that the purpose of Title VII is not "to guarantee a job to every person regardless of qualifications." "Discriminatory preference for any group, minority or majority, is precisely and only what Congress has proscribed."[22]

Summary

Chapter 3 addresses the substantive law of Social Security disability and Title VII of the 1964 Civil Rights Act.

The Substantive Law of Social Security Disability

The Social Security Administration administers several benefits programs. Chapter 3 focuses on Title II disability insurance benefits, a program that provides benefits for persons under age sixty-five who are unable to work.

The Social Security Act provides that there are four requirements for entitlement to disability insurance benefits. The applicant, called a claimant, (1) must be insured for disability insurance benefits, (2) must not have attained retirement age, (3) must file an application, and (4) must be under a disability as defined in the Social Security Act. Essentially, the Social Security Act defines disability as the inability to perform past work *or any other work*. The Act does not require that a job actually be available for a claimant; the claimant need only be capable of performing jobs that exist in significant numbers in the national economy.

The definition of disability stated in the regulations essentially restates the definition in the statute. The regulations, however, provide the procedure formulated by the SSA to determine whether a person is disabled. This procedure is called the sequential evaluation process, which consists of five questions:

Step One: Is the claimant engaging in substantial gainful activity? If so, the claimant is found "not disabled" at the first step. The regulations explain the meaning of substantial gainful activity as work that involves significant physical or mental activities and is usually performed for pay or profit. Earnings of more than $500 per month are generally considered to constitute substantial gainful activity.

Step Two: Does the claimant have impairments that are "severe"? The word "severe" has a specific regulatory meaning that differs from the way people use the word ordinarily. The regulations provide that an impairment is severe if, considered alone or in combination with other impairments, it significantly limits physical or mental ability to do basic work activities. Basic work activities include walking, sitting, standing, and lifting, as well as the ability to understand directions. Interpretation of the term "severe" has been the subject of litigation, and United States Circuit Courts of Appeal have reached somewhat varying conclusions. One interpretation is that an impairment is "not severe" if it is only a slight abnormality that has no more than a minimal effect on the person's ability to work. If a claimant has no severe impairments, the claimant is found "not disabled" at the second step.

Step Three: Does the claimant have an impairment or combination of impairments that meets or equals any of the Secretary's Listing of Impairments? The Listing of Impairments is part of the SSA's regulations, designed to identify impairments so serious that they dictate a finding of disability. The Listings are divided into fourteen body systems, with impairments and their related symptoms listed under each system. If a claimant meets the criteria of one of the impairments, the claimant is found disabled at the third step.

Before progressing to Steps Four and Five in the sequential evaluation process, paralegals must understand the term "residual functional capacity." This is the work capacity that persons retain despite their impairments. The regulations categorize jobs in five levels—sedentary, light, medium, heavy, and very heavy—based on the exertional demands of the job. The level is determined primarily by the amount of weight that must be lifted. Further, sedentary work does not require prolonged standing and walking. Refer to Figure 3–7 for the exertional demands of each of the five levels.

Step Four: Is the claimant able to perform past relevant work? A job performed by a claimant before the claimant became disabled is considered past relevant work if it was performed within the past fifteen years, was performed long enough for the claimant to learn the job, and was performed at a level showing substantial gainful activity. If a claimant retains a residual functional capacity that allows the claimant to perform past relevant work, he or she is found not disabled at Step Four. Thus, if a claimant remains able to perform light work and her past relevant work was performed at the light exertional level, she is found not disabled. However, if she can perform only sedentary work, progress to Step Five.

Step Five: Is the claimant able to perform any other work? The claimant's residual functional capacity remains critical to the outcome at Step Five. Additional vocational factors, however, are now considered, including age and education. Generally speaking, the older a person is and the less formal education he or she has, the more likely the person is to be found disabled. The regulations divide educational levels into four categories and also provide four age categories. These categories are used in applying the Medical-Vocational Guidelines to determine whether a person is disabled. Table No. 1 of the Medical-Vocational Guidelines applies to persons with a residual functional capacity for sedentary work. To apply the rules in Table No. 1 (Figure 3–10), find the rule that has the same age category, education category, and past work experience that the claimant has. That rule applies to the claimant and directs a finding of either "disabled" or "not disabled." Table No. 2 (Figure 3–11) is applied to persons with a residual functional capacity for light work, and Table No. 3 to persons with a residual functional capacity for medium work.

The SSA relies on vocational experts to state whether a claimant has transferable skills. In the text, you will be given the information as to skill level or transferable skills when asked to apply the grids.

To determine whether there are a significant number of jobs a claimant can perform, the SSA may rely on the grids for claimants with exertional limitations, that is, limitations in physical abilities such as standing and lifting. If a claimant has nonexertional limitations— limitations that affect something other than strength—the grids cannot be automatically applied. Nonexertional limitations include mental impairments or restrictions on the work environment such as intolerance of fumes or temperature extremes. If a claimant has non-exertional limitations, the SSA uses a vocational expert to testify as to whether there exist a significant number of jobs which the claimant can perform, taking into consideration nonexertional and exertional limitations.

The Substantive Law of Title VII of the 1964 Civil Rights Act

Title VII prohibits employment discrimination that is based on race, color, religion, sex, or national origin. The EEOC enforces Title VII.

Title VII refers to "employers" as that term is defined in the statute. Employers include private businesses, as well as federal, state, and local governments and other entities discussed in the text. Specifically excluded from Title VII coverage are companies that have fifteen or fewer employees.

Section 703 prohibits discrimination in respect to "compensation, terms, conditions or privileges of employment," which includes discharging, failing to promote, or paying an employee less than others doing similar work. Fringe benefits are also included.

Section 706(g) of Title VII gives courts the power to grant injunctive relief and allows a variety of remedies to make whole a person who has suffered employment discrimination. Remedies include reinstatement to a job and back pay.

The discussion in Chapter 3 focuses on section 704(a) of Title VII, which prohibits employers from retaliating against employees who have opposed activities made unlawful by Title VII. An action can constitute retaliation when the employee has engaged in a protected activity and the employer then takes an unlawful action against the employee as a result. Examples of protected activities include filing formal charges with the EEOC, participating in investigations and hearings, and reporting unlawful activities to the board of directors. The employer must know about the employee's action. Examples of unlawful actions against employees include termination, demotion, unwanted job transfers, harassment, and denial of a promotion, to name a few.

Section 704(a) does not protect employees who make baseless claims (lacking a good faith belief that the activity was unlawful) or who have engaged in criminal or tortious conduct.

Courts have fashioned a sequence of proof for Title VII retaliation cases. Refer to Figure 3–14 for a summary.

Title VII seeks to balance the interests of employees and employers. Title VII does not guarantee a job for persons in protected classes regardless of their qualifications. The person in a protected class must have suffered discrimination or retaliation in order to invoke the relief given in Title VII.

Review Questions

1. Which of the following are nonexertional limitations as described in Social Security regulations? _____
   a. ability to lift
   b. ability to concentrate
   c. ability to stand
   d. none of the above

2. A claimant will be found "not disabled" within the meaning of the Social Security Act in which of the following circumstances? _____
   a. when the claimant can perform past relevant work
   b. when the claimant's impairments do not meet or equal a Listing of Impairments
   c. when the claimant does not have a severe impairment

3. The work capacity that a person retains despite impairments is called _____.
   a. residual functional capacity
   b. past relevant work
   c. sequential evaluation process
   d. none of the above

4. Which of the following are vocational factors used to determine whether a person is disabled? _____
   a. gender
   b. age
   c. education
   d. all of the above
   e. b and c only

5. In assessing a retaliation claim, when an employee engages in a protected activity, it is immaterial whether the employee's supervisor knows of the activity.   True ___ / False ___

6. In order to establish a prima facie case of retaliation, the employee must show a causal connection between his protected action and the adverse treatment he receives.   True ___ / False ___

7. Title VII seeks to protect employees regardless of the interests of the employer.   True ___ / False ___

8. A claimant who completed the eighth grade has a marginal education as defined in the regulations.   True ___ / False ___

9. In a Title VII retaliation case, the plaintiff has the initial burden of proof to establish a prima facie case of retaliation.   True ___ / False ___

10. Once an employer shows a legitimate and nonretaliatory reason for discharging an employee, the plaintiff automatically loses in a Title VII retaliation case.   True ___ / False ___

11. Describe the five steps in the sequential evaluation process.

12. Why has Title VII generated extensive litigation?

Factual Analysis Questions

1. Analyze the following fact situation and discuss whether the employee can establish a prima facie case of retaliation under Title VII: Anita Garry, a black employee at a chemical plant, assisted another employee in filing a charge of race discrimination with the EEOC and participated in a hearing related to the charge. Afterward, she was transferred to a less desirable position in another part of the chemical plant.

2. Assume that Anita Garry has established a prima facie case of retaliation. You now learn that she was not performing her former job adequately and received unsatisfactory performance reviews. How would this affect her chances of establishing retaliation?

3. Assume that a court found the transfer appeared to be based on a legitimate and nonretaliatory reason. Does Anita Garry lose the case?

4. Analyze the following fact situation, and discuss whether the claimant meets the criteria of section 1.11 of the Listing of Impairments: Bill Deal was in an automobile accident in January 1994 and suffered a fracture of his femur. He underwent surgery, and X-rays in March 1994 showed a nonunion. He underwent further treatment, and X-rays in July 1994 revealed that a solid union had been achieved. At this point, Bill Deal's doctor allowed him to return to full weight-bearing status.

5. In January 1995 Bill Deal still has not returned to work. He worked for three years as a cashier in a grocery store, a job classified as light work. Deal's doctor has stated that the claimant is limited to lifting twenty-five pounds and that he can engage in prolonged standing and walking. Is he able to perform his past relevant work?

Practical Applications

Exercise 1

Read the facts of the Lewis case, Sample Case One and answer the following questions.

1. Mrs. Lewis was fifty-two years old on her alleged onset date. How do the regulations define the age category into which she fits?

2. Mrs. Lewis completed the eleventh grade. How do the regulations define the education category into which she fits?

3. Does Mrs. Lewis's past job in the Christmas ornament factory qualify as past relevant work? Explain.

4. Mrs. Lewis's job as a cashier required her to stand most of the time and to lift twenty pounds at a time. How do the regulations define this exertional level—is it sedentary, light, or some other level?

5. If an administrative law judge finds that Mrs. Lewis retains a residual functional capacity for light work, will she be found disabled?

6. If an administrative law judge finds that Mrs. Lewis retains a residual functional capacity for sedentary work, will she be found disabled based on the grids? Assume that her job as a cashier was unskilled work.

7. If Mrs. Lewis were forty-seven years old and the other vocational factors are the same, would she be found disabled based on the grids?

Exercise 2

Read the facts of the Watson case, Sample Case Two and answer the following questions.

1. Title VII prohibits employment discrimination based on one of five factors enumerated in the statute itself. If Watson had a claim for employment discrimination when she failed to receive the promotion, on which of the five enumerated factors would her claim be based?

2. Is Minos an employer within the meaning of Title VII?

3. Is failure to receive a promotion considered a term, condition, or privilege of employment?

4. In regard to the retaliation claim, did Martinez engage in protected activity?

5. What action did Minos take that could be considered retaliatory?

Case Analysis

Read the excerpts below from *Heckler v. Campbell*, 461 U.S. 458 (1983), and answer the following questions.

Justice POWELL delivered the opinion of the Court.

The Social Security Act defines "disability" in terms of the effect a physical or mental impairment has on a person's ability to function in the work place. It provides disability benefits only to persons who are unable "to engage in any substantial gainful activity by reason of any medically determinable physical or mental impairment." And it specifies that a person must "not only [be] unable to do his previous work but [must be unable], considering his age, education, and work experience, [to] engage in any other kind of substantial gainful work which exists in the national economy, regardless of whether such work exists in the immediate area in which he lives, or whether a specific job vacancy exists for him, or whether he would be hired if he applied for work."

In 1978, the Secretary of Health and Human Services promulgated regulations implementing this definition. The regulations recognize that certain impairments are so severe that they prevent a person from pursuing any gainful work. A claimant who establishes that he suffers from one of these impairments will be considered disabled without further inquiry. If a claimant suffers from a less severe impairment, the Secretary must determine whether the claimant retains the ability to perform either his former work or some less demanding employment. If a claimant can pursue his former occupation, he is not entitled to disability benefits. If he cannot, the Secretary must determine whether the claimant retains the capacity to pursue less demanding work.

The regulations divide this last inquiry into two stages. First, the Secretary must assess each claimant's present job qualifications. The regulations direct the Secretary to consider the factors Congress has identified as relevant: physical ability, age, education and work experience. Second, she must consider whether jobs exist in the national economy that a person having the claimant's qualifications could perform.

Prior to 1978, the Secretary relied on vocational experts to establish the existence of suitable jobs in the national economy. After a claimant's limitations and abilities had been determined at a hearing, a vocational expert ordinarily would testify whether work existed that the claimant could perform. Although this testimony often was based on standardized guides, vocational experts frequently were criticized for their inconsistent treatment of similarly situated claimants. To improve both the uniformity and efficiency of this determination, the Secretary promulgated medical-vocational guidelines as part of the 1978 regulations.

These guidelines relieve the Secretary of the need to rely on vocational experts by establishing through rulemaking the types and numbers of jobs that exist in the national economy. They consist of a matrix of the four factors identified by Congress—physical ability, age, education, and work experience—and set forth rules that identify whether jobs requiring specific combinations of these factors exist in significant numbers in the national economy. Where a claimant's qualifications correspond to the job requirements identified by a rule, the guidelines direct a conclusion as to whether work exists that the claimant could perform. If such work exists, the claimant is not considered disabled.

In 1979, Carmen Campbell applied for disability benefits because a back condition and hypertension prevented her from continuing her work as a hotel maid. After her application was denied, she requested a hearing *de novo* before an Administrative Law Judge. He determined that her back problem was not severe enough to find her

disabled without further inquiry, and accordingly considered whether she retained the ability to perform either her past work or some less strenuous job. He concluded that even though Campbell's back condition prevented her from returning to her work as a maid, she retained the physical capacity to do light work. In accordance with the regulations, he found that Campbell was 52-years old, that her previous employment consisted of unskilled jobs and that she had a limited education. He noted that Campbell, who had been born in Panama, experienced difficulty in speaking and writing English. She was able, however, to understand and read English fairly well. Relying on the medical-vocational guidelines, the Administrative Law Judge found that a significant number of jobs existed that a person of Campbell's qualifications could perform. Accordingly, he concluded that she was not disabled.

This determination was upheld by both the Social Security Appeals Council and the District Court for the Eastern District of New York. The Court of Appeals for the Second Circuit reversed. It accepted the Administrative Law Judge's determination that Campbell retained the ability to do light work. And it did not suggest that he had classified Campbell's age, education, or work experience incorrectly.

The court found that the medical-vocational guidelines did not provide the specific evidence that it previously had required. It explained that in the absence of such a showing, "the claimant is deprived of any real chance to present evidence showing that she cannot in fact perform the types of jobs that are administratively noticed by the guidelines." The court concluded that because the Secretary had failed to introduce evidence that specific alternative jobs existed, the determination that Campbell was not disabled was not supported by substantial evidence.

We granted certiorari to resolve a conflict among the Courts of Appeals.

The Social Security Act directs the Secretary to "adopt reasonable and proper rules and regulations to regulate and provide for the nature and extent of the proofs and evidence and the method of taking and furnishing the same" in disability cases. As we previously have recognized, Congress has "conferred on the Secretary exceptionally broad authority to prescribe standards for applying certain sections of the [Social Security] Act." Where, as here, the statute expressly entrusts the Secretary with the responsibility for implementing a provision by regulation, our review is limited to determining whether the regulations promulgated exceeded the Secretary's statutory authority and whether they are arbitrary and capricious.

We do not think that the Secretary's reliance on medical-vocational guidelines is inconsistent with the Social Security Act. It is true that the statutory scheme contemplates that disability hearings will be individualized determinations based on evidence adduced at a hearing. But this does not bar the Secretary from relying on rulemaking to resolve certain classes of issues. The Court has recognized that even where an agency's enabling statute expressly requires it to hold a hearing, the agency may rely on its rulemaking authority to determine issues that do not require case-by-case consideration. A contrary holding would require the agency continually to relitigate issues that may be established fairly and efficiently in a single rule-making proceeding.

In determining whether a claimant can perform less strenuous work, the Secretary must make two determinations. She must assess each claimant's individual abilities and then determine whether jobs exist that a person having the claimant's qualifications could perform. The first inquiry involves a determination of historic facts, and the regulations properly require the Secretary to make these findings on the basis of evidence adduced at a hearing. We note that the regulations afford claimants ample opportunity both to present evidence relating to their own abilities and to offer evidence that the guidelines do not apply to them. The second inquiry requires the Secretary to determine an issue that is not unique to each claimant—the types and numbers of jobs that exist in the national economy. This type of general factual issue may be resolved as fairly through rulemaking as by introducing the testimony of vocational experts at each disability hearing.

As the Secretary has argued, the use of published guidelines brings with it a uniformity that previously had been perceived as lacking. To require the Secretary to relitigate the existence of jobs in the national economy at each hearing would hinder needlessly an already overburdened agency. We conclude that the Secretary's use of medical-vocational guidelines does not conflict with the statute, nor can we say on the record before us that they are arbitrary and capricious.

The Court of Appeals' decision would require the Secretary to introduce evidence of specific available jobs that respondent could perform. It would limit severely her ability to rely on the medical-vocational guidelines. We think the Secretary reasonably could choose to rely on these guidelines in appropriate cases rather than on the testimony of a vocational expert in each case. Accordingly, the judgment of the Court of Appeals is

Reversed.

1. In what year did the SSA promulgate the Medical-Vocational Guidelines?
2. Prior to 1978, what method did the SSA use at each claimant's hearing to establish there were a significant number of jobs that the claimant could perform?
3. The Court mentions at least two reasons why the SSA promulgated the Medical-Vocational Guidelines. State two reasons.
4. Did the Court find that the Medical-Vocational Guidelines were within the authority delegated by Congress to the SSA? Why?
5. The Social Security Act requires that all claimants receive an individualized assessment in determining whether they are disabled. Why did the Court find that the Medical-Vocational Guidelines, with their broad application, nevertheless meet the requirement for individualized assessments?

Notes

[1] 734 F.2d 1012 (4th Cir. 1984).

[2] 493 U.S. 521 (1990).

[3] Title VII applies to the federal government, even though the definition of "employer" in section 701 excludes the federal government. Section 717 of Title VII sets forth different procedures for federal employees to pursue an employment discrimination claim but specifically prohibits the federal government from engaging in discrimination on the basis of race, color, religion, sex, and national origin.

[4] 743 F.2d 612, 616 (8th Cir. 1984).

[5] *Hishon v. King & Spalding,* 467 U.S. 69, at 74–75 (1984).

[6] *Albemarle Paper Co. v. Moody,* 422 U.S. 405 (1975).

[7] *See, e.g., EEOC v. New York Times Broadcasting Serv., Inc.,* 542 F.2d 356, 359 (6th Cir. 1976).

[8] 410 F. Supp. 770 (W.D.N.C. 1975), *aff'd,* 551 F.2d 308 (4th Cir. 1977).

[9] *Pettway v. American Cast Iron Pipe Co.,* 411 F.2d 998 (5th Cir. 1969).

[10] *Eichmann v. Indiana State Univ. Bd. of Trustees,* 597 F.2d 1104 (7th Cir. 1979).

[11] *See* Annotation, *Construction and Application of § 704(a) of Civil Rights Act of 1964 (42 U.S.C. § 2000e-3), Making It Unlawful Employment Practice to Discriminate Against Individual for Participation in Equal Opportunity Proceedings or Activities,* 11 A.L.R. Fed. 316, at 344.

[12] For examples, see 11 A.L.R. Fed. 316.

[13] 411 U.S. 792 (1973).

[14] 411 U.S. at 804. The U.S. Supreme Court remanded the case for retrial, noting that the court below had seriously underestimated the weight to be given to the employer's reason for refusing to rehire Green.

[15] Mack Player, *Federal Law of Employment Discrimination,* 2d ed. (St. Paul: West Publishing Co., 1981), at 136.

[16] 11 A.L.R. Fed. 316, at 334–35.

[17] *Id.*

[18] 663 F.2d at 116 (D.C. Cir. 1980), *cert. denied,* 451 U.S. 985 (1981).

[19] *Id.*

[20] *Donnellon v. Fruehauf Corp.,* 794 F.2d 598, 600–01 (11th Cir. 1986).

[21] 411 U.S. at 800.

[22] 411 U.S. at 800–01 (quoting *Griggs v. Duke Power Co.,* 401 U.S. 430–31 (1971)).

||||

CHAPTER 4

THE SUBSTANTIVE LAW OF NATURALIZATION AND HAZARDOUS WASTE MANAGEMENT

Chapter 4 addresses the substantive law of two additional important areas of administrative law—immigration law and environmental law. In the area of immigration law, the text discusses **naturalization**, the process by which a person becomes a United States citizen. In the area of environmental law, the text discusses hazardous waste management. Both immigration law and environmental law are rapidly growing areas and thus are ripe areas of employment for paralegals.

Before addressing the law of naturalization, an overview of immigration law is necessary to understand how naturalization fits into the entire scheme of immigration law in the United States.

An Overview of Immigration Law

In the Immigration and Nationality Act (INA), Congress has defined the categories that entitle aliens to enter and remain in the United States. Aliens can enter and remain in the United States only if they have a valid immigration status, that is, they fit into one of these designated categories. Immigration attorneys and paralegals identify the approved category into which a client fits and prepare the application and supporting documentation to establish that the client fits in that category.

Recall from Chapter 1 that a visa is a document that allows an alien to enter another country. Some aliens seek nonimmigrant visas, which allow them to remain in the United States for a specific number of years, usually one to five years. Common nonimmigrant visas include the F-1 student visa, which allows aliens to remain in the United States during the course of their studies. Another common nonimmigrant visa is the L-1 intracompany transferee. Suppose a German chemical company has purchased a chemical company in the United States and wishes to send a manager from Germany to the United States for three years to manage its newly acquired operations and set up certain procedures like those used in the German facilities. The manager applies for an L-1 nonimmigrant visa, which allows intracompany transferees to work in their companies' facilities in the United States for several years.

Other aliens seek immigrant visas, which allow aliens to enter the United States and remain here permanently. These aliens become

---

BALLENTINE'S

naturalization The process and the act of conferring nationality and citizenship upon a person who is not a natural-born citizen.

lawful permanent residents, which means that they have a "green card" and can enter and leave the United States freely. After a person has been a lawful permanent resident for the required number of years, he or she may apply to become a United States citizen through the process called naturalization.

Many aliens qualify for immigrant visas because of their relationship to persons who are citizens of the United States. For instance, an alien who marries a United States citizen can become a lawful permanent resident. Other aliens become lawful permanent residents because they have established that they possess certain work skills needed in the United States and that they would not displace an American worker.

Naturalization

Assume that your law firm's client entered the United States and was granted political asylum, a classification that allows her to remain in the United States. One year later, she became a lawful permanent resident. Becoming a lawful permanent resident is not the same as becoming a United States citizen. These terms are frequently confused by persons unfamiliar with immigration law. A lawful permanent resident does not have the same rights and privileges as a U.S. citizen. For instance, a lawful permanent resident does not have the right to vote.

There is no requirement that a lawful permanent resident become a U.S. citizen. Many persons live in the United States for years and never become U.S. citizens. They are allowed to work and to enter and leave the United States as they wish, and simply may not wish to become U.S. citizens.

Acquiring United States Citizenship

There are two ways to become a United States citizen. The first way is by birth. Individuals born in the United States are U.S. citizens. Some individuals born outside the United States also are U.S. citizens at birth. For instance, a child born outside the United States to two U.S. citizen parents becomes a U.S. citizen at birth, provided at least one parent resided in the United States prior to the child's birth.[1] When all other statutory requirements are met, a child born outside the United States to one parent who is a U.S. citizen is also a citizen at birth.[2]

---

lawful permanent resident An alien who has been granted an immigrant visa, allowing the alien to remain in the United States and to enter and leave the United States freely.

The Requirements for Naturalization

The other way to become a United States citizen is through the process called naturalization. The requirements for becoming a naturalized U.S. citizen are set forth in 8 U.S.C. § 1427(a), which is reprinted as Figure 4–1, and 8 CFR 316.2, reprinted as Figure 4–2.

FIGURE 4–1
8 U.S.C. § 1427(a)

§ 1427.   Requirements of naturalization

(a) Residence
No person, except as otherwise provided in this subchapter, shall be naturalized unless such applicant, (1) immediately preceding the date of filing his application for naturalization has resided continuously, after being lawfully admitted for permanent residence, within the United States for at least five years and during the five years immediately preceding the date of filing his application has been physically present therein for periods totaling at least half of that time, and who has resided within the State or within the district of the Service in the United States in which the applicant filed the application for at least three months, (2) has resided continuously within the United States from the date of the application up to the time of admission to citizenship, and (3) during all the period referred to in this subsection has been and still is a person of good moral character, attached to the principles of the Constitution of the United States, and well disposed to the good order and happiness of the United States.

FIGURE 4–2
8 CFR 316.2

316.2   Eligibility.

(a) *General.* Except as otherwise provided in this chapter, to be eligible for naturalization, an alien must establish that he or she:
(1) Is at least 18 years of age;
(2) Has been lawfully admitted as a permanent resident of the United States;
(3) Has resided continuously within the United States, as defined under § 316.5, for a period of at least five years after having been lawfully admitted;
(4) Has been physically present in the United States for at least 30 months of the five years preceding the date of filing the application;
(5) Immediately preceding the filing of an application, or immediately preceding the examination on the application if the application was filed early pursuant to section 334(a) of the Act and the three month period falls within the required period of residence under section 316(a) or 319(a) of the Act, has resided, as defined under § 316.5, for at least three months in a State or Service district having jurisdiction over the applicant's actual

FIGURE 4–2
(continued)

place of residence, and in which the alien seeks to file the application;

(6) Has resided continuously within the United States from the date of application for naturalization up to the time of admission to citizenship;

(7) For all relevant time periods under this paragraph, has been and continues to be a person of good moral character, attached to the principles of the Constitution of the United States, and favorably disposed toward the good order and happiness of the United States; and

(8) Is not a person described in Section 314 of the Act relating to deserters of the United States Armed Forces or those persons who departed from the United States to evade military service in the United States Armed Forces.

(b) *Burden of proof.* The applicant shall bear the burden of establishing that he or she meets all of the requirements for naturalization, including that the applicant was lawfully admitted as a permanent resident to the United States, in accordance with the immigration laws in effect at the time of the applicant's initial entry or any subsequent reentry.

Lawful Admission as a Permanent Resident

The applicant must have been "lawfully accorded the privilege of residing permanently in the United States as an immigrant in accordance with the immigration laws." The statute specifies that the person must have been *lawfully* admitted. Thus, if a person obtained lawful permanent resident status illegally, he or she will be denied naturalization. For instance, suppose that an alien became a permanent resident by misrepresenting facts on his petition for an immigrant visa and that permanent resident status would have been denied if he had told the truth. He did not become a permanent resident lawfully and thus was ineligible for naturalization.[3]

There is one exception. Aliens who served honorably in the United States armed forces in time of war can be naturalized without first becoming permanent residents, if they enlisted or were inducted while in the United States or certain other territories specified in 8 U.S.C. § 1440(a).

Residency Requirements

The INA defines "residence" as the "place of general abode; the place of general abode of a person means his principal, actual dwelling place in fact, without regard to intent."[4] After becoming a permanent resident, an applicant for naturalization must have continuous residence in the United States for at least five years immediately preceding the date the applicant files the application for naturalization. The residency requirement is only three years for spouses of United States citizens.

Further, the applicant must have resided in the state in which the applicant files the application for at least three months immediately before the filing of the application. Finally, the applicant must reside in the United States from the time of filing the application until the time of admission to citizenship.

Extended absences have adverse effects. An absence of one year or more breaks the continuity of residence, as provided in 8 U.S.C. § 1427(b). Absences of less than six months do not break the continuity. Absences of more than six months but less than one year raise a presumption that the applicant has abandoned continuous residence, although the presumption may be rebutted.[5] The statute (8 U.S.C. § 1427(b)) does allow certain persons to apply to preserve their residence, such as employees of the United States government and persons engaged in religious functions.

Physical Presence Requirements

A person may have residence in the United States without being continuously physically present. This is similar to residency determinations made for purposes of jurisdiction and venue with the Rules of Civil Procedure, where a person may be a resident of New York even though the person spends three months each year in Florida.

For at least one-half of the required five-year residency period, the applicant must have been physically present in the United States. Thus, the applicant must have been physically present for an aggregate of thirty months. In the case of a spouse of a United States citizen, with a three-year residency requirement, eighteen months of physical presence is required. Applicants must account for all their absences from the United States. Refer to the Application for Naturalization (Figure 7–5), which requires the applicant to give, for each absence, the date the applicant left the United States, the date he or she returned, the destination, and the reason for going. One task paralegals may perform in connection with naturalization applications is the compilation of the dates during which the applicant was absent from the United States. Frequently the client will not have all the dates recorded, and you will have to examine the stamps in the passport that document a person's entry into a country.

Good Moral Character

An applicant must establish good moral character during the required residency period. The statute does, however, allow the INS to consider conduct prior to the residency period.[6]

The INA (8 U.S.C. § 1101(f)) contains a list of factors that preclude a finding of good moral character, and this is reprinted in Figure 4–3.

This list includes certain criminal convictions, giving false testimony to obtain any benefit under the INA, smuggling a person into the United States, and practicing polygamy, to cite just a few of the grounds.

FIGURE 4–3
8 U.S.C. § 1101(f)

(f)   For the purpose of this chapter—

No person shall be regarded as, or found to be, a person of good moral character who, during the period for which good moral character is required to be established, is, or was—

(1)   a habitual drunkard;

(2)   Repealed. Pub.L. 97–116, § 2(c)(1), Dec. 29, 1981, 95 Stat. 1611.

(3)   a member of one or more of the classes of persons, whether excludable or not, described in paragraphs (2)(D), (6)(E), and (9)(A) of section 1182(a) of this title; or subparagraphs (A) and (B) of section 1182(a)(2) of this title and subparagraph (C) thereof (except as such paragraph relates to a single offense of simple possession of 30 grams or less of marijuana), if the offense described therein, for which such person was convicted or of which he admits the commission, was committed during such period;

(4)   one whose income is derived principally from illegal gambling activities;

(5)   one who has been convicted of two or more gambling offenses committed during such period;

(6)   one who has given false testimony for the purpose of obtaining any benefits under this chapter;

(7)   one who during such period has been confined, as a result of conviction, to a penal institution for an aggregate period of one hundred and eighty days or more, regardless of whether the offense, or offenses, for which he has been confined were committed within or without such period;

(8)   one who at any time has been convicted of an aggravated felony (as defined in subsection (a)(43) of this section).

The list in 8 U.S.C. § 1101(f) is not all inclusive. Applicants may be found to lack good moral character for other reasons, such as failure to pay taxes or to register with the Selective Service, and the question of what type of conduct precludes a finding of good moral character has generated litigation. Conclusions that an alien did not possess good moral character have been based on failure to pay state and federal taxes, although not necessarily on failure to pay child support. An alien who had participated in murder and persecution of civilians while a member of the police in another country was found lacking in good moral character.[7] Some cases are not so clear, and courts look to the mores of the average citizen in the community where the applicant resides.[8] Courts have confirmed the statutory dictate that making intentional false statements to obtain immigration benefits supports a finding of lack of good moral character.[9]

SIDEBAR

Lying to the INS carries serious consequences at any stage. It can preclude obtaining a visa, permanent residence, or naturalization. Attorneys and paralegals must be ever vigilant and ensure that their clients are aware of the serious consequences.

The naturalization application specifically asks whether the applicant has engaged in any of the activities enumerated in the INA. Refer to item 12 on the naturalization application form illustrated in Chapter 7 (Figure 7–5).

Attachment to the Principles of the United States Constitution and Favorable Disposition to the Good Order and Happiness of the United States

The naturalization application asks "Do you believe in the Constitution and form of government of the United States?" Obviously, as a matter of public policy, the United States government does not want to grant citizenship to a person whose aim is to overthrow the government. This requirement seeks to eliminate those applicants who are not committed to the basic form of the United States government. While an applicant is not required to agree with every aspect and every action of the government, people who seek changes through violent means would not be naturalized.

Literacy

An applicant must be able to read, write, and speak words ordinarily used in the English language.[10] There are exceptions to the literacy requirement, including applicants who cannot become literate in English due to a disability, applicants who are over fifty years old and have resided for twenty years in the United States as permanent resident aliens as of the date they filed their applications, and applicants over fifty-five years old who have resided for fifteen years in the United States as permanent resident aliens as of the date of the filing of their applications.

Knowledge of the Fundamentals of the History and Government of the United States

The procedure for naturalization applications is discussed in Chapter 7. For now, it is important to know that one required step is an interview with an **INS examiner,** an INS employee who interviews aliens applying for immigration benefits and determines whether the requested benefit will be granted. The INS examiner asks the applicant questions about the basic structure of the United States government and history, such as who becomes president when both the president and vice president die or are otherwise unable to serve. The examiner may ask the applicant to explain how many stars and stripes are in the United States flag and what they stand for.

The INS has instituted a program for standardized testing for both the literacy and history/government requirements. If an applicant passes a standardized test administered and graded by a testing organization approved by the INS, then the INS examiner does not test the applicant on the ability to read and write English or the knowledge of United States history and government. The standardized test must be passed within one year of the filing date of the naturalization application.

Age Requirements

Generally, a person must be eighteen years old at the time of filing for naturalization. There are certain statutory exceptions. The most notable exception applies to children under age eighteen whose parents are being naturalized. For details, refer to 8 U.S.C. § 1433.

Absolute Bars to Naturalization

The INA precludes naturalization for certain classes of persons, such as anarchists and members of the Communist party. Note, however, that membership in the Communist party is not a bar if membership was involuntary or was necessary to obtain the necessities of life, such as food rations or employment.[11] Persons who deserted the United States armed forces are also barred, unless they receive a pardon from the president.[12] Further, a person may not be naturalized if deportation proceedings are pending.[13]

Part 7 of the naturalization application contains fifteen questions that address various grounds that may result in denial of a naturalization application. For instance, question 12(d) asks "Have you ever knowingly and for gain helped any alien to enter the U.S. illegally?" Chapter

---

INS examiner An INS employee who interviews aliens applying for immigration benefits and determines whether the requested benefits will be granted.

7 discusses how paralegals review the application with clients to ensure that none of the potential grounds of ineligibility apply. For now, the discussion turns to one of the fastest growing areas of law—environmental law.

Hazardous Waste Management

The Environmental Protection Agency (EPA) devotes a significant amount of its resources to research and standard setting as part of its mission to provide an integrated solution to pollution control. The EPA also expends significant resources enforcing the standards it has set. The discussion in this text focuses primarily on the enforcement activities of the EPA.

An Overview of Environmental Law

The EPA enforces numerous statutes, and examination of every statute enforced by the EPA is beyond the scope of this text. The following discussion focuses on the Resource Conservation and Recovery Act (RCRA). Before discussing RCRA, it is useful to have an overview of some of the major environmental control statutes.

Federal Environmental Statutes

Paralegals may already be familiar with some of the major environmental statutes, such as the Clean Air Act[14] or the Federal Water Pollution Control Act, commonly called the Clean Water Act.[15] In addition to the Clean Water Act, numerous other statutes provide protection against water pollution. These include the Safe Drinking Water Act, which sets standards that public drinking water supplies must meet and protects groundwater from contamination.[16] The Marine Protection, Research and Sanctuaries Act protects ocean water from dumping of sewage and other waste.[17] The Oil Pollution Act of 1990 imposes requirements on vessels that transport oil in order to prevent spills and establishes the framework for liability and compensation if spills occur.[18] This statute was passed after the oil spill from the *Exxon Valdez.*

A multitude of statutes address the handling and disposal of hazardous wastes. For instance, RCRA imposes requirements on companies that manufacture, transport, and dispose of hazardous waste. Paralegals should be aware, however, of the other major statutes, which include the Federal Insecticide, Fungicide and Rodenticide Act (FIFRA) and the Toxic Substances Control Act (TSCA).[19] Another major statute is the Comprehensive Environmental Response, Compensation and Liability Act, commonly called CERCLA or Superfund.[20]

There exists a wealth of publications explaining the requirements and liabilities imposed by environmental statutes. Paralegals should first read the statutes themselves and the detailed regulations issued by the EPA, then turn to the secondary sources that help explain the primary sources of environmental law.

State Environmental Statutes and How State and Federal Laws Work Together

You are now famililar with a few of the federal environmental statutes. In environmental law, however, attorneys and paralegals must also be familiar with numerous state laws. The interplay of federal and state laws is an important facet of environmental law.

State Statutes that Implement Federal Statutes. Many federal environmental statutes establish federal-state regulatory programs that give the states "the opportunity to enact and enforce laws . . . to achieve the regulatory objectives which Congress has established."[21] This means that the states have the option to pass and enforce state laws to implement the federal environmental statutes. This is true of major federal statutes including the Clean Air Act, Clean Water Act, and RCRA.

When a state opts to implement its own program, the state legislature passes the necessary laws. Then a state administrative agency becomes the primary enforcement agency and promulgates the necessary regulations. The state agency issues permits, imposes fines for violations, and performs the same duties that the EPA would perform if it were the primary enforcement agency.

When a state opts to implement its own regulatory program, the EPA is not out of the picture. A state must first get its proposed program approved by the EPA. Through its ten regional offices, the EPA also monitors the state programs. If the state program does not effectively enforce the regulatory program, the EPA will intervene. The state program must have standards at least as stringent as those prescribed by federal law and is allowed to implement standards stricter than federal ones.[22] Thus, in its oversight capacity, the EPA must ensure that the state program is at least equivalent to the federal standards and that the state administers the program effectively.

State Statutes that Stand Independent of Federal Statutes. Many states have environmental statutes with no parallel in federal law. For instance, North Carolina has regulatory programs addressing water supply watershed protection, well construction, and dam safety, which have no parallel federal statutes.[23]

Some states, especially New Jersey and California, have enacted numerous environmental protection statutes that go well beyond the protection afforded by federal law.^24 For instance, California Proposition 65 (the California Safe Drinking Water and Toxic Enforcement Act) requires the Governor to publish a list of chemicals "known to the state to cause cancer or reproductive toxicity." If a product contains a detectable quantity of one of the published chemicals, the product must contain a warning. New Jersey imposes labeling requirements on containers that are more stringent than federal standards.

Paralegals must be aware of such statutes in their own states. When the attorney-paralegal team prepares information for clients on how to comply with environmental statutes, both the federal and state statutes must be considered.

Municipal Ordinances

City and county governments also impose restrictions that can affect the daily operations of clients. Local ordinances address issues such as what types of materials may be placed in landfills. Local ordinances restrict the waste that can be emitted into the local water system. Some counties impose strict controls on automobile emissions. The ordinances differ from city to city and county to county, so it is difficult to make general observations that accurately reflect practices nationwide. The attorney-paralegal team that has clients with environmental concerns will deal regularly with local authorities. Paralegals are likely to have as much contact with local officials as with EPA regional officials.

Generally, the federal, state, and local laws operate together without undue interference. Congress does, however, have the power to pass federal statutes that preempt state and local laws. When a federal law specifically preempts state and local laws, the federal law prevails. As a practical matter, many of the major federal environmental laws specify that states may implement their own programs, consistent with the federal programs, and thus the preemption question does not arise as frequently as one might anticipate.

The Resource Conservation and Recovery Act (RCRA)

When Congress enacted RCRA, it acknowledged that the disposal of solid waste is a problem, noting that space for landfills is running out and that inadequate control of waste management "will result in substantial risks to human health and the environment."[25] Congress declared it to be the national policy of the United States that

wherever feasible, the generation of hazardous waste is to be reduced or eliminated as expeditiously as possible. Waste that is nevertheless generated should be treated, stored, or disposed of so as to minimize the present and future threat to human health and the environment.[26]

RCRA was enacted in 1976 and was significantly strengthened by the Hazardous and Solid Waste Amendments of 1984 (HWSA).

The Purpose of RCRA

RCRA regulates the management of hazardous waste from "cradle to grave." After a waste has been identified as hazardous, RCRA imposes standards for handling the waste from the time it is generated to the time it is destroyed. Specifically, RCRA controls the generation, transportation, and disposal of hazardous waste.

The Identification of Hazardous Waste

RCRA governs the handling of hazardous waste. The handling of nonhazardous waste is regulated primarily at the state level. Thus, the starting point in determining whether clients must comply with RCRA is to determine whether any of the substances they handle are identified as hazardous waste. Once a substance is identified as hazardous waste, the requirements of RCRA apply to the generation, transportation, and disposal of the waste.

SIDEBAR

If a material is not considered hazardous under RCRA, the material may nevertheless be regulated under some other statute. The most important example is CERCLA, commonly known as Superfund. CERCLA applies to inactive or abandoned waste sites, in contrast to RCRA, which applies to active waste handlers.[27] Thus, a material not classified as hazardous under RCRA may nevertheless be subject to significant regulation if it is considered hazardous under CERCLA.

EPA Definitions of Hazardous Waste. RCRA delegates to the EPA the authority to define which substances are hazardous waste. The EPA has promulgated lengthy regulations to define hazardous waste, found in 40 CFR part 261. The general definition of hazardous waste is in 40 CFR 261.3. Although the definition is fairly complex, essentially it provides that a substance is hazardous if:

1. it is not specifically excluded from the definition of hazardous waste;

2. it has one of the four characteristics of hazardous wastes described in subpart C of 40 CFR part 261 (ignitability, corrosivity, reactivity, or toxicity); or

3. it is one of the substances specifically listed by the EPA in subpart D of 40 CFR part 261.

Exclusions. The EPA's regulations specifically exempt some substances from classification as hazardous waste. The regulatory exemptions include discharges to sanitary sewers, irrigation water, high-level radioactive waste, and agricultural waste used as fertilizer.[28] Many of these substances are covered by other statutes and regulations.

Substances Designated in EPA's Lists of Hazardous Waste. The EPA has designated specific substances as hazardous waste, and they are contained in lists in subpart D of 40 CFR part 261. The EPA assigns an identification number to each hazardous waste substance. Depending on the source of the waste, its identification number starts with a certain letter. For instance, the "F-List" enumerates hazardous wastes from "nonspecific sources," and the "K-List" enumerates hazardous wastes from "specific sources." Refer to Figure 4–4, which is an excerpt from the "F-List." There is a "U-List" for materials considered to be "toxic" and a "P-List" for materials considered to be "acutely toxic," which are subject to special restrictions.

FIGURE 4–4
Excerpt from 40 CFR 261.31

§ 261.31 Hazardous wastes from non-specific sources.
(a) The following solid wastes are listed hazardous wastes from non-specific sources unless they are excluded under §§ 260.20 and 260.22 and listed in appendix IX.

Industry and EPA hazardous waste No.	Hazardous waste	Hazard code
Generic		
F001	The following spent halogenated solvents used in degreasing: Tetrachlorethylene, trichloroethylene, methylene chloride, 1,1,1-trichloroethene, carbon tetrachloride, and chlorinated fluorocarbons; all spent solvent mixtures/blends used in degressing containing, before use, a total of ten percent or more (by volume) of one or more of the above helogenated solvents or those solvents listed in F002, F004, and F005; and still bottoms from the recovery of these spent solvents and spent solvent mixtures.	(T)
F002	The following spent halogenated solvents: Tetrachloroethylene, methylene chloride, trichloroethylene, 1,1,1-trichloroethane, chlorobenzene, 1,1,2-trichloro-1,2,2-trifluoroethane, ortho-dichlorobenzene, trichlorofluorome- thane, and 1,1,2-trichloroethane; all spent solvent mixtures/blends containing, before use, a total of ten percent or more (by volume) of one or more of the above halogenated solvents or those listed in F001, F004, or F005; and still bottoms from the recovery of these spent solvents and spent solvent mixtures.	(T)
F003	The following spent non-halogenated solvents: X-ylene, acetone, ethyl acetate, ethyl benzene, ethyl ether, methyl isobutyl ketone, n-butyl alcohol, cyclohexanone, and methanol; all spent solvent mixtures/blends containing, before use, only the above spent non-halogenated solvents; and all spent solvent mixtures/blends containing, before use, one or more of the above non-halogenated solvents, and, a total of ten percent or more (by volume) of one or more of those solvents listed in F001, F002, F004, and F005; and still bottoms from the recovery of these spent solvents and spent solvent mixtures.	(I)*
F004	The following spent non-halogenated solvents: Cresols and cresylic acid, and nitrobenzene; all spent solvent mixtures/blends containing, before use, a total of ten percent or more (by volume) of one or more of the above non-halogenated solvents or those solvents listed in F001, F002, and F005; and still bottoms from the recovery of these spent solvents and spent solvent mixtures.	(T)
F005	The following spent non-halogenated solvents: Toluene, methyl ethyl ketone, carbon disulfide, isobutanol, pyridine, benzene, 2-ethoxyethanol, and 2-nitropropane; all spent solvent mixtures/blends containing, before use, a total of ten percent or more (by volume) of one or more of the above non-halogenated solvents or those solvents listed in F001, F002, or F004; and still bottoms from the recovery of these spent solvents and spent solvent mixtures.	(I, T)

Environmental regulations, especially those identifying specific hazardous wastes, are very technical. Most companies that handle hazardous waste employ technical personnel, including chemists and engineers, to ensure compliance with environmental laws. Paralegals may need to consult with the technical experts both in private industry and with the EPA.

Substances that Have Characteristics of Hazardous Waste. Even if a substance is not "listed" in the EPA regulations, it is still covered by RCRA if it has one of four characteristics of hazardous waste as defined in 40 CFR 261, which are:

- ignitability,

- corrosivity,

- reactivity, or

- toxicity.

The policy concerns behind these designated characteristics are not difficult to discern. Special care must be given to materials that ignite easily when handled, corrode their containers, or are extremely unstable and may explode. The fourth characteristic, toxicity, is designed to cover substances that may easily leach into the groundwater.[29]

The regulations describe in detail how to determine whether a substance has one of the four designated characteristics. An excerpt from 40 CFR 261.21, which describes ignitability, is reprinted in Figure 4–5.

FIGURE 4–5
40 CFR 261.21

§ 261.21   **Characteristic of ignitability.**

(a) A solid waste exhibits the characteristic of ignitability if a representative sample of the waste has any of the following properties:

(1) It is a liquid, other than an aqueous solution containing less than 24 percent alcohol by volume and has flash point less than 60°C (140°F), as determined by a Pensky-Martens Closed Cup Tester, using the test method specified in ASTM Standard D-93-79 or D-93-80 (incorporated by reference, see § 260.11), or a Setaflash Closed Cup Tester, using the test method specified in ASTM Standard D-3278-78 (incorporated by reference, see § 260.11), or as determined by an equivalent test method approved by the Administrator under procedures set forth in §§ 260.20 and 260.21.

(2) It is not a liquid and is capable, under standard temperature and pressure, of causing fire through friction, absorption of moisture or spontaneous chemical changes and, when ignited, burns so vigorously and persistently that it creates a hazard. . . .

Hazardous Waste Management

RCRA establishes the structure of the national hazardous waste management program.[30] RCRA sets standards for three groups—those who produce the waste (**generators**), those who transport the waste (**transporters**), and those who dispose of the waste (**TSD facilities**). The statute labels these three groups as generators, transporters, and owners and operators of hazardous waste treatment, storage, and disposal facilities (TSDs). RCRA imposes requirements on each of the three groups.

Notification. One requirement that applies to all three groups is notification. After the EPA has identified a material as hazardous waste, generators, transporters, and owners and operators of TSDs have ninety days to notify the EPA that they handle the identified material. If a facility begins to handle a material already identified by the EPA as hazardous waste, the facility must notify the EPA within ninety days. In either case, the facility files EPA Form 8700-12, and then the EPA issues a facility-specific identification number. This number must then be used on forms and reports used to track the hazardous material. The EPA can then identify each generator, transporter, or owner of a TSD who handled the hazardous waste.

Regulatory Standards for Generators of Hazardous Waste. Generators are producers of hazardous waste. The EPA regulations define generators as "any person, by site, whose act or process produces hazardous waste identified or listed in Part 261 of this chapter or whose act first causes hazardous waste to become subject to regulation."[31] A large chemical company may have several plants throughout the United States. Each plant is a site that must individually meet the RCRA requirements for generators. Thus, each individual plant must obtain its own EPA identification number.

The EPA regulations that describe the standards that generators must follow are much easier to understand than the regulations that identify hazardous wastes. An examination of 40 CFR subparts A through D gives paralegals an overview of the requirements imposed on a typical chemical manufacturing plant. The statutory requirements (42 U.S.C. § 6922) state the requirements very generally and direct the administrator of the EPA to promulgate detailed regulations to implement RCRA.

---

generators In the context of RCRA, generators are producers of hazardous waste.

transporters In the context of RCRA, companies that transport hazardous waste from generators to TSD facilities.

TSD facilities In the context of RCRA, companies that transport, store, and dispose of hazardous waste.

For an overview of the standards applicable to generators, refer to Figure 4–6. This is an excerpt of the table of contents for 40 CFR part 262, the part governing generators of hazardous waste. This will be a helpful reference throughout the discussion.

FIGURE 4–6
Excerpt from Table of Contents, 40 CFR Part 262

PART 262—STANDARDS APPLICABLE TO GENERATORS OF HAZARDOUS WASTE

Subpart A—General

Sec.
262.10 Purpose, scope, and applicability.
262.11 Hazardous waste determination.
262.12 EPA identification numbers.

Subpart B—The Manifest

262.20 General requirements.
262.21 Acquisition of manifests.
262.22 Number of copies.
262.23 Use of the manifest.

Subpart C—Pre-Transport Requirements

262.30 Packaging.
262.31 Labeling.
262.32 Marking.
262.33 Placarding.
262.34 Accumulation time.

Subpart D—Recordkeeping and Reporting

262.40 Recordkeeping.
262.41 Biennial report.
262.42 Exception reporting.
262.43 Additional reporting.
262.44 Special requirements for generators of between 100 and 1000 kg/mo.

SIDEBAR The tables of contents for all parts of CFR are helpful tools. In addition to providing an overview of that part, they also help paralegals identify specific sections of the regulations at a glance.

General Requirements. Subpart A of 40 CFR part 262 sets forth general requirements imposed on generators. The regulations provide that a person who generates a solid waste must determine if that waste is a hazardous waste. In 40 CFR 262.11 the regulations explain how the generator makes that determination. The other major general requirement is that the generator obtain an EPA identification number. The regulations state that a generator is not allowed to treat, store, dispose of, transport, or offer for transportation, hazardous waste without having received an EPA identification number.

SIDEBAR   Each generator has its own EPA identification number. As discussed above, each hazardous waste material has its own identification. Thus, the EPA can track each hazardous waste and its source in order to effectuate the cradle to grave regulation.

The Manifest. The **manifest** is a form that accompanies the hazardous waste at all times.[32] A generator cannot transport a hazardous waste or offer it for transportation without preparing a manifest. See Figure 4–7 for a sample manifest. The manifest has been designated as EPA Form 8700-22, and the EPA provides detailed instructions for completing the manifest in the appendix to 40 CFR part 262. Refer to Figure 4–8 for an excerpt from the instructions.

The manifest describes the hazardous materials being transported. The manifest identifies the generator by name and by EPA identification number. The generator here is Chaco Corporation, the client described in the fourth sample case. Chaco, the generator, lists the TSD facility designated to receive the hazardous waste and the transporter designated to deliver the hazardous waste to the TSD facility. Chaco specifies the TSD facility and the transporter by name and by EPA identification number. Here the transporter is ABC Trucking, Inc., designated on line 5. The TSD facility is Cosmopolitan Environmental, Inc., designated on line 9. The hazardous waste being handled is Toluene, described on line 11a.

The generator must sign the manifest certification, signifying that the contents are properly identified, packaged, and labeled and meet all regulatory requirements for shipment. Large quantity generators must also certify that the best disposal method currently available to minimize future threat to the environment has been chosen and that the generator has a program to reduce the volume and toxicity of waste generated. Before the waste leaves the generator's facility, the generator must obtain the signature of the initial transporter.

---

manifest The document that accompanies hazardous waste from its generation through its disposal, which identifies the waste and the generators, transporters, and TSD facilities that handled the waste.

FIGURE 4–7
A Manifest (EPA
Form 8700-22)

Please print or type   (Form designed for use on elite (12-pitch) typewriter.)   Form approved. OMB No. 2050-0039. Expires 9-30-91

UNIFORM HAZARDOUS WASTE MANIFEST	1. Generator's US EPA ID No. N C D O 6 2 5 6 7 5 5 5	Manifest Document No. 20 2 7 6	2. Page 1 of 1	Information in the shaded areas is not required by Federal law

3. Generator's Name and Mailing Address
Chaco Corp.
P.O. Box 5044   Raleigh, NC   28227

A. State Manifest Document Number

4. Generator's Phone (919) 555-2707

B. State Generator's ID
NCD062567555

5. Transporter 1 Company Name
ABC Trucking, Inc.

6.   US EPA ID Number
I N T 1 9 0 0 1 0 5 5 5

C. State Transporter's ID INT190010555
D. Transporter's Phone 803-555-6000

7. Transporter 2 Company Name

8.   US EPA ID Number

E. State Transporter's ID
F. Transporter's Phone

9. Designated Facility Name and Site Address
Cosmopolitan Environmental, Inc.
308 Washington Industrial Dr.
Charlotte, NC   28222

10.   US EPA ID Number
N C D 0 0 0 0 6 4 8 4 5

G. State Facility's ID
NCD0000648455
H. Facility's Phone 919-555-5100

11. US DOT Description (Including Proper Shipping Name, Hazard Class, and ID Number)	12. Containers		13. Total Quantity	14. Unit Wt/Vol	I. Waste No.
	No.	Type			
a. RQ, Waste Flammable Liquids, N.O.S. (Toluene)	0 0 1	T T	4 0 2 0 7	P	D001 F005
b.					
c.					
d.					

J. Additional Descriptions for Materials Listed Above
Approval #RVBHZ104 - Salt Water/EDTA - Hazardous

K. Handling Codes for Wastes Listed Above

15. Special Handling Instructions and Additional Information
EMERGENCY CONTACT: CHEMTREC 1-800-555-5555

16. GENERATOR'S CERTIFICATION: I hereby declare that the contents of this consignment are fully and accurately described above by proper shipping name and are classified, packed, marked, and labeled, and are in all respects in proper condition for transport by highway according to applicable international and national government regulations.

If I am a large quantity generator, I certify that I have a program in place to reduce the volume and toxicity of waste generated to the degree I have determined to be economically practicable and that I have selected the practicable method of treatment, storage, or disposal currently available to me which minimizes the present and future threat to human health and the environment; OR, if I am a small quantity generator, I have made a good faith effort to minimize my waste generation and select the best waste management method that is available to me and that I can afford.

Printed/Typed Name Darien Tucker	Signature Darien Tucker	Month Day Year 12 14 94

17. Transporter 1 Acknowledgement of Receipt of Materials

Printed/Typed Name Michael Cameron	Signature Michael Cameron	Month Day Year 01 24 24

18. Transporter 2 Acknowledgement of Receipt of Materials

Printed/Typed Name	Signature	Month Day Year

19. Discrepancy Indication Space

20. Facility Owner or Operator: Certification of receipt of hazardous materials covered by this manifest except as noted in Item 19

Printed/Typed Name	Signature	Month Day Year

EPA Form 8700-22 (Rev. 9-88)   Previous editions are obsolete

FIGURE 4–8
Excerpt from
Appendix to 40
CFR Part 262
(Manifest
Instructions)

APPENDIX TO PART 262—UNIFORM HAZARDOUS WASTE MANIFEST AND
INSTRUCTIONS (EPA FORMS 8700-22 AND 8700-22A AND THEIR
INSTRUCTIONS)

U.S. EPA Form 8700-22

Read all instructions before completing this form.

This form has been designed for use on a 12-pitch (elite) typewriter; a firm point pen may also be used—press down hard.

Federal regulations require generators and transporters of hazardous waste and owners or operators of hazardous waste treatment, storage, and disposal facilities to use this form (8700-22) and, if necessary, the continuation sheet (Form 8700-22A) for both inter and intrastate transportation.

Federal regulations also require generators and transporters of hazardous waste and owners or operators of hazardous waste treatment, storage and disposal facilities to complete the following information:

The following statement must be included with each Uniform Hazardous Waste Manifest, either on the form, in the instructions to the form, or accompanying the form:

Public reporting burden for this collection of information is estimated to average: 37 minutes for generators, 15 minutes for transporters, and 10 minutes for treatment, storage and disposal facilities. This includes time for reviewing instructions, gathering data, and completing and reviewing the form. Send comments regarding the burden estimate, including suggestions for reducing this burden, to: Chief, Information/Policy Branch, PM-233, U.S. Environmental Protection Agency, 401 M Street SW., Washington, DC 20460; and to the Office of Information and Regulatory Affairs, Office of Management and Budget, Washington, DC 20503.

GENERATORS

Item 1. Generator's U.S. EPA ID Number—Manifest Document Number

Enter the generator's U.S. EPA twelve digit identification number and the unique five digit number assigned to this Manifest (e.g., 00001) by the generator.

Item 2. Page 1 of __

Enter the total number of pages used to complete this Manifest, i.e., the first page (EPA Form 8700-22) plus the number of Continuation Sheets (EPA Form 8700-22A), if any.

The generator uses the manifest to ensure that the hazardous waste has reached its authorized destination. If the manifest is not returned within thirty-five days of shipment, the generator must investigate and determine what happened to the waste. If after forty-five days, the generator has not received the manifest with signatures showing that the hazardous waste reached the TSD facility, the generator must file an "exception report" with the EPA. The exception report describes the efforts of the generator in tracking the hazardous waste and the results obtained.

Pre-Transport Requirements. The EPA regulations impose packaging, labeling, and marking requirements in 40 CFR 262.30–262.32. When hazardous waste is transported, the regulations of both the EPA and the Department of Transportation (DOT) apply. The EPA has adopted the DOT regulations. The EPA's regulations simply state that the generator must package, label, and mark each package of hazardous waste in accordance with DOT regulations on hazardous waste published in 49 CFR part 172.

SIDEBAR   This is an example of the interplay of administrative agencies. The regulations of one agency often affect, and are sometimes adopted by, other administrative agencies. Thus, the expertise developed by one agency can be used by other agencies.

In addition, EPA regulations (40 CFR 262.32(b)) require that the following warning be placed on containers of 110 gallons or less:

> HAZARDOUS WASTE—Federal Law Prohibits Improper Disposal. If found, contact the nearest police or public safety authority or the U.S. Environmental Protection Agency.

SIDEBAR   Some states require additional warnings or statements. Paralegals must refer to specific state laws and regulations.

Recordkeeping and Reporting. The EPA regulations (40 CFR 262.40) require generators to keep signed manifests received from the designated facilities that received the generators' hazardous waste. The copies must be kept for at least three years, although many generators retain the copies indefinitely.

The EPA regulations (40 CFR 262.41) require generators to submit to the EPA a biennial report to the EPA regional administrator. The biennial report must list the name and EPA identification number of each transporter and TSD facility used by the generator during the previous calendar year. The biennial report must also list and describe the hazardous waste, including the EPA hazardous waste number, and the quantity shipped to off-site facilities.

In 40 CFR 262.42, the regulations detail the information to be included in exception reports. The regulations authorize the EPA to require generators to submit additional reports.

40 CFR part 262 also contains subparts addressing exports and imports of hazardous wastes and regulations specific to farmers. A discussion of these regulations is beyond the scope of this text, but paralegals should be aware of these regulations.

Standards Applicable to Transporters of Hazardous Waste. The regulations governing transporters of hazardous waste are found in 40 CFR part 263. Like generators, transporters must obtain an EPA identification number. Transporters must comply with the manifest system described above. A transporter may not accept hazardous waste unless it is accompanied by a manifest signed by the generator. The regulations (40 CFR 263.20) require the transporter to keep the manifest with the hazardous waste. The regulations also detail the signatures that must be obtained and where the manifest goes after the transporter delivers the hazardous waste to a TSD facility or transfers it to another transporter. If the transporter is unable to deliver the waste in accordance with the generator's instructions, the transporter must contact the generator for further instructions and revise the manifest if necessary.

Like the generator, the transporter must keep copies of manifests for at least three years. The regulations also provide general guidelines for transporters to follow if a discharge of hazardous waste occurs during transportation. As noted above, the EPA has adopted DOT regulations concerning transportation of hazardous waste.

Standards for Owners and Operators of Hazardous Waste Transportation, Storage, and Disposal (TSD) Facilities. The regulations applicable to owners and operators of TSD facilities are extensive, and a detailed discussion is beyond the scope of this text. You will gain an overview of the content of the regulations, but paralegals who work in this area must learn the details of the regulations.

Permits. Like generators and transporters, TSD facilities must obtain EPA identification numbers. TSD facilities, however, must also obtain permits. The purpose of permits is for the EPA to ensure that the facility is able to handle the wastes accepted. The facility notifies the EPA that it is handling hazardous waste and files a "Part A" application to obtain an interim permit and continue operations.[33] The facility then must submit a "Part B" application, which is much more detailed. The procedures for processing the application and issuing the permit are set forth in 40 CFR part 124 and include opportunity for public comment and hearing.[34] The EPA issues the final permit when it is satisfied that the TSD facility will comply with the requirements of RCRA.[35]

Thus, there are two categories of TSD facilities—interim status facilities, which are governed by 40 CFR part 265, and permitted facilities, which are governed by 40 CFR part 264.[36] For both types of facilities, the regulations impose both general standards and standards applicable to specific types of facilities.

General Facility Standards. All TSD facilities must comply with the regulations of general applicability. These regulations require facilities to maintain site security, conduct personnel training, conduct inspections of the facility, and meet certain location and construction standards. Facilities must also maintain emergency preparedness and contingency plans. Before treating, storing, or disposing of a particular hazardous waste, the TSD facility must analyze samples to ensure that it can properly handle the hazardous waste.

TSD facilities must keep the manifest system intact, by returning a completed copy of the manifest to the generator within thirty days of receipt of the shipment. The TSD must keep extensive records, describing the materials handled, how the materials were treated, stored, or disposed of, and results of tests and inspections.[37] The TSD must also file biennial reports with the EPA.

When a TSD facility closes, it must submit a closure plan and obtain certification to close. The facility ceases to accept additional waste and then has a period during which it completes treatment and disposal. The facility must continue to monitor the site, particularly complying with groundwater monitoring requirements.

Standards for Particular Types of TSD Facilities. The EPA regulations contain subparts imposing particular standards on certain types of facilities, such as tank systems, landfills, and incinerators. These subparts define the systems to which they are applicable and then set forth general operating requirements, as well as requirements for waste analysis and monitoring and inspections. Refer to Figure 4–9, which reprints the table of contents for Subpart N—Landfills. This illustrates the standards that RCRA imposes on particular TSD facilities.

FIGURE 4–9
Excerpt from Table of Contents, 40 CFR Part 264 (Landfills)

Subpart N—Landfills

264.300	Applicability.
264.301	Design and operating requirements.
264.302	Action leakage rate.
264.303	Monitoring and inspection.
264.304	Response actions.
264.305–264.308	[Reserved]
264.309	Surveying and recordkeeping.
264.310	Closure and post-closure care.
264.311	[Reserved]
264.312	Special requirements for ignitable or reactive waste.
264.313	Special requirements for incompatible wastes.
264.314	Special requirements for bulk and containerized liquids.
264.315	Special requirements for containers.
264.316	Disposal of small containers of hazardous waste in overpacked drums (lab packs).
264.317	Special requirements for hazardous wastes FO20, FO21, FO22, FO23, FO26, and FO27.

Penalties Under RCRA

Any person who violates RCRA is subject to civil and criminal penalties. The enforcement powers of the EPA are discussed in detail in Chapter 5. Paralegals should be aware from the outset, however, that their law firm's clients are subject to substantial penalties if they violate provisions of RCRA.

Civil penalties of up to $25,000 per day for each violation can be imposed, and there is no maximum penalty amount. Courts may also order injunctive relief. For instance, a hazardous waste treatment facility that is not in compliance with RCRA requirements can be ordered to cease operations. Criminal sanctions include monetary penalties of up to $25,000 per day per violation, as well as imprisonment for individuals.

These severe penalties underscore the importance of compliance with RCRA and other environmental statutes. Thus, the attorney-paralegal team must understand the environmental statutes and regulations and help clients understand how to comply with the laws and the consequences of failure to comply.

State Implementation of RCRA

The RCRA statute allows individual states to implement their own hazardous waste management programs. The state program must meet the standards established by RCRA and must be approved by the EPA. The EPA regulations detail the procedures for obtaining EPA approval. When the state opts to implement its own plan, the state agency is the primary enforcement agency, but the EPA retains oversight and can withdraw approval of state programs.

Most states have opted to implement their own programs. A list of approved state programs is published in 40 CFR part 272.

North Carolina, for example, has opted to implement its own hazardous waste management program. The primary North Carolina statute passed to carry out the requirements of RCRA is the Solid Waste Management Act. The state administrative agency that oversees North Carolina's RCRA program is the Hazardous Waste Branch of the Solid Waste Division of the Department of Environment, Health and Natural Resources.

Paralegals must become familiar with their own state's statutes and regulations for RCRA and for other state-implemented environmental control programs. The environmental statutes and regulations are detailed and require extensive study. Your studies will, however, be worthwhile, in this rapidly expanding area of law.

Summary

Chapter 4 addresses the substantive law of naturalization and hazardous waste management.

An Overview of Immigration Law

Aliens can legally enter and remain in the United States only if they fit into a category designated by Congress in the Immigration and Nationality Act. Some aliens seek permission to remain in the United States for only a certain number of years, and they obtain a nonimmigrant visa such as a student visa. Other aliens seek to be lawful permanent residents, so they acquire an immigrant visa. After being a lawful permanent resident for the requisite number of years, a person can become a United States citizen through the process called naturalization.

Naturalization

There are two ways to acquire United States citizenship—by birth or through naturalization. Persons born in the United States are citizens by birth. Some persons born outside the United States to United States citizen parents are citizens by birth.

A person who seeks to become a naturalized citizen must meet all the statutory and regulatory requirements for naturalization. One requirement is that the applicant was *lawfully* admitted as a permanent resident. Thus, if an alien obtained permanent residence by unlawful means, such as lying on an INS application, this requirement is not met. After becoming a lawful permanent resident, the applicant must have continuous residence in the United States for five years prior to filing application for naturalization. For spouses of U.S. citizens, the residency period is only three years. Extended absences from the United States can break the continuity of residence. In addition, an applicant must have been physically present in the United States for one-half of the required residency period.

Another requirement is good moral character. The INA sets forth certain grounds that preclude a finding of good moral character, such as lying to obtain an immigration benefit. Other past conduct can also preclude a finding of good moral character, as developed in the case law. An applicant must also be attached to the principles of the United States Constitution and must be favorably disposed to the good order and happiness of the United States. This does not mean that the applicant must agree with every decision of Congress. It does mean, however, that the applicant must not support change in government through violent means.

An applicant must able to read, write, and speak words ordinarily used in the English language. There are exceptions to the literacy requirement for older applicants who have been in the United States for a number of years. An applicant must have basic knowledge of the United States government and history. Finally, an applicant must be eighteen years old at the time the applicant files an application. There are some exceptions, most notably children whose parents are being naturalized.

The INA prohibits naturalization for certain classes of people, such as subversives and members of the Communist party. Naturalization must be denied when the applicant is in deportation proceedings.

Hazardous Waste Management

Laws at the federal, state, and local level work together to control pollution. The Resource Conservation and Recovery Act (RCRA) is one of many federal environmental statutes. RCRA governs the manufacture, transport, and disposal of hazardous waste. If a material is not covered by RCRA, it may be covered by some other federal statute.

Many federal environmental statutes allow individual states to implement their own programs to carry out the purpose of the federal statute. RCRA is one such statute. When a state has its own programs, its laws must be at least as stringent as federal law.

Many states have laws with no federal parallel, designed to govern pollution control in areas not covered by federal law. City and county governments also implement ordinances to address local pollution problems, such as discharge into the local water system.

Congress enacted RCRA in recognition that inadequate control of waste management results in substantial risks to the environment. RCRA seeks to minimize damage to the environment by regulating hazardous waste management from the cradle to the grave. Once a material is identified as hazardous waste, RCRA governs the generation, transportation, and disposal of that material. A substance is a hazardous waste if it falls within the definition in the EPA regulations. The identification process is most easily understood by asking three questions. First, is the substance excluded from EPA's definition of hazardous waste? The EPA regulations specifically exclude some substances, such as high-level radioactive waste, from the definition of hazardous waste. Although RCRA does not govern these excluded substances, other laws do. The second question is whether the substance is included in one of EPA's lists of hazardous waste. The EPA regulations contain detailed lists of materials identified by EPA as hazardous waste. The EPA assigns an identification number to each material. The third question concerns materials not on the EPA lists. If a substance is not on the lists, does it have one of the four characteristics of hazardous waste as defined in the regulations? These characteristics are ignitability, corrosivity, reactivity, and toxicity.

Having identified a material as hazardous waste, the EPA regulations dictate how the material is to be handled. RCRA establishes standards that apply to generators of hazardous waste, transporters of hazardous waste, and owners and operators of facilities that treat, store, and dispose of hazardous waste (TSD facilities). Generators produce hazardous waste. They are required to notify the EPA of the hazardous waste they handle and to obtain an EPA identification number.

Generators must complete a manifest, a form that accompanies the hazardous waste at all times. The manifest identifies the generator and the hazardous waste itself. A generator must complete a manifest before it can allow the waste to be transported. The manifest also identifies the transporter and the TSD facility to which the material is to be taken. The generator must track the shipment by means of the manifest, report shipments that do not reach their destination within forty-five days of shipment, and keep copies of manifests for at least three years.

Transporters of hazardous waste must also obtain an EPA identification number and comply with the manifest system and record-keeping requirements.

The requirements for TSD facilities are extensive. A TSD must obtain a permit from the EPA before it can operate. It must also obtain permission to close and monitor sites after they are closed. TSD facilities must also obtain EPA identification numbers, comply with the manifest system, and keep extensive records. The regulations also impose security and training requirements. Further, the regulations impose particular requirements on certain types of TSD facilities, such as landfills and incinerators. These requirements are in addition to the general requirements, such as security and training, imposed on all TSD facilities.

Penalties are stiff for RCRA violations. They include civil and criminal penalties. Finally, it is important to know that most states have exercised the option to implement their own hazardous waste management systems. Their requirements must be consistent with RCRA. The program is administered by the state's designated agency, but the EPA retains oversight to ensure compliance with RCRA.

Review Questions

1. Which of the following precludes a finding of good moral character for purposes of naturalization? _____
   a. making a false statement to gain an immigration benefit
   b. smuggling a person into the United States
   c. practicing polygamy
   d. all of the above
   e. a and b only

2. Which of the following are bars to naturalization? _____
   a. The applicant disagrees with several bills passed during the last session of Congress.
   b. The applicant is a member of a group dedicated to the overthrow of the United States government by violent means.
   c. The applicant is in deportation proceedings.
   d. all of the above
   e. b and c only

3. The EPA has specific requirements for certain types of TSD facilities, including _____.
   a. city sewer systems
   b. tank systems
   c. incinerators
   d. all of the above
   e. b and c only

4. Generators of hazardous waste are required to keep copies of manifests for _____.
    a. one year
    b. two years
    c. three years
    d. six months

5. An F-1 student visa is an immigrant visa, entitling an alien to a green card.   True ___ / False ___

6. In complying with the residence requirements for naturalization, an absence of two months breaks the continuity of residence.
                                                                True ___ / False ___

7. Becoming a lawful permanent resident is the same as becoming a United States citizen.   True ___ / False ___

8. The EPA has adopted Department of Transportation regulations governing the transport of hazardous waste.   True ___ / False ___

9. RCRA allows states to implement their own hazardous waste plans.
                                                                True ___ / False ___

10. The document that accompanies hazardous waste is called a(n) _____.

11. An alien who has been granted an immigrant visa but is not a United States citizen is a(n) _____.

12. Are lawful permanent residents required to become United States citizens?

13. Why is it important for clients to comply with RCRA?

Factual Analysis Questions

1. Suppose that Chaco Corporation is owned by a German corporation. The German parent company wishes to send a manager, Herr Strickmann, to the plant in North Carolina for two years. What type of visa will you and Ms. Garcia recommend that Herr Strickmann obtain?

2. Herr Strickmann worked in North Carolina for two years. He returned to Germany for a year but now Chaco wishes to bring him to work permanently at the Raleigh plant. You and Ms. Garcia assisted him in obtaining an immigrant visa, and he and his wife became lawful permanent residents. Three years after becoming a permanent resident, he asked you and Ms. Garcia whether he can become a United States citizen through naturalization. Is he eligible?

Practical Applications

Exercise 1

Read the facts about Massoud Kazemi in Sample Case 3. Ms. Garcia would like your opinion as to whether Mr. Kazemi meets all the requirements for naturalization. She has the following questions.

1. One requirement is lawful admission as a permanent resident of the United States. Does Mr. Kazemi meet this requirement?

2. Do Mr. Kazemi's absences present a problem with meeting the residency requirements for naturalization?

3. Do Mr. Kazemi's absences present a problem with meeting the physical presence requirements for naturalization?

4. Do you see any other problems Mr. Kazemi might have meeting the naturalization requirements?

5. Mr. Kazemi advocated replacement of the Khomeini regime when he was in Iran. Will this bar him from naturalization?

Exercise 2

Read the facts about Chaco Corporation in Sample Case 4 and answer the following questions.

1. Does RCRA apply to Chaco Corporation? If so, why?

2. Chaco's Raleigh plant has an EPA identification number. Can this number be used by Chaco Corporation's plants at other locations?

3. Suppose that Chaco uses a chemical that was just recently identified by the EPA as a hazardous waste. Must Chaco notify the EPA that it uses this chemical?

4. Chaco has contracted with ABC Trucking Co. to transport hazardous waste to a TSD facility. When ABC's truck arrived one morning, the manifest for that shipment was not ready. An employee of Chaco allowed ABC to take the waste without the manifest, promising to fax a copy later that day. Has Chaco violated EPA regulations?

5. Has ABC violated EPA regulations?

6. Assume that Chaco sent a shipment of hazardous waste, with a completed manifest, to a TSD facility. Four months later, Chaco has not received a copy of the manifest confirming that the waste reached the TSD facility. What are Chaco's obligations?

7. Assume that the hazardous waste did reach the designated TSD facility, and the manifest was returned to Chaco. An employee of Chaco, however, mistakenly threw away the manifest and all copies. Is this a violation of EPA regulations?

Case Analysis

Read the excerpts below from *United States v. Leprich*, 666 F. Supp. 967 (E.D. Mich. 1987), and answer the following questions. Note that this case concerns denaturalization proceedings. As the case explains, if facts surface after a person becomes a naturalized citizen, showing that he was not in fact eligible for naturalization, the United States government can institute denaturalization proceedings. Much of the case law regarding naturalization arises from denaturalization proceedings, yet the cases are instructive regarding the requirements for naturalization.

UNITED STATES

v.

LEPRICH

United States District Court,
E.D. Michigan, S.D.
July 13, 1987.

HACKETT, District Judge.

Facts

1. Johann Leprich was born on July 7, 1925, in Petelea, Romania. Petelea has also been known by the name of Birk in German and Petele in Hungarian.

2. Leprich became a member of the *Waffen* SS in November, 1943.

3. Leprich commenced service as a uniformed SS guard at the Mauthausen concentration camp in November or December, 1943.

4. At Mauthausen, Leprich was a member of the SS *Totenkopf-Sturmbann* (Death's Head Battalion), and wore the skull-and-crossbones symbol on his collar.

(The International Military Tribunal at Nuremberg in 1946 found that the SS, including the Death's Head Battalion, was a criminal organization involved in "the persecution and extermination of Jews, brutalities and killings in concentration camps, excesses in the administration of occupied territories, administration of the slave labor program and the mistreatment and murder of prisoners of war."

5. Leprich continued to serve at the Mauthausen concentration camp until April or May, 1944.

6. Mauthausen was intended as a camp for severe punitive action against enemies of the Reich. . . .

10. Incarcerated at Mauthausen were groups including Jews, Gypsies, Jehovah's Witnesses, and Poles, as well as members of almost every nationality in Europe.

11. Jews were identified as Jews in the camp and were treated especially harshly because they were Jews.

12. Leprich's duty at Mauthausen was to guard the camp inside which the prisoners lived.

13. While performing guard duty at Mauthausen, Leprich carried a rifle on his shoulder and ammunition.

14. At Mauthausen, Leprich was assigned to numerous guard posts around the camp. He stood guard on the ground and in watchtowers.

15. Leprich received pay for his service as a guard at Mauthausen.

16. Leprich was given days off during his service as a guard at Mauthausen.

17. Leprich remained a member of the *Waffen* SS until his capture by the United States Army in June, 1945. . . .

21. Leprich was issued a visa to immigrate to the United States on February 12, 1952, pursuant to the Displaced Persons Act of 1948, as amended.

22. In his signed and sworn visa application, Leprich listed his residences through 1946 as follows: "1939–1943 Birk, Rumania; May, 1945, soldier in Hungarian army; 1946, Sopron, Hungary."

23. The report of Displaced Persons Commission ("DPC") analyst Edward Kelly refers to Leprich's DPC Fragebogen (application), which gave his history as "Service in the Hungarian Army" from 1943 to 1945 and "Farm help in Hungary and Huettenheim, Germany" from 1945 to 1949.

24. It is untrue that Leprich was a soldier in the Hungarian army from 1943 through May 1945 and that he resided in Sopron, Hungary from May, 1945 through 1946.

25. Upon arriving in the United States, Leprich signed and swore in an affidavit that he had "never advocated or assisted in the persecution of any person because of race, religion, or national origin."

26. In seeking to immigrate to the United States, Leprich never informed any United States official that he had been a member of the *Waffen* SS or a guard at Mauthausen.

27. If it had been known that Leprich had been a member of the *Waffen* SS, immigration officials would have commenced an investigation into the nature of that service.

28. If it had been known that Leprich had been a guard at Mauthausen he would not have been granted a visa.

29. Leprich entered this country on March 29, 1952.

30. Leprich became a United States citizen on December 30, 1958.

Evidence and Law

A certificate of naturalization must be revoked if it was illegally procured. Naturalization is illegally procured "if some statutory requirement which is a condition precedent to naturalization is absent at the time the petition for naturalization is granted." Lawful admission into this country, with a valid immigrant visa is a statutory requirement for naturalization.

The evidence establishes that defendant was not eligible for the visa he received under the Displaced Persons Act ("DPA") of 1948. He was ineligible because he was a guard at the Mauthausen concentration camp and because he misrepresented his wartime service by failing to disclose his guard duty in his visa application. Because he was not eligible for the visa he received, he did not have a valid visa and he was not lawfully admitted to this country. He therefore failed to satisfy all the juris-dictional requirements for naturalization. As a consequence, his naturalization was illegally procured and must be revoked.

Defendant's service as an armed guard at a concentration camp rendered his visa illegally procured, even if defendant could prove his service to have been involuntary. The court in *Fedorenko* explicitly found that voluntariness was not a factor in determining whether a guard "assisted in persecution." The court's reasoning relied on the inclusion of a voluntariness requirement in the language of certain exclusionary provisions, but its exclusion from the persecution provisions. In Section 13 of the amended DPA, Congress included a voluntariness requirement in a provision regarding the bearing of arms against the United States, but excluded the requirement from the persecution provision. This court therefore must refuse, as did the court in *Fedorenko*, to "'imply a condition which is opposed to the explicit terms of the statute.'"

Defendant's visa would have been illegally procured under Section 13 even if he had secured it without making misrepresentations. In *Fedorenko* the Court found that: (1) concentration camp guards were ineligible for visas under the DPA, and (2) failure to disclose such service was a misrepresentation making an applicant ineligible for a visa under the DPA. The first finding alone, without proof of misrepresentation, is sufficient to establish that an alien's visa was illegally procured.

Conclusion

Defendant was not eligible for the visa he received because (1) he assisted in the persecution of persons due to their race, religion or national origin; and (2) he willfully made material misrepresentations in order to enter this country. Because he was not eligible for his visa, he was never lawfully admitted to this country and his citizenship was illegally procured. For the foregoing reasons, the government's motion for summary judgment and request that defendant's illegally procured naturalization be revoked are granted.

1. When is naturalization considered to have been illegally procured?
2. Which statutory requirement for naturalization was absent here?
3. Under what circumstances can naturalization be revoked?
4. Why was the defendant's immigrant visa illegally procured?

Notes

[1] 8 U.S.C. § 1401(c).

[2] 8 U.S.C. § 1401. Section 1409 applies to illegitimate children.

[3] *See, e.g., United States v. Leprich*, 666 F. Supp. 967 (E.D. Mich. 1987).

[4] 8 U.S.C. § 1101(a)(33).

[5] See 8 CFR 316.5 for details of consequences of extended absences.

[6] 8 U.S.C. § 1427(e).

[7] *United States v. Kairys*, 782 F.2d 1374 (7th Cir. 1986), *cert. denied*, 476 U.S. 1153 (1986).

[8] *In re Valad*, 465 F. Supp. 120 (E.D. Va. 1979).

[9] *Petition of de la Cruz*, 565 F. Supp. 998 (S.D.N.Y. 1983).

[10] 8 U.S.C. § 1423 and 8 CFR 312.1(a).

[11] 8 U.S.C. § 1424.

[12] 8 U.S.C. § 1425.

[13] 8 U.S.C. § 1429.

[14] 42 U.S.C. §§ 7401–7642.

[15] 33 U.S.C. §§ 1251–1376.

[16] 42 U.S.C. §§ 300–300j.

[17] 17 U.S.C. §§ 1401–1445.

[18] 33 U.S.C. § 2701 *et seq.*

[19] 7 U.S.C. §§ 135–136y and 15 U.S.C. §§ 2601–2629, respectively.

[20] 42 U.S.C. §§ 9601–9657.

[21] J.G. Arbuckle, *et al.*, *Environmental Law Handbook*, 12th ed. (Rockville, MD: Government Institutes, Inc., 1993), at 4.

[22] *Id.*

[23] Daniel McLawhorn, "State Enforcement of Environmental Laws," Environmental Law Handbook 1993 (Wake Forest University School of Law), at 49ff.

[24] Arbuckle, *supra* note 21, at 4.

[25] 42 U.S.C. § 6901.

[26] 42 U.S.C. § 6902(b).

[27] Jan Laitos & Joseph Tomain, *Energy and Natural Resources Law* (St. Paul: West Publishing Co., 1992), at 193.

[28] For more examples, see 40 CFR 261.4.

[29] Arbuckle, *supra* note 21, at 67–68.

[30] *Id.* at 61.

[31] 40 CFR 260.10(a)(26). Note that RCRA defines "person" broadly, including in the definition corporations, partnerships, and local, state, and federal government agencies. 42 U.S.C. § 6903(15).

[32] Arbuckle, *supra* note 21, at 61.

[33] *Id.* at 86.

[34] *Id.*

[35] *Id.*

[36] *Id.* at 78.

[37] *Id.* at 80.

CHAPTER 5

AN OVERVIEW OF AGENCY ACTIONS

The Administrative Procedure Act (APA) sets forth procedural requirements for certain types of agency actions. The APA specifies the procedures only "when the agency is formulating policy for the future through substantive rulemaking (5 U.S.C. § 553), or when the statute being implemented requires that the decision in question be made after a formal trial-type hearing (5 U.S.C. §§ 554, 556–557)."[1] Essentially, all other agency decisions fall within the category of informal action.[2] In this chapter you will gain an overview of the types of actions agencies engage in on a daily basis.

Informal Agency Actions

Most agency actions are informal. In fact, studies have shown that 90 percent of all federal agency decisions are informal.[3]

Administrative agencies make scores of informal determinations every day. For instance, assume that you are self-employed and prepaid part of your federal income tax. The Internal Revenue Service (IRS), however, made a mistake and did not credit the payments to your account. Instead of sending the tax refund you expected, the IRS determines that you owe money. You call the IRS and explain the amounts you paid and the dates the checks were sent. The IRS employee double-checks your records and determines that you did in fact prepay taxes, and three weeks later you receive your refund check. You resolved the problem with the IRS informally, with no need for a hearing or other formal proceedings.

This is just one example of an informal agency action. This chapter discusses numerous other informal actions.

Rule Making

In administrative law, regulations are a critical primary source of law. The discussion now turns to the details of how agencies develop, or **promulgate**, their regulations. As discussed in Chapter 2, the procedure agencies follow to promulgate their regulations is **rule making**.[4]

BALLENTINE'S
---

promulgate 1. To publish, announce, or proclaim and, in particular, to give official notice of a public act, for EXAMPLE, the publication of an executive order in the *Internal Revenue Bulletin*. 2. To enact a law or issue a regulation.

rule making The promulgation by an administrative agency of a rule having the force of law, i.e., a regulation.

Why Agencies Promulgate Regulations

Agencies promulgate regulations to fill in the gaps left by delegation statutes. When Congress enacts a delegation statute, it directs the head of the appropriate agency to promulgate regulations to carry out the provisions of the statute. Refer to Figure 2–5, which illustrates 42 U.S.C. § 405. This delegation statute gives the Social Security Administration the authority to make regulations to carry out the provisions of the Social Security disability benefits statute and directs the agency to adopt regulations to regulate the method for applicants to establish that they are disabled.

When Congress enacts new laws, the appropriate agency must promulgate new regulations. For instance, Congress passed major reforms in immigration law in 1986 and 1990. In turn, the INS had to promulgate regulations to carry out the reforms.

Congress also directs agencies to review periodically certain regulations that they promulgate. The president sometimes issues executive orders, directing administrative agencies to promulgate regulations. Often the agency itself initiates the development of new regulations.

How Agencies Promulgate Regulations—Rule-Making Procedures

The Administrative Procedure Act sets forth the rule-making procedures that federal agencies must follow when they formulate, repeal, or amend their regulations. The APA ensures uniformity among federal agencies.

Exemptions from Rule-Making Requirements

It is important to note at the outset that section 553(a) of the APA exempts certain regulations from the rule-making procedures. Regulations related to "military or foreign affairs functions of the United States" are exempt. Matters related to military and foreign policy are frequently sensitive and often entrusted solely to the president, and thus public participation would not be invited. The APA also exempts matters "relating to agency management or personnel or to public property, loans, grants, benefits, or contracts." Finally, section 553(b)(3)(B) does not require an agency to follow the rule-making procedures when "the agency for good cause finds . . . that notice and public procedure thereon are impracticable, unnecessary, or contrary to the public interest." When an agency makes such a finding, litigation frequently ensues, and courts often view the agency finding with skepticism.[5]

Types of Rule Making

The APA details two methods for rule making—informal and formal. Informal rule making is by far the most commonly used method, but paralegals must also be familiar with formal rule making.

Formal Rule Making

The APA (Section 553(c)) requires formal rule making when statutes require the regulations "to be made on the record after opportunity for an agency hearing." Few statutes contain this language or wording so similar that it is clear that formal rule making is required. One statute that does specifically require formal rule making is the Federal Food, Drug and Cosmetic Act.[6] Thus, the Food and Drug Administration (FDA) regularly uses formal rule making. Some statutes contain language that is ambiguous as to whether formal rule making is required, and this has spawned litigation. The United States Supreme Court held in *United States v. Florida East Coast Railway* that where a statute required a hearing but did not state it had to be "on the record," formal rule making was not required. Generally, if the language is ambiguous, courts have found that formal rule making is not required.[7]

In sections 556 and 557, the APA sets forth detailed requirements for formal rule making. Formal rule making requires the agency to conduct a trial-type hearing. Parties who have an interest in the agency's decision testify, and cross-examination is allowed. The parties submit exhibits, which become part of the record. Section 556 explains that the "transcript of testimony and exhibits, together with all papers and requests filed in the proceeding, constitutes the exclusive record for decision . . . ."

Thus, in a formal rule-making proceeding to determine whether the FDA would allow marketing of a new drug, the manufacturer of the drug, persons opposed to its marketing, and other interested parties would testify. Industry experts may also testify.

The trial-type proceedings vary in length. Perhaps the most infamous formal rule-making proceeding was the Peanut Butter case, where the main issue was whether peanut butter should be 90 percent or 87 percent peanuts. This rule making with the Food and Drug Administration (FDA) lasted several years and generated a transcript of 7,736 pages.[8] This is the exception, not the norm.

Think of a formal rule making as a trial with witnesses, cross-examination, and presentation of exhibits. The proceeding is, however, less formal than a full-blown court trial. For instance, section 556(d) allows submission of written, rather than oral, testimony. At the conclusion of the hearing, the agency considers the evidence and then issues its regulations.

Informal Rule Making

Informal rule making, often called notice and comment rule making, is the most common procedure used by agencies to promulgate regulations. You recall from Chapter 2 the basic procedure required by section 553 of the APA. First, the agency publishes a notice of proposed rule making in the *Federal Register*. Second, the public is given a period of time to submit comments to the agency concerning the proposed regulations. Finally, the agency reviews the comments and then publishes the final regulations in the *Federal Register*. The text now examines these three steps in more detail.

Section 553(b) gives the details that the notice must contain. One important requirement is "reference to the legal authority under which the rule is proposed." This goes back to the fundamental concept in administrative law that agencies can take actions only when they have been delegated proper authority. Section 553(b) also requires "either the terms or substance of the proposed rule or a description of the subjects and issues involved." The purpose of this requirement is to alert affected parties so that they have the opportunity to study the proposed changes and prepare their comments. Refer to Figure 5–1, which reprints excerpts from proposed regulations by the EEOC.

FIGURE 5–1
Excerpts from Proposed Regulations of EEOC in *Federal Register*, Vol. 57, No. 77, April 21, 1992

DEPARTMENT OF JUSTICE

28 CFR Part 37

[AG Order No. 1586-92]

EQUAL EMPLOYMENT OPPORTUNITY COMMISSION

29 CFR Part 1640

Coordination Procedures for Complaints or Charges of Employment Discrimination Based on Disability Subject to the Americans With Disabilities Act and Section 504 of the Rehabilitation Act of 1973

AGENCIES: Department of Justice and Equal Employment Opportunity Commission
ACTION: Proposed rule.
SUMMARY: Section 107(b) of the Americans with Disabilities Act (ADA) requires that the Department of Justice (the Department or DOJ), the Equal Employment Opportunity Commission (the Commission or EEOC), and the Department of Labor's Office of Federal Contract Compliance Programs issue coordination regulations setting forth procedures governing the processing of complaints that fall within the overlapping jurisdiction of both Title I of the ADA and section 504 of the Rehabilitation Act of 1973 to ensure that such complaints are dealt with in a manner that avoids duplication of effort and prevents the imposition of inconsistent or conflicting standards. Pursuant to

**FIGURE 5–1
(continued)**

this mandate, the Department of Justice and EEOC are publishing a proposed joint rule implementing section 107(b) as it pertains to title I of the ADA and section 504 of the Rehabilitation Act of 1973. In addition, this regulation describes coordination procedures for the processing of employment complaints that may fall within the overlapping jurisdiction of title II of the ADA and either, or both, title I or section 504. A joint rule developed by EEOC and the Department of Labor implementing section 107(b) as it pertains to title I and section 503 of the Rehabilitation Act has been published separately in the **Federal Register** of January 24, 1992.

DATES: To be assured of consideration, comments must be in writing and must be received on or before May 21, 1992. Comments that are received after the closing date will be considered to the extent practicable.

ADDRESSES: Written comments should be submitted to Frances M. Hart, Executive Officer, Executive Secretariat, Equal Employment Opportunity Commission, 1801 L Street, NW., Washington, DC 20507.

As a convenience to commenters, the Executive Secretariat will accept public comments transmitted by facsimile ("FAX") machine. The telephone number of the FAX receiver is (202) 663-4114. This is not a toll-free number. Only public comments of six or fewer pages will be accepted via FAX transmittal. This limitation is necessary to assure access to the equipment. Receipt of FAX transmittals will not be acknowledged, except that the sender may request confirmation of receipt by calling the Executive Secretariat Staff at (202) 663-4078. This is not a toll-free number.

Comments received will be available for public inspection in the EEOC Library, room 6502, by appointment only, from 9 a.m. to 5 p.m. Monday through Friday except legal holidays, from May 5, 1992, until the Department and the Commission publish the rule in final form. Persons who need assistance to review the comments will be provided with appropriate auxiliary aids such as readers or print magnifiers. To schedule an appointment, call (202) 663-4630 (voice), (202) 663-4641 (TDD). These are not toll-free numbers.

Copies of this notice of proposed rulemaking are available in the following alternate formats: large print, Braille, electronic file or computer disk, and audio tape. Copies may be obtained from the Office of Equal Employment Opportunity by calling (202) 663-4398 (voice) or (202) 663-4399 (TDD). These are not toll-free numbers.

. . .

Text of Proposed Joint Rule
The text of the proposed joint rule, as adopted by the agencies specified in this document, appears below:

Part_____—COORDINATION PROCEDURES FOR COMPLAINTS OR CHARGES OF EMPLOYMENT DISCRIMINATION BASED ON DISABILITY SUBJECT TO THE AMERICANS WITH DISABILITIES ACT AND SECTION 504 OF THE REHABILITATION ACT OF 1973
Sec.
_____1. Purpose and application.
_____2. Definitions.

FIGURE 5–1
(continued)

____3. Exchange of information.

____4. Confidentiality.

____5. Processing of complaints or charges of employment discrimination against recipients and public entities.

____6. Dual-filed complaints processed by EEOC.

____7. Dual-filed complaints processed by a section 504 agency.

____8. Standards.

§ ____1 Purpose and application.

(a) This part establishes coordination procedures for:

(1) Processing and resolving charges and complaints of employment discrimination filed against recipients of Federal financial assistance where jurisdiction exists under both section 504 and title I; and

(2) Determining which Federal agency shall process and resolve charges and complaints of employment discrimination filed against public entities that may fall within the jurisdiction of title II and either, or both, title I or section 504.

(b) This part does not create rights in any person or confer agency jurisdiction not provided by the ADA or section 504 over any complaint charge.

§ ____2 Definitions.

As used in this part, the term:

Americans with Disabilities Act of 1990 or *ADA* means the Americans with Disabilities Act of 1990 (Pub. L. No. 101-336, 104 Stat. 327, 42 U.S.C. 12101–12213 and 47 U.S.C. 225 and 611).

. . .

Section 504 means section 504 of the Rehabilitation Act of 1973 (Pub. L. No. 93-112, 87 Stat. 394 (29 U.S.C. 794)), as amended.

Section 504 agency means any Federal department or agency that extends Federal financial assistance to programs or activities of recipients.

Title I means title I of the ADA.

Title II means subtitle A of title II of the ADA.

§ ____3 Exchange of information.

EEOC and section 504 agencies shall share any information relating to recipients' employment policies and practices that may assist each office in carrying out its responsibilities. Such information shall include, but is not limited to, complaints, charges, investigative files, compliance review reports and files, annual employment reports, and affirmative action programs.

§ ____4 Confidentiality.

(a) When a section 504 agency receives information obtained by EEOC, the agency shall observe the confidentiality requirements of section 706(b) and section 709(e) of the Civil Rights Act of 1964, as amended (42 U.S.C. 2000e-5(b) and 2000e-8(e)), as incorporated by section 107(a) of the ADA, as would EEOC, except in cases where the agency receives the same information from a source independent of EEOC. Questions concerning the confidentiality requirements of title I shall be directed to the Associate Legal Counsel for Legal Services, Office of Legal Counsel, EEOC.

. . .

In the comment phase of informal rule making, section 553(c) allows interested parties to submit "written data, views, or arguments with or without the opportunity for oral presentation." Thus, agencies are allowed to hold oral hearings as part of the informal rule-making process, but it is not required. The notice in the *Federal Register* provides the name and address of the person to whom written comments should be sent. See Figure 5–1 for an example.

After reviewing the comments, the agency publishes its final regulations in the *Federal Register*. Section 553(c) requires the agency to include with the text "a concise general statement of their basis and purpose." This requirement has generated litigation regarding the amount of detail agencies must include in explaining their reasons for issuing the regulations. The agency is not required to give detailed findings and conclusions like those required in formal rule making. The agency must, however, give sufficient information to enable a reviewing court "to see what major issues of policy were ventilated by the informal proceedings and why the agency reacted to them as it did."[9] The content of the statement of basis and purpose has become a ripe area for litigation, particularly in the area of environmental law. There is a recent trend toward more detailed statements of basis and purpose.[10]

The agency is not bound to accept changes proposed by interested parties. The agency must simply consider the comments received and give a sufficient explanation of why it adopted the final regulations.

SIDEBAR   Parties who oppose an agency's regulations challenge the regulations by trying to find irregularities in the required procedure. Thus, if the notice of proposed rule making or the statement of basis and purpose did not meet the requirements of section 553, a reviewing court would find the resulting regulations invalid. Then the agency would have to start the informal rule-making procedure over again.

Negotiated Rule Making

A recent innovation in rule making is **negotiated rule making**, a procedure that allows the agency and interested parties to meet, exchange ideas and information, and reach a consensus on the text of a proposed regulation.[11] The practice of negotiated rule making was codified in the Negotiated Rulemaking Act of 1990. This method was developed in large part through the research and efforts of the

---

negotiated rule making A procedure in which agencies and interested parties meet, exchange information, and reach a consensus on the text of proposed regulations.

Administrative Conference of the United States (ACUS). The ACUS commentary explains how negotiated rule making fits in with the rule-making provisions of the APA:

> Negotiated rulemaking should be viewed as a supplement to the rulemaking provisions of the Administrative Procedure Act. This means that the negotiation sessions generally take place prior to issuance of the notice and the opportunity for the public to comment on a proposed rule that are required by the Act (5 U.S.C. § 553). In some instances, negotiations may be appropriate at a later stage of the proceeding and have sometimes been used effectively in drafting the text of a final rule based on comments received.[12]

Unlike formal and informal rule making, the use of negotiated rule making is not mandatory. Agencies are given discretion to choose whether they wish to engage in negotiated rule making. The Negotiated Rulemaking Act requires certain procedures, such as publication of notice of planned negotiated rule-making proceedings. The Act allows the agency to appoint a negotiating committee, with no more than twenty-five members, to "consider and discuss issues for the purpose of reaching a consensus in the development of a proposed rule."[13] When an agency decides to form a negotiating committee, it must publish a notice in the *Federal Register* and appropriate trade publications. Persons whose interests will be affected may apply to be a member of the committee.

The Negotiated Rulemaking Act (section 583) sets forth factors for agencies to consider when they determine whether to establish a negotiated rule-making committee. Refer to Figure 5–2, which reprints section 583. These factors are themselves a good explanation of the atmosphere within which negotiated rule making is designed to work and in which it does in fact most effectively work. Negotiated rule making is designed to succeed in a situation where the number of interested parties can be identified and adequately represented by a committee and where the issue is one that can likely be settled by consensus.

FIGURE 5–2
Section 583 of the Negotiated Rulemaking Act

---

§ 583.   Determination of need for negotiated rulemaking committee

(a) **Determination of Need by the Agency.** An agency may establish a negotiated rulemaking committee to negotiate and develop a proposed rule, if the head of the agency determines that the use of the negotiated rulemaking procedure is in the public interest. In making such a determination, the head of the agency shall consider whether—

(1) there is a need for a rule;

(2) there are a limited number of identifiable interests that will be significantly affected by the rule;

**FIGURE 5–2
(continued)**

(3) there is a reasonable likelihood that a committee can be convened with a balanced representation of persons who

(A) can adequately represent the interests identified under paragraph (2); and

(B) are willing to negotiate in good faith to reach a consensus on the proposed rule;

(4) there is a reasonable likelihood that a committee will reach a consensus on the proposed rule within a fixed period of time;

(5) the negotiated rulemaking procedure will not unreasonably delay the notice of proposed rulemaking and the issuance of the final rule;

(6) the agency has adequate resources and is willing to commit such resources, including technical assistance, to the committee; and

(7) the agency, to the maximum extent possible consistent with the legal obligations of the agency, will use the consensus of the committee with respect to the proposed rule as the basis for the rule proposed by the agency for notice and comment.

(b) Use of Conveners.

(1) Purposes of conveners. An agency may use the services of a convener to assist the agency in

(A) identifying persons who will be significantly affected by a proposed rule, including residents of rural areas; and

(B) conducting discussions with such persons to identify the issues of concern to such persons, and to ascertain whether the establishment of a negotiated rulemaking committee is feasible and appropriate in the particular rulemaking.

(2) Duties of conveners. The convener shall report findings and may make recommendations to the agency. Upon request of the agency, the convener shall ascertain the names of persons who are willing and qualified to represent interests that will be significantly affected by the proposed rule, including residents of rural areas. The report and any recommendations of the convener shall be made available to the public upon request.

Negotiated rule making is analogous to reaching an out-of-court settlement in a lawsuit. The parties negotiate and reach a consensus without going through the longer procedures that must be used when a consensus cannot be reached. Negotiated rule making is part of the move in all areas of law toward quicker, less expensive resolution of legal issues.

Alternative Dispute Resolution

Alternative dispute resolution (ADR) is the use of negotiated settlements, arbitration, and similar methods to settle controversies without formal proceedings or litigation. Congress, recognizing the value of ADR, enacted the Administrative Dispute Resolution Act in 1990. The Congressional findings at the beginning of the Act acknowledge that "administrative proceedings have become increasingly formal, costly, and lengthy" and that "alternative means of dispute resolution have been used in the private sector and, in appropriate circumstances, have yielded decisions that are faster, less expensive, and less contentious."[14] Congress then acknowledges that "such alternative means may be used advantageously in a wide variety of administrative programs."[15]

What the Administrative Dispute Resolution Act Requires Agencies to Do

The Act does not require agencies to use ADR, but does provide guidelines when the agencies pursue ADR. The Act does, however, direct agencies to adopt a policy that addresses the use of ADR. Agencies are directed to consult with the Administrative Conference of the United States and the Federal Mediation and Conciliation Service and to examine ADR in connection with formal and informal adjudications, rule making, enforcement actions, issuing and revoking licenses or permits, contract administration, litigation brought by or against the agency, and other agency actions.[16] The Act does not encourage ADR in every action. For instance, the Act states that agencies should consider not using ADR if the matter requires an authoritative resolution for precedential value and an ADR proceeding would not likely be accepted generally as an authoritative precedent.

ADR Methods and Procedures

Section 581(3) of the Act provides that approved ADR methods include "settlement negotiations, conciliation, facilitation, mediation, factfinding, minitrials, and arbitration, or any combination thereof." You may already be familiar with some of these methods, such as settlement negotiations, through your study of litigation. Settlement negotiations work the same way in administrative proceedings as in

---

BALLENTINE'S

alternative dispute resolution (ADR) A term for speedier and less costly methods for resolving disputes than going to court.

civil litigation. For instance, suppose that the INS seeks to deport a client, and a deportation proceeding before an immigration judge is pending. The client has a defense to deportation, but not a strong one. The attorney with whom you work and the INS attorney may reach a compromise by the client agreeing to **voluntary departure.** Here, the alien agrees to leave the United States within a certain period of time, such as thirty days. As the term implies, the departure is voluntary, unlike deportation.

Settlement negotiations are being used increasingly in environmental law. For instance, under CERCLA the EPA can hold liable for the cost of cleanup and remediation of a Superfund site all parties who disposed of waste at that site. Often the parties and the EPA reach a settlement setting out the cost that each party will bear in the cleanup of the site.

Arbitration is another form of alternative dispute resolution. **Arbitration** is similar to a trial or adjudication, with presentation of witnesses and exhibits and cross-examination; however, arbitration has more streamlined procedures and is more informal. Refer to Figure 5–3, which reprints section 589 of the Administrative Dispute Resolution Act, arbitration proceedings. Arbitration pursuant to the Act is voluntary, not mandatory. It may be either binding or nonbinding. A **minitrial** is a "structured settlement process in which each side presents a highly abbreviated summary of its case before senior officials of each party authorized to settle the case."[17] After the minitrial the officials seek to negotiate a settlement, and a neutral adviser may preside over the minitrial and issue an advisory opinion.[18]

---

voluntary departure An agreement for an alien to leave the United States within a certain time limit, as an alternative to deportation.

BALLENTINE'S
---

arbitration A method of settling disputes by submitting a disagreement to a person (an arbitrator) or a group of individuals (an arbitration panel) for decision instead of going to court. If the parties are required to comply with the decision of the arbitrator, the process is called *binding arbitration;* if there is no such obligation, the arbitration is referred to as *nonbinding arbitration.* Compulsory arbitration arbitration required by law, most notably in labor disputes.

---

minitrial A structured settlement process in which each side presents a summary of its case before officials authorized to settle the case.

Figure 5–3
Section 589 of
the
Administrative
Dispute
Resolution Act

§ 589.   Arbitration proceedings

(a) The arbitrator shall set a time and place for the hearing on the dispute and shall notify the parties not less than 5 days before the hearing.

(b) Any party wishing a record of the hearing shall—

(1) be responsible for the preparation of such record;

(2) notify the other parties and the arbitrator of the preparation of such record;

(3) furnish copies to all identified parties and the arbitrator; and

(4) pay all costs for such record, unless the parties agree otherwise or the arbitrator determines that the costs should be apportioned.

(c)(1) The parties to the arbitration are entitled to be heard, to present evidence material to the controversy, and to cross-examine witnesses appearing at the hearing.

(2) The arbitrator may, with the consent of the parties, conduct all or part of the hearing by telephone, television, computer, or other electronic means, if each party has an opportunity to participate.

(3) The hearing shall be conducted expeditiously and in an informal manner.

(4) The arbitrator may receive any oral or documentary evidence, except that irrelevant, immaterial, unduly repetitious, or privileged evidence may be excluded by the arbitrator.

(5) The arbitrator shall interpret and apply relevant statutory and regulatory requirements, legal precedents, and policy directives.

(d) No interested person shall make or knowingly cause to be made to the arbitrator an unauthorized ex parte communication relevant to the merits of the proceeding, unless the parties agree otherwise. If a communication is made in violation of this subsection, the arbitrator shall ensure that a memorandum of the communication is prepared and made a part of the record, and that an opportunity for rebuttal is allowed. Upon receipt of a communication made in violation of this subsection, the arbitrator may, to the extent consistent with the interests of justice and the policies underlying this subchapter, require the offending party to show cause why the claim of such party should not be resolved against such party as a result of the improper conduct.

(e) The arbitrator shall make the award within 30 days after the close of the hearing, or the date of the filing of any briefs authorized by the arbitrator, whichever date is later, unless—

(1) the parties agree to some other time limit; or

(2) the agency provides by rule for some other time limit.

SIDEBAR   The person who presides over arbitration proceedings and other ADR methods is called a **neutral**. The Act defines a neutral as the individual who aids the parties in resolving the controversy.

Mediation is a method of ADR in which a neutral third party directs the settlement negotiations. The parties themselves, however, make the decision, not the mediator.

Facilitating is a similar procedure, where the facilitator coordinates meetings and discussions. The facilitator, however, does not become as involved in substantive issues as does a mediator.[19]

Fact finding involves the parties presenting their information, frequently on technical matters to specialists in that technical area, who make findings that are then used by the parties to reach a settlement or direct further proceedings.

Use of Nonlawyer Representatives

One rewarding aspect of administrative law for paralegals is that statutes and regulations of certain agencies specifically authorize representation by nonlawyers. This is true for Social Security disability, and Chapter 10 discusses this in detail. It is interesting to note at this point, however, that the Administrative Dispute Resolution Act instructs agencies to develop a policy about nonattorney representation in ADR procedures. Agencies are directed to determine which proceedings do not require attorney representation. Agencies are allowed to establish requirements that nonlawyers must meet in order to represent individuals in disputes

---

neutral The person who presides over arbitration proceedings and other ADR methods.

BALLENTINE'S

mediation The voluntary resolution of a dispute in an amicable manner. One of the primary uses of mediators, also called conciliators, is in settling labor disputes. Professional mediators are available for that purpose through the Federal Mediation and Conciliation Service. Mediation differs from arbitration in that a mediator, unlike an arbitrator, does not render a decision.

---

facilitating An ADR method in which a facilitator coordinates meetings and discussions in a manner similar to mediation, but with less involvement with substantive issues than a mediator has.

fact finding An ADR method in which parties present information, usually regarding technical matters, to specialists who make findings used by the parties to reach a settlement.

with the agency. ACUS has formulated a recommendation on Nonlawyer Assistance and Representation, which is reprinted in Figure 5–4.

Figure 5–4
ACUS Recommendation Regarding Nonlawyer Assistance and Representation (1 CFR 305.86-1)

---

§ 305.86-1 Nonlawyer Assistance and Representation (Recommendation No. 86-1).

A substantial number of individuals involved in Federal "mass justice"[1] agency proceedings need and desire assistance[2] in filling out forms, filing claims, and appearing in agency proceedings, but are unable to afford assistance or representation by lawyers. A lack of assistance or representation reduces the probability that an individual will obtain favorable results in dealing with an agency. Further, unassisted individuals are more likely than those who are assisted to cause a loss of agency efficiency by requiring more time, effort, and help from the agency.

Federal agencies currently provide help to persons involved in agency proceedings through information given by agency personnel and through funding of legal aid programs and approval or payment of attorney fee awards. This recommendation does not deal with whether government aid may be needed for persons who cannot afford any form of assistance. This recommendation focuses on the potential for increasing the availability of assistance by nonlawyers. Federal agency experience and statistics indicate that qualified persons who are not lawyers generally are capable of providing effective assistance to individuals in mass justice agency proceedings.

While it is recognized that no established privilege protects the confidentiality of communications between nonlawyers and their clients, agencies may adopt some protections covering their own proceedings. The possible limitation of such protections does not outweigh the benefits of increased assistance and representation.

Agency practices do not currently maximize the potential for free choice of assistance, and, in some instances, may hinder the availability of qualified, low–cost assistance by nonlawyers. Agencies should take the steps necessary to encourage—as well as eliminate inappropriate barriers to—nonlawyer assistance and representation.

Agencies generally have the authority to authorize any person to act as a representative for another person having business with the agency. Where an agency intends to permit nonlawyers to assist individuals in agency matters, the agency needs to state that intention affirmatively in its regulations for two reasons. First, an affirmative statement is essential, under existing case law, to protect a nonlawyer from prosecution—under state "unauthorized practice of law" prohibitions—for assisting and advising a Federal client preparatory to commencing agency proceedings, as well as for advertising the availability of services. Second, an affirmative agency position is needed to overcome a common assumption of nonlawyers that agencies welcome only lawyers as representatives, and thereby to encourage an increase in the provision of nonlawyer services.

**Figure 5–4
(continued)**

RECOMMENDATION

1. The Social Security Administration, the Immigration and Naturalization Service, the Veterans Administration, the Internal Revenue Service, and other Federal agencies that deal with a significant number of unassisted individuals who have personal, family, or personal business claims or disputes before the agency, should review their regulations regarding assistance and representation. The review should be directed toward the goals of authorizing increased assistance by nonlawyers, and of maximizing the potential for free choice of representative to the fullest extent allowed by law.

2. If an agency determines that some subject areas or types of its proceedings are so complex or specialized that only specially qualified persons can adequately provide representation, then the agency may need to adopt appropriate measures to ensure that nonlawyers meet specific eligibility criteria at some or all stages of representation. Agencies should tailor any eligibility requirements so as not to exclude nonlawyers (including nonlawyers who charge fees) as a class, if there are nonlawyers who, by reason of their knowledge, experience, training, or other qualification, can adequately provide assistance or representation.

3. Agencies should declare unambiguously their intention to authorize assistance and representation by nonlawyers meeting agency criteria. Where a declaration by an agency may have the effect of preempting state law (such as "unauthorized practice of law" prohibitions), then the agency should employ the procedures set out in Recommendation 84-5 with regard to notification of and cooperation with the states and other affected groups.

4. Agencies should review their rules of practice that deal with attorney conduct (such as negligence, fee gouging, fraud, misrepresentation, and representation when there is a conflict of interest) to ensure that similar rules are made applicable to nonlawyers as appropriate, and should establish effective agency procedures for enforcing those rules of practice and for receiving complaints from the affected public.

[1] The term "mass justice" is used here to categorize an agency program in which a large number of individual claims or disputes involving personal, family, or personal business matters come before an agency; e.g., the Old Age Survivors and Disability Insurance program administered by the Social Security Administration. To the extent that principles incorporated in this Recommendation may be applicable to other programs in which non-lawyer assistance or representation is (or could be made) available, the Conference recommends the consideration of these principles by the agencies involved.

[2] The term "assistance" is used here to indicate all forms of help, including representation, that may be beneficial to a person in dealing with an agency. The term "representation" is used whenever the most likely form of assistance involves such activities as making an appearance, signing papers, or speaking for the assisted individual. Neither term is meant to be exclusive.

Enforcement and Sanctions

Enforcement of statutes is the primary function of some agencies, such as the EEOC. Enforcement is an important function of the INS and EPA as well. Administrative agencies use various methods to enforce the law, ranging from aggressive litigation to informal administrative hearings or negotiated settlements. As a means of enforcement, agencies assess penalties ranging from interest on overdue tax payments to the large monetary and criminal penalties for environmental violations.

Litigation

Many federal agencies have active litigation sections. The EEOC, for instance, has many trial attorneys in its district offices throughout the country. Other agencies refer their litigation to the Justice Department, which represents the federal government in many types of lawsuits. For instance, the EPA refers litigation to the Environmental Enforcement Section (EES) of the Department of Justice. As environmental litigation has increased, EES had grown in 1994 to the largest litigating section in the Justice Department, with 161 attorneys and 45 paralegals.[20]

On the state level, many administrative agencies are represented in court by the State Attorney General's Office. For instance, in the North Carolina Attorney General's Office there are attorneys and paralegals assigned to litigation involving the University of North Carolina system, state prisons, and state mental hospitals. The North Carolina Attorney General's Office also has attorneys assigned to litigation of environmental violations. In North Carolina, state district attorneys also prosecute many cases involving environmental violations with criminal penalties. Enforcement mechanisms vary from state to state. Thus, paralegals must become familiar with the enforcement mechanisms within administrative agencies in their own states.

Once an action has been filed in court, the Rules of Civil Procedure apply, just as they do in other types of litigation. The same procedure of filing pleadings, conducting discovery, pursuing settlement negotiations, and the actual trial if settlement is not reached proceed as in other civil actions. In criminal prosecutions, the Rules of Criminal Procedure apply.

Pretrial Administrative Procedures

When administrative agencies are involved, there are often appeal procedures within the agency and settlement efforts that must be exhausted before proceeding to court. Further, permission to litigate a case sometimes must be obtained from the agency's central office in Washington, D.C. For instance, when a case is referred to the Environmental Enforcement Section of the Justice Department, each proposed complaint receives five levels of review. Further, each complaint must be signed by the Assistant Attorney General for the Environment and Natural Resources Division.[21]

Presuit Administrative Procedures: The EEOC

People who feel that they have suffered employment discrimination cannot simply file a lawsuit in federal court. Further, the EEOC cannot institute a suit on a person's behalf before certain presuit administrative procedures have been completed. These procedures are set forth in the EEOC's regulations.

In Sample Case Two, Linda Watson felt that her discharge was retaliatory because she had filed a charge with the EEOC. The first step that an aggrieved person, such as Linda Watson, must take is to file a charge of discrimination with the EEOC. The **charge** is a written statement describing the alleged unlawful employment practice, as well as the name and address of the charging party and the person against whom the charge is made. The regulations provide that the EEOC can keep confidential the identity of the charging party. The exact contents of the charge are set forth in 29 CFR 1601.12, which is reprinted as Figure 5–5. Within ten days of the filing of a charge, the EEOC must serve, by mail or in person, a copy of the charge on the person charged, known as the **respondent.** The regulations also state that when serving an actual copy of the charge would "impede the law enforcement functions" of the EEOC, the respondent will receive notice of the charge with a description of the alleged unlawful employment practice (29 CFR 1601.14).

Figure 5–5
29 CFR 1601.12

> **§ 1601.12   Contents of charge; amendment of charge.**
>
> (a) Each charge should contain the following: (1) The full name, address and telephone number of the person making the charge except as provided in § 1601.7;
> (2) The full name and address of the person against whom the charge is made, if known (hereinafter referred to as the respondent);

charge In EEOC presuit procedures, a written statement describing the alleged unlawful employment practice.

respondent In EEOC pretrial procedures, the person charged with engaging in an unlawful employment practice.

(3) A clear and concise statement of the facts, including pertinent dates, constituting the alleged unlawful employment practices: See § 1601.15(b).

(4) If known, the approximate number of employees of the respondent employer or the approximate number of members of the respondent labor organization, as the case may be; and

(5) A statement disclosing whether proceedings involving the alleged unlawful employment practice have been commenced before a State or local agency charged with the enforcement of fair employment practice laws and, if so, the date of such commencement and the name of the agency.

(b) Notwithstanding the provisions of paragraph (a) of this section, a charge is sufficient when the Commission receives from the person making the charge a written statement sufficiently precise to identify the parties, and to describe generally the action or practices complained of. A charge may be amended to cure technical defects or omissions, including failure to verify the charge, or to clarify and amplify allegations made therein. Such amendments and amendments alleging additional acts which constitute unlawful employment practices related to or growing out of the subject matter of the original charge will relate back to the date the charge was first received. A charge that has been so amended shall not be required to be redeferred.

The next step is investigation of the charge. This is discussed in detail below, beginning on page 191.

After the investigation is complete, the EEOC investigator makes a recommendation to the district director explaining whether reasonable cause exists to believe that an unlawful employment practice has occurred. The district director and trial attorneys review the investigator's conclusions. If reasonable cause is not found, the EEOC issues a "no cause determination" and sends a "right to sue" letter, informing the aggrieved party of the right to sue in federal district court within ninety days of receipt of the letter. The EEOC does not represent the aggrieved party, but the aggrieved party is free to retain a private attorney and pursue litigation in federal court.[22]

If the EEOC finds reasonable cause, the parties are notified. Then, the EEOC pursues **conciliation**, a mandatory endeavor to eliminate the unlawful employment practice "by informal methods of conference, conciliation and persuasion" (29 CFR 1601.24). The regulations regarding conciliation direct the EEOC to resolve all violations found and to obtain an agreement that "the respondent will eliminate the unlawful employment practice and provide appropriate affirmative

---

conciliation   A mandatory EEOC presuit procedure in which the parties and the EEOC try to eliminate the alleged unlawful employment practice by informal settlement methods.

relief."[23] If conciliation is successful, the EEOC and the parties sign a conciliation agreement. Refer to Figure 5–6, which reprints 29 CFR 1601.24(a) and (c).

Figure 5–6
29 CFR 1601.24(a)
and (c)

---

§ 1601.24 Conciliation: Procedure and authority.

(a) Where the Commission determines that there is reasonable cause to believe that an unlawful employment practice has occurred or is occurring, the Commission shall endeavor to eliminate such practice by informal methods of conference, conciliation and persuasion. In conciliating a case in which a determination of reasonable cause has been made, the Commission shall attempt to achieve a just resolution of all violations found and to obtain agreement that the respondent will eliminate the unlawful employment practice and provide appropriate affirmative relief. Where such conciliation attempts are successful, the terms of the conciliation agreement shall be reduced to writing and shall be signed by the Commission's designated representative and the parties. A copy of the signed agreement shall be sent to the respondent and the person claiming to be aggrieved. Where a charge has been filed on behalf of a person claiming to be aggrieved, the conciliation agreement may be signed by the person filing the charge or by the person on whose behalf the charge was filed.

. . .

(c) Proof of compliance with title VII or the ADA in accordance with the terms of the agreement shall be obtained by the Commission before the case is closed. In those instances in which a person claiming to be aggrieved or a member of the class claimed to be aggrieved by the practices alleged in the charge is not a party to such an agreement, the agreement shall not extinguish or in any way prejudice the rights of such person to proceed in court under section 706(f)(1) of title VII or the ADA.

If conciliation is unsuccessful, the EEOC notifies the respondent in writing. Conciliation is often unsuccessful, because the EEOC seeks to obtain full relief for the aggrieved party, something the respondent is frequently unwilling to do. The EEOC has then exhausted the presuit administrative procedures. After obtaining approval by a majority of the EEOC commissioners, the trial attorneys at the district office can file suit in federal district court.

Administrative Hearings

Not all enforcement actions take place in federal court. As discussed above, the EEOC's conciliation procedures may produce sufficient relief for the aggrieved party at the agency level, without the necessity of proceeding to federal court. The EPA generally refers the more serious violations to the Department of Justice, but the EPA handles less serious offenses through its own administrative hearings. The INS handles deportation hearings, which are administrative hearings, through its own trial attorneys, not through the Department of Justice. Thus, in administrative law, when paralegals think of litigation, in addition to the traditional notions of courtroom actions, they must also keep in mind the enormous number of administrative hearings and less formal procedures through which much enforcement is accomplished.

Sanctions

Chapter 3 discussed the far-reaching sanctions allowed under Title VII, including reinstatement to a job, back pay, and injunctive relief. A respondent may also agree during the conciliation process to some or all of the sanctions sought by the EEOC. Typical of federal agencies, the sanctions can be imposed both at the agency level or through federal court litigation. Agencies issue orders directing sanctions. For instance, if the INS finds an alien deportable, it issues an order of deportation. The EPA issues orders for violators to clean up sites and pay fines. Courts enter judgments, as in any other civil lawsuit. For instance, if a court finds that a company has violated Title VII, the court enters a judgment, stating the relief to which the plaintiff is entitled.

Agency Information and Advice

Every day administrative agencies answer thousands of questions for the public. As noted in Chapter 1, disseminating information is an important function of many agencies, especially agencies such as the Social Security Administration (SSA) that administer benefits for millions of people. Suppose a woman's husband dies. She needs information from the SSA about benefits as a widow, if she is old enough to meet the requirements, or benefits for minor children. This is important information that she must obtain from the SSA promptly. She can call the SSA and talk to an employee at one of the teleservice centers, or she can go to the local SSA district office to get this information.

The INS also disseminates much information. Many people go to INS offices and ask questions about how to get nonimmigrant or immigrant visas for their relatives who wish to come to the United States.

The EPA disseminates much information, which is critical because many people affected by environmental regulations lack the expertise to understand all the technical information in the regulations. Even environmental engineers who work with environmental compliance issues every day still need to call on the EPA for information and advice.

People who feel that they have suffered employment discrimination contact the EEOC for information on the applicable laws and for instructions on how to file a charge against an employer.

Dissemination of information and advice is a large and critical function of most federal agencies. Agencies dispense information and advice in many forms.

Methods of Giving Information and Advice

Agencies disseminate information in many ways, which vary both in formality and in the extent to which the advice is binding on the agency.

Publications

Many agencies issue their own publications, from brochures to books. For instance, the SSA publishes brochures explaining the basics of certain types of benefits and how to apply for benefits or for a Social Security card. Agency publications range from these informal brochures to detailed texts and surveys. For instance, the United States Department of Justice, Office of Policy and Communications, publishes a book entitled *Freedom of Information Case List*, which includes an alphabetical compilation of judicial decisions, both published and unpublished, addressing issues under the Freedom of Information Act and the Privacy Act.

In the *United States Government Manual*, many agencies list some of their publications. The U.S. Government Printing Office publishes the *Monthly Catalog of U.S. Government Publications*, as well as two catalogs entitled *U.S. Government Books* and *New Books*. Another method for locating government publications is through organizations of professionals who work in one area of administrative law. Refer to the section below on Practical Tips for Paralegals.

SIDEBAR   Publications can be obtained by writing to the Superintendent of Documents, Government Printing Office, Washington, D.C. 20402. It can take four to six weeks to receive orders from the Government Printing Office (GPO). Refer to the U.S. Government Manual for a list of GPO bookstores throughout the country.

Declaratory Orders

Section 554(e) of the APA provides that "[t]he agency, with like effect as in the case of other orders, and in its sound discretion, may issue a declaratory order to terminate a controversy or remove uncertainty." Through your study of civil procedure, you may be familiar with **declaratory judgments,** the procedure in which a party files a complaint seeking a declaration (explanation) of its rights in an actual controversy; the court explains the law in question and the parties' rights under that law, without awarding damages.[24] The administrative counterpart of a declaratory judgment is a **declaratory order.**[25] For example, the Food and Drug Administration (FDA) has issued declaratory orders to withdraw the approval of certain drugs.

Frequently statutes and regulations leave many unanswered questions, and one might imagine that people affected by the laws would seek declaratory orders frequently. Studies, however, have shown that the device is actually not used very often. Professor Burnele Powell has observed that "complete acceptance of the declaratory device as a means of prelitigation dispute resolution has not been realized."[26] One reason that declaratory orders are not used frequently is that the APA gives the agencies discretion to determine whether they wish to use declaratory orders. Agencies are not required to issue declaratory orders merely because a party requests such an order.[27]

Advisory Opinions

A less formal method for an agency to explain the law and a party's rights is through an advisory opinion. An **advisory opinion** is generally defined as an interpretation of the law without binding effect, generally requested by parties before an actual controversy arises.[28] Unlike a declaratory order, an advisory opinion is not binding. Further, it is not reviewable by a court.[29]

————————————————— BALLENTINE'S —————————————————

declaratory judgment A judgment that specifies the rights of the parties but orders no relief. Nonetheless, it is a binding judgment and the appropriate remedy for the determination of an actionable dispute when the plaintiff is in doubt as to his legal rights.

---

declaratory order The administrative equivalent of a declaratory judgment.

————————————————— BALLENTINE'S —————————————————

advisory opinion A judicial interpretation of a legal question requested by the legislative or executive branch of government. Typically, courts prefer not to give advisory opinions.

Federal courts do not render advisory opinions. They address only actual cases and controversies.[30] In contrast, administrative agencies frequently issue advisory opinions. Some advisory opinions are given informally, even over the telephone. Other advisory opinions are more formally rendered. For instance, the IRS issues thousands of revenue rulings each year. Some of the rulings are published, with the approval of the IRS Commissioner.[31]

Informal Advice by Telephone

Attorneys, paralegals, and the public in general frequently contact administrative agency personnel for advice and information. Not all procedures are set forth in agency regulations, and some local offices may have unpublished procedures. Paralegals may have to contact the agency for information and advice on such procedural matters. Paralegals may have to deal with multiple federal agencies to aid one client. For instance, an immigration paralegal may have to contact the local Social Security office to find out how to obtain a Social Security card if the client does not have all the documentation usually required. Paralegals in private law firms and corporations will find that they often need to seek information and advice, formal or informal, from administrative agencies.

Practical Tips for Paralegals on Getting Information

Paralegals and attorneys often need information from agencies on issues ranging from interpretation of new regulations to procedural questions such as where to file a certain document when you are not sure in which of its offices the agency has the client's file. Some agencies, such as the INS, change procedures in their local offices, and this information is not always available in CFR or the *Federal Register*. For instance, the procedure for obtaining employment authorization for applicants for political asylum has varied over the years and procedures have even varied from office to office.

If paralegals work in one area of administrative law, they generally learn the names and phone numbers of agency personnel with expertise in certain areas. If, however, paralegals or attorneys do not know the particular person to ask for and that person's phone number, the quest for specific information can be frustrating. Membership in associations of professionals who work in certain areas of law is very helpful in locating the right agency employees and their telephone numbers. Organizations such as the American Immigration Lawyers Association (AILA) and the National Organization of Social Security Claimants Representatives (NOSSCR) publish newsletters and directories that are helpful. The publications sometimes include the names and phone numbers of agency personnel. Further, the publications can direct you to other professionals who have expertise in a certain area.

Investigations and Monitoring

Most administrative agencies have enforcement duties. Administrative agencies regularly monitor and investigate businesses and individuals as part of their enforcement functions. Paralegals will find that most clients are subject to some type of mandatory record keeping or monitoring. Some types of businesses, however, are subject to more monitoring than others. A clothing store, for instance, is subject to less monitoring and record keeping than a business in a highly regulated industry, such as a chemical plant. The agencies gather information in various ways, but principally through two methods—examining records and conducting on-site investigations.

Record-Keeping and Reporting Requirements

In order to effectuate their investigations and monitoring functions, administrative agencies impose mandatory record-keeping requirements on individuals and businesses. At the most basic level, the IRS requires businesses to keep records of wages paid to their employees. Businesses send each employee a W-2 form, reflecting the wages paid and taxes withheld. Employees must send in their W-2 forms with their tax returns. Individuals and businesses keep other records, in case the IRS wants to audit their tax returns and supporting documentation. Through these records, the IRS monitors businesses and individuals to ensure proper payment of taxes.

The INS also requires employees to keep records. When new employees are hired, employers are required to obtain proof of authorization to work. For United States citizens, the proof may be common documents such as a driver's license and Social Security card. For aliens, a green card or work authorization form may be required. Through these records, the INS can inspect business records to determine whether all employees have proper work authorization. The rationale behind the statute that established these requirements is that illegal aliens will not be able to obtain proper work authorization, will not be hired, and thus will not remain in the United States. The law has not been as effective as envisioned, due in part to a shortage of investigators to visit places of business to check their records.

On a more sophisticated level, pursuant to RCRA, the EPA requires generators, transporters, and owners of TSD facilities to keep copies of manifests for at least three years. Generators must also submit reports to the EPA listing their hazardous wastes and the transporters and TSD facilities they used.

Generators such as Chaco Corporation, in Sample Case Four, must submit a host of reports to federal, state, and local agencies each year. During a typical year, a generator such as Chaco submits reports to the state agency that administers the hazardous waste program. Chaco also submits a yearly report to the EPA describing all toxic emissions into the air and water, with detailed calculations showing the amounts of emissions. Such a report is several inches thick. Chaco also handles a chemical called Toluene, and must submit quarterly reports on this one chemical. Local government agencies monitor air and water quality in Chaco's geographical area, and they require monthly air and water quality reports. Further, when Chaco applies for permits to expand certain operations, such as its research lab, reports on emissions and other technical information must be sent to the appropriate agency. In addition to all the reports required by various administrative agencies, Chaco also compiles monthly reports for internal use to keep track of waste it has generated. A plant such as Chaco may have several employees, including a chemist, who work almost solely on regulatory compliance. Thus, the record-keeping and reporting requirements imposed by administrative agencies can be expensive.

On-Site Investigations

Agency personnel frequently conduct on-site investigations, in which they physically inspect a place of business and examine records. The type of inspection conducted depends on the purpose of the investigation. For instance, the Occupational Safety and Health Administration (OSHA) inspects business facilities to determine whether they are in compliance with safety and health standards and regulations. The INS may arrive unannounced at a restaurant or hotel to determine whether undocumented workers are employed. This may involve questioning the employer and employees and inspecting the business records for documentation of work authorization for employees.

Inspections Required Under RCRA

The EPA has been given authority to conduct on-site inspections of business facilities and their records. In fact, the RCRA statute mandates inspections and specifically gives the EPA authority to enter any establishment "where hazardous wastes are or have been generated, stored, treated, disposed of, or transported from" and to inspect the premises, obtain samples, and review and copy records.[32] Refer to Figure 5–7, which reprints 42 U.S.C. § 6927(a). Note that the statute gives the EPA authority to examine and copy all records relating to wastes. The statute also gives details on how the EPA inspectors obtain samples. The EPA may want samples to determine whether certain types of hazardous wastes are being handled on the premises or to determine whether the emissions of regulated substances are within the required levels.

Figure 5–7
42 U.S.C.
§ 6927(a)

§ 6927. Inspections

(a) Access entry

For purposes of developing or assisting in the development of any regulation or enforcing the provisions of this chapter, any person who generates, stores, treats, transports, disposes of, or otherwise handles or has handled hazardous wastes shall, upon request of any officer, employee or representative of the Environmental Protection Agency, duly designated by the Administrator, or upon request of any duly designated officer, employee or representative of a State having an authorized hazardous waste program, furnish information relating to such wastes and permit such person at all reasonable times to have access to, and to copy all records relating to such wastes. For the purposes of developing or assisting in the development of any regulation or enforcing the provisions of this chapter, such officers, employees or representatives are authorized—

(1) to enter at reasonable times any establishment or other place where hazardous wastes are or have been generated, stored, treated, disposed of, or transported from;

(2) to inspect and obtain samples from any person of any such wastes and samples of any containers or labeling for such wastes.

Each such inspection shall be commenced and completed with reasonable promptness. If the officer, employee or representative obtains any samples, prior to leaving the premises, he shall give to the owner, operator, or agent in charge a receipt describing the sample obtained and if requested a portion of each such sample equal in volume or weight to the portion retained. If any analysis is made of such samples, a copy of the results of such analysis shall be furnished promptly to the owner, operator, or agent in charge.

SIDEBAR

Generators of hazardous waste usually develop internal environmental affairs manuals that explain company policies regarding inspection of records and taking of samples. Paralegals need to be familiar with clients' internal policies. The clients may consult with the law firm while developing their policies.

How a Generator Responds to an On-Site Inspection

Assume that an EPA inspector has just arrived at Chaco Corporation unannounced and seeks to inspect records and take samples. Chaco employees may debate whether to allow the inspector to enter and whether to place any limitations on the inspection. In fact, Chaco has, like most responsible generators, already compiled a compliance manual to guide the employees. If the inspector arrives at a reasonable time, explains the purpose of the inspection, and presents proper credentials, then Chaco will allow the inspection to proceed. In such a case, Chaco's policy is to allow the inspector onto the premises without a search warrant. It is fairly easy for the inspector to obtain a search warrant if Chaco refuses entry, and because this appears to be a routine inspection, Chaco does not request that a warrant be obtained. Chaco might request a warrant under certain circumstances, such as when an inspector refuses to provide information on the authority under which the inspection is being made or refuses to present credentials or identify the purpose of the inspection. A warrant request may also be appropriate if Chaco is operating a daytime shift only, and the inspector arrives late at night when no one is at the facility except for the security guard. Procedures for search warrants are discussed below.

Once the on-site investigation begins, Chaco may make certain reasonable requests to ensure the accuracy of the information obtained and to ensure the protection of confidential business information and proprietary technology. Such protective procedures include reviewing requested documents, marking confidential documents and offering sanitized copies when possible, retaining an identical copy of documents given to the inspector, limiting photographs to the areas that are the subject of the inspection, and taking pictures of all areas photographed by the inspector. Further, Chaco may request that the inspector split the samples taken. This simply means that when inspectors take samples, they give a portion of the sample to Chaco. This allows Chaco to send the sample to an independent lab for analysis to compare to the EPA's analysis.

This is one example of on-site investigations and the informal protective procedures that the facility being inspected may take. The more formal methods, such as requiring a search warrant and resisting a subpoena, are discussed below.

Other Methods of Investigation

Examination of records and on-site inspections are not the only investigative methods used by administrative agencies. Agency personnel may use informal methods such as submitting a list of questions to be answered and returned to the agency within a certain number of days. Agency personnel may arrange meetings in which the involved parties are interviewed in a manner similar to a deposition. The methods used by EEOC investigators illustrate some of these investigative techniques.

The EEOC employs a large number of investigators. When a charge of discrimination is filed, the investigators are the first to gather and analyze information to determine whether there is reasonable cause to believe that an unlawful employment practice has occurred. The district director and a trial attorney then review the investigator's recommendation.

EEOC investigators have the authority to use several different methods to gather information. The EEOC regulations describe the investigative authority given to the investigators and other designated personnel. Refer to Figure 5–8, which reprints 29 CFR 1601.15, describing the EEOC's investigative authority. The first part of the investigation involves getting information from the charging party. To obtain information from the respondent, the EEOC sends a Notice of Charge, briefly explaining the charge, with an attached questionnaire asking the respondent to explain the events that transpired. Subsequently, another questionnaire may be sent asking for more details and requesting pertinent business records. Investigators may require a fact-finding conference, where the respondent is asked questions to help develop the facts. The fact-finding conference may also include informal discussions to help determine which facts are undisputed and to discuss settlement. Refer to 29 CFR 1601.15(c), reprinted in Figure 5–8, for further explanation of the fact-finding conference. As 29 CFR 1601.15(d) notes, the EEOC is not limited to the investigative methods spelled out in the regulations. EEOC investigators may also subpoena records and conduct on-site investigations, which involve interviewing personnel at the respondent's facility and personally inspecting business records on the premises.

FIGURE 5–8
29 CFR 1601.15

> INVESTIGATION OF A CHARGE
> **§ 1601.15 Investigative authority.**
>   (a) The investigation of a charge shall be made by the Commission, its investigators, or any other representative designated by the Commission. During the course of such investigation, the Commission may utilize the services of State and local agencies which are charged with the administration of fair employment practice laws or appropriate Federal agencies, and may utilize the information gathered by such authorities or agencies. As part of each investigation, the Commission will accept any statement of position or evidence with respect to the allegations of the charge which the person claiming to be aggrieved, the person making the charge on behalf of such person, if any, or the respondent wishes to submit.
>   (b) As part of the Commission's investigation, the Commission may

**FIGURE 5–8
(continued)**

require the person claiming to be aggrieved to provide a statement which includes:

(1) A statement of each specific harm that the person has suffered and the date on which each harm occurred;

(2) For each harm, a statement specifying the act, policy or practice which is alleged to be unlawful;

(3) For each act, policy, or practice alleged to have harmed the person claiming to be aggrieved, a statement of the facts which lead the person claiming to be aggrieved to believe that the act, policy or practice is discriminatory.

(c) The Commission may require a fact-finding conference with the parties prior to a determination on a charge of discrimination. The conference is primarily an investigative forum intended to define the issues, to determine which elements are undisputed, to resolve those issues that can be resolved and to ascertain whether there is a basis for negotiated settlement of the charge.

(d) The Commission's authority to investigate a charge is not limited to the procedures outlined in paragraphs (a), (b), and (c) of this section.

Subpoenas and Search Warrants

Subpoenas and search warrants are important tools for administrative agencies, used when an individual or business does not voluntarily allow agency investigators to examine records or inspect the premises. There are, however, limitations on the use of subpoenas and search warrants. The Administrative Procedure Act (APA) states that "[p]rocess, requirement of a report, inspection, or other investigative act or demand may not be issued, made, or enforced except as authorized by law."[33] Thus, the APA states that agencies can use subpoenas and search warrants only when they are carrying out the duties delegated to them.

Subpoenas

A **subpoena** is a document that orders persons to testify or to produce documentary or physical evidence in their possession. An administrative agency can issue a subpoena. If a person does not comply with the subpoena, however, the agency must generally go to court to enforce the subpoena. The restraints on agencies' subpoenas have evolved largely in the context of parties resisting subpoenas. However, the APA and some enabling statutes state guidelines for

---
BALLENTINE'S
---

subpoena A command in the form of written process requiring a witness to come to court to testify; short for subpoena ad testificandum.

issuing and enforcing subpoenas. Refer to 5 U.S.C. § 555(d), the section of the APA addressing subpoenas, which is reprinted in Appendix A. The APA states that agencies may issue and enforce subpoenas only "as authorized by law." Thus, an agency may enforce a subpoena only when it is issued in connection with an investigation that the agency is authorized to undertake. The ever-present theme of delegation arises again; the agency can only act within the authority granted by Congress.

The subpoena must seek information that is relevant to the investigation. Title VII specifies that the EEOC may issue subpoenas only for information relevant to charges under investigation.[34] The question of relevancy is pertinent to all phases of investigation, not just subpoenas. As discussed above, an on-site inspection should cover only areas and records that are relevant to the investigation. The relevancy requirement is crucial to prevent **fishing expeditions,** which are broad, vague requests for large amounts of information without stating a clear purpose for the request. When an agency makes such an ill-defined request, it is said to be going on a fishing expedition, that is, fishing through the information for possible violations, based on vague suspicion rather than a noted violation.

As in all other areas of law, in administrative law, a party is not allowed to obtain privileged information, even with a subpoena. The fifth amendment privilege against self-incrimination applies in administrative law, as do common law privileges such as attorney-client privilege. These privileges are discussed in detail in Chapter 6.

Search Warrants

When an administrative agency seeks to inspect business premises, employees frequently consent to the inspection. Generally, when the scope and time of the inspection are reasonable, consent is given and a search warrant is not necessary. This is not always the case. Thus, paralegals must understand the basic requirements for search warrants and the exceptions, that is, when warrantless searches are allowed.

A **search warrant** is an order authorizing a person to enter property and search for and seize evidence. Unless an exception applies, such as

---

fishing expeditions Broad and ill-defined requests by agencies for large amounts of information, when an agency may not have a firm suspicion of an actual violation.

————————————————— BALLENTINE'S —————————————————

search warrant An order in writing issued by a magistrate or other judicial officer and directed to a law enforcement officer, commanding her to search for and seize stolen, contraband, or illicit property, or other property evidencing the commission of a crime.

giving consent to a search, administrative agencies must obtain warrants to search individuals' homes and businesses. The United States Supreme Court has held that the requirement for a warrant applies to administrative inspections.[35] In *Camara*, the Court determined that a warrant was required for a health inspector to search a private residence.

General Requirements for Search Warrants. The fourth amendment prohibits unreasonable searches and seizures, requiring a finding of probable cause before a warrant will be issued. The United States Supreme Court has required a lesser degree of probable cause for administrative search warrants than for typical criminal search warrants.[36] Perhaps the best known discussion of search warrants involving administrative agencies is the *Barlow* case. Here, the United States Supreme Court held that the Occupational Safety and Health Act's authorization of warrantless searches was unconstitutional. The Court also discussed the level of probable cause needed for warrants in an administrative search. The Court explained that "[p]robable cause in the criminal law sense is not required. For purposes of an administrative search such as this, probable cause justifying the issuance of a warrant may be based not only on specific evidence of an existing violation but also on a showing that reasonable legislative or administrative standards for conducting an . . . inspection are satisfied."[37]

Warrantless Searches. Administrative searches without warrants are allowed in certain circumstances. An exception to the warrant requirement that has evolved in the context of inspections is the *Colonnade-Biswell* exception. The United States Supreme Court upheld the warrantless search of a licensed retail liquor business in *Colonnade* and the warrantless search of a gun shop in *Biswell* on the basis that these are "pervasively regulated" industries.[38] More recent cases have expanded this exception to "closely regulated" industries, such as mines and automobile junkyards.[39]

Warrantless searches are allowed when individuals consent to a search, as noted above. The "plain view" or "open fields" exception to the warrant requirement also applies to administrative searches. Thus, if an EPA inspector in a public area observes unlawful emissions coming from a smoke stack or flowing from a pipe into the city water system, a warrantless inspection would be allowed.

You now have an overview of the actions that administrative agencies take on a daily basis. Agencies are allowed to engage in a wide range of activities; however, their power is not unfettered. The control of agency actions is the subject of Chapter 6.

Summary

Except for procedures that require trial-type hearings, such as adjudications and formal rule making, most agency actions are informal.

Informal Agency Actions

Agencies perform many informal actions every day, ranging from determinations on Social Security disability to calculations of past due taxes. Often disputes with agencies can be resolved through informal means, even as simple as a telephone call.

Rule Making

One of the most important activities agencies perform is rule making, the process through which the agencies promulgate their regulations. This is important because delegation statutes give little detail, and the agencies themselves must fill in the details through their regulations.

There are several reasons why agencies promulgate regulations. First, when Congress enacts a new statute or revises a statute, agencies have to issue regulations to implement the changes in the law. Second, Congress sometimes directs agencies to review certain regulations periodically. Third, the president may issue an executive order directing an agency to take a certain action, and the agency must issue regulations to accomplish the task.

In limited circumstances, agencies are allowed to issue regulations without going through the rule-making procedures generally required by the APA. The exemptions include matters related to military and foreign affairs functions and matters related to agency management and personnel decisions.

Regulations regarding other agency matters must be promulgated according to the procedures set forth in the APA or through the Negotiated Rulemaking Act. The APA establishes two types of rule making—formal and informal. Formal rule making is required when a statute specifies that the regulations are "to be made on the record after opportunity for an agency hearing." Few statutes specify formal rule making, and when the language is ambiguous courts have generally found that formal rule making is not required. The APA sets forth specific procedures for formal rule making, which is a trial-type proceeding with presentation of witnesses, opportunity for cross-examination, and submission of exhibits.

Most regulations are promulgated through informal rule making, often called notice and comment rule making. Section 553 of the APA sets forth the three steps for informal rulemaking—publication of a notice of proposed rule making, a notice and comment period, and publication of final regulations. The notice of proposed rulemaking must include reference to the legal authority under which the regulation is proposed. It must also include the terms or substance of the proposed regulations or a description of the subjects and issues involved. During the notice and comment period, interested parties may submit written data, views, or arguments. After considering the comments, the agency issues final regulations, which must include the text of the final regulations as well as a concise general statement of the regulations' basis and purpose.

A third type of rule making is negotiated rule making, which is not mandatory. The Negotiated Rulemaking Act of 1990, however, does set forth guidelines and procedures. Negotiated rule making is appropriate when the interested parties can be identified and represented on the negotiating committee and issues can likely be settled by consensus. The committee proposes regulations, which are then published in the *Federal Register* in the regular notice and comment procedure.

Alternative Dispute Resolution

In recognition of the advantages of quicker, less expensive agency procedures, Congress enacted the Administrative Dispute Resolution Act. The Act does not require agencies to use alternative dispute resolution (ADR) but does provide guidelines when agencies pursue ADR. In addition to settlement negotiations, the Act's approved ADR methods include arbitration, minitrials, mediation, facilitating, and fact-finding. Review the description of these methods in the text, and you will see that most are analogous to those used in a civil litigation context. In all these methods, an impartial person, called a neutral, presides over the ADR procedure.

Enforcement And Sanctions

One of the obvious and most effective ways that agencies enforce the statutes entrusted to them is through litigation. Many federal and state agencies have active litigation sections. Most agencies must complete certain pretrial administrative procedures before they commence a lawsuit. At the very least, this includes approval from supervisory attorneys or other officials at the agency's regional offices and often at the central office in Washington, D.C. Some agencies must complete more extensive pretrial administrative procedures, and the EEOC offers a good example. After a discrimination charge is filed with the EEOC, the claim is investigated and EEOC personnel determine whether good cause exists to believe that an unlawful employment practice has occurred. If the EEOC determines that good cause does not exist, then the charging party is informed that he or she may pursue a federal court action, but not with the EEOC as counsel. If the EEOC finds good cause, a mandatory conciliation procedure must be followed to try to settle the case and eliminate the unlawful practice. If conciliation is unsuccessful, the EEOC informs the respondent. After these procedures are complete, the EEOC may file suit.

Many agencies handle disputes and enforcement through administrative hearings. These are frequently used for less serious offenses. Many agencies have been given the authority to impose significant civil and criminal sanctions. This is especially true of the EPA and EEOC.

Agency Information And Advice

Agencies share their expertise in a number of informal methods, such as giving advice by telephone. Many agencies publish brochures and books, which can be ordered through the Government Printing Office.

Agencies may issue declaratory orders, which explain the law and its application to the parties in order to terminate a controversy or remove uncertainty. An advisory opinion also interprets the law, but is not binding and is generally sought before a controversy arises.

Paralegals often need to speak with agency personnel to obtain information, and finding the right person can be a challenge. There are numerous sources for locating this information, and resources from organizations of professionals who work in a particular area of law are helpful.

Investigations And Monitoring

Administrative agencies monitor many businesses, especially those in closely regulated industries. Businesses must keep routine records such as wage records, and more closely regulated industries often have to keep extensive records and submit numerous reports to agencies.

In addition to record keeping, on-site investigations are a common method of monitoring. The RCRA statute requires on-site inspections and allows the EPA or state enforcement agency to inspect the premises, examine records, and take samples. Generally, hazardous waste generators allow inspectors to enter the premises without a warrant, unless the inspector refuses to present credentials or explain the purpose of the inspection or comes at an unreasonable time. The generator usually takes precautions to ensure the accuracy of the inspector's results, such as splitting samples and reviewing and copying requested documents.

Agencies use other methods of investigation, such as submitting questionnaires and holding informal meetings. EEOC investigators use these methods and others, because they are given broad investigative authority by the EEOC regulations. Generally, the EEOC sends a Notice of Charge to the respondent and a questionnaire asking for an explanation of the events in question. EEOC investigators also use fact-finding conferences and on-site investigations to obtain information.

Agencies are authorized to issue subpoenas, ordering people to testify or to submit documents. If a person does not respond, the agencies must go to court to enforce subpoenas. Agencies can only seek information in connection with investigations which they are authorized by law to undertake. As in other areas of law, privileged information cannot be obtained, even with a subpoena. Agencies also obtain search warrants when needed. Individuals often consent to searches, making a warrant unnecessary. Unless consent or another exception to the warrant requirement applies, the agency must obtain a warrant to search homes or businesses. Agencies need to establish probable cause to obtain a warrant, although the standard for establishing probable cause is not as stringent as in the criminal law setting. Warrantless searches are permitted when the business is part of a pervasively regulated or closely regulated industry, because of the lessened expectation of privacy. When a violation is seen from plain view off the business's premises, a warrantless search is generally allowed.

Review Questions

1. Which of the following statements about formal rule making are true? _____

   a. Formal rule making is a trial-type procedure.
   b. Formal rule making is the predominant method by which agencies develop their regulations.
   c. Parties are allowed to submit exhibits.
   d. all of the above
   e. a and c only

2. Which of the following statements about informal rule making are true? _____

   a. The procedures for informal rule making are set forth in the Administrative Dispute Resolution Act.
   b. A notice of informal rule making must state the legal authority under which the regulations are proposed.
   c. Agencies must adopt all changes suggested in comments from the public.
   d. none of the above
   e. a and b only

3. Which of the following are ADR methods authorized by the Administrative Dispute Resolution Act? _____
   a. mediation
   b. minitrials
   c. arbitration
   d. all of the above
   e. a and c only

4. In which of the following situations is a warrantless search allowed? _____

   a. An EPA inspector sees a violation while standing off the business's premises.
   b. The business owner consents to a search.
   c. The agency has established probable cause that a violation is taking place.
   d. all of the above
   e. a and b only

5. Declaratory orders are binding on the agency and parties. True ___ / False ___

6. Negotiated rule making is appropriate when there is a reasonable likelihood that a committee can reach a consensus.   True ___ / False ___

7. The Administrative Dispute Resolution Act prohibits nonlawyer representation in administrative proceedings.   True ___ / False ___

8. Regulations regarding agency personnel matters are exempt from rule-making requirements.   True ___ / False ___

9. The procedure for negotiated rule making is set forth in the Administrative Procedure Act.   True ___ / False ___

10. To enforce their subpoenas, administrative agencies generally must go to court.   True ___ / False ___

11. Explain the presuit administrative procedures that the EEOC must follow before filing an action in federal court.

12. How can paralegals locate agency publications?

13. Under what circumstances should a generator of hazardous waste be advised to seek a search warrant before conducting an on-site inspection?

14. Describe appropriate precautions the generator should take to ensure accurate results from the inspection.

Practical Applications

Read the following excerpt from the *Federal Register*, and answer the following questions.

DEPARTMENT OF HEALTH AND HUMAN SERVICES

Social Security Administration

20 CFR Part 416

[Regulations No. 16]

RIN 096Q-AD55

Supplemental Security Income for the Aged, Blind and Disabled; Residence and Citizenship; Temporary Protected Status

AGENCY: Social Security Administration, HHS.
ACTION: Final rule.
SUMMARY: This final rule incorporates into the supplemental security income regulations a provision of the Immigration and Nationality Act (INA) concerning the ineligibility of certain aliens for federal assistance programs. Specifically, this regulation provides that an alien granted temporary protected status (TPS) by the Attorney General of the United States pursuant to section 244A of the INA will not be considered to be permanently residing in the United States under color of law during that period for the purpose of eligibility for Supplemental Security Income (SSI) benefits.
EFFECTIVE DATE: August 3, 1993.
FOR FURTHER INFORMATION CONTACT: Harry J. Short, Legal Assistance, 3-B-1 Operations Building, 6401 Security Boulevard, Baltimore, MD 21235, (410) 965-6243.
SUPPLEMENTARY INFORMATION: The SSI program provides cash assistance to persons who are aged, blind, or disabled and whose income and resources are below specified amounts. A person may be eligible for

SSI benefits if he or she meets all of the eligibility requirements of title XVI of the Social Security Act (the Act) and implementing regulations. Section 1014(a)(1)(B) of the Act provides that an aged, blind or disabled individual, for purposes of the application of title XVI, must be a resident of the United States, and either a citizen or an alien lawfully admitted for permanent residence or otherwise permanently residing in the United States under color of law.

Section 302 of the Immigration Act of 1990, Public Law 101-649 amended the INA on November 29, 1990, by adding a new section 244A entitled "Temporary Protected Status." TPS is an alien status which may be granted temporarily to qualified nationals of designated foreign states. Such designation of a foreign state is based on the existence of an ongoing armed conflict, natural disaster, or other extraordinary and temporary condition which prevents aliens who are nationals of such state from returning safely. Aliens granted TPS may not be deported during the period in which such status is in effect and may work throughout its duration. However, paragraph (f)(1) of section 244A provides that during a period in which an alien is granted TPS, he or she shall not be considered to be permanently residing in the United States under color of law. One effect of this amendment is that individuals will not be eligible for SSI benefits while in TPS, because they have not been admitted for permanent residence and cannot be considered to be permanently residing in the United States under color of law in TPS.

This final regulation adds a new § 416.1819 to subpart P of our regulations to incorporate the provision of section 244A of the INA which states that aliens granted TPS are not considered to be permanently residing in the United States under color of law.

Regulatory Procedures

Justification for Final Rule

The Department, even when not required by statute, as a matter of policy, generally follows the Administrative Procedure Act (APA) notice of proposed rulemaking and public comment procedures specified in 5 U.S.C. 553 in the development of its regulations. The APA provides exceptions to its notice and comment procedures when an agency finds there is good cause for dispensing with such procedures on the basis that they are impracticable, unnecessary, or contrary to the public interest.

We have determined that under 5 U.S.C. 552(b)(B), good cause exists for waiver of notice of proposed rulemaking and public comment procedure on this regulation, because such procedures are unnecessary in this case. This rule merely reflects, without exercise of discretion, section 244A(f)(1) of the INA, 8 U.S.C. 1254a(f)(1), as amended by section 302(a) of Public Law 101-649.

Executive Order No. 12291

The Secretary has determined that this is not a major rule under Executive Order 12291 since the program and administrative impact of the legislation which this regulation implements, is insignificant and the threshold criteria for a major rule are not otherwise met. Therefore, a regulatory impact analysis is not required.

Paperwork Reduction Act
This final regulation imposes no additional reporting and recordkeeping requirements necessitating clearance by the Office of Management and Budget.

Regulatory Flexibility Act
We certify that this final rule will not have a significant economic impact on a substantial number of small entities because it affects only individuals. Therefore, a regulatory flexibility analysis as provided in Public Law 96-354, the Regulatory Flexibility Act, is not required.

(Catalog of Federal Domestic Assistance Program No. 93.807—Supplemental Security Income)

List of Subjects in 20 CFR Part 416
Administrative practice and procedure, Aged, Blind, Disability benefits, Public assistance programs, Supplemental Security Income (SSI), Reporting and recordkeeping requirements.

Dated: April 30, 1993.
Louis D. Enoff,
Principal Deputy Commissioner of Social Security.
Approved: June 15, 1993.
Donna E. Shalala,
Secretary of Health and Human Services.
For the reasons set out in the preamble, part 416 of chapter III of title 20 of the Code of Federal Regulations is amended as follows:
1. The authority citation for subpart P of part 416 is revised to read as follows:
Authority: Secs. 1102, 1614(a)(1)(B) and (e), and 1631 of the Social Security Act; 42 U.S.C. 1302, 1382c(a)(1)(B) and (e) and 1383; sec. 502 of Pub.L. 94-241, 90 Stat. 268; sec. 302 of Pub.L. 101-649, 104 Stat. 4978.
2. A new § 416.1819 is added to read as follows:

§ 416.1819 When you cannot be considered permanently residing in the United States under color of law.

We will not consider you to be permanently residing in the United States under color of law and you are not eligible for SSI benefits during a period in which you have been granted temporary protected status by the Immigration and Naturalization Service under section 244A of the Immigration and Nationality Act.

1. Is this a proposed or a final regulation?

2. The regulation was issued by the Social Security Administration but involves another agency as well. What is the other agency?

3. The SSA issued this regulation because of a change in a statute. What is the name of the statute?

4. The Supplementary Information section explains the circumstances in which a foreign national may be granted temporary protected status in the United States. Explain those circumstances.

5. What benefits does temporary protected status (TPS) grant to qualified individuals?

6. When individuals have been granted TPS, are they considered permanent residents of the United States?

7. What effect does the language in the Immigration and Nationality Act regarding lack of permanent resident status have on eligibility for supplemental security income?

8. What is the CFR cite of the regulation issued in this entry in the *Federal Register*?

9. Here, the SSA issued a final regulation without first issuing a proposed regulation and having a notice and comment period. Why did the SSA state that the notice and comment procedure was not necessary?

Case Analysis

Read the following excerpts from *Marshall v. Barlow's, Inc.*, 437 U.S. 307 (1978), and answer the questions below.

IIII ▬▬▬▬▬▬▬▬▬▬▬▬▬▬▬▬▬▬▬▬▬▬▬▬▬▬▬▬▬▬▬▬▬▬▬▬ IIII

MARSHALL

v.

BARLOW'S

Decided May 23, 1978.

Mr. Justice WHITE delivered the opinion of the Court.

Section 8(a) of the Occupational Safety and Health Act of 1970 (OSHA or Act) empowers agents of the Secretary of Labor (Secretary) to search the work area of any employment facility within the Act's jurisdiction. The purpose of the search is to inspect for safety hazards and violations of OSHA regulations. No search warrant or other process is expressly required under the Act.

On the morning of September 11, 1975, an OSHA inspector entered the customer service area of Barlow's, Inc., an electrical and plumbing installation business located in Pocatello, Idaho. The president and general manager, Ferrol G. "Bill" Barlow, was on hand; and the OSHA inspector, after showing his credentials, informed Mr. Barlow that he wished to conduct a search of the working areas of the business. Mr. Barlow inquired whether any complaint had been received about his company. The inspector answered no, but that Barlow's Inc., had simply turned up in the agency's selection process. The inspector again asked to enter the nonpublic area of the business; Mr. Barlow's response was to inquire whether the inspector had a search warrant. The inspector had none. Thereupon Mr. Barlow refused the inspector admission to the employee area of his business. He said he was relying on his rights as guaranteed by the Fourth Amendment of the United States Constitution.

Three months later, the Secretary petitioned the United States District Court for the District of Idaho to issue an order compelling Mr. Barlow to admit the inspector. The requested order was issued on December 30, 1975, and was presented to Mr. Barlow on January 5, 1976. Mr. Barlow again refused admission, and he sought his own injunctive relief against the warrantless searches assertedly permitted by OSHA. A three–judge court was convened. On December 30, 1976, it ruled in Mr. Barlow's favor. Concluding that *Camara v. Municipal Court* controlled this case, the court held that the Fourth Amendment required a warrant for the type of search involved here and that the statutory authorization for warrantless inspections was unconstitutional. An injunction against searches or inspections was entered. The Secretary appealed, challenging the judgment, and we noted probable jurisdiction.

The Secretary urges that warrantless inspections to enforce OSHA are reasonable within the meaning of the Fourth Amendment. Among other things, he relies on § 8(a) of the Act which authorizes inspection of business premises without a warrant and which the Secretary urges represents a congressional construction of the Fourth Amendment that the courts should not reject. Regretably, we are unable to agree.

The Warrant Clause of the Fourth Amendment protects commercial buildings as well as private homes. To hold otherwise would belie the origin of that Amendment, and the American colonial experience. . . .

This Court has already held that warrantless searches are generally unreasonable, and that this rule applies to commercial premises as well as homes. In *Camara v. Municipal Court, supra* 387 U.S., at 528-529, 87 S.Ct., at 1731, we held:

"[E]xcept in certain carefully defined classes of cases, a search of private property without proper consent is 'unreasonable' unless it has been authorized by a valid search warrant."

On the same day, we also ruled:

"As we explained in *Camara*, a search of private houses is presumptively unreasonable if conducted without a warrant. The businessman, like the occupant of a residence, has a constitutional right to go about his business free from unreasonable official entries upon his private commercial property. The businessman, too, has that right placed in jeopardy if the decision to enter and inspect for violation of regulatory laws can be made and enforced by the inspector in the field without official authority evidenced by a warrant." *See v. City of Seattle.*

These same cases also held that the Fourth Amendment prohibition against unreasonable searches protects against warrantless intrusions during civil as well as criminal investigations. The reason is found in the "basic purpose of this Amendment . . . [which] is to safeguard the privacy and security of individuals against arbitrary invasions by governmental officials." If the government intrudes on a person's property, the privacy interest suffers whether the government's motivation is to investigate violations of criminal laws or breaches of other statutory or regulatory standards. It therefore appears that unless some recognized exception to the warrant requirement applies, *See v. City of Seattle*, would require a warrant to conduct the inspection sought in this case.

The Secretary urges that an exception from the search warrant requirement has been recognized for "pervasively regulated business[es]," and for "closely regulated" industries "long subject to close supervision and inspection." These cases are indeed exceptions, but they represent responses to relatively unique circumstances. Certain industries have such a history of government oversight that no reasonable expectation of privacy could exist for a proprietor over the stock of such an enterprise. Liquor and firearms are industries of this type: when an entrepreneur embarks upon such a business, he has voluntarily chosen to subject himself to a full arsenal of governmental regulation.

Industries such as these fall within the "certain carefully defined classes of cases" referenced in *Camara*. The element that distinguishes these enterprises from ordinary businesses is a long tradition of close government supervision, of which any person who chooses to enter such a business must already be aware. "A central difference between those cases and this one is that businessmen engaged in such federally licensed and regulated enterprises accept the burdens as well as the benefits of their trade, whereas the petitioner here was not engaged in any regulated or licensed business. The businessman in a regulated industry in effect consents to the restrictions placed upon him."

The clear import of our cases is that closely regulated industry is the exception. The Secretary would make it the rule. Invoking the Walsh-Healey Act of 1936, the Secretary attempts to support a conclusion that all businesses involved in interstate commerce have long been subjected to close supervision of employee safety and health conditions. But the degree of federal involvement in employee working circumstances has never been of the order of specificity and pervasiveness that OSHA mandates. It is quite unconvincing to argue that the imposition of minimum wages and maximum hours on employers who contracted with the Government under the Walsh-Healey Act prepared the entirety of American interstate commerce for regulation of working conditions to the minutest detail. Nor can any but the most fictional sense of voluntary consent to later searches be found in the single fact that one conducts a business affecting interstate commerce; under current practice and law, few businesses can be conducted without having some effect on interstate commerce. . . .

Nor do we agree that the incremental protections afforded the employer's privacy by a warrant are so marginal that they fail to justify the administrative burdens that may be entailed. The authority to make warrantless searches devolves almost unbridled discretion upon executive and administrative officers, particularly those in the field, as to when to search and whom to search. A warrant, by contrast, would provide assurances from a neutral officer that the inspection is reasonable under the Constitution, is authorized by statute, and is pursuant to an administrative plan containing specific neutral criteria. Also, a warrant would then and there advise the owner of the scope and objects of the search, beyond which limits the inspector is not expected to proceed. These are important functions for a warrant to perform, functions which underlie the Court's prior decisions that the Warrant Clause applies to inspections for compliance with regulatory statutes. We conclude that the concerns expressed by the Secretary do not suffice to justify warrantless inspections under OSHA or vitiate the general constitutional requirement that for a search to be reasonable a warrant must be obtained.

We hold that Barlow's was entitled to a declaratory judgment that the Act is unconstitutional insofar as it purports to authorize inspections without warrant or its equivalent and to an injunction enjoining the Act's enforcement to that extent. The judgment of the District Court is therefore affirmed.

1. What type of business was Barlow's, Inc.?
2. What was Mr. Barlow's basis for refusing entry to the inspector?
3. Relying on the *Camara* decision, the Court explained that warrantless searches are generally not permitted, and this applies to commercial premises as well as homes. Why is protection afforded to businesses as well as to homes?
4. Did the Court determine that a warrant was necessary for the type of search in question?
5. There is an exception to the warrant requirement for "pervasively regulated" and "closely regulated" businesses. How did the Court explain the reason for this exception?
6. Why did the Court reject the argument that the *Colonnade-Biswell* exception applied to Barlow's?

Notes

[1] Ernest Gellhorn & Ronald Levin, *Administrative Law and Procedure in a Nutshell*, 3d ed. (St. Paul: West Publishing Co., 1990), at 160. For detailed discussion of adjudications, see Chapter 8.

[2] *Id.*

[3] P. Verkuil, "A Study of Informal Adjudication Procedures," 43 *U. Chi. L. Rev.* at 739.

[4] To review the basic characteristics of regulations, refer to Chapter 2.

[5] Gellhorn & Levin, *supra* note 1, at 322.

[6] 21 U.S.C. § 371(e)(3).

[7] 410 U.S. 224 (1973). *See* Lee Modjeska, *Administrative Law Practice and Procedure* (Rochester: Lawyers Co-operative Publishing Co., 1982), at 112.

[8] Kenneth Culp Davis, *Administrative Law and Government* (St. Paul: West Publishing Co., 1975), at 123.

[9] Gellhorn & Levin, *supra* note 1, at 324.

[10] *Id.*

[11] Administrative Conference of the United States, *Federal Administrative Procedure Sourcebook, 2d ed. (Office of the Chairman, 1992), at 792 (hereinafter ACUS Sourcebook).*

[12] *Id.*

[13] *Id.* at 801.

[14] *Id.* at 243.

[15] *Id.*

[16] *Id.* at 246.

[17] *Id.* at 227.

[18] *Id.*

[19] *Id.* at 228.

[20] James Lofton, "Federal Enforcement of Environmental Laws," *Environmental Law Handbook 1993* (Wake Forest University School of Law), at 79.

[21] *Id.* at 80.

[22] *See* 29 CFR 1601.19.

[23] 29 CFR 1601.24.

[24] 28 U.S.C. § 2201; *Black's Law Dictionary* at 368 (5th ed. 1979).

[25] Davis, *supra* note 8, at 289.

[26] B. Powell, "Sinners, Supplicants, and Samaritans: Agency Advice-Giving in Relation to Section 554(e) of the Administrative Procedure Act," 63 *N.C.L. Rev.* at 343 (1985).

[27] ACUS *Sourcebook*, at 125. *See also* Powell, *supra* note 26.

[28] *Black's Law Dictionary* at 50 (5th ed. 1979).

[29] Davis, *supra* note 8, at 289.

[30] U.S. Const., art. III. *See also* Davis, *supra* note 8, at 289.

[31] Gellhorn & Levin, *supra* note 1, at 185.

[32] 42 U.S.C. § 6927.

[33] 5 U.S.C. § 555(c).

[34] 42 U.S.C. § 2000e-8(a).

[35] *Camara v. Municipal Court of San Francisco, 387 U.S. 523 (1967).*

[36] Thomas Sullivan, *Environmental Law Handbook,* 12th ed. (Rockville, MD: Government Institutes, Inc.), at 28.

[37] Marshall v. Barlow's, Inc., 437 U.S. 307, 320 (1978).

[38] *Colonnade Catering Corp. v. United States, 397 U.S. 72 (1970); United States v. Biswell, 406 U.S. 311 (1972).*

[39] Gellhorn & Levin, *supra* note 1, at 146.

IIII

CHAPTER 6

CONTROLS ON AGENCY ACTIONS

Administrative agencies are given very broad powers to accomplish their duties, ranging from rule making to adjudications. Yet the agencies do not operate in a vacuum with complete freedom to do as they wish. All three branches of the government exert significant controls on administrative agencies. Congress, the courts, and the president all exert some control of agency actions.

Executive Control of Agency Actions

The president of the United States exerts control over administrative agencies in many ways.

Appointments

First, the president exercises direct political control by appointing key personnel in federal agencies. Every time a new administration comes to the White House, the president makes high-level appointments, including the heads of the executive agencies, who are members of the president's cabinet. The president also appoints key policy-making federal officials, such as the assistant attorney general for the Civil Rights Division of the Justice Department.

The attitudes and opinions of the president are reflected in appointments to high-level positions in federal agencies. The high-level officials, with views similar to the president, chart the course the agencies will follow. For instance, James Watt was a memorable secretary of the interior in the early years of the Reagan administration. The Department of the Interior has responsibility for most of the public lands in the United States, including national parks. The Bureau of Land Management (BLM), part of the Department of the Interior, controls the use of public lands, including mineral leases, grazing rights, and offshore drilling. As secretary of the interior, James Watt encouraged extensive use of public lands for mining, grazing, and other economic ventures. He was roundly criticized by many citizens who valued public lands for their natural beauty and availability for hiking, fishing, and other recreational activities.

Areas particularly sensitive to presidential direction include environmental issues, such as setting standards for problems such as acid rain, and the vigor with which environmental statutes and regulations will be enforced. Civil rights and human rights issues are also sensitive to changes in the White House, as shown by the contrasting approaches of the Carter administration and Reagan administration.

The heads of agencies, and even high-level agency officials, frequently resign when a new president is elected. The president has the power to remove without cause the heads of the executive agencies. Independent agencies are generally headed by a multimember board whose members have staggered terms. Thus, some members' terms expire in years that do not coincide with presidential elections. This is true of the EEOC, which is headed by five commissioners, one of whom is the chairperson. Usually at least two commissioners are affiliated with the political party that is not in the White House. This arrangement diminishes, but does not eliminate, the president's control over independent agencies.

Most employees of federal agencies are protected by civil service status and can be removed only with cause and extensive proceedings. Many high-level civil servants, however, may be asked to resign by a new president, and they generally comply.

Executive Orders

As noted in Chapter 2, executive orders are formal directives from the president to federal agencies or officials. Executive orders can direct broad actions that affect all federal agencies. For instance, Executive Order 12291 imposes requirements on agency rule making, providing several guidelines to which agencies must adhere. Agencies must base their decisions on adequate information and choose the alternatives "involving the least net cost to society." Executive Order 12291 further provides that agencies may not undertake regulatory action unless "the potential benefits to society for the regulation outweigh the potential costs to society." The general requirements of Executive Order 12291 are reprinted in Figure 6–1. Executive Order 12291 also requires agencies to submit a Regulatory Impact Analysis to the Director of the Office of Management and Budget (OMB) and provides that an agency may not issue a "major rule" without clearance from OMB. A "major rule" is defined as a rule that is likely to have an annual effect on the economy of $100 million or more, or to result in major increase in costs for consumers or the government.

FIGURE 6–1
Excerpt from
Executive Order
12291

> **Sec. 2.** *General Requirements.* In promulgating new regulations, reviewing existing regulations, and developing legislative proposals concerning regulation, all agencies, to the extent permitted by law, shall adhere to the following requirements:

FIGURE 6–1
(continued)

(a) Administrative decisions shall be based on adequate information concerning the need for and consequences of proposed government action;

(b) Regulatory action shall not be undertaken unless the potential benefits to society for the regulation outweigh the potential costs to society;

(c) Regulatory objectives shall be chosen to maximize the net benefits to society;

(d) Among alternative approaches to any given regulatory objective, the alternative involving the least net cost to society shall be chosen; and

(e) Agencies shall set regulatory priorities with the aim of maximizing the aggregate net benefits to society, taking into account the condition of the national economy, and other regulatory actions contemplated for the future.

Executive Order 12498 works in conjunction with Executive Order 12291, requiring executive agencies to submit to OMB annually a "statement of its regulatory policies, goals, and objectives for the coming year and information concerning all significant regulatory actions underway or planned . . . ." Because OMB operates in close conjunction with the president, these executive orders give the president considerable opportunity to influence the actions that administrative agencies plan and implement.

Reorganization Plans

The president may, with the consent of Congress, reorganize agencies. Most frequently, this takes the form of reassigning duties from one agency to another. For instance, the EPA was created by Reorganization Plan No. 3 of 1970 in order to establish coordinated governmental action on matters affecting the environment.[1] Sometimes executive orders and reorganization plans are used in conjunction to place similar duties in one agency. In 1978 Executive Order 12067 abolished the Equal Employment Opportunity Coordinating Council and transferred its duties to the Equal Employment Opportunity Commission.

Congressional Control of Agency Actions

Congress exerts both direct and indirect controls on administrative agencies. Direct controls include enacting and repealing statutes that agencies enforce.

Enactment of Legislation

Enabling statutes are obvious means of direct control. Congress gives agencies the authority to perform certain actions through delegation statutes but also places limitations on them. For instance, in the Immigration and Nationality Act, Congress delegates to the attorney general, who in turns delegates to the INS, broad authority to determine whether applicants qualify for nonimmigrant and immigrant visas. Yet Congress also defines specifically the available visa categories. Thus, the INS is not given the authority to decide the specific visa categories; Congress controls this aspect of immigration law.

Repeal of Legislation

Sometimes Congress passes a statute to enact an idea that seems to be a good idea in the abstract; however, once the designated agency begins to enforce the statute, it may become obvious that the statute was not such a good idea. Some legislation is enacted very quickly and without adequate consideration of the consequences. Because statutes are often lacking in detail, their ramifications may not be clear to Congress. Members of Congress may realize the inadequacies of certain statutes months or years later and pass legislation to repeal or amend the statute.

At times, new laws generate intense controversy and litigation that alert Congress to the laws' inadequacies. One such example was section 5 of the Immigration Marriage Fraud Amendments of 1986, which provided that when a United States citizen married an alien who was in deportation proceedings, a petition enabling the United States citizen's spouse to obtain a green card could not be approved until the spouse had lived outside the United States for two years. Intense litigation challenging the constitutionality of the new law ensued. At the heart of the litigation was the assertion that the law violated due process rights, because the couple was not allowed an opportunity to establish that they had a bona fide marriage, not a marriage of convenience to prevent the spouse's deportation. As part of the Immigration Act of 1990, Congress recognized the due process deficiency and amended the law to allow the couple to have a hearing to prove that they have a bona fide marriage.[2]

Paralegals must follow Congress closely so that they are aware of changes in the law. Familiarity with loose-leaf services, as well as newsletters and publications of organizations for professionals who work in particular areas of law, is critical in keeping up with changes in the law.

Approval of Presidential Appointments

The president must have Congressional approval for certain high-level appointments. Article II, section 2 of the United States Constitution provides that the president makes these appointments with the advice and consent of the Senate. The Senate has occasionally rejected nominees for heads of agencies when the matter came to a vote on the Senate floor. Sometimes the senatorial input is less direct. For instance, in the early months of the Clinton administration, the president would "float" a "trial balloon," making it public knowledge that he was considering certain people for high-level positions. Members of the Senate "shot down" some of these trial balloons by generating such criticism that the president did not nominate these people for the posts.

Control through Funding

Congress holds a very effective, if less publicly obvious, control over administrative agencies—the purse strings. An agency cannot operate without funding, and Congress controls that funding. When Congress passes a budget, every agency has a critical interest in the amount of funding appropriated to it. Some agencies are better funded than others because of the services they provide. Members of Congress are sensitive to complaints by recipients of Social Security disability benefits or retirement benefits if their checks are late or processing of applications is delayed due to staffing shortages in the SSA. Members of Congress may be less sensitive to complaints that processing of nonimmigrant visas by the INS is slow due to staff shortages. Members of Congress may be more inclined to meet the funding needs of some agencies more than others, due to their constituents' concerns.

Other Oversight Mechanisms

Members of Congress, on behalf of their constituents, may make informal inquiries about agency activities. For instance, many people contact their congressmen or senators when they have applied for Social Security disability benefits and feel either that the SSA made an incorrect decision or that the processing of their application is taking too long.

Members of Congress sometimes launch formal investigations of agency activities, such as the hearings surrounding the Iran-Contra scandal in 1987. The hearings often receive extensive coverage by the press and can focus attention on administrative agency personnel. Sometimes the adverse publicity generated by such congressional investigations forces the resignation of agency employees.

An agency under the direct control of Congress is the General Accounting Office (GAO). The *United States Government Manual* states that the GAO is "the investigative arm of Congress and is charged with examining all matters relating to the receipt and disbursement of public funds."[3] The description of the GAO's duties and authority in the *Manual* is instructive, and is reprinted as Figure 6–2. After reading this description, you see that the GAO has been given great authority to investigate many aspects of agencies' operations. When the GAO discovers activities that may constitute civil or criminal misconduct, results of investigations are referred to the Department of Justice or other law enforcement agencies.[4]

FIGURE 6–2
Description of Activities of the General Accounting Office (GAO).

Activities

Audits and Evaluations Supporting the Congress is GAO's fundamental responsibility. In meeting this objective, GAO performs a variety of services, the most prominent of which are audits and evaluations of Government programs and activities. The majority of these reviews are made in response to specific congressional requests. The Office is required to perform work requested by committee chairpersons and, as a matter of policy, assigns equal status to requests from ranking minority Members. GAO also responds to individual Member requests, as possible. Other assignments are initiated pursuant to standing commitments to congressional committees, and some reviews are specifically required by law. Finally, some assignments are independently undertaken in accordance with GAO's basic legislative responsibilities.

The ability to review practically any Government function requires a multidisciplined staff able to conduct assignments wherever needed. GAO's staff has expertise in a variety of disciplines—accounting, law, public and business administration, economics, the social and physical sciences, and others.

The Office is organized so that staff members concentrate on specific subject areas, enabling them to develop a detailed level of knowledge. When an assignment requires specialized experience not available within GAO, outside experts assist the permanent staff. GAO's staff goes wherever necessary on assignments, working onsite to gather data, test transactions, and observe firsthand how Government programs and activities are carried out.

FIGURE 6–2
(continued)

Accounting and Financial Management Policy The Office ensures that the Congress has available for its use current, accurate, and complete financial management data. To do this, GAO
  —prescribes accounting principles and standards for the executive branch;
  —advises other Federal agencies on fiscal and related policies and procedures; and
  —prescribes standards for auditing and evaluating Government programs.
  In addition, the Comptroller General, the Secretary of the Treasury, and the Director of the Office of Management and Budget develop standardized information and data processing systems. This includes standard terminology, definitions, classifications, and codes for fiscal, budgetary, and program-related data and information.

Legal Services The Office provides various legal services to the Congress. In response to inquiries from committees and Members, the Comptroller General provides advice on legal issues involving Government programs and activities. GAO is also available to assist in drafting legislation and reviewing legislative proposals before the Congress. In addition, GAO reviews and reports to the Congress on proposed rescissions and deferrals of Government funds.
  Other legal services include resolving bid protests that challenge Government contract awards, assisting Government agencies in interpreting the laws governing the expenditure of public funds, and adjudicating claims for and against the Government.
  In addition, GAO's staff of trained investigators conducts special investigations and assists auditors and evaluators when they encounter possible criminal and civil misconduct. When warranted, GAO refers the results of its investigations to the Department of Justice and other law enforcement authorities.

Source: United States Government Manual, 1993/94 (Washington, DC: U.S. Government Printing Office), p. 49

Judicial Review of Agency Actions

Judicial review is an important control on agency action, and is discussed in detail in Chapter 9. It is important at the outset, however, for paralegals to have a basic understanding of the scope of judicial review.

The Role of the Courts

The role of the courts is not to substitute their judgment for that of the agencies. The courts' role is much more limited. It is analogous to that of an appellate court reviewing the actions of a trial court. The appellate court does not reverse the decision of a trial judge because it feels that the trial judge should have reached a different conclusion. Instead, the appellate court reviews the actions of trial judges to determine whether they committed a reversible error, such as applying the wrong rule of law or disallowing evidence that should have been admitted.

Similarly, the role of courts that review the decisions of administrative agencies is not to substitute their judgment for that of the agency decision makers. The role of the courts is to ensure fairness, minimum standards, and a well-reasoned explanation of the agency's decision.[5]

The APA: Limitations on Scope of Review

The APA provides limitations that define the scope of the courts' review. Section 706 of the APA provides that courts may review agency decisions to consider whether the agency's action violated the Constitution, whether the agency exceeded its statutory authority, whether the agency's decision is supported by substantial evidence, whether the agency's action is arbitrary and capricious or an abuse of discretion, or whether the agency committed a procedural error. In order to understand fully the courts' role in reviewing agency decisions and actions, these topics are discussed in Chapter 9.

The Role of Discretion

Agency discretion is a fundamental part of administrative law. The amount of control placed on an agency action depends in large part on the amount of discretion that Congress has given to the agency. The level of discretion can differ both according to the agency and according to the particular action.

Often Congress states in the delegation statute itself that the agency has discretion. For instance, in the statute delegating to the attorney general the authority to determine who may be granted political asylum, Congress specified that asylum may be granted "in the discretion of the Attorney General . . . ." Refer to Figure 6–3, which reprints 8 U.S.C. § 1158(a), the delegation statute for political asylum. In contrast, the delegation statute authorizing the secretary of health and human services makes no mention of discretion. Refer to Figure 2–5, which reprints this delegation statute. There is some degree of discretion given to the SSA in determining whether claimants are entitled to disability insurance benefits, but the discretion is not as great as that given to the INS in determining whether applicants are entitled to political asylum in the United States.

FIGURE 6–3
8 U.S.C. § 1158(a)

---

§ 1158. Asylum procedure

(a) Establishment by Attorney General; coverage

 The Attorney General shall establish a procedure for an alien physically present in the United States or at a land border or port of entry, irrespective of such alien's status, to apply for asylum, and the alien may be granted asylum in the discretion of the Attorney General if the Attorney General determines that such alien is a refugee within the meaning of section 1101(a)(42)(A) of this title.

This contrast is typical of the varying degrees of discretion given to agencies in different areas of law. In matters related to foreign policy, such as immigration law, agencies are given broad discretion. In areas such as administration of public benefits, such as Social Security disability, agencies have less discretion.

Administrative Appeals as a Control of Discretion

One way of limiting agency discretion is by allowing multiple levels of administrative appeals. This is well illustrated by the appeals process when a person is denied Social Security disability benefits. In contrast, determinations by other agency officers are subject to virtually no review. These two approaches are illustrated by comparing the determinations made by consular officers with those made by the SSA.

Nonreviewability of Decisions of Consular Officers

Within the State Department is the Bureau of Consular Affairs, whose employees at United States embassies and consular outposts overseas make the day-to-day decisions regarding whether an alien's application for an immigrant or nonimmigrant visa will be approved or denied. Consular officers worldwide process millions of visa applications, and ACUS has reported that about 10 percent of the applications are denied. State Department regulations provide some guidelines for the refusal procedure. Refer to Figure 6–4, which reprints the pertinent regulations (22 CFR 41.121). The regulations do not provide detailed procedures. They state that when consular officers believe that aliens are ineligible for visas, they shall inform the applicants of the provision of law or regulations on which the refusal is based. The officer must then record the reasons for the denial on the visa application and retain the original or copies of the documents on which the denial is based.

FIGURE 6–4
22 CFR 41.121

§ 41.121   Refusal of individual visas.

(a) *Grounds for refusal.* Nonimmigrant visa refusals must be based on legal grounds, that is, one or more provisions of INA 212(a) or (e), INA 214(b), or INA 221(g). Certain classes of nonimmigrant aliens are exempted from specific provisions of INA 212(a) under INA 102, and, upon a basis of reciprocity, under INA 212(d)(8). When a visa application has been properly completed and executed in accordance with the provisions of INA and the implementing regulations, the consular officer must either issue or refuse the visa.

(b) *Refusal procedure.* If a consular officer knows or has reason to believe that an alien is ineligible to receive a visa on grounds of ineligibility which cannot be overcome by the presentation of additional evidence, the officer shall refuse the visa and, if practicable, shall require a nonimmigrant visa application to be executed before the refusal is recorded. In the case of a visa refusal the consular officer shall inform the applicant of the provision of law or regulations upon which the refusal is based. If the alien fails to execute a visa application after being informed by the consular officer of a ground of ineligibility to receive a nonimmigrant visa, the visa shall be considered refused. The officer shall then insert the pertinent data on the visa application, noting the reasons for the refusal, and the application form shall be filed in the consular office. Upon refusing a nonimmigrant visa, the consular officer shall retain the original or a copy of each document upon which the refusal was based as well as each document indicating a possible ground of ineligibility and may return all other supporting documents supplied by the applicant.

(c) *Review of refusal at consular office.* If the ground(s) of ineligibility upon which the visa was refused cannot be overcome by the presentation of additional evidence, the principal consular officer, or a specifically designated alternate, shall review the case without delay, record the review decision, and sign and date the prescribed form. If the ground(s) of ineligibility may be overcome by the presentation of additional evidence, and the applicant has indicated the intention to submit such evidence, a review of the refusal may be deferred for not more than 120 days. If the principal consular officer or alternate does not concur in the refusal, that officer shall either

(1) Refer the case to the Department for an advisory opinion, or

**FIGURE 6–4
(continued)**

> (2) Assume responsibility for the case by reversing the refusal.
>
> (d) *Review of refusal by Department.* The Department may request a consular officer in a specific case or in specified classes of cases to submit a report if a visa has been refused. The Department will review each report and may furnish an advisory opinion to the consular officer for assistance in considering the case further. If the officer believes that action contrary to an advisory opinion should be taken, the case shall be resubmitted to the Department with an explanation of the proposed action. Rulings of the Department concerning an interpretation of law, as distinguished from an application of the law to the facts, shall be binding upon consular officers.

This seems routine enough and not unlike procedures used in other agencies. A remarkable difference, however, is reflected in 22 CFR 41.121(c), which states the procedure for review of a consular officer's unfavorable determination. The regulation provides for review by "the principal consular officer, or a specifically designated alternate." If the principal consular officer does not concur in the refusal, he or she may reverse the refusal and grant the visa, or may refer the case to the State Department for an advisory opinion. Rulings from the State Department are binding in regard to interpretations of law, but not on the application of the facts. After reading the regulations, it may appear to paralegal students that a review mechanism is in place and thus you may wonder why the consular officers' decisions on visa applications are considered virtually unreviewable. ACUS studied the processing and review of visa denials and issued a recommendation that explains why visa denials are seldom reviewed by senior consular officers and are considered unreviewable by the Secretary of State and the courts. Read Figure 6–5, which reprints ACUS Recommendation 89-9 (1 CFR 305.89-9).

**FIGURE 6–5
1 CFR 305.89-9**

> **§ 305.89-9 Processing and Review of Visa Denials (Recommendation 89-9).**
>
> United States consulates around the world complete the processing of some nine million applications for immigrant and nonimmigrant visas each year. Approximately ninety percent are granted; ten percent are denied. Under current practice, the only review of a consular official's denial of a visa may be by a more senior officer in the consulate, or, on points of law, by the Visa Office in the State Department. The Immigration and Nationality Act has been read to preclude administrative review, and the courts, with a few exceptions, have declined to review visa denials.

**FIGURE 6–5
(continued)**

Immigrant visas are available to persons with close family relationships to U.S. citizens and residents, or with particular abilities or skills that are needed but not otherwise available in the United States. Nonimmigrant visas are available in a long list of classes, ranging from tourists to students to certain types of business personnel to diplomats.

Whatever the visas category or class, there clearly are important interests at stake. These interests are not just those of the applicants themselves, but also of citizens and residents of the United States who are sponsoring the applicant or have some other interest in the applicant's presence in the United States. These interests warrant a close look at whether initial decisions in this important program of mass adjudication should be more fully reviewable than at present.

Federal law and State Department regulations give consular officers substantial discretion in adjudicating visa applications. For example, consular officials exercise absolute discretion in determining whether an applicant may be represented by an attorney or other qualified representative at the visa application interview. Furthermore, although current Department regulations, at 22 CFR 41.121(c), require that a denial of a visa application be reviewed by a more senior officer, the high volume of applications at some posts has resulted in only a random sample of denials being reviewed. Review by a senior official may also be a problem in single-officer posts.

Consular posts send a few hundred cases a year presenting significant legal issues to the Visa Office of the State Department for an advisory opinion that is binding only with respect to legal issues. The applicant typically has no notice of this proceeding. Such review affects the results in only a small number of cases, since most visa denials are based on a factual determination.

Current law has been read by some to limit both administrative and judicial review. Section 104(a) of the INA, 8 U.S.C. 1104(a), excepts the Secretary of State from the administration or enforcement of "those powers, duties and functions conferred upon the consular officers relating to the granting or refusal of visas." This language has been considered by some to preclude the establishment of a more formal review mechanism within the State Department. Further, courts have generally limited the extent of available judicial review.

The Conference believes that it is important that there be at least some level of review of consular discretion to deny or grant visas. The availability of such review would not only encourage consistency and care in the initial adjudication, but would serve interests of fairness and legitimacy. On the other hand, a review scheme in this area can be crafted in a fashion that keeps procedure to a minimum, takes account of the extremely high volume of visa applications, and avoids over-judicialization of the process.

The Recommendation reflects a two-pronged approach to administrative review of visa denials, aimed both at improving the review at the consular level and at considering the creation of a level of centralized administrative

FIGURE 6–5
(continued)

review. The suggestions directed at the consular offices are intended to encourage quick, consistently applied, and cost-effective review that would resolve many of the issues on which review might be requested. The Recommendation also asks the State Department to study the issues, and develop and submit to Congress a proposed process for administrative review of consular actions. The Conference recognizes that there are currently competing priorities for resources that might be required by implementation of the Recommendation, but believes that these proposals should be implemented as quickly as is feasible under the circumstances.

RECOMMENDATION

1. The State Department should adopt a regulation ensuring that applicants may be accompanied by an attorney or other authorized representative during the course of the visa application interview process. To the extent practicable, the State Department should take steps to reply promptly to communications from applicants or authorized representatives and to ensure that facilities are available to enable applicants to meet with their representatives during the application interview process.

2. The State Department should require consular officers to provide brief but explicit written statements of the factual and legal bases and reasons for denying a visa application, except where reasons of national security or potential adverse effects of foreign policy dictate otherwise.

3. The State Department should modify its regulations to allow Visa Office advisory opinions to be made available to applicants and their authorized representatives except where national security or potential adverse effects on foreign policy dictate otherwise.

4. The State Department should either comply with its regulation found at 22 CFR 41.121(c) requiring review within a consulate of each denial of a visa application, or examine alternative systems to review visa denials at consular posts. In such a study, the State Department should keep in mind the goal of ensuring consistency in visa adjudications and consider possible alternatives to address exigencies created by busy consular posts, for example, by reviewing random samples of visa denials, or selecting for review certain types of denials.

5. The State Department should, after appropriate study, develop and submit for Congressional review a proposed process for administrative review of consular visa actions.

Further, 8 U.S.C. § 1104(1) has been interpreted as precluding the secretary of state and the attorney general from requiring consular officers to grant or deny visa applications.

Because their decisions are virtually unreviewable, consular officers have been given extremely broad discretion to grant or deny visa applications. Most administrative agency personnel do not enjoy such broad discretion, in part because their decisions are subject to review through both administrative appeals and federal court review. This is certainly true of determinations regarding claimants' eligibility for Social Security disability.

Appeals of Social Security Disability Determinations

This appellate process is discussed in detail in Chapter 7, and you may refer to Figure 7–7, which outlines the administrative appeals for Social Security disability. For now, note that there is a fairly elaborate appeals process within SSA, with three levels of administrative appeal. When an application is denied at the initial level, the claimant can request a reconsideration determination. If this determination is unfavorable, the claimant can request a hearing before an administrative law judge (ALJ). If after the hearing the ALJ finds that the claimant is not disabled, the claimant can request review by the Appeals Council, the highest administrative appellate body, which has authority to reverse or remand cases for further proceedings if an ALJ has erred. This multilevel administrative appeal process is a safeguard and quality control mechanism. The Appeals Council is not bound by the findings of the ALJ, and the ALJ is not bound by determinations made at the initial and reconsideration levels. Frequently, a claimant who has been found "not disabled" at the initial and reconsideration levels is found "disabled" by an ALJ. Thus, the initial determinations in Social Security disability claims are subject to multiple levels of administrative review, and, if this is unsuccessful, the claimant can proceed to federal court to seek judicial review. This procedure reduces the discretion of agency officials because their determinations are subject to so many levels of appeal. This stands in stark contrast to the initial determinations by consular officers, whose actions are virtually unreviewable.

Power to Prosecute

An area in which there is virtually no review and thus broad discretion is the agency's decision whether to prosecute. As noted in Chapter 4, both the EPA and the EEOC require approval from multiple levels within the agency before an action is commenced in federal court. This is typical of federal agencies, requiring at a minimum an opinion from the Office of General Counsel as to whether litigation should be pursued.

Many factors contribute to an agency's decision whether to pursue litigation. Agency personnel consider such factors as the severity of alleged violations, the probability of prevailing in court, and the costs of litigation. Another factor may be the importance of setting an example to deter violations in the future.

Budgetary constraints may be a factor; an agency's budget may accommodate only a limited number of prosecutorial actions, particularly if a hiring freeze has left the agency with an insufficient number of investigators, attorneys, and paralegals.

SIDEBAR

Budgetary constraints cause frustration for both agency employees and those whom the agency is supposed to serve. Hiring freezes are common, particularly in the last few months of the fiscal year. If Congress wishes to increase enforcement in certain areas, such as environmental law, it must appropriate sufficient funding for the personnel to effect the enforcement. If Congress wishes to decrease enforcement, it may decrease the funding.

Paralegals should note that the decision to prosecute and the decision not to prosecute are of equal import. By selecting carefully the cases it chooses to prosecute, the agency sends a message about its agenda and the leeway it is willing to allow with certain violations.

There is, however, no formal mechanism to review an agency's decision not to prosecute alleged violations of the laws entrusted to them. Thus, agencies have been criticized for their failure to pursue certain violations. Prosecutorial discretion is a potent means of controlling an agency's agenda, immune for the most part from judicial review but subject to some political pressure. Thus, agencies such as the EPA and EEOC are more active during the terms of some presidents than others.

Remedies for Failure to Act

In administrative law, inaction can have serious consequences for your law firm's clients. Suppose that your law firm assisted a foreign national in filing an application for naturalization or a petition for an immigrant visa. One year later the INS has not made a decision. Delays of months, even years, are not uncommon with some administrative agencies. A long delay can have a devastating effect on a client, with adverse effects on permission to work or on family unity.

An applicant cannot appeal an unfavorable decision until the agency renders the decision. Thus, the client loses valuable time in pursuing appeals, which themselves can be lengthy.

Informal Methods

How do paralegals and attorneys spur the agencies to act? They can try informal methods such as contacting senators and congressmen and asking them to inquire, hoping that this will spur the agency into action. This approach is of limited effect with some agencies, which either ignore the requests or are so back-logged that even a congressional plea cannot percolate a client's case to the top of the stack.

Often agency inaction has a valid explanation. Some agencies are so understaffed that their employees, working hard and even working overtime, cannot keep up with their workload. Sometimes, however, an agency's dilatoriness is not justified, and attorneys and paralegals invoke the help of federal courts.

Writ of Mandamus

A **writ** is an "order issued from a court requiring the performance of a specific act."[6] Paralegal students may be familiar with the writ of habeas corpus, which is frequently used in criminal law to gain the release of people from unlawful imprisonment. The writ of habeas corpus is sometimes appropriate in an immigration law context, when the INS takes aliens into detention when deportation proceedings are instituted.

A writ that is more commonly used in an administrative law setting is the **writ of mandamus**, a court order "to compel an officer or employee of the United States or any agency thereof to perform a duty owed to the plaintiff."[7] Refer to Figure 6–6, which reprints the mandamus statute in its entirety. There are also state laws that provide similar procedures.

BALLENTINE'S

writ A written order issued by a court directing the person to whom it is addressed to do a specified act. Writs may be addressed to an officer of the court (EXAMPLE: a writ of attachment), to an inferior court (EXAMPLE: a writ of certiorari), to a board (EXAMPLE: a writ of prohibition), to a corporation (EXAMPLE: a writ of mandamus), or to an individual (EXAMPLE: a summons), among others. Writs are also issued by authorities other than courts. EXAMPLES: a commission issued by the governor to a public official; a citation issued to a violator by a police officer.

writ of mandamus A writ issuing from a court of competent jurisdiction, directed to an inferior court, board, or corporation, or to an officer of a branch of government (judicial, executive, or legislative), requiring the performance of some ministerial act. A writ of mandamus is an extraordinary remedy.

FIGURE 6–6
28 U.S.C. § 1361

> ### § 1361. Action to compel an officer of the United States to perform his duty
>
> The district courts shall have original jurisdiction of any action in the nature of mandamus to compel an officer or employee of the United States or any agency thereof to perform a duty owed to the plaintiff.

When a Writ of Mandamus is Appropriate

Courts do not issue writs of mandamus lightly; therefore, this is not a remedy to be sought every time a federal agency is slow to act. The case law has developed three elements that must exist. First, the plaintiff must have a clear right to the relief sought. Second, the defendant must have a plain and absolute duty to perform the act in question. Finally, there must be no other available remedy.[8]

Examples from Case Law

These elements are best understood by examining the case law involving writs of mandamus. The following cases involve the SSA, EEOC, INS, and EPA.

Claimants who appeal the denial of their Social Security disability applications can request a hearing before an administrative law judge, and courts have issued writs of mandamus to order the SSA to hold punctual hearings. In *White v. Mathews*,[9] the court held that a writ of mandamus ordering the SSA to hold prompt hearings was appropriate, noting that the delays were unreasonable and violated both the Social Security Act and the due process clause of the United States Constitution. The court stated that the SSA had a clear statutory duty to conduct hearings with reasonable speed.

In contrast, in *Sunbeam Appliance Co. v. Kelly*, the court found that mandamus was not appropriate because the EEOC had no duty to perform the act that the plaintiff contested. Here, the plaintiff asserted that the EEOC should be compelled to follow the investigatory procedures set forth in the EEOC Compliance Manual. The court held that the plaintiff could not successfully invoke mandamus, because the EEOC Compliance Manual contains internal guidelines. In contrast to statutes and regulations, the internal guidelines did not impose mandatory duties. Thus, the court declined to issue a writ of mandamus, noting that "[t]here can be no mandamus jurisdiction if no 'duty' exists on the part of the defendant."[10] The court stated that mandamus is appropriate "only when a clear, plainly defined and peremptory duty on the federal defendant is shown."[11]

Mandamus is not appropriate when the action in question is discretionary, not mandatory. In *Soler v. Scott*,[12] the Ninth Circuit Court of Appeals addressed the bounds of discretion of the INS, an agency generally given a great deal of discretion. Here, the plaintiff was an illegal alien in a federal prison, convicted of a crime that could make him deportable. The INS had developed a practice of delaying deportation proceedings until after the expiration of the prison sentence, with the result that the aliens remained in prison past the expiration of their sentence while awaiting their deportation hearing. Thus, in 1986 Congress enacted section 701 of the INA, which states that "the Attorney General shall . . . begin any deportation proceeding as expeditiously as possible after the date of conviction." One year after he entered prison, the INS had not held a deportation hearing for the plaintiff, so he requested a writ of mandamus ordering the INS to hold the hearing. The court stated that even in an area generally left to agency discretion, there may exist statutory standards that limit the scope of the agency's discretion. The court examined the language of the INA and the legislative history of section 701 and determined that Congress had imposed a mandatory duty on the INS, that the INS had failed to perform the mandatory duty, and that mandamus was an appropriate remedy.[13]

Cases involving the EPA have addressed the issue of whether other remedies are available. In several cases where plaintiffs have challenged actions of the EPA, courts have found sufficient means of review under environmental statutes, especially CERCLA.[14] Where a gasoline refiner sought mandamus to compel the EPA to comply with a lead banking program, the court found that sufficient review was available under the Clean Air Act.[15]

Due Process

As discussed in Chapter 2, the United States Constitution, particularly the Bill of Rights, provides controls on administrative agencies. The fifth amendment states that no person may "be deprived of life, liberty, or property without due process of law." The fourteenth amendment makes the due process requirement applicable to states as well. Thus, the due process requirement prevents federal and state agencies from taking away a person's life, liberty, or property without a valid reason and adequate procedural protection. In addition, state constitutions have a due process clause, offering yet another source of due process protection.

SIDEBAR   Some state constitutions' due process clauses do not use the term "due process." For instance, the North Carolina Constitution uses the term "law of the land." Case law makes it clear that this term is synonymous with due process. Thus, paralegals should not be confused if a state constitution uses different terminology.

Paralegals must understand that due process does not prevent federal and state agencies from taking away a client's life, liberty, or property. Due process does require, however, that the procedures used are fundamentally fair. Suppose your law firm's clients live on a two-lane road and the state plans to widen the road to four lanes to facilitate traffic flow in a congested area. The widening of the road will deprive the clients of one-half of their front yard. This is a taking of property by the government. There is probably nothing you can do to prevent the state from widening the road at the expense of the clients' front yard. The state must, however, compensate the clients for their property and allow for some type of appeal process if the amount offered for the property is unreasonable.

Analytical Framework for Due Process Claims

It is essential for paralegals to understand the two-step analysis used by courts in assessing due process claims. The analysis was explained well by Justice Powell in *Ingraham v. Wright*,[16] a case in which high school students who had been punished by paddling argued that school officials had violated the fourteenth amendment by not giving them an opportunity for notice and a hearing prior to the disciplinary paddling. Justice Powell, explaining the due process analysis, wrote:

> The Fourteenth Amendment prohibits any state deprivation of life, liberty or property without due process of law. Application of this prohibition requires the familiar two-stage analysis: We must first ask whether the asserted individual interests are encompassed within the Fourteenth Amendment's protection of "life, liberty or property"; if protected interests are implicated, we then must decide what procedures constitute "due process of law."[17]

Thus, in analyzing a due process claim, you ask two questions. First, is a protected interest at stake? If so, you reach the second question—what procedures are necessary to satisfy the due process requirement? In other words, what process is due? This same analysis applies whether you are examining the actions of federal agencies under the fifth amendment, or the actions of state agencies under the fourteenth amendment.

In *Ingraham*, the Court upheld the state law that allowed corporal punishment without prior notice or hearing. To understand more fully what types of interests fall within the liberty and property interests of the due process clause, paralegals must examine more case law. Because the courts have not developed an absolute definition of protected liberty and property interests, paralegals must read the case law to find factual situations similar to the interests of clients.

Interests that Are Protected by Due Process

The fifth and fourteenth amendments state plainly the three types of interests that are protected by due process—life, liberty, and property. It is obvious when a person's life is at stake, and this has not required a body of case law seeking a definition. Actually, administrative actions rarely threaten a person's life.

In contrast, the definitions of protected liberty and property interests have remained somewhat elusive. A considerable body of case law addresses specific fact situations in which the courts have had to determine whether a protected liberty or property interest is at stake. One notion that runs throughout the case law is that not every interest is of sufficient importance to trigger due process protection.

The Courts' Early Approach: Right vs. Privilege

The early approach to determining the interests protected by due process was to determine whether the interest in question was a "right" or a "privilege." Due process protections attached to rights, but not to privileges. This approach is often traced back to Judge Oliver Wendell Holmes, Jr., in a decision rendered in 1892, upholding the firing of a police officer because of his political activities. Judge Holmes stated that a "petitioner may have a constitutional right to talk politics, but he has no constitutional right to be a policeman."[18]

In *Goldberg v. Kelly*,[19] which addressed the termination of public assistance benefits, the United States Supreme Court abandoned the right-privilege distinction. In *Goldberg,* the Court held that due process required an oral hearing prior to termination of public assistance benefits. The procedure that was held to be insufficient allowed only for submission of a written statement explaining why benefits should not be terminated, but no hearing.

Before examining the Court's new approach, it is instructive to note the interests the Court had found to be protected in earlier cases, which were cited in *Goldberg*. Justice Brennan wrote that due process protection applied to public assistance benefits as much as it did to numerous other interests the Court had found to be protected, including disqualification for unemployment compensation, denial of a tax exemption, the right of a certified public accountant to practice before the Board of Tax Appeals, and the right to obtain a retail liquor store license.[20] In some decisions that preceded *Goldberg*, courts had taken the view that public assistance benefits were "mere privileges," not "rights." In an instructive footnote in *Goldberg*, Justice Brennan explained why a more reasonable contemporary approach was to consider welfare entitlements as more like "property" than "gratuities." This footnote is reprinted as Figure 6–7.

FIGURE 6–7
Footnote from
Goldberg v. Kelly

8. It may be realistic today to regard welfare entitlements as more like "property" than a "gratuity." Much of the existing wealth in this country takes the form of rights that do not fall within traditional common-law concepts of property. It has been aptly noted that

"[s]ociety today is built around entitlement. The automobile dealer has his franchise, the doctor and lawyer their professional licenses, the worker his union membership, contract, and pension rights, the executive his contract and stock options; all are devices to aid security and independence. Many of the most important of these entitlements now flow from government: subsidies to farmers and businessmen, routes for airlines and channels for television stations; long term contracts for defense, space, and education; social security pensions for individuals. Such sources of security, whether private or public, are no longer regarded as luxuries or gratuities; to the recipients they are essentials, fully deserved, and in no sense a form of charity. It is only the poor whose entitlements, although recognized by public policy, have not been effectively enforced."

Reich, Individual Rights and Social Welfare: The Emerging Legal Issues, 74 Yale L.J. 1245, 1255 (1965). See also Reich, The New Property, 73 Yale L.J. 733 (1964).

In *Goldberg* the appellant actually had not contended that due process was not applicable to the termination of welfare benefits. The Court nevertheless took the opportunity to disparage the right vs. privilege test. The Court did not, however, delineate a new test, and paralegals must look at post–*Goldberg v. Kelly* case law.

Post-*Goldberg v. Kelly* Cases Addressing Protected Interests

Some commentators have stated that the Court's approach to identifying protected interests has not been particularly clear and consistent.[21] Paralegals must read the Court's major decisions rendered after *Goldberg v. Kelly* to gain an understanding of which interests merit due process protection and which interests do not. The Court has addressed both liberty and property interests, and the discussion below will sample a few of the important cases.

In *Board of Regents of State Colleges v. Roth*,[22] the Court held that an untenured professor at a state university, who had been hired only on a one-year contract, did not have a protected property interest when the university declined to rehire him. The Court stated that due process attached only to "legitimate claims of entitlement" and not to "unilateral expectations." Thus, the professor had no due process right to a hearing on the university's decision not to rehire him.

In *Perry v. Sinderman*,[23] the Court found a protected property interest where a professor did not have tenure or a contract. This professor had been employed at the same college for a number of years, and he argued that the college had an informal tenure system. The Court determined that this professor had an expectation of continued employment and was entitled to a hearing regarding the implied tenure system and his dismissal.

Some interesting cases addressing liberty interests involve the rights of people who are incarcerated. In *Morrissey v. Brewer*,[24] the Court held that revocation of parole was a protected liberty interest.[25] In contrast, where a person in prison is denied parole, the Court did not find a protected liberty interest.[25] The Court found a protected liberty interest when an inmate was to be transferred from prison to a mental hospital, but not when a prisoner was simply to be transferred to a different prison. People sentenced to prison terms expect incarceration, but not treatment in a mental hospital, unless that was part of the sentence imposed by the trial court.[26]

When the government seeks to impose burdens on marriage and marital association, protected liberty interests are at stake. The United States Supreme Court held in 1923 that the right "to marry, establish a home and bring up children" is a central part of the liberty protected by the Due Process Clause.[27] Thus, government restrictions on marriage are subject to "the most exacting scrutiny."[28] This was one of the main arguments asserted by plaintiffs who challenged the constitutionality of the section of the Immigration Marriage Fraud Amendments that imposed a two-year foreign residency requirement on foreign nationals who married United States citizens during deportation proceedings. The law automatically presumed that the marriage was fraudulent and precluded the opportunity for a hearing to prove that the marriage was genuine and based on mutual love and respect, not an effort to avoid deportation. The heart of the plaintiffs' argument was that the law violated their fifth amendment right to due process. In the *Manwani* case, the federal district court agreed that due process required an opportunity for a hearing prior to a forced exile or separation of two years.[29]

The Protections that Are Due

In two of the Court's most important due process cases—*Goldberg v. Kelly*[30] and *Mathews v. Eldridge*[31]—the existence of a protected interest was not in dispute. At issue was the second step in the due process analysis—what procedures are necessary to satisfy the due process requirement?

Prior Notice

Notice is fundamental to the notions of fairness in administrative law, just as in criminal law and civil litigation. In the criminal law context, the accused cannot adequately mount a defense without notice of the charges. In the civil litigation context, defendants must be given notice of the lawsuit by means of a summons and notice of the allegations, stated in the complaint.

In the administrative law context, government agencies must give notice before taking away a protected liberty or property interest. As discussed below, the SSA must give a claimant notice before terminating Social Security benefits, and state agencies that administer benefits such as Aid to Families with Dependent Children (AFDC) must give notice prior to termination of benefits. Similarly, if the city government wished to rezone your neighborhood for business use, you would be given notice. Affected parties cannot have an effective opportunity to respond and to resist actions of administrative agencies without prior notice of those actions. Due process requires such notice.

Further, the notice must be meaningful, that is, it must adequately explain what is at stake. For instance, in *Goldberg v. Kelly*, the Court found that due process required that welfare recipients "have timely and adequate notice detailing the reasons for a proposed termination."[32] The timely and adequate notice requirement applies when people are initially applying for benefits and when they are appealing adverse determinations. For instance, a claimant for Social Security disability benefits who has requested a hearing before an ALJ must receive a notice of the scheduled hearing twenty days before the date of the hearing. To examine the contents of the notice, refer to Figure 8–1, which illustrates such a notice.

A Timely and Meaningful Hearing

In *Goldberg v. Kelly*, the Court observed that "[t]he fundamental requisite of due process of law is the opportunity to be heard."[33] The Court added that "[t]he hearing must be 'at a meaningful time and in a meaningful manner.'"[34] Students might assume that whenever a government agency seeks to terminate benefits, the recipient is entitled to a hearing before the benefits are terminated. This is not the case. The

United States Supreme Court has held that due process "is flexible and calls for such procedural protections as the particular situation demands."[35] Thus, due process does not always require a hearing before benefits are terminated. Further, a full-blown trial-type hearing is not always required. Thus, in *Goss v. Lopez,*[36] the Court held that students suspended from school were not entitled to a trial-type hearing prior to suspension, but only to an oral or written notice of the charges against them and an opportunity to present their side of the story. The Court made it clear that due process did not require a hearing with the opportunity to present witnesses, cross-examine witnesses supporting the charge, and the opportunity to be represented by counsel. A less formal type of hearing was sufficient, and the hearing need not be held before the students were suspended if immediate removal of the students was necessary to prevent danger to persons and property or disruption of the academic process.

The *Mathews v. Eldridge* Balancing Test

In *Mathews v. Eldridge,*[37] the SSA terminated Mr. Eldridge's Social Security disability benefits, and he challenged the SSA's administrative procedures for assessing whether his disability continued, asserting a due process violation. In contrast to *Goldberg v. Kelly,*[38] where the Court held that an evidentiary hearing was necessary before welfare benefits could be terminated, in *Mathews v. Eldridge* the Court held that an evidentiary hearing was not required prior to termination of disability benefits. In fact, the Court explained at length how the interests at stake and the procedures in *Goldberg v. Kelly* differed from those in *Mathews v. Eldridge*.

The heart of Eldridge's argument was that he was entitled to an evidentiary hearing before his disability benefits were terminated. The Court wrote that due process is flexible and that in determining what procedures were constitutionally sufficient, the interests of both the government and the private party had to be analyzed.[39] The Court enunciated three factors that must be considered in balancing private and governmental interests. Refer to Figure 6–8, which reprints the three factors described by the Court.

FIGURE 6–8
Mathews v. Eldridge—The Three Factors in the Due Process Balancing Test

First, the private interest that will be affected by the official action; second, the risk of an erroneous deprivation of such interest through the procedures used, and the probable value, if any, of additional or substitute procedural safeguards; and finally, the Government's interest, including the function involved and the fiscal and administrative burdens that the additional or substitute procedural requirement would entail.

The Court contrasted the private interest at stake to the interest in *Goldberg v. Kelly*, noting that when welfare assistance was terminated, a person was deprived of the "very means by which to live while he waits."[40] The Court noted that disability benefits were not based on financial need and that the recipient may have other sources of income such as earnings of other family members, tort claims awards, or savings. Further, the recipient may qualify for state and local welfare programs.

It is important to note that in *Mathews v. Eldridge* the Court was discussing Title II benefits, which are based on the amount that the worker paid into the Social Security fund while he was still working. In contrast, when only Title XVI benefits were involved, the SSA did not terminate benefits pending appeal and did allow a pretermination evidentiary hearing because Title XVI eligibility requires a low level of income and resources and is essentially a "companion welfare system."[41]

The Court acknowledged that there was a risk of deprivation because a year could elapse between the cutoff of disability benefits and the final decision after a hearing. The Court stated, however, that the degree of potential deprivation in termination of disability benefits is likely to be less than that in termination of welfare benefits and reiterated the other types of aid that the recipient might seek in the interim.

Addressing the second factor, the Court examined the fairness and reliability of the pretermination procedures. The Court emphasized that the decision whether to continue disability benefits was based on "routine, standard, and unbiased medical reports" and contrasted this to *Goldberg*, where the evidence used for a decision was more subjective, written evidence was not sufficient, and credibility determinations were necessary at an earlier stage. The Court found sufficient safeguards in the SSA's procedures, which included detailed questionnaires and doctors' reports and diagnostic studies such as X-rays. Further, the recipient was given a summary of the evidence and the opportunity to submit additional evidence and arguments.

Finally, the Court addressed the administrative burdens that pretermination hearings would impose. The Court noted that additional costs would include the increased number of hearings and the cost of continuing the benefits until appeals were exhausted. The Court did not state a dollar amount, but concluded that "the ultimate additional cost in terms of money and administrative burden would not be insubstantial."[42] The Court added that "the Government's interest, and hence that of the public, in conserving scarce fiscal and administrative resources is a factor that must be weighed."[43] The Court concluded that because the SSA's prescribed procedures were effective and because the recipient was assured the right to a hearing and to judicial review before the denial of his claim became final, a pretermination hearing was not required and that the administrative procedures comported with due process.[44]

Other Protections

Other important protections guaranteed are the right to an impartial decision maker and the right to a written decision, with findings and legal conclusions. The impartial decision maker is most often an administrative law judge, who issues a written decision with appropriate findings of fact and conclusions of law. Administrative law judges and the decisions they issue are addressed in Chapter 8. Due process also guarantees the right to retain counsel in most types of administrative proceedings. This too is discussed in detail in Chapter 8. Paralegals should note at the outset, however, that the representative need not be an attorney in every type of proceeding and that in most cases the representative is not retained at government expense.

Federal Tort Claims

Your law firm may have clients who seek tort damages because they feel they have been injured or otherwise wronged by the actions of administrative agencies. Prior to 1946, it was very difficult to recover damages for governmental wrongdoing, because of the doctrine of **sovereign immunity,** which provided that the governmental could not be sued without its consent. Before 1946, victims of governmental wrongdoing had to seek relief through congressional enactment of a private bill.[45] The defense of sovereign immunity was waived by the Federal Tort Claims Act, which allows individuals to sue the government for money damages. Further, section 702 of the Administrative Procedure Act (APA) waives the sovereign immunity defense for recovery of nonmonetary damages, paving the way for actions seeking equitable remedies such as injunctive relief. Refer to section 702, which is reprinted in Appendix A.

The Federal Tort Claims Act (FTCA)

Commentary on the Federal Tort Claims Act (FTCA) is immense, and a detailed discussion is beyond the scope of this text. Paralegals should, however, be familiar with the basics of the FTCA.[46]

BALLENTINE'S

sovereign immunity The principle that the government—specifically, the United States or any state of the United States—is immune from suit except when it consents to be sued, as, for EXAMPLE, through a statute such as the Federal Tort Claims Act.

The pertinent section of the FTCA allowing damages in tort is reprinted in Figure 6–9. Read the language carefully. The statute renders the government liable for negligent acts or omissions, just as a private individual can be held liable.

FIGURE 6–9
28 U.S.C. § 2674

§2674. Liability of United States

The United States shall be liable, respecting the provisions of this title relating to tort claims, in the same manner and to the same extent as a private individual under like circumstances, but shall not be liable for interest prior to judgment or for punitive damages.

Exceptions to the FTCA

Despite this broad statement of liability, there are, however, numerous exceptions to liability under the FTCA. These exceptions are reprinted in Figure 6–10. Most of the exceptions are self-explanatory, such as claims arising in foreign countries and claims arising from the activities of the Tennessee Valley Authority. Other exceptions have required judicial interpretation, particularly the exception for discretionary functions and duties. This is a broad exception, which has generated litigation. For instance, in *Berkovitz v. United States*,[47] the plaintiff contracted polio after taking a vaccine given under federal supervision. The Court held that the exception applies only to "policy judgments." Thus, if the agency had violated applicable regulations, then there was no discretion involved, and the discretionary function exception did not apply. Thus, not every exercise of judgment is protected; if the agency had exercised purely scientific judgment in deciding that the vaccine met safety standards, the discretionary function exception did not apply.[48]

FIGURE 6–10
28 U.S.C. § 2680

§2680. Exceptions

The provisions of this chapter and section 1346(b) of this title shall not apply to—
(a) Any claim based upon an act or omission of an employee of the Government, exercising due care, in the execution of a statute or regulation, whether or not such statute or regulation be valid, or based upon the exercise or performance or the failure to exercise or perform a discretionary function or duty on the part of a federal agency or an employee of the Government,

**FIGURE 6–10
(continued)**

whether or not the discretion involved be abused.

(b) Any claim arising out of the loss, miscarriage, or negligent transmission of letters or postal matter.

(c) Any claim arising in respect of the assessment or collection of any tax or customs duty, or the detention of any goods or merchandise by any officer of customs or excise or any other law-enforcement officer.

(d) Any claim for which a remedy is provided by sections 741-752, 781-790 of Title 46, relating to claims or suits in admiralty against the United States.

(e) Any claim arising out of an act or omission of any employee of the Government in administering the provisions of sections 1-31 of Title 50, Appendix.

(f) Any claim for damages caused by the imposition or establishment of a quarantine by the United States.

[(g) Repealed Sept. 26, 1950, ch. 1049, §13 (5), 64 Stat. 1043.]

(h) Any claim arising out of assault, battery, false imprisonment, false arrest, malicious prosecution, abuse of process, libel, slander, misrepresentation, deceit, or interference with contract rights: Provided, That, with regard to acts or omissions of investigative or law enforcement officers of the United States Government, the provisions of this chapter and section 1346(b) of this title shall apply to any claim arising, on or after the date of the enactment of this proviso, out of assault, battery, false imprisonment, false arrest, abuse of process, or malicious prosecution. For the purpose of this subsection, "investigative or law enforcement officer" means any officer of the United States who is empowered by law to execute searches, to seize evidence, or to make arrests for violations of Federal law.

(i) Any claim for damages caused by the fiscal operations of the Treasury or by the regulation of the monetary system.

(j) Any claim arising out of the combatant activities of the military or naval forces, or the Coast Guard, during time of war.

(k) Any claim arising in a foreign country.

(l) Any claim arising from the activities of the Tennessee Valley Authority.

(m) Any claim arising from the activities of the Panama Canal Company.

(n) Any claim arising form the activities of a Federal land bank, a Federal intermediate credit bank, or a bank for cooperatives.

Administrative Procedures

As with much litigation involving administrative agencies, before filing an action in federal court, potential plaintiffs must exhaust administrative procedures first. The claim must first be presented in writing to the responsible agency. If the agency either denies the claim outright or takes no action within six months, the claimant may then file a lawsuit.[49] Section 2672 of the FTCA gives the agencies authority to settle claims, with the proviso that settlements in excess of $25,000 must be approved by the attorney general. The Justice Department has issued regulations to guide agencies in settling claims at the administrative level, and some agencies have promulgated more elaborate procedures.[50] If a settlement is not reached, the agency issues a written denial, and the claimant has six months to file an action in federal court.[51]

Court Claims

In FTCA lawsuits, the United States is the defendant, and the attorney general, through the Justice Department, defends the case. The lawsuit proceeds through federal court, using the Federal Rules of Civil Procedure. As to the substantive law regarding liability and damages, the court applies the law of the place where the negligent act occurred. The FTCA, however, does not authorize jury trials, and it limits attorney fees to 25 percent of the judgment or settlement.[52]

Actions Against Individual Government Officers

Sometimes plaintiffs seek damages from government employees personally. The type of action filed depends on the nature of the wrong alleged.

Tort Actions

The long-standing rule was that federal employees were immune from tort liability when acting within the scope of their employment.[53] In a 1988 decision, however, the United States Supreme Court expanded the personal tort liability to federal employees, prompting Congress to amend the FTCA to make it the exclusive remedy for litigants who sue federal employees personally for alleged torts.[54] Thus, section 2679(d) of the FTCA provides that when the attorney general certifies that "the defendant employee was acting within the scope of his office or employment at the time of the incident out of which the claim arose," then the lawsuit is deemed to be against the United States, and the United States is substituted as the party defendant.

Constitutional Violations

The FTCA protection does not extend to employees charged with violating the United States Constitution or a statute.[55] Perhaps the best known case in this area is *Bivens v. Six Unknown Named Agents of the Federal Bureau of Narcotics*,[56] Here, the Court allowed the plaintiff to sue federal narcotics agents for a fourth amendment violation for injuries he sustained when the agents unlawfully searched his apartment. Government officers have also been sued successfully pursuant to 42 U.S.C. § 1983, the

Civil Rights Act of 1871. Although police officers and similar officers have been held liable under section 1983, courts have continued to extend immunity to legislators and judges.[57] There is extensive literature on this subject, and a detailed discussion is beyond the scope of this text. For suggested readings, refer to the ACUS *Sourcebook* (2d ed.) at page 604.

Summary

This chapter examines various controls on administrative agencies. All three branches of the government have certain controls on agency actions. Further, the due process clause places limitations on agency actions. While agencies generally have wide discretion, individuals can seek a writ of mandamus in federal court to order an agency to take a certain action. The Federal Tort Claims Act (FTCA) offers remedies when a government agency's negligent act or omission has injured a person.

Executive Control of Agency Actions

The president influences agencies directly by appointing the heads of executive agencies and other high-level agency employees. The appointees generally reflect the president's own view, influencing the actions that the agency will emphasize and areas that may not see as much enforcement. The president has the authority to issue executive orders, which direct a particular agency or all agencies to take certain actions. An executive order that affects all agencies is Executive Order 12291, which requires agencies to weigh the benefits of proposed regulations against the potential costs to society. Executive Order 12291 also requires agencies to get clearance from the Office of Management and Budget (OMB) before issuing a "major rule." Through reorganization plans the president, with the consent of Congress, can rearrange agencies and reassign duties to different agencies.

Congressional Control of Agency Actions

Congress controls federal agencies by enacting legislation, including enabling statutes, which both give the agencies powers and sometimes state limitations on the agencies. Congress also repeals and amends statutes, thus altering the powers of agencies and the statutes they enforce. Sometimes the inadequacies of a statute are not evident to Congress for months or years, but the power to repeal or amend the statute allows Congress to take corrective measures, which in turn affects the actions of the agency that enforces the statutes. Congress also must approve certain high-level agency officials, and thus can influence the agencies by accepting or rejecting the president's nominees.

Congress allots a budget for each agency and can control agencies by ensuring that they have a big enough budget to carry out their assigned tasks. Members of Congress can contact agency employees to inquire about matters that affect their constituents. Members of Congress can also launch formal investigations of agency actions. Finally, Congress can direct the General Accounting Office (GAO) to investigate agency operations.

Judicial Review of Agency Actions

Federal courts can review agency actions, although the courts' role is not to substitute their judgment for that of the agency decision makers. The APA provides that courts may review agency decisions to consider whether the agency's action violated the Constitution, whether the agency exceeded its statutory authority, whether the agency's decision is supported by substantial evidence, whether the agency's action is arbitrary and capricious or an abuse of discretion, or whether the agency committed a procedural error.

The Role of Discretion

Federal agencies generally enjoy a high degree of discretion in carrying out their duties. Some agencies, however, are given more discretion than others. Agencies that deal with matters related to foreign policy or the military generally have more discretion than agencies that administer public benefits.

One method of limiting agency discretion is to allow multiple levels of administrative appeals. An example is Social Security disability benefits. After an initial unfavorable determination, a claimant can request a reconsideration determination, then a hearing with an administrative law judge, then a review by the Appeals Council. All these levels of review are within the SSA, and after these appeals are exhausted, a claimant can file an action in federal court.

Most agency decisions are subject to some level of review. A few agency decisions, however, are subject to virtually no review. An example is the decision of a consular officer to deny a visa application. Although State Department regulations provide for review by a senior consular officer and allow for an advisory opinion from the State Department, as a practical matter review rarely takes place. Further, the decision of the consular officer is not subject to judicial review, and neither the attorney general nor the secretary of state can order a consular officer to approve or deny a visa application. Thus, the consular officer's decision is virtually unreviewable.

Another area given wide discretion is the decision whether to prosecute a violation of a law that an agency enforces. Most agencies, including the EPA and the EEOC, require approval from high-level officials before a prosecution begins. The decision whether to prosecute or to decline prosecution, however, is not reviewable. Thus, prosecutorial discretion is a powerful tool of agency officials to direct the agency's direction.

Remedies for Failure to Act

Sometimes agencies take months, even years, to make a decision on applications. In the interim, the applicant may face financial and other difficulties. The attorney-paralegal team can try informal methods to try to prod agency action, such as asking a member of Congress to inquire about the status of an application. Sometimes the attorney-paralegal team determines that the case warrants filing an action in federal court to seek a writ of mandamus, which is a court order to compel an agency to perform a duty owed to the plaintiff. Courts do not issue writs of mandamus for every agency delay. Three elements must exist to support a writ of mandamus. The plaintiff must have a clear right to the relief sought, the agency must have a plain duty to perform the act in question, and there must be no other available remedy.

Due Process

The fifth amendment states that the government may not deprive a person of life, liberty, or property without due process of law. The fourteenth amendment makes the due process requirement applicable to state agencies. Further, state constitutions contain due process protections.

The due process requirement does not prevent government agencies from taking individuals' life, liberty, or property. It does, however, require that the procedures used are fundamentally fair.

In analyzing due process claims, the courts have developed a two-step analytical framework. The first question is whether a protected interest is at stake. If so, the second question is what procedures are necessary to satisfy the due process requirement. Case law has developed to define what constitute protected property and liberty interests. The courts' early approach was to classify an interest as either a "right" or a "privilege." Rights were protected interests; privileges were not protected. The United States Supreme Court abandoned the right-privilege distinction in *Goldberg v. Kelly*. Subsequent case law addresses loss of employment, termination of public benefits, and the rights of prisoners, to name a few examples. Case law also addresses government infringement on marriage, which implicates protected liberty interests. Paralegals must be familiar with the case law in order to draw analogies and determine when their clients have protected interests at stake.

The procedures that are generally considered necessary to satisfy due process are prior notice, a timely and meaningful hearing, right to representation, an impartial decision maker, and a written decision with findings of fact and conclusions of law. The hearing does not always precede termination of benefits. In *Goldberg v. Kelly*, the United States Supreme Court held that a pretermination hearing was necessary for welfare benefits, but in *Mathews v. Eldridge* the Court held that a posttermination hearing satisfied the due process requirement when Social Security disability benefits were at stake. In determining what procedures were necessary in *Mathews v. Eldridge*, the Court stated three factors that must be balanced—the private interest that will be affected by the official action; the risk of an erroneous deprivation of such interest through the procedures used, and the probable value, if any, of additional or substitute procedural safeguards; and finally, the government's interest, including fiscal and administrative burdens, that additional or substitute procedures would entail.

Federal Tort Claims

Prior to the enactment of the Federal Tort Claims Act (FTCA), the doctrine of sovereign immunity precluded recovering damages for government wrongdoing. The FTCA waived the defense of sovereign immunity. Under the FTCA, individuals can sue the government for money damages. Nonmonetary damages, such as injunctive relief and other equitable remedies, must be pursued under section 702 of the Administrative Procedure Act (APA). The FTCA renders the government liable for negligent acts or omissions, just as a private individual would be held liable.

There are numerous exceptions to liability under the FTCA, including discretionary acts and claims arising in foreign countries. Refer to Figure 6–10 for the other exceptions.

The FTCA requires plaintiffs to try to settle their claims with the responsible agency through administrative procedures before filing suit in federal court. If a settlement is not reached, the individual has six months to file an action in federal court. The FTCA does not authorize jury trials, and attorney fees are limited to 25 percent of the judgment or court settlement.

Individuals may also sue federal employees personally. If the attorney general certifies that the defendant employee was acting within the scope of his or her office at the time of the incident out of which the claim arose, the United States is substituted as defendant, and the case proceeds under the FTCA. The FTCA protection does not extend to federal employees charged with violating the Constitution or a statute.

Review Questions

1. Which of the following are methods by which the president controls agency actions? _____
   a. appointment of high-level agency officials
   b. executive orders
   c. reorganization plans
   d. all of the above
   e. a and b only

2. Which of the following are methods by which Congress controls agency actions? _____
   a. enactment of statutes that place limitations on agencies
   b. budget appropriations
   c. requesting an investigation of agency matters through the General Accounting Office (GAO)
   d. all of the above
   e. a and b only

3. Once a protected interest has been identified, due process requires which of the following? _____
   a. a written decision with findings of fact and conclusions of law
   b. a full-blown trial-type hearing
   c. prior notice
   d. all of the above
   e. a and c only

4. Which of the following statements about the Federal Tort Claims Act is true? _____
   a. A prerequisite to filing an action in federal court is exhaustion of administrative procedures to try to reach a settlement with the responsible agency.
   b. Plaintiffs can recover only monetary damages under the FTCA.
   c. Plaintiffs are entitled to jury trials under the FTCA.
   d. all of the above
   e. a and b only

5. Which of the following are exceptions to government liability under the FTCA? _____
    a. claims arising out of the loss of letters or postal matter
    b. claims based on discretionary agency functions
    c. claims arising in a foreign country
    d. all of the above
    e. b and c only

6. The APA sets limits on judicial review of agency decisions.

    True ___ / False ___

7. All agency decisions are reviewable by courts.   True ___ / False ___

8. Due process requires a hearing prior to termination of welfare benefits.

    True ___ / False ___

9. When the government seeks to impose burdens on marriage and marital associations, protected liberty interests are at stake.   True ___ / False ___

10. The *Mathews v. Eldridge* balancing test requires consideration of the fiscal burden that additional procedures would place on the government.

    True ___ / False ___

11. The FTCA does not extend protection to federal employees who are sued personally on the basis that they violated the Constitution.

    True ___ / False ___

12. Revocation of parole does not involve a protected liberty interest.

    True ___ / False ___

13. Due process requires notice of intent to terminate Social Security disability benefits before the benefits are actually terminated.

    True ___ / False ___

14. Explain how the president and Congress influence federal agencies through the appointment of high-level officials.

15. Contrast the levels of administrative review of consular officers' decisions whether to approve a visa application with the SSA's determinations of whether claimants are disabled.

Practical Applications

Susan Garcia received a phone call from one of your law firm's clients, Michael Petrenko. Mr. Petrenko explained that he lives on a street that has only private residences. Streets nearby have both private residences and some small office buildings. The office buildings were originally private homes but have been converted to offices. The city posted a notice on Mr. Petrenko's street, stating that it intends to rezone an area that includes Mr. Petrenko's street, to allow for more business use. The notice also stated the time and place for a hearing on the proposed rezoning. Mr. Petrenko is opposed to the rezoning because he and his neighbors wish to continue to live in a residential neighborhood and fear that the value of their property will be adversely affected. Ms. Garcia asked you to consider the due process implications of this situation and to answer the following questions so that she may accurately advise Mr. Petrenko.

1. Does Mr. Petrenko have a protected interest at stake?

2. Does the notice posted on his street give him fair notice of the proposed change?

3. Mr. Petrenko wishes to retain Ms. Garcia to represent him and to present arguments against the rezoning at the hearing. Does due process require that he be allowed to be represented?

4. Mr. Petrenko has learned that one member of the zoning commission owns office buildings on a nearby street and is eager to develop other office buildings in the neighborhood. Is this a due process violation?

Case Analysis

Read the following excerpts from *Garcia v. Baker*, 765 F. Supp. 426 (N.D. Ill. 1990), and answer the questions below. You may not be familiar with the term "exclusion." To exclude a person from the United States means to deny entry. People may be excluded at the border when they try to enter the United States. Here, the consulate in Honduras denied a visa to the plaintiff Garcia, which is another way of excluding an alien from the United States, because a visa is necessary to enter the United States. Aliens may obtain immigrant visas when certain of their relatives are citizens or lawful permanent residents of the United States. The plaintiff sought an immigrant visa based on her mother, who was a lawful permanent resident of the United States.

GRADY, District Judge.

This case, involving the Immigration and Nationality Act ("INA"), is before us on defendants' motion to dismiss the complaint on the grounds that the court lacks subject matter jurisdiction, plaintiffs lack standing, and the complaint fails to state a claim upon which relief can be granted. For the reasons stated below, we dismiss this cause with prejudice.

FACTS

Plaintiff Santa Armida Bendana is a native and citizen of Honduras. Plaintiff Florinda Garcia is her mother and a lawful permanent resident of the United States. Garcia submitted a second preference visa petition on behalf of Bendana which was approved, rendering Bendana eligible to immigrate to the United States as the unmarried, adult daughter of a permanent resident.

Based on the approved second preference petition, Bendana applied to the United States Consulate in Honduras for an immigrant visa. The consulate denied Bendana's petition for an immigrant visa, finding that she was excluded from entering the United States under § 212(a)(19) of the INA. After interviewing Bendana, the consular officer concluded that Bendana had wilfully misrepresented a material fact in securing a tourist visa in 1983. The officer found that Bendana had intended in 1983 to remain in the United States for one year, although she had stated in her 1983 tourist visa interview that she intended to remain in the United States for only two months. Bendana admits that she overstayed the terms of her admission as a tourist in 1983 and did not actually return to Honduras until her interview at the consulate in January 1989.

Plaintiffs allege that State Department regulations required the consular officer to seek a mandatory and binding advisory legal opinion from the Advisory Opinions Division of the State Department regarding the consulate's finding of wilful and material misrepresentations by Bendana. Plaintiffs charge that the Division issued its opinion, concurring with that of the consular officer, in disregard of the Attorney General's controlling interpretation to the contrary. Thus, plaintiffs claim that Bendana's exclusion is not authorized by INA § 212(a)(19) and corresponding regulations and is not in conformity with the Attorney General's interpretation of law.

Plaintiffs seek a declaration that defendants' finding that Bendana made a wilful, material misrepresentation in her 1983 application was unlawful. They further seek an order directing the State Department to communicate to the United States Consulate Office that there is no legal basis to refuse Bendana's immigrant visa and to appoint a General Counsel of the Visa Office as required by § 104(e) of the INA, with a view to secure uniform interpretations of the INA.

DISCUSSION

We lack subject matter jurisdiction to hear plaintiffs' claims. We agree with defendants that this suit begins and ends with the consular officer's denial of Bendana's immigrant visa application. Although the determinations and rulings by the Attorney General regarding all questions of law are controlling, and rulings of the State Department concerning interpretations of law are binding upon consular officers, courts cannot interfere in the visa issuance process.

The law is well settled that a consular officer's denial of a visa application is not subject to judicial review. We cannot review a consular officer's decision even upon allegations that the consular officer acted on erroneous information, that the INA did not authorize the officer's decisions, that the officer erroneously interpreted and applied the INA, or that the State Department failed to follow its own regulations.

Plaintiffs attempt to avoid the consular nonreviewability doctrine by maintaining that they are not seeking review of the consular officer's decision. Rather, they are challenging the State Department's legal opinion, rendered contrary to the law. This argument is unavailing. First, courts have consistently rejected attacks on consular decisions, whatever form they take.

. . .

[A]ny decision we might render ordering the Secretary of State to follow the Attorney General's interpretation of law would not affect consular officers' decisions, because only consular officers can find facts or apply the law to facts with respect to visa applications. Neither the Attorney General nor the Secretary of State can require consular officers to grant or deny visa applications, and they are without power to issue visas. Thus, there is a serious question as to whether granting plaintiffs' prayer for relief would achieve the result they seek.

. . .

CONCLUSION

We lack jurisdiction to hear this case. Accordingly, we grant defendants' motion to dismiss and dismiss this cause with prejudice.

1. Section 212(a)(19) of the Immigration and Nationality Act (INA) provides that aliens are excluded from admission to the United States when they have previously procured or sought to procure a visa or other immigration benefit by fraud or willfully misrepresenting a material fact. What action had the plaintiff taken that the consulate considered to be a willful misrepresentation?
2. Did the court find that the denial of a visa application is subject to judicial review?
3. Is judicial review allowed if the consular officer acted on erroneous information or erroneously interpreted the INA?
4. The court stated that the plaintiff tried to avoid the issue of nonreviewability of consular officers' decisions by arguing that the consular officer's opinion was contrary to the attorney general's interpretation of section 212(a)(19) of the INA and that the attorney general should inform the

consular officer that there was no legal basis for denying the visa. Why did the court reject this approach?

5. On what ground did the court grant the motion to dismiss?

Notes

[1] *U.S. Government Manual, 1993–94*, (Washington, D.C.: U.S. Government Printing Office), at 566.

[2] 8 U.S.C. § 1255(e)(3).

[3] *U.S. Government Manual, supra* note 1, at 47.

[4] *Id.* at 49.

[5] Ernest Gellhorn & Ronald Levin, *Administrative Law and Procedure in a Nutshell*, 3d ed. (St. Paul: West Publishing Co., 1990), at 4.

[6] *Black's Law Dictionary* 1441 (5th ed. 1979).

[7] 28 U.S.C. § 1361.

[8] *See* Annotation, *Mandamus, Under 28 USCS § 1361, to Compel Prompt Hearing in Appeal from Denial of Social Security*, 47 A.L.R. Fed. 929.

[9] 559 F.2d 852 (2d Cir. 1977), cert. denied, 435 U.S. 908 (1978). For more cases addressing this subject, refer to the A.L.R. Annotation cited in note 8, *supra*.

[10] 532 F. Supp. 96, 98 (N.D. Ill. 1982).

[11] *Id.*

[12] 942 F.2d 597 (9th Cir. 1991).

[13] *Id.* at 603.

[14] *See, e.g., Cooper Indus., Inc. v. U.S. EPA*, 774 F. Supp. (W.D. Mich. 1991).

[15] *See, e.g., Farmers Union Cent. Exch., Inc. v. Thomas*, 881 F.2d 757 (1989).

[16] 430 U.S. 651 (1977).

[17] *Id.* at 672.

[18] *McAuliffe v. Mayor of New Bedford*, 155 Mass. 216, 220, 29 N.E. 517 (Sup. Jud. Ct. of Mass. 1892). *See also* Donald Barry & Howard Whitcomb, *The Legal Foundations of Public Administration*, 2d ed. (St. Paul: West Publishing Co., 1987), at 192.

[19] 397 U.S. 254 (1970).

[20] *Id.* at 262.

[21] Barry & Whitcomb, *supra* note 18, at 192.

[22] 408 U.S. 564 (1972).

[23] 408 U.S. 2694 (1972).

[24] 408 U.S. 471 (1972).

[25] Gellhorn & Levin, *supra* note 5, at 210.

[26] For further discussion, *see* Gellhorn & Levin, *supra* note 5, at 208–11.

[27] *Meyer v. Nebraska*, 262 U.S. 390, 399 (1923).

[28] *Manwani v. U.S. Dep't of Justice, INS*, 736 F. Supp. 1376, 1379 (W.D.N.C. 1990).

[29] 736 F. Supp. 1367 (W.D.N.C. 1990). Several courts, however, upheld the statute. *See, e.g., Azizi v. Thornburgh*, 719 F. Supp. 86 (D. Conn. 1989).

[30] 397 U.S. 254 (1970).

[31] 424 U.S. 319 (1976).

[32] 397 U.S. at 267–68.

[33] 397 U.S. at 268.

[34] *Id.*

[35] *Mathews v. Eldridge*, 424 U.S. 319, 335 (1976).

[36] 419 U.S. 565 (1975).

[37] 424 U.S. 319 (1976).

[38] 397 U.S. 254 (1970).

[39] 424 U.S. at 334.

[40] 424 U.S. at 340.

[41] 424 U.S. at 341.

[42] 424 U.S. at 348.

[43] 424 U.S. at 349.

[44] *Id.*

[45] Administrative Conference of the United States, *Federal Administrative Procedure Sourcebook*, 2d ed. (Office of the Chairman, 1992), at 599 (hereinafter ACUS *Sourcebook*).

[46] The ACUS *Sourcebook*, *supra* note 45, at 603ff., has a bibliography on the FTCA, and notes in particular L. Jayson's *Handling Federal Tort Claims*, a three-volume treatise on FTCA legislation.

[47] 486 U.S. 531 (1988).

[48] Gellhorn & Levin, *supra* note 5, at 395.

[49] ACUS *Sourcebook*, at 600.

[50] *Id.*

[51] ACUS *Sourcebook*, at 627.

[52] ACUS *Sourcebook*, at 601.

[53] Gellhorn & Levin, *supra* note 5, at 395.

[54] ACUS *Sourcebook*, at 602, referring to *Westfall v. Erwin*, 484 U.S. 292 (1988).

[55] 28 U.S.C. § 2679(b)(2).

[56] 403 U.S. 388 (1971).

[57] Kenneth Culp Davis, *Administrative Law and Government* (St. Paul: West Publishing Co., 1975), at 110.

IIII

CHAPTER 7

ADMINISTRATIVE PROCEDURES AND APPEALS: HOW TO FILE APPLICATIONS WITH ADMINISTRATIVE AGENCIES AND APPEAL ADMINISTRATIVE DECISIONS

In Chapters 3 and 4, you gained knowledge of the substantive law in four important areas of administrative law. In order to be effective paralegals, you must know both the substantive law and the procedural law of the agencies with which you deal. Only when the attorney-paralegal team knows an agency's procedures can it effectively represent clients.

Chapter 7 discusses in detail the procedure for filing an application for Social Security disability benefits, the content of the application and accompanying forms, and the procedure for appealing unfavorable determinations. The text emphasizes the Social Security disability forms and procedures, but also discusses the same information for an application for naturalization so that paralegal students can become familiar with INS forms and procedures as well.

How to Find an Agency's Procedures

The first question to address is how to find agencies' procedures. There are several valuable sources.

Statutes and Regulations

Paralegals should first look to the primary sources of law—the applicable statutes and regulations. As with substantive law, the statutes contain almost no detail on agency procedures. Paralegals must turn to the agency's regulations for details. Some agencies' regulations are quite clear in explaining the application and accompanying documents necessary to apply for a benefit. For instance, 8 CFR 316.14 identifies the application form and accompanying documents required to file for naturalization. The INS regulations (8 CFR 336.2 and 336.9) explain the procedure necessary to appeal the denial of a naturalization application.

The regulations explaining the procedure for filing applications for Social Security disability benefits are more detailed. The regulations are in subpart G (20 CFR 404.601–404.641). The SSA's regulations regarding the procedure for appealing unfavorable determinations are even more detailed. Subpart J (20 CFR 404.900–404.999d) explains the appeals procedures in much greater detail than the INS regulations regarding naturalization appeals. In order to understand the procedural requirements, both for agencies with detailed regulations and agencies with less detailed regulations, paralegals often need to consult other sources.

Instructions on the Applications

The applications themselves sometimes have helpful instructions attached. This is not true of all applications. For instance, the application for Social Security disability benefits does not have such helpful instructions attached. The application for naturalization and other INS forms, however, have instructions attached to the applications themselves.

Refer to Figure 7–1, which reprints the first page of instructions attached to the application for naturalization. These instructions provide essential information, such as the filing fee, where to file the application, and detailed instructions for the photographs that must accompany the application. Some of this information is found elsewhere in the INS regulations. For instance, the INS lists all its current forms in 8 CFR 299.1 and lists filing fees in 8 CFR 103.7(b). It is, however, convenient to have the information on the instructions that come with the application.

FIGURE 7–1
First Page of
Instructions for
Form N-400

U.S. Department of Justice   OMB #1115-0009
Immigration and Naturalization Service   Application for Naturalization

INSTRUCTIONS

Purpose of This Form.
This form is for use to apply to become a naturalized citizen of the United States.

Who May File.
You may apply for naturalization if:
- you have been a lawful permanent resident for five years;
- you have been a lawful permanent resident for three years, have been married to a United States citizen for those three years, and continue to be married to that U.S. citizen;
- you are a lawful permanent resident child of United States citizen parents; or
- you have qualifying military service.

Children under 18 may automatically become citizens when their parents naturalize. You may inquire at your local Service office for further information. If you do not meet the qualifications listed above but believe that you are eligible for naturalization, you may inquire at your local Service office for additional information.

General Instructions.
Please answer all questions by typing or clearly printing in black ink. Indicate that an item is not applicable with "N/A". If an answer is "none," write "none". If you need extra space to answer any item, attach a sheet of

FIGURE 7–1
(continued)

paper with your name and your alien registration number (A#), if any, and indicate the number of the item.

Every application must be properly signed and filed with the correct fee. If you are under 18 years of age, your parent or guardian must sign the application.

If you wish to be called for your examination at the same time as another person who is also applying for naturalization, make your request on a separate cover sheet. Be sure to give the name and alien registration number of that person.

Initial Evidence Requirements.
You must file your application with the following evidence:

A copy of your alien registration card.

Photographs. You must submit two color photographs of yourself taken within 30 days of this application. These photos must be glossy, unretouched and unmounted, and have a white background. Dimension of the face should be about 1 inch from chin to top of hair. Face should be 3/4 frontal view of right side with right ear visible. Using pencil or felt pen, lightly print name and A#, if any, on the back of each photo. This requirement may be waived by the Service if you can establish that you are confined because of age or physical infirmity.

Fingerprints. If you are between the ages of 14 and 75, you must submit your fingerprints on Form FD-258. Fill out the form and write your Alien Registration Number in the space marked "Your No. OCA" of "Miscellaneous No. MNU". Take the chart and these instructions to a police station, sheriff's office or an office of this Service, or other reputable person or organization for fingerprinting. (You should contact the police or sheriff's office before going there since some of these offices do not take fingerprints for other government agencies.) You must sign the chart in the presence of the person taking your fingerprints and have that person sign his/her name, title, and the date in the space provided. Do not bend, fold, or crease the fingerprint chart.

U.S. Military Service. If you have ever served in the Armed Forces of the United States at any time, you must submit a completed Form G-325B. If your application is based on your military service you must also submit Form N-426, "Request for Certification of Military or Naval Service."

Application for Child. If this application is for a permanent resident child of U.S. citizen parents, you must also submit copies of the child's birth certificate, the parents' marriage certificate, and evidence of the parents' U.S. citizenship. If the parents are divorced, you must also submit the divorce decree and evidence that the citizen parent has legal custody of the child.

FIGURE 7–1
(continued)

Where to File.
File this application at the local Service office having jurisdiction over your place of residence.

Fee.
The fee for this application is $90.00. The fee must be submitted in the exact amount. It cannot be refunded. DO NOT MAIL CASH.

All checks and money orders must be drawn on a bank or other institution located in the United States and must be payable in United States currency. The check or money order should be made payable to the Immigration and Naturalization Service, except that:

- If you live in Guam, and are filing this application in Guam, make your check or money order payable to the "Treasurer, Guam."
- If you live in the Virgin Islands, and are filing this application in the Virgin Islands, make your check or money order payable to the "Commissioner of Finance of the Virgin Islands."

Checks are accepted subject to collection. An uncollected check will render the application and any document issued invalid. A charge of $5.00 will be imposed if a check in payment of a fee is not honored by the bank on which it is drawn.

Government Publications

Often agencies publish manuals or handbooks that offer more details on the programs they administer, including information on procedure. For instance, the *Social Security Handbook 1993* (11th ed.) explains the various programs that the SSA administers and includes a chapter on filing a claim.

Treatises

Often the attorney-paralegal team needs even more information on procedure. This is especially true when legal professionals are fairly new to an area of administrative law.

Many treatises are available to guide the attorney-paralegal team. For instance, the multivolume *Social Security Law and Practice* has several sections on filing applications and appealing unfavorable determinations. Typical of loose-leaf services, this treatise has a running commentary that cites the application statutes and regulations and illustrates forms required by the SSA.

Associations of Legal Professionals in Specific Areas of Law

Organizations such as the American Immigration Lawyers Association (AILA) and the National Organization of Social Security Claimants' Representatives (NOSSCR) publish newsletters to help members keep up with current developments in Social Security and immigration law. Some associations, including AILA, publish treatises as well. Associations also sponsor seminars, including those offered at yearly meetings, that offer important updates on substantive and procedural law. The written materials that accompany each presentation are valuable sources of information, and can be purchased at the meetings or by mail. These materials are a tremendous resource for legal professionals in administrative law, where the law changes so rapidly that sections of CFR are frequently out of date. Further, when paralegals attend the associations' meetings, they meet other professionals and form a network for sharing information on developments in the law throughout the year.

Procedures for Filing an Application for Social Security Disability Benefits

The SSA's regulations in subpart G address the filing of an application for disability benefits. As the introduction in 20 CFR 404.601 explains, "This subpart contains the Social Security Administration's rules for filing a claim for . . . disability . . . insurance benefits. . . . It tells what an application is, who may sign it, where and when it must be signed and filed, the period of time it is in effect and how it may be withdrawn." The text now addresses some of the individual require ments in detail.

A Claimant Must File an Application to Receive Benefits

This requirement may seem too obvious to state. The regulations (20 CFR 404.603) explain, however, why it is necessary to file an application. First, filing an application will "permit a formal decision to be made on [a claimant's] entitlement to benefits." This is important because a claimant has no appeal rights until the SSA issues a formal decision; there is simply nothing to appeal until the SSA renders a decision.

Another important consequence of filing an application is that the regulations allow a claimant to receive benefits for up to twelve months immediately before the month in which the application is filed (20 CFR 404.621(a)). Thus, if a claimant files an application in March 1993, and she is found to have been disabled since January 1992, she may receive retroactive benefits for the twelve months prior to her filing date. If, however, she did not file her application until March 1994, she can receive retroactive benefits only back to March 1993, because of the twelve-month limit on retroactive benefits. Therefore, it is important to establish the filing date of the application so that the claimant can receive these retroactive benefits.

Protective Filings

Before examining the content of the SSA's prescribed application form, it is important for paralegals to know that the regulations allow claimants to submit a statement of their intent to file an application and to submit the prescribed form later. The general rule is that the filing date given to an application is the date that the application is received by an SSA employee at an SSA office, with certain exceptions stated in 20 CFR 404.614. The regulations (20 CFR 404.630) provide, however, that if the written statement indicates an intent to file, and the claimant then files an application on the prescribed form within the required time limit, the date that the claimant informed the SSA of his or her intent to file is used as the filing date of the application. This date is called the **protective filing date.** Thus, if a claimant writes a letter to the SSA stating her intent to file an application for disability benefits on April 9, 1994, and then files the formal application on the SSA's prescribed form on June 10, 1994, the protective filing date for the application is April 9, 1994. Because claimants can receive twelve months in retroactive benefits, this claimant can receive two more months in retroactive benefits than she would have received if her application had been filed in June rather than April.

In order to establish a protective filing date, the claimant must comply with requirements in 20 CFR 404.630. Refer to Figure 7–2, which reprints 20 CFR 404.630. The claimant's written statement must indicate an intent to claim benefits and must be signed by the claimant, the claimant's spouse, or other person described in 20 CFR 404.612. The SSA sends the claimant a written notice advising of the need to file an application, and the claimant must file the actual application within six months of the date of the notice. Finally, the claimant must be alive when the application is filed, with certain exceptions explained in 20 CFR 404.630(d).

---

protective filing date The filing date given to an application for Social Security disability benefits when claimants have informed the Social Security Administration (SSA) of their intent to file an application and then file an application on the prescribed form within the required time limit.

FIGURE 7–2
20 CFR 404.630:
Regulations
Regarding
Protective Filing
Dates

§ 404.630   Use of date of written statement as filing date.

If a written statement, such as a letter, indicating your intent to claim benefits either for yourself or for another person is filed with us under the rules stated in § 404.614, we will use the filing date of the written statement as the filing date of the application, if all of the following requirements are met:

(a) The statement indicates an intent to claim benefits.

(b) The statement is signed by the claimant, the claimant's spouse, or a person described in § 404.612. If you telephone us and advise us that you intend to file a claim but cannot file an application before the end of the month, we will prepare and sign a written statement if it is necessary to prevent the loss of benefits.

(c) The claimant files an application with us on an application form as described in § 404.611, or one is filed for the claimant by a person described in § 404.612, within 6 months after the date of a notice we will send advising of the need to file an application. We will send the notice to the claimant. However, if it is clear from the information we receive that the claimant is a minor or is mentally incompetent, we will send the notice to the person who submitted the written statement.

(d) The claimant is alive when the application is filed; or if the claimant has died after the written statement was filed, an application is filed—

(1) By or for a person who would be eligible to receive benefits on the deceased's earnings record;

(2) By a person acting for the deceased's estate; or

(3) If the statement was filed with a hospital under § 404.632, by the hospital if—

(i) No person described in paragraph (d)(1) or (2) of this section can be located; or

(ii) A person described in paragraphs (d)(1) or (2) of this section is located but refuses or fails to file the application unless the refusal or failure to file is because it would be harmful to the deceased person or the deceased's estate.

Requirements for a Valid Application

The regulations set forth certain requirements that an application must meet in order to be a valid claim for benefits. Those requirements are set out in 20 CFR 404.610, which is reprinted in Figure 7–3.

FIGURE 7–3
20 CFR 404.610:
Requirements for
a Valid
Application for
Social Security
Disability Benefits

---

§ 404.610   What makes an application a claim for benefits.

To be considered a claim for benefits, an application must generally meet all of the following conditions:

(a) It must be on an application form as described in § 404.611.

(b) It must be completed and filed with SSA as described in § 404.611.

(c) It must be signed by the claimant or someone described in § 404.612, who may sign an application for the claimant.

(d) The claimant, with the limited exceptions in § 404.615, must be alive at the time it is filed.

The application must be completed and filed with the SSA, on an application form as prescribed by the SSA. This is the general rule; however, there are certain exceptions which allow filing on forms of the Veterans Administration or Railroad Retirement Act (20 CFR 404.611). Paralegals should be aware of these exceptions, although most clients will not fall within them. It is far more important to remember the general rule that claimants must use the form prescribed by the SSA.

As a general rule, the application must be signed by the claimant. The regulations allow certain exceptions, which can be found in 20 CFR 404.612. Finally, the claimant must be alive at the time the application is filed, although certain exceptions are set forth in 20 CFR 404.615.

Procedure for Filing the Application

The attorney-paralegal team generally is not involved with disability claims until the claim has been denied and the claimant then seeks assistance. It is important, however, for paralegals to understand the procedure for the filing of the application for disability insurance benefits.

Claimants may file their applications in person at the nearest SSA district office. The SSA also allows claimants to phone in their applications. An SSA employee takes down the information, enters it in the computer, generates the application, and sends the application to the claimant to sign. The claimant then signs and dates the application and mails it back to the SSA office. This procedure is convenient for claimants who are too ill to go to the local office.

Employees of the Social Security Administration help claimants fill out their applications. The *Social Security Handbook 1993* explains that "[i]f the claimant finds that help is needed in completing the application form, any Social Security office will provide assistance free of charge."[1] Several forms must be filed along with the application, and SSA employees can assist claimants in completing these forms as well. Thus, the actual filing procedure is fairly simple, SSA employees freely provide help, and there is some flexibility in the filing procedure. Paralegals should be aware that not all agencies provide this much assistance and flexibility in filing applications.

Content of the Application

Throughout the discussion of the application form, refer to Figure 7–4, which illustrates Melinda Lewis's application for disability insurance benefits. This is the standard computer-generated form used by the SSA. Each section of the application has information that serves a specific purpose. The first section states that the claimant is applying for disability insurance benefits (Title II). The application also states that the claimant is applying for benefits under part A of Title XVIII of the Social Security Act. This is Medicare. A person under age sixty-five who has been entitled to disability benefits for twenty-four months becomes eligible for Medicare, which is also called supplementary medical insurance.

FIGURE 7–4
Melinda Lewis's
Application for
Social Security
Disability Benefits

Application For Disability Insurance Benefits

I apply for a period of disability and/or all insurance benefits for which I am eligible under Title II and Part A of Title XVIII of the Social Security Act, as presently amended.

My name is Melinda J. Lewis.

My social security number is 000-00-0000.

My date of birth is January 3, 1940.

I became unable to work because of my disabling condition on March 1, 1992.

I am still disabled.

No previous application has been filed with the Social Security Administration by or for me.

I am not receiving and do not expect to receive workers' compensation, public disability, or black lung benefits.

I am not entitled to nor do I expect to become entitled to a pension or annuity based in whole or in part on work after 1956 not covered by Social Security.

The Social Security Administration and the state agency reviewing my claim does have my permission to contact my employers.

I am married to Michael Lewis. We were married on September 15, 1962, in Charlotte, North Carolina by a clergyman or public official. My spouse's age or birthdate is April 2, 1942 and social security number is 000-00-0001.

I was not previously married.

FIGURE 7–4
(continued)

I do not have any children who may be eligible for Social Security benefits.

I understand that I must provide medical evidence about my disability, or assist the Social Security Administration in obtaining the evidence.

I understand that I may be requested by the State Disability Determination Services to have an independent medical examination at the expense of the Social Security Administration.

I authorize any physician, hospital, agency, or other organization to disclose any medical record or information about my disability to the Social Security Administration or to the state agency that may review my claim or continuing disability.

I authorize the Social Security Administration to release any information about me to a physician or medical facility preparatory to an examination or test. Results of such examination or test may be released to my physician or other treating source.

I authorize that information about my disability may be furnished to any contractor for clerical services by the State Disability Determination Services.

I agree to notify the Social Security Administration of all the events as explained in the rights and responsibilities pamphlet given to me.

I agree to notify the Social Security Administration if:

—My medical condition improves so that I would be able to work, even though I have not yet returned to work.
—I go to work whether as an employee or a self-employed person.
—I apply for or receive a decision on benefits under any Workers' Compensation Law or plan (including black lung benefits from the Department of Labor), or other public benefit based on disability.
—I am imprisoned for conviction of a felony.

The above events may affect my eligibility to disability benefits as provided in the Social Security Act, as amended.

I agree to notify the Social Security Administration if I become entitled to a pension or annuity based on employment after 1956 not covered by Social Security, or if such pension or annuity stops.

My reporting responsibilities have been explained to me.

I know that anyone who makes or causes to be made a false statement or representation of material fact in an application or for use in determining a right to payment under the Social Security Act commits a crime punish-able under federal law by fine, imprisonment or both. I affirm that all information I have given in connection with this claim is true.

My mailing address is   202 Oak St.
                        Charlotte, NC 28212

My telephone number is (area code) 704-555-3524.

Signature _Melinda Lewis_   Date _Jun. 25, 1994_

The next sections identify the claimant by name, together with her Social Security number and date of birth. Next, Ms. Lewis states her alleged onset date and states that she continues to be disabled. The next section states whether the claimant has filed previous applications for disability benefits.[2]

Ms. Lewis indicated that she has not received workers' compensation or the other types of benefits described in the next two sections. Certain types of benefits are an offset to Social Security disability benefits, that is, the Social Security benefits are reduced by the amount of the other benefits. A discussion of the various offsets is beyond the scope of this text, but paralegals may refer to subpart E (20 CFR 404.390–404.469) for a discussion of offsets and reductions.

Next the application has information on the claimant's spouse and dependents. This is important because if a claimant is found disabled, her monthly benefit amount is larger when she has dependents.

Ms. Lewis agrees in the application to give the SSA permission to contact her employers. This may be necessary if there is some question as to when she stopped working or if her earnings record appears to be incorrect and further information about past wages is needed. Ms. Lewis also agrees to provide medical evidence about her condition and authorizes the SSA to obtain information from physicians and hospitals where she has received treatment. This is necessary in order to develop the medical evidence. Ms. Lewis also agrees that information may be released to the State Disability Determination Services (the state agency). The role that the state agency plays in determining whether claimants are disabled is discussed below.

Next Ms. Lewis agrees to notify the SSA if certain events occur. These are events that could show that Ms. Lewis either is not disabled or is not entitled to benefits. For instance, if she returns to work and engages in substantial gainful activity, she may not be disabled. Imprisonment for conviction of a felony is important because the regulations preclude payment of benefits for any month in which a person is confined to jail for a conviction of a felony (20 CFR 404.468).

Next, Ms. Lewis agrees to inform the SSA if she becomes entitled to or stops receiving a pension or annuity from a source other than Social Security. This is important because some government pensions are an offset to Social Security benefits.

Finally, Ms. Lewis acknowledges that she has been informed of her responsibility to report certain events to the SSA. She further acknowledges that the information she has given is true and that she has been informed that giving false information is a federal crime. The application then states her address and telephone number. Ms. Lewis signs and dates the application. Now the SSA has the basic information needed to begin processing Ms. Lewis's application and permission needed to obtain further information from her doctors and former employers.

Forms that Must Be Filed with the Application

After examining the information on the application, you may think back to the factors considered in the sequential evaluation process and note that certain information is not covered on the application. For instance, the exertional requirements of the claimant's past relevant work are not described. This is critical in determining whether a claimant is disabled. Further, while the application gave the SSA permission to obtain information from doctors who have treated the claimant, the application does not reflect the names and addresses of the doctors. Other forms are necessary to provide this important information.

Disability Report

An important form that the claimant completes when applying is the Disability Report (Form SSA 3368). (Throughout the discussion of the Disability Report, refer to Appendix B, where Melinda Lewis's Disability Report is illustrated.) Part I gathers more information about Ms. Lewis's medical condition, especially the functional restrictions that her impairments cause and when her impairments finally made her stop working. The date that the claimant's condition first bothered her and the date that she finally had to stop working (questions 1 and 3A) are the same in some cases, such as when disability is due to a heart attack or injuries in a car accident. Some people, however, work for years after a heart attack or after their back starts hurting. If these dates are different, paralegals should question the client so that the difference in the dates can be explained. Paralegals should pay particular attention to the date given in question 3A, because claimants may attempt to work after their alleged onset date but be unable to sustain the work because of their impairments. Suppose that Melinda Lewis attempted to return to her job as a cashier in July 1992, but was able to work for only two days because of her impairments. This would be an unsuccessful work attempt, not substantial gainful activity. She may, however, have put July 12, 1992, instead of March 1, 1992, as the answer to question 3A. This would require an explanation so that it would not appear that Ms. Lewis worked continuously as a cashier until July 12, 1992.

SIDEBAR   Remember that the attorney-paralegal team generally is not involved when a claimant fills out the application and Disability Report. Paralegals should be alert for any discrepancies in dates and for work activity after the alleged onset date when representation is undertaken and they are reviewing clients' documents.

Part II is a straightforward section. Claimants supply the names and addresses of doctors who have treated them and the names and addresses of hospitals and clinics where they have been treated, together with the dates of treatment. Question 8 asks whether claimants have undergone certain types of tests. This information must be gathered by the SSA so that the claimant's medical condition can be assessed.

Part III requests information about Ms. Lewis's daily activities. The purpose of this section is to find out what types of activities she can no longer perform because of her medical condition. Question 11 requires special attention when paralegals are reviewing claimants' files. Ms. Lewis may state that she cooks, cleans, and shops for groceries, without further explanation. In fact, she may cook only once a week and then prepare a sandwich and soup. She may clean one room in the house per week and have to rest after fifteen minutes, or she may be able to wash dishes but not push a vacuum cleaner. Ms. Lewis may state that she continues to drive, but she may be able to sit for only fifteen minutes at a time due to back pain and thus may drive only when she has to go to the doctor or the pharmacy. Paralegals must be careful in reviewing the claimant's daily activities prior to hearings with administrative law judges so that any discrepancies between statements in the Disability Report and in the claimant's actual daily activities can be explained at the hearing.

Part IV provides information about Ms. Lewis's formal schooling and any other special training she received. Part V describes Ms. Lewis's jobs performed during the past fifteen years. Recall from Chapter 3 that jobs are considered past relevant work only if they were performed within the past fifteen years. Question 15C asks about the physical requirements of Ms. Lewis's past work. These answers indicate the exertional level (sedentary, light, and so forth) at which the claimant's past work was performed. Refer to Ms. Lewis's Disability Report, which shows that her past work as a cashier required lifting up to twenty pounds at a time and standing seven hours a day. When claimants have held several jobs, part VI can be used for additional information, and additional sheets may be necessary to explain adequately the physical requirements of each job.

Part VII is completed by the SSA employee who takes the information about the claimant. Note that in question 18 the SSA employee describes anything unusual observed about the claimant, such as whether she had to stand up during the thirty minutes they spent together because her back hurt or if the claimant displayed any unusual behavior that may indicate a mental impairment.

Authorizations to Release Information

Claimants sign several authorizations to allow doctors and hospitals to release information about them. The form is SSA-827, entitled "Authorization for Source to Release Information to the Social Security Administration (SSA)." Recall from your study of civil procedure and evidence that information exchanged between doctors and patients is privileged. Thus, doctors will not release patients' medical records without the patients' written consent. The SSA, in turn, is bound to protect the medical records from disclosure because of the requirements of the Privacy Act. There are certain exceptions, allowing limited disclosure to other agencies, described in the Privacy Act Notice on the back of the authorization form.

Procedures for Filing an Application for Naturalization

The application for naturalization differs in many respects from the application for Social Security disability and thus serves as a useful example of a different type of application for a benefit from an administrative agency. The application for naturalization is longer and more detailed. It contains many questions regarding grounds that can serve as a basis for denial of the application. A filing fee, photographs of the applicant, and fingerprint cards must accompany the application, requirements not encountered with applications for Social Security disability benefits.

In contrast to applications for Social Security disability benefits, the attorney-paralegal team is usually involved with actual preparation of clients' naturalization applications. Applicants who seek legal representation usually hire an attorney as they prepare to file for naturalization.

Where to File the Naturalization Application

The naturalization application must be filed in the INS office that has jurisdiction over the applicant's place of residence. The attorney-paralegal team must know which INS office has jurisdiction over the geographical area in which its client resides. In comparison to the jurisdiction of SSA offices, which may cross state lines, the bounds of jurisdiction of INS offices frequently do not cross state lines. Thus, a person who resides in Rock Hill, South Carolina, just a few miles from the INS office in Charlotte, North Carolina, may have to file applications and attend interviews at an INS office in South Carolina, much farther from his home.

SIDEBAR   Different types of immigration applications may have to be filed at different INS offices or processing centers, so the attorney-paralegal team must keep abreast of the sometimes complicated filing procedures.

The Content of the Naturalization Application

The information requested on Form N-400 is not difficult to understand. Paralegal students may, however, wonder why some of the information is needed and why certain questions are asked. As you examine Form N-400, refer back to Chapter 4 and review the substantive law of naturalization. This explains, for instance, why the form asks whether an applicant has ever practiced polygamy; the law requires that an applicant have good moral character, and the Immigration and Nationality Act provides that a person who has practiced polygamy cannot be found to have good moral character.

It is often the task of paralegals to go over Form N-400 with clients and to obtain or verify the required information. Form N-400 directly reflects the statutory and regulatory requirements for naturalization. Therefore, the text notes the sections of the application where paralegals should be particularly alert for potential problems with eligibility for naturalization. Refer to Figure 7–5, which illustrates the application of Ms. Garcia's client, Massoud Kazemi, and to Sample Case 3, which states the pertinent facts regarding Mr. Kazemi.

In Part 2, check to ensure that the applicant has in fact been a lawful permanent resident for five years, three years if he became a permanent resident based on marriage to a United States citizen. Paralegals do not want the clients to file applications prematurely.

In Part 3, note that the applicant is a citizen of the country that issued his current passport. The section on absences from the United States can alert paralegals to problems with the residence and physical presence requirements discussed in Chapter 4. Paralegals should be alert for absences of more than six months, and especially absences of more than one year. Further, if the applicant has been absent from the United States for extended periods, add up the total months the applicant was absent to be sure that the applicant meets the requirement that he was physically present for at least one-half of the required five-year residency period (three years for spouses of United States citizens). Paralegals should review the applicant's passport to double check dates that the applicant entered and exited foreign countries.

FIGURE 7–5
Massoud
Kazemi's
Application for
Naturalization

U.S. Department of Justice
Immigration and Naturalization Service

OMB #1115-0009
Application for Naturalization

START HERE - Please Type or Print

FOR INS USE ONLY

Part 1.   Information about you.

Family Name	Given Name	Middle Initial
Kazemi	Massoud	NMN

U.S. Mailing Address - Care of

Street Number and Name	Apt. #
11509 Winding Way	

City	County
Charlotte	Mecklenburg

State	ZIP Code
North Carolina	28226

Date of Birth (month/day/year)	Country of Birth
06/03/58	Iran

Social Security #	A #
000-00-0000	00 000 000

Returned	Receipt
Resubmitted	
Reloc Sent	
Reloc Rec'd	
☐ Applicant Interviewed	
At Interview ☐ request naturalization ceremony at court	
Remarks	

Part 2.   Basis for Eligibility *(check one).*

a. ☒ I have been a permanent resident for at least five (5) years.
b. ☐ I have been a permanent resident for at least three (3) years and have been married to a United States Citizen for those three years.
c. ☐ I am a permanent resident child of United States citizen parent(s).
d. ☐ I am applying on the basis of qualifying military service in the Armed Forces of the U.S. and have attached completed Forms N-426 and G-325B
e. ☐ Other. (Please specify section of law)_____.

Part 3.   Additional information about you.

Date you became a permanent resident (month/day/year)	Port admitted with an immigrant visa or INS Office where granted adjustment of status.
02/04/86	Charlotte, NC

Citizenship
    Iran

Name on alien registration card (if different than in Part 1)
    same as above

Other names used since you became a permanent resident (including maiden name)
    none

Sex ☒ Male ☐ Female	Height 5' 9"	Marital Status:	☐ Single ☒ Married	☐ Divorced ☐ Widowed

Can you speak, read and write English ?   ☐ No ☒ Yes.

Absences from the U.S.:

Have you been absent from the U.S. since becoming a permanent resident?   ☐ No ☒ Yes.

If you answered "Yes" , complete the following. Begin with your most recent absence. If you need more room to explain the reason for an absence or to list more trips, continue on separate paper.

Date left U.S.	Date returned	Did absence last 6 months or more?	Destination	Reason for trip
5/5/90	6/5/90	☐ Yes ☒ No	London	vacation
8/6/91	12/6/91	☐ Yes ☒ No	Dusseldorf	business
		☐ Yes ☐ No		
		☐ Yes ☐ No		
		☐ Yes ☐ No		
		☐ Yes ☐ No		

Action

To Be Completed by
Attorney or Representative, if any

☐ Fill in box if G-28 is attached to represent the applicant

VOLAG#

ATTY State License #

Form N-400 (Rev. 07/17/91)N   *Continued on back*

Part 4. Information about your residences and employment.

A. List your addresses during the last five (5) years or since you became a permanent resident, whichever is less. Begin with your current address. If you need more space, continue on separate paper:

Street Number and Name, City, State, Country, and Zip Code	Dates (month/day/year) From	To
11509 Winding Way Charlotte, NC 28226	10/1/84	present
1611 Bay St., Apt. 4 Charlotte, NC 28212	9/3/81	10/1/84

B. List your employers during the last five (5) years. List your present or most recent employer first. If none, write "None". If you need more space, continue on separate paper.

Employer's Name	Employer's Address Street Name and Number - City, State and ZIP Code	Dates Employed (month/day/year) From	To	Occupation/position
Chaco Corp.	3300 West Ave.,Charlotte, NC28227	3/10/86	present	research chemist
ABC Specialty Chemicals	1100 Steele Rd.,Charlotte, NC28227	1/3/85	3/10/86	chemical technician

Part 5. Information about your marital history.

A. Total number of times you have been married ___1___ . If you are now married, complete the following regarding your husband or wife.

Family name Kazemi	Given name Nancy	Middle initial E.

Address 11509 Winding Way Charlotte, NC 28226

Date of birth (month/day/year) 12/12/58	Country of birth Iran	Citizenship Iran
Social Security # 000-00-0000	A# (if applicable) 00 000 000	Immigration status (if not a U.S. citizen) permanent resident

Naturalization (If applicable)
(month/day/year)   N/A   Place   (City, State)

If you have ever previously been married or if your current spouse has been previously married, please provide the following on separate paper: Name of prior spouse, date of marriage, date marriage ended, how marriage ended and immigration status of prior spouse.

Part 6. Information about your children.

B. Total Number of Children ___0___ . Complete the following information for each of your children. If the child lives with you, state "with me" in the address column; otherwise give city/state/country of child's current residence. If deceased, write "deceased" in the address column. If you need more space, continue on separate paper.

Full name of child	Date of birth	Country of birth	Citizenship	A - Number	Address

Form N-400 (Rev. 07/17/91)N   *Continued on next page*

Continued on back

Part 7. Additional eligibility factors.

Please answer each of the following questions. If your answer is "Yes", explain on a separate paper.

1. Are you now, or have you ever been a member of, or in any way connected or associated with the Communist Party, or ever knowingly aided or supported the Communist Party directly, or indirectly through another organization, group or person, or ever advocated, taught, believed in, or knowingly supported or furthered the interests of communism? ☐ Yes ☒ No

2. During the period March 23, 1933 to May 8, 1945, did you serve in, or were you in any way affiliated with, either directly or indirectly, any military unit, paramilitary unit, police unit, self-defence unit, vigilante unit, citizen unit of the Nazi party or SS, government agency or office, extermination camp, concentration camp, prisoner of war camp, prison, labor camp, detention camp or transit camp, under the control or affiliated with:
   a. The Nazi Government of Germany? ☐ Yes ☒ No
   b. Any government in any area occupied by, allied with, or established with the assistance or cooperation of, the Nazi Government of Germany? ☐ Yes ☒ No

3. Have you at any time, anywhere, ever ordered, incited, assisted, or otherwise participated in the persecution of any person because of race, religion, national origin, or political opinion? ☐ Yes ☒ No

4. Have you ever left the United States to avoid being drafted into the U.S. Armed Forces? ☐ Yes ☒ No

5. Have you ever failed to comply with Selective Service laws? ☐ Yes ☒ No
   If you have registered under the Selective Service laws, complete the following information:
   Selective Service Number:_____ Date Registered:_____
   If you registered before 1978, also provide the following:
   Local Board Number:_____ Classification:_____

6. Did you ever apply for exemption from military service because of alienage, conscientious objections or other reasons? ☐ Yes ☒ No

7. Have you ever deserted from the military, air or naval forces of the United States? ☐ Yes ☒ No

8. Since becoming a permanent resident , have you ever failed to file a federal income tax return? ☐ Yes ☒ No

9. Since becoming a permanent resident , have you filed a federal income tax return as a nonresident or failed to file a federal return because you considered yourself to be a nonresident? ☐ Yes ☒ No

10. Are deportation proceedings pending against you, or have you ever been deported, or ordered deported, or have you ever applied for suspension of deportation? ☐ Yes ☒ No

11. Have you ever claimed in writing, or in any way, to be a United States citizen? ☐ Yes ☒ No

12. Have you ever:
   a. been a habitual drunkard? ☐ Yes ☒ No
   b. advocated or practiced polygamy? ☐ Yes ☒ No
   c. been a prostitute or procured anyone for prostitution? ☐ Yes ☒ No
   d. knowingly and for gain helped any alien to enter the U.S. illegally? ☐ Yes ☒ No
   e. been an illicit trafficker in narcotic drugs or marijuana? ☐ Yes ☒ No
   f. received income from illegal gambling? ☐ Yes ☒ No
   g. given false testimony for the purpose of obtaining any immigration benefit? ☐ Yes ☒ No

13. Have you ever been declared legally incompetent or have you ever been confined as a patient in a mental institution? ☐ Yes ☒ No

14. Were you born with, or have you acquired in same way, any title or order of nobility in any foreign State? ☐ Yes ☒ No

15. Have you ever:
   a. knowingly committed any crime for which you have not been arrested? ☐ Yes ☒ No
   b. been arrested, cited, charged, indicted, convicted, fined or imprisoned for breaking or violating any law or ordinance excluding traffic regulations? ☐ Yes ☒ No

(If you answer yes to 15 , in your explanation give the following information for each incident or occurrence the **city, state,** and **country,** where the offense took place, the **date** and **nature** of the offense, and the **outcome** or **disposition** of the case).

Part 8. Allegiance to the U.S.

If your answer to any of the following questions is "NO", attach a full explanation:
1. Do you believe in the Constitution and form of government of the U.S.? ☒ Yes ☐ No
2. Are you willing to take the full Oath of Allegiance to the U.S.? (see instructions) ☒ Yes ☐ No
3. If the law requires it, are you willing to bear arms on behalf of the U.S.? ☒ Yes ☐ No
4. If the law requires it, are you willing to perform noncombatant services in the Armed Forces of the U.S.? ☒ Yes ☐ No
5. If the law requires it, are you willing to perform work of national importance under civilian direction? ☒ Yes ☐ No

Form N-400 (Rev. 07/17/91)N   *Continued on back*

Part 9. Memberships and organizations.

A. List your present and past membership in or affiliation with every organization, association, fund, foundation, party, club, society, or similar group in the United States or in any other place. Include any military service in this part. If none, write "none". Include the name of organization, location, dates of membership and the nature of the organization. If additional space is needed, use separate paper.

Students for Iran, Iran, 1979-1981

American Association of Textile Chemists, U.S.A.   March 1986-present

Part 10. Complete only if you checked block " C " in Part 2.

How many of your parents are U.S. citizens?   ☐ One   ☐ Both   (Give the following about one U.S. citizen parent:)

Family Name	Given Name	Middle Name

Address

Basis for citizenship:	Relationship to you (check one): ☐ natural parent ☐ adoptive parent
☐ Birth	
☐ Naturalization Cert. No.	☐ parent of child legitimated after birth

If adopted or legitimated after birth, give date of adoption or, legitimation: *(month/day/year)* _____ .

Does this parent have legal custody of you?   ☐ Yes   ☐ No

(Attach a copy of relating evidence to establish that you are the child of this U.S. citizen and evidence of this parent's citizenship.)

Part 11. Signature.   *(Read the information on penalties in the instructions before completing this section).*

I certify or, if outside the United States, I swear or affirm, under penalty of perjury under the laws of the United States of America that this application, and the evidence submitted with it, is all true and correct. I authorize the release of any information from my records which the Immigration and Naturalization Service needs to determine eligibility for the benefit I am seeking.

Signature   *Massoud Kazemi*   Date *April 12, 1994*

Please Note: If you do not completely fill out this form, or fail to submit required documents listed in the instructions, you may not be found eligible for naturalization and this application may be denied.

Part 12. Signature of person preparing form if other than above. *(Sign below)*

I declare that I prepared this application at the request of the above person and it is based on all information of which I have knowledge.

Signature   *Susan Garcia*   Print Your Name *Susan Garcia*   Date *April 12, 1994*

Firm Name and Address   McKethan and Garcia
77 West McDowell St.
Charlotte, NC   28202

DO NOT COMPLETE THE FOLLOWING UNTIL INSTRUCTED TO DO SO AT THE INTERVIEW

I swear that I know the contents of this application, and supplemental pages 1 through_____ , that the corrections , numbered 1 through_____ , were made at my request, and that this amended application, is true to the best of my knowledge and belief.

Subscribed and sworn to before me by the applicant.

_____
(Examiner's Signature)   Date

_____
(Complete and true signature of applicant)

Form N-400 (Rev. 07/17/91)N

In Parts 5 and 6, check that the applicant's spouse and all children are listed, even if they are already United States citizens. Part 7 deserves special attention. If the answer to any of these questions is "yes," the applicant may not be eligible for naturalization. Recall from the discussion in Chapter 4 that there are many classes of people barred from naturalization, such as anarchists, persons who have deserted the United States armed forces, and persons who are under a deportation order. However unlikely it seems that the client may have been affiliated with the Nazi party during the specified period (question 2) or may hold a title of nobility in a foreign state (question 14), ask the client every question as you go over Form N-400. Part 8 addresses the requirement of attachment to the principles of the United States Constitution and favorable disposition to the good order and happiness of the United States, a requirement specified in 8 U.S.C. § 1427(a).

In Part 9, paralegals should be alert for membership in any anarchist or communist organizations, because this raises eligibility problems. Finally, be sure that the client signs and dates the application and is aware that his signature certifies that the information in the application is true and correct.

Documents that Must Accompany the Application

The instructions that come with the N-400 describe the documents that must accompany the application. The regulations (8 CFR 316.4) also describe the required documents. Refer to Figure 7–6, which reprints 8 CFR 316.4. First, the applicant must submit his alien registration card, which is another name for the green card (INS Form I-151). Second, the applicant must submit two photographs, and the photographs must meet all the listed requirements. The INS will only accept photographs that meet these exact specifications. Third, the applicant must submit fingerprints on the specified form—Form FD-258. The fingerprint charts are used to conduct checks of the applicant's background for possible criminal convictions or other grounds that may be a basis for mandatory denial of the application. Finally, the applicant must include a check or money order for the $90 filing fee.

FIGURE 7–6
8 CFR 316.4:
Documents to
File with
Application for
Naturalization

> **§ 316.4 Application; documents.**
>
> (a) The applicant shall apply for naturalization by filing:
> (1) Form N-400 (Application for Naturalization);
> (2) Evidence of lawful permanent residence in the United States in the form of photocopies (front and back) of Forms I-551, or I-151 (Alien Registration Receipt Card), or any other entry document;

FIGURE 7–6
(continued)

(3) Form FD-258 (Fingerprint Card); and

(4) Three (3) photographs as described in § 333.1 of this chapter.

(b) At the time of the examination on the application for naturalization, the applicant may be required to establish the status of lawful permanent resident by submitting the original evidence, issued by the Service, of lawful permanent residence in the United States. The applicant may be also required to submit any passports, or any other documents that have been used to enter the United States at any time after the original admission for permanent residence.

Paralegals must check all the documents, in addition to the N-400, to ensure that all required documents are included and are filled out completely and correctly. The INS rejects applications that are not signed or not accompanied by the proper filing fee. Applications can be corrected, but they are not considered filed until they are complete and meet the requirements established by the INS.

Appeals Procedures for Social Security Disability Benefits and for Naturalization

From the moment that the attorney-paralegal team begins representation of a client in connection with an application for Social Security disability benefits, naturalization, or any other claim before an administrative agency, the team must keep in mind the proper appeal procedures. It is not uncommon for agencies to deny an application, necessitating an appeal. The denial rate is higher for some types of applications than for others. For instance, the percentage of denial of naturalization applications is generally low. This is not surprising when you consider that the applicant has already completed the process for becoming a lawful permanent resident of the United States. In contrast, the percentage of denials of applications for Social Security disability benefits at the initial level is high, and appeals are quite common.

How to Appeal Denials of Applications for Social Security Disability Benefits

The procedure for appealing unfavorable determinations for applications for Social Security Disability benefits is set forth in part 404, subpart J of the Social Security regulations. The regulations provide a multistep appeal procedure, and claimants must follow each step in the prescribed order and must adhere to the prescribed deadlines. The regulations (20 CFR 404.900(a)) give an excellent overview of the nature of the administrative appeal procedure. The regulations state that

> [t]his subpart explains the procedure we follow in determining your rights under Title II of the Social Security Act. The regulations describe the process of administrative review and explain your right to judicial review after you have taken all the necessary administrative steps. . . . The administrative review process consists of several steps which usually must be requested within certain time periods and in the following order . . . .

Throughout the discussion of the appeal procedure, refer to Figure 7–7, which outlines the steps.

FIGURE 7–7
Steps in Appealing Denials of Social Security Disability Benefits

Initial Determination

    determination is based on written record only

    ↓↓

Reconsideration Determination

    determination is based on written record only

    ↓↓

Request for Hearing

    Hearing is held before an administrative law judge in the Office of Hearings and Appeals, which is part of the Social Security Administration

    ↓↓

Appeals Council

    The last step in the appeals within the Social Security Administration. Decision is based on the entire record, including transcript of hearing before the ALJ. The Appeals Council can reverse, affirm, or remand the case.

    ↓↓

ADMINISTRATIVE APPEALS HAVE NOW BEEN EXHAUSTED

Federal Court Appeals:

United States District Court
↓↓

United States Court of Appeals
↓↓

United States Supreme Court

The Initial Determination

After a claimant has filed an application and provided the information requested, the SSA makes an initial determination as to whether the claimant is disabled within the meaning of the Social Security Act. The SSA examines the claimant's application, Disability Report, and medical records, and determines whether the claimant is disabled within the meaning of the Social Security Act. The initial determination is made strictly by examining the written evidence of record. Doctors and agency employees review the documentary evidence, but there is no opportunity for a hearing at this level.

Use of the Sequential Evaluation Process. The SSA uses the five-step sequential evaluation process to make the initial determination. If the initial determination is unfavorable and the claimant appeals, the SSA uses the sequential evaluation process for every stage of administrative appeals. If the claimant appeals to the federal courts, the federal court judges also use the five-step sequential evaluation process.

Written Notice of Denial. Assume that the SSA has made an initial determination that Melinda Lewis is not disabled. The SSA determined that Ms. Lewis retains a residual functional capacity for light work. Her past relevant work as a cashier was performed at the light exertional level. Thus, the SSA determined that Ms. Lewis is not precluded from performing her past relevant work. Accordingly, the SSA found Ms. Lewis not to be disabled.

Ms. Lewis now receives written notice of the denial. The SSA's regulations (20 CFR 404.904) require written notice of the initial determination. The regulations state that "[t]he reasons for the initial determination and the effect of the initial determination will be stated in the notice. The notice also informs you of the right to a reconsideration."

The notice of an unfavorable initial determination typically gives a short, general explanation why the claimant was found not to be disabled, usually about one-half page in length. This stands in contrast to a decision issued by an administrative law judge, which typically provides a multipage rationale explaining why a claimant is found to be not disabled.

The Reconsideration Determination

Melinda Lewis wishes to appeal the denial of her application. Therefore, she pursues the first step in the administrative appeal process—reconsideration.

The regulations (20 CFR 404.909) explain that the request for reconsideration must be in writing. Further, the request must be filed within sixty days after the date that the claimant receives notice of the initial determination. The SSA has a standard form for requesting reconsideration (Form SSA-561-U2). Refer to Figure 7–8, which illustrates Melinda Lewis's request for reconsideration. The SSA does not require that the request for reconsideration be filed on its standard form. A handwritten request on a piece of notebook paper would be accepted. The use of approved forms, however, is the best approach.

Often claimants are not yet represented at the reconsideration level, and they may make a very general statement explaining why they disagree with the initial determination and seek reconsideration. The reason given is less important than the fact that the reconsideration request be filed in a timely manner.

The claimant has the opportunity to present additional evidence at the reconsideration level. Often claimants have updated medical evidence since the time of the initial determination, and submission of the new evidence may enhance the chances of a favorable determination at the reconsideration level. Unless there is some remarkable new evidence, the reconsideration determination is often unfavorable.

SIDEBAR   It is important for paralegals to understand that new evidence can be submitted at every step in the administrative appeal process. In fact, new evidence should be submitted at every step in order to update the claimant's medical records and to prove that the claimant meets the twelve-month duration requirement.

The SSA seeks updated information on the claimant's condition, in part through the Reconsideration Disability Report. Part I, "Information About Your Condition," asks whether the claimant's illness or injury has worsened, whether there are additional illnesses or injuries that the SSA should know about, and whether doctors have placed restrictions on the claimant since she filed her claim. Part II requests updated information on the doctors the claimant has seen and any hospitals where she has been treated. Part III asks whether the claimant has worked since filing her claim, and Part IV asks whether the claimant's activities have changed since the claim was filed. The first page of Melinda Lewis's Reconsideration Disability Report is illustrated in Figure 7–9.

FIGURE 7–8
Melinda Lewis's
Request for
Reconsideration

DEPARTMENT OF HEALTH AND HUMAN SERVICES
SOCIAL SECURITY ADMINISTRATION   TOE 710

REQUEST FOR RECONSIDERATION

(Do not wirte in this space)

The information on this form is authorized by regulation (20 CFR 404.907 – 404.921 and 416.1407 – 416.1421). While your responses to these questions is voluntary, the Social Security Administration cannot reconsider the decision on this claim unless the information is furnished.

NAME OF CLAIMANT	NAME OF WAGE EARNER OR SELF-EMPLOYED PERSON *(If different from claimant.)*
Melinda Lewis	

SOCIAL SECURITY CLAIM NUMBER	SUPPLEMENTAL SECURITY INCOME (SSI) CLAIM NUMBER
000-00-0000	

SPOUSE'S NAME *(Complete ONLY in SSI cases)*	SPOUSE'S SOCIAL SECURITY NUMBER *(Complete ONLY in SSI cases)*

CLAIM FOR *(Specify type, e.g., retirement, disability, hospital insurance, SSI, etc.)*
Title II Disability

I do not agree with the determination made on the above claim and request reconsideration. My reasons are:
I am unable to do any work because of back pain and a heart condition.

SUPPLEMENTAL SECURITY INCOME RECONSIDERATION ONLY *(See reverse of claimant's copy)*

"I want to appeal your decision about my claim for supplemental security income, SSI. I've read the back of this form about the three ways to appeal. I've checked the box below."

☐ Case Review   ☐ Informal Conference   ☐ Formal Conference

EITHER THE CLAIMANT OR REPRESENTATIVE SHOULD SIGN – ENTER ADDRESSES FOR BOTH

SIGNATURE OR NAME OF CLAIMANT'S REPRESENTATIVE	CLAIMANT SIGNATURE
☐ NON-ATTORNEY ☐ ATTORNEY	*Melinda Lewis*

STREET ADDRESS	STREET ADDRESS *202 Oak St.*

CITY	STATE	ZIP CODE	CITY *Charlotte*	STATE *NC*	ZIP CODE *28212*

TELEPHONE NUMBER *(Include area code)* (— — —)	DATE	TELEPHONE NUMBER *(Include area code)* *(704)* *555- 3524*	DATE *March 16, 1994*

TO BE COMPLETED BY SOCIAL SECURITY ADMINISTRATION

See reverse of claim folder copy for list of initial determinations

1. HAS INITIAL DETERMINATION BEEN MADE?	☐ YES ☐ NO	2. CLAIMANT INSISTS ON FILING	☐ YES ☐ NO

3. IS THIS REQUEST FILED TIMELY? *(If "NO", attach claimant's explanation for delay and attach only pertinent letter, material, or information in social security office.)*	☐ YES ☐ NO

RETIREMENT AND SURVIVORS RECONSIDERATIONS ONLY (CHECK ONE) REFER TO (GN 03102.125)	SOCIAL SECURITY OFFICE ADDRESS

☐ NO FURTHER DEVELOPMENT REQUIRED   (GN 03102.125)

☐ REQUIRED DEVELOPMENT ATTACHED

☐ REQUIRED DEVELOPMENT PENDING, WILL FORWARD OR ADVISE STATUS WITHIN 30 DAYS

ROUTING INSTRUCTIONS (CHECK ONE)	☐ DISABILITY DETERMINATION SERVICES *(ROUTE WITH DISABILITY FOLDER)*	☐ ODO, BALTIMORE	☐ PROGRAM SERVICE CENTER
	☐ INTPSC, BALTIMORE	☐ DISTRICT OFFICE RECONSIDERATION	☐ OCRO BALTIMORE

NOTE: TAKE OR MAIL COMPLETED COPIES TO YOUR SOCIAL SECURITY OFFICE

FORM **SSA-561-U2** (9-85)   **CLAIMS FOLDER**

FIGURE 7–9
First Page of
Melinda Lewis's
Reconsideration
Disability Report

DEPARTMENT OF HEALTH AND HUMAN SERVICES
Social Security Administration

Form Approved
OMB No. 0960-0144

For SSA Use Only - Do NOT Complete This Item.	
Name of Wage Earner	Social Security Number
Name of Claimant *Melinda Lewis*	Social Security Number *000–00–0000*
Type of Claim:	

Title II — ☐ Freeze ☒ DIB ☐ DWB ☐ CDB   Title XVI — ☐ Disability ☐ Blind ☐ Child

RECONSIDERATION DISABILITY REPORT

PLEASE PRINT, TYPE OR WRITE CLEARLY AND ANSWER ALL ITEMS TO THE BEST OF YOUR ABILITY. If you are filing on behalf of someone else, answer all questions. COMPLETE ANSWERS WILL AID IN PROCESSING THE CLAIM.

PRIVACY ACT/PAPERWORK REDUCTION ACT NOTICE: The Social Security Administration is authorized to collect the information on this form under sections 205(a), 223(d) and 1633(a) of the Social Security Act. The information on this form is needed by Social Security to make a decision on your claim. While giving us the information on this form is voluntary, failure to provide all or part of the requested information could prevent an accurate or timely decision on your claim and could result in the loss of benefits. Although the information you furnish on this form is almost never used for any purpose other than making a determination on your disability claim, such information may be disclosed by the Social Security Administration as follows: (1) To enable a third party or agency to assist Social Security in establishing rights to Social Security benefits and/or coverage; (2) to comply with Federal laws requiring the release of information from Social Security records (e.g., the General Accounting Office and the Veterans Administration); (3) to facilitate statistical research and audit activities necessary to assure the integrity and improvement of the Social Security programs (e.g., to the Bureau of the Census and private concerns under contract to Social Security). These and other reasons why information about you may be used or given out are explained in the **Federal Register**. If you would like more information about this, any Social Security office can assist you.

Date Claim Filed   *1/25/94*

PART I — INFORMATION ABOUT YOUR CONDITION

1. Has there been any change (for better or worse) in your illness or injury since you filed your claim? .... ☒ Yes   ☐ No
   If "Yes," describe any changes in your symptoms.

   I have more shortness of breath, chest pain, and back pain.

2. Describe any physical or mental limitations you have as a result of your condition since you filed your claim.

   I still cannot lift much or stand for a long time.

3. Have any restrictions been placed on you by a physician since you filed your claim? .... ☒ Yes   ☐ No
   If "Yes," give name, address, and telephone number of the physician and show what kinds of restrictions have been imposed.

   My doctors told me to rest a lot and not to lift more than 10 pounds.

4. Do you have any additional illness or injury that you feel we should know about? .... ☐ Yes   ☒ No
   If "Yes," describe the kind of illness or injury and the date that it occurred.

FORM **SSA-3441-F6** (2-88)

As with the initial determination, the reconsideration determination is based on the documentary evidence. The claimant is not interviewed or seen by the personnel who make the reconsideration determination. The *Social Security Handbook* describes the reconsideration process as "a thorough and independent reexamination of all evidence of record related to the case."[3] The *Handbook* explains that the reconsideration determination "is made by a member of a different staff from the one that made the initial determination and who is specially trained in the handling of reconsiderations."[4]

The SSA issues a written Notice of Reconsideration, stating whether or not the claimant has been found disabled at the reconsideration level. An unfavorable notice looks very much like the initial denial notice, and the explanation of why the claimant was found not to be disabled is not detailed.

The Role of the State Agency

The SSA regulations provide that individual states may request permission from the SSA to carry out disability determination functions. If permission is given, a state agency makes the initial and reconsideration determinations. The regulations (20 CFR 404.1602) define a **state agency** as "that agency of a State which has been designated by the State to carry out the disability determination function." The regulations explain the administrative duties of the state agency as follows: "The State will provide the organizational structure, qualified personnel, medical consultant services, and a quality assurance function sufficient to ensure that disability determinations are made accurately and promptly."

The state agency must comply with all applicable Social Security statutes and regulations. Further, the SSA provides standards for processing time and for accuracy with which the state agency must comply (CFR 404.1640–404.1643). If the state agency substantially fails to perform disability determination functions in accordance with the SSA's standards, then the SSA assumes the functions (20 CFR 404.1690). The SSA's regulations provide for appeals by state agencies when they are notified that the SSA has made a finding of substantial failure. This arrangement is analogous to the RCRA statute, which allows states to implement their own hazardous waste programs under the supervision of the EPA.[5]

The state agency employs disability examiners to review claimants' applications and medical records and determine whether claimants are disabled. The state agency contracts with medical and psychological

---

state agency   The agency designated by a particular state to carry out the disability determination function at the initial and reconsideration levels.

consultants who evaluate the evidence and advise the state agency whether they consider the claimant to be disabled. The medical and psychological consultants complete forms explaining their opinions regarding the claimant's residual functional capacity, and the state agency examiners use these recommendations in determining whether the claimant is disabled.

Throughout, the text refers to the SSA's determinations, but paralegals should be aware that the function of determining whether a claimant is disabled, at the initial and reconsideration levels, is often performed by the state agency on behalf of the SSA.

The state agency is responsible only for initial and reconsideration determinations. When claimants file a Request for Hearing by an administrative law judge, the file is sent to the component of the SSA called the Office of Hearings and Appeals (OHA), which is discussed in detail below.

Request for Hearing Before an Administrative Law Judge

Melinda Lewis wishes to continue her administrative appeals, and the next step is the Request for Hearing before an administrative law judge (ALJ). Often claimants do not seek representation until this step in the appeal process.

Procedure for the Request for Hearing. The regulations (20 CFR 404.933) provide that claimants must file a written Request for Hearing within sixty days of receipt of the reconsideration determination. The SSA has a standard Request for Hearing form (HA 501-U5), which is illustrated by Melinda Lewis's Request for Hearing in Figure 7–10. Claimants also file Form HA-4486, entitled "Claimant's Statement When Request for Hearing Is Filed and the Issue Is Disability." This form asks whether the claimant has worked since the date of reconsideration and also requests updated information on the claimant's condition and medical treatment.

The Office of Hearings and Appeals. The claimant's file is sent at this step of the appeal process to the Office of Hearings and Appeals (OHA). OHA has offices throughout the United States, and each office has a staff of administrative law judges (ALJs) who hear claims within their geographical region. In Florida, for instance, there are OHA offices in Tampa, Orlando, Miami, Fort Lauderdale, and Jacksonville. The ALJs conduct hearings and make decisions as to whether claimants are disabled within the meaning of the Social Security Act. The ALJs' support staff includes OHA staff attorneys in each office and considerable clerical support from OHA employees who keep the docket records updated, work up the files when they reach the office, record the hearings, type and mail decisions.

FIGURE 7–10
Melinda Lewis's
Request for
Hearing

DEPARTMENT OF HEALTH AND HUMAN SERVICES
SOCIAL SECURITY ADMINISTRATION
OFFICE OF HEARINGS AND APPEALS

Form Approved
OMB No. 0960-0269

REQUEST FOR HEARING BY ADMINISTRATIVE LAW JUDGE
[Take or mail original and all copies to your local Social Security Office]

**PRIVACY ACT NOTICE
ON REVERSE SIDE OF FORM.**

1. CLAIMANT Melinda Lewis	2. WAGE EARNER, IF DIFFERENT	3. SOC. SEC. CLAIM NUMBER 000–00–0000	SPOUSE's CLAIM NUMBER

5. I REQUEST A HEARING BEFORE AN ADMINISTRATIVE LAW JUDGE. I disagree with the determination made on my claim because:
I am unable to perform substantial gainful activity on a sustained

basis due to my multiple impairments.

You have a right to be represented at the hearing. If you are not represented but would like to be, your Social Security Office will give you a list of legal referral and service organizations. (If you are represented, complete form SSA-1696.)

An Administrative Law Judge of the Office of Hearings and Appeals will be appointed to conduct the hearing or other proceedings in your case. You will receive notice of the time and place of a hearing at least 20 days before the day set for a hearing.

6 Check one of these blocks.	7. Check one of the blocks:
☐ I have no additional evidence to submit.	☒ I wish to appear at a hearing.
☒ I have additional evidence to submit. (Please submit it to the Social Security Office within 10 days.)	☐ I do not wish to appear and I request that a decision be made based on the evidence in my case (Complete Waiver Form HA-4608)

[You should complete No. 8 and your representative (if any) should complete No. 9. If you are represented and your representative is not available to complete this form. you should also print his or her name, address, etc. in No. 9.]

8. (CLAIMANT'S SIGNATURE) *Melinda Lewis*	9. (REPRESENTATIVE'S SIGNATURE/NAME) *Susan Garcia*
ADDRESS 202 Oak St.	(ADDRESS) ☒ ATTORNEY; ☐ NON ATTORNEY 77 West McDowell St.
CITY STATE ZIP CODE Charlotte, NC 28212	CITY STATE ZIP CODE Charlotte, NC 28202
DATE AREA CODE AND TELEPHONE NUMBER 704–555–3524	DATE AREA CODE AND TELEPHONE NUMBER 704–555–5210

TO BE COMPLETED BY SOCIAL SECURITY ADMINISTRATION—ACKNOWLEDGMENT OF REQUEST FOR HEARING

10.
Request for Hearing RECEIVED for the Social Security Administration on _____ by: _____

(TITLE)	ADDRESS	·	Servicing FO Code	PC Code

11.
☐ Request timely filed

☐ Request not timely filed-Attach (1) claimant's explanation for delay, (2) any pertinent letter, material, or information in the Social/Security Office.

12. Claimant not represented –
☐ list of legal referral and service organizations provided

13. Interpreter needed –
☐ enter language (including sign language): _____

14.
Check one: ☐ Initial Entitlement Case
☐ Disability Cessation Case
☐ Other Postentitlement Case

15.
Check claim type(s):
☐ RSI only . . . . (RSI)
☐ Disability—worker or child only . . . . (DIWC)
☐ Disability—Widow(er) only . . . . (DIWW)
☐ SSI Aged only . . . . (SSIA)
☐ SSI Blind only . . . . (SSIB)
☐ Disability only . . . . (SSID)
☐ SSI Aged/Title II . . . . (SSAC)
☐ SSI Blind/Title II . . . . (SSBC)
☐ SSI Disability/Title II . . . . (SSDC)
☐ HI Entitlement . . . . (HIE)
☐ Other—Specify: (_____)

16.
HO COPY SENT TO: _____ HO on _____.
☐ CF Attached: ☐ Title II; ☐ Title XVI; or
☐ Title II CF held in FO to establish CAPS ORBIT; or
☐ CF requested: ☐ Title II; ☐ Title XVI
(Copy of teletype or phone report attached).

17.
CF COPY SENT TO: _____ HO on _____.
☐ CF attached: ☐ Title II; ☐ Title XVI
☐ Other attached _____

FORM **HA-501-U5** (5-88)
Issue old stock

CLAIMS FOLDER

The hearing before an ALJ is a formal adjudication, and Chapter 8 discusses preparation for hearing and ALJs' written decisions in detail. For now, it is sufficient to know that OHA notifies claimants when it receives their files. Attorneys and paralegals should notify OHA when they represent a claimant by filing Form 1696, which is illustrated in Figure 7–11. Then OHA will send copies of all correspondence and will contact you directly, as the claimant's representative, if additional information is needed. As soon as the file is ready, paralegals should go to the OHA office and make a copy of the claimant's file in order to review the evidence and to begin immediately to obtain any additional medical evidence that may be needed.

After the hearing, the ALJ issues a written decision explaining in detail why the claimant is found to be disabled or not disabled. If the ALJ decision is unfavorable, the claimant may pursue the last step in the administrative appeal process—the Appeals Council.

Request for Review Before the Appeals Council

The Appeals Council is located in Arlington, Virginia, and hears the appeals of ALJ decisions nationwide. The Appeals Council consists of administrative appeal judges, who review the ALJs' decisions.

Procedure for Requesting Review Before the Appeals Council. To request Appeals Council review, the claimant must file a written request within sixty days of receipt of the ALJ's decision. The regulations (20 CFR 404.968) provide that the written request may be mailed directly to the Appeals Council or filed in an SSA office, including an OHA office.

There is a standard Request for Review form (HA 520-U5). Typically, representatives attach to the form a letter or brief explaining why the Appeals Council should grant the request for review. Such a letter or brief delineates the errors allegedly made by the ALJ. Representatives are also allowed to submit new evidence, and if important medical evidence becomes available after the ALJ decision, the new evidence should definitely be sent along with the Request for Review.

Review on Its Own Motion. The regulations provide that the Appeals Council may review an ALJ's decision even if the claimant does not request review (20 CFR 404.969). This is generally referred to as "own motion review," and must be initiated by the Appeals Council within sixty days of the date of the ALJ's decision. The Appeals Council notifies all parties when it initiates an own motion review. The Appeals Council may initiate own motion review of both favorable and unfavorable ALJ decisions.

FIGURE 7–11
Appointment of
Representative
Form

DEPARTMENT OF
HEALTH AND HUMAN SERVICES
SOCIAL SECURITY ADMINISTRATION

NAME (Claimant) (Print or Type)	SOCIAL SECURITY NUMBER
Melinda Lewis	000–00–0000
WAGE EARNER (if different)	SOCIAL SECURITY NUMBER

Section I   APPOINTMENT OF REPRESENTATIVE

I appoint this individual _Susan Garcia_

(Name and Address)

to act as my representative in connection with my claim or asserted right under:

[XX] Title II (RSDI)   [ ] Title XVI (SSI)   [ ] Title IV FMSHA (Black Lung)   [ ] Title XVIII (Medicare Coverage)

I authorize this individual to make or give any request or notice; to present or elicit evidence; to obtain information; and to receive any notice in connection with my pending claim or asserted right wholly in my stead.

SIGNATURE (Claimant)	ADDRESS 202 Oak St.
Melinda Lewis	Charlotte, NC 28212
TELEPHONE NUMBER	DATE
(Area Code) 704–555–3524	*April 12, 1994*

Section II   ACCEPTANCE OF APPOINTMENT

I, _Susan Garcia_ , hereby accept the above appointment. I certify that I have not been suspended or prohibited from practice before the Social Security Administration; that I am not, as a current or former officer or employee of the United States, disqualified from acting as the claimant's representative; and that I will not charge or receive any fee for the representation unless it has been authorized in accordance with the laws and regulations referred to on the reverse side hereof. In the event that I decide not to charge or collect a fee for the representation, I will notify the Social Security Administration. (Completion of Section III satisfies this requirement.)

I am a / an _Attorney_

(Attorney, union representative, relative, law student, etc.)

SIGNATURE (Representative)	ADDRESS 77 West McDowell
Susan Garcia	Charlotte, NC 28202
TELEPHONE NUMBER	DATE
(Area code) 704–555–5210	*april 12, 1994*

Section III (Optional)   WAIVER OF FEE

I waive my right to charge and collect a fee under Section 206 of the Social Security Act, and I release my client (the claimant) from any obligations, contractual or otherwise, which may be owed to me for services I have performed in connection with my client's claim or asserted right.

SIGNATURE (Representative)	DATE

WAIVER OF DIRECT PAYMENT

I ONLY waive my right to direct certification of a fee from the withheld past-due benefits of my client (the claimant). I do NOT, however, waive my right to petition for and be authorized to charge and collect a fee directly from my client.

SIGNATURE (Representative)	DATE

Form SSA-1696-U4 (3-88)   *(See Important Information on Reverse)*   FILE COPY

Grounds for Granting the Request for Review. The Appeals Council may either accept or decline a request for review. The grounds that support review are set forth in 20 CFR 404.970, which is reprinted in Figure 7–12. If the Appeals Council decides to review a case, it sends notice to all parties.

FIGURE 7–12
20 CFR 404.970:
Cases that the
Appeals Council
Will Review

---

§ 404.970   Cases the Appeals Council will review.

(a) The Appeals Council will review a case if—
(1) There appears to be an abuse of discretion by the administrative law judge;
(2) There is an error of law;
(3) The action, findings or conclusions of the administrative law judge are not supported by substantial evidence; or
(4) There is a broad policy or procedural issue that may affect the general public interest.

(b) If new and material evidence is submitted, the Appeals Council shall consider the additional evidence only where it relates to the period on or before the date of the administrative law judge hearing decision. The Appeals Council shall evaluate the entire record including the new and material evidence submitted if it relates to the period on or before the date of the administrative law judge hearing decision. It will then review the case if it finds that the administrative law judge's action, findings, or conclusion is contrary to the weight of the evidence currently of record.

Procedure After the Request for Review Is Granted. Representatives may request an opportunity for oral argument, but this is generally granted only when a significant question of law or policy is at issue (20 CFR 404.976(c)). Most frequently, the Appeals Council members, sitting in two-member panels, review the documentary evidence and then issue a written decision explaining their action and the basis therefor.

Actions that the Appeals Council May Take. The Appeals Council may remand the case to the ALJ with instructions, such as instructions to hold another hearing to obtain the testimony of a vocational expert. The Appeals Council sometimes remands cases with instructions to obtain additional medical evidence from treating physicians or to obtain consultative examinations. When a case is remanded, the ALJ holds another hearing and issues a new decision, following the instructions given by the Appeals Council.

The Appeals Council may uphold (affirm) the ALJ's decision. If the Appeals Council affirms the ALJ's decision, notice is sent to the claimant and the claimant's representative, and the notice explains the right to appeal to the federal court.

The Appeals Council may issue an outright reversal, finding that the claimant is disabled and should begin receiving benefits. Outright reversals have been uncommon in recent years.

Federal Court Appeals

After the Appeals Council issues an unfavorable decision, the claimant has exhausted administrative remedies. Now the claimant may file an action in the federal district court. If unsuccessful with the federal trial court, the claimant may then appeal to the Circuit Court of Appeals and, if that appeal is unsuccessful, to the United States Supreme Court. Chapter 9 addresses the federal court appeal process in the discussion of judicial review.

Good Cause for Missing the SSA's Filing Deadlines

Claimants and their representatives should make every effort to file all requests at all levels of appeal in a timely manner. There are, however, instances in which the claimant cannot file a written request within the time allotted in the regulations. If the SSA determines that a claimant had good cause for late filing, the SSA may grant an extension of time. The SSA's regulations state several reasons that constitute good cause for late filing in 20 CFR 404.911, which is reprinted as Figure 7–13. Perhaps the most common reasons for late filing are that an unrepresented claimant was in the hospital or too ill to file or the claimant did not receive the notice.

FIGURE 7–13
20 CFR 404.911:
Circumstances
that May Establish
Good Cause for
Late Filing of
Appeals

> ### § 404.911   Good cause for missing the deadline to request review.
>
>   (a) In determining whether you have shown that you had good cause for missing a deadline to request review we consider—
>   (1) What circumstances kept you from making the request on time;
>   (2) Whether our action misled you;
>   (3) Whether you did not understand the requirements of the Act resulting from amendments to the Act, other legislation, or court decisions.
>   (b) Examples of circumstances where good cause may exist include, but are not limited to, the following situations:
>   (1) You were seriously ill and were prevented from contacting us in person, in writing, or through a friend, relative, or other person.
>   (2) There was a death or serious illness in your immediate family.

**FIGURE 7–13
(continued)**

(3) Important records were destroyed or damaged by fire or other accidental cause.

(4) You were trying very hard to find necessary information to support your claim but did not find the information within the stated time periods.

(5) You asked us for additional information explaining our action within the time limit, and within 60 days of receiving the explanation you requested reconsideration or a hearing, or within 30 days of receiving the explanation you requested Appeal Council review or filed a civil suit.

(6) We gave you incorrect or incomplete information about when and how to request administrative review or to file a civil suit.

(7) You did not receive notice of the determination or decision.

(8) You sent the request to another Government agency in good faith within the time limit and the request did not reach us until after the time period had expired.

(9) Unusual or unavoidable circumstances exist which show that you could not have known of the need to file timely, or which prevented you from filing timely.

The examples of good cause in 20 CFR 404.911 apply at every step of administrative appeal. The decision whether to grant an extension is made "by the office responsible for making reconsideration, the ALJ, or the Appeals Council depending upon who has jurisdiction of the case."[6] Paralegals should be alert for deadlines and ensure that clients meet the filing deadlines. If, however, a client has missed a deadline before seeking representation, it is still possible to submit a written explanation of why the deadline was missed and to receive an extension because good cause has been established.

How to Appeal Denials of Naturalization Applications

The discussion of the appeal procedures for naturalization applications is less detailed than applications for Social Security benefits. This is because denials of naturalization applications are far less common.

Administrative Remedies

After the application for naturalization is filed, an INS examiner interviews the applicant and determines whether the requirements for naturalization have been met. As noted in Chapter 4, the INS examiner tests the applicant's knowledge of United States history and government and ability to speak and write English, unless the applicant has already passed a standardized test. If, after completing the examination procedures (as prescribed in part 335 of 8 CFR), the INS determines that the naturalization application should be denied, the INS must serve written notice of the denial upon the applicant. The regulations (8 CFR 336.1(a)) require that the INS issue a decision within 120 days of the applicant's initial interview with the INS examiner. If no decision is issued within 120 days, the applicant may proceed to federal court, as discussed below.

If the INS denies the application within the 120-day period, the applicant may request a hearing before an immigration officer (8 CFR 336.2). The applicant must file his request for hearing within thirty days of receipt of the notice of denial. The INS must schedule the review hearing within "a reasonable period of time not to exceed 180 days from the date upon which the appeal is filed." The regulations require that the officer who conducts the hearing be an officer other than the one who conducted the original examination. The reviewing officer may affirm the original decision or redetermine the original in whole or in part. The regulations (8 CFR 336.2) allow the reviewing officer flexibility in conducting the review and specifically allow the officer to take new testimony and evidence and conduct a full **de novo** hearing or to use a less formal review procedure.

If the reviewing officer issues a favorable decision, there is no need for further appeals. If, however, the reviewing officer denies the application, the applicant has now exhausted administrative remedies and may file an action in federal court.

Judicial Review

There are two avenues to reach the federal courts for review of the INS action, or inaction, on an application for naturalization. First, if the decision of the INS examiner is unfavorable, and the applicant also receives an unfavorable decision from the reviewing officer, then the applicant has exhausted administrative appeals and may file an action in federal court for review of the hearing officer's decision.

The second avenue to reach federal court, as noted above, is available when the INS does not issue a decision within 120 days of the initial examination. If the INS misses this deadline, the applicant may file an action in federal court, requesting a hearing on the matter. The court "may either determine the matter or remand the matter, with appropriate instructions, to the Service to determine the matter."[7] Thus, the court may issue a favorable decision, granting the application for naturalization. In the alternative, the court may remand the case to the INS with instructions. If on remand the INS denies the application, the applicant appeals for a hearing before an immigration officer. If the

de novo   Anew; over again; a second time. USAGE: "de novo review."

hearing officer's decision is unfavorable, the applicant has exhausted administrative remedies and may file an action in federal court for review of the hearing officer's decision.

These two routes to federal court direct your attention back to a fundamental concept in administrative law—exhaustion of administrative remedies before filing actions in federal court. If the initial decision of the INS is unfavorable, the applicant must exhaust the administrative remedies by requesting a hearing before an immigration officer. The alternative route implicitly recognizes an exception to the exhaustion of administrative remedies—there is no requirement to exhaust administrative remedies if those remedies are ineffective.

SUMMARY

Chapter 7 addresses the procedure for filing applications for Social Security disability benefits and for naturalization. It also explains the procedure for appealing denials of the applications.

How to Find an Agency's Procedures

To find the procedures, paralegals look first to primary sources of law—statutes and regulations. The statutes offer little or no details, but the regulations contain the details for filing applications and for appeals. Some types of applications, such as the application for naturalization, have instructions attached that explain the procedure, including where to file and other documentation that must be attached. Some administrative agencies publish brochures or books that explain procedure. There are treatises and loose-leaf services that explain procedure and sometimes give sample forms. Associations such as the American Immigration Lawyers Association and the National Organization of Social Security Claimants' Representatives offer publications on procedure and a wide range of information, including seminar materials, which are helpful in keeping up with rapidly changing areas of law.

Procedures for Filing an Application for Social Security Disability Benefits

Subpart G of 20 CFR 404 contains the SSA's rather detailed regulations on how to file an application for disability benefits.

One requirement is that the claimant file an application. The filing date given to the application is important because the regulations allow payment of retroactive benefits for twelve months prior to the filing date. A prompt filing ensures the opportunity to receive all the months of retroactive benefits allowed. The general rule is that the filing date is the date that the application was received in an SSA office by an SSA employee. An application can be given a protective filing date if the claimant informs the SSA of his or her intent to file an application and then files the application on the prescribed form within six months of receiving the SSA's notice that it is necessary to file the actual application. With certain exceptions, in order to preserve a protective filing date, the application must be signed by the claimant and the claimant must be alive when the application is filed.

SSA regulations (20 CFR 404.610) explain the requirements that must be met for an application to be considered valid. The application must be completed and filed with the SSA, on an application form prescribed by the SSA. Limited exceptions allow filing on forms of the Veterans Administration or Railroad Retirement Act, at those agencies' offices. With certain exceptions, the application must be signed by the claimant and filed while the claimant is alive.

Claimants may file their applications in person at local SSA offices. Claimants are also allowed to give the information to an SSA employee by telephone and then to sign the application mailed to them by the employee, and mail it back to SSA.

The content of the application for Social Security disability is illustrated in Figure 7–4. Important information that the claimant must give includes the alleged onset date of disability, identification of spouse and dependent children, and disclosure of workers' compensation benefits and other benefits that are an offset to Social Security disability benefits. The claimant also agrees to inform the SSA if he or she returns to work, is imprisoned for conviction of a felony, and other events that can terminate payment of Social Security disability benefits.

With the application, the claimant files a Disability Report, which contains information on the claimant's past relevant work, sources of medical treatment, and daily activities. There is much information on the Disability Report that paralegals must review when representation is undertaken to determine whether certain information needs further explanation. The claimant also signs several forms authorizing the SSA to obtain her medical records.

Procedures for Filing an Application for Naturalization

Disability claimants often do not seek representation until well into the appeal process. In contrast, paralegals are often involved in naturalization applications from the outset, helping to prepare the forms to be filed with the INS. The application for naturalization (Form N-400) is filed in the local INS office having jurisdiction over the geographical area in which the applicant resides. Form N-400 reflects the substantive law of naturalization because the questions address the eligibility requirements, including residency in the United States for the required length of time and physical presence in the United States for the required length of time. The long list of questions in part 7 address factors that render an applicant ineligible for naturalization, such as conviction of certain crimes or membership in communist or anarchist organizations.

Together with Form N-400, the applicant must also file a copy of his or her alien registration form (green card), photographs that meet INS specifications, fingerprint cards, and the filing fee. If all these are not included, the INS will reject the application.

Appeals Procedures for Social Security Disability Benefits and for Naturalization

Applications for Social Security disability benefits are frequently denied initially, in part because it may not be clear whether the claimant will be disabled for twelve months. The percentage of denials of naturalization applications is lower, because the applicants have already completed the rather rigorous process of becoming lawful permanent residents, which detects potential ineligibility factors at an earlier stage.

After the application is filed, the SSA reviews the documentary evidence and issues an initial determination. If this is unfavorable, the SSA sends a written notice of denial briefly explaining the rationale for the denial and explaining the claimant's appeal rights. The claimant can file a request for reconsideration. At this level, the SSA again reviews the documentary evidence, and if the determination is unfavorable, sends a written notice of denial. Social Security regulations allow the SSA to contract with a state agency to make the initial and reconsideration determinations.

The next step is to file a request for hearing before an administrative law judge. This stage of the appeal is handled by the Office of Hearings and Appeals (OHA), a component of the SSA. At the hearing the claimant meets the decision maker face to face; the details of those hearings are discussed in Chapter 8. The ALJ issues a written decision. If the decision is unfavorable, the claimant may request review before the Appeals Council, which reviews ALJ decisions from across the country. If the Appeals Council reviews a case, it may affirm the decision of the ALJ or remand the case to the ALJ with instructions for further medical development and a new hearing or other instructions. Occasionally the Appeals Council reverses an ALJ decision outright and finds that the claimant is disabled and entitled to benefits. The Appeals Council occasionally reviews an ALJ decision even if no request for review has been filed; this is called "own motion review."

If the Appeals Council decision is unfavorable, the claimant has exhausted administrative remedies and may file an action in federal court. If the trial court decision is unfavorable, the decision may be appealed to the United States Circuit Court of Appeals and then to the United States Supreme Court.

An applicant for naturalization has an interview with an INS examiner to go over the application and, unless the applicant has passed the standardized tests, to test knowledge of United States government and history and knowledge of the English language. If the INS examiner has not issued a decision within 120 days of this initial interview, then the applicant may file an action in federal court. If the INS examiner issues a decision within 120 days and the decision is unfavorable, there is one level of administrative appeal—review by a review officer. The review officer is authorized to take new testimony and evidence. If the review officer's decision is unfavorable, the applicant has exhausted administrative remedies and may file an action in federal court for review of the INS decision.

REVIEW QUESTIONS

1. Which of the following may indicate a problem with eligibility for naturalization? _____
    a. membership in a communist organization
    b. an absence from the United States of four months
    c. the applicant holds a title of nobility in a foreign State.
    d. all of the above
    e. a and c only

2. What is the highest level of administrative appeal of a denial of Social Security disability? _____
   a. a hearing before an ALJ
   b. Appeals Council review
   c. reconsideration
   d. none of the above

3. Which of the following are sources for finding the procedure for filing naturalization applications? _____
   a. the instructions attached to the application
   b. the INS regulations
   c. materials published by the American Immigration Lawyers Association
   d. all of the above
   e. a and b only

4. Which of the following are claimants required to disclose to the SSA after filing their applications? _____
   a. imprisonment for conviction of a felony
   b. receipt of workers' compensation benefits
   c. a return to work which lasted several months
   d. all of the above
   e. b and c only

5. Which of the following are filed together with the application for Social Security disability benefits? _____
   a. Disability Report
   b. authorizations for doctors to release medical records
   c. $90 filing fee
   d. all of the above
   e. a and b only

6. Social Security regulations prohibit SSA employees from helping claimants complete their applications.   True ___ / False ___

7. The rationale given in the written notice of denial at the reconsideration level informs claimants of the right to appeal.   True ___ / False ___

8. The Appeals Council has the authority to reverse the decision of an ALJ and find that the claimant is disabled.   True ___ / False ___

9. The state agency is responsible only for initial and reconsideration determinations.   True ___ / False ___

10. If an INS examiner denies an application for naturalization, the regulations require written notice of denial.   True ___ / False ___

11. Describe the documents that must be filed with an application for naturalization.

12. Describe the two different ways to reach federal court for review of INS actions in regard to an application for naturalization.

PRACTICAL APPLICATIONS

Exercise 1

Susan Garcia began representing Melinda Lewis after Ms. Lewis received a notice of denial at the reconsideration level. Ms. Lewis is going to file a Request for Hearing, as shown in Figure 7–10. You have been asked to get the information from Ms. Lewis necessary to complete a form that is filed with the Request for Hearing. The blank form is in the Instructor's Guide and will be provided to you. Your interview with Ms. Lewis revealed that she has not been hospitalized since March 16, 1994, the date of her Request for Reconsideration. She has continued to see Dr. Emami and Dr. Pearson once a month. She last saw Dr. Emami on April 5, 1994, and Dr. Pearson on April 4, 1994. Ms. Lewis stated that her condition continues to deteriorate, and she has more back pain and fatigue. She does even less housework than described in her Disability Report. Ms. Lewis also reported that she tried to return to work as a cashier on March 31, 1994, but was able to work only for two days because of her impairments. Ms. Lewis forgot to bring her medications to the interview, so you will have to get this information from her later. She takes no nonprescription medications. Based on this information, complete the form entitled "CLAIMANT'S STATEMENT WHEN REQUEST FOR HEARING IS FILED AND THE ISSUE IS DISABILITY" so that it will be ready for Ms. Lewis's signature. You do not have to fill in question 7, but note in your office tickler system that you must obtain this information soon.

Exercise 2

Refer to Figure 7–5 in the text, which illustrates Massoud Kazemi's application for naturalization, and answer the following questions. You may need to refer back to Chapter 4, regarding the substantive law of naturalization.

1. Do you see any problems with Mr. Kazemi's meeting the requirement of residing for five years in the United States after he became a lawful permanent resident?

2. Do you see any problems with Mr. Kazemi's meeting the physical presence requirement?

3. Mr. Kazemi was born in 1958. Why was it necessary to answer question 2 in Part 7?

4. In Part 9, Mr. Kazemi stated that during the period 1979–1981, he belonged to an organization called Students for a Free Iran. Should paralegals find out more about this organization? Explain.

5. Do you see any unanswered questions on the N-400?

CASE ANALYSIS

Read the excerpts below from *Sinatra v. Heckler,* 566 F. Supp. 1354 (E.D.N.Y. 1983), and answer the following questions. This exercise focuses on the part of the case addressing good cause for late filing of a request for hearing in a Social Security disability appeal.

IIII ▬▬▬ IIII

Sinatra v. Heckler
566 F. Supp. 1354
(E D.N.Y. 1983)

. . .

By letter dated December 21, 1979, plaintiff was informed that his request for reconsideration had been reviewed by the state agency and the prior determination had been upheld. The letter stated that plaintiff could request a hearing before an administrative law judge "not later than *60 days from the date you receive this notice.*" (Emphasis added.)

December 21, 1979 was the Friday just before the year-end holiday period. The following Monday, December 24th, was Christmas Eve and Tuesday, December 25th, was Christmas Day. The balance of that week, Wednesday, Thursday and Friday, December 26th through December 28th, comprised the only full working days between Christmas and New Year's. Monday of the following week, December 31, 1979, was New Year's Eve. Tuesday was New Year's Day.

The court takes judicial notice that a substantial number of federal employees take vacations at this time of year and that there is a general slowing down of office operations during this period. The court also takes judicial notice that the mails are heavily burdened during and in the aftermath of the holiday season and that delivery is sometimes slowed.

Notices of denial of benefits upon reconsideration are mailed from the Bureau of Disability Determinations in Baltimore, Maryland. The Postal Service applies a two-day delivery standard from Baltimore to claimant's postal district 117 in Suffolk County. But the Post Office's Origin-Destination Information System reported that for the period December 29, 1979 through January 25, 1980,

on-time delivery to district 117 from two-day delivery areas was down to 49%, the worst on Long Island.

. . .

When plaintiff received the December 21st notice is in dispute. Plaintiff claims he received the notice on January 15, 1980. Relying on a presumption, the government contends that the letter must have been delivered on or before December 26th.

A request for a hearing was not filed until March 3, 1980, 73 days after the December 21st notice is dated. Had the letter been received on or after January 3, 1980, the request would have been timely. By decision of June 2, 1980, the hearing request was dismissed as untimely. Given the administrative presumption that a notice is received by a claimant five days after it is dated, the time to request a hearing expired on February 25th. (The sixtieth day from presumed day of receipt was February 24, 1980. Since that day was a Sunday, the request period was extended by one day pursuant to 20 C.F.R. § 404.3(c).

By order dated May 24, 1981, this court remanded the case to the Appeals Council for findings on the timeliness of plaintiff's hearing request. A hearing was held before an administrative law judge in July, 1982, at which time apparently the only evidence taken on the timeliness issue was plaintiff's testimony. A transcript of the hearing is not available. The original tape has been misplaced and a back-up tape is not accessible.

The administrative law judge, in a decision dated August 11, 1982, declared that he did not find plaintiff's arguments credible and recommended that plaintiff's hearing request be dismissed as untimely. The Appeals Council concurred by letter of December 16, 1982. A second appeal to this court followed.

. . .

These regulations are grounded in section 205(b) of the Social Security Act, which at all times relevant to this case provided that a hearing request "must be filed within sixty days after notice of such decision is received by the individual making such request."

Since the period runs from date of receipt rather than date of mailing, the Secretary has established a presumption that a notice is received five days after it is dated. At the time plaintiff received his notice of adverse determination, the regulations stated that "the date of receipt of notice of the reconsidered determination notice shall be presumed to be five days after the date of such notice, unless there is a reasonable showing to the contrary." The regulations currently offer a general definition of "Date you receive notice" as "5 days after the date on the notice, unless you show us that you did not receive it within the 5-day period."

. . .

A consideration of the position of the parties in the processing of a disability claim and the equities involved support an interpretation of the regulations that places upon a claimant only the burden of going forward with evidence rebutting the presumption of receipt. Understandably, orderly functioning of the social security office and the mails should be assumed if content is to be given to the limit on filing hearing requests within 60 days after receipt of the challenged notice. But whether a notice has been mailed on its purported date is ultimately a fact within the province of the Secretary. Since notices are given without a request for verification of delivery, it would be difficult for a claimant to prove that he did not receive a timely notice, no matter how long the mailing was deferred. To force a claimant to negotiate the bureaucratic maze of the social security and postal systems to uncover an administrative mishap would place upon him an inordinate burden. The responsibility of ultimate proof, once a claimant has presented plausible evidence to rebut the presumption of receipt, should rest with the Secretary who has easier access to whatever facts may be available.

. . .

In order to rebut the presumption that a notice of reconsideration is received five days after it is dated, the claimant must adduce evidence that would be sufficient to overcome a directed verdict for the Secretary in a jury trial. Whether the bare affidavit of the claimant that he did not receive the notice within the prescribed time would be sufficient need not now be decided. One court has held that where no copy of the notice was mailed to a claimant's attorney of record, there was no evidence in the record that a copy was mailed to the claimant, and claimant signed an affidavit of non-receipt, the presumption of receipt was rebutted.

The facts of this case are suggestive of untimely receipt. A glance at the calendar provides a credible explanation for delay. The notice was dated on the eve of the Christmas-New Year's holiday period. Many government employees take vacation at this time of the year, and office operations slow considerably. Not implausibly, January 2, 1981 was the first day a complete staff was available to clean desks of the remains of the previous year's work. In addition, the mails move more slowly during and after this period, because of the large holiday postal volume.

Given these factors, it is not unreasonable that a letter dated December 21, 1979 would be belatedly dispatched and then delayed in the mail so that it would not have been received before January 3, 1980. Had it been received on that date, the March 3, 1980 filing of a request for a hearing would have been timely. Were this a jury trial plaintiff's case would be more than sufficient to defeat a directed verdict against him on the issue of timely receipt. It more than meets a claimant's burden of coming forward under 20 C.F.R. § 404.901 (1982).

CONCLUSION

On the facts of this case, the Secretary has the burden of persuading the Administrative Judge that the notice was received before January 3, 1980. The Secretary has apparently produced no evidence to this effect on the prior remand to the Appeals Council or in this court. Since, however, there is no record of the hearing on this point there can be no assurance that the Secretary did not prove her present contention of prompt delivery of the notice. The case is remanded for the purpose of conducting a hearing not inconsistent with this memorandum.

The Clerk of Court shall send a copy of this Memorandum and Order to the parties.

So ordered.

1. The claimant (plaintiff) received a letter dated December 21, 1979, stating that the reconsideration determination in his case was unfavorable. What is the next level of administrative appeal, and what is the filing deadline?
2. The SSA regulations stated a presumption regarding the date that notices are received by claimants. What is that presumption and what is the CFR citation?
3. Why is the date of receipt of the notice difficult to prove?
4. The court stated that Mr. Sinatra, the plaintiff, must state "plausible evidence to rebut the presumption of receipt." Did the court state that the claimant or the SSA has the ultimate burden of proof to show the date that the notice was actually mailed?
5. On what facts did the court rely in deciding that Mr. Sinatra had presented plausible evidence that he did not receive the notice five days after the date on the notice?

Notes

[1] *Social Security Handbook, 1993,* 11th ed. (Washington, D.C.: U.S. Government Printing Office), at 256.

[2] The regulations provide that under certain circumstances, previous applications can be reopened. This means that the claimant can receive benefits based on an earlier application, which can result in a substantial increase in the amount of retroactive benefits. The regulations for reopening are found in 20 CFR 404.987–404.989.

[3] *Social Security Handbook, 1993,* at 339.

[4] *Id.*

[5] Refer to the discussion of state management of hazardous waste disposal in Chapter 4.

[6] *Social Security Handbook, 1993,* at 343.

[7] 8 U.S.C. § 1447(b).

IIII
CHAPTER 8

ADJUDICATIONS: A CLOSER LOOK AT ADMINISTRATIVE HEARINGS

In Chapter 7 you learned how to find and follow procedures for appeals of unfavorable agency decisions. Administrative appeals frequently involve hearings, which afford an opportunity to present witnesses and exhibits and to offer oral arguments. There is a great variety of administrative hearings, ranging from informal to formal and from nonadversarial to highly adversarial. Because of the great diversity in administrative hearings, it is difficult to state rules that apply to every type of hearing. There are, however, elements common to most hearings, and Chapter 8 discusses these common elements.

Paralegals must also know how to prepare for hearings, so the text discusses how to gather the facts and prepare documentary evidence and witnesses. Chapter 8 concentrates on two types of hearings—Social Security disability hearings before administrative law judges and deportation hearings before immigration judges. In Chapter 8 the emphasis switches from naturalization to deportation because deportation hearings are common and serve well as a contrast to Social Security disability hearings, which are less formal and less adversarial.

Types of Hearings

Administrative agencies hold hearings in connection with many types of agency actions. Trial-type hearings are part of the formal rule-making process, as noted in Chapter 5. Hearings in connection with rule making affect large numbers of people. In contrast, many agency hearings involve the adjudication of individual cases, such as entitlement to Social Security benefits or relief from deportation. When the EPA prosecutes a company or individual for violations of environmental laws, the agency often holds administrative hearings.

Just as the subject matter of hearings is quite diverse, so is the nature of various agencies' hearings. Paralegals can gain a better appreciation for the types of hearings by examining more closely two types of hearings that paralegals often work to prepare.

A Closer Look at a Social Security Disability Hearing

As discussed in Chapter 7, claimants who have received unfavorable determinations at the initial and reconsideration levels may request a hearing before an administrative law judge. When the claimant files a request for hearing, the claimant's file is forwarded to the Office of Hearings and Appeals (OHA) that serves the geographical district where he or she resides.

A typical hearing room is fairly small, with the ALJ seated at a raised desk at the front of the hearing room. In front of the ALJ is a large table where the claimant and the claimant's representative sit. A hearing clerk also sits at the table and tape records the hearing. Generally, claimants do not bring a large number of witnesses. If there are witnesses other than the claimant, they may be the claimant's spouse, parent, or child. Usually the witnesses' testimony is brief, corroborating the claimant's testimony and offering observations about the claimant's daily activities. A vocational expert testifies if the ALJ has decided while reviewing the file that the claimant has nonexertional limitations that reduce the range of work the claimant can perform. Sometimes the ALJ decides that the testimony of a medical advisor is necessary, particularly in cases involving complex medical questions regarding cardiac or mental conditions. Medical advisors review the claimant's medical records, ask the claimant questions if necessary, and answer questions directed to them by the ALJ. Generally, the ALJ asks the medical advisor questions such as whether the claimant meets a Listing of Impairments.

The ALJ usually elicits general information from the claimant such as name, address, names and ages of children, and so forth. Often the ALJ turns over the questioning to the representative at this point, although some ALJs ask most of the questions throughout the course of the hearing. Speaking broadly, the claimant is asked to describe the physical demands of past relevant work. The claimant is then asked to describe the claimant's medical problems and the limitations that they impose on him or her. This includes a description of daily activities. After the claimant and the witnesses testify, if a vocational expert (VE) has been called, the VE is then questioned by the ALJ. The ALJ asks the VE to describe the exertional level of the claimant's past relevant jobs and whether the claimant has skills transferable to lighter exertional levels. The ALJ then asks the VE a hypothetical question—whether there exists a significant number of jobs in the regional and national economy that the claimant can perform, taking into consideration the claimant's age, education, past relevant work experience, transferable skills or lack thereof, and assuming that the claimant can perform work at a certain exertional level. For instance, the ALJ may have determined that the claimant can perform "light" work that allows the claimant to sit and stand as necessary to alleviate back pain.

The claimant's representative then cross-examines the VE. Although the cross-examination of the VE is sometimes vigorous, overall Social Security disability hearings are not adversarial. Unless the case has complex and novel issues, the SSA attorneys are not generally present during the hearing. The SSA attorneys do not as a rule attend the hearings and cross-examine witnesses or make opening or closing arguments.

Claimants' representatives often make brief closing arguments, essentially explaining their theory of the case—why the claimant is disabled. For instance, Susan Garcia may argue that Melinda Lewis is limited to sedentary work and disabled pursuant to Rule 201.09 of the Medical-Vocational Guidelines.

A Closer Look at a Deportation Hearing

Refer back to the facts of Sample Case 3. Assume that instead of applying for political asylum while he still had a valid tourist visa, Mr. Kazemi allowed his tourist visa to expire and that he had not yet applied for political asylum. Mr. Kazemi would have been **out of status**, that is, he would not have had a valid visa allowing him to remain in the United States. Without a valid immigration status, a foreign national is subject to deportation because one of the statutory grounds for deportation is violation of immigration status (8 U.S.C. § 1251(a)). Assume that Mr. Kazemi went to the INS to inquire about applying for political asylum. In the course of asking questions, the INS employee determined that Mr. Kazemi was out of status, and Mr. Kazemi was placed in deportation proceedings. The INS commences deportation proceedings by issuing an **order to show cause (OSC)**, a document that identifies the alien who is allegedly subject to deportation, states the statutory section alleged to have been violated, and states the nature of a deportation proceeding. The OSC also states that the alien must respond and "show cause why he should not be deported." Thus, aliens who are placed in deportation proceedings are called **respondents.**

Mr. Kazemi was released from INS custody and retained Susan Garcia to represent him at his deportation hearing. You and Ms. Garcia prepare Mr. Kazemi's request for political asylum. Assume that all the preparation is complete, all documents are filed, and it is time for the deportation hearing. The goal of the attorney-paralegal team is to assert

---

out of status The term used to describe aliens who do not have valid visas allowing them to be in the United States.

BALLENTINE'S

order to show cause An order of court directing a party to appear before the court and to present facts and legal arguments showing cause why the court should not take a certain action adversely affecting that party's interests. Orders to show cause are often granted *ex parte*. A party's failure to appear or, having appeared, his failure to show cause, will result in a final judgment unfavorable to him.

---

respondent The term used for an alien who has been placed in deportation proceedings.

a defense to deportation, that is, to establish a ground of relief from deportation. If the immigration judge finds that Mr. Kazemi is entitled to a grant of political asylum, then Mr. Kazemi is allowed to remain in the United States even though he overstayed his tourist visa and thus violated his immigration status.

At deportation hearings, the respondent and his attorney, as well as his witnesses, are present. The INS is represented by a trial attorney. The role of the INS trial attorney is much like that of an assistant district attorney, objecting to evidence and presenting the INS's argument as to why the requested relief should not be granted.

After introductory remarks by the immigration judge (IJ), the respondent presents evidence. Generally the first witness is the respondent himself. The point of our evidence in Mr. Kazemi's case is to establish that he is a refugee within the statutory meaning. As you recall from Chapter 1, a person is a refugee if the person is unable or unwilling to return to his or her country of nationality because of persecution or a well-founded fear of persecution on account of race, religion, nationality, membership in a particular social group, or political opinion. Mr. Kazemi's claim is based on a well-founded fear of persecution because of his political opinion. The first witness is Mr. Kazemi. After preliminary questions about his name, address, and identification of his country of nationality, Ms. Garcia asks questions to elicit the facts to establish a well-founded fear of persecution based on Mr. Kazemi's political opinion. Mr. Kazemi explains that he opposed the Khomeini government through membership in Students for Iran and participation in anti-Khomeini demonstrations. He also explains how he knows that the government seeks to imprison and torture him. Part of this proof is evidence that other people who opposed the government were imprisoned, tortured, and even executed.

The INS attorney cross-examines Mr. Kazemi. As in cross-examination in a state or federal court proceeding, the opposing attorney focuses on any discrepancies in the testimony, especially any testimony that is contradictory to earlier written statements of Mr. Kazemi. The INS attorney may question the foundation of some of Mr. Kazemi's testimony, such as how Mr. Kazemi knows that others opposed to the government were persecuted. The INS attorney also asks questions about any ground of mandatory denial that may apply to the respondent. In Mr. Kazemi's case, there are no such grounds. If, however, a respondent had a criminal conviction that would preclude a grant of asylum or if there were an issue regarding third-country resettlement, the INS attorney would address pertinent questions to Mr. Kazemi on cross-examination.

After cross-examination of Mr. Kazemi, Ms. Garcia may ask questions on redirect, if necessary. The same procedure of direct examination, cross-examination, and redirect follows for all other witnesses. The IJ also enters exhibits into the record, after hearing arguments on any exhibits to which there are objections. The INS attorney, for instance, may object to the admission of an affidavit from a person who is not present for cross-examination. Finally, the attorney for the respondent and the INS attorney make closing arguments. While the closing arguments are not as lengthy as in state and federal court trials, each side presents a summary of the evidence and an argument as to why the requested relief should or should not be granted. The IJ decides whether the relief from deportation is granted and issues a written order and explanation of the decision whether to grant or deny the requested relief.

The length of deportation hearings varies, depending on the complexities of the issues. A deportation hearing, however, will generally last at least an hour. Compare this to the less adversarial Social Security disability hearings, which frequently last about thirty minutes.

Elements Common to Administrative Hearings: Sources of Law and Required Elements

From the overview of Social Security disability hearings and deportation hearings, you can discern elements common to administrative hearings. These include prior notice of the hearing, the opportunity to examine and cross-examine witnesses, the opportunity to present documentary evidence, an impartial decision maker, and a written explanation of why the requested relief is granted or denied. Further, in both of these types of hearings, the party seeking relief or benefits had the right to representation.

Not every element described above is part of every administrative hearing. Hearing procedures can differ, depending on the subject matter of the hearing. Hearing procedures are shaped not only by the subject matter of the controversy, but also by the applicable statutes and regulations and the requirements imposed by reviewing courts.[1] There are several sources of law that determine the required elements for a particular type of hearing.

The Requirements of the Administrative Procedure Act

The APA provides minimum standards for certain types of administrative hearings.[2] The APA's procedural requirements apply to adjudications "required by statute to be determined on the record after opportunity for an agency hearing."[3] Thus, where a statute directs an agency to issue a decision only after holding a hearing, then the agency's hearing procedures must provide the minimum procedural requirements of the APA. It is important for paralegals to understand that even when a certain type of hearing is not covered by the APA, the minimum requirements of the APA are frequently afforded.

Notice

Section 554(b) provides that "persons entitled to notice of an agency hearing shall be timely informed of—(1) the time, place, and nature of the hearing; (2) the legal authority and jurisdiction under which the hearing is to be held; and (3) the matters of fact and law asserted." These requirements are not onerous. They are logical, and reflect what attorneys and paralegals familiar with the concept of due process expect. Examine the notice of hearing for a Social Security disability hearing, illustrated in Figure 8–1. The notice informs the claimant of all the elements required by the APA. The Social Security Administration has various preprinted notices, with the statement of issues tailored to the issues in controversy. Thus, a different Notice is used for a hearing in which only Title II benefits are at issue than for a hearing in which only Title XVI benefits are at issue because some of the requirements for receiving Title II benefits are different from Title XVI. For instance, a claimant must be insured for purposes of Title II benefits, and there is no such requirement for Title XVI benefits, which are available even for claimants who have never worked.[4]

The SSA fills in the facts specific to the particular claimant, such as the claimant's name and the date, time, and location of the hearing. This is just one example of a notice. Formats for notices vary depending on the agency and the subject matter. Generally, where hearings are covered by the APA, the agencies have developed notices that comply with the APA requirements. Paralegals will not find that every time they receive a notice of hearing they have to review it carefully for APA compliance. If an agency changes a form it has used for many years, however, attorneys and paralegals should review the forms to be sure they comply with APA requirements.

Right to Representation

Section 555(b) of the APA states that "[a] person compelled to appear in person before an agency or representative thereof is entitled to be accompanied, represented, and advised by counsel or, if permitted by the agency, by other qualified representative." This simply states that a person who must appear before an agency is entitled to have a representative. Thus, when the SSA sends a claimant notice that the

FIGURE 8–1
Notice of Hearing
for Social Security
Disability Hearing

DEPARTMENT OF HEALTH AND HUMAN SERVICES
SOCIAL SECURITY ADMINISTRATION
OFFICE OF HEARINGS AND APPEALS

NOTICE OF HEARING

Claim for Period of Disability and
Disability Insurance Benefits (Title II)

000–00–0000

(Social Security Number)

Melinda Lewis

(Claimant—Wage Earner)

TO:

Melinda Lewis
202 Oak St.
Charlotte, NC 28212

> NOTE: IF YOU DO NOT APPEAR AT THE SCHEDULED HEARING AND I FIND THAT YOU DO NOT HAVE GOOD CAUSE FOR NOT APPEARING, I MAY DISMISS YOUR REQUEST FOR HEARING WITHOUT FURTHER NOTICE.

THE HEARING YOU REQUESTED WILL BE HELD BY ME ON:

Tuesday	,	May 31, 1994	at 9:00 a.m. o'clock in Room	400
(Day of Week)		(Full Date)		
Federal Building		1100 West McDowell St.	Charlotte	, NC
(Building)		(Number and Street)	(City)	(State)

PLEASE COMPLETE THE ENCLOSED ACKNOWLEDGMENT CARD AND RETURN IT TO ME AT ONCE in the envelope provided. (No postage is required on this envelope.) **IF YOU CAN NOT ATTEND THE HEARING AS SCHEDULED,** you must telephone me at once or state your reasons on the enclosed acknowledgment card and mail it to me immediately. I WILL ADVISE YOU WHETHER OR NOT I FIND GOOD CAUSE TO GRANT YOUR REQUEST FOR A CHANGE IN THE TIME OR PLACE OF HEARING. I will find good cause where the evidence shows that you or your representative are unable to attend the scheduled hearing because of a serious injury or illness, or death in the family, or severe weather conditions which make it impossible for you to travel to the hearing. I WILL CONSIDER OTHER REASONS you give for requesting a change and will determine the impact of the change on the efficient administration of the hearing process, including the effect on the processing of other scheduled hearings, delays which might occur in rescheduling your hearing, and whether any prior requests for changes were granted to you. If an emergency arises after you mail the acknowledgment card stating you will be present, notify me promptly.

ISSUES: The general issue to be decided is whether you are entitled to a period of disability under section 216(i) of the Social Security Act and to disability insurance benefits under 223(a). The specific issues to be decided are (1) whether you have enough Social Security earnings to be "insured for disability" and, if so, as of what date; (2) the nature and extent of your impairment: (3) whether your impairment has lasted or can be expected to last for at least 12 months, or can be expected to result in death; (4) your ability to engage in substantial gainful activity since your impairment began; and (5) when your disability, if any, began. If I find that you are entitled to disability insurance benefits, I will also decide whether your disability continues. This depends on whether there has been any medical improvement in your impairment(s) or whether one of the exceptions to medical improvement applies and whether (except for certain limited situations) you can again engage in substantial gainful activity.

The hearing involves your application(s) filed January 25, 1994   .
                                                        (Date)

You should be prepared to prove that you were under disability on or before March 1, 1992   .
                                                        (Date)

REMARKS:

   NOTE: **READ THE OTHER SIDE OF THIS NOTICE FOR FURTHER INFORMATION REGARDING YOUR HEARING.**

Enclosure
Administrative Law Judge

(Signature): _Russell H. Osborne_

(Type name in full): Russell H. Osborne
Date
          April 29, 1994   704-555-6100
                         Area Code and Telephone Number
cc: Representative (Name and Address)

        Susan Garcia
        McKethan and Garcia
        77 West McDowell St.
        Charlotte, NC 28202

Hearing Office Mailing Address
        1100 West McDowell St.
        Charlotte, NC 28202

cc: Social Security Office (Street Address)

        Social Security Office
        P.O. Box 0000
        Charlotte, NC 28202

Form **HA-5071-U4** (11-90)   CLAIMANT

claimant's application has been denied at the initial or reconsideration level, the notice states that the claimant has a right to have a representative.

The APA states that the representative can be an attorney or other qualified representative. The APA itself does not authorize nonattorneys to serve as representatives. Section 555(b) states that "[t]his subsection does not grant or deny a person who is not a lawyer the right to appear for or represent others before an agency or in an agency proceeding." Paralegals must look to the particular agency's regulations to determine whether nonattorney representation is allowed. Social Security regulations (20 CFR 404.1705) specifically provide that a claimant may have as a representative either an attorney or a person other than an attorney.

Paralegals must understand one important aspect of the right to representation in administrative hearings. The APA and agency regulations provide the right to representation. They do not, however, provide that the agency will pay the representative's fee. This stands in contrast to criminal law, where a person accused of certain offenses has the right to representation and the government pays the attorney fees. In Social Security disability cases, the representative's fee is usually 25 percent of past due benefits. The fee is, however, contingent on approval of the claimant's application. Thus, if the claimant is found not to be disabled, the representative does not receive a fee.

An Impartial Decision Maker

Section 556(b) of the APA provides that persons who preside over "the taking of the evidence" shall perform their functions "in an impartial manner." Further, section 554(d) prohibits agency employees who are involved in investigating or prosecuting a case from participating in the decision making, except as a witness or counsel in a public proceeding. The purpose of these provisions is to ensure that the decision makers are impartial, not agency employees who have been involved in the case to the extent that they cannot be objective.

Administrative law judges preside over many types of agency hearings. Claimants and their representatives seldom assert that the ALJ in a Social Security disability hearing has a personal stake in the outcome of the decision. In contrast, some hearings before agencies such as the Federal Trade Commission (FTC) lend themselves more readily to assertions that the members of the boards making the decisions have personal stakes or have preconceived notions and have made up their minds before hearing the evidence. For instance, in *FTC v. Cement Institute*,[5] the FTC issued a complaint against a company that used a certain pricing system, asserting that the system violated antitrust laws. The company claimed that previous publications and testimony by the FTC had condemned this type of pricing system and this showed that the FTC had prejudged the issues. The United States Supreme Court declined to disqualify the FTC commissioners, noting that Congress intended for those with expertise like the commissioners' to make such decisions and that there was no provision for substitution of commissioners and thus no other agency authorized to bring a cease and desist order.[6]

Just as with state and federal court judges, attorneys and other representatives should be alert for decision makers who truly have conflicts of interest. The most obvious factor that could support disqualification is a personal, financial stake.

Powers of Decision Makers. Section 556(c) of the APA lists the powers of the decision makers who preside at hearings. These powers include administering the oath to witnesses, ruling on the admissibility of evidence and receiving relevant evidence, regulating the course of the hearing, holding settlement conferences, disposing of procedural requests, and making a decision on the issues that the hearing addresses. It is important for paralegals to note that the list of powers is preceded by the statement that these powers are "[s]ubject to published rules of the agency and within its powers." Thus, the APA does not confer powers on decision makers beyond those allowed by the regulations of the agency. Section 556(c)(9) of the APA, however, does provide that decision makers may take actions in addition to those enumerated, as long as the actions are consistent with the APA.

A Written Decision

The APA requires that decision makers explain in writing the decision they reach and the basis for the decision. If the decision is unfavorable, a written explanation is necessary so that appellate bodies within the agency, as well as the courts, can give meaningful review. Section 557(c) of the APA requires that all decisions include "a statement of—(A) findings and conclusions, and the reasons or basis therefor, on all the material issues of fact, law, or discretion presented on the record; and (B) the appropriate rule, order, sanction, relief or denial thereof." Thus, the APA requires the decision maker to address every issue of fact and law and to explain why the relief sought was denied or granted. By requiring such an explanation, the APA forces decision makers to think through their decisions and give sufficient explanation to withstand scrutiny by administrative appellate bodies and the federal courts.

The APA refers to initial decisions and recommended decisions. A **recommended decision** is one that must be reviewed at a higher level in the agency before it becomes the agency's final decision. An **initial decision** is one that becomes the agency's final decision without review at a higher level in the agency. The decisions issued by ALJs after Social Security disability hearings are usually initial decisions. Thus, at the time the decision is issued by the ALJ, it is the agency's final decision and is ready for appeal if it is unfavorable to the claimant. In some instances, however, the ALJ must issue a recommended decision, which does not become the final decision of the SSA until the Appeals Council approves it. Consider a decision that was appealed to the federal district court and remanded to the SSA with instructions to hold a supplemental hearing and to develop certain evidence more completely. After the court remands the case, the Appeals Council then issues an order to the ALJ specifying the precise actions the ALJ must take at the supplemental hearing, such as obtain the testimony of a vocational expert. Sometimes the Appeals Council further instructs the ALJ to issue a recommended decision after the supplemental hearing. Thus, the ALJ is required to send a recommended decision to the Appeals Council for approval before the ALJ's decision becomes the SSA's decision of whether the claimant is disabled. Agencies frequently require recommended decisions when there are sensitive policy issues involved. This ensures that persons at high levels in the agency concur with the ALJ's decision before it is issued.

Prohibition of Ex Parte Contacts

As in a court trial, formal agency adjudications must be decided solely on the evidence of record.[7] In civil litigation, the record consists of pleadings, depositions and other discovery, testimony at trial, and the written documents admitted into evidence at trial. The record in an agency adjudication is similar. Section 556(e) of the APA defines the **record** as the "transcript and exhibits, together with all papers and requests filed in the proceeding." In a Social Security disability

---

recommended decision A recommended decision is one that must be reviewed at a higher level in the agency before it becomes the agency's final decision.

initial decision An initial decision is one that is the agency's final decision, unless an appeal is taken to a higher level in the agency.

record As defined in the APA, the record includes the transcript and exhibits, together with all papers and requests filed in a proceeding. Speaking generally, it is the evidence, both documentary and oral, that is presented to the decision maker.

adjudication, the record includes the claimant's applications, the state agency's explanations of the initial and reconsideration determinations, Disability Reports and other reports completed by the claimant, the Request for Hearing, the claimant's medical records, and the testimony at the hearing. The ALJ's decision must be limited to this evidence of record.

One purpose of the prohibition against ex parte contacts is to ensure cross-examination of adverse statements. Suppose that Melinda Lewis's sister-in-law did not like her, phoned the Office of Hearings and Appeals, and reported that Ms. Lewis really runs three miles a day and maintains a large garden. If an ALJ were to rely on this statement without allowing cross-examination, it would be fundamentally unfair.

SIDEBAR   Paralegals will hear the word "record" used in many contexts in administrative law. For instance, an ALJ may review a claimant's file before a hearing is scheduled and decide that based on the evidence already in the record, the claimant is disabled. The ALJ issues a decision "on the record," that is based on the record as is, without need for a hearing or further evidence.

Statutes Specific to an Agency or Type of Controversy

For some types of controversies, statutes specify the type of hearing to which a party is entitled. This is true for deportation hearings. Deportation proceedings are not governed by the Administrative Procedure Act. Courts have held that the Immigration and Nationality Act (INA) provides the sole and exclusive procedures governing deportation hearings. In so holding, the courts have recognized the specific intent of Congress stated in the INA that the procedures described in the INA "shall be the sole and exclusive procedure for determining the deportability of an alien. . . ."[8] Respondents in deportation proceedings are not, however, left without procedural protections. The INA (8 U.S.C. § 1252(b)) specifically requires that the alien must be given reasonable notice of the nature of the charges against him or her and the time and place of the hearing, that the alien shall have the privilege of being represented by counsel, that the alien shall have reasonable opportunity to examine evidence against him or her and to present evidence on the alien's behalf, and to cross-examine witnesses. Refer to Figure 8–2, which reprints pertinent sections of 8 U.S.C. § 1252(b).

FIGURE 8–2
Excerpts from 8
U.S.C. § 1252(b)

(b) Proceedings to determine deportability; removal expenses

A special inquiry officer shall conduct proceedings under this section to determine the deportability of any alien, and shall administer oaths, present and receive evidence, interrogate, examine, cross-examine the alien or witnesses, and, as authorized by the Attorney General, shall make determinations, including orders of deportation. Determination of deportability in any case shall be made only upon a record made in a proceeding before a special inquiry officer, at which the alien shall have reasonable opportunity to be present, unless by reason of the alien's mental incompetency it is impracticable for him to be present, in which case the Attorney General shall prescribe necessary and proper safeguards for the rights and privileges of such alien. If any alien has been given a reasonable opportunity to be present at a proceeding under this section, and without reasonable cause fails or refuses to attend or remain in attendance at such proceeding, the special inquiry officer may proceed to a determination in like manner as if the alien were present. In any case or class of cases in which the Attorney General believes that such procedure would be of aid in making a determination, he may require specifically or by regulation that an additional immigration officer shall be assigned to present the evidence on behalf of the United States and in such case such additional immigration officer shall have authority to present evidence, and to interrogate, examine and cross-examine the alien or other witnesses in the proceedings. Nothing in the preceding sentence shall be construed to diminish the authority conferred upon the special inquiry officer conducting such proceedings. No special inquiry officer shall conduct a proceeding in any case under this section in which he shall have participated in investigative functions or in which he shall have participated (except as provided in this subsection) in prosecuting functions. Proceedings before a special inquiry officer acting under the provisions of this section shall be in accordance with such regulations, not inconsistent with this chapter, as the Attorney General shall prescribe. Such regulations shall include requirements that are consistent with section 1252b of this title and that provide that—

(1) the alien shall be given notice, reasonable under all the circumstances, of the nature of the charges against him and of the time and place at which the proceedings will be held,

(2) the alien shall have the privilege of being represented (at no expense to the Government) by such counsel, authorized to practice in such proceedings, as he shall choose,

(3) the alien shall have a reasonable opportunity to examine the evidence against him, to present evidence on his own behalf, and to cross-examine witnesses presented by the Government, and

(4) no decision of deportability shall be valid unless it is based upon reasonable, substantial, and probative evidence.

The procedure so prescribed shall be the sole and exclusive procedure for determining the deportability of an alien under this section.

Do not expect radical differences between deportation hearings, which are not governed by the APA, and those hearings that are governed by the APA. From the description of deportation hearings above, you see that deportation hearings are just as formal as Social Security disability hearings. In fact, deportation hearings, in part because of their adversarial nature, are generally more formal than Social Security disability hearings.

Due Process

Many of the protections provided by the APA, other statutes, and regulations sound familiar to paralegals. They are the same protections discussed in Chapter 6. The case law regarding due process has defined whether hearings are required and at what point the hearing must be held. For instance, in *Mathews v. Eldridge,*[9] the Court held that due process required a hearing in connection with the termination of Social Security disability benefits, a protected property interest, but that holding the hearing after the benefits had been ceased comported with the requirements of due process.

In many areas of administrative law, the issues of whether due process requires a hearing and the elements of the hearing have long since been established, in part through the case law. Paralegals and attorneys must, however, be alert for due process concerns when agencies change their procedures. For instance, when the INS issued proposed regulations for political asylum procedures in 1987, the proposed regulations essentially cut immigration judges out of the decision-making process, leaving applicants only with hearings before INS employees. During the notice and comment period, the INS received scores of comments expressing due process concerns over this proposal. The final regulations, issued in July 1990, addressed the due process concerns and restored the immigration judges as the decision makers when political asylum is asserted as a defense to deportation.

By this point in the study of administrative law, paralegals are aware that the major themes in administrative law really do affect their daily work. Paralegals should be ever vigilant for due process concerns and assert their concerns through the rule-making notice and comment procedures. With the more routine, established agency regulations, many of these concerns may already have been addressed and worked out, through rule making or even litigation. However, anytime that an agency proposes changes in procedure that alter the type of hearing or the decision maker, the attorney-paralegal team must be alert for due process problems.

Regulations

It comes as no surprise to paralegal students that they must turn to the agency's regulations to find the details of the prehearing and hearing procedures. The regulations have been shaped by rule making as well as due process considerations. For an example of the topics that agency regulations cover in regard to hearings, refer to Figure 8–3, which reprints the headings of 20 CFR 404.929 through 404.941, governing prehearing and hearing procedures with administrative law judges.

FIGURE 8–3
Headings from Regulations Regarding Hearings Before Administrative Law Judges (20 CFR 404.929–404.941)

	HEARING BEFORE AN ADMINISTRATIVE LAW JUDGE
404.929	Hearing before an administrative law judge—general.
404.930	Availability of a hearing before an administrative law judge.
404.932	Parties to a hearing before an administrative law judge.
404.933	How to request a hearing before an administrative law judge.
404.935	Submitting evidence prior to a hearing before an administrative law judge.
404.936	Time and place for a hearing before an administrative law judge.
404.938	Notice of a hearing before an administrative law judge.
404.939	Objections to the issues.
404.940	Disqualification of the administrative law judge.
404.941	Prehearing case review.

How Administrative Hearings Differ from Federal Court Trials

Administrative hearings are different from federal and state court trials in many ways. To simplify and focus our discussion, we will discuss federal court trials only.

The Federal Rules of Civil Procedure Do Not Apply

The Federal Rules of Civil Procedure govern federal court trials but do not govern administrative hearings. The agency's regulations govern the procedure instead. This results in many differences between administrative hearings and federal court procedures. In many types of administrative hearings, such as Social Security disability, there are no formal pleadings.

There is generally no formal discovery, which is such a large and critical part of federal court litigation. Aside from Freedom of Information Act (FOIA) requests, the APA provides no mechanism for gaining information from the government agency. The attorney-paralegal team must look to the agency's regulations. Sometimes the regulations do not actually address the exchange of information, and paralegals must simply learn the informal procedures from attorneys and paralegals who have practiced before the agency.

The Federal Rules of Evidence Do Not Apply

The Federal Rules of Evidence likewise do not apply in administrative hearings. Because the formal rules of evidence do not apply, much evidence is admitted into the record in administrative hearings that would not be admissible in a court trial. Social Security regulations (20 CFR 404.949(c)) specify that "[t]he administrative law judge may receive evidence at the hearing even though the evidence would not be admissible in court under the rules of evidence used by the court."

The Hearings Are Not Always Adversarial

Many administrative hearings are nonadversarial and actually fairly informal. The attorney-paralegal team should explain to clients the nature of the hearing in which they will participate. This may relieve some of the clients' anxiety because many clients think that witnesses are always subjected to rigorous cross-examination, as in the trials they have seen on television and in movies. On the other hand, in deportation hearings, clients should be prepared for rigorous cross-examination.

There Can Be Significant Differences in Procedures Among Various Offices of the Same Agency

An agency's regulations explain some of the procedure for adjudications, but many aspects of procedure are not addressed by regulations. Thus, local practices emerge that can vary from office to office. For instance, some Office of Hearings and Appeals (OHA) offices call the representatives and confirm a time and date for which the representative is available. This cuts down on postponement of hearings due to scheduling conflicts. Other OHA offices send out Notices of Hearings without contacting the representatives first. Procedures for rescheduling hearings for a later date can also differ. Some agencies require the filing of a motion to continue. With other agencies, the representative may telephone a hearing clerk, who speaks with the judge and then lets the representative know whether the hearing will be rescheduled. In this type of informal arrangement, all communications are by telephone and no written requests are required.

SIDEBAR Some agencies have local operating rules that supplement the procedures set forth in the agency's regulations. These are similar to the local rules of court in federal and state court litigation. Local operating rules address topics such as the procedure for certain motions, how many days before the hearing documents must be submitted, and how many copies of documents must be submitted. Like local court rules, the local operating rules also address ministerial topics, such as special requirements for the format of documents presented. For instance, the Executive Office of Immigration Review has local operating rules that require documents submitted to the immigration judge to be two-hole punched at the center of the top of the page with holes $2^3\!/_4$ inches apart.

Evidence and the Exchange of Information in Administrative Hearings

Before discussing how paralegals gather evidence and perform other prehearing tasks for Social Security disability hearings and deportation hearings, it is important to have an overview of the procedures generally applicable to adjudications. As in civil litigation, most of the work takes place prior to the hearing. Paralegals perform many of the prehearing tasks, including gathering evidence and exchanging information with the government.

Evidence in Administrative Hearings

One of the major differences between civil litigation and administrative hearings is that hearsay evidence is frequently admitted into the record. Further, the use of written evidence rather than oral testimony is common in administrative hearings. Thus, in a Social Security disability hearing, a statement from the claimant's treating physician is admissible without the physician being present at the hearing for cross-examination.

Despite the fact that the Federal Rules of Evidence do not apply, an administrative hearing is not an unfettered forum for the receipt of any type of evidence a claimant or an applicant wishes to present. Statutes, regulations, and case law establish general standards for the admission of evidence in adjudications.

Some statutes alter the general rule that the Federal Rules of Evidence do not apply. For instance, the National Labor Relations Act states that proceedings regarding unfair labor practices "shall, so far as practicable, be conducted in accordance with the rules of evidence applicable in the district courts of the United States under the rules of civil procedure for the district courts of the United States. . . ."[10]

Relevancy

Despite the relaxed rules, evidence must nevertheless be relevant and material. Section 556(d) of the APA provides that "[a]ny oral or documentary evidence may be received, but the agency as a matter of policy shall provide for the exclusion of irrelevant, immaterial, or unduly repetitious evidence." The Immigration and Nationality Act provides that "no decision of deportability shall be valid unless it is based upon reasonable, substantial and probative evidence."[11]

Some agencies' regulations also address the admissibility of evidence. For instance, the EPA regulations (40 CFR) include Part 22, Consolidated Rules of Practice Governing the Administrative Assessment of Civil Penalties and the Revocation or Suspension of Permits. The regulations address relevancy, stating that the "Presiding Officer shall admit all evidence which is not irrelevant, immaterial, unduly repetitious, or otherwise unreliable or of little probative value. . . ."[12]

Although the Social Security regulations contain no such precise statements regarding the relevancy of evidence, ALJs nevertheless may question the relevancy of certain evidence. Suppose, for instance, that Melinda Lewis has a mental impairment, posttraumatic stress disorder, which stems from an event that occurred many years before her alleged onset. When Ms. Lewis testifies about that distant event, the ALJ may ask why this evidence is relevant. The representative would then have to explain the relevancy of the distant event before the ALJ would allow Ms. Lewis to continue with this testimony.

To prevent unduly repetitious evidence, decision makers sometimes limit the number of witnesses who testify at a hearing. Generally the testimony of the claimant and perhaps one other witness is sufficient at a Social Security disability hearing. If a representative brings eight witnesses and the first three witnesses all say exactly the same thing, the ALJ may well inform counsel that sufficient evidence has been presented because further repetition by the other witnesses would be unduly repetitious.

Credibility

Administrative law judges and other administrative decision makers assess the credibility of witnesses. For instance, in a Social Security disability hearing the claimant may testify that she has such severe daily headaches that she spends all her time, day and night, lying in bed in a dark room, with a cool washcloth on her forehead. Close perusal of the claimant's medical records may reveal treatment for poison ivy and sunburn, indicating that the claimant does not in fact spend all her time lying in a dark room.

Consider a deportation hearing in which an Iranian national asserts a claim for political asylum on the basis that he converted from Islam to Christianity and, therefore, has a well-founded fear of persecution because of his religious beliefs. At the deportation hearing, the witness states on direct examination that he has joined the Presbyterian Church and attends services regularly. The INS attorney asks questions on cross-examination that address knowledge of the beliefs associated with the Presbyterian Church and further details about how he chose this denomination and details about his involvement with the church he attends. The INS attorney is exploring the credibility of the statements regarding conversion from Islam to Christianity.

Cross-Examination

Cross-examination does take place in administrative hearings. Expert witnesses are subject to cross-examination. As noted in the description of Social Security disability hearings, the claimant's representative cross-examines vocational experts and medical experts. Further, the ALJ often asks the claimant to clarify statements made during direct examination by the representative, and the ALJ's questions are essentially cross-examination. As noted above, the INS attorneys regularly cross-examine all witnesses, often vigorously.

The Exchange of Information

The exchange of information varies considerably among agencies, both in procedure and extent. One commentator observed that a few agencies, such as the Federal Trade Commission, have broad discovery provisions modeled on the discovery procedure used in federal court, while other agencies such as the National Labor Relations Board offer very little opportunity to discover evidence before the hearing.[13]

The Office of Hearings and Appeals allows claimants' representatives to copy the exhibits in the file, including applications, Disability Reports, medical records, and records of telephone conversations with the claimant. The exchange of information with the INS during deportation hearings is more limited. The attorney-paralegal team must file a FOIA request to get information from the client's file.

Informal Exchange

Some agencies are willing to disclose certain types of information informally, that is, without the necessity of a FOIA request. As noted, the Office of Hearings and Appeals allows claimant's representatives to copy exhibits prior to the hearing. The amount of information that agencies disclose voluntarily is to some extent related to the degree to which the proceedings are adversarial, with less exchange in the adversarial setting of deportation hearings and more exchange in the less formal setting of Social Security disability hearings. Further, the claimant has independent access to many of the documents, such as doctors' records, so it would not make sense for the SSA to try to block access to those records that are in its possession.

Informal exchange is part of the EEOC conciliation process, discussed in Chapter 3. Here, the EEOC and the lawyer for the respondent exchange information by telephone and during conferences. Further, the respondent gives written replies to the charges made, although this is not part of a formal discovery process, such as would occur during the actual litigation. Paralegals must become familiar with the particular agency's procedures to know what types of information the agency will disclose informally.

The Freedom of Information Act (FOIA)

The most common method for obtaining information that an administrative agency will not voluntarily disclose is through a FOIA request. As you recall from Chapter 2, FOIA is section 552 of the APA (8 U.S.C. § 552).

Information that the Government Must Disclose Under FOIA. Section 552(a)(3) provides that an agency must make records promptly available to any person, on receiving a request that reasonably describes such records, when the request is made in accordance with the agency's published rules and procedures, unless the information is exempt from disclosure. The exemptions are discussed below.

Paralegals should note that the agency is not limited to disclosing records only to the person whom the records are about. Thus, attorneys and paralegals make requests on their clients' behalf. Further, many groups that monitor agency actions file FOIA requests. For instance, a consumer protection group or a group that works on environmental issues may request certain agency records in order to monitor agency actions and policies.

Procedure for FOIA Requests. Section 552(a)(3) requires agencies to publish their regulations "stating the time, place, fees (if any), and procedures to be followed" for FOIA requests. Refer to Figure 8–4, which illustrates excerpts from the SSA's regulations addressing FOIA requests. The regulations (20 CFR 422.428(a)), provide that the addresses where FOIA requests should be sent. Thus, a paralegal's first step is to locate the applicable regulations and submit the request to the correct person and place.

FIGURE 8–4
20 CFR
422.428(a)

> ### § 422.428   Where to send a request.
>
> (a) You may send your request for a record to: (1) The Director, Office of Public Inquiries, Social Security Administration, 6401 Security Boulevard, Baltimore, Maryland 21235, or (2) the Public Affairs Director of the appropriate HHS Regional Office. The locations and service areas of these offices are as follows:
>
> Region I—John F. Kennedy Federal Building, Government Center, Boston, MA 02203. Connecticut, Maine, Massachusetts, New Hampshire, Rhode Island, Vermont. . . .

SIDEBAR   These regulations were issued before the SSA became an independent agency. The information is thus subject to change, which is typical in administrative law and a reminder that paralegals must keep up with the latest regulations.

The procedure varies from agency to agency. Compare a FOIA request submitted in connection with a deportation hearing. The attorney-paralegal team sends a FOIA request both to the immigration judge and to the INS trial attorney because each has a file on the client.

The form of the FOIA request may also vary. The statute requires that the request "reasonably describe" the records sought. A simple letter describing the records is sufficient for some requests. Some agencies, however, require use of their own forms for FOIA requests. Refer to Figure 8–5, which illustrates the form designated by the INS for FOIA and Privacy Act requests. Figure 8–5 illustrates the FOIA request submitted to the INS trial attorney by Susan Garcia in connection with Mr. Kazemi's deportation hearing.

Time Limits and Fees. Section 552(a)(6)(A)(i) requires agencies to determine within ten working days after receipt of the request whether the agency intends to comply with or deny the request. The agency must promptly notify the requester who, in the case of a denial, may appeal to the head of the agency. The agency must

FIGURE 8–5
FOIA Request Filed
in Deportation
Proceeding

U.S. Department of Justice
Immigration and Naturalization Service

OMB No. 1115-0087
Freedom of Information/Privacy Act Request

START HERE - Please Type or Print and read instructions on the reverse before completing this form.

1. Type of Request: *(Check appropriate box)*   a. ☒ Freedom of Information Act *(FOIA) (complete all items except 6)*

   b. ☐ Privacy Act *(PA) (Item 6 **Must** be completed in addition to all other applicable items)* c. ☐ Amendment *(PA only)*

2. List below, the name and telephone number of the person to whom the information should be released. By my signature, I consent to the following *(check applicable boxes)*:

   a. ☒ Pay all costs incurred for search, duplication and review of materials up to $25.00, when applicable. *(see reverse)*

   b. ☐ Allow the person name below to see *(my record/a portion)* **(Specify)** _____
   (Consent is required for records for USC and Lawful Permanent Residents)

   c. ☐ Proof of Death is attached for deceased subject *(obituary or death certificate)*

   Name of person authorized to see record: Signature of person giving consent:

Name: Susan Garcia	Day time phone number: (704) 555-5544
Address *(street number and name)*: 77 West McDowell St.	Apt. No.:
City: Charlotte	State: NC	Zip Code: 28202

3. Action Request *(check one)*:   a. ☒ Copy   b. ☐ In-person Review

4. **Information needed to search for record (s):**

   Specific information, document(s), or record(s) desired. *(Identify by name, date subject matter and location of information)*

   All documents beginning with the investigation that culminated in issuance of Order to Show Cause on May 31, 1994.

   Purpose *(optional) (You are not required to state the purpose for your request. However, doing so may assist the INS in locating the records needed to respond to you.)*
   Prepare for deportation hearing

5. Data **NEEDED** on **SUBJECT** of Record (*If not provided records may not be located):

* Family Name: Kazemi	Given Name: Massoud	Middle Name: N/A
* Other names used, if any: none	* Name at time of Entry in U.S.: Massoud Kacemi	I-94 Admissions#: 00-000
* Alien Registration #: 00 000 000	* Petition#: N/A	* Country of Birth: Iran	* Date of Birth or Age: 6/3/58

   Names of other Family Members that may appear on requested record *(i.e., daughter, son, spouse)*:
   Nancy Kazemi

Country of Origin: Iran	Port of Entry into U.S.: Charlotte, NC		Date of Entry: 2/4/86
Manner of Entry *(air, sea, land)*: air	Mode of Travel *(name of carrier)*: U.S.Air		SSAN: 000-00-0000
*Name on Naturalization Certification: N/A		Certificate #: N/A	Naturalization Date: N/A
Address at time of Naturalization: N/A			Court and Location: N/A

6. Verification of Subject's Identity: *(See reverse for explanation) (check one)*:

   a. ☒ In person with ID   b. ☐ Notarized Affidavit of Identity c. ☐ Other (Specify)_____

   | Signature of Requester: *Susan Garcia* | Date: June 10, 1994 | Telephone Number: (704) 555-5210 |

Form G-639 (Rev. 10-30-92) N

determine the appeal within twenty working days. The FOIA statute does allow for some extension of these time limits.[14]

Section 552(a)(4)(A) allows agencies to charge fees for FOIA requests. When a request is for "commercial use," an agency may charge for search time, duplication, and review costs. When the records are not for commercial use and are sought by an educational or noncommercial scientific institution, or a representative of the news media, the agency's fees are limited to reasonable standard charges for document duplication. If the request does not fall within these two categories, the statute allows fees for document search and duplication. Certain agencies provide some information free of charge.

Judicial Review of FOIA Requests.   If an agency wrongfully withholds records or fails to comply with time limits, the requester may file an action in the federal district court.[15] Agencies often do not respond to FOIA requests within ten days. Courts have allowed actions against agencies if they were "responding with due diligence and exceptional circumstances exist."[16] Courts have found "exceptional circumstances" when an agency had an extremely large volume of requests, and have found "due diligence" when an agency has committed a large amount of resources to respond to requests on a first come, first served basis.[17]

Exemptions. Nine categories of information are exempt from mandatory disclosure under FOIA. If the information you request falls within one of the exemptions, the agency is not required to give you the information. Thus, the issue of whether requested information falls within an exemption is frequently the subject of litigation. We discuss only highlights of the exemptions. For an extensive listing of FOIA litigation, paralegals may refer to the *Freedom of Information Case List,* which is published by the Justice Department and available through the Government Printing Office.

The nine exemptions are stated in 5 U.S.C. § 552(b), reprinted in Appendix A. Read the nine exemptions, and you see that the attorney-paralegal team may rarely encounter some of them, such as geological information concerning wells. Several of the exemptions, however, deserve paralegals' special attention.

The third exemption covers records that are specifically exempted from disclosure by a statute other than section 552(b). For instance, the Internal Revenue Service provides information on individuals' earnings to the SSA so that the SSA can maintain accurate records of yearly earnings. The Internal Revenue Code prohibits the SSA from disclosing the tax return information.[18] Paralegals do not want to waste their time on information that is forbidden from disclosure by statute.

The fourth exemption covers trade secrets and commercial or financial information that is obtained from a person (i.e., not from the government) and is privileged or confidential. One purpose of this exemption is to preclude competitors from gaining information about each other through a government agency's records. For instance, if a company has developed a new drug and seeks approval from the FDA to market the drug, this exemption precludes a competitor from gaining information about the new drug from the FDA. In the context of the fourth exemption, paralegals may encounter "reverse FOIA" cases. A **reverse FOIA case** involves a request from the submitter of the information to enjoin the agency from releasing information.[19] Thus, if the company that developed the new drug wished to enjoin the FDA from releasing its information, that company would file a "reverse FOIA" action.

The fifth exemption covers intragency communications which "would not be available by law to a party . . . in litigation with the agency." This exemption applies to the agency's communications that are protected by the attorney-client privilege and the work product privilege. In the context of administrative law, paralegals encounter the "executive privilege," which protects "internal deliberative documents that contain advice or recommendations."[20] The executive privilege applies only to documents written before the agency makes a decision; when the agency reaches a decision and writes a memorandum explaining the decision it has reached, this memorandum is not exempted from disclosure.[21]

The sixth exemption covers "personnel and medical files and similar files the disclosure of which would constitute a clearly unwarranted invasion of personal privacy." The policy behind this exemption is clear—people should not be able to obtain from administrative agencies information about other people that they could not otherwise obtain. FOIA is not a tool to seek embarrassing information about adversaries or even family members.

Agencies sometimes release documents that have been **redacted**, that is, some information in the documents has been deleted. Often a person's name has been deleted. For instance, in *U.S. Dep't. of State v. Ray,*[22] the State Department had released, pursuant to a FOIA request, documents containing information about Haitian nationals who had attempted to enter the United States illegally and were involuntarily returned to Haiti, but had deleted the names of most of the individuals. In cases addressing the withholding of information under the sixth exemption, courts have balanced the individual's right of privacy against the public interest in disclosure. In *Ray*, the Supreme Court held that the

---

reverse FOIA case A case in which a party who submitted information to an agency seeks to enjoin the agency from releasing the information.

redacted A redacted document is one in which information that cannot be disclosed has been deleted.

public interest in disclosure had been met by releasing the reports without identifying the persons who were the subjects of the reports and that to identify the persons would constitute an unwarranted invasion of privacy, in light of the highly personal information involved.[23]

The Privacy Act

As noted in Chapter 2, the Privacy Act (5 U.S.C. § 552a) requires agencies to keep accurate information about individuals and allows individuals access to the information kept about them, to request amendment of erroneous information, and to request an accounting from the agency of the disclosures made about them. The Privacy Act also prohibits disclosure of information about individuals without their consent.

The Privacy Act provides another avenue for obtaining information from administrative agencies. The Privacy Act allows individuals access to information about them maintained in an agency's system of records, unless an exemption to disclosure applies. The Privacy Act differs from FOIA, because the Privacy Act allows individuals only to get information about themselves, not about other people.

As with FOIA, paralegals must become familiar with individual agencies' regulations regarding procedures for obtaining information and forms designated by the agency. Refer to Figure 8–6, which reprints an excerpt from the regulations of the Department of Health and Human Services (HHS) concerning Privacy Act requests. Note that HHS requires verification of the requester's identity. HHS also has specific regulations regarding release of medical records. These regulations (45 CFR 5b.6) require that individuals who request their medical records must designate a representative, who "may be a physician other health professional, or other responsible individual, who would be willing to review the record and inform the subject individual of its contents at the representative's discretion." This is an example of a specific agency's regulations, designed to safeguard the use and interpretation of sensitive materials.

FIGURE 8–6
5 CFR 5b.5(a)

§ 5b.5   Notification of or access to records.

(a) *Times, places, and manner of requesting notification of or access to a record.* (1) Subject to the provisions governing medical records in § 5b.6 of this part, any individual may request notification of a record. He may at the same time request access to any record pertaining to him. An individual may be accompanied by another individual of his choice when he requests access to a record in person; *Provided,* That he affirmatively authorizes the presence

FIGURE 8–6
(continued)

of such other individual during any discussion of a record to which access is requested.

(2) An individual making a request for notification of or access to a record shall address his request to the responsible Department official and shall verify his identity when required in accordance with paragraph (b)(2) of this section. At the time the request is made, the individual shall specify which systems of records he wishes to have searched and the records to which he wishes to have access. He may also request that copies be made of all or any such records. An individual shall also provide the responsible Department official with sufficient particulars to enable such official to distinguish between records on subject individuals with the same name. The necessary particulars are set forth in the notices of systems of records.

(3) An individual who makes a request in person may leave with any responsible Department official a request for notification of or access to a record under the control of another responsible Department official; *Provided,* That the request is addressed in writing to the appropriate responsible Department official.

Exemptions. If information is exempt from disclosure under the Privacy Act, the agency does not have to provide the information to the requester. Refer to section 552a(j) and (k) of the Privacy Act, reprinted in Appendix A. Section 552a(j) exempts from disclosure records maintained by the Central Intelligence Agency or by criminal law enforcement agencies, unless the records are compiled for a noncriminal or administrative purpose.[24] Some of the records exempted from disclosure under section 552a(k) are statistical records required by statute, and information maintained to provide protective service to the president. As with FOIA, if the agency declines to furnish the requested records, the requester may file an action in federal court.

The Jencks Act

Government attorneys often prosecute criminal violations of statutes enforced by administrative agencies. When the government is actually prosecuting a person, the Jencks Act entitles the person to request prior statements made by government witnesses. A request pursuant to the Jencks Act has its origin in criminal law, but applies in an administrative setting when the government attorneys are serving in a prosecutorial capacity.[25]

The Jencks Act provides that "[a]fter a witness called by the United States has testified on direct examination, the court shall on motion of the defendant, order the United States to produce any statement . . . of the witness in the possession of the United States which relates to the subject matter to which the witness has testified." Thus, the witness' statement or report is discoverable, but only after the witness has testified. Seeing the written statement can be useful to find inconsistencies between the written statement and the witness's testimony.

Privileges

Paralegals must always be mindful not to disclose information that is privileged. The privileges that apply in civil litigation and criminal law apply in administrative law as well. This includes attorney-client privilege, doctor-patient privilege, and work product privilege. Further, the fifth amendment privilege against self-incrimination applies when clients face criminal penalties. This may occur with agencies such as the Environmental Protection Agency and Internal Revenue Service, which have the authority to impose criminal penalties. A detailed discussion of each privilege is beyond the scope of this text. Paralegals should, however, consult texts on civil procedure and criminal law when questions about these privileges arise.

Administrative Hearings and Appeals of Decisions

Preparation for administrative hearings is similar to preparation for trials. The attorney-paralegal team identifies and prepares witnesses, gathers all necessary documentary evidence, and sometimes prepares a trial brief or other form of written argument to present to the decision maker.

With any type of administrative hearing, the attorney-paralegal team should review the evidence and develop a "theory of the case," that is, an explanation of why the client should be granted the benefits or relief sought. Although administrative hearings are often less formal than court trials, the attorney-paralegal team must prepare carefully and be ready to answer the decision maker's questions, including the question of why a client should receive a favorable decision.

Gathering the Facts to Present

In general, gathering the facts for an administrative hearing is similar to gathering the facts for a court trial. The attorney-paralegal team ensures that all necessary documentary evidence is a part of the record and interviews the witnesses who may testify at the hearing.

Types of Evidence in Deportation Hearings

In connection with administrative hearings, the attorney-paralegal team may gather types of evidence that may not readily come to mind in preparation for a court trial. Consider Mr. Kazemi's claim for political asylum as a defense to deportation. The witnesses will include Mr. Kazemi, as well as other people he knows who have been subjected to persecution for similar reasons. The documentary evidence will be more expansive than paralegal students may readily envision. The documentary evidence will include an affidavit of Mr. Kazemi explaining in detail why he has a well-founded fear of persecution if forced to return to Iran. Affidavits of persons who have been persecuted for similar reasons may also be included, especially if those persons are available for cross-examination at the hearing. Each year the State Department prepares a report on human rights conditions country by country. The State Department report on Iran would typically be an exhibit. Amnesty International publishes reports annually as well, and the section of the *Amnesty International Report* for Iran would also be submitted. Amnesty International has many other publications, including those directed at human rights abuses in particular countries, which may also be submitted. Another source of information is the *Handbook on Procedures and Criteria for Determining Refugee Status,* published by the United Nations High Commissioner on Refugees. Further, political asylum claims are frequently supported by newspaper and magazine articles documenting human rights abuses in the country in question. Thus, paralegals must be open to types of evidence that they may not have encountered in proceedings other than administrative hearings.

Types of Evidence in Social Security Disability Hearings

In regard to Melinda Lewis's claim for Social Security disability, by the time her file reaches OHA, it will contain much of her medical records. Paralegals must, however, ensure that the most up-to-date information on her medical condition is in the file. For instance, she may have been hospitalized just weeks before the hearing, and that hospital report must be submitted. The most up-to-date treatment notes must also be submitted. Often treating physicians are asked to summarize their treatment of the claimant and to specify her physical restrictions. For instance, Ms. Lewis's treating orthopedist and treating cardiologist may state that she is limited to lifting no more than ten pounds and cannot engage in prolonged standing and walking. Thus, she is limited to "sedentary" work.

SIDEBAR Some agencies have regulations or local operating rules that specify how far in advance documentary evidence must be submitted. For instance, the Executive Office for Immigration Review requires that evidence be submitted ten days prior to the hearing, with certification of service of the documents on the opposing party. Although other agencies have no such definite deadlines, it is best to submit evidence well before the hearing so that the decision maker has time to review it.

Preparing Witnesses

The preparation of witnesses for administrative adjudications is similar to the preparation for court trials. The attorney-paralegal team explains to the witnesses the nature of the hearing, that is, who presides, how formal the hearing is, and so forth. The attorney-paralegal team then goes over the questions they will ask the witness at the hearing. Finally, paralegals ensure that the witnesses know the date, time, and location of the hearing.

Preparing Written Arguments

For some types of administrative hearings, the attorney-paralegal team prepares a trial brief. The format of such a brief may vary depending on the type of adjudication. The trial brief may be less formal and may be shorter than, for instance, a brief submitted in a complex civil trial. In connection with Social Security disability hearings, representatives may simply present a one-page letter explaining the claimant's age, education, past relevant work experience, and residual functional capacity; highlighting doctors' conclusion to support their contentions; and stating why this supports a finding that the claimant is disabled. Paralegals can become familiar with the appropriate format by consulting with the attorneys with whom they work and other legal professionals familiar with agency practices.

Presentation of the Case

You already have an overview of the presentation of a case through the description of a Social Security disability hearing and a deportation hearing at the beginning of Chapter 8. As those descriptions illustrate, examination of witnesses is similar to that in a court trial—direct examination, cross-examination, and if necessary, redirect examination. The exhibits are entered into the record, and the representative generally makes a closing argument. The closing arguments in administrative hearings are generally briefer than those in a civil trial, especially in less formal hearings such as Social Security disability adjudications. In adversarial hearings, such as deportation hearings, both the respondent's attorney and the INS attorney make closing statements. In some hearings, decision makers state their conclusions after closing statements, and you know before you leave whether the relief requested will be granted. Frequently, the decision maker takes the case under advisement and issues a written decision at a later time.

The Written Decision

The length, format, and amount of detail in a written decision can vary greatly depending on the type of adjudication. Immigration judges often enter a one-page order to grant relief from deportation. The regulations (8 CFR 3.37) allow immigration judges to state their decision orally, provided they stated the decision in the presence of the parties, and issue a memorandum summarizing the oral decision, which is then served on the parties.

When ALJs find that a claimant is disabled, they issue fairly short decisions. On the other hand, an unfavorable decision is much longer and has a much lengthier rationale. Even a short decision explains the issues, reviews the evidence, states the rationale for the judge's decisions, and contains findings of facts and conclusions of law. Suppose that the ALJ found that Melinda Lewis was limited to sedentary work and thus disabled under the Medical-Vocational Guidelines. The ALJ's decision in this favorable case is shown in Appendix C. Read the decision, and note that the sections cover procedure, issues, rationale, findings, and conclusions.

Note that the ALJ addresses credibility even in a fully favorable decision. An assessment of credibility is important in administrative decisions just as in court trials.

Due process is a particular concern when a decision is unfavorable. The judge's decision must contain adequate rationale, findings, and conclusions to allow effective review by higher administrative bodies and reviewing courts.

Appealing the Decision

If a decision is unfavorable, the attorney-paralegal team must follow the designated procedures for appeal. The attorney-paralegal team must be ever mindful of the need to exhaust administrative remedies before filing actions in federal court. Thus, familiarity with the regulations explaining the administrative review procedures is critical.

Regulatory Procedures and Deadlines

Paralegals must read the regulations to determine the administrative review body to whom the appeal is made. Equally critical to sending the request for review to the appropriate body is the need to meet the designated deadlines. Chapter 7 examined the procedures for exhausting administrative appeals for unfavorable decisions in Social Security disability hearings and also discussed administrative appeals of denials of naturalization applications. The text now examines the procedure for appealing an adverse decision in a deportation hearing.

Appeals of Immigration Judges' Decisions

Decisions of immigration judges are appealed to the Board of Immigration Appeals (BIA). The BIA is a component of the Executive Office for Immigration Review (EOIR). Although the INS and the EOIR are both components of the Justice Department, they are separate and independent components.

The regulations (8 CFR 3.38) explain that the proper procedure is to file a Notice of Appeal with the office of the immigration judge having administrative jurisdiction over the case. Refer to Figure 8–7, which reprints 8 CFR 3.38. You see that the regulations state the deadline for filing the appeal (ten days), allow for filing of briefs, and require use of the appropriate form for filing the Notice of Appeal. Once the Notice of Appeal has been properly filed, the BIA takes jurisdiction of the case, and the immigration judge no longer has jurisdiction. This is the same as in appeals from decisions of state court judges; once the appeal has been filed properly with the appellate court, the appellate court takes jurisdiction of the case.

FIGURE 8–7
8 CFR 3.38

§ 3.38 Appeals.

(a) Decisions of Immigration Judges may be appealed to the Board of Immigration Appeals as authorized by 8 CFR 3.1(b).

(b) The notice of appeal of the decision shall be filed with the Office of the Immigration Judge having administrative control over the Record of Proceeding within ten (10) calendar days after service of the decision. Time will be 13 days if mailed. If the final date for filing falls on a Saturday, Sunday, or legal holiday, this appeal time shall be extended to the next business day.

(c) Briefs may be filed by both parties pursuant to 8 CFR 3.3(c).

(d) In any proceeding before the Board wherein the respondent/applicant is represented, the attorney or representative shall file a notice of appearance on the appropriate form. Withdrawal or substitution of an

FIGURE 8–7
(continued)

> attorney or representative may be permitted by the Board during proceedings only upon written motion submitted without fee.

The BIA is authorized to affirm the IJ's decision, reverse the decision, remand the decision, or dismiss the appeal.[26] If the BIA affirms the IJ's decision, the attorney-paralegal team has exhausted administrative remedies and is ready to pursue judicial review, which is the subject of the next chapter.

Summary

Chapter 8 presents an overview of adjudications, also called administrative hearings. In addition to the general principles regarding adjudications, Chapter 8 gives a practical understanding of the nature of adjudications by examining Social Security disability hearings and deportation hearings.

Types of Hearings

There are many types of administrative hearings, ranging from formal to informal and from nonadversarial to adversarial. Social Security hearings are a good example of less formal, less adversarial hearings. Deportation hearings are a good example of more formal, more adversarial hearings. After reading the descriptions of these two types of hearings, try to apply this practical knowledge to the general principles discussed in the remainder of the chapter.

Elements Common to Administrative Hearings: Sources of Law and Required Elements

Elements common to most administrative hearings include prior notice of the hearing, the opportunity to examine and cross-examine witnesses, the opportunity to present documentary evidence, an impartial decision maker, and a written explanation of why the requested relief is granted or denied. These elements are required by various sources of law. The Administrative Procedure Act (APA) requires these elements for all the hearings to which it applies. The APA sets forth specific factors that must be covered in the notice of hearing. Review the factors specified in the text, and examine Figure 8–1, a Notice of Hearing for a Social Security disability hearing. The APA provides that a person compelled to attend a hearing is entitled to representation. The APA does not, however, provide that the representative is paid by the government. Further, the APA does not directly authorize nonattorney representation, but does state that nonattorney representation is allowed when permitted by the particular agency's regulations.

The APA requires that decision makers be impartial. Paralegals should be alert for conflicts of interest such as a financial interest in the outcome of the case. The powers of decision makers are similar to those of judges in court trials, such as swearing witnesses and directing the course of the hearing. The APA requires a written decision that addresses every issue of fact and law and explains the decision maker's rationale. The APA prohibits ex parte contacts in order to ensure that the decision is based only on the evidence of record.

The APA does not cover every type of hearing. Congress has exempted some types of hearings by providing a specific statute that describes the required procedures and rights afforded. This is true of deportation hearings, which are governed by the Immigration and Nationality Act (INA) rather than the APA.

In addition to the minimum requirements imposed by the APA or other statutes, agencies' regulations may provide additional procedures and protections. Paralegals must always read the specific agency's regulations.

How Administrative Hearings Differ from Federal Court Trials

The Federal Rules of Civil Procedure do not govern administrative hearings; rather, the agencies' regulations govern the procedures. The Federal Rules of Evidence do not apply. Administrative hearings are not always adversarial, and procedures can differ significantly among various offices of the same agency.

Evidence and the Exchange of Information in Administrative Hearings

Although hearsay and other types of evidence that may not be admissible in federal court trials may be admitted into the record in administrative hearings, there are limitations on the types of evidence on which a decision can be based in administrative hearings. The evidence must be relevant and credible. The opportunity for cross-examination to clarify statements is available to aid the decision maker in determining what evidence is relevant and credible.

Although formal discovery procedures do not generally exist in administrative proceedings, the parties do exchange information prior to the hearing. Some agencies will provide copies of exhibits and other information by an informal request such as a simple letter or going to the office and requesting to copy the file. When an agency requires a more formal approach, the most common method for obtaining information is a FOIA request. The government must disclose the requested information if it is adequately described and the agencies' procedures are followed, unless the information falls within one of the nine exemptions in the FOIA statute. Refer to 5 U.S.C. § 552a(b). Exemptions frequently encountered include trade secrets and information that another statute, such as the Internal Revenue Code, forbids from disclosure. Paralegals should be familiar with all nine exemptions.

A request pursuant to the Privacy Act is a method for individuals to get information about themselves that is in federal agencies' records. Paralegals should also be familiar with exemptions to disclosure, found in 5 U.S.C. § 552a(j) and (k). The Jencks Act provides access to prior statements made by government witnesses when clients are being prosecuted.

Paralegals should always be careful during the exchange of information not to disclose any privileged information about clients. The attorney-client privilege and work product privilege are particularly important.

Administrative Hearings and Appeals of Decisions

In gathering the facts in preparation for hearings, paralegals should be aware that there are many types of evidence used in administrative hearings that may not be encountered elsewhere. Review the types of evidence used in political asylum requests as an example. Remember that affidavits are sometimes admissible even when the affiant is not available for cross-examination, although this is not always the case. Witnesses are prepared for administrative hearings in the same way they are prepared for a trial—by reviewing the questions they will be asked. Paralegals should ensure that witnesses are familiar with the procedure for the hearing and that they know the date, time, and location of the hearing.

The attorney-paralegal team often prepares written arguments in support of their clients' requests. The written arguments may be shorter or less formal than in court trials. The procedure for presenting a case differs depending on the type of case, and paralegals should observe hearings to become familiar with the procedure. Review the descriptions of Social Security disability hearings and deportation hearings at the beginning of Chapter 8 to become more familiar with two common types of hearings.

If the client receives an unfavorable decision, follow the proper procedures for administrative appeals. Consult the regulations to identify the administrative body to whom the appeal goes and the proper procedure. For instance, decisions of immigration judges in deportation hearings go to the Bureau of Immigration Appeals (BIA). All administrative appeals must be exhausted before review in federal court can be pursued.

Review Questions

1. Which of the following are required in adjudications governed by the APA? _____
   a. prior notice of the hearing
   b. an impartial decision maker
   c. the right to representation
   d. all of the above

2. Which of following does the APA authorize decision makers to do?
   _____
   a. administer oaths to witnesses
   b. regulate the course of the hearing
   c. make a decision on the issues that the hearing addresses
   d. all of the above
   e. b and c only

3. The APA requires that notices of hearings contain which of the following? _____
   a. the legal authority under which the hearing is being held
   b. the time, place, and nature of the hearing
   c. the matters of fact and law asserted
   d. all of the above

4. Which of the following are exempt from disclosure under FOIA? _____
   a. trade secrets obtained from a person, which are privileged or confidential
   b. geophysical data concerning wells
   c. information forbidden from disclosure by another statute, such as the Internal Revenue Code
   d. all of the above
   e. a and c only

5. Which of the following must be included in the decision of an administrative law judge explaining why a claimant is not disabled? _____
   a. a statement of the issues
   b. the rationale for the ALJ's decision
   c. conclusions of law
   d. all of the above

6. Cross-examination is not allowed in administrative hearings.
   True ___ /False ___

7. Deportation hearings are generally nonadversarial in nature.
   True ___ /False ___

8. Administrative agencies may have local operating rules that address matters such as how many days before a hearing the documentary evidence must be filed.   True ___ /False ___

9. The Social Security Administration is not allowed to provide copies of exhibits to claimants' representatives without a formal FOIA request.
   True ___ /False ___

10. Due process has helped to shape the elements common to adjudications.
    True ___ /False ___

11. The INS has trial attorneys who participate in deportation hearings.
    True ___ /False ___

12. The document by which the INS commences deportation proceedings is called a(n)_____.

13. The statute that entitles a person to request prior statements made by government witnesses when the government is prosecuting the person is called _____.

14. Does the APA authorize nonattorneys to serve as representatives in administrative hearings?

15. Name three types of evidentiary privileges that apply in administrative proceedings as well as in court trials.

Practical Applications

Exercise 1

Read the following statement from Dr. Mark Pearson, one of Melinda Lewis's treating physicians, and answer the following questions. You will most likely need to refer to the discussion of Social Security disability in Chapter 3, at least to review the various levels of residual functional capacity.

TREATING PHYSICIAN'S STATEMENT

RE Melinda Lewis

1. For what medical conditions have you treated Ms. Lewis?

coronary artery disease status post myocardial infarction and triple bypass grafting, with associated fatigue and shortness of breath

2. Please describe the treatment administered to Ms. Lewis and her response to date.

On March 1, 1992, Melinda Lewis suffered a myocardial infarction. Cardiac catheterization revealed extensive stenoses, and she underwent triple bypass grafting. I performed the surgery and have followed Ms. Lewis monthly since March 1992. She had continued to have shortness of breath and persistent fatigue, despite continued treatment and adjustment of her multiple medications.

3. Based on your medical findings, what limitations, if any, would you place on Ms. Lewis' ability to sustain standing and walking over an 8-hour period?

STAND/WALK 0 (1) 2 3 4 5 6 7 8 Total Hours

4. Based on your medical findings, what limitations, if any, would you place on Ms. Lewis' ability to sit over an 8-hour period?

SIT 0 1 2 3 4 5 6 (7) 8 Total Hours

5. Based on your medical findings, what limitations, if any, would you place on Ms. Lewis' ability to lift?

0–5 lbs.	Occasionally____	Frequently _X_
6–10 lbs.	Occasionally _X_	Frequently____
11–20 lbs.	Occasionally____	Frequently____

Mark Pearson, M.D.
Mark Pearson, M.D.

May 15, 1994
Date

1. Dr. Pearson concluded that Ms. Lewis can sit for seven hours during an eight-hour work day. State the residual functional capacity with which this restriction is compatible.

2. Dr. Pearson concluded that Ms. Lewis can lift no more than ten pounds. State the residual functional capacity with which this restriction is compatible.

3. Based on the residual functional capacity described by Dr. Pearson, can Ms. Lewis perform her past relevant work as a cashier, which was performed at the "light" exertional level?

4. Based on the Medical-Vocational Guidelines, is Ms. Lewis disabled?

5. What reasons did Dr. Pearson state for the limitations he described?

Exercise 2

Refer to Judge Osborne's decision in the Melinda Lewis case, which is reprinted in Appendix C. You may also need to refer to Chapter 3, particularly Figure 3–4, which illustrates the sequential evaluation process.

1. The statement of Issues in Judge Osborne's decision actually names four issues. What are the issues in Ms. Lewis's case?

2. Ms. Lewis alleged that she has been disabled since March 1, 1992. Did Judge Osborne find that she has been disabled since March 1, 1992?

3. What residual functional capacity did Judge Osborne conclude that Ms. Lewis has?

4. Did Judge Osborne rely on Dr. Pearson's statement?

5. Did Judge Osborne conclude that Ms. Lewis's testimony was credible?

6. At which step in the sequential evaluation process did Judge Osborne find Ms. Lewis to be disabled?

7. On which Medical-Vocational Rule did he rely?

8. Is there any conclusion in Judge Osborne's decision that should be appealed?

Case Analysis

Read the following excerpts from *U.S. Dep't. of State v. Ray,* 112 S.Ct. 541 (1991), and answer the following questions.

U.S. Dep't. of State

v.

Ray

112 S.Ct. 541 (1991)

In response to a Freedom of Information Act (FOIA) request, the Department of State produced 25 documents containing information about Haitian nationals who had attempted to emigrate illegally to the United States and were involuntarily returned to Haiti. Names of individual Haitians had been deleted from 17 of the documents. The question presented is whether these deletions were authorized by FOIA Exemption 6, which provides that FOIA disclosure requirements do not apply to "personnel and medical files and similar files the disclosure of which would constitute a clearly unwarranted invasion of personal privacy." 5 U.S.C. § 552(b)(6).

The Freedom of Information Act was enacted to facilitate public access to Government documents. *John Doe Agency v. John Doe Corp.,* 493 U.S. 146, 151, 110 S.Ct. 471, 475, 107 L.Ed.2d 462 (1989). The statute was designed "'to pierce the veil of administrative secrecy and to open agency action to the light of public scrutiny.'" *Department of Air Force v. Rose,* 425 U.S. 352, 361, 96 S.Ct. 1592, 1599, 48 L.E.2d 11 (1976). Consistently with this purpose, as well as the plain language of the Act, the strong presumption in favor of disclosure places the burden on the agency to justify the withholding of any requested documents. *Ibid.; Department of Justice v. Reporters Committee,* 489 U.S. at 755, 109 S.Ct., at 1472. That burden remains with the agency when it seeks to justify the redaction of identifying information in a particular document as well as when it seeks to withhold an entire document. See 5 U.S.C. § 552(a)(4)(B).

The redaction procedure is, however, expressly authorized by FOIA. Congress thus recognized that the policy of informing the public about the operation of its Government can be adequately served in some cases without unnecessarily compromising individual interests in privacy. Accordingly, in the leading case interpreting Exemption 6, we held that the statute required disclosure of summaries of Air Force Academy disciplinary proceedings "with personal references or other identifying information deleted." *Rose,* 425 U.S., at 380, 96 S.Ct., at 1607–08. The question in this case is whether the Government has discharged its burden of demonstrating that the disclosure of the contents of the interviews with the Haitian returnees adequately served the statutory purpose and that the release of the information identifying the particular interviewees would constitute a clearly unwarranted invasion of their privacy.

As we held in *Rose,* the text of the exemption requires the Court to balance "the individual's right of privacy" against the basic policy of opening "agency action to the light of public scrutiny," *id.,* at 372, 96 S.Ct., at 1604. The District Court and the Court of Appeals properly began their analysis by considering the significance of the privacy interest at stake. We are persuaded, however, that several factors, when considered together, make the privacy interest more substantial than the Court of Appeals recognized.

First, the Court of Appeals appeared to assume that respondents sought only the names and addresses of the interviewees. But respondents sought—and the District Court ordered that the Government disclose—the unredacted interview summaries. As the

Government points out, many of these summaries contain personal details about particular interviewees. Thus, if the summaries are released without the names redacted, highly personal information regarding marital and employment status, children, living conditions, and attempts to enter the United States, would be linked publicly with particular, named individuals. Although disclosure of such personal information constitutes only a *de minimis* invasion of privacy when the identities of the interviewees are unknown, the invasion of privacy becomes significant when the personal information is linked to particular interviewees. Cf. *id.*, at 380–381, 96 S.Ct., at 1607–1608.

In addition, disclosure of the unredacted interview summaries would publicly identify the interviewees as people who cooperated with a State Department investigation of the Haitian Government's compliance with its promise to the United States Government not to prosecute the returnees. The Court of Appeals failed to acknowledge the significance of this fact. As the State Department explains, disclosure of the interviewees' identities could subject them or their families to "embarrassment in their social and community relationships." App. 43. More importantly, this group of interviewees occupies a special status: they left their homeland in violation of Haitian law and are protected from prosecution by their government's assurance to the State Department. . . .

Finally, we cannot overlook the fact that respondents plan to make direct contact with the individual Haitian returnees identified in the reports. As the Court of Appeals properly recognized, the intent to interview the returnees magnifies the importance of maintaining the confidentiality of their identities.

Although the interest in protecting the privacy of the redacted information is substantial, we must still consider the importance of the public interest in its disclosure. For unless the invasion of privacy is "clearly unwarranted," the public interest in

disclosure must prevail. As we have repeatedly recognized, FOIA's "basic policy of 'full agency disclosure unless information is exempted under clearly delineated statutory language,' . . . focuses on the citizens' right to be informed about 'what their government is up to.' Official information that sheds light on an agency's performance of its statutory duties falls squarely within that statutory purpose." *Department of Justice v. Reporters Committee,* 489 U.S, at 773, 109 S.Ct., at 1481 (quoting *Department of Air Force v. Rose,* 425 U.S., at 360–61, 96 S.Ct., at 1598–1599) (internal citations omitted). Thus, the Court of Appeals properly recognized that the public interest in knowing whether the State Department has adequately monitored Haiti's compliance with its promise not to prosecute returnees is cognizable under FOIA. We are persuaded, however, that this public interest has been adequately served by disclosure of the redacted interview summaries and that disclosure of the unredacted documents would therefore constitute a clearly unwarranted invasion of the interviewees' privacy.

The unredacted portions of the documents that have already been released to respondents inform the reader about the State Department's performance of its duty to monitor Haitian compliance with the promise not to prosecute the returnees. The documents reveal how many returnees were interviewed, when the interviews took place, the contents of individual interviews, and details about the status of the interviewees. The addition of the redacted identifying information would not shed any additional light on the Government's conduct of its obligation. . . .

On the record before us, we are satisfied that the proposed invasion of the serious privacy interest of the Haitian returnees is "clearly unwarranted."

The judgment of the Courts of Appeals is *Reversed.*

1. Which exemption to disclosure under FOIA does *Ray* address?
2. What documents did the respondents request from the State Department?
3. Which party has the burden of proof when an agency withholds documents?
4. The State Department had redacted the names and other identifying information from seventeen of the documents. Does the FOIA statute authorize redaction?
5. In determining whether information is exempt from FOIA disclosure, what are the two factors that courts balance?
6. Did the Supreme Court conclude that disclosure of unredacted information would constitute an unwarranted invasion of privacy?
6. Did the U.S. Supreme Court conclude that disclosure of unredacted information would constitute an unwarranted invasion of privacy?

Notes

[1] Ernest Gellhorn & Ronald Levin, *Administrative Law and Procedure in a Nutshell,* 3d ed. (St. Paul: West Publishing Co., 1990), at 242.

[2] *Id.*

[3] 5 U.S.C. § 554(a).

[4] Refer to Chapter 3 for a reminder of insured status.

[5] 333 U.S. 200 (1980).

[6] Gellhorn & Levin, *supra,* note1, at 291.

[7] Gellhorn & Levin, *supra,* note1, at 278.

[8] *See, e.g., Kaczmarczyk v. INS,* 933 F.2d 588 (7th Cir. 1991).

[9] 424 U.S. 319 (1976).

[10] 29 U.S.C. § 166(b).

[11] 8 U.S.C. § 1252(b)(4).

[12] 40 CFR 22.22(a).

[13] Gellhorn & Levin, *supra,* note 1, at 255.

[14] 5 U.S.C. § 552(a)(6)(B).

[15] Refer to section 552(a)(4)(B)–(G), which is reprinted in Appendix A.

[16] Administrative Conference of the United States, *Federal Administrative Procedure Sourcebook,* 2d ed. (Office of the Chairman, 1992), at 643 (hereinafter ACUS *Sourcebook).*

[17] *Id.*

[18] *Social Security Law and Practice* § 48:3 (Clark, Boardman, Callaghan).

[19] ACUS *Sourcebook,* at 639.

[20] Gellhorn & Levin, *supra,* note 1, at 151.

[21] *Id.*

[22] 112 S.Ct. 541 (1991).

[23] *Id.* at 550.

[24] ACUS *Sourcebook,* at 867.
[25] 18 U.S.C. § 3500.
[26] 8 CFR 3.1(d)(2).

CHAPTER 9

JUDICIAL REVIEW: UNDERSTANDING THE EXTENT TO WHICH COURTS CONTROL AGENCY ACTIONS

CHAPTER OUTLINE

Distinguish De Novo Litigation from Judicial Review

Issues Common to All Types of Litigation

The Right to Judicial Review

Scope of Judicial Review

Procedure for Pursuing Judicial Review

In Chapter 8 you learned how to appeal agency decisions within the agency itself. Thus far, the text has followed the administrative procedure for appealing adverse decisions in deportation hearings and Social Security disability hearings, learning how to exhaust administrative appeals. Chapter 9 explains how to pursue judicial review of such adverse decisions by administrative agencies. The text also examines judicial review of agency actions generally, ranging from agencies' interpretation of the statutes they administer to questions regarding the constitutionality of those statutes.

Distinguish De Novo Litigation from Judicial Review

Litigation with administrative agencies usually arises in one of two contexts. With judicial review, the agency has already made a decision, such as whether a person is disabled within the meaning of the Social Security Act. If an ALJ found the claimant was not disabled, and the Appeals Council declined review, then the SSA has made a final administrative decision. The attorney-paralegal team may now seek judicial review, asking a federal district court to review the ALJ's decision to determine whether the conclusions reached are supported by substantial evidence, whether the ALJ made procedural errors, in short, whether the ALJ made any reversible errors. In this instance, the federal trial court's role is like that of an appellate court, reviewing the record to determine whether the agency has made any mistakes that warrant a reversal or remand of the agency's decision.

In contrast to judicial review, there are instances in which the attorney-paralegal team is involved in a "regular" trial, just like any other federal court litigation, except that the opposing party is an administrative agency. For instance, suppose that your law firm represents a corporation which is the defendant in a Title VII case. The mandatory conciliation process failed, and the EEOC filed an action in federal district court, naming your law firm's client as the defendant. This litigation is a trial de novo. Each side will participate in discovery and at trial present testimony, introduce exhibits, and go through all the stages of a trial, through closing arguments. The trial will result in a judgment for or against the client. The federal court is not simply reviewing a prior administrative decision; it is conducting an actual trial. The failed conciliation process was not a final decision of the agency; it was simply a mandatory attempt at settlement.

When clients deal with enforcement agencies such as the EPA and the EEOC, you will frequently be involved in federal court trials, as the attorney-paralegal team defends clients who have been charged with violations of environmental statutes or employment laws. In contrast, when clients seek benefits from federal agencies, such as Social Security disability benefits, or relief from deportation, the attorney-paralegal team's federal court litigation will involve judicial review of agency decisions which are adverse to clients.

Issues Common to All Types of Litigation

Regardless of the basis of the litigation, every lawsuit involving a federal agency has common concerns. The attorney-paralegal team must ensure that the timing of the lawsuit is appropriate, in particular that all administrative appeals have been exhausted. While exhaustion of administrative appeals is peculiar to litigation with administrative agencies, the attorney-paralegal team faces other concerns that are common to every type of lawsuit in federal court. The lawsuit must be commenced in the proper court, so jurisdiction is an issue. If the client is the plaintiff, the attorney-paralegal team must check to be sure that the client has standing to bring a lawsuit. The attorney-paralegal team must follow the Federal Rules of Civil Procedure and local court rules. Service of process must be proper, and there are specific requirements for obtaining proper service on a federal agency. Chapter 9 discusses all these issues, using your knowledge of Social Security disability, immigration law, Title VII, and environmental law as a vehicle to gain a practical understanding that paralegals can apply to all types of litigation they encounter.

The Right to Judicial Review

The right to judicial review is not automatic. When the client's application has been denied by a federal administrative agency, the attorney-client team must clear several hurdles in order to obtain federal court review. Failure to clear these hurdles will result in dismissal at a very early stage, not to mention an unhappy client.

Agency Actions that Are Not Subject to Judicial Review

There is a strong presumption that agency actions are reviewable by courts. This presumption may, however, be overcome. There are two exceptions to judicial review, which are recognized in the Administrative Procedure Act (APA).

SIDEBAR

Paralegals must know from the outset that the APA is an important source for the rules regarding the right to judicial review and other important aspects of judicial review, discussed below.

Section 701(a) states that the provisions regarding judicial review do not apply "to the extent that (1) statutes preclude judicial review; or (2) agency action is committed to agency discretion by law." If a decision is unreviewable, you do not reach issues such as jurisdiction and scope of review, because the road to federal court has been blocked.

Statutes that Preclude Judicial Review

Congress can, by statute, preclude judicial review of certain agency actions and decisions. Congress must, however, pass statutes that clearly state the preclusion of judicial review. The United States Supreme Court has held that the APA's "generous review provision must be given a hospitable interpretation" and that "only upon a showing of 'clear and convincing evidence' of a contrary legislative intent should the courts restrict access to judicial review."[1] Statutes that unequivocally preclude judicial review are rare. Generally, the statute is open to some interpretation and, applying the strong language of *Abbott,* courts find in favor of reviewability.

Actions Committed to Agency Discretion by Law

Even if the statute does not state outright that an agency decision is unreviewable, Congress may give the agency such broad discretion that the decision is virtually unreviewable. As noted in Chapter 6, Congress has granted great discretion to certain agencies in regard to certain decisions they make, rendering those decisions unreviewable. Chapter 6 noted that consular officers are given extremely broad discretion to grant or deny visa applications, and the denial of applications by consular officers is for all intents and purposes unreviewable.

Standing for Judicial Review

Standing to sue means that a plaintiff has sufficient stake in a justiciable controversy to obtain judicial resolution of that controversy.[2] Without standing, a plaintiff is not allowed to pursue federal court litigation. The requirement that the plaintiff has standing has its origin in article III, section 2 of the United States Constitution, which "restricts judicial power to 'cases' and 'controversies.'"[3] The purpose of the standing doctrine is to ensure that plaintiffs have a sufficient interest at stake in the litigation.[4] Suppose that your best friend was found not to be disabled within the meaning of the Social Security Act, and she appealed the adverse decision through the Appeals Council level. She does not wish to seek review in federal court, but you think it is so outrageous that she was not found to be disabled, that you think you might file a lawsuit yourself challenging the SSA's decision. You do not have standing to file a lawsuit, because you were not harmed by the agency decision. You are not the proper party to pursue federal court litigation; your friend is.

Congress Can Confer Standing by Statute

Much litigation has ensued on the issue of standing. Paralegals, however, do not always have to research the case law to determine whether a client has standing to sue an agency, challenging its decision. This is because Congress has passed statutes that directly confer standing for some types of federal court review. For instance, section 205(g) of the Social Security Act confers standing on persons who were a party to "any final decision of the Secretary made after a hearing." Refer to Figure 9–1, which reprints Section 205(g).

FIGURE 9–1
Section 205(g) of the Social Security Act (42 U.S.C. § 405(g))

(g) Any individual, after any final decision of the Secretary made after a hearing to which he was a party, irrespective of the amount in controversy, may obtain a review of such decision by a civil action commenced within sixty days after the mailing to him of notice of such decision or within such further time as the Secretary may allow. Such action shall be brought in the district court of the United States for the judicial district in which the

---

BALLENTINE'S

standing to sue The legal capacity to bring and to maintain a lawsuit. A person is without standing to sue unless some interest of hers has been adversely affected or unless she has been injured by the defendant. The term "standing to sue" is often shortened simply to "standing."

FIGURE 9–1
(continued)

plaintiff resides, or has his principal place of business, or, if he does not reside or have his principal place of business within any such judicial district, in the United States District Court for the District of Columbia. As part of his answer the Secretary shall file a certified copy of the transcript of the record including the evidence upon which the findings and decision complained of are based. The court shall have power to enter, upon the pleadings and transcript of the record, a judgment affirming, modifying, or reversing the decision of the Secretary, with or without remanding the cause for a rehearing. The findings of the Secretary as to any fact, if supported by substantial evidence, shall be conclusive, and where a claim has been denied by the Secretary or a decision is rendered under subsection (b) hereof which is adverse to an individual who was a party to the hearing before the Secretary, because of failure of the claimant or such individual to submit proof in conformity with any regulation prescribed under subsection (a) hereof, the court shall review only the question of conformity with such regulations and the validity of such regulations. The court may, on motion of the Secretary made for good cause shown before he files his answer, remand the case to the Secretary for further action by the Secretary, and it may at any time order additional evidence to be taken before the Secretary, but only upon a showing that there is new evidence which is material and that there is good cause for the failure to incorporate such evidence into the record in a prior proceeding; and the Secretary shall, after the case is remanded, and after hearing such additional evidence if so ordered, modify or affirm his findings of fact or his decision, or both, and shall file with the court any such additional and modified findings of fact and decision, and a transcript of the additional record and testimony upon which his action in modifying or affirming was based. Such additional or modified findings of fact and decision shall be reviewable only to the extent provided for review of the original findings of fact and decision. The judgment of the court shall be final except that it shall be subject to review in the same manner as a judgment in other civil actions. Any action instituted in accordance with this subsection shall survive notwithstanding any change in the person occupying the office of Secretary or any vacancy in such office.

SIDEBAR   You may wonder when a person other than the claimant may be a party to the agency's final decision. The Social Security Act governs other types of benefits in addition to disability benefits, including retirement benefits, widow's benefits, and so forth. Thus, many different people have interests that may be affected by the SSA's decision, including spouses, divorced spouses, or children. If any of these people are parties to the SSA's final decision, then they have standing to pursue federal court review.

Numerous other statutes confer standing on parties adversely affected by agency decisions. For instance, the Immigration and Nationality Act provides for federal court appeals of BIA decisions to deport an alien.[5] When an individual is directly and adversely affected by an agency's decision, standing generally does not arise as an issue.

Standing in the Absence of a Statutory Provision

In the absence of a statute that confers standing, plaintiffs may have to prove that they have standing. Otherwise, the case may be dismissed. In such cases, the attorney-paralegal team must turn to the case law that has evolved on the issue of standing.

In many areas of administrative law, individuals and groups may wish to challenge an agency's regulations and policies and other types of agency decisions that affect large numbers of people. This has been particularly true in the area of environmental law, where many organizations engage in litigation to challenge the actions of agencies such as the EPA, the Department of the Interior (which includes the Fish and Wildlife Service, the National Park Service, and the Bureau of Land Management), and the Forest Service.

Many environmental statutes confer standing on "any person" or "citizen" to challenge agency actions.[6] The provisions of environmental statutes that allow individuals to file lawsuits to compel agencies to enforce the statutes delegated to them are called **"citizen suit"** provisions. Environmental statutes that contain citizen suit provisions include RCRA, the Clean Water Act, the Clean Air Act, CERCLA, and the Endangered Species Act of 1973, to name just a few.[7] Frequently environmental protection groups, such as the Sierra Club, file citizen suits on behalf of their members to compel enforcement of statutes. Standing is not, however, automatic just because a statute contains a citizen suit provision. Much of the case law regarding standing has evolved in lawsuits involving citizen suits where environmental protection groups have sued on behalf of their members to enjoin agency action or to force the agency to take action against a polluter when the agency has failed to act.

The United States Supreme Court has developed a two-pronged test to determine whether a person has standing to seek judicial review of agency decisions. One of the seminal cases did not involve environmental issues, but has been cited in various types of citizen suits. In *Association of Data Processing Service Organizations v. Camp,* the Court framed the test as: (1) whether the challenged action has caused the plaintiff injury in fact; and (2) whether the interest the plaintiff

---

citizen suits Lawsuits brought by individuals, not an enforcement agency, to compel agencies to enforce the statutes delegated to them.

seeks to protect is "arguably within the zone of interests to be protected or regulated by the statute or constitutional guarantee in question."[8]

In formulating the test, the Court was interpreting section 702 of the APA, which provides that persons "adversely affected or aggrieved by agency action within the meaning of a relevant statute" are entitled to judicial review.[9] In *Data Processing,* the Court concluded that the sellers of data processing services to businesses had standing to challenge a ruling by the Comptroller of the Currency that authorized banks to compete with them in providing data processing services. In regard to the first part of the test, the Court held that there was no doubt that the sellers had established economic injury in fact. In regard to the second part of the test, the Court held that the statute in question "arguably brings a competitor within the zone of interests protected by it. . . ."[10]

Many of the leading cases addressing "injury in fact" involve the National Environmental Policy Act (NEPA). A leading case is *Sierra Club v. Morton.*[11] Here, the Sierra Club sued the Secretary of the Department of the Interior (Morton), seeking to block the development of a ski resort in a national forest area in California. The Supreme Court recognized that threats to "aesthetic and environmental well-being" could constitute sufficient injury in fact to satisfy the standing requirement. However, the Sierra Club had not alleged that any of its members used the area of the proposed development. The Court held that the Sierra Club had not alleged an injury in fact and thus did not have standing. This defect in pleadings has been easily overcome in subsequent lawsuits by the plaintiffs' alleging an actual aesthetic or other noneconomic interest.[12] For instance, a Sierra Club member may allege that she could no longer hike or camp in the wilderness area if it were developed.

In *Students Challenging Regulatory Agency Proceedings v. United States*[13] (commonly called the *SCRAP* case), the United States Supreme Court found that SCRAP had standing to challenge approval by the Interstate Commerce Commission (ICC) of a rate increase on recyclable commodities. The law students in *SCRAP* alleged that their enjoyment of camping and hiking in forests or parks in the Washington, D.C. area would be diminished by increased litter and depletion of minerals in the park areas because the rate decreased the use of recyclable materials.

The Court has, however, been more stringent in finding that the plaintiffs have standing in some more recent lawsuits.[14] When preparing a lawsuit where an organization asserts standing to sue on behalf of its members, the attorney-paralegal team must research the case law and find similar cases. As in so many areas of administrative law, the law is constantly evolving.

The Timing of Judicial Review

The timing of filing a lawsuit is critical. This is true in lawsuits involving administrative law, just as it is in any type of lawsuit. If the lawsuit is filed too early, such as before administrative appeals have been exhausted, the action may be dismissed. A lawsuit is also subject to dismissal if it is filed too late. Many statutes set deadlines for filing lawsuits seeking judicial review of agency actions. Before filing a personal injury lawsuit, the attorney-paralegal team checks the statute of limitations. Likewise, before filing a lawsuit for judicial review of agency action, the attorney-paralegal team checks the applicable statutes to ensure that the required deadlines are met.

Statutory Deadlines

The Social Security Act (42 U.S.C. § 205(g)) requires that an action seeking judicial review of the secretary's final decision regarding Social Security disability benefits must be commenced within sixty days of the date that the SSA mails the claimant notice of its final decision "or within such further time as the Secretary may allow." The SSA's regulations (20 CFR 422.210(c)) have expanded the sixty-day deadline slightly by providing that the federal court action must be commenced within sixty days *of receipt* of the Appeals Council's denial of the request to review the ALJ's decision. The regulations then explain that the notice is presumed to have been received within five days after the date of the notice, unless there is a reasonable showing to the contrary. Thus, in the case of Melinda Lewis, Susan Garcia has sixty-five days from the receipt of the Appeals Council's notice that it has denied the request for review to commence an action in the federal district court.

The Immigration and Nationality Act (INA) also imposes deadlines for commencing federal court review. Suppose that the immigration judge found that Mr. Kazemi was not eligible for political asylum and ordered his deportation. The BIA upheld the IJ's decision and ordered Mr. Kazemi's deportation. The lawsuit seeking judicial review of the BIA decision is filed directly with the United States Court of Appeals in the circuit in which the alien resides or in the circuit in which the deportation hearing was held. The INA (8 U.S.C. § 1105a(a)(1)) requires the petition for review in the United States Circuit Court of Appeals to be filed within ninety days of the BIA's order. If, however, the alien has been convicted of an "aggravated felony" as defined in the INA, then the petition must be filed within thirty days.

Extensions of the Filing Deadlines. It is always preferable to file the lawsuit well ahead of the deadline to avoid later problems. If, however, an extension of time for commencing a lawsuit becomes necessary, the attorney-paralegal team must carefully review the statutes and regulations that address extensions. Consider the filing of an action in federal district court for review of the SSA's final decision that Ms. Lewis is not disabled. SSA regulations (20 CFR 404.982) provide that a request for an extension of time may be filed with the Appeals Council, stating "good cause" for an extension. Refer to Figure 9–2, which reprints 20 CFR 404.982. Note that for a definition of "good cause" you are referred to 20 CFR 404.911, which explains "good cause" for missing filing deadlines during the administrative appeals process. This section was discussed in Chapter 7.

FIGURE 9–2
20 CFR 404.982

§ 404.982   Extension of time to file action in Federal district court.

Any party to the Appeals Council's decision or denial of review, or to an expedited appeals process agreement, may request that the time for filing an action in a Federal district court be extended. The request must be in writing and it must give the reasons why the action was not filed within the stated time period. The request must be filed with the Appeals Council, or if it concerns an expedited appeals process agreement, with one of our offices. If you show that you had good cause for missing the deadline, the time period will be extended. To determine whether good cause exists, we use the standard explained in § 404.911.

The request for an extension of time is filed with the Appeals Council, not the federal court. The court does not yet have jurisdiction.

Suppose that your worst nightmare were recognized. You and Ms. Garcia missed the sixty-five-day deadline, and the Appeals Council denied your request for an extension of time to file a court action. All may not be lost. The SSA may waive the requirement for timely filing. The United States Supreme Court has held that the requirement of timely filing for review is a statute of limitations requirement and is waivable by the parties.[15] Do not count on the SSA's waiving the requirement for timely filing. The SSA may choose instead to file a motion to dismiss. Timely filing or securing an extension of time from the Appeals Council is far preferable and will save the attorney-paralegal team and the client much concern.

Exhaustion of Administrative Remedies

Just as it is important not to file the lawsuit too late, it is also important not to file the lawsuit prematurely. Throughout, the text has emphasized the importance of exhausting administrative appeals before seeking judicial review. The Supreme Court has long recognized that it is a "long-settled rule of judicial administration that no one is entitled to judicial relief for a supposed or threatened injury until the prescribed administrative remedy has been exhausted."[16] Many statutes addressing judicial review of particular agencies' decisions reflect the requirement of exhaustion of administrative remedies. Thus, section 205(g) allows judicial review only of "final orders" of SSA. The APA also reflects the exhaustion requirement, stating in section 704 that "final agency action" is subject to judicial review. Thus, the exhaustion requirement is pervasive in administrative law, and is a prerequisite for judicial review, unless an exception applies.

Principles Underlying the Requirement of Exhaustion of Administrative Remedies. The exhaustion requirement is similar to the "final decision rule" stated in 28 U.S.C. § 1291, which provides that a party may not appeal a trial court's rulings until the court enters a final decision and thus precludes the appeal of interlocutory orders. The exhaustion of administrative appeals requirement is a corollary of the final decision rule, refined for imposition in lawsuits seeking review of agency actions. The purpose of the exhaustion requirement, like the final decision rule, is in part to shield the federal courts from "piecemeal" litigation. Instead of appealing each error as it occurs, the plaintiff must appeal all errors in one lawsuit. The effect in the context of court review of agency actions is that the agency will have refined and developed its position and its rulings through the course of administrative appeals, so that the agency's position is clear to the court.

In fact, during the course of administrative appeals, an administrative appellate body may modify or even reverse the decision made by the agency at a lower level, negating the need for judicial review. Thus, if the Appeals Council vacates an ALJ's decision and remands the case for further action, there is no need to file an action in federal court seeking remand of the case.

Further, the record for review becomes more fully developed as the case proceeds through administrative appeals. For instance, the record contains much more information about a claimant's impairments by the time the case reaches the Appeals Council than it did at the initial determination level. This can be beneficial for a claimant, who can develop the medical evidence and may have a better opportunity to establish that the claimant has been unable to work for a period of twelve continuous months. The Supreme Court observed in *Weinberger v. Salfi*[17] that the exhaustion requirement is essential to permit the SSA to function efficiently, to have an opportunity to correct its errors, to afford the parties and the courts the benefit of the agency's experience, and to compile a record adequate for judicial review.

Waiver of the Requirement of Exhaustion of Administrative Remedies. Despite the importance of the exhaustion requirement in preventing premature interference with the actions of administrative agencies, courts sometimes waive the exhaustion requirement. Because waiver is highly discretionary, it is difficult to predict when courts will waive the exhaustion requirement. There are certain instances, however, in which courts are more likely to waive the requirement. The requirement may be waived when further exhaustion of administrative remedies would be futile or the remedies are inadequate. Courts have found the pursuit of administrative remedies to be futile "by virtue of a preannounced decision by the final administrative decision maker" or where there is "objective and undisputed evidence of administrative bias."[18]

Administrative remedies may be futile or inadequate where the only issue is a constitutional question. Constitutional issues are considered to be beyond the scope of the agency to decide; they are entrusted to the courts. In some cases both of these bases for waiver apply; in fact, the two may overlap. Consider the *Manwani*[19] case, which challenged the constitutionality of the Immigration Marriage Fraud Amendments of 1986. The issues before the court were purely constitutional—whether the proposed administrative procedures violated the fifth amendment right to due process and the fourteenth amendment's requirement of equal protection. Further, exhaustion of the administrative procedures of the INS, if unconstitutional, would have been futile.

Courts have waived the exhaustion requirement where the plaintiff would suffer irreparable harm while pursuing administrative remedies. In *Mathews v. Eldridge*,[20] a recipient of Social Security disability benefits asserted that he would suffer irreparable harm if his administrative hearing were held after the termination of his benefits, rather than before the termination. While the Court ultimately upheld the constitutionality of the posttermination hearing, the lawsuit was allowed to proceed without exhaustion of administrative remedies because of the risk of irreparable harm alleged by the plaintiff.

Although courts have waived the exhaustion requirement in some cases, the attorney-paralegal team should not rely on such waivers as a rule. Courts are not eager to waive the exhaustion requirement, because one purpose of the requirement is to keep out of the courts cases in which the agencies have not had the opportunity to address the technical issues fully and to correct administrative actions if necessary, thereby obviating the need for a lawsuit.

Ripeness

Article III of the United States Constitution allows only "cases and controversies" to be resolved by the federal courts. Thus, if only a potential problem exists, one that has not evolved into a full-blown controversy, the case is not "ripe" for review by the courts. A case is **ripe** when the agency has reached a final decision, or at least a decision that is concrete enough that a court can determine whether an actual problem exists. In a leading case on the issue of ripeness, the Supreme Court explained the reasons for the ripeness requirement, noting that "its basic rationale is to prevent the courts, through avoidance of premature adjudication, from entangling themselves in abstract disagreements over administrative policies, and also to protect the agencies from judicial interference until an administrative decision has been formalized and its effects felt in a concrete way by the challenging parties."[21]

The requirements of ripeness and exhaustion of administrative remedies overlap to an extent. The purpose of both requirements is to keep out of court cases that are not ready for judicial review. There are differences, however between the two doctrines, which are well explained by one commentator:

> The ripeness doctrine and the law requiring that plaintiffs exhaust their chances for administrative remedies are sometimes virtually indistinguishable. A difference does exist, however. A case that is unripe is somehow incomplete. Further facts need to be developed or rules interpreted, and thus the court does not have the final problem necessarily before it. Exhaustion is narrower. A decision is final. A potential or actual harm has taken clear shape. Yet the agency itself may provide relief from the harm the plaintiff fears. Exhaustion is thus primarily a gatekeeping rule, one designed to avoid work for courts unless and until it becomes unavoidable.[22]

Paralegals should understand the difference between ripeness and exhaustion of administrative remedies. As a practical matter, however, the important task is to analyze carefully cases before lawsuits are commenced, to ensure that all prefiling requirements are met, even if those requirements overlap.

Other Prefiling Requirements

Ripeness, exhaustion of administrative remedies, and standing are requirements for all lawsuits addressing agency actions. In addition to these general requirements, some types of lawsuits have specific prefiling requirements required by statute or regulation. For instance, before filing a citizens suit, a notice letter must be sent to the defendants. The defendants generally include the polluter, as well as relevant federal and state agencies. Regulations set forth the information that must be in the notice and the method for service of the notice.[23]

---

ripeness A case is ripe for court review when the agency has reached a final decision, or at least a decision concrete enough that the court can determine whether an actual problem exists.

The attorney-paralegal team must be aware of all such specific requirements and comply with them. As in all aspects of administrative law, there are many details contained in statutes and regulations, specific not just to that particular area of law but to a specific type of lawsuit, with which the attorney-paralegal team must be familiar.

Scope of Judicial Review

The attorney-paralegal team has cleared all the hurdles and has successfully commenced an action for judicial review of an agency action in the proper federal court. It is critical for paralegals to understand the role the court will now play in reviewing agency actions and decisions.

An Introduction to Scope of Review

The court's role is defined by its **scope of review**, that is, the extent to which the court is allowed to examine the particular agency action at issue. In some types of cases, courts have a very limited scope of review. The scope of review is more expansive in other types of cases. As one commentator observed, "[t]he scope of judicial review of administrative action ranges from zero to one hundred per cent."[24] Thus, the court's review can range from no review at all to a de novo review. For instance, some agency actions, particularly those addressing sensitive issues of foreign policy, are unreviewable. Thus, if the State Department decides to evacuate personnel from a United States embassy in a country where a civil war has erupted, this decision is not subject to judicial review. In contrast, if the issue is purely a question of law, such as whether a statute or regulation the agency has enforced is unconstitutional, the court reviews the case de novo.

Most often, the scope of review lies between these two extremes. The issue before the court frequently is not the agency's interpretation or application of a law, but its conclusions regarding the facts of a case. For instance, in reviewing the SSA's decision as to whether a claimant is disabled, the issue is generally not whether the SSA has applied the

---

BALLENTINE'S

scope of review A phrase referring to the nature and extent of the jurisdiction of an appellate court when reviewing the decision of a lower court, or the jurisdiction of any court when reviewing the decision of an administrative agency. The issues the reviewing tribunal may address, and the action it is entitled to take, are prescribed by state and federal constitutional and statutory provisions.

correct statute and regulations. Rather, the issue is whether the SSA's findings of fact are reasonable and supported by the evidence. The court's scope of review in examining agencies' determinations of fact is whether the determinations of fact are supported by substantial evidence. The "substantial evidence" standard of review has been refined through the case law and is discussed in detail below.

The Purpose of Limitations on Judicial Review

Before examining in more detail the various standards of review, it is important to understand the purpose of judicial review of agency actions and decisions. Judicial review is an important limitation on the power of administrative agencies, designed to protect individuals from agency action that is unconstitutional, beyond the authority delegated to the agency, or otherwise defective. Judicial review helps to ensure that administrative decision makers have adequate reasons for their decisions and are not just acting arbitrarily. Perhaps the main purpose of judicial review is "to foster reasoned decision making by requiring the agencies to produce supporting facts and rational explanations."[25]

Yet the role of the courts in reviewing agency actions has been limited by defining the courts' scope of review. The purpose of the limitation is to prevent the courts from substituting their own judgment for that of the administrative decision makers. It is the administrative decision makers who have had the opportunity to observe the demeanor of witnesses and assess their credibility. Further, they generally have expertise in the area of administrative law in which they work every day. Speaking generally, the scope of judicial review has evolved so that the "main idea" is "that courts should decide questions of law but should limit themselves to determining whether findings of fact are reasonable."[26]

The Judicial Review Provisions of the Administrative Procedure Act

Judicial review is an area that is constantly evolving through the case law, and generalizations are difficult because the subject is vast and subject to change. Some general rules are, however, available, and a good starting point is the Administrative Procedure Act (APA), which presents a "good summary of the law of judicial review."[27]

Sections 701 through 706 of the APA address judicial review. The text has already discussed section 701, which provides that there is a presumption that judicial review is available unless precluded by statute or unless an agency action has been committed to agency discretion by law. The text has also discussed section 702 on standing, that persons who have suffered legal wrongs or have been adversely affected by an agency action are entitled to judicial review. Section 703 addresses the proper court in which to file a lawsuit for judicial review, and is discussed below in the section on Procedure for Pursuing Judicial Review. Section 705 authorizes courts to postpone the effective date of the agency action in question, pending judicial review.[28] Thus, courts may issue a stay of a deportation order pending judicial review. Section 706 addresses scope of review.

Application of Section 706 of the APA: Six Commandments

Refer to Figure 9–3, which reprints section 706. Section 706(2) lists six categories, which describe the types of agency actions that courts must "hold unlawful and set aside."

FIGURE 9–3
Section 706 of the APA

> **§706. Scope of review**
>
> To the extent necessary to decision and when presented, the reviewing court shall decide all relevant questions of law, interpret constitutional and statutory provisions, and determine the meaning or applicability of the terms of an agency action. The reviewing court shall—
>   (1) compel agency action unlawfully withheld or unreasonably delayed; and
>   (2) hold unlawful and set aside agency action, findings, and conclusions found to be—
>
>   (A) arbitrary, capricious, an abuse of discretion, or otherwise not in accordance with law;
>
>   (B) contrary to constitutional right, power, privilege, or immunity;
>
>   (C) in excess of statutory jurisdiction, authority, or limitations, or short of statutory right;
>
>   (D) without observance of procedure required by law;
>
>   (E) unsupported by substantial evidence in a case subject to sections 556 and 557 of this title or otherwise reviewed on the record of an agency hearing provided by statute; or
>
>   (F) unwarranted by the facts to the extent that the facts are subject to trial de novo by the reviewing court.
>
> In making the foregoing determinations, the court shall review the whole record or those parts of it cited by a party, and due account shall be taken of the rule of prejudicial error.

In analyzing a case to determine whether judicial review is worth seeking, the attorney-paralegal team may wish to consider the categories in section 706 of the APA as a checklist of potential reversible errors. Actually, the APA categories reflect not only the body of case law on judicial review, but common sense as well. Think of things that the attorney-paralegal team does not want administrative agencies to do. Think of the six categories in section 706(2) as "six commandments" for administrative agencies to follow. Simplifying the language of section 706(2), you have the following "six commandments" for agencies:

1. Do not abuse the discretion Congress has given you, and do not engage in actions so outrageous that your actions appear to be arbitrary or capricious.

2. Do not contravene the United States Constitution.

3. Do not exceed the statutory authority Congress has given you or wrongly apply or interpret the applicable statutes.

4. Do not fail to follow the procedures prescribed by law.

5. Do not make decisions that are unsupported by substantial evidence.

6. Do not make decisions that are so unsupported by the facts that a court will find that de novo review is necessary.

An Analytical Framework for Identifying Agency Errors

Before addressing specific cases that illustrate a court's scope of review for particular agency actions, it is useful to consider an analytical framework to guide the attorney-paralegal team in identifying the errors they wish to present to the reviewing court. An administrative agency may make more than one reversible error, and the errors may fall within more than one of the categories in section 706. To identify potential reversible errors, the attorney-paralegal team may find it useful to ask four questions. First, did the agency apply the correct law and interpret that law correctly? Second, does the evidence of record support the agency's findings of fact? Third, was the agency action arbitrary, capricious, or an abuse of its discretion? Fourth, did the agency commit procedural errors?

The analytical framework is derived from section 706 of the APA, which is "the principal statutory authority governing judicial review of agency action."[29] The goal is to take the language of section 706 and apply it in a practical and understandable manner. Refer to Figure 9–4, which shows the four-question analytical framework, with the appropriate segments of section 706 matched to each of the four questions.

FIGURE 9–4
Framework for
Identifying
Reversible Errors

1. Did the agency apply a valid law and interpret that law correctly?

    Section 706(2)(B): contrary to constitutional right, power, privilege, or immunity; and

    Section 706(2)(C): in excess of statutory jurisdiction, authority, or limitation, or short of statutory right.

2. Does the evidence of record support the agency's findings of fact?

    Section 706(2)(E): unsupported by substantial evidence . . .

    Section 706(2)(F): unwarranted by the facts to the extent that the facts are subject to trial de novo by the reviewing court.

3. Was the agency action arbitrary, capricious, or an abuse of its discretion?

    Section 706(2)(A): arbitrary, capricious, an abuse of discretion, or otherwise not in accordance with law.

4. Did the agency commit procedural errors?

    Section 706(2)(D): without observance of procedure required by law.

Questions of Law and Questions of Fact

One of the first and most obvious conclusions is that courts review both questions of law and questions of fact. A **question of law** addresses the interpretation of the statutes that agencies administer. For instance, if an immigration judge misinterpreted the meaning of a "well-founded fear of persecution" in the Immigration and Nationality Act (INA) and as a result had found that Mr. Kazemi was not a "refugee" within the statutory meaning, this would present a question of law to a reviewing court. A **question of fact** addresses the resolution of a factual dispute. Thus, if an immigration judge had interpreted the INA correctly but had found that the evidence did not support a finding that Mr. Kazemi had a well-founded fear of persecution, this would present a question of fact to a reviewing court.

Questions of law must be distinguished from questions of fact because the scope of review differs. Courts review agency conclusions on questions of law de novo.[30] Courts review most agency determinations

---
BALLENTINE'S
---

question of law A question to be decided by the judge; that is, a question as to the appropriate law to be applied in a case, or its correct interpretation.

question of fact A question to be decided by the jury in a trial by jury or by the judge in a bench trial; that is, a question of what is the truth when the evidence is in conflict.

of fact under the "substantial evidence" test, although the "arbitrary and capricious/abuse of discretion" test is sometimes used.[31] The distinction between questions of fact and questions of law is not always clear cut. When the distinction blurs, so does the proper scope of review. In such cases, the attorney-paralegal team can face tough issues requiring extensive legal research. The text focuses on the more clear-cut categories. Using the four-question analytical framework, examine actual cases in order to grasp a basic and practical understanding of reversible errors and the proper scope of review.

Did the Agency Apply a Valid Law and Interpret that Law Correctly?

Questions of law presented to the courts frequently involve the agencies' interpretation of the statutes they administer. The attorney-paralegal team may, however, challenge the validity of a law that an agency seeks to enforce, particularly when Congress has passed a new statute.

Challenging the Constitutionality of the Law. Courts will not allow administrative agencies to engage in unconstitutional activities. Thus, if an agency seeks to enforce statutes or regulations that are arguably unconstitutional, this is an appropriate ground for judicial review.

How the Standard of Review Affects the Outcome of the Case. In considering the validity of statutes, courts recognize that Congress has broad legislative powers, particularly in certain areas of law, including immigration law. Thus, in *Fiallo v. Bell*,[32] the Supreme Court stated that courts have a "limited scope of judicial inquiry into immigration legislation." The Court cited a line of cases that recognized "the power to expel or exclude aliens as a fundamental sovereign attribute exercised by the Government's political departments largely immune from judicial control" and that "the power over aliens is of a political character and therefore subject only to narrow judicial review."[33] In *Fiallo*, the plaintiffs challenged sections of the Immigration and Nationality Act which gave special preference to illegitimate alien children whose natural mothers were United States citizens but denied special preference to illegitimate alien children whose natural fathers were United States citizens. The plaintiffs brought first, fifth, and ninth amendment challenges to the statute, arguing that the statutes denied them of equal protection and due process and infringed upon their right to mutual association and privacy. In *Fiallo* the Court upheld the statute, despite assertions that it was unconstitutional, largely because the Court at the outset narrowed its scope of review.

In cases challenging the constitutionality of section 5(b) of the Immigration Marriage Fraud Amendments of 1986 (IMFA), different federal district courts reached different conclusions. The courts' conclusions were shaped in large part by the standard of review they chose to apply to section 5. In *Azizi v. Thornburgh*,[34] a federal district court adopted the narrow scope of review used in *Fiallo*, accepting the INS's assertion that "judicial review of immigration legislation may proceed only within a narrowly drawn field of inquiry."[35] The court in *Azizi* concluded that "a heightened standard of review is inappropriate when analyzing constitutional challenges to immigration provisions" and thus applied the rational basis standard to section 5. The *Azizi* court found that section 5 had a rational basis and thus was constitutional.

In contrast, in *Manwani v. U.S. Dep't of Justice, INS*,[36] a federal district court rejected the INS's contention that the court must apply *Fiallo* and uphold section 5. The *Manwani* court distinguished *Fiallo* on several grounds and concluded that "the deferential standard of review applied in *Fiallo*" did not apply to section 5. Having rejected the narrow standard of review, the court held that section 5 "must be reviewed in light of established due process principles." The court went on to recognize the long line of cases that establish that marriage is a fundamental right, applied the strict scrutiny standard, and struck down section 5 as unconstitutional.

A comparison of the courts' approaches in *Azizi* and *Manwani* teaches paralegals some important principles. First, two federal courts can address the same statute and disagree on the standard of review that is appropriate. Second, courts may grant more deference and thus limit their scope of review in areas of law traditionally entrusted to Congress as policy areas with which courts are hesitant to interfere. Finally, as a practical matter, the more limited the scope of review, the more likely the court is to uphold the statute.

SIDEBAR   The *Manwani* decision was issued after the plaintiffs and the defendant had filed cross-motions for summary judgment. The first court hearing, which resulted in a memorandum decision, was on a rule 12(b)(6) motion to dismiss. At the time that motion was argued, all the federal court decisions had adopted the *Fiallo* deferential standard of review and had upheld section 5. Paralegals should be mindful that different courts can reach different conclusions. Thus, the attorney-paralegal team can continue to advance a claim, emphasizing differences between their clients' cases and precedential cases, when the claimant is supported by good faith argument for a different outcome or interpretation of the law.

When Constitutional Challenges Are Most Likely to Arise. When Congress passes new, controversial statutes for agencies to enforce, and when the agencies then promulgate regulations for the enforcement of those statutes, the attorney-paralegal team should be alert for challenges to the validity of the statutes and regulations. Paralegals may have the opportunity to participate in such litigation, which can be very exciting, often placing the attorney-paralegal team in the spotlight regionally, if not nationally. Even if paralegals are not directly involved with litigation challenging statutes and regulations, they must keep up with such litigation, because the outcome will affect their clients.

Challenging the Agency's Interpretation of the Law. Frequently the question of law presented to courts is not whether a statute is valid, but whether the agency has interpreted and applied the statute correctly. One purpose of judicial review is to ensure that the agencies apply reasonable interpretations of the statutes they administer. The courts' role, however, is not to substitute their own interpretation of a statute just because the court may disagree with the agency's interpretation. The role of the courts has been well summarized as follows:

> When a court reviews an agency's construction of the statute it administers the court is required to uphold Congress' intent where Congress has directly spoken to the precise statutory question at issue. If the statute is silent or ambiguous with respect to the specific issue, however, the agency's interpretation of the statute must be upheld if the agency's construction of the statute is permissible.[37]

This is a summary of a long line of decisions addressing agencies' interpretation of the statutes they administer. Perhaps the "grandparent" of the recent line of cases is *Chevron v. Natural Resources Defense Council, Inc.*[38] *Chevron* involved the EPA's interpretation of a term in the Clean Air Act. Paralegals can find a long line of cases regarding judicial deference to agencies' interpretations of the statutes they administer by Shepardizing *Chevron*.

A look at some fairly straightforward cases involving agency interpretation of statutes is useful to understand the principles enunciated in *Chevron*. In *Wheeler v. Heckler*,[39] the issue involved the construction of a provision of the Social Security Act addressing payment of attorney fees in connection with Title XVI benefits. The Third Circuit Court of Appeals, citing *Chevron*, explained its role, or scope of review, in examining SSA's interpretation of the Social Security Act. The court explained:

> As the Supreme Court and this Court have emphasized frequently, our role is not to impose upon the SSA our own interpretation of the Social Security legislation. Rather, because congress has delegated to the Secretary the responsibility for administering the complex programs, we must defer to her construction, as long as it is reasonable and not arbitrary and capricious.[40]

Thus, the court made it clear that it would not substitute its own interpretation for that of the SSA's interpretation of the Social Security Act. Rather, it limited its scope of review to whether the agency had given the statute a reasonable interpretation.

In *INS v. Cardoza Fonseca*,[41] the Supreme Court addressed the statutory construction of the term "well-founded fear of persecution." As you recall, an alien may be granted political asylum only if a refugee within the meaning of the Immigration and Nationality Act (INA). In order to meet the definition, the alien must establish that the alien has a well-founded fear of persecution if he or she is forced to return to his or her country of nationality. The INS had interpreted "well-founded fear of persecution" as requiring an alien to show "that it is more likely than not that he or she will be persecuted in his or her home country." The Court stated that its task was not to set forth a detailed description of how the well-founded fear test should be applied. It merely held that the interpretation the INS had been using was too high a standard of proof. In reaching this conclusion, the Court used "ordinary canons of statutory construction," focusing on an examination of the plain language of the INA and on its legislative history. The Court concluded that "Congress did not intend to restrict eligibility . . . to those who could prove that it is more likely than not that they will be persecuted if deported."[42]

Challenging Agencies' Regulations. In reviewing agencies' interpretation of the statutes they administer, the courts look to the intent of Congress. This hearkens back to the ever-present theme in administrative law that agencies are authorized to do only the tasks Congress has delegated to them. After Congress gives agencies broad directives through statutes, the agencies promulgate regulations to fill in the details on both substance and procedure. The attorney-paralegal team must be alert for regulations that are so inconsistent with the statute that they go beyond the authority delegated to the agency. Such regulations are fair game for judicial review.

In Chapter 3, you read excerpts from *Heckler v. Campbell*.[43] Here, the respondent had asserted that the Medical-Vocational Guidelines were inconsistent with the Social Security Act and thus had exceeded the SSA's statutory authority to promulgate regulations to implement the Social Security Act. The Supreme Court defined its scope of review as follows:

> Where, as here, the statute expressly entrusts the Secretary with the responsibility for implementing a provision by regulation, our review is limited to determining whether the regulations promulgated exceeded the Secretary's statutory authority and whether they are arbitrary and capricious.[44]

The Court found that the Medical-Vocational Guidelines did not conflict with the Social Security Act and that they were not arbitrary and capricious. Accordingly, the Court upheld the use of the Medical-Vocational Guidelines.

The Court considered, in addition to whether the SSA had exceeded its authority, whether the regulations in question were arbitrary and capricious. Courts look for more than one type of reversible error. Just as the courts do, look for types of reversible error in addition to application of invalid laws or incorrect interpretations of laws. Following the four-question analytical framework, turn to a common question—whether the evidence supports the agency's findings of fact.

Does the Evidence of Record Support the Agency's Findings of Fact?

Section 706(2)(E) provides that when an agency issues a decision after a hearing, which was required by statute, then the agency's decision must be supported by substantial evidence. The "substantial evidence" standard of review thus applies to an ALJ's decision that a claimant is not disabled. In fact, section 205(g) of the Social Security Act imposes the "substantial evidence" standard of review on courts reviewing disability decisions. Section 205(g) states that "[t]he findings of the Secretary as to any fact, if supported by substantial evidence, shall be conclusive . . . ."

What Constitutes Substantial Evidence? Paralegals who work in the area of Social Security disability will find that their research includes reading numerous decisions to find cases similar to clients' cases, in which courts found that ALJ decisions were not supported by substantial evidence. In fact, you must turn to the case law to find a definition of "substantial evidence" to begin with.

Substantial evidence has been defined by the Supreme Court as "more than a mere scintilla. It means such relevant evidence as a reasonable mind might accept as adequate to support a conclusion."[45]

If after reading this definition, you think it is open to interpretation, you are right. What may constitute substantial evidence to one federal court may not constitute substantial evidence to another federal court. There is simply no substitute for reading the case law to understand what may constitute substantial evidence.

Perhaps the most helpful guide to understanding what "substantial evidence" means is an examination of the court's purpose in reviewing a decision. As the Sixth Circuit Court of Appeals has pointed out, the reviewing court "may not try the case *de novo*, nor resolve conflicts in the evidence, nor decide questions of credibility."[46] That is the administrative agency's job. The court's job is to review the entire

---

BALLENTINE'S

substantial evidence Evidence that a reasonable person would accept as adequate to support the conclusion or conclusions drawn from it; evidence beyond a scintilla.

record to determine whether the agency considered all the pertinent evidence and made findings that are supported by that evidence. One important principle is that the agency's decision must be based on the entire record. The agency may not just look at the unfavorable evidence and reach a decision based on a discussion of that evidence alone. Rather, the agency must consider favorable and unfavorable evidence, weigh the conflicting evidence, resolve conflicts in the evidence, and make credibility assessments. If an agency performs all these tasks, there is a good chance that its decision, if reasonable, will be found to be supported by substantial evidence.

De Novo Review of the Facts. Section 706(2)(F) of the APA provides for de novo review, with the court making independent findings of fact, only when the agencies' findings are unwarranted by the facts. The Supreme Court explained, in *Citizens to Preserve Overton Park, Inc. v. Volpe,*[47] that this standard of review is appropriate in only two circumstances. One is when "the action is adjudicatory in nature and the agency factfinding procedures are inadequate." The second circumstance is when "issues that were not before the agency are raised in a proceeding to enforce nonadjudicatory agency action."[48] These are narrow circumstances, and it is a "fairly unusual situation in which the facts are subject to trial de novo by the reviewing court."[49]

The substantial evidence standard applies when an agency's interpretation of the facts is at issue, but only when the agency decision is reviewed on the record of an agency hearing required by statute.[50] Very few agency findings are subject to de novo review. Thus, some agency determinations of fact are not subject either to substantial evidence or de novo review. Even if neither of these standards of review is applicable, the findings may be reviewed to ensure that they are not arbitrary and capricious or an abuse of discretion.

Was the Agency Action Arbitrary, Capricious, or an Abuse of Its Discretion?

The "arbitrary and capricious or abuse of discretion" standard of review can be applied both to agencies' findings of fact and interpretations of the laws they administer. In fact, it can be applied to all agency actions. It is difficult to find case law that states squarely and definitively what types of agency actions are arbitrary, capricious, or an abuse of discretion. This standard of review has been described as "a highly deferential standard of review which presumes the validity of agency action and requires affirmance if the action is supported by a rational basis."[51] In *Citizens to Preserve Overton Park, Inc. v. Volpe,*[52] the Supreme Court gave some direction on this standard of review, stating that "[t]o make this finding the court must consider whether the decision was based on a consideration of the relevant factors and whether there has been a clear error of judgment." This statement by the Supreme Court still leaves much room for debate and interpretation. One commentator has offered some concrete situations that could be considered arbitrary, capricious, or an abuse of discretion, including actions that are inconsistent with the agency's own regulations, departure from agency precedents without adequate explanation for failure to follow precedent, or imposition of a harsh penalty without adequate explanation of why a less drastic sanction was not chosen.[53]

SIDEBAR

As discussed earlier, the APA provides that some agency actions are committed by law to the agency's discretion and are not subject to judicial review. This is a very narrow exception, precluding judicial review. Do not confuse it with the abuse of discretion standard of judicial review. Further, remember that some agencies, such as the INS, are given great discretion; an argument that such agencies abused their discretion is less likely to be successful than with agencies that are generally given less discretion.

Did the Agency Commit Procedural Errors?

Section 706(2)(D) allows courts to set aside agency findings, conclusions, and actions that were reached without observance of procedure required by law. Procedural errors are more concrete and are easier to identify than some of the more nebulous standards of review. The attorney-paralegal team must, of course, know all the required procedures throughout the administrative process in order to raise this issue with a reviewing court.

A defect in notice of a hearing could be a procedural error. For instance, the SSA's regulations require that claimants receive written notice twenty days before their hearing before an ALJ. If the claimant received notice just two days before the hearing, this could be a reversible procedural error. Proper prior notice is important because some claimants may not seek representation until they receive their notice of hearing.

Procedure for Pursuing Judicial Review

Filing suit against an administrative agency is like filing suit against any other defendant in many respects. There are, however, some significant differences which the attorney-paralegal team must remember.

Follow the Federal Rules of Civil Procedure

A lawsuit against a federal agency will proceed under the Federal Rules of Civil Procedure. The plaintiff files a complaint and obtains service of process, the defendant files an answer, both parties file motions, and so forth. There are, however, some important ways in which actions against federal agencies differ from other lawsuits. One important difference is that actions for judicial review of agency decisions are often decided by means of dispositive motions, such as motions for judgment on the pleadings and motions for summary judgment. This is not surprising, when you consider the federal court's role in reviewing agency decisions. Consider an action seeking review of the SSA's decision that Melinda Lewis is not disabled. The court reviews the record to determine whether the SSA's decision is supported by substantial evidence or whether the SSA applied an erroneous standard of law. The court does not generally need to take additional testimony. Rather, it reviews the medical records, testimony from the hearing with an ALJ, and the other evidence to determine whether the SSA's decision is supported by substantial evidence. There may well be no material issues of fact, and thus summary judgment is an appropriate mechanism to dispose of the lawsuit.

Check Applicable Statutes and Regulations for Requirements Specific to Certain Administrative Agencies

Procedurally, lawsuits against administrative agencies are commenced just like other lawsuits. There are, however, some important considerations for the attorney-paralegal team prior to filing a complaint.

Deadlines for Filing the Complaint

Statutes addressing judicial review for a particular agency may require that the federal court action must be commenced within a certain number of days after receipt of the final decision from the agency. For instance, 42 U.S.C. § 405(g) requires that a plaintiff commence a lawsuit for review of SSA's final decision "within sixty days after the mailing to him of [the final] decision or within such further time as the Secretary may allow." A petition for review of a final order of deportation must be filed within ninety days of the date of the final order, unless the alien has been convicted of an "aggravated felony," in which case the petition must be filed within thirty days. The attorney-paralegal team must note all such filing deadlines and enter them into the office "tickler" system.

Jurisdiction

As with any lawsuit, the complaint must be filed in the proper court. Otherwise, the lawsuit is subject to dismissal pursuant to rule 12 of the Federal Rules of Civil Procedure. The attorney-paralegal team must check the appropriate statutes to determine whether the lawsuit should be filed in the United States District Court or in the United States Circuit Court of Appeals. Actions for judicial review of the SSA's decision denying disability benefits are filed in the district court, pursuant to 42 U.S.C. § 405(g). In contrast, after an immigration judge has denied a respondent's request for political asylum and ordered deportation, and that order of deportation has been affirmed by the BIA, then an action is filed directly with the federal circuit court of appeals, pursuant to 8 U.S.C. § 1105a(a)(2).

Read the applicable statutes very carefully to ensure that the attorney-paralegal team in fact files the action with the federal court that has jurisdiction. Allege jurisdiction in the complaint, as you would with any type of lawsuit.

The Complaint: Special Considerations

Complaints commencing actions for judicial review are often quite short. This is consistent with the notice pleading requirements of the Federal Rules of Civil Procedure. The details are generally reserved for the memoranda of law in support of or in opposition to the dispositive motions so common in lawsuits involving judicial review. Refer to the sample complaint in Figure 9–5, which illustrates the complaint that would be filed if Melinda Lewis had been found not to be disabled, and the Appeals Council had declined her request for review.

FIGURE 9–5
Complaint
Seeking Judicial
Review of the
Social Security
Administration
(SSA)'s Final
Decision

IN THE UNITED STATES DISTRICT COURT
FOR THE WESTERN DISTRICT OF NORTH CAROLINA
CHARLOTTE DIVISION
CIVIL NUMBER C-C-94-776-M

Melinda Lewis,
Social Security #000-00-0000,
      Plaintiff,

    vs.   COMPLAINT

Donna Shalala,
Secretary of Health and
Human Services,
      Defendant,

FIGURE 9–5
(continued)

The plaintiff, complaining of the defendant, alleges and says that:

1. This court has jurisdiction pursuant to 42 U.S.C. § 405(g).

2. The plaintiff is a resident of Charlotte, Mecklenburg County, North Carolina.

3. The plaintiff filed a claim for a period of disability and disability insurance benefits under title II of the Social Security Act.

4. The plaintiff's claim was denied, and the plaintiff has exhausted all administrative remedies in this matter.

5. The decision of the defendant that the plaintiff is not disabled is not supported by substantial evidence and applies an erroneous standard of law.

WHEREFORE, the plaintiff prays the Court that:

1. The decision of the defendant be reviewed, reversed, and set aside and that the plaintiff's claim for a period of disability and disability insurance benefits be allowed; or in the alternative,

2. The Court remand this cause to the defendant for a fair hearing.

3. The costs of this action, including reasonable attorney fees for plaintiff's counsel, be assessed against the defendant.

4. The Court grant such other and further relief as may be just and proper.

This the _10th_ day of August, 1994.

Susan Garcia
Susan Garcia
Attorney for the Plaintiff
77 West McDowell St.
Charlotte, NC 28202
704-555-5210

The format of the complaint is just like complaints filed in other federal court actions. Paragraph 1 establishes the court's jurisdiction. Paragraph 2 is for purposes of venue. Refer to Figure 9–1, which reprints 42 U.S.C. § 405(g), containing the venue specifications for lawsuits involving judicial review of SSA's decision regarding disability benefits.

Paragraph 3 describes in simple terms the type of claim that is being appealed. Paragraph 4 states the important requirement that administrative remedies have been exhausted. Section 5 states the applicable standard of review. As with any lawsuit, the prayer for judgment states the relief that the plaintiff requests. Finally, the complaint contains the attorney's name, address, and telephone number.

Name the Appropriate Defendant

Sometimes the named defendant is stated simply by the agency's name, such as "United States Department of Justice, Immigration and

Naturalization Services." More frequently, the named defendant is the head of the agency that is being sued. Consider the titles of some of the well-known cases discussed earlier in this chapter. In *Sierra Club v. Morton*, Rogers Morton was the secretary of the Department of the Interior, the agency that was being sued. In *Citizens to Preserve Overton Park, Inc. v. Volpe*, John Volpe was the secretary of the Department of Transportation, the agency that was being sued.

In Social Security disability cases, the named defendant was the secretary of health and human services, prior to March 31, 1995, when the SSA became an independent agency. Some plaintiffs stated the defendant simply as "Secretary of Health and Human Services," while others named the person who was secretary at the time the lawsuit was filed. Thus, Melinda Lewis's complaint named as the defendant Donna Shalala, who was secretary of health and human services, at the time the complaint was filed. Lawsuits filed after March 31, 1995, will name the commissioner of the SSA as the defendant.

SIDEBAR   A lawsuit, particularly if it is a class action, may stay in court for several years before it is resolved. Thus, the name of the defendant may change over the years. A class action that was pending in the United States District Court for the Western District of North Carolina for several years was captioned *Hyatt v. Heckler*, although the final order had the caption *Hyatt v. Shalala*, because the secretary of HHS changed.

Other Documents that Must Be Filed with the Complaint

An important task for paralegals is to ensure that all documents that must accompany the complaint are properly filed. These include the summons and civil cover sheet, a requirement with all federal court actions. Ensure that a check for the required filing fee is included. For instance, the filing fee for Melinda Lewis would be $120, unless she qualifies to proceed in forma pauperis, in which case the filing fee is waived.

Service of Process on a Federal Administrative Agency

Rule 4 of the Federal Rules of Civil Procedure contains special requirements to obtain effective service of process when the United States government is the defendant. Refer to Figure 9–6, which reprints rule 4(d)(4), which explains how to serve process when the United States is the defendant. Applying this to Melinda Lewis's court action, the attorney-paralegal team serves process on the United States attorney for the district in which the action is filed, the United States Attorney General, and the secretary of health and human services. The complaint and summons are sent to the United States Attorney General and to the secretary of HHS by certified mail, return receipt requested, in Washington, D.C.

FIGURE 9–6
Rule 4(d)(4) of the
Federal Rules of
Civil Procedure

(4) Upon the United States, by delivering a copy of the summons and complaint to the United States attorney for the district in which the action is filed or a clerical employee designated by the United States attorney to accept service. A copy of the summons and complaint must also be served upon the Attorney General in Washington, D.C., by registered or certified mail. If the lawsuit attacks the validity of an action of a United States agency or officer, the agency or officer must also be served by certified or registered mail.

Settlement

Paralegals should be mindful that settlements can be reached in lawsuits involving judicial review of agency decisions, just as in any other type of lawsuit. For instance, it is not uncommon for the plaintiff and the defendant to agree to a joint order to remand a case to the SSA for further proceedings, when both sides acknowledge a procedural or legal deficiency that should have been addressed. Even lawsuits that have been pending for many months and have involved numerous, hotly contested motions may eventually be settled.

Disposition by Pretrial Motions

As noted, lawsuits involving judicial review are often disposed of by motions for judgment on the pleadings or motions for **summary judgment.** In fact, cross-motions for summary judgment or judgment on the pleadings are common. As with other types of lawsuits involving dispositive motions, the parties file their motions, supported by memoranda of law explaining why the motion should be granted or denied. The memoranda of law are generally detailed and cite numerous precedential cases. A typical memorandum of law in support of the plaintiff's motion for summary judgment in an action against

──────────────── BALLENTINE'S ────────────────

summary judgment A method of disposing of an action without further proceedings. Under the Federal Rules of Civil Procedure, and the rules of civil procedure of many states, a party against whom a claim, counterclaim, or cross-claim is asserted, or against whom a declaratory judgment is sought, may file a motion for summary judgment seeking judgment in her favor if there is no genuine issue as to any material fact.

the secretary of HHS contains an Introduction, Procedural History, Statement of the Issues, Statement of the Applicable Provisions of Law, Statement of Facts, Argument and Conclusion. Refer to Figure 9–7, which illustrates the Conclusion in Melinda Lewis's Memorandum of Law in Support of Motion for Summary Judgment. Note that she requests either that her case be reversed outright by the court or remanded to the secretary (SSA) for further proceedings.

FIGURE 9–7
Conclusion in Memorandum of Law in Support of Motion for Summary Judgment

<u>CONCLUSION</u>

The plaintiff respectfully submits that the Administrative Law Judge, as affirmed by the Secretary, applied an incorrect standard of law, that the decision is not supported by substantial evidence, and that in the event the decision of the Secretary is not reversed, the case should be remanded to the Secretary for such further proceedings as may be just and proper.

Respectfully submitted this the _10th_ day of October, 1994.

Susan Garcia

Susan Garcia
Attorney for the Plaintiff
77 West McDowell St.
Charlotte, NC 28202
704-555-5210

The Court's Disposition of Actions for Judicial Review

The court essentially has three choices of how to dispose of the case. First, it may affirm the agency's decision. If this happens, the attorney-paralegal team must then decide whether to pursue appeal with the appropriate federal appellate court. Second, the court may reverse the agency's decision and order the agency to grant the requested benefits, such as payment of Social Security disability benefits or granting a request for political asylum. If this happens, the case is sent back to the agency for implementation of the relief ordered by the court. The court may choose a third option, to remand the case to the agency for further proceedings. If this happens, the court issues an order that tells the agency the mistakes it made that warrant the remand and instructs the agency on the procedures it must now take. Assume that the federal district court finds that the SSA made a reversible error by failing to have a vocational expert testify at Melinda Lewis's hearing. The court remands the case for a supplemental hearing, which must include vocational expert testimony. The SSA may again decide, after the supplemental hearing, that Ms. Lewis is not disabled. If this happens, the attorney-paralegal team may again exhaust their administrative remedies and then seek judicial review in the federal district court.

Appeals to Federal Appellate Courts

As with other types of federal court action, an unfavorable decision can be appealed. If the action was filed in federal district court, appeal is taken to the United States Circuit Court of Appeals and then to the United States Supreme Court. Some lawsuits for judicial review are filed originally in the circuit court of appeals, so the next and only level of appeal is to the Supreme Court. In filing appeals to either the circuit court of appeals or the Supreme Court, follow the Federal Rules of Appellate Procedure and the individual courts' internal operating procedures, which are published in Title 28 of the United States Code.

SIDEBAR   Some federal appellate courts, and in particular the United States Supreme Court, have detailed rules that must be followed exactly. The attorney-paralegal team must review all the applicable rules carefully and allow plenty of time for preparation of all documents, especially appellate briefs, which require extensive preparation. Appellate courts have detailed requirements for the format and number of copies to be filed. Appellate courts also tend to enforce their filing deadlines strictly.

Lawsuits seeking judicial review of agency decisions and appeals, if necessary, are generally interesting and exciting work. The attorney-paralegal team does, however, work under considerable pressure during the course of these actions. It is all worthwhile when your law firm's client prevails. The client's case may even result in a published decision, and you can proudly point to the decision published in *Federal Supplement*, *Federal Reporter*, or even *United States Reports*.

Summary

Chapter 9 addresses one of the most important topics in administrative law—judicial review of agency actions. The courts' oversight is one of the most important controls on agency actions.

Distinguish De Novo Litigation from Judicial Review

The attorney-paralegal team litigates against federal agencies primarily in two circumstances. One is when an agency has named the client as a defendant, for instance in an employment discrimination lawsuit. This is de novo litigation, which involves presentation of witnesses and introduction of exhibits as in any other type of civil litigation. The second circumstance is judicial review of an agency's final decision that is adverse to your client. Here, the federal court's role is like that of an appellate court, reviewing the record to determine whether the agency committed reversible errors.

Issues Common to All Types of Litigation

There are concerns that are common to both types of lawsuits. These include following the Federal Rules of Civil Procedure, filing the action in the proper court (jurisdiction), service of process, and standing to sue. These common concerns are addressed at the end of Chapter 9, after the discussion of issues particular to lawsuits involving judicial review, such as scope of review and exhaustion of administrative remedies.

The Right to Judicial Review

The right to judicial review is not automatic. The attorney-paralegal team must clear several obstacles to obtain federal court review. These obstacles include nonreviewable agency actions, standing to sue, exhaustion of administrative remedies, ripeness, and agency-specific prefiling requirements.

The APA recognizes two instances in which agency actions are not subject to judicial review. One is when a statute precludes judicial review. The statute must, however, state specifically that the action is not subject to review. Because there is a strong presumption of reviewability, courts require clear and convincing evidence of the intent of Congress to make an action nonreviewable.

The second type of nonreviewable action is one that is committed to agency discretion. This applies when Congress has given an agency such great discretion that its decisions in that area are virtually nonreviewable, as with consular officers' decisions to deny visas.

Another potential obstacle to judicial review is standing to sue. Plaintiffs are not allowed to sue agencies unless they have sufficient stake in a justiciable controversy to obtain judicial resolution of that controversy. The idea is that the plaintiff must be sufficiently affected by the agency action to have a legitimate complaint. Standing is not an issue when Congress has conferred standing by statute. For instance, the Social Security Act provides that claimants have standing to seek court review of the SSA's final decision that they are not disabled. In the absence of a statutory provision for standing, the attorney-paralegal team must turn to the case law. The United States Supreme Court has developed a two-prong test to determine whether plaintiffs have standing to sue in the absence of a statutory provision. The first question is whether the plaintiffs have suffered injury in fact. The second question is whether the plaintiffs are "arguably within the zone of interest to be protected or regulated by the statute or constitutional guarantee in question." Many of the lawsuits involving standing issues are citizen suits, in which individuals file lawsuits to compel agencies to enforce the statutes delegated to them. Often groups such as environmental protection organizations file citizen suits, in which the plaintiffs are members of the organization who have suffered injury in fact.

Further obstacles to judicial review involve the timing of the lawsuit. Premature filing can lead to dismissal of the lawsuit. Some statutes require that plaintiffs file their lawsuits seeking judicial review within a certain number of days after receipt of the agency's final decision. Failure to comply with this deadline can result in dismissal. Agencies are generally authorized to waive the deadline if it is missed, but this is discretionary. Thus, the attorney-paralegal team should not rely on waiver of the deadline.

A lawsuit is also subject to dismissal if the plaintiff has not exhausted administrative remedies. Thus, the plaintiff must have followed through with all administrative appeals. With Social Security disability claims, this means appealing all the way through the Appeals Council. There are several purposes behind the exhaustion requirement, including to ensure that all agency errors are reviewed by the court at the same time, to allow full development of the administrative record, and to give agencies the opportunity to correct their errors. The exhaustion requirement may be waived when pursuit of administrative appeals would be futile or inadequate. This may be appropriate when the decision maker is obviously biased or when a constitutional issue exists.

A lawsuit must also be ripe for judicial review. The concept of ripeness is closely akin to exhaustion of administrative remedies and shares a common goal of preventing cases from reaching federal court prematurely. A case is not ripe for review if it has not developed into a full-blown case or controversy for the court to review.

A final obstacle to consider is that of prefiling requirements specific to a certain agency or a certain type of lawsuit. For instance, notice must be given to potential defendants before the filing of a citizen's suit. The attorney-paralegal team must check statutes and regulations carefully to identify such requirements.

Scope of Judicial Review

A court's scope of review is the extent to which it is allowed to examine the particular agency action at issue. The extent of the review varies, depending on the type of issue. When an action has been committed to the agency's discretion, the court employs a narrow scope of review. In contrast, if the constitutionality of the action is at issue, the court adopts an expansive scope of review. Generally, courts have a wider scope of review of questions of law than questions of fact. The purpose of having limitations on courts' scope of review is to ensure that the courts do not substitute their own judgment for that of the agencies' decision makers.

Section 706 of the APA is the principal statutory authority that governs judicial review of agency action. Section 706 lists the types of agency actions that courts must hold unlawful and set aside. Section 706 lists six such types of actions, referred to in the text as the "Six Commandments." Section 706 essentially instructs agencies not to abuse their discretion or to engage in actions that are arbitrary and capricious, not to contravene the United States Constitution, not to exceed their statutory authority, and not to make decisions unsupported by substantial evidence. Section 706 also requires agencies to follow the procedures prescribed by law.

Paralegals must understand the difference between questions of law and questions of fact because the scope of review is wider for questions of law than for questions of fact. A question of law addresses the interpretation of the statutes that agencies administer, while a question of fact addresses the resolution of a factual dispute.

In reviewing a case for reversible errors, the attorney-paralegal team can use four questions, derived from section 706 of the APA. First, did the agency apply a valid law and interpret that law correctly? Courts do not allow agencies to enforce unconstitutional statutes and regulations, and courts have a wide scope of review to examine constitutional questions. Courts can, however, reach different conclusions. Review the text's discussion of the cases challenging the constitutionality of the Immigration Marriage Fraud Amendments of 1986 for an example. Courts also have a fairly wide scope of review when examining agencies' interpretations of statutes. Courts are not, however, allowed to substitute their own interpretation of a statute just because the court disagrees with the agency's interpretation. Rather, courts examine whether the agency has upheld the legislative intent of the statute and whether the agency's construction of the statute is permissible. If an agency's interpretation is reasonable, courts generally uphold the agency's conclusions. The same principles regarding validity and interpretation apply equally to agencies' regulations.

The second question is whether the evidence of record supports the agency's findings of fact. The general rule is that the agency's findings of fact must be supported by substantial evidence. Paralegals must read the case law to understand what the courts will find to constitute substantial evidence. The general rule is that substantial evidence is "more than a scintilla" and "such relevant evidence as a reasonable mind might accept as adequate." Although section 706 provides for de novo review of factual findings, with the court making independent findings of fact, this occurs rarely, only when the agencies' findings are unwarranted by the facts.

The third question is whether the agency action was arbitrary, capricious, or an abuse of discretion. In order to understand what the courts consider to be arbitrary and capricious, paralegals must read the case law and identify cases similar to their clients' facts. Some actions that may fall within this category are decisions that are contrary to the agency's regulations or decisions with similar facts but wildly different outcomes. Whether an action constitutes an abuse of discretion depends in part upon the degree of discretion committed to the agency for the particular type of action in question.

The fourth question is whether the agency committed procedural errors. The attorney-paralegal team must become very familiar with the agency's regulations to identify procedural errors. Be alert for lack of proper notice or other procedures required by due process.

Procedure for Pursuing Judicial Review

This section addresses the concerns common to all types of civil litigation in federal court, with special note of requirements peculiar to lawsuits seeking judicial review of agency actions. The attorney-paralegal team must follow the Rules of Civil Procedure, but must be alert for additional rules peculiar to certain types of lawsuits. For instance, an action for judicial review of the SSA's decision that a claimant is not disabled must be commenced within sixty days of notice of the SSA's final decision. Jurisdiction is always a concern with federal court litigation, and the attorney-paralegal team must check the applicable statutes to determine the proper court in which to file a lawsuit. The format of the complaint is like that in other types of lawsuits, but some special allegations must be made, including a statement that the plaintiff has exhausted administrative remedies or an explanation as to why an exception to this requirement applies. Name the appropriate defendant, who is usually the head of the agency you are suing.

Rule 4(d)(4) of the Federal Rules of Civil Procedure sets forth the specific requirements for service of process on a federal agency. The summons and complaint must be served on the United States Attorney for the district in which the action is filed, the head of the agency, and the United States Attorney General.

Actions against federal agencies can be settled, just as other lawsuits can. For instance, the agency may agree to remand the case for further administrative proceedings, such as a new hearing. Actions seeking judicial review are frequently disposed of by motions such as summary judgment, judgment on the pleadings, or a motion to dismiss.

Courts have basically three options for disposition of cases involving judicial review. The court may affirm the agency's decision. The court may reverse the agency's decision outright and award the benefits requested. The court may remand the case to the agency with instructions for further actions to take before issuing a new decision. Finally, if the first level of judicial review produces a result unfavorable to the client, the attorney-paralegal team may choose to appeal to the next level federal court, all the way to the United States Supreme Court.

Review Questions

1. The principal statutory authority that governs judicial review of agency action is _____.
   a. the Freedom of Information Act
   b. section 706 of the Administrative Procedure Act
   c. the National Environmental Policy Act
   d. the Federal Tort Claims Act

2. Which of the following can constitute an injury in fact to satisfy the standing requirement? _____
   a. threats to environmental well-being
   b. threats to aesthetic well-being
   c. threats to economic interests
   d. all of the above
   e. a and c only

3. The interpretation of the Social Security Act is _____.

   a. a question of law
   b. a question of fact
   c. not subject to judicial review
   d. none of the above

4. Which of the following are appropriate grounds for challenging agency regulations? _____
   a. The regulations are unconstitutional.
   b. The regulations exceed the authority granted to the agency in the delegation statute.
   c. The regulations are arbitrary and capricious.
   d. all of the above
   e. a and b only

5. When a federal administrative agency is the defendant, the summons and complaint must be served on which of the following? _____
   a. the United States Attorney for the district in which the action is filed
   b. the United States Attorney General
   c. the head of the agency being sued
   d. all of the above
   e. a and c only

6. Which of the following are exceptions to the strong presumption that agency actions are reviewable by the courts? _____
   a. A statute shows by clear and convincing evidence that Congress intended to preclude judicial review.
   b. Congress has given the agency such broad discretion that the action is not reviewable.
   c. A statute implies that Congress intended to preclude judicial review.
   d. all of the above
   e. a and b only

7. Which of the following may result in dismissal of a lawsuit seeking judicial review of an agency action? _____
   a. The issue is not ripe for judicial review.
   b. The plaintiff did not exhaust administrative appeals.
   c. The plaintiff failed to comply with agency-specific prefiling requirements.
   d. all of the above
   e. a and b only

8. Administrative agencies are not given the discretion to waive the timely filing of a lawsuit seeking judicial review.   True ___ / False ___

9. Exhaustion of administrative remedies is required even when the only issue is the constitutionality of a statute the agency has enforced.
   True ___ / False ___

10. The Social Security Act confers standing to seek judicial review on claimants when SSA's final decision was adverse to them.
    True ___ / False ___

11. Standing is not precluded even when Congress has not directly conferred standing by means of a statute.   True ___ / False ___

12. When a court decides that a narrow scope of review is appropriate, it is more likely to uphold the agency action.   True ___ / False ___

13. Name three reasons that administrative remedies must be exhausted before filing an action for judicial review.

14. Describe three ways that a court is allowed to dispose of a lawsuit for judicial review of the SSA's decision that a claimant is not disabled.

15. What allegations regarding exhaustion of administrative remedies should be included in a complaint seeking judicial review of agency decisions?

Practical Applications

Section 205(g) of the Social Security Act (42 U.S.C. § 405(g)) governs many aspects of judicial review of SSA's decision that a claimant is not disabled. Refer to section 205(b), which is in Figure 9–1, and answer the following questions.

1. What amount must be in controversy in order for the federal court to have jurisdiction?

2. What is the statutory deadline for commencing the action? Is the SSA allowed to grant an extension?

3. Is the action brought in a federal district court or in a federal circuit court of appeals?

4. In which judicial district does section 205(g) instruct the plaintiff to file the lawsuit?

5. Section 205(g) gives the federal district court authority to take three different actions when it review the SSA's final decision. What are those actions?

6. When are the SSA's findings of fact conclusive?

7. Is the federal district court's judgment final when it reviews the SSA's decision?

8. Assume that a lawsuit was filed in 1994 and thus named Donna Shalala, the secretary of health and human services, as the defendant. Assume further that in 1995 Donna Shalala had resigned and there was a new secretary of HHS. Does the lawsuit survive the appointment of a new secretary of HHS?

Case Analysis

Read the following excerpt from *Coffman v. Bowen*, 829 F.2d 514 (4th Cir. 1987), and answer the following questions.

|||| ||||

COFFMAN
v.
BOWEN

United States Court of Appeals,
Fourth Circuit.
Decided Sept. 23, 1987.

VAN GRAAFEILAND, Circuit Judge:
Hallie Coffman, as Executrix of Estate of Junior R. Coffman, appeals from a judgment of the United States District Court for the Northern District of West Virginia (Kidd, J.), which affirmed the Secretary of Health and Human Services' denial of Junior Coffman's claim for Social Security disability benefits. For the reasons that follow, we reverse the district court's judgment with instructions to remand to the Secretary for a computation and award of benefits.

On May 7, 1981, Junior Coffman, then fifty-six years of age, applied for disability benefits under sections 216(i) and 223 of the Social Security Act, alleging an onset date of August 19, 1980. In the

Secretary's initial Disability Determination, Coffman was held to have retained residual functional capacity to perform light work that did not include stooping, kneeling, crouching and crawling, and his claim for benefits was denied. Coffman's request for reconsideration was denied. At the request of Coffman's counsel, a hearing was held on July 23, 1982, before an administrative law judge, who determined that Coffman was not under a disability as that term is defined in the Act. The Appeals Council of the Social Security Administration affirmed. Coffman commenced his district court action on December 22, 1982. On February 9, 1986, "so tired of this kind of living", Coffman committed suicide. His wife was substituted as plaintiff, and, on November 21, 1986, her complaint was dismissed.

The only witness at the administrative hearing was Coffman himself. Coffman testified that his schooling had terminated at the eighth grade and that he had worked in the coal mines for over thirty years. He said that he was hospitalized on August 20, 1980 because of a work-related injury to his back and that his attending physician at the time of hearing was Dr. Louis Groves, whom he was seeing regularly. . . .

Dr. Groves reported that Coffman had far advanced degenerative changes throughout his spine, rheumatoid arthritis with pain in multiple joints that varied in intensity and location, and x-ray evidence of pneumoconiosis. Dr. Groves concluded that "without any question this man is totally and permanently disabled for any occupation [the Secretary] might reasonably expect him to pursue."

A district court's primary function in reviewing an administrative finding of no disability is to determine whether the ALJ's decision was supported by substantial evidence. However, the court's duty does not end there. A factual finding by the ALJ is not binding if it was reached by means of an improper standard or misapplication of the law. Our review of the record has convinced us that the ALJ applied erroneous legal standards in making several factual findings in the instant case.

A well established rule followed with minor variations in almost every circuit is the so-called attending physicians rule. As applied in the Fourth Circuit, that rule requires that the opinion of a claimant's treating physician be given great weight and may be disregarded only if there is persuasive contradictory evidence. The ALJ, in the instant case, after acknowledging Dr. Groves' conclusion that Coffman was disabled from gainful employment, said:

> The weight to be given such conclusionary statement depends on the extent to which it is supported by specific and completed clinical findings and other evidence. I find that this conclusionary statement does not have the required support in the record.

The first quoted sentence was a misstatement of the legal principles and standards that should have guided the ALJ in making his factual findings. "A treating physician's testimony is ignored *only* if there is persuasive contradictory evidence." There was no persuasive contradictory evidence in the instant case. For this reason, if for no other, the denial of benefits must be reversed.

Indeed, not only was there no persuasive contradictory evidence, there was in fact substantial supportive evidence. Dr. Groves forwarded fifteen pages of medical reports with his opinion letter, including clinical notes of seven examinations of Coffman, a treadmill workload and physical performance text, a radiological examination of Coffman's lumbar, dorsal, and cervical spine, an ecg analysis, and the results of a rheumatoid arthritis test. The findings of Dr. Hunter and Dr. Thompson already have been noted. Finally, there was the testimony of Coffman himself.

Finally, we conclude that the ALJ applied improper standards in making his determination that, although Coffman could not return to work in the mines, there were other kinds of "substantial gainful work which exists in the national economy" that Coffman could perform. Once a claimant has made a prima facie showing of a physical impairment that precludes him from performing past work, the Secretary has the burden of going forward and showing that the claimant, considering his age, education, work experience, skills and physical shortcomings, has the capacity to perform an alternate job and that this type of job exists in the national economy. The Secretary can meet this burden by proper reference to the medical-vocational guidelines set forth in 20 C.F.R. Pt. 404, Subpt. P, App. 2. However, in cases such as Coffman's reference which routinely and mechanically follows the provisions of the guidelines is not proper. The guidelines provide an ALJ with administrative notice of classes of jobs available in the national economy for persons who have, among other things, certain disability characteristics such as strength or exertional limitations. The guidelines do not take into account nonexertional limitations such as pain, loss of hearing, loss of manual dexterity, postural limitations and pulmonary impairment. When nonexertional limitations such as these occur in conjunction with exertional limitations, the guidelines are not to be treated as conclusive.

Without any substantial supportive evidence, the ALJ found that Coffman had functional capacity to perform medium work as defined in 20 C.F.R. § 404.1567(c), *i.e.,* "lifting no more than 50 pounds at a time with frequent lifting or carrying of objects weighing up to 25 pounds." He then found:

> Considering the claimant's age, education, prior work experience and residual functional capacity to perform medium work, Rule 203.04 of Appendix 2, Subpart P, Social Security Administration Regulations No. 4 applies and the claimant is found "not disabled."

This mechanical application of the guidelines, where, as here, substantial nonexertional impairments existed, constituted reversible error.

Having determined for the reasons above expressed that the Secretary's denial of benefits cannot stand, we must decide what course to follow. Over six years have elapsed since Junior Coffman filed his claim for disability benefits, and over five years have elapsed since they were wrongfully denied. Three years ago, Coffman, who was being medicated for heart pain at the time of his administrative hearing, had triple bypass heart surgery, and last year he committed suicide. Coffman's widow has asked that we either reverse and direct an award of benefits or remand to the Secretary for a rehearing. We, of course, have the statutory authority to do either. We are convinced, however, that if the matter were to be remanded to the Secretary for redetermination and the Secretary were to conclude again that Coffman was not disabled, his decision would not withstand judicial review. It is time to bring this matter to a close. We reverse the district court's judgment with instructions to remand to the Secretary for a computation of appropriate statutory benefits due and owing to Junior Coffman based on a total permanent disability commencing on August 20, 1980.

REVERSED AND REMANDED FOR AN AWARD OF BENEFITS.

1. How did the Fourth Circuit Court of Appeals describe the district court's primary function in the judicial review of an ALJ's decision finding that a claimant is not disabled?
2. A finding of fact must be set aside if it is not supported by substantial evidence. The Fourth Circuit describes another circumstance in which an ALJ's factual finding is not binding. Explain that circumstance.
3. What weight must an ALJ give to the opinion of a treating physician?
4. When can an ALJ disregard the opinion of a treating physician?
5. What is the claimant's burden of proof to establish that he is disabled?

Notes

[1] *Abbott Laboratories v. Gardner,* 387 U.S. 136 (1967).

[2] *Sierra Club v. Morton,* 405 U.S. 727, 731 (1972).

[3] *Association of Data Processing Serv. Organizations v. Camp,* 397 U.S. 150 (1970).

[4] *Black's Law Dictionary* 1260 (5th ed. 1979).

[5] 8 U.S.C. § 1105a(a)(2).

[6] Stephen Berlin, "Litigation, Settlement and Insurance Issues," *Environmental Law Handbook 1993* (Wake Forest Univ. School of Law), at 139.

[7] J. David Farren, "Citizens Suits and Public Interest Issues," *Environmental Law Handbook 1993* (Wake Forest Univ. School of Law), at 184.

[8] *Association of Data Processing Serv. Organizations v. Camp,* 397 U.S. 150, 152–53 (1970).

[9] Ernest Gellhorn & Ronald Levin, *Administrative Law and Procedure in a Nutshell,* 3d ed. (St. Paul: West Publishing Co., 1990), at 371.

[10] 397 U.S. at 156.

[11] 405 U.S. 727 (1972).

[12] J.G. Arbuckle, *et al., Environmental Law Handbook,* 12th ed. (Rockville, MD: Government Institutes, Inc., 1993), at 26.

[13] 412 U.S. 669 (1973).

[14] J.G. Arbuckle, *et al., Environmental Law Handbook,* 12th ed. (Rockville, MD: Government Institutes, Inc., 1993), at 26. *See, e.g., Lujan v. Defenders of Wildlife,* 110 S. Ct. 3177 (1990).

[15] *Mathews v. Eldridge,* 424 U.S. 319 (1976); *Social Security Law and Practice* § 55:31 (New York: Clark Boardman Callaghan, 1987).

[16] *Myers v. Bethlehem Shipbuilding Corp.,* 303 U.S. 41, 50–51 (1938).

[17] 422 U.S. 749 (1975).

[18] *White Mountain Apache Tribe v. Hodel,* 840 F.2d 675 (9th Cir. 1988).

[19] *Manwani v. U.S. Dep't of Justice, INS,* 736 F. Supp. 1367 (W.D.N.C. 1990).

[20] 424 U.S. 319 (1976).

[21] *Abbott Laboratories v. Gardner,* 387 U.S. 136, 148–49 (1967).

[22] Lief Carter, *Administrative Law and Politics* (Glenview, IL: Scott, Foresman and Company, 1983), at 222.

[23] Farren, *supra* note 7, at 187 (citing 40 CFR 54 (Clean Air Act), 40 CFR 135.1 (Clean Water Act), and 40 CFR 254 (RCRA)).

[24] Kenneth Culp Davis, *Administrative Law and Government* (St. Paul: West Publishing Co., 1975), at 59.

[25] Gellhorn & Levin, *supra* note 9, at 73.

[26] Davis, *supra* note 24, at 59.

[27] Davis, *supra* note 24, at 60.

[28] Administrative Conference of the United States, *Federal Administrative Procedure Sourcebook,* 2d ed. (Office of the Chairman, 1992), at 209 (hereinafter ACUS *Sourcebook*).

[29] *Id.* at 207.

[30] *Id.* at 209.

[31] *Id.*

[32] 430 U.S. 792 (1977).

[33] *Id.*

[34] 419 F. Supp. 86 (D. Conn. 1989).

[35] *Id.* at 90.
[36] 436 F. Supp. 1367 (W.D.N.C. 1990).
[37] ACUS *Sourcebook, supra* note 28, at 209.
[38] 467 U.S. 837, *reh'g denied,* 468 1227 (1984).
[39] 787 F.2d 101 (3d Cir. 1986).
[40] *Id.* at 104.
[41] 480 U.S. 421 (1987).
[42] *Id.* at 450.
[43] 461 U.S. 458 (1983).
[44] Refer to the *Resource Manual,* Chapter 3.
[45] *Richardson v. Perales,* 402 U.S. 389 (1971).
[46] *Garner v. Heckler,* 745 F.2d 383, 387 (6th Cir. 1984).
[47] 401 U.S. 402 (1971).
[48] *Id.* at 416.
[49] ACUS *Sourcebook, supra* note 28, at 210.
[50] *Id.* at 209.
[51] Lee Modjeska, *Administrative Law Practice and Procedure* (Rochester, NY: The Lawyers Co-operative Publishing Co., 1982), at 218.
[52] 401 U.S. 402, 416 (1971).
[53] Gellhorn & Levin, *supra* note 9, at 100–01.

||||

CHAPTER 10

LEGAL ETHICS: GENERAL RULES AND STANDARDS OF CONDUCT SPECIFIC TO FEDERAL GOVERNMENT EMPLOYEES

By now you are familiar with the rules of ethics that govern attorneys' conduct, including each state's rules of ethics and the Model Rules of the American Bar Association, on which many states' rules are based. Ethics rules, such as the duty to preserve client confidences and to avoid conflicts of interest, apply in the area of administrative law, as in all other areas of law. In addition to the rules of ethics common to every state, there are specific laws that govern the conduct of government employees. These laws deserve special attention also, because they apply not only to attorneys, but to every employee of the executive branch of government.

How State Rules of Professional Conduct and Rules Specific to Government Employees' Conduct Differ

There are two important differences between state rules of professional conduct and rules specific to federal government employees. First, the rules specific to government employees apply directly not just to attorneys but to all employees. Second, paralegals are subject to direct imposition of sanctions for violating rules that apply to all government employees. A state bar generally has the authority to impose disciplinary penalties only on attorneys, and not on paralegals. In contrast, regulations and statutes that apply to federal employees can impose penalties on all government employees to whom the restrictions apply. For instance, title 18 of the United States Code provides for imposition of criminal penalties not just on attorneys who violate federal conflict of interest statutes, but on other federal employees as well.

Suppose a paralegal who is an employee of a federal administrative agency commits an act that violates a conflict of interest statute. The paralegal is subject to direct imposition of criminal penalties. This contrasts with a paralegal who works with a private law firm and commits an act that violates a state's rules of professional conduct. Here, the sanction is imposed on the attorney for whom the paralegal works, because the state bar has the authority to impose sanctions only on attorneys.

Why It Is Important for Paralegals to Be Familiar with State Rules of Professional Conduct and Rules Specific to Government Employees

Paralegals must be familiar both with state rules of professional conduct and with the statutes and regulations that apply specifically to federal employees. They must be alert for potential ethics problems, especially in the area of conflicts of interest, that have their source both in state rules of professional conduct and in federal law. Paralegals who are employees of federal administrative agencies must comply with these laws. Paralegals who work with private law firms that deal with federal agencies must also be familiar with these laws in order to avoid putting federal employees in an awkward position and to avoid giving the impression of trying to influence the federal employee. For instance, there are very specific regulations governing federal employees' acceptance of gifts. An innocent gesture of appreciation could be misinterpreted as an attempt at undue influence if acceptance of the gift would cause the federal employee to contravene federal law. Thus, knowledge of the ethics laws specific to federal employees allows a smoother working relationship with federal agencies.

The restrictions on paralegals who are employees of federal agencies are extensive. Many people do not realize the extent of the restrictions on their actions until they begin employment with a federal agency. The regulations impose a duty on federal employees to recognize potential conflicts of interest. If paralegals are unaware of the applicable statutes and regulations, they are unable to recognize potential conflicts.

Chapter 10 addresses some of the rules of professional conduct that are particularly important to attorneys and paralegals who work in the area of administrative law. A detailed discussion of the rules would fill volumes, and there are texts available solely on the subject of legal ethics. The purpose of Chapter 10 is to gain an overview of the applicable rules so that paralegals know the applicable sources of law to consult when ethics questions arise.

Ethics Rules of General Applicability

The following discussion focuses on the Model Rules of Professional Conduct (Model Rules) developed by the American Bar Association (ABA). The ABA Model Rules themselves do not directly regulate lawyers. Rather, they serve as the model for the state rules of ethics. Because the ABA Model Rules have been adopted in some form by the majority of states, they provide common ground for a discussion of rules of ethics of general applicability.[1]

The Duty to Supervise Nonlawyer Assistants

Model rule 5.3 imposes on lawyers the duty to supervise the conduct of nonlawyer assistants. Lawyers have a duty to ensure that their nonlawyer assistants' "conduct is compatible with the professional obligations of the lawyer." As the comment to model rule 5.3 explains, "[a] lawyer should give such assistants appropriate instruction and supervision concerning the ethical aspects of their employment, particularly regarding the obligation not to disclose information relating to representation of the client, and should be responsible for their work product."

In many areas of administrative law, particularly immigration law, paralegals may prepare crucial legal documents, such as visa petitions. In fact, the paralegal may gather the facts and documentation from the client, complete the INS application, draft supporting affidavits, and assemble the supporting documentation, before giving the entire package to the attorney for review. The work product of experienced paralegals may require little rewriting or change. Attorneys must, however, review a paralegal's work product and sign the documents. This is an ethical obligation.

Rule 5.3 provides that lawyers are responsible for the conduct of nonlawyer employees that is incompatible with the Rules of Professional Conduct if the lawyer instructs the employee to take the incompatible action or has knowledge of the action but fails to take appropriate measures to stop the conduct and mitigate its consequences. In order to achieve proper oversight, attorneys must keep abreast of their nonlawyer assistants' work and provide proper training so that the employees are aware of ethical obligations.

The Duty to Assist in Preventing the Unauthorized Practice of Law

Closely related is model rule 5.5, which prohibits lawyers from assisting nonlawyers "in the performance of activity that constitutes the unauthorized practice of law." The comment to rule 5.5 explains that the rule does not prohibit lawyers from employing nonlawyer assistants and delegating functions to them, "so long as the lawyer supervises the delegated work and retains responsibility for their work." In order to satisfy model rules 5.3 and 5.5, the attorney-paralegal team must work closely together and keep each other well-informed about their work.

Special Considerations in Administrative Law

In some areas of administrative law, specific regulations allow paralegals to represent clients and to work without attorney supervision. For instance, paralegals often represent Social Security claimants and appear at the disability hearings, questioning the witnesses and presenting written and oral arguments as to why the ALJ should find their clients disabled. Remember, however, that the Social Security regulations (20 CFR 404.1705) specifically provide that a claimant's representative may be either an attorney or a person who is not an attorney. Refer to Figure 10–1, which reprints 20 CFR 404.1705.

FIGURE 10–1
20 CFR 404.1705

> **§ 404.1705 Who may be your representative.**
>
> (a) *Attorney.* You may appoint as your representative in dealings with us, any attorney in good standing who—
> (1) Has the right to practice law before a court of a State, Territory, District, or Island possession of the United States, or before the Supreme Court or a lower Federal court of the United States;
> (2) Is not disqualified or suspended from acting as a representative in dealings with us; and
> (3) Is not prohibited by any law from acting as a representative.
> (b) *Person other than attorney.* You may appoint any person who is not an attorney to be your representative in dealings with us if he or she—
> (1) Is generally known to have a good character and reputation;
> (2) Is capable of giving valuable help to you in connection with your claim;
> (3) Is not disqualified or suspended from acting as a representative in dealings with us; and
> (4) Is not prohibited by any law from acting as a representative.

INS regulations also allow for representation by both attorneys and nonattorneys in some instances. Refer to the portions of 8 CFR 292.1 and 292.2 reprinted in Figure 10–2. The INS regulations state that attorneys and law students supervised by attorneys may serve as representatives for foreign nationals in proceedings before the INS and the Board of Immigration Appeals (BIA). Certain nonlawyers are also authorized to serve as representatives. These include "reputable individuals" who serve without remuneration, who had a preexisting relationship with the foreign national, and who have obtained permission to appear from the INS or BIA. The regulations provide, however, that "such permission shall not be granted with respect to any individual who regularly engages in immigration and naturalization practice or preparation, or holds himself out to the public as qualified to do so." The INS regulations also allow for "accredited representatives." These are individuals who work with nonprofit organizations recognized by the BIA. As the regulations state, to be a recognized organization, the BIA must be satisfied that the organization charges only a nominal fee and has adequate knowledge, information, and experience.

FIGURE 10–2
8 CFR 292.1 and
292.2(a)

---

§ 292.1   Representation of others.

(a) A person entitled to representation may be represented by any of the following:

(1) *Attorneys in the United States.* Any attorney as defined in § 1.1(f) of this chapter.

(2) *Law students and law graduates not yet admitted to the bar.* A law student who is enrolled in an accredited law school, or a law graduate who is not yet admitted to the bar, provided that:

(i) He or she is appearing at the request of the person entitled to representation;

(ii) In the case of a law student, he or she has filed a statement that he or she is participating, under the direct supervision of a faculty member or an attorney, in a legal aid program or clinic conducted by the law school, and that he or she is appearing without direct or indirect remuneration;

(iii) In the case of a law graduate, he or she has filed a statement that he or she is appearing under the supervision of a licensed attorney or accredited representative and that he or she is appearing without direct or indirect remuneration; and

(iv) The law student's or law graduate's appearance is permitted by the official before whom he or she wishes to appear (namely an Immigration Judge, district director, officer-in-charge, regional commissioner, the Commissioner, or the Board). The official or officials may require that a law student be accompanied by the supervising faculty member or attorney.

(3) *Reputable individuals.* Any reputable individual of good moral character, provided that:

(i) He is appearing on an individual case basis, at the request of the person entitled to representation;

(ii) He is appearing without direct or indirect remuneration and files a written declaration to that effect;

(iii) He has a pre-existing relationship or connection with the person entitled to representation (e.g., as a relative, neighbor, clergyman, business associate or personal friend), provided that such requirement may be waived, as a matter of administrative discretion, in cases where adequate representation would not otherwise be available; and

(iv) His appearance is permitted by the official before whom he wished to appear (namely, a special inquiry officer, district director, officer-in-charge,

**FIGURE 10-2
(continued)**

regional commissioner, the Commissioner, or the Board), provided that such permission shall not be granted with respect to any individual who regularly engages in immigration and naturalization practice or preparation, or holds himself out to the public as qualified to do so.

(4) *Accredited representatives.* A person representing an organization described in § 292.2 of this chapter who has been accredited by the Board.

(5) *Accredited officials.* An accredited official, in the United States, of the government to which an alien owes allegiance, if the official appears solely in his official capacity and with the alien's consent.

(6) Attorneys outside the United States. An attorney other than one described in § 1.1(f) of this chapter who is licensed to practice law and is in good standing in a court of general jurisdiction of the country in which he/she resides and who is engaged in such practice. Provided that he/she represents persons only in matters outside the geographical confines of the United States as defined in section 101(a)(38) of the Act, and that the Service official before whom he/she wishes to appear allows such representation as a matter of discretion.

(b) *Persons formerly authorized to practice.* A person, other than a representative of an organization described in § 292.2 of this chapter, who on December 23, 1952, was authorized to practice before the Board and the Service may continue to act as a representative, subject to the provisions of § 292.3 of this chapter.

(c) *Former employees.* No person previously employed by the Department of Justice shall be permitted to act as a representative in any case in violation of the provisions of 28 CFR 45.735–7.

(d) *Amicus curiae.* The Board may grant permission to appear, on a case-by-case basis, as amicus curiae, to an attorney or to an organization represented by an attorney, if the public interest will be served thereby.

(e) Except as set forth in this section, no other person or persons shall represent others in any case.

[40 FR 23271, May 29, 1975 as amended at 53 FR 7728, Mar. 10, 1988; 55 FR 49251, Nov. 27, 1990]

§ 292.2   Organizations qualified for recognition; requests for recognition; withdrawal of recognition; accreditation of representatives; roster.

(a) *Qualifications of organizations.* A non-profit religious, charitable, social service, or similar organization established in the United States and recognized as such by the Board may designate a representative or representatives to practice before the Service and the Board. Such organization must establish to the satisfaction of the Board that:

(1) It makes only nominal charges and assesses no excessive membership dues for persons given assistance; and

(2) It has at its disposal adequate knowledge, information and experience.

Thus, paralegals have opportunities to serve as representatives in procedures before administrative agencies that are not available in state and federal court proceedings. Paralegals, like attorneys, must, however, meet the agencies' regulatory criteria. Further, paralegals, like attorneys, are subject to sanctions for misconduct in connection with representation in agency proceedings.

Agencies' Power to Sanction Representatives. Social Security regulations do not require that a nonattorney representative be accredited to appear before the Social Security Administration. Social Security regulations do, however, contain rules governing representatives. These regulations are a good example of an agency's power to sanction representatives. Refer to Figure 10–3, which reprints 20 CFR 404.1740, describing conduct that is forbidden of both attorney and nonattorney representatives. The SSA is authorized to institute disciplinary proceedings against representatives whose conduct contravenes rules of conduct set forth in the regulations. The SSA has the authority to suspend a representative for "a specified period of not less than 1 year, nor more than 5 years" or to disqualify the representative, although reinstatement at a later time may be possible (20 CFR 404.1770(a)). SSA regulations (20 CFR 404.1745–404.1799) detail the procedure for bringing charges, holding a hearing, and appealing adverse decisions. A representative who has been sanctioned has the right to appeal to the Appeals Council, but the regulations do not provide for judicial review. A substantial constitutional claim or a claim for mandamus may support an action in federal court for review, and courts may examine whether the SSA acted arbitrarily or exceeded its authority.[2]

FIGURE 10–3
20 CFR 404.1740

404.1740 Rules governing representatives.

No attorney or other person representing a claimant shall—

(a) With intent to defraud, in any manner willfully and knowingly deceive, mislead, or threaten by word, circular, letter, or advertisement, either oral or written, any claimant or prospective claimant or beneficiary regarding benefits, or other initial or continued right under the Act;

(b) Knowingly charge or collect, or make any agreement to charge or collect, directly or indirectly, any fee in any amount in excess of that allowed by us or by the court;

(c) Knowingly make or participate in the making or presentation of any false statement, representation, or claim about any material fact affecting the rights of any person under title II of the Act; or

(d) Divulge, except as may be authorized by regulations prescribed by us, any information we furnish or disclose about the claim or prospective claim of another person.

Thus, paralegals must also be familiar with specific agencies' regulations governing the conduct of representatives. In administrative law, there is no substitute for in-depth knowledge of the regulations of the agencies with whom paralegals deal.

The Duty to Preserve Client Confidences

Model rule 1.6 prohibits lawyers from disclosing information relating to the representation of clients unless an exception, permitting disclosure, applies. In the course of representation, clients must disclose much personal information to their attorneys, including financial data and potentially embarrassing or legally damaging information. Only with the assurance that the attorneys will keep the information confidential will clients be comfortable with full disclosure. Model rule 1.6 defines broadly information that is considered confidential. As the comments to rule 1.6 explain, the "confidentiality rule applies not merely to matters communicated in confidence by the client but also to all information relating to the representation, whatever its source." As noted, the ethics rules require attorneys to ensure that nonlawyer assistants preserve clients' confidential information.

SIDEBAR   Closely connected with the ethical duty to preserve confidential client information are the evidentiary privileges, including work product privilege, attorney-client privilege, and so forth. Paralegals must bear in mind *all* types of privileged and confidential information in order to avoid improper disclosure.

Exceptions: When Disclosure Is Allowed

There are exceptions to the prohibition against disclosing confidential client information, embodied in model rule 1.6. The language of the exceptions may vary somewhat from state to state, but there are four generally recognized exceptions. The first exception provides that disclosure is proper when clients have consented, after being fully informed of the consequences of disclosure. The second exception allows disclosure in the context of a dispute about the lawyer's conduct, such as when a client accuses an attorney of wrongdoing or raises a dispute about the amount of the attorney's fee. Third, an attorney may reveal a client's intention to commit a crime and information necessary to prevent the crime. Be careful to distinguish client information about a crime that has already been committed, which is protected from disclosure. Finally, attorneys may disclose information when permitted under other ethics rules or required by court order.

Application to Government Employees

There is no question that attorneys who work for government agencies must preserve confidential information. A comment to rule 1.6 makes it clear, however, that government attorneys must maintain the confidentiality of information even when they "may disagree with the policy goals that their representation is designed to advance." Suppose that a lawyer with the Army Corps of Engineers disagrees fundamentally with the Corps' plan to dam a scenic river. The Corps' plans have been challenged in court by an environmental protection group, and the attorney's sentiments lie with the environmental group. The attorney nevertheless has a duty to preserve the Corps' confidential information.

Successive Government and Private Employment

Model rule 1.11 addresses "successive government and private employment." The provisions of model rule 1.11 and related state ethics rules reflect concerns about conflicts of interest, protection of confidential information, and avoidance of the appearance of impropriety. All these concerns arise when an attorney either leaves a government agency to go into private practice in a related area of law or leaves private practice to work for an administrative agency in a related area of law.

To people who have not been involved with administrative law, this may seem like a long and complicated rule for a narrow concern. When you consider, however, that the federal government is the largest employer in the United States and that state governments also employ huge numbers of people, including many lawyers, you realize that the concern is actually a broad one. Looking simply at the four federal agencies on which the text has concentrated, consider that an attorney may leave the EEOC and go to work with a private law firm that concentrates on labor law or that a lawyer with the EPA may go to work for a law firm and concentrate practice in environmental law. An INS trial attorney may leave the INS and open her own immigration law practice. An attorney with the SSA's Office of Hearings and Appeals (OHA) may leave OHA and begin a private law practice with a concentration in the representation of claimants seeking Social Security disability benefits. Likewise, attorneys with experience in labor law, immigration law, or Social Security disability may leave private practice and go to work for the EEOC, the INS, or the SSA. This phenomenon of attorneys changing from private practice to government employment and vice versa is often referred to as "the revolving door."

The restrictions on attorneys involved in successive government and private employment, and the attorneys with whom they work, are addressed in model rule 1.11, which can be found in any publication that includes the ABA's Model Rules. In order to compare model rule 1.11 with a similar state ethics rule, the following discussion focuses on rule 9.1 of the North Carolina Rules of Professional Conduct. North Carolina rule 9.1 is similar to model rule 1.11 and illustrates its major points. Rule 9.1, however, has one variation from model rule 1.11, which serves as an interesting example of how state ethics rules can vary in narrow but important ways from the ABA's Model Rules.

Read North Carolina rule 9.1 and its comments, printed in Figure 10–4. Parts A and B apply to attorneys who have left government employment and entered private employment.

FIGURE 10–4
Rule 9.1 of the North Carolina Rules of Professional Conduct

CANON IX. A LAWYER SHOULD AVOID EVEN THE APPEARANCE OF PROFESSIONAL IMPROPRIETY

RULE 9.1 SUCCESSIVE GOVERNMENT AND PRIVATE EMPLOYMENT

(A) Except as law may otherwise expressly permit, a lawyer shall not represent a private client in connection with a matter in which the lawyer participated personally and substantially as a public officer or employee, unless the appropriate government agency consents after full disclosure. No lawyer in a firm with which that lawyer is associated may knowingly undertake or continue representation in such a matter without the consent of the public agency involved.

(B) Except as law may otherwise expressly permit, a lawyer having information that the lawyer knows is confidential government information about a person acquired when the lawyer was a public officer or employee may not represent a private client whose interests are adverse to that person on a matter in which the information could be used to the material disadvantage of that person. A firm with which that lawyer is associated may undertake or continue representation in the matter only with the consent of the person about whom the information was obtained.

(C) Except as law may otherwise expressly permit, a lawyer serving as a public officer or employee shall not:

(1) Participate in a matter in which the lawyer participated personally and substantially while in private practice or non-governmental employment, unless under applicable law no one is, or by lawful delegation may be, authorized to act in the lawyer's stead in the matter; or

(2) Negotiate for private employment with any person who is involved as a party or as attorney for a party in a matter in which the lawyer is participating personally and substantially.

(D) As used in this Rule, the term "matter" includes:

(1) Any judicial or other proceeding, application, request for a ruling or other determination, contract, claim, controversy, investigation, charge,

FIGURE 10–4
(continued)

accusation, arrest or other particular matter involving a specific party or parties; and

(2) Any other matter covered by the conflict of interest rules of the appropriate government agency.

(**E**) As used in this Rule, the term "confidential government information" means information which has been obtained under governmental authority and which, at the time this Rule is applied, the government is prohibited by law from disclosing to the public or has a legal privilege not to disclose, and which is not otherwise available to the public.

Comment

This Rule prevents a lawyer from exploiting public office for the advantage of a private client.

A lawyer representing a government agency, whether employed or specially retained by the government, is subject to the Rules of Professional Conduct, including the prohibition against representing adverse interests stated in Rule 5.1.

Where the successive clients are a public agency and a private client, the risk exists that power or discretion vested in public authority might be used for the special benefit of a private client. A lawyer should not be in a position where benefit to a private client might affect performance of the lawyer's professional functions on behalf of public authority. Also, unfair advantage could accrue to the private client by reason of access to confidential government information about the client's adversary obtainable only through the lawyer's government service.

When the client is an agency of one government, that agency should be treated as a private client for purposes of this Rule if the lawyer thereafter represents an agency of another government, as when a lawyer represents a city and subsequently is employed by a federal agency.

Paragraph (B) operates only when the lawyer in question has knowledge of the information, which means actual knowledge; it does not operate with respect to information that merely could be imputed to the lawyer.

Paragraphs (A) and (C) do not prohibit a lawyer from jointly representing a private party and a government agency when doing so is permitted by Rule 5.1 and is not otherwise prohibited by law.

Paragraph (C) does not disqualify other lawyers in the agency with which the lawyer in question has become associated.

Restrictions on the Former Government Attorney

The essential prohibition in part A is that an attorney is not allowed to "represent a private client in connection with a matter in which the lawyer participated personally and substantially as a public officer or employee. . . ." Part D defines "matter" broadly to include not just a judicial or administrative proceeding, but also contract negotiations, investigations, and other activities in which administrative agencies frequently engage. The term "personally and substantially" is not defined in North Carolina rule 9.1 or ABA model rule 1.11. Thus, in uncertain situations, attorneys should consult case law, ethics opinions from the ABA, and ethics opinions from the appropriate state bar. There are, however, some situations that clearly would violate this prohibition. For instance, suppose that an INS trial attorney participated in a deportation hearing that resulted in Mr. Kazemi's deportation. After the requisite waiting period expired, Mr. Kazemi wished to apply for a visa to live and work in the United States. The INS trial attorney had left the INS and was now in private practice. He could not represent Mr. Kazemi in connection with his efforts to enter the United States.

Similarly, suppose that an attorney with the SSA's Office of Hearing and Appeals (OHA) wrote a decision for an ALJ finding that Melinda Lewis was not disabled. The attorney subsequently went into private practice, and Ms. Lewis decided to file a new application for disability benefits. The former OHA attorney could not represent Ms. Lewis. Consider another OHA attorney who worked at OHA while Ms. Lewis's application was being considered but who never worked on the case or had any knowledge of it. If this attorney went into private practice, she could represent Ms. Lewis.

Restrictions on the Lawyers in the Firm with Whom the Former Government Attorney Is Associated

Part A of North Carolina rule 9.1 provides that when the former government lawyer herself would be prohibited from providing representation because of her past government employment, another lawyer in the firm may provide representation, provided the public agency involved consents. Here, the North Carolina rule differs from the ABA model rule. Model rule 1.11 does not require consent from the government. Rather, it allows the other lawyers in the firm to undertake representation if "the disqualified lawyer is screened from any participation in the matter and is apportioned no part of the fee therefrom" and prompt written notice is given to the appropriate government agency. This insulation of the disqualified lawyer is often referred to as erecting a "chinese wall" or "chinese screen."

Prohibition on the Use of Confidential Government Information

Part B of North Carolina rule 9.1 prohibits former government attorneys from using confidential government information gained about a person "to the material disadvantage of that person." Thus, if a former government attorney knows confidential government information about

Mr. Smith, that attorney may not represent a person whose interests are adverse to those of Mr. Smith and use that information to Mr. Smith's "material disadvantage." Other attorneys in the former government attorney's law firm may represent the person with interests adverse to Mr. Smith if, under the North Carolina rule, Mr. Smith consents. Under model rule 1.11, the other attorneys may represent the person if the former government attorney is screened from participation in the case and is apportioned no part of the fee.

Prohibitions on Private Attorneys Who Move into Government Employment

Part C of North Carolina rule 9.1 applies to attorneys who have left private employment to work for the government. Part C prohibits government attorneys from participating in matters in which they "participated personally and substantially while in private practice or non-governmental employment," with one narrow exception. This is the flip side of part A, which prohibits participation as a private attorney in matters in which the attorney participated personally and substantially while working for the government. These restrictions prevent the use of confidential client information, whether the attorney's former client was a government agency or a private individual.

The comments to North Carolina rule 9.1 and model rule 1.11 specify that if a government attorney is disqualified from participation in a particular matter, this does not disqualify the other attorneys in the agency from participation in the matter. Such a prohibition would put an undue burden on government agencies.

Part C also provides that government attorneys may not negotiate for private employment with a party or an attorney for a party "in a matter in which the lawyer is participating personally and substantially." Suppose that an EEOC lawyer was trying a lawsuit against a company charged with a title VII violation. The general counsel for the corporation was so impressed with the EEOC attorney's abilities that she asked the attorney to consider a position as assistant counsel for the defendant corporation. While that lawsuit was active, the EEOC lawyer could not negotiate for employment with the defendant corporation.

Comment 2 to model rule 1.11 states that in addition to the restrictions in rule 1.11, lawyers representing government agencies are also subject to the prohibition against representing adverse interests stated in model rule 1.7 and the protections afforded former clients in rule 1.9. The comment further notes that in addition, lawyers for government agencies are subject "to statutes and government regulations regarding conflict of interest." Lawyers for government agencies are indeed subject not just to general ethics rules, but also to regulations and statutes that govern the conduct of all government employees. Thus, it is important to consider the laws that address the conduct of all government employees, not just lawyers for government agencies.

Statutes and Regulations Specific to Government Employees

Federal government personnel deal with huge numbers of people, and in light of the sheer mass of these interactions, situations that present conflicts of interest are bound to arise. For instance, government employees negotiate contracts worth billions of dollars. Suppose that a potential contractor has lunch with the government employee who will decide who gets a large contract, and the potential contractor offers to pay for the government employee's lunch. Is the government employee allowed to accept? Regulations address this specific question. Before addressing this and other laws that guide the conduct of government employees, a brief overview of the sources of the law of the standards of ethical conduct is instructive.

The Sources of Law of the Standards of Conduct of Government Employees

The governmentwide standards of conduct have their source in statutes, regulations, and executive orders dating back to the 1960s. The "bribery, graft, and conflict of interest" statutes (18 U.S.C. §§ 201–209) that set forth criminal penalties for certain conduct have been in effect since 1963.[3] In October 1978 the Ethics in Government Act was signed into law, but the responsibility for administering the ethics programs remained with individual agencies.[4]

The Ethics Reform Act of 1989 added significant amendments, pertaining in large part to the solicitation and receipt of gifts from outside sources. The Ethics Reform Act of 1989, together with Executive Order 12731, authorized the Office of Government Ethics to promulgate "regulations that establish a single, comprehensive, and clear set of executive-branch standards of conduct that shall be objective, reasonable, and enforceable."[5] The final regulations were published at 57 *Federal Register* 35006–35067 (August 7, 1992) and became effective on February 3, 1993. The regulations may now be found in 5 CFR part 2635.

There are other statutes affecting the conduct of employees of the federal government, such as the Hatch Act (5 U.S.C. § 7321 *et seq.*), which governs federal employees' participation in the political process. Thus, although the Standards of Ethical Conduct in 5 CFR part 2635 provide uniform guidance for employees, federal government employees must also be aware of a host of other federal statutes that govern their conduct. The detailed regulations, together with the other applicable statutes, may cause confusion and raise questions as to whether a federal employee can engage in certain conduct. There are designated people in the federal government to whom employees may turn for ethics advice.

Sources of Ethics Advice for Federal Agency Employees

Paralegals who work for federal administrative agencies will at times have questions on whether they are allowed to do certain things, ranging from accepting a gift from a coworker to the propriety of having an additional part-time job.

The Office of Government Ethics

The Ethics Reform Act of 1989 created the Office of Government Ethics (OGE) as an executive agency, separating it from the Office of Personnel and Management (OPM), of which it was formerly a part. In addition to promulgating the regulations pertaining to standards of ethical conduct, OGE also has responsibility for "providing ethics program assistance and information to executive branch agencies through a desk officer system" and "providing guidance on and promoting understanding of ethical standards in executive agencies through an extensive program of Government ethics advice, education, and training."[6] OGE provides advisory letters and formal advisory opinions. Thus, OGE is a major source of ethics advice.

Agency Ethics Officials

The Standards of Ethical Conduct require each agency to have a "designated agency ethics official who, on the agency's behalf, is responsible for coordinating and managing the agency's ethics programs. . . ." (5 CFR 2635.17). The Standards of Ethical Conduct direct employees with questions to seek advice from an agency ethics official. The regulations (5 CFR 2635.107(b)) provide for reliance on this advice, stating that

> [d]isciplinary action for violating . . . agency regulations will not be taken against an employee who has engaged in conduct in good faith reliance upon the advice of an agency ethics official, provided that the employee, in seeking such advice, has made full disclosure of all relevant circumstances.

The regulations further note, however, that reliance on an agency ethics official's advice will not necessarily shield the employee from prosecution when the employee's conduct violates a criminal statute.

Paralegals who work for federal administrative agencies have a duty to seek advice about ethics questions. Paralegals may consult their agency's ethics officials and personnel in the Office of Government Ethics. Note, however, that it may be a good idea to first consult with your immediate supervisor. Chain of command has an important place in federal agencies, and your immediate supervisor may either know the answer to your question or readily direct you to an agency ethics official.

A Closer Look at the Standards of Ethical Conduct for Employees of the Executive Branch

The following discussion gives an overview of the actual contents of the Standards of Ethical Conduct for employees of administrative agencies in the executive branch of the federal government.

To Whom the Standards of Ethical Conduct Apply

To answer this question, paralegals must take the logical first step in reading any regulations. Look at the definitions set forth in the regulations themselves. The standards apply to agency employees, and the regulations define "agency" as "an executive agency as defined in 5 U.S.C. § 105 and the Postal Service and the Postal Rate Commission" (5 CFR 2635.102(a)).[7]

Principles Underlying the Standards of Ethical Conduct

One commentator has observed that the Standards of Ethical Conduct embody three basic principles. The first is that the ethics regulations "are to remain substantially uniform throughout the executive branch."[8] Thus, any supplemental regulations can be adopted by an individual agency only with OGE's approval and will generally be confined to "areas in which an agency may have unique interest because of its statutory mission."[9] The second principle is that employees have a responsibility to recognize conflicts of interest and to seek advice regarding compliance. Finally, the Standards of Ethical Conduct provide objective standards by which employees' conduct can be judged.[10]

Summary of the Standards of Ethical Conduct

There is no better place to look for the summary of new regulations than in the summary that accompanies final regulations when they are published in the *Federal Register*. Read the summary published with these final regulations, which is reprinted in Figure 10–5.

FIGURE 10–5
Summary of the Standards of Ethical Conduct for Employees of the Executive Branch, 57 FR 35009 (August 7, 1992)

OFFICE OF GOVERNMENT ETHICS

5 CFR Part 2635

RIN 3209-AA04

Standards of Ethical Conduct for Employees of the Executive Branch

AGENCY: Office of Government Ethics.
ACTION: Final rule.

SUMMARY: The Office of Government Ethics is issuing a final rule which establishes uniform standards of ethical conduct for officers and employees of the executive branch of the Federal Government (hereinafter Government). When effective in 180 days, part 2635 will supersede most of subparts A, B and C of 5 CFR part 735 and agency regulations thereunder, as well as 5 CFR 2635.101 of the Office of Government Ethics regulations.

The final rule establishes standards relating to the receipt of gifts, whether from prohibited sources, because of official position, or between employees. It establishes standards for dealing with the employee's own and other financial interests that conflict with an employee's official duties. These include disqualification requirements that apply when a matter to which the employee is assigned affect a person with whom he or she is seeking employment. In addition to standards relating to use of official position and time, Government property and nonpublic information, it establishes specific standards for application to outside activities in which an employee may participate, including fundraising and outside employment.

The Standards of Ethical Conduct are divided into subparts, which provide a framework for a brief overview of the contents of the Standards. Refer to Figure 10–6, which reprints the table of contents of 5 CFR part 2635, the Standards of Ethical Conduct.

FIGURE 10–6
Table of
Contents of
5 CFR part 2635

Table of Contents

Subpart A—General Provisions

§ 2635.101	Basic obligation of public service
§ 2635.102	Definitions
§ 2635.103	Applicability to members of the uniformed services
§ 2635.104	Applicability to employees on detail
§ 2635.105	Supplemental agency regulations
§ 2635.106	Disciplinary and corrective action
§ 2635.107	Ethics advice

Subpart B—Gifts From Outside Sources

§ 2635.201	Overview
§ 2635.202	General standards
§ 2635.203	Definitions
§ 2635.204	Exceptions
§ 2635.205	Proper disposition of prohibited gifts

Subpart C—Gifts Between Employees

§ 2635.301	Overview
§ 2635.302	General standards
§ 2635.303	Definitions
§ 2635.304	Exceptions

Subpart D—Conflicting Financial Interests

§ 2635.401	Overview
§ 2635.402	Disqualifying financial interests
§ 2635.403	Prohibited financial interests

Subpart E—Impartiality in Performing Official Duties

§ 2635.501	Overview
§ 2635.502	Personal and business relationships
§ 2635.503	Extraordinary payments from former employers

Subpart F—Seeking Other Employment

§ 2635.601	Overview
§ 2635.602	Applicability and related considerations
§ 2635.603	Definitions
§ 2635.604	Disqualification while seeking employment

**FIGURE 10–6
(continued)**

§ 2635.605   Waiver or authorization permitting participation while
             seeking employment
§ 2635.606   Disqualification based on an arrangement concerning
             prospective employment or otherwise after negotiations

Subpart G—Misuse of Position

§ 2635.701   Overview
§ 2635.702   Use of public office for private gain
§ 2635.703   Use of nonpublic information
§ 2635.704   Use of Government property
§ 2635.705   Use of official time

Subpart H—Outside Activities

§ 2635.801   Overview
§ 2635.802   Conflicting outside employment and activities
§ 2635.803   Prior approval for outside employment and activities
§ 2635.804   Outside earned income limitations applicable to certain
             Presidential appointees and other noncareer employees
§ 2635.805   Service as an expert witness
§ 2635.806   Participation in professional associations [Reserved]
§ 2635.807   Teaching, speaking and writing
§ 2635.808   Fundraising activities
§ 2635.809   Just financial obligations

Subpart I—Related Statutory Authorities

§ 2635.901   General
§ 2635.902   Related statutes

In subpart A, paralegals should take special note of the basic obligations of public service (5 CFR 2635.101). The fourteen general principles that apply to every employee are reprinted in Figure 10–7. These principles are actually a restatement of the principles published in Executive Order 12731.

FIGURE 10–7
Principles of
Ethical Conduct
(Executive Order
12731)

By virtue of the authority vested in me as President by the Constitution and the laws of the United States of America, and in order to establish fair and exacting standards of ethical conduct for all executive branch employees, it is hereby ordered as follows:

Part I—Principles of Ethical Conduct

Section 101. *Principles of Ethical Conduct.* To ensure that every citizen can have complete confidence in the integrity of the Federal Government, each Federal employee shall respect and adhere to the fundamental principles of ethical service as implemented in regulations promulgated under sections 201 and 301 of this order:

(a) Public service is a public trust, requiring employees to place loyalty to the Constitution, the laws, and ethical principles above private gain.

(b) Employees shall not hold financial interests that conflict with the conscientious performance of duty.

(c) Employees shall not engage in financial transactions using nonpublic Government information or allow the improper use of such information to further any private interest.

(d) An employee shall not, except pursuant to such reasonable exceptions as are provided by regulation, solicit or accept any gift or other item of monetary value from any person or entity seeking official action from, doing business with, or conducting activities regulated by the employee's agency, or whose interests may be substantially affected by the performance or nonperformance of the employee's duties.

(e) Employees shall put forth honest effort in the performance of their duties.

(f) Employees shall make no unauthorized commitments or promises of any kind purporting to bind the Government.

(g) Employees shall not use public office for private gain.

(h) Employees shall act impartially and not give preferential treatment to any private organization or individual.

(i) Employees shall protect and conserve Federal property and shall not use it for other than authorized activities.

(j) Employees shall not engage in outside employment or activities, including seeking or negotiating for employment, that conflict with official Government duties and responsibilities.

(k) Employees shall disclose waste, fraud, abuse, and corruption to appropriate authorities.

FIGURE 10–7
(continued)

(l) Employees shall satisfy in good faith their obligations as citizens, including all just financial obligations, especially those—such as Federal, State, or local taxes—that are imposed by law.

(m) Employees shall adhere to all laws and regulations that provide equal opportunity for all Americans regardless of race, color, religion, sex, national origin, age, or handicap.

(n) Employees shall endeavor to avoid any actions creating the appearance that they are violating the law or the ethical standards promulgated pursuant to this order.

Subparts B through H address specific areas of ethical concerns in more detail. These areas include gifts from outside sources, gifts between employees, conflicting financial interests, impartiality in performing official duties, seeking other employment, misuse of an employee's public position, and restrictions on outside activities. Although an in-depth discussion of each subpart is beyond the scope of the text, the following discussion examines a few sections from the subparts.

Gifts from Outside Sources

The purpose of subpart B is "to prohibit an employee from soliciting or accepting any gift from a prohibited source or given because of the employee's official position," unless an exception applies. Paralegals must read subpart B carefully to understand the meaning of the key terms, including "prohibited source" and "gift." Read the definition of gift from subpart B (5 CFR 2635.203(b)), which is reprinted in Figure 10–8. The regulations give a broad definition of "gift," followed by nine exceptions, that is, things that are not defined as "gifts." Note the detailed description of the exceptions. This is typical of the regulations, which provide great detail and numerous examples to guide federal employees. Because of the detail of the regulations, employees are alert to potential problems on which they need to seek ethics advice.

FIGURE 10–8
5 CFR
2635.203(b)

(b) Gift includes any gratuity, favor, discount, entertainment, hospitality, loan, forbearance, or other item having monetary value. It includes services as well as gifts of training, transportation, local travel, lodgings and meals, whether provided in-kind, by purchase of a ticket, payment in advance, or reimbursement after the expense has been incurred. It does not include:

(1) Modest items of food and refreshments, such as soft drinks, coffee and donuts, offered other than as part of a meal;

(2) Greeting cards and items with little intrinsic value, such as plaques, certificates, and trophies, which are intended solely for presentation;

(3) Loans from banks and other financial institutions on terms generally available to the public;

(4) Opportunities and benefits, including favorable rates and commercial discounts, available to the public or to a class consisting of all Government employees or all uniformed military personnel, whether or not restricted on the basis of geographic considerations;

(5) Rewards and prizes given to competitors in contests or events, including random drawings, open to the public unless the employee's entry into the contest or event is required as part of his official duties;

(6) Pension and other benefits resulting from continued participation in an employee welfare and benefits plan maintained by a former employer;

(7) Anything which is paid for by the Government or secured by the Government under Government contract;

Note: Some airlines encourage those purchasing tickets to join programs that award free flights and other benefits to frequent fliers. Any such benefit earned on the basis of Government-financed travel belongs to the agency rather than to the employee and may be accepted only insofar as provided under 41 CFR 301-1.6(b).

(8) Any gift accepted by the Government under specific statutory authority including:

(i) Travel, subsistence, and related expenses accepted by an agency under the authority of 31 U.S.C. 1353 in connection with an employee's attendance at a meeting or similar function relating to his official duties which takes place away from his duty station. The agency's acceptance must be in accordance with the implementing regulations at 41 CFR part 304-1; and

(ii) Other gifts provided in-kind which have been accepted by an agency under its agency gift acceptance statute; or

(9) Anything for which market value is paid by the employee.

Gifts Between Employees

Paralegals may wish to give their supervisors a birthday gift. This seemingly innocent gesture can cause problems. If the value of the gift is $50, the giving and accepting of the gift is prohibited. If the value of the birthday gift is less than $10, there is no problem, because the regulations allow giving gifts other than cash, with an aggregate market value of $10 or less per occasion, on an occasional basis, including any occasion on which gifts are traditionally given or exchanged. The regulations give several specific examples of acceptable gifts.

Conflicting Financial Interests

Subpart D contains two limitations on federal employees' financial interests. The first limitation actually incorporates the prohibitions set forth in 18 U.S.C. § 208, the criminal conflict of interest statute. An employee is prohibited from "participating personally and substantially in an official capacity in any particular matter in which, to his knowledge, he or any person whose interests are imputed to him . . . has a financial interest, if the particular matter will have a direct and predictable effect on that interest." The second limitation is that agency employees must comply with statutes and regulations that prohibit employees of specific federal agencies from holding certain types of financial interests.

Impartiality in Performing Official Duties

Subpart E "provides a mechanism for employees to deal with situations in which the interest of someone close to the employee would be affected by a matter to which the employee is assigned."[11] The regulations provide that employees may not participate, without prior authorization from the agency, in matters likely to have a direct and predictable effect on the financial interest of a household member, where a reasonable person with knowledge of the relationship would question the employee's impartiality. The regulations provide examples for guidance, and these are illustrated in Figure 10–9. Example 1 illustrates a situation in which the employee's impartiality would likely be questioned, and Example 2 illustrates a situation in which impartiality does not appear to be a problem.

FIGURE 10–9
Excerpt from
5 CFR
2635.502(b)(3)

Example 1: An employee of the General Services Administration has made an offer to purchase a restaurant owned by a local developer. The developer has submitted an offer in response to a GSA solicitation for lease of office space. Under the circumstances, she would be correct in concluding that a reasonable person would be likely to question her impartiality if she were to participate in evaluating that developer's or its competitor's lease proposal.

Example 2: An employee of the Department of Labor is providing technical assistance in drafting occupational safety and health legislation that will affect all employers of five or more persons. His wife is employed as an administrative assistant by a large corporation that will incur additional costs if the proposed legislation is enacted. Because the legislation is not a particular matter involving specific parties, the employee may continue to work on the legislation and need not be concerned that his wife's employment with an affected corporation would raise a question concerning his impartiality.

Seeking Other Employment

Subpart F prohibits employees from participating in matters affecting the financial interest of a prospective employer. The prohibition applies even when "an employee's actions in seeking employment fall short of actual employment negotiations" (5 CFR 2635.601). Individual waivers permitting participation may be sought by an employee. As with other subparts, the regulations provide numerous examples for guidance.

Misuse of Position

Subpart G prohibits federal employees from using public office for private gain. Thus, federal employees may not use their position or title for private gain for themselves or family members. Federal employees also may not take actions that give the appearance that the federal government endorses their personal activities or those of others. Thus, if a federal employee gives a speech expressing personal opinions on a matter of government policy, the employee must make a disclaimer to ensure that the audience is aware that this is personal opinion and not the opinion of the agency for which the employee works. Further, federal employees may not use nonpublic information for personal gain. Subpart G also prohibits the use of government property except for authorized purposes. The term "government property" is defined to include use of government vehicles, office supplies, telephones, and government mails. Thus, if a paralegal used an envelope with postage paid by the government to mail a car payment, this would be an ethical violation. Finally, federal employees must use their time at work only to perform official duties.

Outside Activities

Subpart H describes limitations on the activities of federal employees outside their jobs. To paralegals and other federal employees, this may be the most surprising set of prohibitions, because of their broad scope. Further, many people are unaware that their activities outside their government work are subject to restrictions. Many agencies require written approval before employees can engage in outside activities, regardless of whether the employee will receive compensation. Subpart H is long and detailed. For a summary, refer to Figure 10–10. This is a synopsis of subpart H prepared by the Office of Government Ethics. OGE prepared a synopsis of all the subparts of the Standards of Ethical Conduct to accompany the publication of the final regulations in August 1992. The synopses can be found in the *Federal Administrative Procedure Sourcebook* published by the Administrative Conference of the United States (ACUS).

FIGURE 10–10
Synopsis of
subpart H
of 5 CFR
part 2635

SYNOPSIS OF SUBPART H - OUTSIDE ACTIVITIES

GENERALLY. In addition to the standards set forth in subpart H, an employee's outside employment and other activities must comply with all ethical requirements set forth in the subparts A through G of the regulation, including the requirement to avoid even the appearance of using public office for private gain. For example, the prohibition against use of Government property for unauthorized purposes would prohibit an employee from using the agency photocopier to reproduce documents for his outside organization.

RESTRICTIONS IMPOSED BY OTHER LAWS. An employee's outside employment and other activities must comply with applicable laws other than the Standards of Ethical Conduct. Several are listed in subparts H and I. Outside activities frequently raise questions about the following:

The restrictions in 18 U.S.C. 203 and 205 on employees engaging in representational activities before the United States:

The constitutional prohibition against accepting any office, title or compensation from a foreign government; and

The Hatch Act, which prohibits most employees' participation in certain partisan political activities.

FIGURE 10–10
(continued)

PRIOR APPROVAL FOR OUTSIDE ACTIVITIES. When required by supplemental agency regulation, an employee shall obtain approval before engaging in outside employment or activities.

CONFLICTING OUTSIDE ACTIVITIES. An employee shall not engage in outside employment or activities prohibited by statute or by supplemental agency regulation, or that would materially impair the ability to perform his official duties by requiring his disqualification under subpart D or E.

RESTRICTIONS ON RECEIPT OF COMPENSATION. With certain exceptions, Presidential appointees to full-time noncareer positions shall not receive any outside earned income for outside employment or other outside activities performed during that appointment. Higher-level noncareer employees may not, in any calendar year, receive outside earned income which exceeds 15 percent of the rate of pay for Level II of the Executive Schedule. These noncareer employees also are prohibited from receiving any compensation for teaching without prior approval, serving as officers or board members of outside entities, practicing certain professions or being affiliated with firms or other entities that practice those professions.

SERVICE AS AN EXPERT WITNESS. In the absence of specific authorization, an employee shall not represent anyone other than the United States as an expert witness in any proceeding before a court or agency of the United States if the United States is a party or has a direct and substantial interest. The restriction applies even though no compensation is received. A less restrictive standard applies to special Government employees.

TEACHING, SPEAKING AND WRITING. An employee shall not receive compensation for teaching, speaking or writing that is related to his official duties.

DEFINITION OF RELATED TO DUTIES: Teaching, speaking or writing is "related to an employee's official duties" if:

The activity is undertaken as part of his official duties;

The invitation to engage in the activity was extended primarily because of his official position;

The invitation or the offer of compensation was extended by a person whose interests may be affected by the employee's official duties;

The information draws substantially on nonpublic information; or

For most employees, the subject of the teaching, speaking or writing deals in significant part with any matter presently assigned to the employee, any matter to which the employee had been assigned in the previous one-year period, or to any ongoing or announced policy, program or operation of his agency. Certain noncareer employees are subject to additional restrictions and special Government employees are subject to less restrictive standards.

FIGURE 10–10
(continued)

EXCEPTION FOR TEACHING. An employee may receive compensation for teaching certain courses, notwithstanding that the subject matter is related to his official duties and notwithstanding that he may have been offered the opportunity because of his official position.

FUNDRAISING. Provided that he does not otherwise violate the Standards of Ethical Conduct, an employee may engage in charitable fundraising activities in a personal capacity if he does not use his official title, position or authority to further that effort or personally solicit funds or other support from subordinates or from anyone known to him to be a prohibited source for purposes of the gift restrictions in subpart B. A special Government employee, however, may solicit charitable contributions from a prohibited source as long as that person does not have interests affected by the performance of his official duties.

JUST FINANCIAL OBLIGATIONS. Employees shall satisfy in good faith all just financial obligations.

Source: Administrative Conference of the United States, *Federal Administrative Procedure Sourcebook*, 2d ed. (1992), at 515.

Some of the prohibitions of subpart H, such as the prohibition of outside activities that conflict with the employee's official duties, are not surprising. The scope of some of the limitations in subpart H may, however, surprise paralegals and other government employees. Thus, before engaging in any outside activities, paralegals should consult with their immediate supervisors and designated ethics officials.

Summary

In administrative law, as in all other areas of law, attorneys are governed by the ethics rules of the state in which they are licensed to practice. In the area of administrative law, however, paralegals must also be familiar with the statutes and regulations that impose restrictions on the conduct of all employees of administrative agencies.

How State Rules of Professional Conduct and Rules Specific to Government Employees' Conduct Differ

First, rules specific to government employees apply directly to all employees, not just attorneys. Second, unlike state bars, the federal government can impose sanctions directly on all employees, not just attorneys. Thus, paralegals are subject to direct sanctions if they are federal employees and contravene ethics rules for federal employees.

Why It Is Important for Paralegals to Be Familiar with State Rules of Professional Conduct and Rules Specific to Government Employees

Paralegals must be alert for potential ethics problems arising both from state rules and rules for federal employees. Otherwise, a paralegal may take a seemingly innocent action, such as offering a gift, which will put a federal employee in an awkward position or give the appearance of trying to exert undue influence. Paralegals must be familiar with the statutes and regulations that govern the conduct of federal employees, because they may not otherwise be aware of the extent of these laws.

Ethics Rules of General Applicability

This section focuses on the ABA Model Rules of Professional Conduct, which serve as the model for the ethics rules in most states. Paralegals should, however, always be aware of differences between their own state's rules and those of the ABA Model Rules.

Model rule 5.3 imposes on lawyers the duty to supervise the conduct of nonlawyer assistants. Attorneys must instruct their assistants on matters of ethics and supervise their work. By doing so, attorneys will ensure that they also comply with the ethical obligation to assist in preventing the unauthorized practice of law. There are some tasks paralegals are authorized to perform by virtue of agency regulations that, without the regulatory authority, could be considered unauthorized practice. Both the SSA and the INS have regulations permitting nonlawyers to represent clients, if certain conditions are met. The qualifications required in the INS regulations are more extensive than those in the SSA's regulations. Both agencies have the authority to impose sanctions, such as disqualification from future representation of clients before them, on both attorneys and nonattorney representatives.

In all areas of law, there is an ethical duty to preserve confidential client information. There are exceptions, which allow disclosure, including information to prevent the commission of a planned future crime, information in connection with a dispute between lawyers and clients, disclosure with the client's consent, and disclosure allowed by other ethics rules or a court. The duty to preserve confidential information applies equally to attorneys who work for administrative agencies, even when attorneys disagree with their agencies' policies.

Lawyers often switch between working for government agencies and private law firms, and this phenomenon is called the revolving door. Certain restrictions apply in order to preserve the confidential information of former clients. A former government attorney who enters private practice is not allowed to represent a private client in connection with a matter in which the lawyer participated personally and substantially as a public employee. Other lawyers in the firm may participate in representation if the former government employee is screened from participation and receives none of the fee. The ABA Model Rule also requires that the agency be notified, while the North Carolina rule requires the agency's consent. Attorneys who leave private practice to work with a government agency are not allowed to participate in matters in which they participated personally and substantially while in private practice or nongovernmental employment. Other attorneys within the agency may participate.

Statutes and Regulations Specific to Government Employees

The sources of law for governmentwide standards of conduct include numerous statutes, such as the Hatch Act and the Ethics Reform Act of 1989, as well as regulations and executive orders. The Office of Government Ethics (OGE) is responsible for providing ethics assistance and promulgating regulations for conduct of federal employees. OGE is a source of ethics advice for federal employees, as are ethics officials within each agency.

The Standards of Ethical Conduct, found in 5 CFR part 2635, apply to all employees of executive agencies, not just attorneys. The principles underlying the standards include having regulations that are uniform from agency to agency, imposing a responsibility to seek ethics advice, and providing objective standards to judge conduct.

The Standards of Ethical Conduct are divided into subparts addressing different topics. Subpart A contains the fourteen general obligations of public servants, adopted from Executive Order 12731. Subparts B through H address gifts from outside sources, gifts between employees, conflicting financial interests, impartiality in performing official duties, seeking other employment, misuse of an employee's public position, and restrictions on outside activities. Paralegals should read these regulations carefully and study the examples contained in the regulations.

Review Questions

1. The Board of Immigration Appeals allows which of the following to represent persons in appeals before it? _____
   a. accredited representatives who work for nonprofit organizations that meet the BIA's regulatory qualifications
   b. a business associate who has a preexisting relationship with the represented person and receives no remuneration
   c. law students who are under an attorney's supervision
   d. all of the above
   e. a and b only

2. SSA regulations prohibit representatives from doing which of the following? _____
   a. knowingly charging a fee in excess of that allowed by the SSA or a court
   b. divulging, except as allowed by regulation, information disclosed by the SSA about a claimant
   c. knowingly making a false statement of material fact
   d. all of the above
   e. a and b only

3. The Standards of Ethical Conduct for Employees of the Executive Branch cover which of the following topics? _____
   a. gifts between employees
   b. obtaining permission to hold part-time jobs outside the government
   c. use of government property
   d. all of the above
   e. a and b only

4. The regulations regarding misuse of position define "government property" to include which of the following? _____
   a. government telephones
   b. government automobiles
   c. envelopes with postage paid by the federal agency
   d. all of the above
   e. a and b only

5. Which of the following are sources of ethics advice for federal agency employees? _____
   a. the Office of Government Ethics
   b. an ethics official in the employee's agency
   c. the employee's supervisor
   d. all of the above
   e. a and b only

6. Which of the following are sources of law for prohibitions on the actions of federal agency employees? _____
   a. the Hatch Act
   b. 5 CFR part 2635
   c. the Ethics Reform Act of 1989
   d. all of the above
   e. b and c only

7. The SSA, but not the BIA, has the authority to impose sanctions on nonattorney representatives.   True ___ / False ___

8. If the SSA disqualifies a representative, the SSA has the authority to reinstate the representative subsequently.   True ___ / False ___

9. Employees of federal administrative agencies are prohibited from participating in matters affecting the financial interests of a prospective employee.   True ___ / False ___

10. The federal agency given authority to promulgate regulations governing the conduct of executive agency employees is the Office of Personnel and Management.   True ___ / False ___

11. The Standards of Conduct for Employees of the Executive Branch allow a paralegal to give her supervisor $10 in cash for her birthday.
                                                           True ___ / False ___

12. Federal employees may have to obtain permission to participate in outside activities even if they receive no compensation for the activities.   True ___ / False ___

13. Federal employees must use their time at work only to perform official duties.   True ___ / False ___

14. Describe four exceptions to the general prohibition against disclosure of confidential client information.

15. If a paralegal who works for a federal agency relies on the advice of an ethics officer and the advice turns out to be wrong, is the paralegal likely to be disciplined?

Practical Applications

The Standards of Ethical Conduct for Employees of the Executive Branch address in detail the giving and receipt of gifts between employees. The exercises below will help you to understand the general prohibitions and the numerous exceptions.

Exercise 1

The general rules prohibit an employee from giving a gift to a superior or accepting a gift from an employee receiving less pay. Based on your reading of section 2635.302 addressing General Standards, answer the following questions.

---

§2635.302

General standards.

(a) Gifts to superiors. Except as provided in this subpart, an employee may not:

(1) Directly or indirectly, give a gift to or make a donation toward a gift for an official superior; or

(2) Solicit a contribution from another employee for a gift to either his own or the other employee's official superior.

(b) Gifts from employees receiving less pay. Except as provided in this subpart, an employee may not, directly or indirectly, accept a gift from an employee receiving less pay than himself unless:

(1) The two employees are not in a subordinate-official superior relationship; and

(2) There is a personal relationship between the two employees that would justify the gift.

(c) Limitation on use of exceptions. Notwithstanding any exception provided in this subpart, an official superior shall not coerce the offering of a gift from a subordinate.

---

1. Do the general standards allow paralegals to chip in together to buy a gift for their supervisor?

2. Suppose that a secretary, who is not your subordinate and was a friend of yours before you began working together, gives you a birthday gift. Your salary is higher than hers. May you accept the gift?

3. Suppose that your supervisor tells you that tomorrow is her birthday and that she expects a nice gift from you. Has your supervisor violated the general standards in section 2635.302?

Exercise 2

Section 2635.304 provides several exceptions to general gift-giving prohibitions. Read the following excerpts, which include five examples. There are two examples in (a) and three examples in (b). For each of the five examples, explain why the gift either is or is not acceptable.

---

§2635.304

Exceptions.

The prohibitions set forth in §2635.302(a) and (b) do not apply to a gift given or accepted under the circumstances described in paragraph (a) or (b) of this section. A contribution or the solicitation of a contribution that would otherwise violate the prohibitions set forth in §2635.302(a) and (b) may only be made in accordance with paragraph (c) of this section.

(a) General exceptions. On an occasional basis, including any occasion on which gifts are traditionally given or exchanged, the following may be given to an official superior or accepted from a subordinate or other employee receiving less pay:

(1) Items, other than cash, with an aggregate market value of $10 or less per occasion;

(2) Items such as food and refreshments to be shared in the office among several employees;

(3) Personal hospitality provided at a residence which is of a type and value customarily provided by the employee to personal friends;

(4) Items given in connection with the receipt of personal hospitality if of a type and value customarily given on such occasions; and

(5) Leave transferred under subpart I of part 630 of this title to an employee who is not an immediate supervisor, unless obtained in violation of §630.912 of this title.

Example 1: Upon returning to work following a vacation at the beach, a claims examiner with the Department of Veterans Affairs may give his supervisor, and his supervisor may accept, a bag of saltwater taffy purchased on the boardwalk for $8.

Example 2: An employee of the Federal Deposit Insurance Corporation whose bank examination responsibilities require frequent travel may not bring her supervisor, and her supervisor may not accept, souvenir coffee mugs from each of the cities she visits in the course of performing her duties, even though each of the mugs costs less than $5. Gifts given on this basis are not occasional.

. . .

(b) Special, infrequent occasions. A gift appropriate to the occasion may be given to an official superior or accepted from a subordinate or other employee receiving less pay:

(1) In recognition of infrequently occurring occasions of personal significance such as marriage, illness, or the birth or adoption of a child; or

(2) Upon occasions that terminate a subordinate-official superior relationship, such as retirement, resignation, or transfer.

Example 1: The administrative assistant to the personnel director of the Tennessee Valley Authority may send a $30 floral arrangement to the personnel director who is in the hospital recovering from surgery. The personnel director may accept the gift.

Example 2: A chemist employed by the Food and Drug Administration has been invited to the wedding of the lab director who is his official superior. He may give the lab director and his bride, and they may accept, a place setting in the couple's selected china pattern purchased for $70.

Example 3: Upon the occasion of the supervisor's retirement from Federal service, an employee of the Fish and Wildlife Service may give her supervisor a book of wildlife photographs which she purchased for $19. The retiring supervisor may accept the book.. . .

Case Analysis

Read the excerpt below from *Ezell v. Bowen*, 849 F.2d 844 (4th Cir. 1988), and answer the following questions.

PER CURIAM:

Sheryl Ezell appeals the district court dismissal of her complaint challenging the decision of the Secretary of Health and Human Services prohibiting her from representing claimants seeking benefits pursuant to the Social Security Act and the Federal Coal Mine Health and Safety Act. We affirm.

Section 206(a) of the Social Security Act provides that non-attorneys may represent claimants if "they are of good character [sic] and in good repute." Ezell, a non-attorney representative of claimants, was notified in August 1984 that the Secretary was initia-

ting proceedings to suspend or disqualify her from further representation of claimants. The Secretary's actions were based upon Ezell's September 1983 felony conviction of two counts of filing false claims for job-related expenses.

Following a hearing an administrative law judge suspended Ezell from representing claimants for a period of five years. The Social Security Administration's Appeals Council affirmed that decision, but found disqualification rather than suspension to be warranted. Ezell then filed suit in district court challenging the constitutionality of section 206(a) and the statutory authority for her disqualification. She contended that in addition to the lack of authority for the disqualification, the standard of good character and reputation required of non-attorney representatives denied her equal protection and due process. She based her equal protection argument on the claim that the good character requirement unconstitutionally distinguishes between attorneys and non-attorneys. Due process was allegedly denied because the requirement was ambiguous and vague. Ezell also alleged that the Secretary's actions were arbitrary and exceeded statutory authority because the actions for which she was disqualified did not involve representation of a claimant.

The district court dismissed Ezell's complaint finding that the court lacked subject matter jurisdiction. The court held that judicial review of the Secretary's decision was precluded by section 205(h) of the Social Security Act, which provides:

> The findings and decision of the Secretary after a hearing shall be binding upon all individuals who were parties to such hearing. No findings of fact or decision of the Secretary shall be reviewed by any person, tribunal, or governmental agency except as herein provided. No action against the United States, the Secretary, or any officer or employee thereof shall be brought under Section 1331 or 1346 of Title 28 to recover on any claim arising under this subchapter.

The district court rejected Ezell's argument that section 205(h) does not foreclose judicial review of the action due to the presence of her constitutional questions, stating that Ezell's "constitutional claims [were] 'inextricably intertwined' with her challenge to the Secretary's decision to suspend her."

Ezell contends that section 205(h) does not apply because it only pertains to claimants seeking recovery of benefits under the Social Security Act and not to disqualification of representatives. We need not address this argument because we find subject matter jurisdiction lacking due to Ezell's failure to raise a colorable statutory or constitutional claim.

As the district court noted, the regulations implementing section 206(a) do not provide for judicial review of the disqualification decision. And, judicial review of a decision of the Secretary is foreclosed unless it is an "initial determination." One administrative action which is not an "initial determination" subject to judicial review is "[d]isqualifying or suspending a person from acting as [a] representative in a proceeding before [the Social Security Administration]."

These regulations do not absolutely foreclose judicial review because federal courts are always free to examine whether the Secretary has acted arbitrarily or exceeded his authority. However, before subject matter jurisdiction arises for review of the propriety of the Secretary's actions, there must be more than a bare allegation of unconstitutional action. The court in *Thomason* determined that the district court had properly dismissed an action for lack of subject matter jurisdiction where there was no "colorable" claim on constitutional, statutory or regulatory grounds. This result is consistent with the Supreme Court's declaration that a "substantial" constitutional claim is required for invocation of federal subject matter jurisdiction.

Ezell's contentions fail to meet these requirements. She entered a guilty plea for two counts of filing false claims for expenses following her dismissal from employment with the federal government. The action of the Secretary disqualifying Ezell for lack of good character was clearly warranted in light of this felony conviction and Ezell failed to assert a colorable statutory challenge to this decision. Further, her claims of violations of constitutional protections are clearly unsubstantiated.

AFFIRMED.

1. What was the basis of the secretary's proceedings to suspend or disqualify Sheryl Ezell from further representation of claimants?
2. What sanctions did the administrative law judge impose on Sheryl Ezell?
3. Did the Appeals Council affirm the ALJ's decision?

4. Explain the basis of Ezell's constitutional argument to the federal court that the requirement of "good character" denied her equal protection.
5. Although the trial court dismissed Ezell's complaint, the Fourth Circuit Court of Appeals did not foreclose the possibility of judicial review. Under what circumstances would judicial review be allowed?

Notes

[1] Although the majority of states have adopted some version of the Model Rules, it is important that paralegals also be familiar with the ABA's Model Code of Professional Responsibility, which preceded the Model Rules, because some states' ethics rules also contain some elements of the Model Code.

[2] *See, e.g., Ezell v. Bowen*, 849 F.2d 844 (4th Cir. 1988), which is used in the Case Analysis at the end of Chapter 10.

[3] Myrna Siegel, "The New Federal Standards of Conduct," *The Public Lawyer* 22 (Spring 1993).

[4] *Id.*

[5] Executive Order 12731 (3 CFR 306 (1991)).

[6] *U.S. Government Manual, 1993–94* (Washington, D.C.: U.S. Government Printing Office), at 699.

[7] The statute to which the regulations refer (5 U.S.C. § 105) lists the executive agencies, which include the Departments of State, the Treasury, Defense, Justice, the Interior, Agriculture, Commerce, Labor, Health and Human Services, Housing and Urban Development, Transportation, Energy, Education, and Veterans Affairs.

[8] Siegel, *supra* note 3, at 23.

[9] *Id.*

[10] *Id.*

[11] *Id.* at 23.

APPENDIX A

ADMINISTRATIVE PROCEDURE ACT
Title 5, U.S. Code
Chapter 5-Administrative Procedure

§ 551.   Definitions

For the purpose of this subchapter—

(1) "agency" means each authority of the Government of the United States, whether or not it is within or subject to review by another agency, but does not include:

  (A) the Congress;

  (B) the courts of the United States;

  (C) the governments of the territories or possessions of the United States;

  (D) the government of the District of Columbia; or except as to the requirements of section 552 of this title;

  (E) agencies composed of representatives of the parties or of representatives of organizations of the parties to the disputes determined by them;

  (F) courts martial and military commissions;

  (G) military authority exercised in the field in time of war or in occupied territory; or

  (H) functions conferred by sections 1738, 1739, 1743, and 1744 of title 12; chapter 2 of title 41; or sections 1622, 1884, 1891-1902, and former section 1641(b)(2), of title 50, appendix;

(2) "person" includes an individual, partnership, corporation, association, or public or private organization other than an agency;

(3) "party" includes a person or agency named or admitted as a party, or properly seeking and entitled as of right to be admitted as a party, in an agency proceeding, and a person or agency admitted by an agency as a party for limited purposes;

(4) "rule" means the whole or a part of an agency statement of general or particular applicability and future effect designed to implement, interpret, or prescribe law or policy or describing the organization, procedure, or practice requirements of an agency and includes the approval or prescription for the future of rates, wages, corporate or financial structures or reorganizations thereof, prices, facilities, appliances, services or allowances therefor or of valuations, costs, or accounting, or practices bearing on any of the foregoing;

(5) "rule making" means agency process for formulating, amending, or repealing a rule;

(6) "order" means the whole or a part of a final disposition, whether affirmative, negative, injunctive, or declaratory in form, of an agency in a matter other than rule making but including licensing;

(7) "adjudication" means agency process for the formulation of an order;

(8) "license" includes the whole or a part of an agency permit, certificate, approval, registration, charter, membership, statutory exemption or other form of permission;

(9) "licensing" includes agency process respecting the grant, renewal, denial, revocation, suspension, annulment, withdrawal, limitation, amendment, modification, or conditioning of a license;

(10) "sanction" includes the whole or a part of an agency—

(A) prohibition, requirement, limitation, or other condition affecting the freedom of a person;

(B) withholding a relief;

(C) imposition of penalty or fine;

(D) destruction, taking, seizure, or withholding of property;

(E) assessment of damages, reimbursement, restitution, compensation, costs, charges, or fees;

(F) requirement, revocation, or suspension of a license; or

(G) taking other compulsory or restrictive action;

(11) "relief" includes the whole or a part of an agency—

(A) grant of money, assistance, license, authority, exemption, exception, privilege, or remedy;

(B) recognition of a claim, right, immunity, privilege, exemption, or exception; or

(C) taking of other action on the application or petition of, and beneficial to, a person;

(12) "agency proceeding" means an agency process as defined by paragraphs (5), (7), and (9) of this section;

(13) "agency action" includes the whole or a part of an agency rule, order, license, sanction, relief, or the equivalent or denial thereof, or failure to act; and

(14) "ex parte communication" means an oral or written communication not on the public record with respect to which reasonable prior notice to all parties is not given, but it shall not include requests for status reports on any matter or proceeding covered by this subchapter.

§ 552. Public information; agency rules, opinions, orders, records, and proceedings

(a) Each agency shall make available to the public information as follows:

(1) Each agency shall separately state and currently publish in the Federal Register for the guidance of the public—

(A) descriptions of its central and field organization and the established places at which, the employees (and in the case of a uniformed service, the members) from whom, and the methods whereby, the public may obtain information, make submittals or requests, or obtain decisions;

(B) statements of the general course and method by which its functions are channeled and determined, including the nature and requirements of all formal and informal procedures available;

(C) rules of procedure, descriptions of forms available or the places at which forms may be obtained, and instructions as to the scope and contents of all papers, reports, or examinations;

(D) substantive rules of general applicability adopted as authorized by law, and statements of general policy or interpretations of general applicability formulated and adopted by the agency; and

(E) each amendment, revision, or repeal of the foregoing.

Except to the extent that a person has actual and timely notice of the terms thereof, a person may not in any manner be required to resort to, or be adversely affected by, a matter required to be published in the Federal Register and not so published. For the purpose of this paragraph, matter reasonably available to the class of persons affected thereby is deemed published in the Federal Register when incorporated by reference therein with the approval of the Director of the Federal Register.

(2) Each agency, in accordance with published rules, shall make available for public inspection and copying—

(A) final opinions, including concurring and dissenting opinions, as well as orders, made in the adjudication of cases;

(B) those statements of policy and interpretations which have been adopted by the agency and are not published in the Federal Register; and

(C) administrative staff manuals and instructions to staff that affect a member of the public; unless the materials are promptly published and copies offered for sale. To the extent required to prevent a clearly unwarranted invasion of personal privacy, an agency may delete identifying details when it makes available or publishes an opinion, statement of policy, interpretation, or staff manual or instruction. However, in each case the justification for the deletion shall be explained fully in writing. Each agency shall also maintain and make available for public inspection and copying current indexes providing identifying information for the public as to any matter issued, adopted, or promulgated after July 4, 1967, and required by this paragraph to be made available or published. Each agency shall promptly publish, quarterly or more frequently, and distribute (by sale or otherwise) copies of each index or supplements thereto unless it determines by order published in the Federal Register that the publication would be unnecessary and impracticable, in which case the agency shall nonetheless provide copies of such index on request at a cost not to exceed the direct cost of duplication. A final order, opinion, statement of policy, interpretation, or staff manual or instruction that affects a member of the public may be relied on, used, or cited as precedent by an agency against a party other than an agency only if—

    (i) it has been indexed and either made available or published as provided by this paragraph; or

    (ii) the party has actual and timely notice of the terms thereof.

(3) Except with respect to the records made available under paragraphs (1) and (2) of this subsection, each agency, upon any request for records which (A) reasonably describes such records and (B) is made in accordance with published rules stating the time, place, fees (if any), and procedures to be followed, shall make the records promptly available to any person.

(4)(A)(i) In order to carry out the provisions of this section, each agency shall promulgate regulations, pursuant to notice and receipt of public comment, specifying the schedule of fees applicable to the processing of requests under this section and establishing procedures and guidelines for determining when such fees should be waived or reduced. Such schedule shall conform to the guidelines which shall be promulgated, pursuant to notice and receipt of public comment, by the Director of the Office of Management and Budget and which shall provide for a uniform schedule of fees for all agencies.

    (ii) Such agency regulations shall provide that—

        (I) fees shall be limited to reasonable standard charges for document search, duplication, and review, when records are requested for commercial use;

        (II) fees shall be limited to reasonable standard charges for document duplication when records are not sought for commercial use and the request is made by an educational or noncommercial scientific institution, whose purpose is scholarly or scientific research; or a representative of the news media; and

        (III) for any request not described in (I) or (II), fees shall be limited to reasonable standard charges for document search and duplication.

  (iii) Documents shall be furnished without any charge or at a charge reduced below the fees established under clause (ii) if disclosure of the information is in the public interest because it is likely to contribute significantly to public understanding of the operations or activities of the government and is not primarily in the commercial interest of the requester.

  (iv) Fee schedules shall provide for the recovery of only the direct costs of search, duplication, or review. Review costs shall include only the direct costs incurred during the initial examination of a document for the purposes of determining whether the documents must be disclosed under this section and for the purposes of withholding any portions exempt from disclosure under this section. Review costs may not include any costs incurred in resolving issues of law or policy that may be raised in the course of processing a request under this section. No fee may be charged by any agency under this section—

    (I) if the costs of routine collection and processing of the fee are likely to equal or exceed the amount of the fee; or

    (II) for any request described in clause (ii) (II) or (III) of this subparagraph for the first two hours of search time or for the first one hundred pages of duplication.

  (v) No agency may require advance payment of any fee unless the requester has previously failed to pay fees in a timely fashion, or the agency has determined that the fee will exceed $250.

(vi) Nothing in this subparagraph shall supersede fees chargeable under a statute specifically providing for setting the level of fees for particular types of records.

(vii) In any action by a requester regarding the waiver of fees under this section, the court shall determine the matter de novo: Provided, That the court's review of the matter shall be limited to the record before the agency.

(B) On complaint, the district court of the United States in the district in which the complainant resides, or has his principal place of business, or in which the agency records are situated, or in the District of Columbia, has jurisdiction to enjoin the agency from withholding agency records and to order the production of any agency records improperly withheld from the complainant. In such a case the court shall determine the matter de novo, and may examine the contents of such agency records in camera to determine whether such records or any part thereof shall be withheld under any of the exemptions set forth in subsection (b) of this section, and the burden is on the agency to sustain its action.

(C) Notwithstanding any other provision of law, the defendant shall serve an answer or otherwise plead to any complaint made under this subsection within thirty days after service upon the defendant of the pleading in which such complaint is made, unless the court otherwise directs for good cause shown.

[(D) Repealed. Pub. L. No. 98-620, title IV, § 402(2), Nov. 8, 1984, 98 Stat. 3357.]

(E) The court may assess against the United States reasonable attorney fees and other litigation costs reasonably incurred in any case under this section in which the complainant has substantially prevailed.

(F) Whenever the court orders the production of any agency records improperly withheld from the complainant and assesses against the United States reasonable attorney fees and other litigation costs, and the court additionally issues a written finding that the circumstances surrounding the withholding raise questions whether agency personnel acted arbitrarily or capriciously

with respect to the withholding, the Special Council shall promptly initiate a proceeding to determine whether disciplinary action is warranted against the officer or employee who was primarily responsible for the withholding. The Special Counsel, after investigation and consideration of the evidence submitted, shall submit his findings and recommendations to the administrative authority of the agency concerned and shall send copies of the findings and recommendations to the officer or employee or his representative. The administrative authority shall take the corrective action that the Special Counsel recommends.

(G) In the event of noncompliance with the order of the court, the district court may punish for contempt the responsible employee, and in the case of a uniformed service, the responsible member.

(5) Each agency having more than one member shall maintain and make available for public inspection a record of the final votes of each member in every agency proceeding.

(6)(A) Each agency, upon any request for records made under paragraph (1), (2), or (3) of this subsection, shall—

(i) determine within ten days (excepting Saturdays, Sundays, and legal public holidays) after the receipt of any such request whether to comply with such request and shall immediately notify the person making such request of such determination and the reasons therefor, and of the right of such person to appeal to the head of the agency any adverse determination; and

(ii) make a determination with respect to any appeal within twenty days (excepting Saturdays, Sundays, and legal public holidays) after the receipt of such appeal. If on appeal the denial of the request for records is in whole or in part upheld, the agency shall notify the person making such request of the provisions for judicial review of that determination under paragraph (4) of this subsection.

(B) In unusual circumstances as specified in this subparagraph, the time limits prescribed in either clause (i) or clause (ii) of subparagraph (A) may be extended by written notice to the person making such request setting forth the reasons for such extension and the date on which a determination is expected to be dispatched. No such notice shall specify a date that would result in an extension for more than ten working days. As used in this subparagraph, "unusual circumstances" means, but only to the extent reasonably necessary to the proper processing of the particular request—

    (i) the need to search for and collect the requested records from field facilities or other establishments that are separate from the office processing the request;

    (ii) the need to search for, collect, and appropriately examine a voluminous amount of separate and distinct records which are demanded in a single request; or

    (iii) The need for consultation, which shall be conducted with all practicable speed, with another agency having a substantial interest in the determination of the request or among two or more compon- ents of the agency having substantial subject-matter interest therein.

(C) Any person making a request to any agency for records under paragraph (1), (2), or (3) of this subsection shall be deemed to have exhausted his administrative remedies with respect to such request if the agency fails to comply with the applicable time limit provisions of this paragraph. If the Government can show exceptional circumstances exist and that the agency is exercising due diligence in responding to the request, the court may retain jurisdiction and allow the agency additional time to complete its review of the records. Upon any determination by an agency to comply with a request for records, the records shall be made promptly available to such person making such request. Any notification of denial of any request for records under this subsection shall set forth the names and titles or positions of each person responsible for the denial of such request.

(b) This section does not apply to matters that are—

(1)(A) specifically authorized under criteria established by an Executive order to be kept secret in the interest of national defense or foreign policy and (B) are in fact properly classified pursuant to such Executive order:

(2) related solely to the internal personnel rules and practices of an agency;

(3) specifically exempted from disclosure by statute (other than section 552b of this title), provided that such statute (A) requires that the matters be withheld from the public in such a manner as to leave no discretion on the issue, or (B) establishes particular criteria for withholding or refers to particular types of matters to be withheld;

(4) trade secrets and commercial or financial information obtained from a person and privileged or confidential;

(5) inter-agency or intra-agency memorandums or letters which would not be available by law to a party other than an agency in litigation with the agency;

(6) personnel and medical files and similar files the disclosure of which would constitute a clearly unwarranted invasion of personal privacy;

(7) records or information compiled for law enforcement purposes, but only to the extent that the production of such law enforcement records or information (A) could reasonably be expected to interfere with enforcement proceedings, (B) would deprive a person of a right to a fair trial or an impartial adjudication, (c) could reasonably be expected to constitute an unwarranted invasion of personal privacy, (D) could reasonably be expected to disclose the identity of a confidential source, including a State, local, or foreign agency or authority or any private institution which furnished information on a confidential basis, and, in the case of a record or information compiled by criminal law enforcement authority in the course of a criminal investigation or by an agency conducting a lawful national security intelligence investigation, information furnished by a confidential source, (E) would disclose techniques and procedures for law enforcement investigations or prosecutions, or would disclose guidelines for law enforcement investigations or prosecutions if such disclosure could reasonably be expected to risk circumvention of the law, or (F) could reasonably be expected to endanger the life or physical safety of any individual;

(8) contained in or related to examination, operating, or condition reports prepared by, on

behalf of, or for the use of an agency responsible for the regulation or supervision of financial institutions; or

(9) geological and geophysical information and data, including maps, concerning wells.

Any reasonably segregable portion of a record shall be provided to any person requesting such record after deletion of the portions which are exempt under this subsection.

(c)(1) Whenever a request is made which involves access to records described in subsection (b)(7)(A) and—

(A) the investigation or proceeding involves a possible violation of criminal law; and

(B) there is reason to believe that (i) the subject of the investigation or proceeding is not aware of its pendency, and (ii) disclosure of the existence of the records could reasonably be expected to interfere with enforcement proceedings, the agency may, during only such time as that circumstance continues, treat the records as not subject to the requirements of this section.

(2) Whenever informant records maintained by a criminal law enforcement agency under an informant's name or personal identifier are requested by a third party according to the informant's name or personal identifier, the agency may treat the records as not subject to the requirements of this section unless the informant's status as an informant has been officially confirmed.

(3) Whenever a request is made which involves access to records maintained by the Federal Bureau of Investigation pertaining to foreign intelligence or counterintelligence, or international terrorism, and the existence of the records is classified information as provided in subsection (b)(1), the Bureau may, as long as the existence of the records remains classified information, treat the records as not subject to the requirements of this section.

(d) This section does not authorize withholding of information or limit the availability of records to the public, except as specifically stated in this section. This section is not authority to withhold information from Congress.

(e) On or before March 1 of each calendar year, each agency shall submit a report covering the preceding calendar year to the Speaker of the House of Representatives and President of the Senate for referral to the appropriate committees of the Congress. The report shall include—

(1) The number of determinations made by such agency not to comply with requests for records made to such agency under subsection (a) and the reasons for each such determination;

(2) the number of appeals made by persons under subsection (a)(6), the result of such appeals, and the reason for the action upon each appeal that results in a denial of information;

(3) the names and titles or positions of each person responsible for the denial of records requested under this section, and the number of instances of participation for each;

(4) the results of each proceeding conducted pursuant to subsection (a)(4)(F), including a report of the disciplinary action taken against the officer or employee who was primarily responsible for improperly withholding records or an explanation of why disciplinary action was not taken;

(5) a copy of every rule made by such agency regarding this section;

(6) a copy of the fee schedule and the total amount of fees collected by the agency for making records available under this section; and

(7) such other information as indicates efforts to administer fully this section.

The Attorney General shall submit an annual report on or before March 1 of each calendar year which shall include for the prior calendar year a listing of the number of cases arising under this section, the exemption involved in each case, the disposition of such case, and the cost, fees, and penalties assessed under subsections (a)(4)(E), (F), and (G). Such report shall also include a description of the efforts undertaken by the Department of Justice to encourage agency compliance with this section.

(f) For purposes of this section, the term "agency" as defined in section 551(1) of this title includes an executive department, military deartment, Government corporation, Government controlled corporation, or other establishment in the executive branch of the Government (including the Executive Office of the President), or any independent regulatory agency.

§ 552a. Records maintained on individuals

(a) Definitions.

For purposes of this section—

(1) the term "agency" means agency as defined in section 552(e) of this title;

(2) the term "individual" means a citizen of the United States or an alien lawfully admitted for permanent residence;

(3) the term "maintain" includes maintain, collect, use, or disseminate;

(4) the term "record" means any item, collection, or grouping of information about an individual that is maintained by an agency, including, but not limited to, his education, financial transactions, medical history, and criminal or employment history and that contains his name, or the identifying number, symbol, or other identifying particular assigned to the individual, such as a finger or voice print or a photograph;

(5) the term "system of records" means a group of any records under the control of any agency from which information is retrieved by the name of the individual or by some identifying number, symbol, or other identifying particular assigned to the individual;

(6) the term "statistical record" means a record in a system of records maintained for statistical research or reporting purposes only and not used in whole or in part in making any determination about an identifiable individual, except as provided by section 8 of title 13;

(7) the term "routine use" means, with respect to the disclosure of a record, the use of such record for a purpose which is compatible with the purpose for which is was collected;

(8) the term "matching program"—

  (A) means any computerized comparison of—

    (I) two or more automated systems of records or a system of records with non-Federal records for the purpose of—

      (i) establishing or verifying the eligibility of, or continuing compliance with statutory and regulatory requirements by, applicants for, recipients or beneficiaries of, participants in, or providers of services with respect to, cash or in-kind assistance or payments under Federal benefit programs, or

      (II) recouping payments or delinquent debts under such Federal benefit programs, or

    (ii) Two or more automated Federal personnel or payroll systems of records or a system of Federal personnel or payroll records with non-Federal records,

(B) but does not include:

    (i) matches performed to produce aggregate statistical data without any personal identifiers;

    (ii) matches performed to support any research or statistical project, the specific data of which may not be used to make decisions concerning the rights, benefits, or privileges of specific individuals;

    (iii) matches performed, by an agency (or component thereof) which performs as its principal function any activity pertaining to the enforcement of criminal laws, subsequent to the initiation of a specific criminal or civil law enforcement investigation of a named person or persons for the purpose of gathering evidence against such person or persons;

    (iv) matches of tax information (I) pursuant to section 6103(d) of the Internal Revenue Code of 1986, (II) for purposes of tax administration as defined in section 6103(b)(4) of such Code, (III) for the purpose of intercepting a tax refund due an individual under authority granted by section 464 or 1137 of the Social Security Act; or (IV) for the purpose of intercepting a tax refund due an individual under any other tax refund intercept program authorized by statute which has been determined by the Director of the Office of Management and Budget to contain verification, notice, and hearing requirements that are substantially similar to the procedures in section 1137 of the Social Security Act;

    (v) matches—

      (I) using records predominantly relating to Federal personnel, that are performed for routine administrative purposes (subject to guidance provided by the Director of the Office of Management and Budget pursuant to subsection (v)); or

(II) conducted by an agency using only records from systems of records maintained by that agency;

if the purpose of the match is not to take any adverse financial, personnel, disciplinary, or other adverse action against Federal personnel; or

(vi) matches performed for foreign counterintelligence purposes or to produce background checks for security clearances of Federal personnel or Federal contractor personnel;

(9) the term "recipient agency" means any agency, or contractor thereof, receiving records contained in a system of records from a source agency for use in a matching program;

(10) the term "non-Federal agency" means any State or local government, or agency thereof, which receives records contained in a system of records from a source agency for use in a matching program;

(11) the term "source agency" means any agency which discloses records contained in a system of records to be used in a matching program, or any State or local government, or agency thereof, which discloses records to be used in a matching program;

(12) the term "Federal benefit program" means any program administered or funded by the Federal Government, or by any agent or State on behalf of the Federal Government, providing cash or in-kind assistance in the form of payments, grants, loans, or loan guarantees to individuals; and

(13) the term "Federal personnel" means officers and employees of the Government of the United States, members of the uniformed services (including members of the Reserve Components), individuals entitled to receive immediate or deferred retirement benefits under any retirement program of the Government of the United States (including survivor benefits).

(b) Conditions of Disclosure.

No agency shall disclose any record which is contained in a system of records by any means of communication to any person, or to another agency, except pursuant to a written request by, or with the prior written consent of, the individual to whom the record pertains, unless disclosure of the record would be—

(1) to those officers and employees of the agency which maintains the record who have a need for the record in the performance of their duties;

(2) required under section 552 of this title;

(3) for a routine use as defined in subsection (a)(7) of this section and described under subsection (e)(4)(D) of this section;

(4) to the Bureau of the Census for purposes of planning or carrying out a census or survey or related activity pursuant to the provisions of title 13;

(5) to a recipient who has provided the agency with advance adequate written assurance that the record will be used solely as a statistical research or reporting record, and the record is to be transferred in a form that is not individually identifiable;

(6) to the National Archives and Records Administration as a record which has sufficient historical or other value to warrant its continued preservation by the United States Government, or for evaluation by the Archivist of the United States or the designee of the Archivist to determine whether the record has such value;

(7) to another agency or to an instrumentality of any governmental jurisdiction within or under the control of the United States for a civil or criminal law enforcement activity if the activity is authorized by law, and if the head of the agency or instrumentality has made a written request to the agency which maintains a record specifying the particular portion desired and the law enforcement activity for which the record is sought;

(8) to a person pursuant to a showing of compelling circumstances affecting the health or safety of an individual if upon such disclosure notification is transmitted to the last known address of such individual;

(9) to either House of Congress, or, to the extent of matter within its jurisdiction, any committee or subcommittee thereof, any joint committee of Congress or subcommittee of any such joint committee;

(10) to the Comptroller General, or any of his authorized representatives, in the course of the performance of the duties of the General Accounting Office;

(11) pursuant to the order of a court of competent jurisdiction; or

(12) to a consumer reporting agency in accordance with section 3711(f) of title 31.

(c) Accounting of Certain Disclosures.

Each agency, with respect to each system of records under its control, shall—

(1) except for disclosures made under subsections (b)(1) or (b)(2) of this section, keep an accurate accounting of—

(A) the date, nature, and purpose of each disclosure of a record to any person or to another agency made under subsection (b) of this section; and

(B) the name and address of the person or agency to whom the disclosure is made;

(2) retain the accounting made under paragraph (1) of this subsection for at least five years or the life of the record, whichever is longer, after the disclosure for which the accounting is made;

(3) except for disclosures made under subsection (b)(7) of this section, make the accounting made under paragraph (1) of this subsection available to the individual named in the record at his request; and

(4) inform any person or other agency about any correction or notation of dispute made by the agency in accordance with subsection (d) of this section of any record that has been disclosed to the person or agency if an accounting of the disclosure was made.

(d) Access to Records.

Each agency that maintains a system of records shall—

(1) upon request by any individual to gain access to his record or to any information pertaining to him which is contained in the system, permit him and upon his request, a person of his own choosing to accompany him, to review the record and have a copy made of all or any portion thereof in a form comprehensible to him,

except that the agency may require the individual to furnish a written statement authorizing discussion of that individual's record in the accompanying person's presence;

(2) permit the individual to request amendment of a record pertaining to him and—

(A) not later than 10 days (excluding Saturdays, Sundays, and legal public holidays) after the date of receipt of such request, acknowledge in writing such receipt; and

(B) promptly, either—

(i) make any correction of any portion thereof which the individual believes is not accurate, relevant, timely, or complete; or

(ii) inform the individual of its refusal to amend the record in accordance with his request, the reason for the refusal, the procedures established by the agency for the individual to request a review of that refusal by the head of the agency or an officer designated by the head of the agency, and the name and business address of that official;

(3) permit the individual who disagrees with the refusal of the agency to amend his record to request a review of such refusal, and not later than 30 days (excluding Saturdays, Sundays, and legal public holidays) from the date on which the individual requests such review, complete such review and make a final determination unless, for good cause shown, the head of the agency extends such 30-day period; and if, after his review, the reviewing official also refuses to amend the record in accordance with the request, permit the individual to file with the agency a concise statement setting forth the reasons for his disagreement with the refusal of the agency, and notify the individual of the provisions for judicial review of the reviewing official's determination under subsection (g)(1)(A) of this section;

(4) in any disclosure, containing information about which the individual has filed a statement of disagreement, occurring after the filing of the statement under paragraph (3) of this subsection, clearly note any portion of the record which is disputed and provide copies of the statement and, if the agency deems it appropriate, copies of a concise statement of the reasons of the agency for not making the amendments requested, to persons or other agencies to whom the disputed record has been disclosed; and

(5) nothing in this section shall allow an individual access to any information compiled in reasonable anticipation of a civil action or proceeding.

(e) Agency Requirements.

Each agency that maintains a system of records shall—

(1) maintain in its records only such information about an individual as is relevant and necessary to accomplish a purpose of the agency required to be accomplished by statute or by executive order of the President;

(2) collect information to the greatest extent practicable directly from the subject individual when the information may result in adverse determinations about an individual's rights, benefits, and privileges under Federal programs;

(3) inform each individual whom it asks to supply information, on the form which it uses to collect the information or on a separate form that can be retained by the individual—

(A) the authority (whether granted by statute, or by executive order of the President) which authorizes the solicitation of the information and whether disclosure of such information is mandatory or voluntary;

(B) the principal purpose or purposes for which the information is intended to be used;

(C) the routine uses which may be made of the information, as published pursuant to paragraph (4)(D) of this subsection; and

(D) the effects on him, if any, of not providing all or any part of the requested information;

(4) subject to the provisions of paragraph (11) of this subsection, publish in the Federal Register upon establishment or revision a notice of the existence and character of the system of records, which notice shall include—

(A) the name and location of the system;

(B) the categories of individuals on whom records are maintained in the system;

(C) the categories of records maintained in the system;

(D) each routine use of the records contained in the system, including the categories of users and the purpose of such use;

(E) the policies and practices of the agency regarding storage, retrievability, access controls, retention, and disposal of the records;

(F) the title and business address of the agency official who is responsible for the system of records;

(G) the agency procedures whereby an individual can be notified at his request if the system of records contains a record pertaining to him;

(H) the agency procedures whereby an individual can be notified at his request how he can gain access to any record pertaining to him contained in the system of records, and how he can contest its content; and

(I) the categories of sources of records in the system;

(5) maintain all records which are used by the agency in making any determination about any individual with such accuracy, relevance, timeliness, and completeness as is reasonably necessary to assure fairness to the individual in the determination;

(6) prior to disseminating any record about an individual to any person other than an agency, unless the dissemination is made pursuant to subsection (b)(2) of this section, make reasonable efforts to assure that such records are accurate, complete, timely, and relevant for agency purposes;

(7) maintain no record describing how any individual exercises rights guaranteed by the First Amendment unless expressly authorized by statute or by the individual about whom the record is maintained or unless pertinent to and within the scope of an authorized law enforcement activity;

(8) make reasonable efforts to serve notice on an individual when any record on such individual is made available to any person under compulsory legal process when such process becomes a matter of public record;

(9) establish rules of conduct for persons involved in the design, development, operation, or maintenance of any system of records, or in maintaining any record, and instructing each such person with respect to such rules and the requirements of this section, including any other rules and procedures adopted pursuant to this section and the penalties for noncompliance;

(10) establish appropriate administrative, technical, and physical safeguards to insure the security and confidentiality of records and to protect against any anticipated threats or hazards to their security or integrity which could result in substantial harm, embarrassment, inconvenience, or unfairness to any individual on whom information is maintained;

(11) at least 30 days prior to publication of information under paragraph (4)(D) of this subsection, publish in the Federal Register notice of any new use or intended use of the information in the system, and provide an opportunity for interested persons to submit written data, views, or arguments to the agency; and

(12) if such agency is a recipient agency or a source agency in a matching program with a non-Federal agency, with respect to any establishment or revision of a matching program, at least 30 days prior to conducting such program, publish in the Federal Register notice of such establishment or revision.

(f) Agency Rules.

In order to carry out the provisions of this section, each agency that maintains a system of records shall promulgate rules, in accordance with the requirements (including general notice) of section 553 of this title, which shall—

(1) establish procedures whereby an individual can be notified in response to his request if any system of records named by the individual contains a record pertaining to him;

(2) define reasonable times, places, and requirements for identifying an individual who requests his record or information pertaining to him before the agency shall make the record or information available to the individual;

(3) establish procedures for the disclosure to an individual upon his request of his record or information pertaining to him, including special procedure, if deemed necessary, for the disclosure to an individual of medical records, including psychological records, pertaining to him;

(4) establish procedures for reviewing a request from an individual concerning the amendment of any record or information pertaining to the individual, for making a determination on the request, for an appeal within the agency of an initial adverse agency determination, and for whatever additional means may be necessary for each individual to be able to exercise fully his rights under this section; and

(5) establish fees to be charged, if any, to any individual for making copies of his record, excluding the cost of any search for and review of the record.

The Office of the Federal Register shall biennially compile and publish the rules promulgated under this subsection and agency notices published under subsection (e)(4) of this section in a form available to the public at low cost.

(g)(1) Civil Remedies.

Whenever any agency—

(A) makes a determination under subsection (d)(3) of this section not to amend an individual's record in accordance with his request, or fails to make such review in conformity with that subsection;

(B) refuses to comply with an individual request under subsection (d)(1) of this section;

(C) fails to maintain any record concerning any individual with such accuracy, relevance, timeliness, and completeness as is necessary to assure fairness in any determination relating to the qualifications, character, rights, or opportunities of, or benefits to the individual that may be made on the basis of such record, and consequently a determination is made which is adverse to the individual; or

(D) fails to comply with any other provision of this section, or any rule promulgated thereunder, in such a way as to have an adverse effect on an individual, the individual may bring a civil action against the agency, and the district courts of the United States shall have jurisdiction in the matters under the provisions of this subsection.

(2)(A) in any suit brought under the provisions of subsection (g)(1)(A) of this section, the court may order the agency to amend the individuals' record in accordance with his request or in such other way as the court may direct. In such a case the court shall determine the matter de novo.

(B) The court may assess against the United States reasonable attorney fees and other litigation costs reasonably incurred in any case under this paragraph in which the complainant has substantially prevailed.

(3)(A) in any suit brought under the provisions of subsection (g)(1)(B) of this section, the court may enjoin the agency from withholding the records and order the production to the complainant of any agency records improperly withheld from him. In such a case the court shall determine the matter de novo, and may examine the contents of any agency records in camera to determine whether the records or any portion thereof may be withheld under any of the exemptions set forth in subsection (k) of this section, and the burden is on the agency to sustain its action.

(B) the court may assess against the United States reasonable attorney fees and other litigation costs reasonably incurred in any case under this paragraph in which the complainant has substantially prevailed.

(4) In any suit brought under the provisions of subsection (g)(1)(C) or (D) of this section in which the court determines that the agency acted in a manner which was intentional or willful, the United States shall be liable to the individual in an amount equal to the sum of—

(A) actual damages sustained by the individual as a result of the refusal or failure, but in no case shall a person entitled to recovery receive less than the sum of $1,000; and

(B) the costs of the action together with reasonable attorney fees as determined by the court.

(5) an action to enforce any liability created under this section may be brought in the district court of the United States in the district in which the complainant resides, or has his principal place of business, or in which the agency records are situated, or in the District of Columbia, without regard to the amount in controversy, within two years from the date on which the cause of action arises, except that where an agency has materially and willfully misrepresented any information required under this section to be disclosed to an individual and the information so misrepresented is material to establishment of the liability of the agency to the individual under this section, the action may be brought at any time within two years after discovery by the individual of the misrepresentation. Nothing in this section shall be construed to authorize any civil action by reason of any injury sustained as the result of a disclosure of a record prior to September 27, 1975.

(h) Rights of Legal Guardians.

For the purposes of this section, the parent of any minor, or the legal guardian of any individual who has been declared to be incompetent due to physical or mental incapacity or age by a court of competent jurisdiction, may act on behalf of the individual.

(i) Criminal Penalties.

(1) Any officer or employee of an agency, who by virtue of his employment or official position, has possession of, or access to, agency records which contain individually identifiable information the disclosure of which is prohibited by this section or by rules or regulations established thereunder, and who knowing that disclosure of the specific material is so prohibited, willfully discloses the material in any manner to any person or agency not entitled to receive it, shall be guilty of a misdemeanor and fined not more than $5,000.

(2) Any officer or employee of any agency who willfully maintains a system of records without meeting the notice requirements of subsection (e)(4) of this section shall be guilty of a misdemeanor and fined not more than $5,000.

(3) Any person who knowingly and willfully requests or obtains any record concerning an individual from an agency under false pretenses shall be guilty of a misdemeanor and fined not more than $5,000.

(j) General Exemptions.

The head of any agency may promulgate rules, in accordance with the requirements (including general notice) of sections 533(b)(1), (2), and (3), (c), and (e) of this title, to exempt any system of records within the agency from any part of this section except subsections (b), (c)(1) and (2), (e)(4)(A) through (F), (e)(6), (7), (9), (10), and (11), and (i) if the system of records is—

(1) maintained by the Central Intelligence Agency; or

(2) maintained by an agency or component thereof which performs as its principal function any activity pertaining to the enforcement of criminal laws, including police efforts to prevent, control, or reduce crime or to apprehend criminals, and the activities of prosecutors, courts, correctional, probation, pardon, or parole authorities, and which consists of (A) information compiled for the purpose of identifying individual criminal offenders and alleged offenders and consisting only of identifying data and notations of arrests, the nature and disposition of criminal charges, sentencing, confinement, release, and parole and probation status; (B) information compiled for the purpose of a criminal investigation, including reports of inform- ants and investigators, and associated with an identifiable individual; or (c) reports identifiable to an individual compiled at any stage of the process of enforcement of the criminal laws from arrest or indictment through release from supervision.

At the time rules are adopted under this subsection, the agency shall include in the statement required under section 553(c) of this title, the reasons why the system of records is to be exempted from a provision of this section.

(k) Specific Exemptions.

The head of any agency may promulgate rules, in accordance with the requirements (including general notice) of sections 553(b)(1), (2), and (3), (c), and (e) of this title, to exempt any system of records within the agency from subsections (c)(3), (d), (e)(1), (e)(4)(G), (H), and (I), and (f) of this section of the system if records is—

(1) subject to the provisions of section 552(b)(1) of this title;

(2) investigatory material compiled for law enforcement purposes, other than material within the scope of subsection (j)(2) of this section: Provided, however, that if any individual is denied any right, privilege, or benefit that he would otherwise be entitled by Federal law, or for which he would otherwise be eligible, as a result

of the maintenance of such material, such material shall be provided to such individual, except to the extent that the disclosure of such material would reveal the identity of a source who furnished information to the Government under an express promise that the identity of the source would be held in confidence, or, prior to the effective date of this section, under an implied promise that the identity of the source would be held in confidence;

(3) maintained in connection with providing protective services to the President of the United States or other individuals pursuant to section 3056 of title 18;

(4) required by statute to be maintained and used solely as statistical records;

(5) investigatory material compiled solely for the purpose of determining suitability, eligibility, or qualifications for Federal civilian employment, military service, Federal contracts, or access to classified information, but only to the extent that the disclosure of such material would reveal the identity of a source who furnished information to the Government under an express promise that the identity of the source would be held in confidence, or, prior to the effective date of this section, under an implied promise that the identity of the source would be held in confidence;

(6) testing or examination material used solely to determine individual qualifications for appointment or promotion in the Federal service the disclosure of which would compromise the objectivity or fairness of the testing or examination process; or

(7) evaluation material used to determine potential for promotion in the armed services, but only to the extent that the disclosure of such material would reveal the identity of a source who furnished information to the Government under an express promise that the identity of the source would be held in confidence.

At the time rules are adopted under this subsection, the agency shall include in the statement required under section 553(c) of this title, the reasons why the system of records is to be exempted from a provision of this section.

(l) Archival Records.

(1) Each agency record which is accepted by the Archivist of the United States for storage, processing, and servicing in accordance with section 3101 of title 44 shall, for the purposes of this section, be considered to be maintained by the agency which deposited the record and shall be subject to the provisions of this section. The Archivist of the United States shall not disclose the record except to the agency which maintains the record, or under rules established by that agency which are not inconsistent with the provisions of this section.

(2) Each agency record pertaining to an identifiable individual which was transferred to the National Archives of the United States as a record which has sufficient historical or other value to warrant its continued preservation by the United States Government, prior to the effective date of this section, shall, for the purposes of this section, be considered to be maintained by the National Archives and shall not be subject to the provisions of this section, except that a statement generally describing such records (modeled after the requirements relating to records subject to subsections (e)(4)(A) through (G) of this section) shall be published in the Federal Register.

(3) Each agency record pertaining to an identifiable individual which is transferred to the National Archives of the United States as a record which has sufficient historical or other value to warrant its continued preservation by the United States Government, on or after the effective date of this section, shall, for the purposes of this section, be considered to be maintained by the National Archives and shall be exempt from he requirements of this section except subsections (e)(4)(A) through (G) and (e)(9) of this section.

(m) Government Contractors.

(1) When an agency provides by a contract for the operation by or on behalf of the agency of a system of records to accomplish an agency function, the agency shall, consistent with its authority, cause the requirements of this section to be applied to such system. for purposes of subsection (i) of this section any such contractor and any employee of such contractor, if such contract is agreed to on or after the effective date of this section, shall be considered to be an employee of an agency.

(2) A consumer reporting agency to which a record is disclosed under section 3711(f) of title 31 shall not be considered a contractor for the purposes of this section.

(n) Mailing Lists.

An individual's name and address may not be sold or rented by an agency unless such action is specifically authorized by law. This provision shall not be construed to require the withholding of names and addresses otherwise permitted to be made public.

(o) Matching Agreements.

(1) No record which is contained in a system of records may be disclosed to a recipient agency or non-Federal agency for use in a computer matching program except pursuant to a written agreement between the source agency and the recipient agency or non-Federal agency specifying—

(A) the purpose and legal authority for conducting the program;

(B) the justification for the program and the anticipated results, including a specific estimate of any savings;

(C) a description of the records that will be matched, including each data element that will be used, the approximate number of records that will be matched, and the projected starting and completion dates of the matching program;

(D) procedures for providing individualized notice at the time of application, and notice periodically thereafter as directed by the Data Integrity Board of such agency (subject to guidance provided by the Director of the Office of Management and Budget pursuant to subsection (v)), to—

(i) applicants for and recipients of financial assistance or payments under Federal benefit programs, and

(ii) applicants for and holders of positions as Federal personnel, that any information provided by such applicants, recipients, holders, and individuals may be subject to verification through matching programs;

(E) procedures for verifying information produced in such matching program as required by subsection (p);

(F) procedures for the retention and timely destruction of identifiable records created by a recipient agency or non-Federal agency in such matching program;

(G) procedures for ensuring the administrative, technical, and physical security of the records matched and the results of such programs;

(H) prohibitions on duplication and redisclosure of records provided by the source agency within or outside the recipient agency or the non-Federal agency, except where required by law or essential to the conduct of the matching program;

(I) procedures governing the use by a recipient agency or non-Federal agency of records provided in a matching program by a source agency, including procedures governing return of the records to the source agency or destruction of records used in such program;

(J) information on assessments that have been made on the accuracy of the records that will be used in such matching program; and

(K) that the Comptroller General may have access to all records of a recipient agency or a non-Federal agency that the Comptroller General deems necessary in order to monitor or verify compliance with the agreement.

(2)(A) A copy of each agreement entered into pursuant to paragraph (1) shall—

(i) be transmitted to the Committee on Governmental Affairs of the Senate and the Committee on Government Operations of the House of Representatives; and

(ii) be available upon request to the public.

(B) No such agreement shall be effective until 30 days after the date on which such a copy is transmitted pursuant to subparagraph (A)(i).

(C) Such an agreement shall remain in effect only for such period, not to exceed 18 months, as the Data Integrity Board of the agency determines is appropriate in light of the purposes, and length of time necessary for the conduct, of the matching program.

(D) Within 3 months prior to the expiration of such an agreement pursuant to subparagraph (C), the Data Integrity Board of the agency may, without additional review, renew the matching agreement for a current, ongoing matching program for not more than one additional year if—

(I) such program will be conducted without any change; and

(ii) each party to the agreement certifies to the Board in writing that the program has been conducted in compliance with the agreement.

(p) Verification and Opportunity to Contest Findings.

(1) In order to protect any individual whose records are used in a matching program, no recipient agency, non-Federal agency, or source agency may suspend, terminate, reduce, or make a final denial of any financial assistance or payment under a Federal benefit program to such individual, or take other adverse action against such individual, as a result of information produced by such matching program, until—

(A)(I) the agency has independently verified the information; or

(ii) the Data Integrity Board of the agency, or in the case of a non-Federal agency the Data Integrity Board of the source agency, determines in accordance with guidance issued by the Director of the Office of Management and Budget that—

(I) the information is limited to identification and amount of benefits paid by the source agency under a Federal benefit program; and

(II) there is a high degree of confidence that the information provided to the recipient agency is accurate;

(B) the individual receives a notice from the agency containing a statement of its findings and informing the individual of the opportunity to contest such findings; and

(C)(i) the expiration of any time period established for the program by statute or regulation for the individual to respond to that notice; or

(ii) in the case of a program for which no such period is established, the end of the 30-day period beginning on the date on which notice under subparagraph (B) is mailed or otherwise provided to the individual.

(2) Independent verification referred to in paragraph (1) requires investigation and confirmation of specific information relating to an individual that is used as a basis for an adverse action against the individual, including where applicable investigation and confirmation of—

(A) the amount of any asset or income involved;

(B) whether such individual actually has or had access to such asset or income for such individual's own use; and

(C) the period or periods when the individual actually had such asset or income.

(3) Notwithstanding paragraph (1), an agency may take any appropriate action otherwise prohibited by such paragraph if the agency determines that the public health or public safety may be adversely affected or significantly threatened during any notice period required by such paragraph.

(q) Sanctions.

(1) Notwithstanding any other provision of law, no source agency may disclose any record which is contained in a system of records to a recipient agency or non-Federal agency for a matching program if such source agency has reason to believe that the requirements of subsection (p), or any matching agreement entered into pursuant to subsection (o), or both, are not being met by such recipient agency.

(2) No source agency may renew a matching agreement unless—

(A) the recipient agency or non-Federal agency has certified that it has complied with the provisions of that agreement; and

(B) the source agency has no reason to believe that the certification is inaccurate.

(r) Report on New Systems and Matching Programs.

Each agency that proposes to establish or make a significant change in a system of records or a matching program shall provide adequate advance notice of any such proposal (in duplicate) to the Committee on Government Operations of the House of Representatives, the Committee on Governmental Affairs of the Senate, and the Office of Management and Budget in order to permit an evaluation of the probable or potential effect of such proposal on the privacy or other rights of individuals.

(s) Biennial Report.

The President shall biennially submit to the Speaker of the House of Representatives and the President pro tempore of the Senate a report—

(1) describing the actions of the Director of the Office of Management and Budget pursuant to section 6 of the Privacy Act of 1974 during the preceding 2 years;

(2) describing the exercise of individual rights of access and amendment under this section during such years;

(3) identifying changes in or additions to systems of records;

(4) containing such other information concerning administration of this section as may be necessary or useful to the Congress in reviewing the effectiveness of this section in carrying out the purpose of the Privacy Act of 1974.

(t) Effect of Other Laws.

(1) No agency shall rely on any exemption contained in section 552 of this title to withhold from an individual any record which is otherwise accessible to such individual under the provisions of this section.

(2) No agency shall rely on any exemption in this section to withhold from an individual any record which is otherwise accessible to such individual under the provisions of section 552 of this title.

(u) Data Integrity Boards.

(1) Every agency conducting or participating in a matching program shall establish a Data Integrity Board to oversee and coordinate among the various components of such agency the agency's implementation of this section.

(2) Each Data Integrity Board shall consist of senior officials designated by the head of the agency, and shall include any senior official designated by the head of the agency as responsible for implementation of this section, and the inspector general of the agency, if any. The inspector general shall not serve as chairman of the Data Integrity Board.

(3) Each Data Integrity Board—

(A) shall review, approve, and maintain all written agreements for receipt or disclosure of agency records for matching programs to ensure compliance with subsection (o), and all relevant statutes, regulations, and guidelines;

(B) shall review all matching programs in which the agency has participated during the year, either as a source agency or recipient agency, determine compliance with applicable laws, regulations, guidelines, and agency agreements, and assess the costs and benefits of such programs;

(C) shall review all recurring matching programs in which the agency has participated during the year, either as a source agency or recipient agency, for continued justification for such disclosures;

(D) shall compile an annual report, which shall be submitted to the head of the agency and the Office of Management and Budget and made available to the public on request, describing the matching activities of the agency, including—

(i) matching programs in which the agency has participated as a source agency or recipient agency;

(ii) matching agreements proposed under subsection (o) that were disapproved by the Board;

(iii) any changes in membership or structure of the Board in the preceding year;

(iv) the reasons for any waiver of the requirement in paragraph (4) of this section for completion and submission of a cost-benefit analysis prior to the approval of a matching program;

(v) any violations of matching agreements that have been alleged or identified and any corrective action taken; and

(vi) any other information required by the Director of the Office of Management and Budget to be included in such report;

(E) shall serve as a clearing house for receiving and providing information on the accuracy, completeness, and reliability of records used in matching programs;

(F) shall provide interpretation and guidance to agency components and personnel on the requirements of this section for matching programs;

(G) shall review agency record keeping and disposal policies and practices for matching programs to assure compliance with this section; and

(H) may review and report on any agency matching activities that are not matching programs.

(4)(A) Except as provided in subparagraphs (B) and (C), a Data Integrity Board shall not approve any written agreement for a matching program unless the agency has completed and submitted to such Board a cost-benefit analysis of the proposed program and such analysis demonstrates that the program is likely to be cost effective.

(B) The Board may waive the requirements of subparagraph (A) of this paragraph if it determines in writing, in accordance with guidelines prescribed by the Director of the Office of Management and Budget, that a cost-benefit analysis is not required.

(C) A cost-benefit analysis shall not be required under subparagraph (A) prior to the initial approval of a written agreement for a matching program that is specifically required by statute. Any subsequent written agreement for such a program shall not be approved by the Data Integrity Board unless the agency has submitted a cost-benefit analysis of the program as conducted under the preceding approval of such agreement.

(5)(A) If a matching agreement is disapproved by a Data Integrity Board, any party to such agreement may appeal the disapproval to the Director of the Office of Management and Budget. Timely notice of the filing of such an appeal shall be provided by the Director of the Office of Management and Budget to the Committee on Governmental Affairs of the Senate and the Committee on Government Operations of the House of Representatives.

(B) The Director of the Office of Management and Budget may approve a matching agreement notwithstanding the disapproval of a Data Integrity Board if the Director determines that—

(i) the matching program will be consistent with all applicable legal, regulatory, and policy requirements;

(ii) there is adequate evidence that the matching agreement will be cost-effective; and

(iii) the matching program is in the public interest.

(C) The decision of the Director to approve a matching agreement shall not take effect until 30 days after it is reported to committees described in subparagraph (A).

(D) If the Data Integrity Board and the Director of the Office of Management and Budget disapprove a matching program proposed by the inspector general of an agency, the inspector general may report the disapproval to the head of the agency and to the Congress.

(6) The Director of the Office of Management and Budget shall, annually during the first 3 years after the date of enactment of this subsection and biennially thereafter, consolidate in a report to the Congress the information contained in the reports from the various Data Integrity Boards under paragraph (3)(D). Such report shall include detailed information about costs and benefits of matching programs that are conducted during the period covered by such consolidated report, and shall identify each waiver granted by a Data Integrity Board of the requirement for completion and submission of a cost-benefit analysis and the reasons for granting the waiver.

(7) In the reports required by paragraphs (3)(D) and (6), agency matching activities that are not matching programs may be reported on an aggregate basis, if and to the extent necessary to protect ongoing law enforcement or counterintelligence investigations.

(v) Office of Management and Budget Responsibilities.

The Director of the Office of Management and Budget shall—

(1) develop and, after notice and opportunity for public comment, prescribe guidelines and regulations for the use of agencies in implementing the provisions of this section; and

(2) provide continuing assistance to and oversight of the implementation of this section by agencies.

§ 522b. Open meetings

(a) For purposes of this section—

(1) the term "agency" means any agency, as defined in section 522(e) of this title, headed by a collegial body composed of two or more individual members, a majority of whom are appointed to such position by the President with the advice and consent of the Senate, and any subdivision thereof authorized to act on behalf of the agency;

(2) the term "meeting" means the deliberations of at least the number of individual agency members required to take action on behalf of the agency where such deliberations determine or result in the joint conduct or disposition of official agency business, but does not include deliberations required or permitted by subsection (d) or (e); and

(3) the term "member" means an individual who belongs to a collegial body heading an agency.

(b) Members shall not jointly conduct or dispose of agency business other than in accordance with this section. Except as provided in subsection (c), every portion of every meeting of an agency shall be open to public observation.

(c) Except in a case where the agency finds that the public interest requires otherwise, the second sentence of subsection (b) shall not apply to any portion of an agency meeting, and the requirements of subsections (d) and (e) shall not apply to any information pertaining to such meeting otherwise required by this section to be disclosed to the public, where the agency properly determines that such portion or portions of its meeting or the disclosure of such information is likely to—

(1) disclose matters that are (A) specifically authorized under criteria established by an Executive order to be kept secret in the interests of national defense or foreign policy and (B) in fact

properly classified pursuant to such Executive order;

(2) relate solely to the internal personnel rules and practices of an agency;

(3) disclose matters specifically exempted from disclosure by statute (other than section 552 of this title), provided that such statute (A) requires that the matters be withheld from the public in such a manner as to leave no discretion on the issue, or (B) establishes particular criteria for withholding or refers to particular types of matters to be withheld;

(4) disclose trade secrets and commercial or financial information obtained from a person and privileged or confidential;

(5) involve accusing any person of a crime, or formally censuring any person;

(6) disclose information of a personal nature where disclosure would constitute a clearly unwarranted invasion of personal privacy;

(7) disclose investigatory records compiled for law enforcement purposes, or information which if written would be contained in such records, but only to the extent that the production of such records or information would (A) interfere with enforcement proceedings, (B) deprive a person of a right to a fair trial or an impartial adjudication, (C) constitute an unwarranted invasion of personal privacy, (D) disclose the identity of a confidential source and, in the case of a record compiled by a criminal law enforcement authority in the course of a criminal investigation, or by an agency conducting a lawful national security intelligence investigation, confidential information furnished only by the confidential source, (E) disclose investigative techniques and procedures, or (F) endanger the life or physical safety of law enforcement personnel;

(8) disclose information contained in or related to examination, operating, or condition reports prepared by, on behalf of, or for the use of an agency responsible for the regulation or supervision of financial institutions;

(9) disclose information the premature disclosure of which would—

(A) in the case of an agency which regulates currencies, securities, commodities, or financial institutions, be likely to (i) lead to significant financial speculation in currencies, securities, or commodities, or (ii) significantly endanger the stability of any financial institution; or

(B) in the case of any agency, be likely to significantly frustrate implementation of a proposed agency action,

except that subparagraph (B) shall not apply in any instance where the agency has already disclosed to the public the content or nature of its proposed action, or where the agency is required by law to make such disclosure on its own initiative prior to taking final agency action on such proposal; or

(10) specifically concern the agency's issuance of a subpoena, or the agency's participation in a civil action or proceeding, an action in a foreign court or international tribunal, or an arbitration or the initiation, conduct, or disposition by the agency of a particular case of formal agency adjudication pursuant to the procedures in section 554 of this title or otherwise involving a determination on the record after opportunity for a hearing.

(d)(1) Action under subsection (c) shall be taken only when a majority of the entire membership of the agency (as defined in subsection (a)(1)) votes to take such action. A separate vote of the agency members shall be taken with respect to each agency meeting a portion or portions of which are proposed to be closed to the public pursuant to subsection (c), or with respect to any information which is proposed to be withheld under subsection (c). A single vote may be taken with respect to a series of meetings, a portion or portions of which are proposed to be closed to the public, or with respect to any information concerning such series of meetings, so long as each meeting in such series involves the same particular matters and is scheduled to be held no more than thirty days after the initial meeting in such series. The vote of each agency member participating in such vote shall be recorded and no proxies shall be allowed.

(2) Whenever any person whose interests may be directly affected by a portion of a meeting requests that the agency close such portion to the public for any of the reasons referred to in paragraph (5), (6), or (7) of subsection (c), the agency, upon request of any one of its members,

shall vote by recorded vote whether to close such meeting.

(3) Within one day of any vote taken pursuant to paragraph (1) or (2), the agency shall make publicly available a written copy of such vote reflecting the vote of each member on the question. If a portion of a meeting is to be closed to the public, the agency shall, within one day of the vote taken pursuant to paragraph (1) or (2) of this subsection, make publicly available a full written explanation of its action closing the portion together with a list of all persons expected to attend the meeting and their affiliation.

(4) Any agency, a majority of whose meetings may properly be closed to the public pursuant to paragraph (4), (8), (9)(A), or (10) of subsection (c), or any combination thereof, may provide by regulation for the closing of such meetings or portions thereof in the event that a majority of the members of the agency votes by recorded vote at the beginning of such meeting, or portion thereof, to close the exempt portion or portions of the meeting, and a copy of such vote, reflecting the vote of each member on the question, is made available to the public. The provisions of paragraphs (1), (2), and (3) of this subsection and subsection (e) shall not apply to any portion of a meeting to which such regulations apply; Provided, That the agency shall, except to the extent that such information is exempt from disclosure under the provisions of subsection (c), provide the public with public announcement of the time, place, and subject matter of the meeting and of each portion thereof at the earliest practicable time.

(e)(1) In the case of each meeting, the agency shall make public announcement, at least one week before the meeting, of the time, place, and subject matter of the meeting, whether it is to be open or closed to the public, and the name and phone number of the official designated by the agency to respond to requests for information about the meeting. Such announcement shall be made unless a majority of the members of the agency determines by a recorded vote that agency business requires that such meeting be called at an earlier date, in which case the agency shall make public announcement of the time, place, and subject matter of such meeting,

and whether open or closed to the public, at the earliest practicable time.

(2) The time or place of a meeting may be changed following the public announcement required by paragraph (1) only if the agency publicly announces such change at the earliest practicable time. The subject matter of a meeting, or the determination of the agency to open or close a meeting, or portion of a meeting, to the public, may be changed following the public announcement required by this subsection only if (A) a majority of the entire membership of the agency determines by a recorded vote that agency business so requires and that no earlier announcement of the change was possible, and (B) the agency publicly announces such change and the vote of each member upon such change at the earliest practicable time.

(3) Immediately following each public announcement required by this subsection, notice of the time, place, and subject matter of a meeting, whether the meeting is open or closed, any change in one of the preceding, and the name and phone number of the official designated by the agency to respond to requests for information about the meeting, shall also be submitted for publication in the Federal Register.

(f)(1) For every meeting closed pursuant to paragraphs (1) through (10) of subsection (c), the General Counsel or chief legal officer of the agency shall publicly certify that, in his or her opinion, the meeting may be closed to the public and shall state each relevant exemptive provision. A copy of such certification, together with a statement from the presiding officer of the meeting setting forth the time and place of the meeting, and the persons present, shall be retained by the agency. The agency shall maintain a complete transcript or electronic recording adequate to record fully the proceedings of each meeting, or portion of a meeting, closed to the public, except that in the case of a meeting, or portion of a meeting, closed to the public pursuant to paragraph (8), (9)(A), or (10) of subsection (c), the agency shall maintain either such a transcript or recording, or a set of minutes. Such minutes shall fully and clearly describe all matters discussed and shall provide a full and accurate summary of any actions taken, and the reasons therefor, including a description of each of the views expressed on any item and the record of any rollcall vote (reflecting the vote of each member on the question.) All documents considered in connection with any action shall be identified in such minutes.

(2) The agency shall make promptly available to the public, in a place easily accessible to the public, the transcript, electronic recording, or minutes (as required by paragraph (1)) of the discussion of any item on the agenda, or of any item of the testimony of any witness received at the meeting, except for such item or items of such discussion or testimony as the agency determines to contain information which may be withheld under subsection (c). Copies of such transcript, or minutes, or a transcription of such recording disclosing the identity of each speaker, shall be furnished to any person at the actual cost of duplication or transcription. The agency shall maintain a complete verbatim copy of the transcript, a complete copy of the minutes, or a complete electronic recording of each meeting, or portion of a meeting, closed to the public, for a period of at least two years after such meeting, or until one year after the conclusion of any agency proceeding with respect to which the meeting or portion was held, whichever occurs later.

(g) Each agency subject to the requirements of this section shall, within 180 days after the date of enactment of this section, following consultation with the Office of the Chairman of the Administrative Conference of the United States and published notice in the Federal Register of at least thirty days and opportunity for written comment by any person, promulgate regulations to implement the requirements of subsections (b) through (f) of this section. Any person may bring a proceeding in the United States District Court for the District of Columbia to require an agency to promulgate such regulations if such agency has not promulgated such regulations within the time period specified herein. Subject to any limitations of time provided by law, any person may bring a proceeding in the United States Court of Appeals for the District of Columbia to set aside agency regulations issued pursuant to this subsection that are not in accord with the requirements of subsections (b)

through (f) of this section and to require the promulgation of regulations that are in accord with such subsections.

(h)(1) The district courts of the United States shall have jurisdiction to enforce the requirements of subsections (b) through (f) of this section by declaratory judgment, injunctive relief, or other relief as may be appropriate. Such actions may be brought by any person against an agency prior to, or within sixty days after, the meeting out of which the violation of this section arises, except that if public announce- ment of such meeting is not initially provided by the agency in accordance with the requirements of this section, such action may be instituted pursuant to this section at any time prior to sixty days after any public announce- ment of such meeting. Such actions may be brought in the district court of the United States for the district in which the agency meeting is held or in which the agency in question has its headquarters, or in the District Court for the District of Columbia. In such actions a defendant shall serve his answer within thirty days after the service of the complaint. The burden is on the defendant to sustain his action. In deciding such cases the court may examine in camera any portion of the transcript, electronic recording, or minutes of a meeting closed to the public, and may take such additional evidence as it deems necessary. The court, having due regard for orderly administration and the public interest, as well as the interests of the parties, may grant such equitable relief as it deems appropriate, including granting an injunction against future violations of this section or ordering the agency to make available to the public such portion of the transcript, recording, or minutes of a meeting as is not authorized to be withheld under subsection (c) of this section.

(2) Any Federal court otherwise authorized by law to review agency action may, at the application of any person properly participating in the proceeding pursuant to other applicable law, inquire into violations by the agency of the requirements of this section and afford such relief as it deems appropriate. Nothing in this section authorizes any Federal court having jurisdiction solely on the basis of paragraph (1) to set aside,

enjoin, or invalidate any agency action (other than an action to close a meeting or to withhold information under this section) taken or discussed at any agency meeting out of which the violation of this section arose.

(i) The court may assess against any party reasonable attorney fees and other litigation costs reasonably incurred by any other party who substantially prevails in any action brought in accordance with the provisions of subsection (g) or (h) of this section, except that costs may be assessed against the plaintiff only where the court finds that the suit was initiated by the plaintiff primarily for frivolous or dilatory purposes. In the case of assessment of costs against an agency, the costs may be assessed by the court against the United States.

(j) Each agency subject to the requirements of this section shall annually report to Congress regarding its compliance with such require- ments, including a tabulation of the total number of agency meetings open to the public, the total number of meetings closed to the public, the reasons for closing such meetings, and a description of any litigation brought against the agency under this section, including any costs assessed against the agency in such litigation (whether or not paid by the agency).

(k) Nothing herein expands or limits the present rights of any person under section 552 of this title, except that the exemptions set forth in subsection (c) of this section shall govern in the case of any request made pursuant to section 552 to copy or inspect the transcripts, recordings, or minutes described in subsection (f) of this section. The requirements of chapter 33 of title 44, United States Code, shall not apply to the transcripts, recordings, and minutes described in subsection (f) of this section.

(l) This section does not constitute authority to withhold any information from Congress, and does not authorize the closing of any agency meeting or portion thereof required by any other provision of law to be open.

(m) Nothing in this section authorizes any agency to withhold from any individual any record, including transcripts, recordings, or minutes required by this section, which is otherwise

accessible to such individual under section 552a of this title.

§ 553.   Rulemaking

(a) This section applies, according to the provisions thereof, except to the extent that there is involved—

(1) a military or foreign affairs function of the United States; or

(2) a matter relating to agency management or personnel or to public property, loans, grants, benefits, or contracts.

(b) General notice of proposed rule making shall be published in the Federal Register, unless persons subject thereto are named and either personally served or otherwise have actual notice thereof in accordance with law. The notice shall include—

(1) a statement of the time, place, and nature of public rule making proceedings;

(2) reference to the legal authority under which the rule is proposed; and

(3) either the terms or substance of the proposed rule or a description of the subjects and issues involved. Except when notice or hearing is required by statute, this subsection does not apply—

(A) to interpretative rules, general statements of policy, or rules of agency organization, procedure, or practice; or

(B) when the agency for good cause finds (and incorporates the finding and a brief statement of reasons therefor in the rules issued) that notice and public procedure thereon are impracticable, unnecessary, or contrary to the public interest.

(c) After notice required by this section, the agency shall give interested persons an opportunity to participate in the rule making through submission of written data, views, or arguments with or without opportunity for oral presentation. After consideration of the relevant matter presented, the agency shall incorporate in the rules adopted a concise general statement of their basis and purpose. When rules are required by statute to be made on the record after opportunity for an agency hearing, sections 556 and 557 of this title apply instead of this subsection.

(d) The required publication or service of a substantive rule shall be made not less than 30 days before its effective date, except—

(1) a substantive rule which grants or recognizes an exception or relieves a restriction;

(2) interpretative rules and statements of policy; or

(3) as otherwise provided by the agency for good cause found and published with the rule.

(e) Each agency shall give an interested person the right to petition for the issuance, amendment, or repeal of a rule.

§ 554.   Adjudications

(a) This section applies, according to the provisions thereof, in every case of adjudication required by statute to be determined on the record after opportunity for an agency hearing, except to the extent that there is involved—

(1) a matter subject to a subsequent trial of the law and the facts de novo in a court;

(2) the selection or tenure of an employee, except an administrative law judge appointed under section 3105 of this title;

(3) proceedings in which decisions rest solely on inspections, tests, or elections;

(4) the conduct of military or foreign affairs functions;

(5) cases in which an agency is acting as an agent for a court; or

(6) the certification of worker representatives.

(b) Persons entitled to notice of an agency hearing shall be timely informed of—

(1) the time, place, and nature of the hearing;

(2) the legal authority and jurisdiction under which the hearing is to be held; and

(3) the matters of fact and laws asserted.

When private persons are the moving parties, the other parties to the proceeding shall give prompt notice of issues controverted in fact or law; and in other instances agencies may by rule require responsive pleading. In fixing the time and place for hearings, due regard shall be had for the convenience and necessity of the parties or their representatives.

(c) The agency shall give all interested parties opportunity for—

(1) the submission and consideration of facts, arguments, offers of settlement, or proposals of adjustment when time, the nature of the proceeding, and the public interest permit; and

(2) to the extent that the parties are unable so to determine a controversy by consent, hearing and decision on notice and in accordance with sections 556 and 557 of this title.

(d) The employee who presides at the reception of evidence pursuant to section 556 of this title shall make the recommended decision or initial decision required by section 557 of this title, unless he becomes unavailable to the agency. Except to the extent required for the disposition of ex parte matters as authorized by law, such an employee may not—

(1) consult a person or party on a fact in issue, unless on notice and opportunity for all parties to participate; or

(2) be responsible to or subject to the supervision or direction of an employee or agent engaged in the performance of investigative or prosecuting functions for an agency.

An employee or agent engaged in the performance of investigative or prosecuting functions for an agency in a case may not, in that or a factually related case, participate or advise in the decision, recommended decision, or agency review pursuant to section 557 of this title, except as witness or counsel in public proceedings. This subsection does not apply—

(A) in determining applications for initial licenses;

(B) to proceedings involving the validity or application of rates, facilities, or practices of public utilities or carriers; or

(C) to the agency or a member or members of the body comprising the agency.

(e) The agency, with like effect as in the case of other orders, and in its sound discretion, may issue a declaratory order to terminate a controversy or remove uncertainty.

§ 555.   Ancillary matters

(a) This section applies, according to the provisions thereof, except as otherwise provided by this subchapter.

(b) A person compelled to appear in person before an agency or representative thereof is entitled to be accompanied, represented, and advised by counsel or, if permitted by the agency, by other qualified representative. A party is entitled to appear in person or by or with counsel or other duly qualified representative in an agency proceeding. So far as the orderly conduct of public business permits, an interested person may appear before an agency or its responsible employees for the presentation, adjustment, or determination of an issue, request, or controversy in a proceeding, whether interlocutory, summary, or otherwise, or in connection with an agency function. With due regard for the convenience and necessity of the parties or their representatives and within a reasonable time, each agency shall proceed to conclude a matter presented to it. This subsection does not grant or deny a person who is not a lawyer the right to appear for or represent others before an agency or in an agency proceeding.

(c) Process, requirement of a report, inspection, or other investigative act or demand may not be issued, made, or enforced except as authorized by law. A person compelled to submit data or evidence is entitled to retain or, on payment of lawfully prescribed costs, procure a copy or transcript thereof, except that in a nonpublic investigatory proceeding the witness may for good cause be limited to inspection of the official transcript of his testimony.

(d) Agency subpoenas authorized by law shall be issued to a party on request and, when required by rules of procedure, on a statement or showing of general relevance and reasonable scope of the evidence sought. On contest, the court shall sustain the subpoena or similar process or demand to the extent that it is found to be in accordance with law. In a proceeding for enforcement, the court shall issue an order requiring the appearance of the witness or the production of the evidence or data within a reasonable time under penalty of punishment for contempt in case of contumacious failure to comply.

(e) Prompt notice shall be given of the denial in whole or in part of a written application, petition, or other request of an interested person made in connection with any agency proceeding. Except in affirming a prior denial or when the denial is self-explanatory, the notice shall be accompanied by a brief statement of the grounds for denial.

§ 556.   Hearings; presiding employees; powers and duties; burden of proof; evidence; record as basis of decision

(a) This section applies, according to the provisions thereof, to hearings required by section 553 or 554 of this title to be conducted in accordance with this section.

(b) There shall preside at the taking of evidence—

(1) the agency;

(2) one or more members of the body which comprises the agency; or

(3) one or more administrative law judges appointed under section 3105 of this title.

This subchapter does not supersede the conduct of specified classes of proceedings, in whole or in part, by or before boards or other employees specially provided for by or designated under statute. The functions of presiding employees and of employees participating in decisions in accordance with section 557 of this title shall be conducted in an impartial manner. A presiding or participating employee may at any time disqualify himself. On the filing in good faith of a timely and sufficient affidavit of personal bias or other disqualification of a presiding or participating employee, the agency shall determine the matter as a part of the record and decision in the case.

(c) Subject to published rules of the agency and within its powers, employees presiding at hearings may—

(1) administer oaths and affirmations;

(2) issue subpoenas authorized by law;

(3) rule on offers of proof and receive relevant evidence;

(4) take depositions or have depositions taken when the ends of justice would be served;

(5) regulate the course of the hearing;

(6) hold conferences for the settlement or simplification of the issues by consent of the parties or by the use of alternative means of dispute

resolution as provided in subchapter IV of this chapter;

(7) inform the parties as to the availability of one or more alternative means of dispute resolution, and encourage use of such methods;

(8) require the attendance at any conference held pursuant to paragraph (6) of at least one representative of each party who has authority to negotiate concerning resolution of issues in controversy;

(9) dispose of procedural requests or similar matters;

(10) make or recommend decisions in accordance with section 557 of this title; and

(11) take other action authorized by agency rule consistent with this subchapter.

(d) Except as otherwise provided by statute, the proponent of a rule or order has the burden of proof. Any oral or documentary evidence may be received, but the agency as a matter of policy shall provide for the exclusion of irrelevant, immaterial, or unduly repetitious evidence. A sanction may not be imposed or rule or order issued except on consideration of the whole record or those parts thereof cited by a party and supported by and in accordance with the reliable, probative, and substantial evidence. The agency may, to the extent consistent with the interests of justice and the policy of the underlying statutes administered by the agency, consider a violation of section 557(d) of this title sufficient grounds for a decision adverse to a party who has knowingly committed such violation or knowingly caused such violation to occur. A party is entitled to present his case or defense by oral or documentary evidence, to submit rebuttal evidence, and to conduct such cross-examination as may be required for a full and true disclosure of the facts. In rule making or determining claims for money or benefits or applications for initial licenses an agency may, when a party will not be prejudiced thereby, adopt procedures for the submission of all or part of the evidence in written form.

(e) The transcript of testimony and exhibits, together with all papers and requests filed in the proceeding, constitutes the exclusive record for decision in accordance with section 557 of this title and, on payment of lawfully prescribed costs, shall be made available to the parties. When an agency decision rests on official notice of a material fact not appearing in the evidence in the record, a party is entitled, on timely request, to an opportunity to show the contrary.

§ 557.   Initial decisions; conclusiveness; review by agency; submissions by parties; contents of decisions; record

(a) This section applies, according to the provisions thereof, when a hearing is required to be conducted in accordance with section 556 of this title.

(b) When the agency did not preside at the reception of the evidence, the presiding employee or, in cases not subject to section 554(d) of this title, an employee qualified to preside at hearings pursuant to section 556 of this title, shall initially decide the case unless the agency requires, either in specific cases or by general rule, the entire record to be certified to it for decision. When the presiding employee makes an initial decision, that decision then becomes the decision of the agency without further proceedings unless there is an appeal to, or review on motion of, the agency within time provided by rule. On appeal from or review of the initial decision, the agency has all the powers which it would have in making the initial decision except as it may limit the issues on notice or by rule. When the agency makes the decision without having presided at the reception of the evidence, the presiding employee or an employee qualified to preside at hearings pursuant to section 556 of this title shall first recommend a decision, except that in rule making or determining applications for initial licenses—

(1) instead thereof the agency may issue a tentative decision or one of its responsible employees may recommend a decision; or

(2) this procedure may be omitted in a case in which the agency finds on the record that due and timely execution of its functions imperatively and unavoidably so requires.

(c) Before a recommended, initial, or tentative decision, or a decision on agency review of the decision of subordinate employees, the parties are entitled to a reasonable opportunity to submit for the consideration of the employees participating in the decisions—

(1) proposed findings and conclusions; or

(2) exceptions to the decisions or recommended decisions of subordinate employees or to tentative agency decisions; and

(3) supporting reasons for the exceptions or proposed findings or conclusions.

The record shall show the ruling on each finding, conclusion, or exception presented. All decisions, including initial, recommended, and tentative decisions, are a part of the record and shall include a statement of—

(A) findings and conclusions, and the reasons or basis therefor, on all the material issues of fact, law, or discretion presented on the record; and

(B) the appropriate rule, order, sanction, relief, or denial thereof.

(d)(1) In any agency proceeding which is subject to subsection (a) of this section, except to the extent required for the disposition of ex parte matters as authorized by law—

(A) no interested person outside the agency shall make or knowingly cause to be made to any member of the body comprising the agency, administrative law judge, or other employee who is or may reasonably be expected to be involved in the decisional process of the proceeding, an ex parte communication relevant to the merits of the proceeding;

(B) no member of the body comprising the agency, administrative law judge, or other employee who is or may reasonably be expected to be involved in the decisional process of the proceeding, shall make or knowingly cause to be made to any interested person outside the agency an ex parte communication relevant to the merits of the proceeding;

(C) a member of the body comprising the agency, administrative law judge, or other employee who is or may reasonably be expected to be involved in the decisional process of such proceeding who receives, or who makes or knowingly causes to be made, a communication prohibited by this subsection shall place on the public record of the proceeding:

(i) all such written communications;

(ii) memoranda stating the substance of all such oral communications; and

(iii) all written responses, and memoranda stating the substance of all oral responses, to the materials described in clauses (i) and (ii) of this subparagraph;

(D) upon receipt of a communication knowingly made or knowingly caused to be made by a party in violation of this subsection, the agency, administrative law judge, or other employee presiding at the hearing may, to the extent consistent with the interests of justice and the policy of the underlying statutes, require the party to show cause why his claim or interest in the proceeding should not be dismissed, denied, disregarded, or otherwise adversely affected on account of such violation; and

(E) the prohibitions of this subsection shall apply beginning at such time as the agency may designate, but in no case shall they begin to apply later than the time at which a proceeding is noticed for hearing unless the person responsible for the communication has knowledge that it will be noticed, in which case the prohibitions shall apply beginning at the time of his acquisition of such knowledge.

(2) This subsection does not constitute authority to withhold information from Congress.

§ 558.   Imposition of sanctions; determination of applications for licenses; suspension, revocation, and expiration of licenses

(a) This section applies, according to the provisions thereof, to the exercise of a power or authority.

(b) A sanction may not be imposed or a substantive rule or order issued except within jurisdiction delegated to the agency and as authorized by law.

(c) When application is made for a license required by law, the agency, with due regard for the rights and privileges of all the interested parties or adversely affected persons and within a reasonable time, shall set and complete proceedings required to be conducted in accordance with sections 556 and 557 of this title or other proceedings required by law and shall make its decision. Except in cases of willfulness or those in which public health, interest, or safety requires otherwise, the withdrawal, suspension, revocation, or annulment of a license is lawful only if, before the institution of agency proceedings therefor, the licensee has been given—

(1) notice by the agency in writing of the facts or conduct which may warrant the action; and

(2) opportunity to demonstrate or achieve compliance with all lawful requirements.

When the licensee has made timely and sufficient application for a renewal or a new license in accordance with agency rules, a license with reference to an activity of a continuing nature does not expire until the application has been finally determined by the agency.

§ 559. Effect on other laws; effect of subsequent statute

This subchapter, chapter 7, and sections 1305, 3105, 3344, 4301(2)(E), 5372, and 7521 of this title, and the provisions of section 5335(a)(B) of this title that relate to administrative law judges, do not limit or repeal additional requirements imposed by statute or otherwise recognized by law. Except as otherwise required by law, requirements or privileges relating to evidence or procedure apply equally to agencies and persons. Each agency is granted the authority necessary to comply with the requirements of this subchapter through the issuance of rules or otherwise. Subsequent statute may not be held to supersede or modify this subchapter, chapter 7, sections 1305, 3105, 3344, 4301(2)(E), 5372, or 7521 of this title, or the provisions of section 5335(a)(B) of this title that relate to administrative law judges, except to the extent that it does so expressly.

§ 701. Application; definitions

(a) This chapter applies, according to the provisions thereof, except to the extent that—

(1) statutes preclude judicial review; or

(2) agency action is committed to agency discretion by law.

(b) For the purpose of this chapter—

(1) "agency" means each authority of the Government of the United States, whether or not it is within or subject to review by another agency, but does not include—

(A) the Congress;

(B) the courts of the United States;

(C) the governments of the territories or possessions of the United States;

(D) the government of the District of Columbia;

(E) agencies composed of representatives of the parties or of representatives of organizations of the parties to the disputes determined by them;

(F) courts martial and military commissions;

(G) military authority exercised in the field in time of war or in occupied territory; or

(H) functions conferred by sections 1738, 1739, 1743, and 1744 of title 12; chapter 2 of title 41; or sections 1622, 1884, 1891-1902, and former section 1641(b)(2) of title 50, appendix; and

(2) "person", "rule", "order", "license", "sanction", "relief", and "agency action" have the meanings given them by section 551 of this title.

§ 702. Right of review

A person suffering legal wrong because of agency action, or adversely affected or aggrieved by agency action within the meaning of a relevant statute, is entitled to judicial review thereof. An action in a court of the United States seeking relief other than money damages and stating a claim that an agency or an officer or employee thereof acted or failed to act in an official capacity or under color of legal authority shall not be dismissed nor relief therein be denied on the ground that it is against the United States or that the United States is an indispensable party. The United States may be named as a defendant in any such action, and a judgment or decree may be entered against the United States: Provided, That any mandatory or injunctive decree shall specify the Federal officer or officers (by name or by title), and their successors in office, personally responsible for compliance. Nothing herein (1) affects other limitations on judicial review or the power or duty of the court to dismiss any action nor deny relief on any other appropriate legal or equitable ground; or (2) confers authority to grant relief if any other statute that grants consent to suit expressly or impliedly forbids the relief which is sought.

§ 703.   Form and venue of proceeding

The form of proceeding for judicial review is the special statutory review proceeding relevant to the subject matter in a court specified by statute or, in the absence or inadequacy thereof, any applicable form of legal action, including actions for declaratory judgments or writs of prohibitory or mandatory injunction or habeas corpus, in a court of competent jurisdiction. If no special statutory review proceeding is applicable, the action for judicial review may be brought against the United States, the agency by its official title, or the appropriate officer. Except to the extent that prior, adequate, and exclusive opportunity for judicial review is provided by law, agency action is subject to judicial review in civil or criminal proceedings for judicial enforcement.

§ 704.   Actions reviewable

Agency action made reviewable by statute and final agency action for which there is no other adequate remedy in a court are subject to judicial review. A preliminary, procedural, or intermediate agency action or ruling not directly reviewable is subject to review on the review of the final agency action. Except as otherwise expressly required by statute, agency action otherwise final is final for the purposes of this section whether or not there has been presented or determined an application for a declaratory order, for any form of reconsiderations, or, unless the agency otherwise requires by rule and provides that the action meanwhile is inoperative, for an appeal to superior agency authority.

§ 705.   Relief pending review

When an agency finds that justice so requires, it may postpone the effective date of action taken by it, pending judicial review. On such conditions as may be required and to the extent necessary to prevent irreparable injury, the reviewing court, including the court to which a case may be taken on appeal from or on application for certiorari or other writ to a reviewing court, may issue all necessary and appropriate process to postpone the effective date of an agency action or to preserve status or rights pending conclusion of the review proceedings.

§ 706.   Scope of review

To the extent necessary to decision and when presented, the reviewing court shall decide all relevant questions of law, interpret constitutional and statutory provisions, and determine the meaning or applicability of the terms of an agency action. The reviewing court shall—
(1) compel agency action unlawfully withheld or unreasonably delayed; and
(2) hold unlawful and set aside agency action, findings, and conclusions found to be—
  (A) arbitrary, capricious, an abuse of discretion, or otherwise not in accordance with law;
  (B) contrary to constitutional right, power, privilege, or immunity;
  (C) in excess of statutory jurisdiction, authority, or limitations, or short of statutory right;
  (D) without observance of procedure required by law;
  (E) unsupported by substantial evidence in a case subject to sections 556 and 557 of this title or otherwise reviewed on the record of an agency hearing provided by statute; or
  (F) unwarranted by the facts to the extent that the facts are subject to trial de novo by the reviewing court.
In making the foregoing determinations, the court shall review the whole record or those parts of it cited by a party, and due account shall be taken of the rule of prejudicial error.

§ 1305.   Administrative law judges

For the purpose of section 3105, 3344, 4301(2)(D), and 5372 of this title and the provisions of section 5335(a)(B) of this title that relate to administrative law judges, the Office of Personnel Management may, and for the purpose of section 7521 of this title, the Merit Systems Protection Board may investigate, require reports by agencies, issue reports, including an annual report to Congress, prescribe regulations, appoint advisory committees as necessary, recommend legislation, subpoena witnesses and records, and pay witness fees as established for the courts of the United States.

§ 3105. Appointment of administrative law judges

Each agency shall appoint as many administrative law judges as are necessary for proceedings required to be conducted in accordance with sections 556 and 557 of this title. Administrative law judges shall be assigned to cases in rotation so far as practicable, and may not perform duties inconsistent with their duties and responsibilities as administrative law judges.

§ 3344. Details; administrative law judges

An agency as defined by section 551 of this title which occasionally or temporarily is insufficiently staffed with administrative law judges appointed under section 3105 of this title may use administrative law judges selected by the Office of Personnel Management from and with the consent of other agencies.

§ 5372. Administrative law judges

(a) For the purposes of this section, the term "administrative law judge" means an administrative law judge appointed under section 3105.

(b)(1) There shall be 3 levels of basic pay for administrative law judges (designated as AL-1, 2, and 3, respectively), and each such judge shall be paid at 1 of those levels, in accordance with the provisions of this section. The rates of basic pay for those levels shall be as follows:

AL-3, rate A 65 percent of the rate of basic pay for level IV of the Executive Schedule.

AL-3, rate B 70 percent of the rate of basic pay for level IV of the Executive Schedule.

AL-3, rate C 75 percent of the rate of basic pay for level IV of the Executive Schedule.

AL-3, rate D 80 percent of the rate of basic pay for level IV of the Executive Schedule.

AL-3, rate E 85 percent of the rate of basic pay for level IV of the Executive Schedule.

AL-3, rate F 90 percent of the rate of basic pay for level IV of the Executive Schedule.

AL-2, 95 percent of the rate of basic pay for level IV of the Executive Schedule.

AL-1 The rate of basic pay for level IV of the Executive Schedule.

(2) the Office of Personnel Management shall determine, in accordance with procedures which the Office shall by regulation prescribe, the level in which each administrative-law-judge position shall be placed and the qualifications to be required for appointment to each level.

(3)(A) Upon appointment to a position in AL-3, an administrative law judge shall be paid at rate A of AL-3, and shall be advanced successively to rates B, C, and D of that level upon completion of 52 weeks of service in the next lower rate, and to rates E and F of that level upon completion of 104 weeks of service in the next lower rate.

(B) The Office of Personnel Management may provide for appointment of an administrative law judge in AL-3 at an advanced rate under such circumstances as the Office may determine appropriate.

(c) The Office of Personnel Management shall, prescribe regulations necessary to administer this section.

§ 7521. Actions against administrative law judges

(a) An action may be taken against an administrative law judge appointed under section 3105 of this title by the agency in which the administrative law judge is employed only for good cause established and determined by the Merit Systems Protection Board on the record after opportunity for hearing before the Board.

(b) The actions covered by this section are—

(1) a removal;

(2) a suspension;

(3) a reduction in grade;

(4) a reduction in pay; and

(5) a furlough of 30 days or less;

but do not include:

(A) a suspension or removal under section 7532 of this title;

(B) a reduction-in-force action under section 3502 of this title; or

(C) any action initiated under section 1215 of this title.

APPENDIX B

DEPARTMENT OF HEALTH AND HUMAN SERVICES
Social Security Administration

Form Approved
OMB No. 0960-0141

DISABILITY REPORT

PLEASE PRINT, TYPE, OR WRITE CLEARLY AND ANSWER ALL ITEMS TO THE BEST OF YOUR ABILITY. If you are filing on behalf of someone else, enter his or her name and social security number in the space provided and answer all questions. **COMPLETE ANSWERS WILL AID IN PROCESSING THE CLAIM.**

PRIVACY ACT/PAPERWORK REDUCTION ACT NOTICE: The Social Security Administration is authorized to collect the information on this form under sections 205(a), 223(d) and 1633(a) of the Social Security Act. The information on this form is needed by Social Security to make a decision on your claim. While giving us the information on this form is voluntary, failure to provide all or part of the requested information could prevent an accurate or timely decision on your claim and could result in the loss of benefits. Although the information you furnish on this form is almost never used for any purpose other than making a determination on your disability claim, such information may be disclosed by the Social Security Administration as follows: (1) To enable a third party or agency to assist Social Security in establishing rights to Social Security benefits and/or coverage; (2) to comply with Federal laws requiring the release of information from Social Security records (e.g., to the General Accounting Office and the Veterans Administration); and (3) to facilitate statistical research and audit activities necessary to assure the integrity and improvement of the Social Security programs (e.g., to the Bureau of the Census and private concerns under contract to Social Security). These and other reasons why information about you may be used or given out are explained in the Federal Register. If you would like more information about this, any Social Security office can assist you.

A. NAME OF CLAIMANT	B. SOCIAL SECURITY NUMBER	C. TELEPHONE NUMBER where you can be reached (include area code)
Melinda Lewis	0 0 0 / 0 0 / 0 0 0 0	704-555-3524

D. WHAT IS YOUR DISABLING CONDITION? *(Briefly explain the injury or illness that stops you from working.)*

Heart condition and back pain

PART I — INFORMATION ABOUT YOUR CONDITION

1. When did your condition first bother you	MONTH	DAY	YEAR
	March	1	1992

2A. Did you work after the date shown in item 1? (If "no", go on to items 3A and 3B.)   ☐ YES   ☒ NO

2B. If you did work since the date in item 1, did your condition cause you to change —

Your job or job duties?	☐ YES	☐ NO
Your hours of work?	☐ YES	☐ NO
Your attendance?	☐ YES	☐ NO
Anything else about your work?	☐ YES	☐ NO

(If you answered "no" to **all** of these, go to items 3A and 3B.)

2C. If you answered "yes" to **any** item in 2B, explain below what the changes in your work circumstances were, the dates they occurred, and how your condition made these changes necessary.

3A. When did your condition finally make you stop working?	MONTH	DAY	YEAR
	March	1	1992

3B. Explain how your condition now keeps you from working.

I had a heart attack in March 1992. Since then I have been very tired and short of breath. I also have back pain and pain in my leg. I can only stand up for 30 minutes. I cannot lift a gallon of milk.

Form **SSA-3368-BK** (1-89)

1

♻ Printed on recycled paper

A-31

PART II — INFORMATION ABOUT YOUR MEDICAL RECORDS

4. List the name, address and telephone number of the doctor who has the latest medical records about your disabling condition.

If you have **no** doctor check ☐

NAME	ADDRESS
Dr. Mark Pearson	Cardiology Associates 5100 Randolph Rd. Charlotte, NC 28207

TELEPHONE NUMBER (include area code)
704-555-1612

HOW OFTEN DO YOU SEE THIS DOCTOR?	DATE YOU **FIRST** SAW THIS DOCTOR	DATE YOU **LAST** SAW THIS DOCTOR
once a month	March 1, 1992	two weeks ago

REASONS FOR VISITS *(show illness or injury for which you had an examination or treatment)*

To check heart and medications

TYPE OF TREATMENT OR MEDICINES RECEIVED (such as surgery, chemotherapy, radiation, and the medicines you take for your illness or injury, if known. If no treatment or medicines, show "NONE".)

I had bypass surgery and I take multiple medications.

5A. Have you seen any other doctors since your disabling condition began?
If "yes", show the following:

☑ YES   ☐ NO

NAME	ADDRESS
Dr. Tahereh Emami	6221 Randolph Rd. Charlotte, NC 28207

TELEPHONE NUMBER (include area code)
704-555-9000

HOW OFTEN DO YOU SEE THIS DOCTOR?	DATE YOU **FIRST** SAW THIS DOCTOR	DATE YOU **LAST** SAW THIS DOCTOR
once a month	1987	last week

REASONS FOR VISITS *(show illness or injury for which you had an examination or treatment)*

back & leg pain

TYPE OF TREATMENT OR MEDICINES RECEIVED (such as surgery, chemotherapy, radiation, and the medicines you take for your illness or injury, if known. If no treatment or medicines, show "NONE".)

pain medicine, stretching exercises

5B. Identify below any other doctor you have seen since your illness or injury began.

NAME	ADDRESS

TELEPHONE NUMBER (include area code)

HOW OFTEN DO YOU SEE THIS DOCTOR?	DATE YOU **FIRST** SAW THIS DOCTOR	DATE YOU **LAST** SAW THIS DOCTOR

REASONS FOR VISITS *(show illness or injury for which you had an examination or treatment.)*

TYPE OF TREATMENT OR MEDICINES RECEIVED (such as surgery, chemotherapy, radiation, and the medicines you take for your illness or injury, if known. If no treatment or medicines, show "NONE".)

6A. Have you been hospitalized or treated at a clinic for your disabling condition?   ☒ YES ☐ NO
If "yes", show the following:

NAME OF HOSPITAL OR CLINIC	ADDRESS
Charlotte Hospital	4100 Randolph Rd. Charlotte, NC 23207
PATIENT OR CLINIC NUMBER	

WERE YOU AN INPATIENT? (stayed at least overnight?) ☒ YES ☐ NO (If "yes", show:)	WERE YOU AN OUTPATIENT? ☐ YES ☐ NO (If "yes", show:)
DATES OF ADMISSIONS	DATES OF DISCHARGES	DATES OF VISITS
March 1, 1992	March 7, 1992	

REASON FOR HOSPITALIZATION OR CLINIC VISITS (show illness or injury for which you had an examination or treatment.)

heart attack and heart surgery

TYPE OF TREATMENT OR MEDICINES RECEIVED (such as surgery, chemotherapy, radiation, and the medicines you take for your illness or injury, if known. If no treatment or medicines, show "NONE".)

bypass surgery, x-rays, cardiac catheterization, medications for my heart

6B. If you have been in other hospital or clinic for your illness or injury, identify it below.

NAME OF HOSPITAL OR CLINIC	ADDRESS
PATIENT OR CLINIC NUMBER	

WERE YOU AN INPATIENT? (stayed at least overnight?) ☐ YES ☐ NO (If "yes", show:)	WERE YOU AN OUTPATIENT? ☐ YES ☐ NO (If "yes", show:)
DATES OF ADMISSIONS	DATES OF DISCHARGES	DATES OF VISITS

REASON FOR HOSPITALIZATION OR CLINIC VISITS (show illness or injury for which you had an examination or treatment.)

TYPE OF TREATMENT OR MEDICINES RECEIVED (such as surgery, chemotherapy, radiation, and the medicines you take for your illness or injury, if known. If no treatment or medicines, show "NONE".)

If you have been in other hospitals or clinics for your illness or injury, list the names, addresses, patient or clinic numbers, dates and reasons for hospitalization or clinic visits in Part VI.

7. Have you been seen by other agencies for your disabling condition?
(VA, Workmen's Compensation, Vocational Rehabilitation, Welfare, etc.)
(If "yes," show the following:)   ☐ YES ☐ NO

NAME OF AGENCY	ADDRESS
YOUR CLAIM NUMBER	
DATE OF VISITS	

TYPE OF TREATMENT, EXAMINATION OR MEDICINES RECEIVED (such as surgery, chemotherapy, radiation, and the medicines you take for your illness or injury, if known. If no treatment or medicines, show "NONE".)

If more space is needed, list the other agencies, their addresses, your claim numbers, dates, and treatment received in Part VI.

Form **SSA-3368-BK** (1-89)

8. Have you had any of the following tests in the last year?

TEST	CHECK APPROPRIATE BLOCK OR BLOCKS	IF "YES" SHOW	
		WHERE DONE	WHEN DONE
Electrocardiogram	☒ YES ☐ NO	Charlotte Hosp.	3/92
Chest X-Ray	☒ YES ☐ NO	"	"
Other X-Ray (name body part here) _____back_____	☒ YES ☐ NO		1987- present
Breathing Tests	☐ YES ☒ NO	Charlotte Hosp.	
Blood Tests	☒ YES ☐ NO		3/92
Other (Specify)	☐ YES ☒ NO		

9. If you have a medicaid card, what is your number (some hospitals and clinics file your records by your medicaid number.)

PART III — INFORMATION ABOUT YOUR ACTIVITIES

10. Has your doctor told you to cut back or limit your activities in any way?   ☒ YES   ☐ NO
If "yes", give the name of the doctor below and tell what he or she told you about cutting back or limiting your activities.

Both my doctors told me not to lift more than ten pounds

11. Describe your daily activities in the following areas and state what and how much you do of each and how often you do it:
- **Household maintenance** (including cooking, cleaning, shopping, and odd jobs around the house as well as any other similar activities):

I fix cereal for breakfast and a sandwich for lunch. I dust, but the heavy work is done by my husband. I must rest often during the day.

- **Recreational activities and hobbies** (hunting, fishing, bowling, hiking, musical instruments, etc.):

I read and watch TV.

- **Social contacts** (visits with friends, relatives, neighbors):

church on Sunday

- **Other** (drive car, motorcycle, ride bus, etc.)

Drive short distances

PART IV — INFORMATION ABOUT YOUR EDUCATION

12. What is the highest grade of school that you completed and when?

11th grade in 1955

13. Have you gone to trade or vocational school or had any type of special training? *If "yes", show:*   ☐ YES   ☒ NO

- The type of trade or vocational school or training:

- Approximate dates you attended:

- How this schooling or training was used in any work you did:

PART V — INFORMATION ABOUT THE WORK YOU DID

14. List all jobs you have had in the last 15 years before you stopped working, beginning with your usual job. Normally, this will be the kind of work you did the longest. (If you have a 6th grade education or less, AND did only heavy unskilled labor for 35 years or more, list all of the jobs you have had since you began to work. If you need more space, use Part VI.)

JOB TITLE (Be sure to begin with your usual job)	TYPE OF BUSINESS	DATES WORKED (Month and Year) FROM	TO	DAYS PER WEEK	RATE OF PAY (Per hour, day, week, month or year)
cashier	small grocery store	6/63	3/1/92	5	$6.50/hr

15A. Provide the following information for your usual job shown in item 14, line 1.

In your job did you:
- Use machines, tools, or equipment of any kind?   ☒ Yes   ☐ No
- Use technical knowledge or skills?   ☐ Yes   ☒ No
- Do any writing, complete reports, or perform similar duties?   ☐ Yes   ☒ No
- Have supervisory responsibilities?   ☐ Yes   ☒ No

15B. Describe your basic duties (explain what you did and how you did it) below. Also, explain all "Yes" answers by giving a FULL DESCRIPTION of: the types of machines, tools, or equipment you used and the exact operation you performed; the technical knowledge or skills involved; the type of writing you did, and the nature of any reports; and the number of people you supervised and the extent of your supervision:

I used a cash register

15C. Describe the kind and amount of physical activity this job involved during typical day in terms of:

- **Walking** (circle the number of hours a day spent walking) — 0 1 2 3 4 5 6 ⑦ 8
- **Standing** (circle the number of hours a day spent standing) — 0 1 2 3 4 5 6 ⑦ 8
- **Sitting** (circle the number of hours a day spent sitting) — 0 ① 2 3 4 5 6 7 8
- **Bending** (circle how often a day you had to bend) — Never · Occasionally · (Frequently) · Constantly
- **Reaching** (circle how often a day you had to reach) — Never · Occasionally · (Frequently) · Constantly
- **Lifting and Carrying:** Describe below what was lifted, and how far it was carried. Check heaviest weight lifted, and weight frequently lifted and/or carried:

HEAVIEST WEIGHT LIFTED	WEIGHT FREQUENTLY LIFTED/CARRIED
☐ 10 lbs.	☒ Up to 10 lbs.
☒ 20 lbs.	☐ Up to 25 lbs.
☐ 50 lbs.	☐ Up to 50 lbs.
☐ 100 lbs.	☐ Over 50 lbs.
☐ Over 100 lbs.	

PART VI — REMARKS

Use this section for additional space to answer any previous questions. Also use this space to give any additional information that you think will be helpful in making a decision in your disability claim, (such as information about other illnesses or injuries not shown in Parts I and II.) Please refer to the previous items by number.

Public reporting burden for this collection of information is estimated to average 30 minutes per response, including the time for reviewing instructions, searching existing data sources, gathering and maintaining the data needed, and completing and reviewing the collection of information. Send comments regarding this burden estimate or any other aspect of this collection of information, including suggestions for reducing this burden to the Social Security Administration ATTN: Reports Clearance Officer, 1-A-21 Operations Bldg., Baltimore, MD 21235 and to the Office of Management and Budget, Paperwork Reduction Project (OMB #0960-0141), Washington, D.C. 20503.

Knowing that anyone making a false statement or representation of a material fact for use in determining a right to payment under the Social Security Act commits a crime punishable under Federal law, I certify that the above statements are true.

NAME (Signature of claimant or person filing on the claimant's behalf)

SIGN HERE ▶ *Melinda Lewis*   DATE *January 25, 1994*

Witnesses are required ONLY if this statement has been signed by mark (X) above. If signed by mark (X), two witnesses to the signing who know the person making the statement must sign below, giving their full addresses.

1. Signature of Witness	2. Signature of Witness
Address (Number and street, city, state, and ZIP code)	Address (Number and street, city, state, and ZIP code)

Form **SSA-3368-BK** (1-89)   6

PART VII — FOR SSA USE ONLY - DO NOT WRITE BELOW THIS LINE

NAME OF CLAIMANT	SOCIAL SECURITY NUMBER
Melinda Lewis	0 0 0 / 0 0 / 0 0 0 0

16. Check any of the following categories which apply to this case:

PRESUMPTIVE DISABILITY CONSIDERATION
(If any of these boxes are checked, DO's (and DDS's) should be alert to the possibility of a presumptive disability determination in SSI claims per DI 11055.240 and 23535.005.

A. ☐ Amputation of two limbs

B. ☐ Amputation of a leg at the hip

C. ☐ Allegation of total deafness

D. ☐ Allegation of total blindness

E. ☐ Allegation of bed confinement or immobility without a wheelchair, walker, or crutches, allegedly due to a longstanding condition — exclude recent accident and recent surgery.

F. ☐ Allegation of a stroke (cerebral vascular accident) more than 3 months in the past and continued marked difficulty in walking or using a hand or arm.

G. ☐ Allegation of cerebral palsy, muscular dystrophy or muscular atrophy and marked difficulty in walking (e.g., use of braces), speaking or coordination of the hands or arms.

H. ☐ Allegation of diabetes with amputation of a foot.

I. ☐ Allegation of Down's Syndrome (Mongolism).

J. ☐ An applicant filing on behalf of another individual alleges severe mental deficiency for claimant who is at least 7 years of age. The applicant alleges that the individual attends (or attended) a special school, or special classes in school, because of his mental deficiency, or is unable to attend any type of school (or if beyond school age was unable to attend), and requires care and supervision of routine daily activities.

L. ☐ Allegation of Acquired Immune Deficiency Syndrome (AIDS)

17A. Does the claimant speak English? . . . .   ☒ Yes   ☐ No
If "no," what language does he speak?

17B. Does the claimant need assistance in prosecuting his or her claim? . . . .   ☐ Yes   ☒ No
If "yes," show name, address, relationship, and telephone number of an interested party willing to assist the claimant.

NAME	ADDRESS	RELATIONSHIP	TELEPHONE NUMBER (area code)

17C. Can the claimant (or his representative) be readily reached by telephone with no communication problems due to language, speech or hearing difficulties? If "no" DO should complete SSA-3369-F6.   ☒ Yes   ☐ No

Form SSA-3368-BK (1-89)

7

18A. Check each item to indicate if any difficulty was observed:

Reading	☐ Yes	☒ No	Using Hands	☐ Yes	☒ No
Writing	☐ Yes	☒ No	Breathing	☒ Yes	☐ No
Answering	☐ Yes	☒ No	Seeing	☐ Yes	☒ No
Hearing	☒ Yes	☐ No	Walking	☐ Yes	☒ No
Sitting	☒ Yes	☐ No			
Understanding	☐ Yes	☒ No	Other (Specify): _____		

18B. If any of the above items were checked "yes," describe the exact difficulty involved:

    The claimant had to stand up after 30 minutes. Her breathing
    was labored.

18C. Describe the claimant fully (e.g., general build, height, weight, behavior, any difficulties that add to or supplement those noted above, etc.):

    short, somewhat obese

19. Medical Development — Initiated by District or Branch Office

SOURCE	DATE REQUESTED	DATE(S) OF FOLLOW-UP	CAPABILITY DEVELOPMENT REQUESTED

20. DO or BO curtailed completion of Parts III - V per DI 11005.035 (DI 20501.005)	☐ YES	☒ NO
21. Is capability development by the DDS necessary? If "yes", show "DDS capability development needed" in item 11 of the SSA-831-U5	☐ YES	☒ NO
22. Is development of work activity necessary?	☐ YES	☒ NO
If "yes", is an SSA-820-F4 or SSA-821-F4..	☐ Pending	☐ In File

23. SSA-3368-BK taken by:			24. Form supplemented: If "yes" by:	☐ Yes	☐ No
☐ Personal Interview	☐ Telephone	☐ Mail	☐ Personal Interview ☐ Telephone	☐ Mail	

SIGNATURE OF DO OR BO INTERVIEWER OR REVIEWER	TITLE	DATE
Maria Endoza		1/25/94

Form SSA-3368-BK (1-89)　　　　　　8　　　　　　*U.S. Government Printing Office: 1994 — 364-202/90705

APPENDIX C

ADMINISTRATIVE LAW JUDGE DECISION FOR MELINDA LEWIS

SOCIAL SECURITY ADMINISTRATION
OFFICE OF HEARINGS AND APPEALS

DECISION

IN THE CASE OF

Melinda Lewis
_____
(Claimant)

_____
(Wage Earner)

CLAIM FOR

Period of Disability
and Disability Insurance
_____

000-00-0000
_____

PROCEDURAL HISTORY

This case is before the Administrative Law Judge on a request for hearing filed by the claimant, who is dissatisfied with the previous determinations finding that she is not disabled.

The claimant appeared and testified at the hearing, represented by Susan Garcia, attorney at law.

ISSUES

The issues in this case are whether the claimant is under a disability as defined by the Social Security Act and if so, when her disability commenced, the duration of the disability, and whether the insured status requirements of the Act are met for the purpose of entitlement to a period of disability and disability insurance benefits.

EVALUATION OF THE EVIDENCE

After a thorough evaluation of the entire record, it is concluded that the claimant has been disabled since March 1, 1992. She met the insured status requirements of the Social Security Act on that date and thereafter, through the date of this decision.

The claimant was 52 years old on the date her disability began. She has an eleventh grade education. The claimant has not engaged in substantial gainful activity since the disability onset date.

The claimant has the following impairments which are considered to be "severe" under the Social Security Act and Regulations: coronary artery disease, degenerative disc disease and associated pain. These impairments prevent the claimant from performing more than "sedentary" work.

On March 1, 1992, the claimant suffered a myocardial infarction. Cardiac catheterization revealed significant stenoses of three coronary arteries, and the claimant underwent triple bypass grafting. The surgery was performed by Dr. Mark Pearson, a cardiologist, who has followed the claimant regularly since March 1992. Dr. Pearson concluded in May 1994 that despite surgery and multiple medications, the claimant is unable to lift more than 10 pounds or stand for more than 1 hour in an 8-hour day. Thus, he has placed restrictions on the claimant that limit her to "sedentary" work. Dr. Pearson's conclusions are supported by his own treatment notes and the other medical evidence of record. The undersigned is persuaded that the combined effect of the claimant's coronary artery disease and degenerative disc disease, with associated pain, limits her to "sedentary" work.

The claimant's description of her limitations is consistent with the record when considered in its entirety. The claimant cannot perform her past relevant work and does not have transferable skills to perform other work within her residual functional capacity.

Given the claimant's residual functional capacity, and the vocational factors of her age, education and past relevant work experience, there are no jobs existing in significant numbers that the claimant is capable of performing. The claimant is under a disability as defined by the Social Security Act and Regulations.

FINDINGS

After consideration of the entire record, the Administrative Law Judge makes the following findings:

1. The claimant met the insured status requirements of the Act on March 1, 1992. The claimant has not performed substantial gainful activity since March 1, 1992.

2. The claimant's impairments which are considered to be "severe" under the Social Security Act are coronary artery disease, degenerative disc disease and associated pain.

3. The claimant's impairments do not meet or equal in severity the appropriate medical findings contained in 20 CFR Part 404, Appendix 1 to Subpart P (Listing of Impairments).

4. The claimant's allegations are found to be credible.

5. The claimant's impairments prevent her from performing more than "sedentary" work.

6. The claimant is unable to perform her past relevant work.

7. As of her alleged onset date, the claimant was 52 years old, which is defined as closely approaching advanced age. The claimant has a limited education.

8. The claimant does not have transferable skills to perform other work within her physical and mental residual functional capacity.

9. Based upon the claimant's residual functional capacity, and vocational factors, there are no jobs existing in significant numbers which she can perform. This finding is based upon Medical-Vocational Rule 201.09, 20 CFR Part 404, Appendix 2 to Subpart P.

10. The claimant has been under a disability as defined by the Social Security Act and Regulations since March 1, 1992.

DECISION

Based on the Title II application filed on January 25, 1994, the claimant is entitled to a period of disability beginning on March 1, 1992, and to disability insurance benefits under sections 216(i) and 223, respectively, of the Social Security Act, and the claimant's disability has continued through at least the date of this decision.

Russell H. Osborne

Russell H. Osborne
Administrative Law Judge

June 15, 1994

Date

GLOSSARY

adjudication The final decision of a court, usually made after trial of the case; the court's final judgment.

administrative law 1. The body of law that controls the way in which administrative agencies operate. 2. Regulations issued by administrative agencies.

advisory opinion A judicial interpretation of a legal question requested by the legislative or executive branch of government. Typically, courts prefer not to give advisory opinions.

alien 1. Any person present within the borders of the United States who is not a U.S. Citizen. 2. Any foreigner.

alternative dispute resolution (ADR) A term for speedier and less costly methods for resolving disputes than going to court.

annotation 1. A notation, appended to any written work, which explains or comments upon its meaning. 2. A commentary that appears immediately following a printed statute and describes the application of the statute in actual cases. Such annotations, with the statutes on which they comment, are published in volumes known as annotated statutes or annotated codes. 3. A notation that follows an opinion of court printed in a court report, explaining the court's action in detail.

arbitration A method of settling disputes by submitting a disagreement to a person (an arbitrator) or a group of individuals (an arbitration panel) for decision instead of going to court. If the parties are required to comply with the decision of the arbitrator, the process is called *binding arbitration;* if there is no such obligation, the arbitration is referred to as *nonbinding arbitration.* Compulsory arbitration arbitration required by law, most notable in labor disputes.

basic work activities In the context of Social Security disability, basic work activities include walking, standing, sitting, and lifting, as well as mental skills such as the ability to understand directions and use appropriate judgment.

Bill of Rights The first 10 amendments to the United States Constitution. The Bill of Rights is the portion of the Constitution that sets forth the rights which are the fundamental principles of the United States and the foundation of American citizenship.

charge In EEOC presuit procedures, a written statement describing the alleged unlawful employment practice.

checks and balances The principle that each branch of government will perform its duties and in doing so will provide restraints on the exercise of power by the other two branches.

citizen suits Lawsuits brought by individuals, not an enforcement agency, to compel agencies to enforce the statutes delegated to them.

conciliation A mandatory EEOC presuit procedure in which the parties and the EEOC try to eliminate the alleged unlawful employment practice by informal settlement methods.

declaratory judgment A judgment that specifies the rights of the parties but orders no relief. Nonetheless, it is a binding judgment and the appropriate remedy for the determination of an actionable dispute when the plaintiff is in doubt as to his legal rights.

declaratory order The administrative equivalent of a declaratory judgment.

delegation 1. The act of conferring authority upon, or transferring it to, another. USAGE: "By virtue of the delegation of powers contained in the Constitution, Congress is the branch of the federal government empowered to make laws." 2. The delegates from a particular state or other unit represented at a convention. USAGE: "She was an elected member of the Idaho delegation to the national convention of the Democratic Party."

de novo Anew; over again; a second time. USAGE: "de novo review."

disabled In the context of Social Security disability, persons are disabled if they cannot perform their past relevant work or any substantial gainful activity because of medically determinable impairments which can be expected to result in death or to last for a period of twelve continuous months.

due process of law Law administered through courts of justice, equally applicable to all under established rules that do not violate fundamental principles of fairness. Whether a person has received due process of law can only be determined on a case-by-case basis. In all criminal cases, however, it involves, at the very least, the right to be heard by a fair and impartial tribunal, the defendant's right to be represented by counsel, the right to cross-examine witnesses against him, the right to offer testimony on his own behalf, and the right to have advance notice of trial and of the charge sufficient in detail and in point of time to permit adequate preparation for trial. Due process requirements for criminal prosecutions are considerably more rigorous than those for civil cases. "Due process of law" is guaranteed by both the Fifth Amendment and the Fourteenth Amendment.

enabling statutes Statutes by which Congress delegates to agencies the authority to carry out their mission and sets out the substantive law that the agency enforces.

executive agency An agency that operates directly under the President (chief of the executive branch of government), with one head, who can be terminated without cause.

executive order An order issued by the chief executive officer (EXAMPLES: the president of the United States; the governor of a state; the mayor of a city) of government, whether national, state, or local.

facilitating An ADR method in which a facilitator coordinates meetings and discussions in a manner similar to mediation, but with less involvement with substantive issues than a mediator has.

fact finding An ADR method in which parties present information, usually regarding technical matters, to specialists who make findings used by the parties to reach a settlement.

federal statutes Statutes enacted by Congress.

regulation 1. The act of regulating. 2. A rule having the force of law, promulgated by an administrative agency; the act of rulemaking. 3. a rule of conduct established by a person or body in authority for the governance of those over whom they have authority.

fishing expeditions Broad and ill-defined requests by agencies for large amounts of information, when an agency may not have a firm suspicion of an actual violation.

generator In the context of RCRA, generators are producers of hazardous waste.

grids A term synonymous with Medical-Vocational Guidelines.

independent agency An agency that does not operate under a specific branch of government, usually headed by multi-member board, and considered less subject to direct Presidential control.

initial decision An initial decision is one that is the agency's final decision, unless an appeal is taken to a higher level in the agency.

informal rule making A process for developing regulations that consists of publication of proposed regulations (notice), comment from the public, and publication of final regulations.

INS examiner An INS employee who interviews aliens applying for immigration benefits and determines whether the requested benefits will be granted.

juducial review 1. Review by a court of a decision or ruling of an administrative agency. 2. Review by an appellate court of a determination by a lower court.

judicial review 1. Review by a court of a decision or ruling of an administrative agency. 2. Review by an appellate court of a determination by a lower court.

lawful permanent resident An alien who has been granted an immigrant visa, allowing the alien to remain in the United States and to enter and leave the United States freely.

Listing of Impairments The section of the Social Security regulations that describes, for each of the major body systems, impairments that are considered severe enough to prevent a person from doing any substantial gainful activity.

loose-leaf service A set of volumes that gathers the sources of law, with explanatory text, for one particular area of law.

mandamus A writ issuing from a court of competent jurisdiction, directed to an inferior court, board, or corporation, or to an officer of a branch of government (judicial, executive, or legislative), requiring the performance of some ministerial act. A writ of mandamus is an extraordinary remedy.

manifest the document that accompanies hazardous waste from its generation through its disposal, which identifies the waste and the generators, transporters, and TSD facilities that handled the waste.

mediation The voluntary resolution of a dispute in an amicable manner. One of the primary uses of mediators, also called conciliators, is in settling labor disputes. Professional mediators are available for that purpose through the Federal Mediation and Conciliation Service. Mediation differs from arbitration in that a mediator, unlike an arbitrator, does not render a decision.

Medical-Vocational Guidelines Tables promulgated by the SSA which categorize the vocational factors—residual functional capacity, age, education, and past work experience—and direct a conclusion of "not disabled" or "disabled" when all the factors coincide.

minitrial A structured settlement process in which each side presents a summary of its case before officials authorized to settle the case.

naturalization The process and the act of conferring nationality and citizenship upon a person who is not a natural-born citizen.

negotiated rule making A procedure in which agencies and interested parties meet, exchange information, and reach a consensus on the text of proposed regulations.

neutral The person who presides over arbitration proceedings and other ADR methods.

order making Another term for adjudications.

order to show cause An order of court directing a party to appear before the court and to present facts and legal arguments showing cause why the court should not take a certain action adversely affecting that party's interests. Orders to show cause are often granted *ex parte*. A party's failure to appear or, having appeared, his failure to show cause, will result in a final judgment unfavorable to him.

out of status The term used to describe aliens who do not have valid visas allowing them to be in the United States.

past relevant work Work performed within the past fifteen years, which lasted long enough for the person to learn the job and generated wages high enough to indicate substantial gainful activity.

police power 1. The power of government to make and enforce laws and regulations necessary to maintain and enhance the public welfare and to prevent individuals from violating the rights of others. 2. The sovereignty of each of the states of the United States that is not surrendered to the federal government under the Constitution.

primary authority The mandatory enforceable law, including federal and state constitutions, statues, and court decisions.

procedural law The law governing the manner in which rights are enforced; the law prescribing the procedure to be followed in a case. Also called adjective law, procedural law dictates *how* rights are *presented* for interpretation and enforcement, as distinguished from substantive law, which *creates* legal rights. The Federal Rules of Civil Procedure, the Federal Rules of Criminal Procedure, and rules of court are EXAMPLES of procedural laws.

promulgate 1. To publish, announce, or proclaim and, in particular, to give official notice of a public act, for EXAMPLE, the publication of an executive order in the *Internal Revenue Bulletin*. 2. To enact a law or issue a regulation.

protective filing date The filing date given to an application for Social Security disability benefits when claimants have informed the Social Security Administration (SSA) of their intent to file an application and then file an application on the prescribed form within the required time limit.

question of fact A question to be decided by the jury in a trial by jury or by the judge in a bench trial; that is, a question of what is the truth when the evidence is in conflict.

question of law A question to be decided by the judge; that is, a question as to the appropriate law to be applied in a case, or its correct interpretation.

recommended decision A recommended decision is one that must be reviewed at a higher level in the agency before it becomes the agency's final decision.

record As defined in the Administrative Procedure Act (ADMINISTRATIVE PROCEDURE ACT (APA)), the record includes the transcript and exhibits, together with all papers and requests filed in a proceeding. Speaking generally, it is the evidence, both documentary and oral, that is presented to the decision maker.

redacted A redacted document is one in which information that cannot be disclosed has been deleted.

refugee A person who cannot return to his or her country of nationality because "of persecution or a well-founded fear of persecution on account of race, religion, nationality, membership in a particular social group or political opinion."

regulation 1. The act of regulating. 2. A rule having the force of law, promulgated by an administrative agency; the act of rulemaking. 3. A rule of conduct established by a person or body in authority for the governance of those over whom they have authority.

residual functional capacity The work capacity that a person retains despite his or her impairments, categorized as the capacity for sedentary, light, medium, heavy, or very heavy work.

respondent The term used for an alien who has been placed in deportation proceedings.

respondent In EEOC pretrial procedures, the person charged with engaging in an unlawful employment practice.

retaliation In the context of title VII, retaliation occurs when an employee has engaged in a protected activity and an employer takes an unlawful action against the employee because of his or her action.

reverse FOIA Case A case in which a party who submitted information to an agency seeks to enjoin the agency from releasing the information.

ripeness A case is ripe for court review when the agency has reached a final decision, or at least a decision concrete enough that the court can determine whether an actual problem exists.

rulemaking The promulgation by an administrative agency of a rule having the force of law, i.e., a regulation.

rule making The procedure agencies follow in formulating, amending, or repealing their regulations.

scope of review A phrase referring to the nature and extent of the jurisdiction of an appellate court when reviewing the decision of a lower court, or the jurisdiction of any court when reviewing the decision of an administrative agency. The issues the reviewing tribunal may address, and the action it is entitled to take, are prescribed by state and federal constitutional and statutory provisions.

search warrant An order in writing issued by a magistrate or other judicial officer and directed to a law enforcement officer, commanding her to search for and seize stolen, contraband, or illicit property, or other property evidencing the commission of a crime.

secondary authority Sources other than primary authority, which can be persuasive, though not mandatory, in interpreting a primary source of law.

separation of powers A fundamental principle of the Constitution, which gives exclusive power to the legislative branch to make the law, exclusive power to the executive branch to administer it, and exclusive power to the judicial branch to enforce it. The authors of the Constitution believed that the separation of powers would make abuse of power less likely.

sequential evaluation process The five-step evaluation process used by SSA to determine whether claimants are disabled within the meaning of the Social Security Act.

severe impairment As used in the context of Social Security disability, an impairment that significantly limits a person's physical or mental ability to perform basic work activities; defined by courts as an impairment that has more than a minimal effect on a person's ability to work.

sovereign immunity The principle that the government—specifically, the United States or any state of the United States—is immune from suit except when it consents to be sued, as for EXAMPLE, through a statute such as the Federal Tort Claims Act.

standing to sue The legal capacity to bring and to maintain a lawsuit. A person is without standing to sue unless some interest of hers has been adversely affected or unless she has been injured by the defendant. The term "standing to sue" is often shortened simply to "standing."

state agency The agency designated by a particular state to carry out the disability determination function at the initial and reconsideration levels.

subpart A section of regulations addressing a common subject.

subpoena A command in the form of written process requiring a witness to comt to court to testify; short for subpoena ad testificandum.

substantial evidence Evidence that a reasonable person would accept as adequate to support the conclusion or conclusions drawn from it; evidence beyond a scintilla.

substantial gainful activity A Social Security regulatory term which means work that involves significant mental or physical activity and is usually performed for pay or profit.

substantive law Area of the law that defines right conduct, as opposed to procedural law, which governs the process by which rights are adjudicated.

summary judgment A method of disposing of an action without further proceedings. Under the Federal Rules of Civil Procedure, and the rules of civil procedure of many states, a party against whom a claim, counterclaim, or cross-claim is asserted, or against whom a declaratory judgment is sought, may file a motion for summary judgment seeking judgment in her favor if there is no genuine issue as to any material fact.

transporters In the context of RCRA, companies that transport hazardous waste from generators to TSD facilities.

TSD facilities In the context of RCRA, companies that transport, store, and dispose of hazardous waste.

visa A stamp affixed to a passport by an official of a country one wishes to visit. It is a recognition of the validity of the passport and approval to enter the country.

vocational experts Person relied on by the SSA, when the grids cannot be directly applied, to state whether there exists a significant number of jobs a claimant can perform, considering the claimant's vocational factors.

voluntary departure An agreement for an alien to leave the United States within a certain time limit, as an alternative to deportation.

writ A written order issued by a court directing the person to whom it is addressed to do a specified act. Writs may be addressed to an officer of the court (EXAMPLE: a writ of attachment), to an inferior court (EXAMPLE: a writ of certiorari), to a board (EXAMPLE: a writ of prohibition), to a corporation (EXAMPLE: a writ of mandamus), or to an individual (EXAMPLE: a summons), among others. Writs are also issued by authorities other than courts. EXAMPLES: a commission issued by the governor to a public official; a citation issued to a violator by a police officer.

Index

(References in bold indicate illustrations.)